ANTHROPOLOGICAL THEORY FOR THE TWENTY-FIRST CENTURY

ANTHROPOLOGICAL THEORY

FOR THE TWENTY-FIRST CENTURY
A CRITICAL APPROACH

Edited by A. Lynn Bolles, Ruth Gomberg-Muñoz,
Bernard C. Perley, and Keri Vacanti Brondo

UNIVERSITY OF TORONTO PRESS
Toronto Buffalo London

ISBN 978-1-4875-0884-5 (cloth)   ISBN 978-1-4875-3907-8 (EPUB)
ISBN 978-1-4875-2637-5 (paper)   ISBN 978-1-4875-3906-1 (PDF)

Library and Archives Canada Cataloguing in Publication

Title: Anthropological theory for the twenty-first century : a critical approach / edited by A. Lynn Bolles, Ruth Gomberg-Muñoz, Bernard C. Perley, and Keri Vacanti Brondo.
Names: Bolles, Augusta Lynn, editor. | Gomberg-Muñoz, Ruth, editor. | Perley, Bernard C., editor. | Brondo, Keri Vacanti, editor.
Description: Includes bibliographical references and index.
Identifiers: Canadiana (print) 20210391154 | Canadiana (ebook) 20210391219 | ISBN 9781487526375 (paper) | ISBN 9781487508845 (cloth) | ISBN 9781487539078 (EPUB) | ISBN 9781487539061 (PDF)
Subjects: LCSH: Anthropology – Philosophy.
Classification: LCC GN33 .A42 2022 | DDC 301.01 – dc23

We welcome comments and suggestions regarding any aspect of our publications – please feel free to contact us at news@utorontopress.com or visit us at utorontopress.com.

Every effort has been made to contact copyright holders; in the event of an error or omission, please notify the publisher.

We wish to acknowledge the land on which the University of Toronto Press operates. This land is the traditional territory of the Wendat, the Anishnaabeg, the Haudenosaunee, the Métis, and the Mississaugas of the Credit First Nation.

University of Toronto Press acknowledges the financial support of the Government of Canada and the Ontario Arts Council, an agency of the Government of Ontario, for its publishing activities.

ONTARIO ARTS COUNCIL
CONSEIL DES ARTS DE L'ONTARIO
an Ontario government agency
un organisme du gouvernement de l'Ontario

Funded by the   Financé par le
Government   gouvernement
of Canada   du Canada

Canadä

For our students – the future ancestors

* * *

The editors' proceeds will be donated to the American Anthropological Association undergraduate internship program. For more information about the internship, please visit www.americananthro.org.

Contents

Section Five: On Writing Cultures   113

Section Six: On Colonialism and Anthropological "Others"   147

Contents

Provocation: Going Native – A Satirical End to Anthropology Theory   420

Timeline

1492	October 12, Columbus makes landfall at Guanahaní
1513	Free Black soldier with Ponce de Leon sets foot on native North America (Florida)
1550–1551	*Valladolid Debate* on Aristotelian justification for the *natural slavery* of "Indians"
1552	Fra Bartolomé de las Casas publishes *A Short Account of the Destruction of the Indies*
1619	Arrival of Africans in Virginia
1640–1865	US chattel slavery
1754–1763	French and Indian War
1763	Royal Proclamation of 1763 designating land west of the Appalachian Mountains "Indian Reserve"
1775–1783	American Revolutionary War
1798	Kant's first edition publication of *Anthropology from a Pragmatic Point of View*
1812–1815	War of 1812
1830	Indian Removal Act
1833	William Apess publishes "An Indian's Looking Glass for the White Man"

1854	Frederick Douglass publishes "The Claims of the Negro Ethnologically Considered"
1859	Charles Darwin publishes *On the Origin of Species*
1861–1865	US Civil War
1865	First Jim Crow laws mandating racial segregation
1872	Karl Marx and Friedrich Engels publish the *Communist Manifesto*
1877	Lewis Henry Morgan publishes *Ancient Society*
1884	Chinese Exclusion Act
1886	May Day uprising, for which Lucy Parsons's husband, Albert Parsons, was executed
1888	First issue of *American Anthropologist*
1890	Wounded Knee I
1893	World's Columbian Exposition
1896	*Plessy v. Ferguson* decision legalizing racial segregation in the US
1902	Boas founds anthropology department at Columbia University
1903	W.E.B. Du Bois publishes *The Souls of Black Folk*
1905	Lucy Parsons speaks at the Founding Convention of the Industrial Workers of the World
1905	Max Weber publishes *The Protestant Ethic and the Spirit of Capitalism*
1912	Edward Sapir publishes "Language and Environment"
1914–1918	World War I
1916	Arthur Caswell Parker publishes "The Origin of the Iroquois"
1917–1923	Russian Revolution
1920	Franz Boas publishes "Methods of Ethnology"
1922	Bronislaw Malinowski publishes *Argonauts of the Western Pacific*
1924	Native Americans gain access to US citizenship
1925	Marcel Mauss publishes *The Gift*
1926	Margaret Mead publishes "The Methodology of Racial Testing"

1935	●	W.E.B. Du Bois publishes *Black Reconstruction in America, 1860–1880*
1935	●	Ruth Benedict publishes *Patterns of Culture*
1935	●	Zora Neale Hurston publishes *Mules and Men*
1938	●	Jomo Kenyatta publishes *Facing Mt. Kenya*
1939–1945	●	World War II
1940	●	Fernando Ortiz publishes *Cuban Counterpoint: Tobacco and Sugar*
1941	●	Elsie Clews Parsons elected first woman president of AAA
1944	●	The Bretton Woods Agreement
1946	●	Katherine Dunham publishes *Journey to Accompong*
1948–1968	●	Civil Rights Movement
1951	●	Claude Levi Strauss publishes "Language and the Analysis of Social Laws"
1954	●	*Brown v. Board of Education* decision
1955–1975	●	Vietnam War
1955	●	Julian Steward publishes *Theory of Culture Change*
1960–1996	●	Guatemalan Civil War
1963	●	Birmingham church bombing
1964	●	US Civil Rights Act
1967	●	AAA resolution on Vietnam
1968	●	End of Jim Crow laws
1969	●	Stonewall Riots
1969	●	Vine Deloria Jr. publishes *Anthropologists and Other Friends*
1971	●	Rodolfo Stavenhagen publishes "Decolonializing Applied Social Sciences"
1972	●	Eleanor Burke Leacock publishes the Introduction to Engles's *The Origin of the Family, Private Property and the State: In the Light of the Researches of Lewis H. Morgan*
1973	●	Clifford Geertz publishes *The Interpretation of Cultures*

1973	Wounded Knee II
1975	Sally Slocum publishes "Woman the Gatherer: Male Bias in Anthropology"
1976	Michel Foucault publishes *The History of Sexuality, Vol. I*
1978	Beatrice Medicine publishes "Learning to Be an Anthropologist and Remaining 'Native'"
1979	Edward Said publishes *Orientalism*
1979–1992	El Salvadoran Civil War
1982	Eric Wolf publishes *Europe and the People without History*
1986	Arjun Appadurai publishes "Theory in Anthropology: Center and Periphery"
1986	George Marcus and Michael Fischer publish *Anthropology as Cultural Critique*
1987	Sylvia Yanagisako and Jane Fishburne Collier publish "Toward a Unified Analysis of Gender and Kinship"
1987	Gloria Anzaldúa publishes *Borderlands/La Frontera: The New Mestiza*
1987	Ifi Amadiume publishes *Male Daughters, Female Husbands: Gender and Sex in an African Society*
1988	Donna Haraway publishes "Situated Knowledges"
1989	Renato Rosaldo publishes "Grief and a Headhunter's Rage"
1989	Ann Stoler publishes "Making Empire Respectable"
1989	Karen Brodkin Sacks publishes "Toward a Unified Theory of Class, Race, and Gender"
1990	The passage of NAGPRA
1991	Lila Abu-Lughod publishes "Writing against Culture"
1991	Faye V. Harrison publishes *Decolonizing Anthropology*
1992	Akhil Gupta and James Ferguson publish "Beyond 'Culture'"
1992	Pierre Bourdieu publishes "Symbolic Power"
1993	Epeli Hau'ofa publishes "Our Sea of Islands"
1994	Formal end of apartheid in South Africa

1995	●	Nancy Scheper-Hughes publishes "The Primacy of the Ethical"
1995	●	Delmos Jones publishes "Anthropology and the Oppressed"
1995	●	Yolanda T. Moses elected first Black woman president of AAA
1996	●	Philippe Bourgois publishes "In Search of Masculinity"
1997	●	Esteban Krotz publishes "Anthropologies of the South"
1997	●	Michael Blakey publishes "Man and Nature, White and Other"
1998	●	Begoña Aretxaga publishes "What the Border Hides"
2001	●	World Trade Center/Pentagon attacks
2001	●	Lynn Bolles publishes "Seeking the Ancestors"
2002	●	Evan B. Towle and Lynn M. Morgan publish "Romancing the Transgender Native"
2002	●	Katherine Verdery publishes "Seeing like a Mayor"
2003	●	Dána-Ain Davis publishes "What Did You Do Today?"
2003	●	Michel-Rolph Trouillot publishes *Global Transformations: Anthropology and the Modern World*
2003	●	Achille Mbembé publishes *Necropolitics*
2004	●	Tsunami strikes Indonesia
2004	●	Paul Farmer publishes "An Anthropology of Structural Violence"
2005	●	Heike Becker, Emile Boonzaier, and Joy Owen publish "Fieldwork in Shared Spaces"
2005	●	Paige West publishes "Translation, Value, and Space"
2005	●	Saba Mahmood publishes "The Subject of Freedom"
2005	●	Leith Mullings publishes "Interrogating Racism"
2005	●	Aihwa Ong publishes "Mutations in Citizenship"
2007	●	UN Declaration on the Rights of Indigenous Peoples
2008	●	Faye V. Harrison publishes *Outsider Within: Reworking Anthropology in the Global Age*
2008	●	Shalini Shankar publishes "Speaking like a Model Minority"
2008	●	Susan Stryker publishes "Transgender History, Homonormativity, and Disciplinarity"

2008	The Great Recession and Occupy Wall Street movement
2009	Gustavo Lins Riberio publishes "Non-hegemonic Globalizations"
2010	AAA omits "science" from long-range plan
2012	Jafari Allen publishes "One Way or Another"
2013	Bernard Perley publishes "Gone Anthropologist"
2013	Christen Smith publishes "Strange Fruit"
2013	Victoria Redclift publishes "Abjects or Agents?"
2014	Laquan MacDonald is killed by police
2014	Michael Brown is killed by police
2015	US legalizes same-sex marriage
2015	Zoe Todd publishes "Indigenizing the Anthropocene"
2015	Jonathan Rosa and Yarimar Bonilla publish "#Ferguson"
2015	Jeff Maskovsky writes "At Home in the End Times"
2016–2017	Standing Rock protests
2016	Audra Simpson publishes "Consent's Revenge"
2016	Ghassan Hage publishes "Towards an Ethics of the Theoretical Encounter"
2016	Rosabelle Boswell publishes "Sensuous Stories in the Indian Ocean Islands"
2017	Deborah Thomas becomes the first editor of color of *American Anthropologist*
2017	Arturo Escobar publishes *Designs for the Pluriverse*
2018	Savannah Shange publishes "Play Aunties and Dyke Bitches"
2019	Kim TallBear publishes "Caretaking Relations, Not American Dreaming"
2020	George Floyd and Breonna Taylor are killed by police
2020	Alaka Wali publishes "Complicity and Resistance in the Indigenous Amazon"
2020–	COVID-19 pandemic
2021	Insurrection to take over the US Capitol

Introduction: A Contested Canon

What is anthropology as an academic discipline, as a way of understanding the world? Anthropologists have approached this question with different visions of our discipline that develop over time and in response to changing ideological and social conditions. This ongoing conversation mostly takes place through published articles and books, as well as presentations at academic conferences. Perhaps inevitably, some publications and presentations become more influential than others: they reach a wider audience, are discussed more, are cited more often, and ultimately form a cornerstone of anthropological scholarship. These cornerstone publications comprise the anthropological "canon," a collection of scholarship considered especially influential or paradigmatic in the field. Theory volumes such as this one present a version of the canon, in that they communicate to readers that the pieces within are central to anthropological thought.

This process appears fairly straightforward and even intellectually mundane, but canonization, like everything else, is profoundly shaped by social, political, and economic relationships. *Why* do some scholarly works reach wider publics than others? What does it take to publish in prestigious journals and with academic presses? How are decisions made about publishing and citing? More broadly, what factors influence academic achievements like the attainment of advanced degrees, the allocation of research funds, and the distribution of academic jobs that allow scholars time to publish? And perhaps most importantly, who gets to decide?

We take as the starting point for this volume the notion that the anthropological canon is contested and mired in the sociopolitical contexts in which scholars live and work. Indeed, canonization is messy, political, and disputed, and this begs the question of whether canonization, as an academic process, should be attempted in the first place. After all, if the canon is a product of unequal access to academic resources, doesn't putting together a canon reproduce academic and social inequities? And doesn't curating certain pieces of scholarship *make* them more authoritative, thereby suppressing divergent views? We take these questions seriously, and we hope you do, too. Nevertheless, we believe that a volume such as this has both pedagogical and intellectual usefulness, and we offer it as a fodder for discussion rather than as the last authority on anthropological scholarship.

Indeed, it is precisely the sociopolitical nature of canonization that has driven the creation of this volume. As theorists and teachers of theory, we found ourselves frustrated with existing theory volumes that present the anthropological canon as an established scholarly collection principally authored by scholars from elite Western institutions. We found ourselves supplementing theory texts in our classrooms with key pieces of scholarship written by anthropologists who have largely been erased from the US canon: scholars from the "Global South," colonized places, and marginalized communities within the United States and Europe, such as Black and Indigenous scholars, and especially marginalized women. This supplementation catalyzed conversations with our students about *why* key scholars from racialized, marginalized, and non-Western communities are largely absent from anthropological theory volumes. These questions often go unaddressed in the volumes themselves, which treat "the canon" as politically unproblematic and decontextualized.

Before we go further, we want to acknowledge that this volume addresses but does not resolve these issues. Our selections are limited, both in number and range. By reproducing only theoretical writings that have had outsize influence in the discipline, we do not incorporate the perspectives of people without access to academic outlets. And while we include non-US scholars in every section, ultimately the volume reflects our theoretical and pedagogical concerns with US hegemony. This volume *does*, however, attend to the theoretical, geopolitical, and sociocultural diversity of anthropological scholars and scholarship, and we additionally incorporate pieces that comment on representation, positionality, solidarity, and politics in the discipline. We also ask students to consider the sociopolitical contexts in which scholars are working and to which they are responding in their thinking and writing. More broadly, we put scholars working from and in different sociopolitical contexts in conversation with each other to illuminate the contested, ongoing, and dynamic conversation that builds anthropological theory.

WHAT IS THEORY?

Theory is a key element of scientific knowledge production that comprises a plausible, general explanation for a phenomenon, typically based on robust empirical evidence. The degree to which this definition applies to anthropology is, as you may have guessed, contested, but it is still a helpful place to start.

First and foremost, a theory is an explanation of something. As you read the selections in the volume, ask yourself: What is the puzzle here? What elements of human society are being addressed? What explanation is offered, and how does it advance our understanding of humanity? Anthropological theory is notoriously difficult to understand, so also ask yourself: Does the argument being presented clarify, does it actually explain, and how can you tell?

Second, theory is generalizable. The degree to which explanations for human culture can be generalized is disputed in anthropology, and some of the selections herein imply that no general theory of human society is plausible (itself arguably a theoretical generalization). As you read, ask yourself: In what way does this explanation apply to humans broadly? Is the argument universal or particular? Can you ascertain any explanatory limits?

Finally, theory is based on the premise that a knowable reality exists, and we can all observe it in roughly the same way. Studying our observations produces explanations that can be tested, challenged, and replicated by others. This process of testing, replication, and argumentation can give rise to explanations that are so well evidenced and generally accepted that they rise to the level of theory. Again, the degree to which this is applicable to anthropology is disputed. Many anthropological arguments are philosophical in nature and are not tested, challenged, or replicated by others; furthermore, there is ongoing disagreement about what kinds of observations, and whose observations, "count" in academic production. Relatedly, many critical anthropologists have suggested that we forgo claims to scientific knowledge production all together, as science itself is a product of a particular (Western, elite) ideology, and all anthropological analyses are necessarily partial and subjective. Others have noted the prevalence of scientific practices in non-Western contexts and argued for their utility in addressing social problems in marginalized communities. These arguments will be fleshed out in subsequent readings, and as you read, ask yourself: What evidence is offered to support the explanation? How might the social position of the scholar affect their observations, assumptions, and arguments? As some explanations are advanced, which others are foreclosed?

We invite readers of this volume to think about theory, to critique it and work with it. That is, we believe that theoretical arguments in anthropology are only valuable insofar as they are helpful in explaining elements of human (and other-than-human) worlds; their mere publication (even in prestigious venues) does not confer any inherent authority. Thus, it is up to readers to do the work of discerning the utility and limitations of anthropological scholarship. Undertaking this work is a key part of the intellectual development of the next generation of anthropological theorists.

HONORING THE ANCESTORS

To put together the selections for this volume, we called upon a wide range of anthropologists who have long been thinking and writing about anthropological theory and canonical diversity. We also combed a host of anthropological websites that present curated lists of texts, "syllabi," which provide critical insights into social issues. A list of these websites can be found in an appendix at the end of the text. We reached out to our colleagues and mentors, who offered thoughtful suggestions for the content and organization of the volume. And reviewers of the proposal for the reader also provided helpful feedback and made a host of productive suggestions. We also drew on our teaching experiences and have been inspired by students who plunge into theoretical critique with passion and insight.

Ultimately, we chose pieces that (1) are recognized as influential in anthropological theory; (2) comprise a range of approaches to and perspectives on common anthropological problems; (3) represent a diversity of social and geopolitical positions of scholars and the contexts in which they live and work; and (4) reflect the contemporaneous direction and concerns of critical anthropology. To keep the reader affordable, we cut selections to about 2,000 words each (omitted text is indicated by bracketed ellipses, except at the beginning of the readings) and eliminated original footnotes, which allowed us to include more than 70 pieces of scholarship here. Still, there are many worthy pieces that could not be included. Again, this book should be read as a starting point, not an end, to thinking about anthropological scholarship.

This volume is organized into 14 sections; each section includes five pieces that contribute to a common anthropological conversation (except for Section One, which has six essays). Sections are roughly chronological, representative of how anthropological scholarship develops over time as scholars respond to each other in their writing. Each section opens with a brief introduction that describes the sociopolitical context in which the pieces were written and to which many of them explicitly respond. Section introductions also include three guiding questions to help readers think through the interactions of the texts with each other and the broader concerns that they address; a glossary of terms can be found at the end of most sections.

By the time you reach the end of this volume, you will be more conversant in a range of anthropological issues, including how the discipline of anthropology has been shaped over time through scholarly conversation; the utility and limitations of thinking with theory; the interaction of anthropological thought with broader political economic contexts; and the politics of science, position, and advocacy in anthropological scholarship. We hope that these understandings will help enrich upcoming generations of anthropology students – the future anthropological ancestors.

SECTION ONE

On Roots of Social Difference

THE SOCIAL CONTEXT

Anthropology, like evolutionary theory, was informed by principles of the European Enlightenment such as rationality, progress, and science. The assumption of human progress exemplified by European civilization was used to justify the conquest and enslavement of non-Europeans by rising capitalists throughout the nineteenth century. Indeed, while wars for independence had expelled imperial powers from most of the Western hemisphere by this time, Western European elites were carving up the resources of Africa, Southeast Asia, and the Indian subcontinent amongst themselves. Meanwhile, US leaders, enriched by chattel slavery, waged predatory wars against Indigenous Peoples and Mexican ranchers to expand US territory to the Pacific Coast by 1848. These wars of conquest spread the capitalist form of labor exploitation, the wage system, alongside older systems of slavery in mines and plantations. By the late nineteenth century, capitalist industrialization was catalyzing displacement, migration, and urbanization, profoundly shifting social and material life.

As disparate human groups encountered each other on this highly unequal terrain, questions about the character of their interactions, and about the nature of humankind itself, preoccupied Western intellectuals. Were these vastly different peoples related to one another? And if so, how? Eschewing explanations rooted in biblical stories, Western intellectuals began turning to evolutionary theory to explain the similarities and differences, as well as inequalities, among people around the world. These scholars are known as **social or cultural evolutionists**.

Many early social evolutionists drew on Darwinian concepts such as "fitness" to explain and justify colonial and racial inequality, a conceptual model known as **social Darwinism**. **Herbert Spencer**, for example, is attributed with coining the term "survival of the fittest" to explain dominance (manifested as conquest and displacement of others) by way of putatively evolutionary traits. And while Darwinian evolutionary theory makes no claims

Credit: Bernard C. Perley

to directionality or progress, early social evolutionists sketched out human "evolutionary" schemes in which people were thought to progress through successive stages from "savagery" (exemplified by non-Western, small-scale, and unbureaucratic forms of organization) to "civilization" (exemplified by Western European societies). Some, such as John Wesley Powell, Nathaniel Southgate Shaler, and Frederic Ward Putnam, argued that these differences were inherently hierarchical and attributable to the racial inferiority of non-white peoples. As founders of cornerstone anthropological projects at prestigious museums and universities, these scholars molded early anthropological understandings of human sameness and difference. By promoting schemes of racial hierarchy while eliding the roles of colonialism, slavery, and capitalist exploitation in cultivating categorical inequality, these

Credit: Bernard C. Perley

scholars placed early anthropological theory squarely in service to **white supremacist** ideologies and practices. We did not have the space to include writings of these earliest anthropologists here, and we are reluctant to legitimize them, but we provide links to discussions of their work on the companion website (www.anthropologicaltheory.com). Instead, in this section we begin with theorists who draw on highly divergent worldviews to reckon with this context and make sense of social difference and inequality.

THE CONVERSATION

Our first piece in this section, Reading 1.1 by William Apess, challenges race-based explanations for inequality. Apess, himself a member of the Pequot community who today would be called "mixed race," begins by describing impoverishment of "Indian" communities in New England. He goes on to build an argument that degradation of Indigenous Peoples is based on a "bad principle" – the pretext of skin color to justify pervasive rape, land dispossession, and legal disenfranchisement of Native and African-descended people in the United States. Apess calls particular attention to the hypocrisy of colonial agents who strip non-whites of rights and resources even as they "[claim] they think as much of us [Indians] as they do of themselves."

A former slave and abolitionist in the United States, Frederick Douglass was also deeply concerned with developing theoretical models to address social inequalities. In Reading 1.2, Douglass refutes claims that Black people are less fully human than whites – challenging prevailing theoretical paradigms of the nineteenth-century United States. Drawing on evolutionary theory and ethnological comparisons between Black people and other humans, as well as on his own intellectual powers as a Black man, Douglass discredits racialized evolutionary schemes, and the racial classifications of Dr. Samuel Morton in particular, that deny non-whites' claims to equality.

While many social theorists were naturalizing and legitimizing sociopolitical inequality, others were seeking to challenge it. Karl Marx and Friedrich Engels, authors of the third piece, used social evolutionary theory as a tool to address political and economic inequalities of the time, developing the argument that capitalism would eventually give way to communism through a revolutionary overthrow of the capitalist system. In this piece, Marx and Engels develop a **materialist** worldview, in which they argue that political economic conditions of a society – in this case, capitalism – give rise to social classes with conflicting interests, the bourgeoisie and proletariat, ultimately leading the oppressed class, the proletariat, to revolt.

Some social evolutionists, such as Lewis Henry Morgan, who is the author of the fourth essay, rejected the notion that evolutionary stages were fixed by race. Instead, Morgan, a materialist and anthropologist, sought to categorize human groups based on political and economic characteristics. These politico-economic categories, he argued in social evolutionist fashion, developed from simple to more complex over time. As technologies and societies became more complex, all groups would evolve along similar trajectories toward civilization. In surmising that "savage" peoples would eventually reach civilization, Morgan's theory was progressive for its time. Nevertheless, as Lee Baker (1998) argues, Morgan held deeply racist worldviews that informed his evolutionary model and, in particular, his assumption that Western civilization symbolizes the height of human "progress."

Our fifth author, Lucy Parsons, drew on Marxist theory to build an international feminist perspective on capitalism, the family, and labor organizing. Growing up as a "mixed race" woman during Reconstruction, Parsons became a radical labor organizer who was famously characterized by Chicago police as "more dangerous than a thousand rioters."

Parsons wrote extensively about labor, class interests, and women; in Reading 1.5, she describes gendered exploitation within the capitalist system and the labor movement itself. Referring to women as the "slaves of slaves," Parsons contextualized gender inequality in households and workplaces within broader political and economic processes associated with capitalism.

Our final selection in this section, written by Max Weber, moves away from materialist conceptions of social organization to advance a more **idealist** understanding of human social worlds. In his exploration of the influence of religious ideas on economy, Weber argued that the emergence of capitalism in Europe – along with the "highest" human achievements in arts, sciences, and architecture, among other things – is ultimately attributable to the Reformation, which encouraged Protestants to pursue economic gain. In particular, Weber argues that elements of Protestant religion led adherents to develop a particular rationalized work ethic and, eventually, to build enterprises and invest their wealth, leading to affluence relative to Catholics and non-Europeans.

THREE QUESTIONS FOR THE READINGS

1 What is the underlying explanation for human social organization in each piece? How does the social position of the scholar inform the analysis that is advanced?
2 How are these pieces in conversation with each other? What assumptions do they hold in common, and where do they diverge?
3 Most of these pieces were written more than 100 years ago, yet the social problems they address – racial and gendered inequality and violence, in particular – persist. How are the arguments presented here relevant to how we understand inequality and movements for social change today?

ON THE COMPANION WEBSITE

More Dangerous Than a Thousand Rioters, a documentary about Lucy Parsons, plus suggested readings and more.

www.anthropologicaltheory.com

REFERENCE

Baker, Lee. 1998. *From Savage to Negro: Anthropology and the Construction of Race 1986–1954.* Berkeley: University of California Press.

1.1. An Indian's Looking-Glass for the White Man (1833)

William Apess

It may be that many are ignorant of the situation of many of my [Indian] brethren within the limits of New England. Let me for a few moments turn your attention to the reservations in the different states of New England, and, with but few exceptions, we shall find them as follows: The most mean, abject, miserable race of beings in the world – a complete place of prodigality and prostitution.

Let a gentleman and lady, of integrity and respectability visit these places, and they would be surprised; as they wandered from one hut to the other they would view the females who are left alone, children half starved, and some almost as naked as they came into the world. And it is a fact that I have seen them as much so – while the females are left without protection, and are seduced by white men, and are finally left to be common prostitutes for them, and to be destroyed by that burning, fiery curse, that has swept millions, both of red and white men, into the grave with sorrow and disgrace – Rum. One reason why they are left so is because their most sensible and active men are absent at sea. Another reason is because they are made to believe they are minors and have not the abilities given them from God to take care of themselves. […] Their land is in common stock, and they have nothing to make them enterprising.

Another reason is because those men who are [Government] Agents, many of them are unfaithful, and care not whether the Indians live or die [or whether] they are much imposed upon by their neighbors who have no principle. They would think it no crime to go upon Indian lands and cut and carry off their most valuable timber, or anything else they chose; and I doubt not but they think it clear gain. Another reason is because they have no education to take care of themselves; if they had, I would risk them to take care of their property.

Now I will ask, if the Indians are not called the most ingenious people amongst us? And are they not said to be men of talents? And I would ask, could there be a more efficient way to distress and murder them by inches than the way they have taken? And there is no people in the world but who may be destroyed in the same way. Now if these people are what they are held up in our view to be, I would take the liberty to ask why they are not brought forward and pains taken to educate them? To give them all a common education, and those of the brightest and first-rate talents put forward and held up to office. Perhaps some unholy, unprincipled men would cry out, the skin was not good enough; but stop friends – I am not talking about the skin, but about principles. I would ask if there cannot be as good feelings and principles under a red skin as there can be under a white? And let me ask, is it not on the account of a bad principle, that we who are red children have had to suffer so much as we have? And let me ask, did not this bad principle proceed from the whites or their forefathers? And I would ask, is it worthwhile to nourish it any longer? If not then let us have a change; although some men no doubt will spout their corrupt principles against it, [men who] are in the halls of legislation and elsewhere. [For them] I presume this kind of talk will seem surprising and horrible. I do not see why it should so long as they (the whites) say that they think as much of us as they do of themselves. [...]

I know that many say that they are willing, perhaps the majority of the people, that we should enjoy our rights and privileges as they do. If so, I would ask why are not we protected in our persons and property throughout the Union? Is it not because there reigns in the breast of many who are leaders, a most unrighteous, unbecoming and impure black principle, and as corrupt and unholy as it can be – while these very same unfeeling, self-esteemed characters pretend to take the skin as a pretext to keep us from our unalienable and lawful rights? I would ask you if you would like to be disfranchised from all your rights, merely because your skin is white, and for no other crime? I'll venture to say, these very characters who hold the skin to be such a barrier in the way, would be the first to cry out, injustice! awful injustice! [...]

[...] Now suppose these skins were put together, and each skin had its national crimes written upon it – which skin do you think would have the greatest? I will ask one question more. Can you charge the Indians with robbing a nation almost of their whole Continent, and murdering their women and children, and then depriving the remainder of their lawful rights, that nature and God require them to have? And to cap the climax, rob another nation [for African slaves] to till their grounds, and welter out their days under the lash with hunger and fatigue under the scorching rays of a burning sun? I should look at all the skins, and I know that when I cast my eye upon that white skin, and if I saw those crimes written upon it, I should enter my protest against it immediately, and cleave to that which is more honorable. And I can tell you that I am satisfied with the manner of my creation, fully – whether others are or not.

But we will strive to penetrate more fully into the conduct of those who profess to have pure principles, and who tell us to follow Jesus Christ and imitate him and have his Spirit. Let us see if they come anywhere near him and his ancient disciples. The first thing we are to look at, are his precepts, of which we will mention a few. "Thou shalt love the Lord thy God with all thy heart, with all thy soul, with all thy mind, and with all thy strength." The second is like unto it. "Thou shalt love thy neighbor as thyself." On these two precepts hang all the law and the prophets. [...]

Did you ever hear or read of Christ teaching his disciples that they ought to despise one because his skin was different from theirs? Jesus Christ being a Jew, and those of his

Apostles certainly were not whites – and did not he who completed the plan of salvation complete it for the whites as well as for the Jews, and others? And were not the whites the most degraded people on the earth at that time, and none were more so; for they sacrificed their children to dumb idols! And did not St. Paul labor more abundantly for building up a Christian nation amongst you than any of the Apostles. And you know as well as I that you are not indebted to a principle beneath a white skin for your religious services, but to a colored one. [...]

I will refer you to St. Peter's precepts – Acts 10. "God is no respecter of persons" – &c. Now if this is the case, my white brother, what better are you than God? And if no better, why do you profess his gospel and to have his spirit, act so contrary to it? Let me ask why the men of a different skin are so despised, why are not they educated and placed in your pulpits? I ask if his services well performed are not as good as if a white man performed them? I ask if a marriage or a funeral ceremony, or the ordinance of the Lord's house would not be as acceptable in the sight of God as though he was white? And if so, why is it not to you? I ask again, why is it not as acceptable to have men to exercise their office in one place as well as in another?

Perhaps you will say that if we admit you to all of these privileges you will want more. I expect that I can guess what that is – Why, say you, there would be intermarriages. How that would be I am not able to say – and if it should be, it would be nothing strange or new to me; for I can assure you that I know a great many that have intermarried, both of the whites and the Indians – and many are their sons and daughters – and people too of the first respectability. And I could point to some in the famous city of Boston and elsewhere. You may now look at the disgraceful act in the city of Boston and elsewhere. You may now look at the disgraceful act in the statute law passed by the Legislature of Massachusetts, and behold the fifty pound fine levied upon any Clergyman or Justice of the Peace that dare to encourage the laws of God and nature by a legitimate union in holy wedlock between the Indians and whites. I would ask how this looks to your law makers. I would ask if this corresponds with your sayings – that you think as much of the Indians as you do of the whites. I do not wonder that you blush many of you while you read; for many have broken the ill-fated laws made by man to hedge up the laws of God and nature. I would ask if they who have made the law have not broken it – but there is no other state in New England that has this law but Massachusetts; and I think as many of you do not, that you have done yourselves no credit. [...]

By what you read, you may learn how deep your principles are, I should say they were skin deep. I should not wonder if some of the most selfish and ignorant would spout a charge of their principles now and then at me. But I would ask, how are you to love your neighbors as yourself? Is it to cheat them? Is it to wrong them in anything? Now to cheat them out of any of their rights is robbery. And I ask, can you deny that you are not robbing the Indians daily, and many others? But at last you may think I am what is called a hard and uncharitable man. But not so. I believe there are many who would not hesitate to advocate our cause; and those too who are men of fame and respectability – as well as ladies of honor and virtue. There is a Webster, and Everett, and a Wirt, and many others who are distinguished characters – besides an host of my fellow citizens, who advocate our cause daily. And how I congratulate such noble spirits – how they are to be prized and valued; for they are well calculated to promote the happiness of mankind. They well know that man was made for society, and not for hissing stocks and outcasts. And when such a principle as this lies within the hearts of men, how much it is like its God – and how it honors its Maker – and how it imitates the feelings of the good Samaritan, that had his wounds bound up, who had been among thieves and robbers.

Do not get tired, ye noble-hearted – only think how many poor Indians want their wounds done up daily; the Lord will reward you, and pray you stop not till this tree of distinction shall be leveled to the earth, and the mantle of prejudice torn from every American heart – then shall peace pervade the Union.

1.2. The Claims of the Negro, Ethnologically Considered (1854)

Frederick Douglass

I propose to submit to you a few thoughts on the subject of the Claims of the Negro, suggested by ethnological science, or the natural history of man. [...]

The first general claim which may here be set up, respects the manhood of the negro. This is an elementary claim, simple enough, but not without question. It is fiercely opposed. A respectable public journal, published in Richmond, Va., bases its whole defense of the Slave system upon a denial of the negro's manhood.

> The white peasant is free, and if he is a man of will and intellect, can rise in the scale of society; or at least his offspring may. He is not deprived by law of those "inalienable rights" "liberty and the pursuit of happiness," by the use of it. But here is the essence of slavery – that we do declare the negro destitute of these powers. We bind him by law to the condition of the laboring peasant forever, without his consent, and we bind his posterity after him. Now, the true question is, have we a right to do this? If we have not, all discussions about his comfortable situation, and the actual condition of free laborers elsewhere, are quite beside the point. If the negro has the same right to his liberty and the pursuit of his own happiness that the white man has, then we commit the greatest wrong and robbery to hold him a slave – an act at which the sentiment of justice must revolt in every heart – and negro slavery is an institution which that sentiment must sooner or later blot from the face of the *earth. – Richmond Examiner*

After stating the question thus, the *Examiner* boldly asserts that the negro has no such right – BECAUSE HE IS NOT A MAN!

[...] To know whether negro is a man, it must first be known what constitutes a man. Here, as well as elsewhere, I take it, that the "coat must be cut according to the cloth." It is not necessary, in order to establish the manhood of any one making the claim, to prove that such an one equals Clay in eloquence, or Webster and Calhoun in logical force and directness; for, tried by such standards of mental power as these, it is apprehended that very few could claim the high designation of *man*. Yet something like this folly is seen in the arguments directed against the humanity of the negro. His faculties and powers, uneducated and unimproved, have been contrasted with those of the highest cultivation; and the world has then been called upon to behold the immense and amazing difference between the man admitted, and the man disputed. The fact that these intellects, so powerful and so controlling, are almost, if not quite as exceptional to the general rule of humanity, in one direction, as the specimen negroes are in the other, is quite overlooked.

Man is distinguished from all other animals, by the possession of certain definite faculties and powers, as well as by physical organization and proportions. He is the only two-handed animal on the earth – the only one that laughs, and nearly the only one that weeps. Men instinctively distinguish between men and brutes. Common sense itself is scarcely needed to detect the absence of manhood in a monkey, or to recognize its presence in a negro. His speech, his reason, his power to acquire and to retain knowledge, his heaven-erected face, his habitudes, his hopes, his fears, his aspirations, his prophecies, plant between him and the brute creation, a distinction as eternal as it is palpable. Away, therefore, with all the scientific moonshine that would connect men with monkeys; that would have the world believe that humanity, instead of resting on its own characteristic pedestal – gloriously independent – is a sort of sliding scale, making one extreme brother to the orangutan, and the other to angels, and all the rest intermediates![1] Tried by all the usual, and all the unusual tests, whether mental, moral, physical, or psychological, the negro is a MAN – considering him as possessing knowledge, or needing knowledge, his elevation or his degradation, his virtues, or his vices – whichever road you take, you reach the same conclusion, the negro is a MAN. His good and his bad, his innocence and his guilt, his joys and his sorrows, proclaim his manhood in speech that all mankind practically and readily understand.

A very recondite author says, that "man is distinguished from all other animals, in that he resists as well as adapts himself to his circumstances." He does not take things as he finds them, but goes to work to improve them. Tried by this test, too, the negro is a man. You may see him yoke the oxen, harness the horse, and hold the plow. He can swim the river; but he prefers to fling over it a bridge. The horse bears him on his back – admits his mastery and dominion. The barn-yard fowl know his step, and flock around to receive their morning meal from his sable hand. The dog dances when he comes home, and whines piteously when he is absent. All these know that the negro is a MAN. Now, presuming that what is evident to beast and to bird, cannot need elaborate argument to be made plain to men, I assume, with this brief statement, that the negro is a man.

The first claim conceded and settled, let us attend to the second, which is beset with some difficulties, giving rise to many opinions, different from my own, and which opinions I propose to combat. There was a time when, if you established the point that a particular being is a man, it was considered that such a being, of course, had a common ancestry with

---

1 This is a response to social Darwinism and probably Darwinism, as well.

the rest of mankind. But it is not so now. This is, you know, an age of science, and science is favorable to division.

[…] I say it is remarkable – nay, it is strange that there should arise a phalanx of learned men – speaking in the name of *science* – to forbid the magnificent reunion of mankind in one brotherhood.

[… S]laveholders, not a few, like the *Richmond Examiner* to which I have referred, have admitted, that the whole argument in defense of slavery, becomes utterly worthless the moment the African is proved to be equally a man with the Anglo-Saxon. The temptation, therefore, to read the negro out of the human family is exceedingly strong, and may account somewhat for the repeated attempts on the part of Southern pretenders to science, to cast a doubt over the Scriptural account of the origin of mankind. […] Pride and selfishness, combined with mental power, never want for a theory to justify them – and when men oppress their fellow-men, the oppressor ever finds, in the character of the oppressed, a full justification for his oppression. Ignorance and depravity, and the inability to rise from degradation to civilization and respectability, are the most usual allegations against the oppressed. The evils most fostered by slavery and oppression, are precisely those which slaveholders and oppressors would transfer from their system to the inherent character of their victims. Thus, the very crimes of slavery become slavery's best defense. By making the enslaved a character fit only for slavery, they excuse themselves for refusing to make the slave a freeman.

[…] The proposition to which I allude, and which I mean next to assert, is this, that what are technically called the negro race, are a part of the human family, and are descended from a common ancestry, with the rest of mankind. […] Dr. Samuel George Morton may be referred to as a fair sample of American Ethnologists. His very able work *"Crania Americana,"* published in Philadelphia in 1839, is widely read in this country. In this great work his contempt for negroes is ever conspicuous. I take him as an illustration of what had been alleged as true of his class.

[Drawing on Morton's work we may conclude] that Egypt was one of the earliest abodes of learning and civilization; [this claim] is as firmly established as are the everlasting hills, defying, with a calm front the boasted mechanical and architectural skill of the nineteenth century – smiling serenely on the assaults and the mutations of time, there she stands in overshadowing grandeur, riveting the eye and the mind of the modern world – upon her, in silent and dreamy wonder – Greece and Rome – and through them Europe and America have received their civilization from the ancient Egyptians. This fact is not denied by anybody. But Egypt is in Africa. Pity that it had not been in Europe, or in Asia, or better still, in America! Another unhappy circumstance is, that the ancient Egyptians were not white people; but were, undoubtedly, just about as dark in complexion as many in this country who are considered genuine negroes; and that is not all, their hair was far from being of that graceful lankness which adorns the fair Anglo-Saxon head. But the next best thing, after these defects, is a positive unlikeness to the negro. Accordingly, our learned author [Morton] enters into an elaborate argument to prove that the ancient Egyptians were totally distinct from the negroes, and to deny all relationship between. Speaking of the "Copts and Fellahs," whom everybody knows are descendants of the Egyptians, he says, *"The Copts, though now remarkably distinct from the people that surround them, derive from their remote ancestors some mixture of Greek, Arabian, and perhaps even negro blood.*" Now, mark the description given of Egyptians in this same work: "*Complexion brown. The nose is straight, excepting the end, where it is rounded and wide; the lips are rather thick, and the hair black and curly.*" This description would certainly seem to make it safe to suppose the presence of "*even* negro blood." A man, in our day, with brown complexion, "nose rounded and wide, lips thick, hair black and curly," would, I think, have no difficulty in getting himself recognized as a negro!!

[...] In everything touching the negro, Dr. Morton, in his "Crania Americana," betrays the same spirit. He thinks that the *Sphinx* was not the representative of an Egyptian Deity, but was a shrine, worshiped at by the degraded *negroes* of Egypt; and this fact he alleges as the secret of the mistake made by Volney, in supposing that the Egyptians were real negroes. The absurdity of this assertion will be very apparent, in view of the fact that the great Sphinx in question was the chief of a series, full two miles in length. Our author again repels the supposition that the Egyptians were related to negroes, by saying there is no mention made of *color* by the historian, in relating the marriage of Solomon with Pharaoh's daughter; and with genuine American feeling, he says, such a circumstance as the marrying of an European monarch with the daughter of a negro would not have been passed over in silence in our day. This is a sample of the reasoning of men who reason from *prejudice* rather than from *fact*. It assumes that a *black skin* in the *East* excites the same prejudice which we see here in the West. Having denied all relationship of the negro to the ancient Egyptians, with characteristic American assumption, he says, "It is easy to prove, that whatever may have been the hue of their skin, they belong to the same race with ourselves." Of course, I do not find fault with Dr. Morton, or any other American, for claiming affinity with Egyptians. All that goes in that direction belongs to my side of the question, and is really right.

The leaning here indicated is natural enough, and may be explained by the fact, that an educated man in Ireland ceases to be an Irishman; and an intelligent black man is always supposed to have derived his intelligence from his connection with the white race. To be intelligent is to have one's negro blood ignored.

1.3. Bourgeois and Proletarians (1872)

Karl Marx and Friedrich Engels

The history of all hitherto existing society is the history of class struggles.

Freeman and slave, patrician and plebeian, lord and serf, guild-master and journeyman, in a word, oppressor and oppressed, stood in constant opposition to one another, carried on an uninterrupted, now hidden, now open fight, a fight that each time ended, either in a revolutionary reconstitution of society at large, or in the common ruin of the contending classes.

In the earlier epochs of history, we find almost everywhere a complicated arrangement of society into various orders, a manifold gradation of social rank. In ancient Rome we have patricians, knights, plebeians, slaves; in the Middle Ages, feudal lords, vassals, guild-masters, journeymen, apprentices, serfs; in almost all of these classes, again, subordinate gradations.

The modern bourgeois society that has sprouted from the ruins of feudal society has not done away with class antagonisms. It has but established new classes, new conditions of oppression, new forms of struggle in place of the old ones.

Our epoch, the epoch of the bourgeoisie, possesses, however, this distinct feature: it has simplified class antagonisms. Society as a whole is more and more splitting up into two great hostile camps, into two great classes directly facing each other – Bourgeoisie and Proletariat.

From the serfs of the Middle Ages sprang the chartered burghers of the earliest towns. From these burgesses the first elements of the bourgeoisie were developed.

The discovery of America, the rounding of the Cape, opened up fresh ground for the rising bourgeoisie. The East-Indian and Chinese markets, the colonization of America, trade with the colonies, the increase in the means of exchange and in commodities generally, gave to commerce, to navigation, to industry, an impulse never before known, and thereby, to the revolutionary element in the tottering feudal society, a rapid development.

The feudal system of industry, in which industrial production was monopolized by closed guilds, now no longer sufficed for the growing wants of the new markets. The manufacturing system took its place. The guild-masters were pushed on one side by the manufacturing middle class; division of labor between the different corporate guilds vanished in the face of division of labor in each single workshop.

Meantime the markets kept ever growing, the demand ever rising. Even manufacturer no longer sufficed. Thereupon, steam and machinery revolutionized industrial production. The place of manufacture was taken by the giant, Modern Industry; the place of the industrial middle class by industrial millionaires, the leaders of the whole industrial armies, the modern bourgeois.

Modern industry has established the world market, for which the discovery of America paved the way. This market has given an immense development to commerce, to navigation, to communication by land. This development has, in its turn, reacted on the extension of industry; and in proportion as industry, commerce, navigation, railways extended, in the same proportion the bourgeoisie developed, increased its capital, and pushed into the background every class handed down from the Middle Ages.

We see, therefore, how the modern bourgeoisie is itself the product of a long course of development, of a series of revolutions in the modes of production and of exchange.

Each step in the development of the bourgeoisie was accompanied by a corresponding political advance of that class. An oppressed class under the sway of the feudal nobility, an armed and self-governing association in the medieval commune: here independent urban republic (as in Italy and Germany); there taxable "third estate" of the monarchy (as in France); afterwards, in the period of manufacturing proper, serving either the semi-feudal or the absolute monarchy as a counterpoise against the nobility, and, in fact, cornerstone of the great monarchies in general, the bourgeoisie has at last, since the establishment of Modern Industry and of the world market, conquered for itself, in the modern representative State, exclusive political sway. The executive of the modern state is but a committee for managing the common affairs of the whole bourgeoisie.

[...] Constant revolutionizing of production, uninterrupted disturbance of all social conditions, everlasting uncertainty and agitation distinguish the bourgeois epoch from all earlier ones. All fixed, fast-frozen relations, with their train of ancient and venerable prejudices and opinions, are swept away, all new-formed ones become antiquated before they can ossify. All that is solid melts into air, all that is holy is profaned, and man is at last compelled to face with sober senses his real conditions of life, and his relations with his kind.

The need of a constantly expanding market for its products chases the bourgeoisie over the entire surface of the globe. It must nestle everywhere, settle everywhere, establish connexions everywhere.

The bourgeoisie has through its exploitation of the world market given a cosmopolitan character to production and consumption in every country. To the great chagrin of Reactionists, it has drawn from under the feet of industry the national ground on which it stood. All old-established national industries have been destroyed or are daily being destroyed. They are dislodged by new industries, whose introduction becomes a life and death question for all civilized nations, by industries that no longer work up indigenous raw material, but raw material drawn from the remotest zones; industries whose products are consumed, not only at home, but in every quarter of the globe. In place of the old wants, satisfied by the production of the country, we find new wants, requiring for their satisfaction the products of distant lands and climes. In place of the old local and national seclusion and self-sufficiency, we have intercourse in every direction, universal inter-dependence of nations. And as in material, so also in intellectual production. The intellectual creations of individual nations become common property. National one-sidedness and narrow-mindedness become more and more impossible, and from the numerous national and local literatures, there arises a world literature.

The bourgeoisie, by the rapid improvement of all instruments of production, by the immensely facilitated means of communication, draws all, even the most barbarian, nations into civilization. The cheap prices of commodities are the heavy artillery with which it batters down all Chinese walls, with which it forces the barbarians' intensely obstinate hatred of foreigners to capitulate. It compels all nations, on pain of extinction, to adopt the bourgeois mode of production; it compels them to introduce what it calls civilization into their midst, i.e., to become bourgeois themselves. In one word, it creates a world after its own image.

The bourgeoisie has subjected the country to the rule of the towns. It has created enormous cities, has greatly increased the urban population as compared with the rural, and has thus rescued a considerable part of the population from the idiocy of rural life. Just as it has made the country dependent on the towns, so it has made barbarian and semi-barbarian countries dependent on the civilized ones, nations of peasants on nations of bourgeois, the East on the West.

The bourgeoisie keeps more and more doing away with the scattered state of the population, of the means of production, and of property. It has agglomerated population, centralized the means of production, and has concentrated property in a few hands. The necessary consequence of this was political centralization. Independent, or but loosely connected provinces, with separate interests, laws, governments, and systems of taxation, became lumped together into one nation, with one government, one code of laws, one national class-interest, one frontier, and one customs-tariff.

The bourgeoisie, during its rule of scarce one hundred years, has created more massive and more colossal productive forces than have all preceding generations together. Subjection of Nature's forces to man, machinery, application of chemistry to industry and agriculture, steam-navigation, railways, electric telegraphs, clearing of whole continents for cultivation, canalization of rivers, whole populations conjured out of the ground – what earlier century had even a presentiment that such productive forces slumbered in the lap of social labor?

We see then: the means of production and of exchange, on whose foundation the bourgeoisie built itself up, were generated in feudal society. At a certain stage in the development of these means of production and of exchange, the conditions under which feudal society produced and exchanged, the feudal organization of agriculture and manufacturing industry, in one word, the feudal relations of property became no longer compatible with the already developed productive forces; they became so many fetters. They had to be burst asunder; they were burst asunder.

Into their place stepped free competition, accompanied by a social and political constitution adapted in it, and the economic and political sway of the bourgeois class.

A similar movement is going on before our own eyes. Modern bourgeois society, with its relations of production, of exchange and of property, a society that has conjured up such gigantic means of production and of exchange, is like the sorcerer who is no longer able to control the powers of the nether world whom he has called up by his spells. For many a decade past the history of industry and commerce is but the history of the revolt of modern productive forces against modern conditions of production, against the property relations that are the conditions for the existence of the bourgeois and of its rule. [...]

The weapons with which the bourgeoisie felled feudalism to the ground are now turned against the bourgeoisie itself.

But not only has the bourgeoisie forged the weapons that bring death to itself; it has also called into existence the men who are to wield those weapons – the modern working class – the proletarians.

In proportion as the bourgeoisie, i.e., capital, is developed, in the same proportion is the proletariat, the modern working class, developed – a class of laborers, who live only so long as they find work, and who find work only so long as their labor increases capital. These laborers, who must sell themselves piecemeal, are a commodity, like every other article of commerce, and are consequently exposed to all the vicissitudes of competition, to all the fluctuations of the market.

Owing to the extensive use of machinery, and to the division of labor, the work of the proletarians has lost all individual character, and, consequently, all charm for the workman. He becomes an appendage of the machine, and it is only the most simple, most monotonous, and most easily acquired knack, that is required of him. Hence, the cost of production of a workman is restricted, almost entirely, to the means of subsistence that he requires for maintenance, and for the propagation of his race. But the price of a commodity, and therefore also of labor, is equal to its cost of production. In proportion, therefore, as the repulsiveness of the work increases, the wage decreases. Nay more, in proportion as the use of machinery and division of labor increases, in the same proportion the burden of toil also increases, whether by prolongation of the working hours, by the increase of the work exacted in a given time or by increased speed of machinery, etc.

Modern Industry has converted the little workshop of the patriarchal master into the great factory of the industrial capitalist. Masses of laborers, crowded into the factory, are organized like soldiers. As privates of the industrial army they are placed under the command of a perfect hierarchy of officers and sergeants. Not only are they slaves of the bourgeois class, and of the bourgeois State; they are daily and hourly enslaved by the machine, by the overlooker, and, above all, by the individual bourgeois manufacturer himself. The more openly this despotism proclaims gain to be its end and aim, the more petty, the more hateful and the more embittering it is.

The less the skill and exertion of strength implied in manual labor, in other words, the more modern industry becomes developed, the more is the labor of men superseded by that of women. Differences of age and sex have no longer any distinctive social validity for the working class. All are instruments of labor, more or less expensive to use, according to their age and sex. [...]

But with the development of industry, the proletariat not only increases in number; it becomes concentrated in greater masses, its strength grows, and it feels that strength more. The various interests and conditions of life within the ranks of the proletariat are more and more equalized, in proportion as machinery obliterates all distinctions of labor, and nearly everywhere reduces wages to the same low level. The growing competition among the bourgeois, and the resulting commercial crises, make the wages of the workers ever more fluctuating. The increasing improvement of machinery, ever more rapidly developing, makes their livelihood more and more precarious; the collisions between individual workmen and individual bourgeois take more and more the character of collisions between two classes. Thereupon, the workers begin to form combinations (Trades' Unions) against the bourgeois; they club together in order to keep up the rate of wages; they found permanent associations in order to make provision beforehand for these occasional revolts. Here and there, the contest breaks out into riots.

Now and then the workers are victorious, but only for a time. The real fruit of their battles lies, not in the immediate result, but in the ever expanding union of the workers. This union is helped on by the improved means of communication that are created by modern industry, and that place the workers of different localities in contact with one another. It was just this contact that was needed to centralise the numerous local struggles, all of the same character, into one national struggle between classes. But every class struggle is a political struggle. And that union, to attain which the burghers of the Middle Ages, with their miserable highways, required centuries, the modern proletarian, thanks to railways, achieve in a few years.

This organization of the proletarians into a class, and, consequently into a political party, is continually being upset again by the competition between the workers themselves. But it ever rises up again, stronger, firmer, mightier. It compels legislative recognition of particular interests of the workers, by taking advantage of the divisions among the bourgeoisie itself. Thus, the ten-hours' bill in England was carried.

Altogether collisions between the classes of the old society further, in many ways, the course of development of the proletariat. The bourgeoisie finds itself involved in a constant battle. At first with the aristocracy; later on, with those portions of the bourgeoisie itself, whose interests have become antagonistic to the progress of industry; at all time with the bourgeoisie of foreign countries. In all these battles, it sees itself compelled to appeal to the proletariat, to ask for help, and thus, to drag it into the political arena. The bourgeoisie itself, therefore, supplies the proletariat with its own elements of political and general education, in other words, it furnishes the proletariat with weapons for fighting the bourgeoisie.

1.4. Ethnical Periods (1877)

Lewis Henry Morgan

The latest investigations respecting the early condition of the human race are tending to the conclusion that mankind commenced their career at the bottom of the scale and worked their way up from savagery to civilization through the slow accumulations of experimental knowledge.

As it is undeniable that portions of the human family have existed in a state of savagery, other portions in a state of barbarism, and still other portions in a state of civilization, it seems equally so that these three distinct conditions are connected with each other in a natural as well as necessary sequence of progress. Moreover, that this sequence has been historically true of the entire human family, up to the status attained by each branch respectively, is rendered probable by the conditions under which all progress occurs, and by the known advancement of several branches of the family through two or more of these conditions. An attempt will be made in the following pages to bring forward additional evidence of the rudeness of the early condition of mankind, of the gradual evolution of their mental and moral powers through experience, and of their protracted struggle with opposing obstacles while winning their way to civilization. It will be drawn in part, from the great sequence of inventions and discoveries which stretches along the entire pathway of human progress; but chiefly from domestic institutions, which express the growth of certain ideas and passions. As we re-ascend along the several lines of progress toward the primitive ages of mankind, and eliminate one after the other, in the order in which they appeared, inventions and discoveries on the one hand, and institutions on the other, we are enabled to perceive that the former stand to each other in progressive, and the latter in unfolding relations. While the former class have had a connection, more or less direct, the latter have been developed from a few primary germs of thought. Modern institutions plant their roots in the period of barbarism, into which their germs were transmitted from the previous period of savagery. They have had a lineal descent through the ages, with the streams of the blood, as well as a logical development. Two independent lines of investigations thus invite our attention. The one leads through inventions and discoveries, and the other through primary institutions. With the knowledge gained therefrom, we may hope to indicate the principal stages of human development. The proofs to be adduced will be drawn chiefly from domestic institutions; the references to achievements more strictly intellectual being general as well as subordinate.

The facts indicate the gradual formation and subsequent development of certain ideas, passions, and aspirations. Those which hold the most prominent positions may be generalized as growths of the particular ideas with which they severally stand connected. Apart from inventions and discoveries they are the following:

I. *Subsistence*	IV. *The Family*	VII. *Property*
II. *Government*	V. *Religion*	
III. *Language*	VI. *House Life and Architecture*	

First. Subsistence has been increased and perfected by a series of successive arts, introduced at long intervals of time, and connected more or less directly with inventions and discoveries.

Second. The germ of government must be sought in the organization into gentes in the Status of savagery; and followed down, through advancing forms of this institution, to the establishment of political society.

Third. Human speech seems to have been developed from the rudest and simplest forms of expression. Gesture or sign language, as intimated by Lucretius, must have preceded articulate language, as thought, preceded speech. The monosyllabical preceded the syllabical, as the latter did that of concrete words. Human intelligence, unconscious of design, evolved articulate language by utilizing the vocal sounds. This great subject, a department of knowledge by itself, does not fall within the scope of the present investigation.

Fourth. With respect to the family, the stages of its growth are embodied in systems of consanguinity and affinity, and in usages relating to marriage, by means of which, collectively, the family can be definitely traced through several successive forms.

Fifth. The growth of religious ideas is environed with such intrinsic difficulties that it may never receive a perfectly satisfactory exposition. Religion deals so largely with the imaginative and emotional nature, and consequently with such uncertain elements of knowledge, that all primitive religions are grotesque and to some extent unintelligible. This subject also falls without the plan of this work excepting as it may prompt incidental suggestions.

Sixth. House architecture, which connects itself with the form of the family and the plan of domestic life, affords a tolerably complete illustration of progress from savagery to civilization. Its growth can be traced from the hut of the savage, through the communal houses of the barbarians, to the house of the single family of civilized nations, with all the successive links by which one extreme is connected with the other. This subject will be noticed incidentally.

Lastly. The idea of property was slowly formed in the human mind, remaining nascent and feeble through immense periods of time. Springing into life in savagery, it required all the experience of this period and of the subsequent period of barbarism to develop the germ, and to prepare the human brain for the acceptance of its controlling influence. Its dominance as passion over all other passions marks the commencement of civilization. It not only led mankind to overcome the obstacles which delayed civilization, but to establish political society on the basis of territory and property. A critical knowledge of the evolution of the idea of property would embody, in some respects, the most remarkable portion of the mental history of mankind. [...]

It may be further observed that the domestic institutions of the barbarous, and even of the savage ancestors of mankind, are still exemplified in portions of the human family with such completeness that, with the exception of the strictly primitive period, the several stages of this progress are tolerably well preserved. They are seen in the organization of society upon the basis of sex, then upon the basis of kin, and finally upon the basis of territory; through the successive forms of marriage and of the family, with the systems of consanguinity thereby created; through house life and architecture; and through progress in usages with respect to the ownership and inheritance of property. [...]

The theory of human degradation to explain the existence of savages and of barbarians is no longer tenable. It came in as a corollary from the Mosaic cosmogony, and was acquiesced in from a supposed necessity which no longer exists. As a theory, it is not only incapable of explaining the existence of savages, but it is without support in the facts of human experience.

The remote ancestors of the Aryan nations presumptively passed through an experience similar to that of existing barbarous and savage tribes. Though the experience of these nations embodies all the information necessary to illustrate the periods of civilization, both ancient and modern, together with a part of that in the later period of barbarism, their anterior experience must be deduced, in the main, from the traceable connection between the elements of their existing institutions and inventions, and similar elements still preserved in those of savage and barbarous tribes.

It may be remarked finally that the experience of mankind has run in nearly uniform channels; that human necessities in similar conditions have been substantially the same; and that the operations of the mental principle have been uniform in virtue of the specific identity of the brain of all the races of mankind. This, however, is but a part of the explanation of uniformity in results. The germs of the principal institutions and arts of life were developed while man was still a savage. To a very great extent the experience of the subsequent periods of barbarism and of civilization has been expended in the further development of these original conceptions. Wherever a connection can be traced on different continents between a present institution and a common germ, the derivation of the people themselves from a common original stock is implied. [...]

The period of savagery, of the early part of which very little is known, may be divided, provisionally, into three sub-periods. These may be named respectively the *Older,* the *Middle,* and the *Later* period of savagery; and the condition of society in each, respectively, may be distinguished as the *Lower,* the *Middle,* and the *Upper Status* of savagery.

In like manner, the period of barbarism divides naturally into three sub-periods, which will be called, respectively, the *Older,* the *Middle,* and the *Later* period of barbarism; and the condition of society in each, respectively, will be distinguished as the *Lower,* the *Middle,* and the *Upper Status* of barbarism.

It is difficult, if not impossible, to find such tests of progress to mark the commencement of these several periods as will be found absolute *in* their application, and without exceptions upon all the continents. Neither is it necessary, for the purpose in hand, that exceptions should not exist. It will be sufficient if the principal tribes of mankind can be classified, according to the degree of their relative progress, into conditions which can be recognized as distinct. [...]

Another advantage of fixing definite ethnical periods is the direction of special investigation to those tribes and nations which afford the best exemplification of each *status,* with the view of making each both standard and illustrative. Some tribes and families have been left in geographical isolation to work out the problems of progress by original mental effort; and have, consequently, retained their arts and institutions pure and homogeneous; while those of other tribes and nations have been adulterated through external influence. Thus, while Africa was and is an ethnical chaos of savagery and barbarism, Australia and Polynesia were in savagery, pure and simple, with the arts and institutions belonging to that condition. In the like manner, the Indian family of America, unlike any other existing family, exemplified the condition of mankind in three successive ethnical periods. In the undisturbed possession of a great continent, of common descent, and with homogeneous institutions, they illustrated, when discovered, each of these conditions, and especially those of the Lower and of the Middle Status of barbarism, more elaborately and completely than any other portion of mankind. The far northern Indians and some of the coast tribes of North and South America were in the Upper Status of savagery; the partially Village Indians east of the Mississippi were in the Lower Status of barbarism, and the Village Indians of North and South America were in the Middle Status. Such an opportunity to recover full and minute information of the course of human experience and progress in developing their arts and institutions through these successive conditions has not been offered within the historical period. It must be added that it has been indifferently improved. Our greatest deficiencies relate to the last period named. [...]

Commencing, then, with the Australians and Polynesians, following with the American Indian tribes, and concluding with the Roman and Grecian, who afford the highest exemplifications respectively of the six great stages of human progress, the sum of their united experiences may be supposed fairly to represent that of the human family from the Middle Status of savagery to the end of ancient civilization. Consequently, the Aryan nations will find the type of the condition of their remote ancestors, when in savagery, in that of the Australians and Polynesians; when in the Lower Status of barbarism in that of the partially Village Indians of America; and when in the Middle Status in that of the Village Indians, with which their own experience in the Upper Status directly connects. So essentially identical are the arts, institutions and mode of life in the same status upon all the continents, that the archaic form of the principal domestic institutions of the Greeks and Romans must even now be sought in the corresponding institutions of the American aborigines, as will be shown, in the course of this volume. This fact forms a part of the accumulating evidence tending to show that the principal institutions of mankind have been developed from a few primary germs of thought; and that the course and *manner* of their development was predetermined, as well as restricted within narrow limits of divergence, by the natural logic of the human mind and the necessary limitations of its powers. Progress has been found to be substantially the same in kind in tribes and nations inhabiting different and even disconnected continents, while in the same status, with deviations from uniformity *in* particular instances produced by special causes. The argument when extended tends to establish the unity of origin of mankind.

In studying the condition of tribes and nations in these several ethnical periods, we are dealing substantially with the ancient history and condition of our own remote ancestors.

1.5. Afternoon Session, June 29: Speeches at the Founding Convention of the Industrial Workers of the World (1905)

Lucy E. Parsons

I wish to state to you that I have taken the floor because no other woman has responded, and I feel that it would not be out of place for me to say in my poor way a few words about this movement. We, the women of this country, have no ballot even if we wished to use it, and the only way that we can be represented is to take a man to represent us. You men have made such a mess of it in representing us that we have not much confidence in asking you; and I for one feel very backward in asking the men to represent me. We have no ballot, but we have our labor. I think it is August Bebel, in his Woman in the Past, Present and Future – a book that should be read by every woman that works for wages – Bebel says that men have been slaves throughout all the ages, but that woman's condition has been worse, for she has been the slave of a slave.

There was never a greater truth uttered. We are the slaves of the slaves. We are exploited more ruthlessly than men. Wherever wages are to be reduced the capitalist class use women to reduce them, and if there is anything that you men should do in the future it is to organize the women. And I say that if the women had inaugurated a boycott of the State Street stores since the teamsters' strike, the stores would have surrendered long ago. I do not stand before you to brag. I had no man connected with that strike to make it of interest to me to boycott the stores, but I have not bought one penny's worth there since that strike was inaugurated. I intended to boycott all of them as one individual at least, so it is important to educate the women.

Now, I wish to show my sisters here that we fasten the chains of slavery upon our sisters, sometimes unwittingly, when we go down to the department store and look around so cheap. When we come to reflect it simply means the robbery of our sisters, for we know that the things cannot be made for such prices and give women who made them fair wages. I wish to say that I have attended many conventions in the twenty-seven years since I came here to Chicago, a young girl, so full of life and animation and hope. [...]

But when you go out of this hall, when you have laid aside your enthusiasm, then comes the solid work. Are you going out of here with your minds made up that the class which we call ourselves, revolutionary Socialists so-called – that class, is organized to meet organized capital with the millions at its command? It has many weapons to fight us. First, it has money. Then, it has legislative tools. Then, it has armories; and last, it has the gallows. We call ourselves revolutionists. Do you know what the capitalists mean to do to you revolutionists? I simply throw these hints out that you, young people may become reflective and know what you have to face at the first, and then it will give you strength. I am not here to cause any discouragement, but simply to encourage you to go on in your grand work.

Now, that is the solid foundation that I hope this organization will be built on; that it may be built not like a house upon the sand, that when the waves of adversity come it may go over into the ocean of oblivion; but that it shall be built upon a strong, granite, hard foundation; a foundation made up of the hearts and aspirations of the men and women of this twentieth century, who have set their minds, their hands, their hearts and their heads against the past with all its miserable poverty, with its wage-slaves, with its children ground into dividends, with its miners away down under the earth and with never the light of sunshine, and with its women selling the holy name of womanhood for a day's board. I hope we understand that this organization has set its face against that iniquity, and that it has set its eyes to the rising star of liberty, that means fraternity, solidarity, the universal brotherhood of man. I hope that while politics have been mentioned here – I am not one of those who, because a man or woman disagrees with me, cannot act with them – I am glad and proud to say I am too broad-minded to say they are a fakir or fool or a fraud because they disagree with me.

My view may be narrow and theirs may be broad; but I do say to those who have intimated politics here as being necessary or a part of this organization, that I do not impute to them dishonesty or impure motives. But as I understand the call for this convention, politics had no place here; it was simply to be an economic organization, and I hope for the good of this organization that when we go away from this hall, and our comrades go some to the west, some to the east, some to the north and some to the south, while some remain in Chicago, and all spread this light over this broad land and carry the message of what this convention has done, that there will be no room for politics at all.

There may be room for politics; I have nothing to say about that; but it is a bread and butter question, an economic issue, upon which the fight must be made. Now, what do we mean when we say revolutionary Socialist? We mean that the land shall belong to the landless, the tools to the toiler, and the products to the producers. Now, let us analyze that for just a moment, before you applaud me. First, the land belongs to the landless. Is there a single land owner in this country who owns his land by the constitutional rights given by the constitution of the United States who will allow you to vote it away from him? I am not such a fool as to believe it. We say, "The tools belong to the toiler." They are owned by the capitalist class. Do you believe they will allow you to go into the halls of the legislature and simply say, "Be it enacted that on and after a certain day the capitalist shall no longer own the tools and the factories and the places of industry, the ships that plow the ocean and our lakes?"

Do you believe that they will submit? I do not. We say, "The product belongs to the producers." It belongs to the capitalist class as their legal property. Do you think that they will allow you to vote them away from them by passing a law and saying, "Be it enacted that on and after a certain day Mr. Capitalist shall be dispossessed?" You may, but I do not believe it. Hence, when you roll under your tongue the expression that you are revolutionists, remember what that word means. It means a revolution that shall turn all these things over where they belong – to the wealth producers.

Now, how shall the wealth-producers come into possession of them? I believe that if every man and every woman who works, or who toils in the mines, the mills, the workshops, the fields, the factories and the farms in our broad America should decide in their minds that they shall have that which of right belongs to them, and that no idler shall live upon their toil, and when your new organization, your economic organization, shall declare as man to man and woman to woman, as brothers and sisters, that you are determined that you will possess these things, then there is no army that is large enough to overcome you, for you yourselves constitute the army. Now, when you have decided that you will take possession of these things, there will not need to be one gun fired or one scaffold erected.

[…] Nature has been lavish to her children. She has placed in this Earth all the material of wealth that is necessary to make men and women happy. She has given us brains to go into her storehouse and bring from its recesses all that is necessary. She has given us these two hands and these brains to manufacture them on a parallel with all other civilizations.

There is just one thing we lack, and we have only ourselves to blame if we do not become free. We simply lack the intelligence to take possession of that hope, and I feel that the men and women who constitute a convention like this can come together and organize that intelligence. I feel that you will at least listen to me, and maybe you will disagree with it.

I wish to say that my conception of the future method of taking possession of this Earth is that of the general strike; that is my conception of it. The trouble with all the strikes in the past has been this: the workingmen, like the teamsters of our cities, these hard-working teamsters, strike and go out and starve. Their children starve. Their wives get discouraged. Some feel that they have to go out and beg for relief, and to get a little coal to keep the children warm, or a little bread to keep the wife from starving, or a little something to keep the spark of life in them so that they can remain wage-slaves. That is the way with the strikes in the past.

My conception of the strike of the future is not to strike and go out and starve, but to strike and remain in and take possession of the necessary property of production. If anyone is to starve – I do not say it is necessary – let it be the capitalist class. They have starved us long enough, while they have had wealth and luxury and all that is necessary. You men and women should be imbued with the spirit that is now displayed in far-off Russia and far-off Siberia where we thought the spark of manhood and womanhood had been crushed out of them. Let us take example from them.

[…] They know that where the red flag has been raised whoever enroll themselves beneath that flag recognize the universal brotherhood of man; they recognize that the red current that flows through the veins of all humanity is identical, that the ideas of all humanity are identical; that those who raise the red flag, it matters not where, whether on the sunny plains of China, or on the sun-beaten hills of Africa, or on the far-off snow-capped shores of the north, or in Russia or America – that they all belong to the human family and have an identity of interest. That is what they know.

So when we come to decide, let us sink such differences as nationality, religion, politics, and set our eyes eternally and forever toward the rising star of the industrial republic of labor; remembering that we have left the old behind and have set our faces toward the future. There is no power on Earth that can stop men and women who are determined to be free at all hazards. There is no power on Earth so great as the power of intellect. It moves the world and it moves the Earth.

1.6. The Protestant Ethic and the Spirit of Capitalism (1905)

Max Weber

INTRODUCTION

A product of modern European civilization, studying any problem of universal history, is bound to ask himself to what combination of circumstances the fact should be attributed that in Western civilization, and in Western civilization only, cultural phenomena have appeared which (as we like to think) lie in a line of development having *universal* significance and value.

Only in the West does science exist at a stage of development which we recognize today as valid. Empirical knowledge, reflection on problems of the cosmos and of life, philosophical and theological wisdom of the most profound sort, are not confined to it, though in the case of the last the full development of a systematic theology must be credited to Christianity under the influence of Hellenism, since there were only fragments in Islam and in a few Indian sects. In short, knowledge and observation of great refinement have existed elsewhere, above all in India, China, Babylonia, Egypt. But in Babylonia and elsewhere astronomy lacked – which makes its development all the more astounding – the mathematical foundation which it first received from the Greeks. The Indian geometry had no rational proof; that was another product of the Greek intellect, also the creator of mechanics and physics. The Indian natural sciences, though well developed in observation, lacked the method of experiment, which was, apart from beginnings in antiquity, essentially a product of the Renaissance, as was the modern laboratory. Hence medicine, especially in India, though highly developed in empirical technique, lacked a biological and particularly a biochemical foundation. A rational chemistry has been absent from all areas of culture except the West. [...]

[Not only science, but also law, art, architecture, and government have all reached their highest stages only in Europe.] And the same is true of the most fateful force in our modern life, capitalism. The impulse to acquisition, pursuit of gain, of money, of the greatest possible amount of money, has in itself nothing to do with capitalism. This impulse exists and has existed among waiters, physicians, coachmen, artists, prostitutes, dishonest officials, soldiers, nobles, crusaders, gamblers, and beggars. One may say that it has been common to all sorts and conditions of men at all times and in all countries of the earth, wherever the objective possibility of it is or has been given. It should be taught in the kindergarten of cultural history that this naïve idea of capitalism must be given up once and for all. Unlimited greed for gain is not in the least identical with capitalism, and is still less its spirit. Capitalism *may* even be identical with the restraint, or at least a rational tempering, of this irrational impulse. But capitalism is identical with the pursuit of profit, and forever *renewed* profit, by means of continuous, rational, capitalistic enterprise. For it must be so: in a wholly capitalistic order of society, an individual capitalistic enterprise which did not take advantage of its opportunities for profitmaking would be doomed to extinction. [...]

CHAPTER 1: RELIGIOUS AFFILIATION AND SOCIAL STRATIFICATION

A glance at the occupational statistics of any country of mixed religious composition brings to light with remarkable frequency a situation which has several times provoked discussion in the Catholic press and literature, and in Catholic congresses in Germany, namely, the fact that business leaders and owners of capital, as well as the higher grades of skilled labor, and even more the higher technically and commercially trained personnel of modern enterprises, are overwhelmingly Protestant. This is true not only in cases where the difference in religion coincides with one of nationality and thus of cultural development, as in Eastern Germany between Germans and Poles. The same thing is shown in the figures of religious affiliation almost wherever capitalism, at the time of its great expansion, has had a free hand to alter the social distribution of the population in accordance with its needs, and to determine its occupational structure. The more freedom it has had, the more clearly is the effect shown. It is true that the greater relative participation of Protestants in the ownership of capital, in management, and the upper ranks of labor in great modern industrial and commercial enterprises, may in part be explained in terms of historical circumstances which extend far back into the past, and in which religious affiliation is not a cause of the economic conditions, but to a certain extent appears to be a result of them. Participation in the above economic function usually involves some previous ownership of capital; and generally an expensive education; often both. These are today largely dependent on the possession of inherited wealth, or at least on a certain degree of material well-being. A number of those sections of the old Empire which were most highly developed economically and most favored by natural resources and situation, in particular a majority of the wealthy towns, went over to Protestantism in the sixteenth century. The results of that circumstance favor the Protestants even today in their struggle for economic existence. There arises thus the historical question: why were the districts of highest economic development at the same time particularly favorable to a revolution in the Church? The answer is by no means so simple as one might think.

The emancipation from economic traditionalism appears, no doubt, to be a factor which would greatly strengthen the tendency to doubt the sanctity of the religious tradition, as of all traditional authorities. But it is necessary to note, what has often been forgotten, that the Reformation meant not the elimination of the Church's control over everyday life, but rather the substitution of a new form of control for the previous one. It meant the repudiation of a control which was very lax, at that time scarcely perceptible in practice, and hardly more than formal, in favor of a regulation of the whole of conduct which, penetrating to all departments of private and public life, was infinitely burdensome and earnestly enforced. [...]

CHAPTER 2: THE SPIRIT OF CAPITALISM

[...] "For six pounds a year you may have the use of one hundred pounds, provided you are a man of known prudence and honesty.

"He that spends a groat a day idly, spends idly above six pounds a year, which is the price for the use of one hundred pounds.

"He that wastes idly a groat's worth of his time per day, one day with another, wastes the privilege of using one hundred pounds each day.

"He that idly loses five shillings' worth of time, loses five shillings, and might as prudently throw five shillings into the sea.

"He that loses five shillings, not only loses that sum, but all the advantage that might be made by turning it in dealing, which by the time that a young man becomes old, will amount to a considerable sum of money."[1]

It is Benjamin Franklin who preaches to us in these sentences [...]. That is the spirit of capitalism which here speaks in characteristic fashion, no one will doubt, however little we may wish to claim that everything which could be understood as pertaining to that spirit is contained in it. Let us pause a moment to consider this passage, the philosophy of which [Ferdinand] Kürnberger sums up in the words, "They make tallow out of cattle and money out of men." The peculiarity of this philosophy of avarice appears to be the ideal of the honest man of recognized credit, and above all the idea of a duty of the individual toward the increase of his capital, which is assumed as an end in itself. Truly what is here preached is not simply a means of making one's way in the world, but a peculiar ethic. The infraction of its rules is treated not as foolishness but as forgetfulness of duty. That is the essence of the matter. It is not mere business astuteness, that sort of thing is common enough, it is an ethos. *This* is quality which interests us. [...]

In fact, the *summum bonum* of this ethic, the earning of more and more money, combined with the strict avoidance of all spontaneous enjoyment of life, is above all completely

---

1 The final passage is from *Necessary Hints to Those That Would Be Rich* (written 1736, Works, Sparks edition, II, p. 80), the rest from *Advice to a Young Tradesman* (written 1748, Sparks edition, II, pp. 87 ff.). The italics in the text are Franklin's.

devoid of any eudæmonistic, not to say hedonistic, admixture. It is thought of so purely as an end in itself, that from the point of view of the happiness of, or utility to, the single individual, it appears entirely transcendental and absolutely irrational. Man is dominated by the making of money, by acquisition as the ultimate purpose of his life. Economic acquisition is no longer subordinated to man as the means for the satisfaction of his material needs. This reversal of what we should call the natural relationship, so irrational from a naïve point of view, is evidently as definitely a leading principle of capitalism as it is foreign to all peoples not under capitalistic influence. At the same time it expresses a type of feeling which is closely connected with certain religious ideas. If we thus ask, *why* should "money be made out of men," Benjamin Franklin himself, although he was a colourless deist, answers in his autobiography with a quotation from the Bible, which his strict Calvinistic father drummed into him again and again in his youth: "Seest thou a man diligent in his business? He shall stand before kings" (Prov. xxii. 29). The earning of money within the modern economic order is, so long as it is done legally, the result and the expression of virtue and proficiency in a calling; and this virtue and proficiency are, as it is now not difficult to see, the real Alpha and Omega of Franklin's ethic, as expressed in the passages we have quoted, as well as in all his works without exception. [...]

[The] origin and history of such ideas [are] much more complex than the theorists of the superstructure [such as Marx and Engels] suppose. The spirit of capitalism, in the sense in which we are using the term, had to fight its way to supremacy against a whole world of hostile forces. A state of mind such as that expressed in the passages we have quoted from Franklin, and which called forth the applause of a whole people, would both in ancient times and in the Middle Ages have been proscribed as the lowest sort of avarice and as an attitude entirely lacking in self-respect. [...]

The universal reign of absolute unscrupulousness in the pursuit of selfish interests by the making of money has been a specific characteristic of precisely those countries whose bourgeois-capitalistic development, measured according to Occidental standards, has remained backward. As every employer knows, the lack of *coscienziosità* of the labourers of such countries, for instance Italy as compared with Germany, has been, and to a certain extent still is, one of the principal obstacles to their capitalistic development. Capitalism cannot make use of the labor of those who practice the doctrine of undisciplined *liberum arbitrium*, any more than it can make use of the business man who seems absolutely unscrupulous in his dealings with others, as we can learn from Franklin. Hence the difference does not lie in the degree of development of any impulse to make money. The *auri sacra fames* is as old as the history of man. But we shall see that those who submitted to it without reserve as an uncontrolled impulse, such as the Dutch sea-captain who "would go through hell for gain, even though he scorched his sails," were by no means the representatives of that attitude of mind from which the specifically modern capitalist spirit as a mass phenomenon is derived, and that is what matters. At all periods of history, wherever it was possible, there has been ruthless acquisition, bound to no ethical norms whatever. Like war and piracy, trade has often been unrestrained in its relations with foreigners and those outside the group. The double ethic has permitted here what was forbidden in dealings among brothers.

Section One Glossary

Herbert Spencer   A leading figure in social evolutionary theory, Spencer is attributed with the phrase "survival of the fittest" to explain inequality by way of putatively evolutionary processes.

idealist   An approach to understanding human society that prioritizes human psychology as the basis for cultural beliefs and sociopolitical organization.

materialist   An approach to understanding human society that prioritizes economic processes as the bases for cultural beliefs and sociopolitical organization.

social Darwinism   The belief that "less fit" social groups and cultural practices would eventually die off due to the evolutionary force of natural selection. In anthropology, this idea was promulgated most notably by English anthropologist Herbert Spencer.

social or cultural evolutionists   Promoters of the belief that Darwinian principles of biological evolution could be applied to human societies and cultures. Social and cultural evolutionists largely believed that not only did societies change over time but they changed in a linear, progressive, predictable direction. This belief is called unilineal cultural evolution. Unilineal cultural evolution has been largely discredited in anthropology, though there is a strong popular tendency to view human societies as naturally progressive over time.

white supremacism   The belief that people are divisible into races and that the white race is superior to all other races, and the creation of social structures based on that premise. White supremacist ideologies have historically been used to justify dispossession, enslavement, and subjugation of non-white groups.

SECTION TWO

On Methods of Fieldwork

THE SOCIAL CONTEXT

The nineteenth-century writings of William Apess, Karl Marx, Frederick Douglass, and Lucy Parsons envisioned social change, and the first three decades of the twentieth century wrought profound changes – just not necessarily those they had predicted. In the "West," mass migrations of Europeans, World War I (1914–1918), the Russian Revolution (1917–1923), and the Great Depression (1929–1930s) threw **hegemonic** assumptions about the fixity of culture, power, and capitalism into doubt. Meanwhile, the women's suffrage movement won voting rights for (at least some) women in scores of countries by the 1920s and 1930s. In the United States, millions of southern Blacks fled extreme poverty and violence in the Jim Crow South to seek manufacturing work in burgeoning industrial cities of the North. And European imperialists, temporarily stymied by wars for national independence in the Western Hemisphere, seized land and people across Africa, the Middle East, and Southern and Eastern Asia.

Scientific racism not only survived such changes but thrived in the West, particularly in the United States. An emergent science of **eugenics** drew on the most pernicious claims of social evolutionism to specify and strengthen racial classifications that were hierarchically ordered from superior to inferior. For example, US eugenicists determined that immigrants from Italy, Poland, Hungary, and Russia were "defective stock" inferior to the "Nordic races" of Northern and Western Europe, and they used this classification system to extensively limit US immigration in 1924. The scholars in this section intervened in this sociopolitical landscape to challenge eugenicist ideology and introduce both scientific rigor and relative perspective to anthropological study.

THE CONVERSATION

Often known as "the Boasians" or "the ethnographers," these writers were part of a new generation of US anthropologists who rejected social evolutionary theory and advocated for a "four-field" approach to anthropological study. While they retained a concern with explaining human sameness and difference, ethnographers emphasized the importance of prolonged fieldwork, communicating with people in their first language, and understanding the particular histories of social groups. A logical extension of this approach is **cultural relativism** – an emphasis on understanding cultural practices from the point of view of those who practice them, rather than through the anthropologist's worldview. Relatedly, the ethnographers preferred to work inductively from in-depth knowledge of particular human societies rather than deductively from grand theory. While Arthur C. Parker was not an ethnographer but an archaeologist, you will see that his attention to historic specificity and cultural detail complements Boasian thought. All five scholars we include here also belonged to communities targeted by scientific racism and dedicated much of their professional life to challenging racist ideologies and structures in the United States.

In the pieces we have chosen for this section, anthropologists emphasize the importance of rigorous methodology in anthropological research and/or the historic and cultural specificities of the contexts in which they work. Reading 2.1, by linguist Edward Sapir, argues that linguistic symbols are arbitrary and that languages are shaped by people's meaningful interactions with their environments. In contrast with social evolutionist classifications of languages from savage to civilized, then, Sapir shows that language develops in a particular cultural context and that linguistic similarities are due not to parallel evolution but to descent from a common language, diffusion, or coincidence. This approach is known as linguistic relativism, or the Sapir-Whorf hypothesis, and is named for Sapir and his student, Benjamin Whorf. Sapir's work on linguistic relativism developed under the influence of Boas at Columbia, and Sapir was a central figure in the establishment of linguistic anthropology as one of the four fields of American anthropology.

Our second selection is written by Arthur C. Parker, an archaeologist who provides detailed description of elements of Iroquois culture, including pottery, tools, mythology, and social organization (we had to cut much of the detail to fit it here). Parker's attention to Iroquois history and material culture allows Iroquois society to stand on its own as an anthropological case without attribution to a particular stage in an evolutionist system.

Our third piece is by Franz Boas, who is often considered the father of American anthropology. In this selection from "The Methods of Ethnology," Boas discredits social evolution for its faulty reasoning, unproven claims, **ethnocentrism,** and ultimately scientific invalidity. He asserts, "As soon as we admit that the hypothesis of a uniform evolution has to be proved before it can be accepted, the whole structure loses its foundation." We like to imagine Boas scoffing at the evolutionists: "You didn't *discover* stages of social evolution – you just made them up!" In contrast, Boas advocates for an ethnographic approach to understanding human cultures.

Reading 2.4 is by Boas's student Margaret Mead, who challenges the validity of intelligence testing based on race, also by taking on its faulty methodology. Mead argues that while the complications inherent to testing "intelligence" are well known, less known but at least as problematic is the notion that one can classify test-takers according to their "race." While Mead became well known for challenging hegemonic perspectives on gender, this piece represents an example of how ethnographers used anthropological methods to challenge pervasive racist ideologies, as well.

Our final piece by Zora Neale Hurston, also a student of Boas, exemplifies one of the main tenets of Boasian ethnography: in-depth cultural and linguistic familiarity. This essay, excerpted from Neale Hurston's book *Mules and Men*, is also a pioneering example of what today we would call "native anthropology" or "auto-ethnography," in which anthropologists study a community they belong to and use their experiences as a meaningful source of ethnographic data. As you read, pay special attention to how Neale Hurston conveys African-American language and dialect to communicate a particular cultural ambience of her hometown of Eatonville, Florida.

THREE QUESTIONS FOR THE READINGS

1 What do these scholars suggest about anthropology as a science? What qualities make for good, reliable research?
2 Given these methods, what is knowable about human societies? What is unknowable?
3 Boas and Mead were critiqued, even attacked, for their work. What about the arguments they make render them so politically threatening?

ON THE COMPANION WEBSITE

An Ojibwe perspective on the Great Lakes, more about Zora Neale Hurston, additional readings, and more.

www.anthropologicaltheory.com

2.1. Language and Environment (1912)

Edward Sapir

[W]e may expect to find two sets of environmental factors reflected in language, assuming for the moment that language is materially influenced by the environmental background of its speakers. Properly speaking, of course, the physical environment is reflected in language only in so far as it has been influenced by social factors. The mere existence, for instance, of a certain type of animal in the physical environment of a people does not suffice to give rise to a linguistic symbol referring to it. It is necessary that the animal be known by the members of the group in common and that they have some interest, however slight, in it before the language of the community is called upon to make reference to this particular element of the physical environment. In other words, so far as language is concerned, all environmental influence reduces at last analysis to the influence of social environment. Nevertheless, it is practical to keep apart such social influences as proceed more or less directly from the physical environment, and those that cannot be easily connected with it. Language may be influenced in one of three ways: in regard to its subject matter or content, i.e., in regard to the vocabulary; in regard to its phonetic system, i.e., the system of sounds with which it operates in the building of words; and in regard to its grammatical form, i.e., in regard to the formal processes and the logical or psychological classifications made use of in speech. Morphology, or the formal structure of words, and syntax, or the methods employed in combining words into larger units or sentences, are the two main aspects of grammatical form.

It is the vocabulary of a language that most clearly reflects the physical and social environment of its speakers. The complete vocabulary of a language may indeed be looked upon as a complex inventory of all the ideas, interests, and occupations that take up the attention of the community, and were such a complete thesaurus of the language of a given tribe at our disposal, we might to a large extent infer the character of the physical environment and the characteristics of the culture of the people making use of it. It is not difficult to find examples of languages whose vocabulary thus bears the stamp of the physical environment in which the speakers are placed. This is particularly true of the languages of primitive peoples, for among these, culture has not attained such a degree of complexity as to imply practically universal interests. From this point of view the vocabulary of primitive languages may be compared to the vocabularies of particular sections of the population of civilized peoples. The characteristic vocabulary of a coast tribe, such as the Nootka Indians, with its precise terms for many species of marine animals, vertebrate and invertebrate, might be compared to the vocabulary of such European fisher-folk as the Basques of southwestern France and northern Spain. In contrast to such coast peoples may be mentioned the inhabitants of a desert plateau, like the Southern Paiute of Arizona, Nevada, and Utah. In the vocabulary of this tribe we find adequate provision made for many topographical features that would in some cases seem almost too precise to be of practical value. Some of the topographical terms of this language that have been collected are: divide, ledge, sand flat, semicircular valley, circular valley or hollow, spot of level ground in mountains surrounded by ridges, plain valley surrounded by mountains, plain, desert, knoll, plateau, canyon without water, canyon with creek, wash or gutter, gulch, slope of mountain or canyon wall receiving sunlight, shaded slope of mountain or canyon wall, rolling country intersected by several small hill-ridges, and many others.

In the case of the specialized vocabularies of both Nootka and Southern Paiute, it is important to note that it is not merely the fauna or topographical features of the country as such that are reflected, but rather the interest of the people in such environmental features. Were the Nootka Indians dependent for their food supply primarily on land hunting and vegetable products, despite their proximity to the sea, there is little doubt that their vocabulary would not be as thoroughly saturated as it is with sea lore. Similarly, it is quite evident from the presence in Paiute of such topographical terms as have been listed, that accurate reference to topography is a necessary thing to dwellers in an inhospitable semiarid region; so purely practical a need as definitely locating a spring might well require reference to several features of topographical detail. [...] Another instructive example of how largely interest determines the character of a vocabulary is afforded by the terms in several Indian languages for sun and moon. While we find it necessary to distinguish sun and moon, not a few tribes content themselves with a single word for both, the exact reference being left to the context. If we complain that so vague a term fails to do justice to an essential natural difference, the Indian might well retaliate by pointing to the *omnium gatherum* character of our term "weed" as contrasted with his own more precise plant vocabulary. Everything naturally depends on the point of view as determined by interest. Bearing this in mind, it becomes evident that the presence or absence of general terms is to a large extent dependent on the negative or positive character of the interest in the elements of environment involved. The more necessary a particular culture finds it to make distinctions within a given range of phenomena, the less likely the existence of a general term covering the range. On the other hand, the more indifferent culturally are the elements, the more likely that they will all be embraced in a single term of general application. [...]

We have just seen that the careful study of a vocabulary leads to inferences as to the physical and social environment of those who use the vocabulary; furthermore, that the relatively transparent or untransparent character of the vocabulary itself may lead us to infer as to the degree of familiarity that has been obtained with various elements of this environment. Several students, notably Schrader, in dealing with Indo-Germanic material, have attempted to make a still more ambitious use of the study of vocabularies of related languages. By selecting such words as are held in common by all, or at least several, of a group of genetically related languages, attempts have been made to gather some idea of the vocabulary of the hypothetical language of which the forms of speech investigated are later varieties, and in this way to get some idea of the range of concepts possessed by the speakers of the reconstructed language. We are here dealing with a kind of linguistic archeology. [...] The only pity is that in comparing languages that have diverged very considerably from each other, and the reconstructed prototype of which must therefore point to a remote past, too little material bearing on the most interesting phases of culture can generally be obtained. We do not need extended linguistic comparison to convince us that at a remote period in the past people had hands and fathers, though it would be interesting to discover whether they knew of the use of salt, for instance. Naturally the possibility of secondary borrowing of a word apparently held in common must always be borne in mind. Yet, on the whole, adequate knowledge of the phonology and morphology of the languages concerned will generally enable a careful analyst to keep apart the native from the borrowed elements. [...]

[...] There is a difference between the rich, conceptually ramified vocabulary of a language like English or French and that of any typical primitive group, corresponding in large measure to that which obtains between the complex culture of the English-speaking or French-speaking peoples of Europe and America with its vast array of specialized interests, and the relatively simple undifferentiated culture of the primitive group. Such variability of vocabulary, as reflecting social environment, obtains in time as well as place; in other words, the stock of cultural concepts and therefore also the corresponding vocabulary become constantly enriched and ramified with the increase within a group of cultural complexity. That a vocabulary should thus to a great degree reflect cultural complexity is practically self-evident, for a vocabulary, that is, the subject matter of a language, aims at any given time to serve as a set of symbols referring to the culture background of the group. [...]

[...] There are many cases, to be sure, of distinct languages with comparable phonetic systems spoken over a continuous territory of fairly uniform physical characteristics, yet in all such cases it can readily be shown that we are dealing not with the direct influence of the environment itself, but with psychological factors of a much subtler character, comparable perhaps to such as operate in the diffusion of cultural elements. Thus, the phonetic systems of Tlingit, Haida, Tsimshian, Kwakiutl, and Salish are not similar because [they belong] to languages whose speakers are placed in about the same set of environmental conditions, but merely because these speakers are geographically contiguous to each other and hence capable of exerting mutual psychological influence.

Leaving these general considerations on the lack of correlation between physical environment and a phonetic system as a whole we may point to several striking instances, on the one hand, of phonetic resemblances between languages spoken by groups living in widely different environments and belonging to widely different cultural strata, on the other hand, of no less striking phonetic differences that obtain between languages spoken in adjoining regions of identical or similar environment and sharing in the same culture. These examples will serve to emphasize the point already made. The use of pitch accent as a significant element of speech is found in Chinese and neighboring languages of southeastern Asia, Ewe and other languages of western Africa, Hottentot in South Africa, Swedish, Tewa in New Mexico, and Takelma in southwestern Oregon. In this set of instances, we have illustrated practically the whole gamut of environmental and cultural conditions. Nasalized vowels occur not only in French and Portuguese, but also in Ewe, Iroquois, and Siouan. "Fortis" consonants, i.e., stop consonants pronounced with simultaneous closure and subsequent release of glottal cords, are found not only in many languages of America west of the Rockies, but also in Siouan, and in Georgian and other languages of the Caucasus. Glottal stops as significant elements of speech are found not only plentifully illustrated in many, perhaps most, American Indian languages, but also in Danish and in Lettish, one of the Letto-Slavic languages of Western Russia. [...]

[...] We seem then, perhaps reluctantly, forced to admit that, apart from the reflection of environment in the vocabulary of a language, there is nothing in the language itself that can be shown to be directly associated with environment. One wonders why, if such be the case, so large a number of distinct phonetic systems and types of linguistic morphology are found in various parts of the world. Perhaps the whole problem of the relation between culture and environment generally, on the one hand, and language, on the other, may be furthered somewhat by a consideration simply of the rate of change or development of both. Linguistic features are necessarily less capable of rising into the consciousness of the speakers than traits of culture. Without here attempting to go into an analysis of this psychological difference between the two sets of phenomena, it would seem to follow that changes in culture are the result, to at least a considerable extent, of conscious processes or of processes more easily made conscious, whereas those of language are to be explained, if explained at all, as due to the more minute action of psychological factors beyond the control of will or reflection. If this be true, and there seems every reason to believe that it is, we must conclude that cultural change and linguistic change do not move along parallel lines and hence do not tend to stand in a close causal relation. This point of view makes it quite legitimate to grant, if necessary, the existence at some primitive stage in the past of a more definite association between environment and linguistic form than can now be posited anywhere, for the different character and rate of change in linguistic and cultural phenomena, conditioned by the very nature of those phenomena, would in the long run very materially disturb and ultimately entirely eliminate such an association.

2.2. The Origin of the Iroquois as Suggested by Their Archeology (1916)

Arthur C. Parker

The centers of prehistoric Iroquoian occupations, recognized as such by the objects known to archeologists as Iroquoian, are: (1) the St. Lawrence basin with Montreal as a center; (2) the region between Georgian bay and Ontario with Lake Simcoe as a center; (3) the Niagara peninsula in Ontario following the Grand river; (4) the Genesee river-Finger lake region; (5) Chautauqua county, stretching across the Pennsylvania neck into Ohio; (6) the highlands east of Lake Ontario in Jefferson county; (7) Oneida, Madison, and Onondaga counties; and (8) the Susquehanna about Elmira. Circles of various circumferences may be drawn from these centers intercepting smaller centers. This plan of approximating areas is only a scheme to fix the localities in our minds, and no attempt is made to make them independent localities with definite boundaries. The contour of the land, streams, lakes, lines of travel, and danger from enemies largely determined the early limitations of occupied territory.

With these data in mind, we wish now to inquire which of these centers are the oldest and if there is any possible means of determining the causes that made Iroquoian material culture differ from the surrounding Algonkian. We wish to inquire, as others have before us, whence the Iroquois stock came into these centers and what clue may be found showing a migration from earlier centers. We wish to inquire just how definitely valuable are Iroquoian objects, as they are now recognized, in determining a migration from other regions. [...]

The older theory that all the Iroquois originated or had their early home along the St. Lawrence about Montreal is not entirely without serious flaws. I believe from archeological evidence that certain Iroquoian tribes never came from the St. Lawrence region, for example the Seneca. The Seneca and Erie divisions seem to have been as closely allied in western New York as the Onondaga and Mohawk were in northern and eastern New York. The Mohawk (or Laurentian Iroquois) never agreed with the Senecan division and there indeed seems to have been a long period of separation which made these two dialects more unlike than all the others of the five. It would seem that the early band of Iroquois had divided at the Detroit or the Niagara river, one passing over and coursing the northern shores and the other continuing on the southern shores of Erie and Ontario. It would seem that the northern branch became the Huron and Mohawk-Onondaga; that those who coursed south of these lakes became the Seneca-Erie, the Conestoga (Andaste) and the Susquehannock. It also appears that the Cherokee and Tuscarora separated earlier than the Senecan and Huron-Mohawk divisions.

In the analysis that follows we shall briefly consider the material culture of the Iroquois. In the topical discussion we have repeated certain facts under one topic mentioned in another, not for the sake of emphasis only but to obtain another view of the same facts when differently correlated. [...]

Polished Stone Implements. – The celt, better termed the ungrooved axe, and the flat-bellied adze were used by the Iroquois who seem never to have used the grooved axe. Their ungrooved axes, however, are well made and both types are, in many instances, carefully polished. The Iroquoian adze on the top or back is either beveled in flat planes or rounded. The small celts and adzes are common and seem to have been used as chisels and scrapers rather than as axes. In many instances these are simply waterwashed stones, suitably shaped by nature, and rubbed to a cutting edge. The Iroquois seem never or rarely to have used gouges. They had perforated polished stone beads in abundance, but never seem to have used gorgets, stone tubes, birdstones, or banner stones. This is so common an observation on the part of the archeologist that it may be safely said that no polished stone implement with a hole drilled straight through it is Iroquoian. There were, indeed, polished stone pipes but no straight pipes. We except also stone beads and occasional small stone faces.

Stone Tools. – The Iroquois along the Susquehanna may have used stone hoes but the various overlapping occupations render this doubtful. It is certain, however, that the Iroquois did not generally use the long cylindrical roller pestle, but some have been found on early sites. They did use a flattened muller and a shallow flattened mortar or meal-stone, and these are common on nearly all Iroquoian sites.

Notched sinkers are very common and generally were made of a flattened water-washed stone, about the size and shape of the palm of the hand, though various sizes larger or smaller are found. Pitted stones are abundant. Some appear to have been hammers, judging from the battered edges, but others are pitted on either side and show no battering on the edges. Some of the pits are neatly and symmetrically drilled, others roughly picked in as if a flint had been pounded against the stone. This is especially noticeable in the softer stones. Other hammers are of diabase, granite, or other hard rock and have no pits. Their battered sides, some with flattened planes or faces, others rounded, give evidence of hard and prolonged use.

Anvils, that is flat stones upon which stone was hammered, are fairly common. Now and then an arrow shaft rubber is found and plenty of scratched stones, or "awl sharpeners" are in evidence and occasionally a "sinew stone" comes to light.

Shell Ornaments. – The later Iroquois loved shell ornaments such as beads, perforated shells, runtees and disks, masketts, and variously formed effigies, but they did not have them in any abundance until the coming of the white man. Shell beads of spherical shape, cylindrical, or even discoidal appear on early sites, most of them from the columella of the conch. Perforated periwinkles also were used but only a few beads small enough to be similar to the wampum of the colonial period have been found, compared with the abundance that later appeared. Large conch shells have been found on certain Neuter sites, especially in Erie and Genesee counties. Now and then a clam shell is found, used possibly as a potter's tool. The fresh water univalve was frequently employed for this purpose and they are sometimes found in pits filled with clay.

Pottery. – The most strikingly characteristic product of Iroquoian manufacture is pottery. Both in form and decoration, generally speaking, Huron-Iroquois pottery differs from that found in other regions. At the same time we must qualify a statement of an absolute difference from all others, for on certain sites pottery is found that resembles, in many respects, the pottery of the Ohio village sites, as of Baum and Gartner, and even certain pottery of Tennessee but this is the exception and not the rule.

Typical Iroquoian pottery is known both by its shape and by its decoration. The typical pot [h]as a globular body that as it turns inward toward the top, turns upward and outward into a constricted neck, and a flaring or overhanging collar respectively. The width of the neck at its base is about one sixth of the circumference of the body and it rises as if from the top of an imaginary hexagon drawn inside the globe. From the top of the neck, which turns outward like the bell of a trumpet, rises a collar, sometimes round but as often four-sided and having an upward turn at each corner. This collar is frequently decorated by a series of triangles within which have been drawn lines close together and parallel with one side of the triangle. [...] These triangles contrast with one another as the parallel lines slant obliquely, either right or left, in the adjacent space. At the corners figures are often drawn having three round dots punched in to make a conventional human face (eyes and mouth). In a few instances the face stands out in effigy, or an entire human figure more or less conventionalized is drawn.

Pipes. – Equally, if not more striking than the pottery vessels, are the clay pipes. These are usually gracefully modeled and have stems from three to ten inches in length. The general base line of these pipes is one that follows the line formed by the forefinger and thumb, when the thumb is extended at right angles to the hand and the ball turned back. This is the lower line of the trumpet pipe, for example. Iroquois pipes sometimes have bowls imitating the tops of pots. In other instances the bowls imitate the bodies or heads of birds, mammals, or snakes. Many have the chevron pattern, or parallel lines, arranged in triangles about the bowl top. Some of the forms widely found throughout the Iroquoian area are: the trumpet form, the square-topped flaring bowl, the cylindrical bowl having a wide collar decorated with parallel rings, the bird body with the bowl in the bird's back, the effigy of a man with his hands to his mouth blowing through his lips, animal heads as of the bear, raccoon, or fox, and pipes having a human head modeled on the bowl. [...]

Miscellaneous Observations. – [...] Iroquois houses were of bark, and there were large communal dwellings. Many of them held from five to twelve families or more. They had either a rounded or pitched roof with openings at the top, as a vent for each fire beneath. The Iroquois did not ordinarily employ the conical skin tipi.

The permanency of their village life is indicated in a measure by their vast fields of corn and other vegetables. Agriculture exercised an immense influence over their national life, and it was pursued with method and on a large scale. There are accounts of expeditions sent out to procure new seeds and vegetable foods.

The Iroquois system of consanguinity was matriarchal. There were various clans having animal symbols and names. The women nominated the civil sachems and could veto the acts of the tribal council.

Cosmogony. – The Iroquois cosmogony relates that a pregnant woman fell from the heaven world. She fell upon the back of a great turtle and gave birth to a female child. This child grew quickly to maturity and gave birth to two sons, good-minded and evil-minded, or more properly, Light one and Dark one. The Light or shiny one molded man after seeing his reflection in the water. He found his father dwelling on the top of a mountain that rose from the sea "to the east" and begged from him certain gifts tied up in bags which were given. Reaching his home land again, he opened them and found animals and birds of all kinds, trees and plants. The mother of the two boys died in giving them birth, killed by Dark one or The Warty (Flinty) one, who insisted on emerging through her armpit. The grandmother nursed the boys and bade them watch their mother's grave. The food plants and tobacco sprang from her grave. The sun and moon in other versions were made from her face, eyes, and limbs. [...]

[In the] middle of the colonial period [c]ame the golden age of the Five Nations. This was from 1650 to 1755. Before the earlier date their foes had been Indians, and after that date they battled with the white man, it is true, but they lost no power. By 1755 however, the colonists had come in such numbers that the Five Nations saw the end of their ascendancy as an imperial power. They had come, they had conquered, and now they became engulfed in a complex of cultural elements of which their ancestors never dreamed. More than five thousand Iroquois remain in New York State; more than fifteen thousand reside in the United States and in Canada, but whence they came in the dim distant past, not one remains to tell. The secret may only be solved by the student of Iroquois mythology and of archeology. Our present knowledge, as we have argued points to a southern origin, "down the Ohio."

2.3. The Methods of Ethnology (1920)

Franz Boas

During the last ten years the methods of inquiry into the historical development of civilization have undergone remarkable changes. During the second half of the last century evolutionary thought held almost complete sway and investigators like Spencer, Morgan, Tylor, Lubbock, to mention only a few, were under the spell of the idea of a general, uniform evolution of culture in which all parts of mankind participated. The newer development goes back in part to the influence of Ratzel whose geographical training impressed him with the importance of diffusion and migration. The problem of diffusion was taken up in detail particularly in America, but was applied in a much wider sense by Foy and Graebner, and finally seized upon in a still wider application by Elliot Smith and Rivers, so that at the present time, at least among certain groups of investigators in England and also in Germany, ethnological research is based on the concept of migration and dissemination rather than upon that of evolution.

A critical study of these two directions of inquiry [evolution and diffusion] shows that each is founded on the application of one fundamental hypothesis. The evolutionary point of view presupposes that the course of historical changes in the cultural life of mankind follows definite laws which are applicable everywhere, and which bring it about that cultural development is, in its main lines, the same among all races and all peoples. This idea is clearly expressed by Tylor in the introductory pages of his classic work "Primitive Culture." As soon as we admit that the hypothesis of a uniform evolution has to be proved before it can be accepted, the whole structure loses its foundation. It is true that there are indications of parallelism of development in different parts of the world, and that similar customs are found in the most diverse and widely separated parts of the globe. The occurrence of these similarities which are distributed so irregularly that they cannot readily be explained on the basis of diffusion is one of the foundations of the evolutionary hypothesis, as it was the foundation of Bastian's psychologizing treatment of cultural phenomena. On the other hand, it may be recognized that the hypothesis implies the thought that our modern Western

European civilization represents the highest cultural development toward which all other more primitive cultural types tend, and that, therefore, retrospectively, we construct an orthogenetic development toward our own modern civilization. It is clear that if we admit that there may be different ultimate and coexisting types of civilization, the hypothesis of one single general line of development cannot be maintained.

Opposed to these assumptions is the modern tendency to deny the existence of a general evolutionary scheme which would represent the history of the cultural development the world over. The hypothesis that there are inner causes which bring about similarities of development in remote parts of the globe is rejected and in its place it is assumed that identity of development in two different parts of the globe must always be due to migration and diffusion. On this basis historical contact is demanded for enormously large areas. The theory demands a high degree of stability of cultural traits such as is apparently observed in many primitive tribes, and it is furthermore based on the supposed correlation between a number of diverse and mutually independent cultural traits which reappear in the same combinations in distant parts of the world In this sense, modern investigation takes up anew Gerland's theory of the persistence of a number of cultural traits which were developed in one center and carried by man in his migrations from continent to continent.

It seems to me that if the hypothetical foundations of these two extreme forms of ethnological research arc broadly stated as I have tried to do here, it is at once clear that the correctness of the assumptions has not been demonstrated, but that arbitrarily the one or the other has been selected for the purpose of obtaining a consistent picture of cultural development. These methods are essentially forms of classification of the static phenomena of culture according to two distinct principles, and interpretations of these classifications as of historical significance, without, however, any attempt to prove that this interpretation is justifiable. To give an example: It is observed that in most parts of the world there arc resemblances between decorative forms that are representative and others that are more or less geometrical. According to the evolutionary point of view, their development is explained in the following manner: the decorative forms are arranged in such order that the most representative forms are placed at the beginning. The other forms are so placed that they show a gradual transition from representative forms to purely conventional geometric forms, and this order is then interpreted as meaning that geometric designs originated from representative designs which gradually degenerated. [...] While I do not mean to deny that this development may have occurred, it would be rash to generalize and to claim that in every case the classification which has been made according to a definite principle represents an historical development. The order might as well be reversed and we might begin with a simple geometric element which, by the addition of new traits, might be developed into a representative design, and we might claim that this order represents an historical sequence. Both of these possibilities were considered by Holmes as early as 1885. Neither the one nor the other theory can be established without actual historical proof.

The opposite attitude, namely, origin through diffusion, is exhibited in Heinrich Schurtz's attempt to connect the decorative art of Northwest America with that of Melanesia. The simple fact that in these areas elements occur that may be interpreted as eyes, induced him to assume that both have a common origin, without allowing for the possibility that the pattern in the two areas – each of which shows highly distinctive characteristics – may have developed from independent sources. In this attempt Schurtz followed Ratzel who had already tried to establish connections between Melanesia and Northwest America on the basis of other cultural features.

While ethnographical research based on these two fundamental hypotheses seems to characterize the general tendency of European thought, a different method is at present pursued by the majority of American anthropologists. The difference between the two directions of study may perhaps best be summarized by the statement that American scholars are primarily interested in the dynamic phenomena of cultural change, and try to elucidate cultural history by the application of the results of their studies; and that they relegate the solution of the ultimate question of the relative importance of parallelism of cultural development in distant areas, as against worldwide diffusion, and stability of cultural traits over long periods to a future time when the actual conditions of cultural change are better known. The American ethnological methods are analogous to those of European, particularly of Scandinavian, archaeology, and of the researches into the prehistoric period of the eastern Mediterranean area.

It may seem to the distant observer that American students are engaged in a mass of detailed investigations without much bearing upon the solution of the ultimate problems of a philosophic history of human civilization. I think this interpretation of the American attitude would be unjust because the ultimate questions are as near to our hearts as they are to those of other scholars, only we do not hope to be able to solve an intricate historical problem by a formula.

First of all, the whole problem of cultural history appears to us as a historical problem. In order to understand history it is necessary to know not only how things are, but how they have come to be. In the domain of ethnology, where, for most parts of the world, no historical facts are available except those that may be revealed by archaeological study, all evidence of change can be inferred only by indirect methods. Their character is represented in the researches of students of comparative philology. The method is based on the comparison of static phenomena combined with the study of their distribution. What can be done by this method is well illustrated by Dr. Lowie's investigations of the military societies of the Plains Indians, or by the modern investigation of American mythology. It is, of course, true that we can never hope to obtain incontrovertible data relating to the chronological sequence of events, but certain general broad outlines can be ascertained with a high degree of probability, even of certainty.

As soon as these methods are applied, primitive society loses the appearance of absolute stability which is conveyed to the student who sees a certain people only at a certain given time. All cultural forms rather appear in a constant state of flux and subject to fundamental modifications. [...]

The further pursuit of these inquiries emphasizes the importance of a feature which is common to all historic phenomena. While in natural sciences we are accustomed to consider a given number of causes and to study their effects, in historical happenings we are compelled to consider every phenomenon not only as effect but also as cause. This is true even in the particular application of the laws of physical nature, as, for instance, in the study of astronomy in which the position of certain heavenly bodies at a given moment may be considered as the effect of gravitation, while, at the same time, their particular arrangement in space determines future changes. This relation appears much more clearly in the history of human civilization. To give an example: a surplus of food supply is liable to bring about an increase of population and an increase of leisure, which gives opportunity for occupations that are not absolutely necessary for the needs of everyday life. In turn the increase of population and of leisure, which may be applied to new inventions, give rise to a greater food supply and to a further increase in the amount of leisure, so that a cumulative effect results.

[…] In short then, the method which we try to develop is based on a study of the dynamic changes in society that may be observed at the present time. We refrain from the attempt to solve the fundamental problem of the general development of civilization until we have been able to unravel the processes that are going on under our eyes.

Certain general conclusions may be drawn from this study even now. First of all, the history of human civilization does not appear to us as determined entirely by psychological necessity that leads to a uniform evolution the world over. We rather see that each cultural group has its own unique history, dependent partly upon the peculiar inner development of the social group, and partly upon the foreign influences to which it has been subjected. There have been processes of gradual differentiation as well as processes of leveling down differences between neighboring cultural centers, but it would be quite impossible to understand, on the basis of a single evolutionary scheme, what happened to any particular people. […]

Studies of the dynamics of primitive life also show that an assumption of long continued stability such as is demanded by Elliot Smith is without any foundation in fact. Wherever primitive conditions have been studied in detail, they can be proved to be in a state of flux, and it would seem that there is a close parallelism between the history of language and the history of general cultural development. Periods of stability are followed by periods of rapid change. It is exceedingly improbable that any customs of primitive people should be preserved unchanged for thousands of years.

2.4. The Methodology of Racial Testing: Its Significance for Sociology (1926)

Margaret Mead

The unquestioning quotation of the results in one field of research by workers in another field carries with it at least tacit approval of the methodology which produced those results. The sociologist is, therefore, very much concerned with the methods employed in experimental psychology, which furnishes him with so much of the raw material for generalization. Perhaps no results of experimental psychology have been utilized so widely and so uncritically as the results of intelligence testing, and particularly of the intelligence testing of different racial and nationality groups. In the discussion of race problems, a controversy so encumbered by worn-out dogmas and hot partisanships, this quantitative type of material was particularly welcome.

The first research to be generally exploited was the army testing. But here so many opponents of the resulting generalizations came forward with destructive criticism, and so many defenders of the tests carefully tried to warn the layman against unjustified conclusions, that the mischief became too public to be dangerous. No discussions today which pretend to scientific caution quote the army tests without many explicit reservations. But the criticisms of the army tests were in great part devoted to the deficiencies of all intelligence tests, of verbal tests, or of group tests as such. Far less attention was devoted to the special problems inherent in racial and nationality testing.[1] Thus, while the writer on general social problems has learned that the methodology of intelligence testing is still in swaddling clothes, he is not so conscious that a methodology adequate to deal with racial and nationality testing has not even been born. And, unwarned, he draws freely and uncritically upon the findings of special studies which appear from time to time in the scientific journals. [...]

---

1 Here, Mead is pointing out that while there has been critical questioning of what we mean by intelligence and how it might be measured, scholars had yet to question what we mean by race and how racial and national categories might be measured.

The special problems involved in this type of testing are three in number: (1) the practicability and validity of attempts to equate test score and amount of racial admixture; (2) the effect which social status has on the results of such tests – the problem here is threefold: Does social status influence test score? Is it particularly influential in the case of immigrant groups or groups which suffer from social discrimination because of their race? What methods are adequate to evaluate the social status of the children so tested? (3) What effect does linguistic disability have on the test results? These three aspects of the matter will be considered in turn.

RACIAL ADMIXTURE

On the face of it, no method of determining race differences in intelligence seems more promising than this attempt to equate test scores with the amount of Negro or Indian blood, as the case may be, when it is possible, as it often is in this country, to study such a mixed group. In such an instance it seems highly probable that language and social status might be controlled, and the effect of race as such isolated and studied. But here we are confronted with two difficulties: one technological, the other theoretical. Does a quantitative expression of degree of admixture have any qualitative significance and, if so, how may this quantitative expression be arrived at? Garth suggests: "If the genetic law works in mental traits as it does in physical traits, possibly we ought to get multimodal effects in one distribution of mixed bloods' performance in a mental test; particularly should we get at least bimodal effects in a distribution of performances of an F2 population." But this is not enough. We cannot use either degree of variability or a multimodal distribution first as hypothesis and then as proof. And while increased variability is generally recognized by physical anthropologists as an index of racial admixture, it is not so specifically developed a concept as to make possible exact equations between the expression of intelligence in a test and exact degree of intermixture involved.

If, however, we lay aside this theoretical objection as incapable of solution on the basis of our present knowledge of the laws of heredity, and an attempt is made to establish a purely empirical relationship between degrees of racial admixture and intelligence scores, what methods can be used? Garth and Hunter used the official records of the government schools. Subject to the accuracy of these genealogical records, this method is thorough and valid. But here Garth admits that his results are quite indeterminate because the social conditions for his various groups were probably extremely varied before the children entered the government schools. Methodologically however, the procedure is sound.

In his studies on the American Negro, Ferguson has made a less objective method the basis of his determination of amount of admixture. In 1916 he tested 907 school children in several Virginia cities, 421 of whom were colored. He made his estimate of amount of Negro blood on the basis of skin color graded by an eye judgment, and finds an increasingly high score with increased amount of white blood. From which result he generalizes as follows:

Such considerations indicate that it is a native ability and not an acquired capacity that differentiates the mixed from the pure negroes, and that *skin color is its outward sign*. [Italics Mead's.] They also indicate that the tests used are primarily tests of native capacity, and the consequent differences found between whites and negroes as a whole are innate differences. The average performance of the colored people of this country in such intelligence work as that represented by the tests of higher capacity appears to be only about three-fourths as efficient as the performance of the white with the same amount of training.

This is obviously reasoning in a circle; he divides his group according to skin color, finds differences between these divisions, then assumes that this proves skin color a valid index and that, therefore, the differences so found are innate. In 1919 Ferguson made a similar analysis of the results of the army testing of 5,425 Negroes at Camp Lee. Again on the basis of an eye judgment he divided 1,132 of these Negroes into a "darker" and a "lighter" group, and found that the median Alpha score for the "lighter" group was 51, for the "darker," 40; on the Stenquist combination test the group classified as "lighter" made a median score of 19; those called "darker," a median score of 17. Eight additional companies were classified by other observers and gave results comparable to these. Ferguson has severely criticized a similar attempt, made by Morse and Strong, as "rough," yet his own methods are open to the same criticism. There is no conclusive evidence that skin color, *accurately determined,* is a reliable index of racial admixture. Such a classification is even less admissible when unchecked by any such quantitative device as the color top. The methods of Garth and Hunter on one hand, and that of Ferguson and Strong on the other, are illustrations of a scientific and unscientific approach to this problem. If the genealogical method could be subjected to extensive verification and supplemented by some technique for holding the other factors constant it might be productive of valuable results.

SOCIAL STATUS

Several careful attempts have been made to ascertain the influence which social status has in this type of testing. Very often the conclusions of these experimenters have to be rejected because they have concentrated upon this one problem and neglected other complicating conditions, but they are none the less valuable as illustrations of the particular methodological point.

In 1912 Phillips made an investigation of the intelligence of white and Negro children in the Philadelphia public schools, using the Binet scale. His treatment of the social status factor was a specific attempt to hold it constant. The homes of the children were visited and rated on a four-division scale. Only those children, twenty-nine from each race, whose homes were rated "good" were used in the final comparisons. This method of elimination of all cases of incomparable social status is open to two objections. In the first place, strict comparability is exceedingly difficult to determine, and the final use of only one status group prevents the utilization of other status groups as checks. And in the second place, it is enormously unpractical in that it pares down the number of cases, and the more exact the classification, the more cases there are which will have to be eliminated. [...]

LANGUAGE DISABILITY

Perhaps no complicating factor in appraising the results of this kind of intelligence testing has been so neglected as the question of language disability. With the exception of the work of two investigators, the whole matter has usually been dismissed with statements that the child was under no language handicap beyond the first grade if he had gone to an American kindergarten, or that "all the Italians spoke English without difficulty," or that the children were selected by the principal of the school as having no language handicap. [...]

[...] From these various attempts to elaborate a methodology of racial and nationality testing it is clearly evident that test scores are affected, to a degree not yet determined, by social status and by language disabilities. No attempt has yet been made to analyze the effects of that more subtle and less measurable aspect of environment which may determine the attitude of the subject toward the tests and profoundly affect his score. The method of equating test score and amount of racial admixture is subject to modification in terms of these other complicating factors, and also to the inherent weaknesses of the method in the present state of ignorance concerning the laws regulating the inheritance of mental traits.

All these considerations should suggest extreme caution in any attempt to draw conclusions concerning the relative intelligence of different racial or nationality groups on the basis of tests, unless a careful consideration is given the factors of language, education, and social status, and a further allowance is made for an unknown amount of influence which may be logically attributed to different attitudes and different habits of thought.

REFERENCES

Ferguson Jr., G.O. 1916. "Psychology of the Negro." *Archives of Psychology* 32.
Ferguson Jr., G.O. 1919. "Intelligence of the Negroes at Camp Lee." *School and Society* 9: 721–6.
Garth, T.R. 1921. "Results of Some Tests on Full and Mixed Blood Indians." *Journal of Applied Psychology* 4: 359–72.
Garth, T.R. 1922. "Comparison of the Mental Ability of Mixed and Full-Blood Indians on the Basis of Education." *Psychological Review* 29: 221–36.
Garth, T.R. 1922a. "Mental Fatigue of Mixed and Full-Blooded Indians." *Journal of Applied Psychology* 6: 333–41.
Garth, T.R. 1922b. "National Intelligence Tests Given to Mixed and FullBlood Indians." *Science,* December 1.
Hunter, W.S. 1920. "A Relation of Degree of Indian Blood to Score on Otis Intelligence Test." *Proceedings of the American Psychological Association.*
Phillips, B.A. 1914. "Binet Tests Applied to Colored School Children." *Psych. Clinic*: 190–6.

2.5. Mules and Men (1935)

Zora Neale Hurston

INTRODUCTION

I was glad when somebody told me, "You may go and collect Negro folklore."

In a way it would not be a new experience for me. When I pitched headforemost into the world I landed in the crib of negroism. From the earliest rocking of my cradle, I had known about the capers Brer Rabbit is apt to cut and what the Squinch Owl says from the house top. But it was fitting me like a tight chemise. I couldn't see it for wearing it. It was only when I was off in college, away from my native surroundings, that I could see myself like somebody else and stand off and look at my garment. Then I had to have the spy-glass of Anthropology to look through at that.

Dr. Boas asked me where I wanted to work and I said, "Florida," and gave, as my big reason, that "Florida is a place that draws people – white people from all over the world, and Negroes from every Southern state surely and some from the North and West." So I knew that it was possible for me to get a cross section of the Negro South in the one state. And then I realized that I was new myself, so it looked sensible for me to choose familiar ground.

First place I aimed to stop to collect material was Eatonville, Florida. And now, I'm going to tell you why I decided to go to my native village first. I didn't go back there so that the home folks could make admiration over me because I had been up North to college and come back with a diploma and a Chevrolet. I knew they were not going to pay either one of these items too much mind. I was just Lucy Hurston's daughter, Zora, and even if I had – to use one of our down-home expressions – had a Kaiser baby, and that's something that hasn't been done in this Country yet, I'd still be just Zora to the neighbors. If I had exalted myself to impress the town, somebody would have sent me word in a match-box that I had been up North there and had rubbed the hair off of my head against some college wall, and then come back there with a lot of form and fashion and outside show to the world. But they'd stand flat-footed and tell me that they didn't have me, neither my sham-polish, to study 'bout. And that would have been that.

I hurried back to Eatonville because I knew that the town was full of material and that I could get it without hurt, harm or danger. As early as I could remember it was the habit of the men folks particularly to gather on the store porch of evenings and swap stories. Even the women folks would stop and break a breath with them at times. As a child when I was sent down to Joe Clarke's store, I'd drag out my leaving as long as possible in order to hear more.

Folklore is not as easy to collect as it sounds. The best source is where there are the least outside influences and these people, being usually underprivileged, are the shyest. They are most reluctant at times to reveal that which the soul lives by. And the Negro, in spite of his open-faced laughter, his seeming acquiescence, is particularly evasive. You see we are a polite people and we do not say to our questioner, "Get out of here!" We smile and tell him or her something that satisfies the white person because, knowing so little about us, he doesn't know what he is missing. The Indian resists curiosity by a stony silence. The Negro offers a feather-bed resistance. That is, we let the probe enter, but it never comes out. It gets smothered under a lot of laughter and pleasantries.

The theory behind our tactics: "The white man is always trying to know into somebody else's business. All right, I'll set something outside the door of my mind for him to play with and handle. He can read my writing but he sho' can't read my mind. I'll put this play toy in his hand, and he will seize it and go away. Then I'll say my say and sing my song."

I knew that even I was going to have some hindrance among strangers. But here in Eatonville I knew everybody was going to help me. So below Palatka I began to feel eager to be there and I kicked the little Chevrolet right along.

I thought about the tales I had heard as a child. How even the Bible was made over to suit our vivid imagination. How the devil always outsmarted God and how that over-noble hero Jack or John – not John Henry, who occupies the same place in Negro folklore that Casey Jones does in white lore and if anything is more recent – outsmarted the devil. Brer Fox, Brer Deer, Brer 'Gator, Brer Dawg, Brer Rabbit, Ole Massa and his wife were walking the earth like natural men way back in the days when God himself was on the ground and men could talk with him. Way back there before God weighed up the dirt to make the mountains. When I was rounding Lily Lake I was remembering how God had made the world and the elements and people. He made souls for people, but he didn't give them out because he said:

"'Folks ain't ready for souls yet. De clay ain't dry. It's de strongest thing Ah ever made. Don't aim to waste none thru loose cracks. And then men got to grow strong enough to stand it. De way things is now, if Ah give it out it would tear them shackly bodies to pieces. Bimeby, Ah give it out.'

So folks went round thousands of years without no souls. All de time de soul-piece, it was setting 'round covered up wid God's loose raiment. Every now and then de wind would blow and hist up de cover and then de elements would be full of lightning and de winds would talk. So people told one 'nother that God was talking in de mountains.

De white man passed by it way off and he looked but he wouldn't go close enough to touch. De Indian and de Negro, they tipped by cautious too, and all of 'em seen de light of diamonds when de winds shook de cover, and de wind dat passed over it sung songs. De Jew come past and heard de song from de soul-piece then he kept on passin' and all of a sudden he grabbed up de soul-piece and hid it under his clothes, and run off down de road. It burned him and tore him and throwed him down and lifted him up and toted him across de mountain and he tried to break loose but he couldn't do it. He kept on hollerin' for help but de rest of 'em run hid 'way from him. Way after while they come out of holes and corners and picked up little chips and pieces that fell back on de ground. So God mixed it up wid feelings and give it out to 'em. 'Way after while when He ketch dat Jew, He's goin' to 'vide things up more ekal."

So I rounded Park Lake and came speeding down the straight stretch into Eatonville, the city of five lakes, three croquet courts, three hundred brown skins, three hundred good swimmers, plenty guavas, two schools, and no jail-house. [...]

ONE

As I crossed the Maitland-Eatonville township line I could see a group on the store porch. I was delighted. The town had not changed. Same love of talk and song. So I drove on down there before I stopped. Yes, there was George Thomas, Calvin Daniels, Jack and Charlie Jones, Gene Brazzle, B. Moseley and "Seaboard." Deep in a game of Florida-flip. All of those who were not actually playing were giving advice – "bet straightening" they call it.

"Hello, boys," I hailed them as I went into neutral.

They looked up from the game and for a moment it looked as if they had forgotten me. Then B. Moseley said, "Well, if it ain't Zora Hurston!" Then everybody crowded around the car to help greet me.

"You gointer stay awhile, Zora?"

"Yep. Several months."

"Where you gointer stay, Zora?"

"With Mett and Ellis, I reckon."

"Mett" was Mrs. Armetta Jones, an intimate friend of mine since childhood and Ellis was her husband. Their house stands under the huge camphor tree on the front street.

"Hello, heart-string," Mayor Hiram Lester yelled as he hurried up the street. "We heard all about you up North. You back home for good, I hope."

"Nope, Ah come to collect some old stories and tales and Ah know y'all know a plenty of 'em and that's why Ah headed straight for home."

"What you mean, Zora, them big old lies we tell when we're jus' sittin' around here on the store porch doin' nothin'?" asked B. Moseley.

"Yeah, those same ones about Ole Massa, and colored folks in heaven, and – oh, y'all know the kind I mean."

"Aw shucks," exclaimed George Thomas doubtfully. "Zora, don't you come here and tell de biggest lie first thing. Who you reckon want to read all them old-time tales about Brer Rabbit and Brer Bear?"

"Plenty of people, George. They are a lot more valuable than you might think. We want to set them down before it's too late."

"Too late for what?"

"Before everybody forgets all of 'em."

"No danger of that. That's all some people is good for – set 'round and lie and murder groceries."

"Ah know one right now," Calvin Daniels announced cheerfully. "It's a tale 'bout John and de frog."

"Wait till she get out her car, Calvin. Let her get settled at 'Met's' and cook a pan of ginger bread then we'll all go down and tell lies and eat ginger bread. Dat's de way to do. She's tired now from all dat drivin'."

"All right, boys," I agreed. "But Ah'll be rested by night. Be lookin' for everybody."

So I unloaded the car and crowded it into Ellis's garage and got settled. Armetta made me lie down and rest while she cooked a big pan of ginger bread for the company we expected.

Section Two Glossary

cultural relativism   The notion that there is no single natural, right, or normal way to think or behave; all cultural beliefs and practices are relative. The methodological implication of cultural relativism is the emphasis on understanding culture from the perspective of those who are part of it.

ethnocentrism   Belief in the singular importance, normality, or centrality of one's own ethnocultural group. Cultural relativism poses a challenge to ethnocentrism.

eugenics   The pseudoscientific study of human difference based on categorizing people into distinct racial groups and ranking those groups in order from superior to inferior. Eugenics has played an important role in propping up colonialist and white supremacist ideologies and shaping legal and social institutions.

hegemony/hegemonic   Hegemony is a term coined by Italian communist Antonio Gramsci to analyze ideo-cultural dimensions of power. I like to think of "hegemony" as a way to describe rule via common sense: the internalization of normative assumptions that prop up capitalist power structures – e.g., "We should participate in democratic elections; everyone should have freedom; we ought to respect private property." Hegemony is often analytically applied to the global spread of capitalism and Western cultural norms.

On Hidden Logics of Culture

THE SOCIAL CONTEXT

The essays in this section bookend World War II (1939–1945), a deadly, globalized conflict among imperial powers that cost tens of millions of human lives. After the war, much of Europe was destroyed, and wealthy imperial nations created two global financial institutions – the International Bank for Reconstruction and Development and the International Monetary Fund – to bankroll its rebuilding. These institutions would play key roles in global transitions from formal colonial relationships to neocolonial ones, in which "development" loans would compel former colonies to open their markets to global capitalism. Later sections explore the subsequent penetration of global capitalism in more depth, but the shifting geopolitical relationships wrought by world war and its aftermath provide the social context for the essays in this section.

While most of these essays do not directly address war or colonialism (itself a ground for critique), the work lives of the authors in this section were deeply embedded in globalized conflicts. Bronislaw Malinowski, for example, conducted fieldwork while exiled from England during World War II and notoriously championed anthropology's utility for imperial rule, even as he trained and encouraged Jomo Kenyatta, an anti-colonial activist, anthropologist, and the first Indigenous president of independent Kenya. Ruth Benedict dedicated much of her anthropological career to promoting the principle of cultural relativism, which she used to critique Western hegemony in the selection we include here. Marcel Mauss, born in France to a Jewish family, served in World War I and was active in challenging anti-Semitic and racist ideologies during and after World War II (Mauss was also sociologist Émile Durkheim's nephew and student). Mauss influenced Claude Lévi-Strauss, also French and Jewish, who fled Nazi-occupied France during World War II and spent the rest of his career in the United States, where he worked closely with Franz Boas. These experiences shaped these scholars' interests and contributions – and, in particular, their shared emphasis on discovering human universals that underlie observable cultural practices.

THE CONVERSATION

These scholars advanced distinct theoretical paradigms, and they are typically allotted different sections in anthropological theory texts (except for Kenyatta, who has largely been erased from the Western canon altogether). We chose to group them together to draw out their theoretical commonalities and focus on the dynamic conversation in which their work engages.

Our first essay, Reading 3.1, exemplifies Malinowski's theory of **psychological functionalism.** It is taken from his well-known book, *Argonauts of the Western Pacific* (the work conducted during his exile), in which Malinowski argues that ritualized exchange of non-utilitarian items among Trobriand Islanders functions to help circulate utilitarian goods and solidify far-flung relationships, thereby addressing Trobrianders' psychological needs. Importantly, Malinowski also makes a methodological intervention here, in which he urges the ethnographer to identify the hidden logic of function among cultural practices that "Natives" are unable to perceive.

If you have ever been in the awkward position of getting a holiday gift from someone for whom you have no gift in return, you will relate to Reading 3.2, by Marcel Mauss. In it, Mauss advances his well-known argument that gifting has less to do with generosity or charity than with deepening interpersonal relationships through social obligation. Thus, when your friend gave you a gift and you had nothing for them in return, you felt awkward because you violated a social norm of reciprocal peer exchange. Moreover, you will likely be sure to have a gift for your friend in the future, deepening your relationship with them through exchange. Mauss argues that these social laws, of which the gift is but an example, underlie our cultural practices but are not often consciously discerned.

Our third piece, by Ruth Benedict, exemplifies anthropological analysis associated with the "**culture and personality school**" – pioneered by Benedict and Margaret Mead. In this selection, Benedict argues that people are shaped by their culture from the time of their infancy. "By the time [a child] can talk," Benedict writes, "he [*sic*] is the little creature of his culture." The influence of culture on personhood leads people to naturalize their own cultural particularities – a tendency that reached new heights under Western imperialism and has driven the spread of Western hegemony. "Our" inability to perceive our own cultural bias, Benedict argues, obscures the role that ethnocentrism plays in shaping global relationships and anthropological analyses alike.

Our fourth essay is by Jomo Kenyatta, most known in anthropology for his study of the Gikuyu, the community to which Kenyatta belonged. Rather than include one of Kenyatta's ethnographic descriptions of Gikuyu "culture," we chose a piece that illustrates how Kenyatta sought to use anthropology as a tool to challenge colonialism. Here, Kenyatta relates a Gikuyu fable about structures of imperial governance in colonial Kenya. The fable both reveals veiled fictions of imperial rule and pokes fun at colonial officials too ignorant of the dangers of their own greed to stop it from destroying them in the end.

In Reading 3.5, Claude Lévi-Strauss advances the argument that hidden cultural logics are a product of universal structures of the human mind. This approach, termed **French structuralism,** understands everything from language, to kinship patterns, to myths, to religious belief as separable into detectable patterns that reveal underlying structures of thought. Structuralism is probably the broadest of anthropological theories concerned with revealing hidden cultural logics.

THREE QUESTIONS FOR THE READINGS

1   What are the broader implications of Malinowski's argument that "Natives" cannot perceive the underlying functions of our own cultural practices? How does this claim reconcile with the work of Jomo Kenyatta, a "**native**" anthropologist and Malinowski's mentee?

2   The logical extension of these arguments is that what we think and say about our culture is different from its "real" meanings. If, as Benedict and Malinowksi argue, it's hard for us to even perceive these real meanings, how can we gauge the veracity and helpfulness of these theories? What are the political and methodological implications of a hidden universality of culture?

3   Think of the example of "gifting" as a behavior that has underlying, often unperceived, social functions. Does this interpretation of gifting rob gift exchange of its sentimental value? What about other social behaviors – generosity, conspicuous consumption, romance, and sex – that can be anthropologically explained as functional? How can we reconcile competing interpretations of these practices?

ON THE COMPANION WEBSITE

Andy and Dwight trade favors, why we love surprises, additional readings, and more.

www.anthropologicaltheory.com

3.1. The Essentials of the Kula (1922)

Bronislaw Malinowski

Having thus described the scene, and the actors, let us now proceed to the performance. The Kula is a form of exchange, of extensive, inter-tribal character; it is carried on by communities inhabiting a wide ring of islands, which form a closed circuit. This circuit […] is represented by the lines joining a number of islands to the North and East of the East end of New Guinea. Along this route, articles of two kinds, and these two kinds only, are constantly traveling in opposite directions. In the direction of the hands of a clock, moves constantly one of these kinds – long necklaces of red shell, called *soulava* […]. In the opposite direction moves the other kind – bracelets of white shell called *mwali* […]. Each of these articles, as it travels in its own direction on the closed circuit, meets on its way articles of the other class, and is constantly being exchanged for them. Every movement of the Kula articles, every detail of the transactions is fixed and regulated by a set of traditional rules and conventions, and some acts of the Kula are accompanied by an elaborate magical ritual and public ceremonies.

On every island and in every village, a more or less limited number of men take part in the Kula – that is to say, receive the goods, hold them for a short time, and then pass them on. Therefore every man who is in the Kula, periodically though not regularly, receives one or several *mwali* (arm-shells) or a *soulava* (necklace of red shell discs), and then has to hand it on to one of his partners, from whom he receives the opposite commodity in exchange. Thus no man ever keeps any of the articles for any length of time in his possession. One transaction does not finish the Kula relationship, the rule being "once in the Kula, always in the Kula," and a partnership between two men is a permanent and lifelong affair. Again, any given *mwali* or *soulava* may always be found traveling and changing hands, and there is no question of its ever settling down, so that the principle "once in the Kula, always in the Kula" applies also to the valuables themselves.

The ceremonial exchange of the two articles is the main, the fundamental aspect of the Kula. But associated with it, and done under its cover, we find a great number of secondary activities and features. Thus, side by side with the ritual exchange of arm-shells and necklaces, the natives carry on ordinary trade, bartering from one island to another a great number of utilities, often unprocurable in the district to which they are imported, and indispensable there. Further, there are other activities, preliminary to the Kula, or associated with it, such as the building of sea-going canoes for the expeditions, certain big forms of mortuary ceremonies, and preparatory taboos. The Kula is thus an extremely big and complex institution, both in its geographical extent, and in the manifoldness of its component pursuits. It welds together a considerable number of tribes, and it embraces a vast complex of activities, interconnected, and playing into one another, so as to form one organic whole.

Yet it must be remembered that what appears to us an extensive, complicated, and yet well ordered institution is the outcome of ever so many doings and pursuits, carried on by savages, who have no laws or aims or charters definitely laid down. They have no knowledge of the *total outline* of any of their social structure. They know their own motives, know the purpose of individual actions and the rules which apply to them, but how, out of these, the whole collective institution shapes, this is beyond their mental range. Not even the most intelligent native has any clear idea of the Kula as a big, organized social construction, still less of its sociological function and implications. If you were to ask him what the Kula is, he would answer by giving a few details, most likely by giving his personal experiences and subjective views on the Kula, but nothing approaching the definition just given here. Not even a partial coherent account could be obtained. For the integral picture does not exist in his mind; he is in it, and cannot see the whole from the outside.

The integration of all the details observed, the achievement of a sociological synthesis of all the various, relevant symptoms, is the task of the Ethnographer. First of all, he has to find out that certain activities, which at first sight might appear incoherent and not correlated, have a meaning. He then has to find out what is constant and relevant in these activities, and what accidental and inessential, that is, to find out the laws and rules of all the transactions. Again, the Ethnographer has to *construct* the picture of the big institution, very much as the physicist constructs his theory from the experimental data, which always have been within reach of everybody, but which needed a consistent interpretation. I have touched on this point of method in the Introduction (Divisions V and VI), but I have repeated it here, as it is necessary to grasp it clearly in order not to lose the right perspective of conditions as they really exist among the natives.

In giving the above abstract and concise definition, I had to reverse the order of research, as this is done in ethnographic fieldwork, where the most generalized inferences are obtained as the result of long inquiries and laborious inductions. The general definition of the Kula will serve as a sort of plan or diagram in our further concrete and detailed descriptions. And this is the more necessary as the Kula is concerned with the exchange of wealth and utilities, and therefore it is an economic institution, and there is no other aspect of primitive life where our knowledge is more scanty and our understanding more superficial than in Economics. Hence misconception is rampant, and it is necessary to clear the ground when approaching any economic subject.

Thus in the Introduction we called the Kula a "form of trade," and we ranged it alongside other systems of barter. This is quite correct, if we give the word "*trade*" a sufficiently wide interpretation, and mean by it any exchange of goods. But the word "trade" is used in current Ethnography and economic literature with so many different implications that a whole lot of misleading, preconceived ideas have to be brushed aside in order to grasp the facts correctly. Thus the aprioric current notion of primitive trade would be that of an exchange of indispensable or useful articles, done without much ceremony or regulation, under stress of dearth or need, in spasmodic, irregular intervals – and this done either by direct barter, everyone looking out sharply not to be done out of his due, or, if the savages were too timid and distrustful to face one another, by some customary arrangement, securing by means of heavy penalties compliance in the obligations incurred or imposed. Waiving for the present the question how far this conception is valid or not in general – in my opinion it is quite misleading – we have to realize clearly that the Kula contradicts in almost every point the above definition of "savage trade." It shows to us primitive exchange in an entirely different light.

The Kula is not a surreptitious and precarious form of exchange. It is, quite on the contrary, rooted in myth, backed by traditional law, and surrounded with magical rites. All its main transactions are public and ceremonial, and carried out according to definite rules. It is not done on the spur of the moment, but happens periodically, at dates settled in advance, and it is carried on along definite trade routes, which must lead to fixed trysting places. Sociologically, though transacted between tribes differing in language, culture, and probably even in race, it is based on a fixed and permanent status, on a partnership which binds into couples some thousands of individuals. This partnership is a lifelong relationship, it implies various mutual duties and privileges, and constitutes a type of inter-tribal relationship on an enormous scale. As to the economic mechanism of the transactions, this is based on a specific form of credit, which implies a high degree of mutual trust and commercial honor – and this refers also to the subsidiary, minor trade, which accompanies the Kula proper. Finally, the Kula is not done under stress of any need, since its main aim is to exchange articles which are of no practical use. [...]

This negative description leaves us with the questions: why, then, are these objects valued, what purpose do they serve? The full answer to this question will emerge out of the whole story contained in the following chapters, but an approximate idea must be given at once. As it is always better to approach the unknown through the known, let us consider for a moment whether among ourselves we have not some type of objects which play a similar role and which are used and possessed in the same manner. When, after a six years' absence in the South Seas and Australia, I returned to Europe and did my first bit of sight-seeing in Edinburgh Castle, I was shown the Crown jewels. The keeper told many stories of how they were worn by this or that king or queen on such and such occasion, of how some of them had been taken over to London, to the great and just indignation of the whole Scottish nation, how they were restored, and how now everyone can be pleased, since they are safe under lock and key, and no one can touch them. As I was looking at them and thinking how ugly, useless, ungainly, even tawdry they were, I had the feeling that something similar had been told to me of late, and that I had seen many other objects of this sort, which made a similar impression on me.

And then arose before me the vision of a native village on coral soil, and a small, rickety platform temporarily erected under a pandanus thatch, surrounded by a number of brown, naked men, and one of them showing me long, thin red strings, and big, white, worn-out objects, clumsy to sight and greasy to touch. With reverence he also would name them, and tell their history, and by whom and when they were worn, and how they changed hands, and how their temporary possession was a great sign of the importance and glory of the village. The analogy between the European and the Trobriand *vaygu'a* (valuables) must be delimited with more precision. The Crown Jewels, in fact, any heirlooms too valuable and too cumbersome to be worn, represent the same type as *vaygu'a* in that they are merely possessed for the sake of possession itself, and the ownership of them with the ensuing renown is the main source of their value. Also both heirlooms and *vaygu'a* are cherished because of the historical sentiment which surrounds them. However ugly, useless, and – according to current standards – valueless an object may be, if it has figured in historical scenes and passed through the hands of historic persons, and is therefore an unfailing vehicle of important sentimental associations, it cannot but be precious to us. This historic sentimentalism, which indeed has a large share in our general interest in studies of past events, exists also in the South Seas. Every really good Kula article has its individual name, round each there is a sort of history and romance in the traditions of the natives. Crown jewels or heirlooms are insignia of rank and symbols of wealth respectively, and in olden days with us, and in New Guinea up till a few years ago, both rank and wealth went together. The main point of difference is that the Kula goods are only in possession for a time, whereas the European treasure must be permanently owned in order to have full value. [...]

The *vaygu'a* – the Kula valuables – in one of their aspects are overgrown objects of use. They are also, however, *ceremonial* objects in the narrow and correct sense of the word. This will become clear after perusal of the following pages, and to this point we shall return in the last chapter.

3.2. The Gift (1925)

Marcel Mauss

I have never found a man so generous and hospitable that he would not receive a present, nor one so liberal with his money that he would dislike a reward if he could get one.

Friends should rejoice each others' hearts with gifts of weapons and raiment, that is clear from one's own experience. That friendship lasts longest – if there is a chance of its being a success – in which friends both give and receive gifts.

A man ought to be a friend to his friend and repay gift with gift. People should meet smiles with smiles and lies with treachery.

Know – if you have a friend in whom you have sure confidence and wish to make use of him, you ought to exchange ideas and gifts with him and go to see him often.

If you have another in whom you have no confidence yet will make use of him, you ought to address him with fair words but crafty heart and repay treachery with lies.

Further, with regard to him in whom you have no confidence and of whose motives you are suspicious, you ought to smile upon him and dissemble your feelings. Gifts ought to be repaid in like coin.

Generous and bold men have the best time in life and never foster troubles. But the coward is apprehensive of everything and a miser is always groaning over his gifts.

Better there should be no prayer than excessive offering; a gift always looks for recompense. Better there should be no sacrifice than an excessive slaughter.

– *Havamal*, vv. 39, 41–2, 44–6, 48, and 145, from the translation by D.E. Martin Clarke in *The Havamal, with Selections from Other Poems in the Edda*, Cambridge, 1923

GIFTS AND RETURN GIFTS

The foregoing lines from the *Edda* outline our subject matter. In Scandinavian civilization and many other civilizations contracts are fulfilled and exchanges of goods are made by means of gifts. In theory such gifts are voluntary but in fact they are given and repaid under obligation.

This work is part of a wider study. For some years our attention has been drawn to the realm of contract and the system of economic prestations between the component sections or subgroups of "primitive" and what we might call "archaic" societies. On this subject there is a great mass of complex data. For, in these "early" societies, social phenomena are not discrete; each phenomenon contains all the threads of which the social fabric is composed. In these *total* social phenomena, as we propose to call them, all kinds of institutions find simultaneous expression: religious, legal, moral, and economic. In addition, the phenomena have their aesthetic aspect and they reveal morphological types.

We intend in this book to isolate one important set of phenomena: namely, prestations which are in theory voluntary, disinterested, and spontaneous, but are in fact obligatory and interested. The form usually taken is that of the gift generously offered; but the accompanying behavior is formal pretense and social deception, while the transaction itself is based on obligation and economic self-interest. We shall note the various principles behind this necessary form of exchange (which is nothing less than the division of labor itself), but we shall confine our detailed study to the inquiry: *In primitive or archaic types of society what is the principle whereby the gift received has to be repaid? What force is there in the thing given which compels the recipient to make a return?* We hope, by presenting enough data, to be able to answer this question precisely, and also to indicate the direction in which answers to cognate questions might be sought. We shall also pose new problems. Of these, some concern the morality of the contract: for instance, the manner in which today the law of things remains bound up with the law of persons; and some refer to the forms and ideas which have always been present in exchange and which even now are to be seen in the idea of individual interest.

Thus we have a double aim. We seek a set of more or less archaeological conclusions on the nature of human transactions in the societies which surround us and those which immediately preceded ours, and whose exchange institutions differ from our own. We describe their forms of contract and exchange. It has been suggested that these societies lack the economic market, but that is not true; for the market is a human phenomenon which we believe to be familiar to every known society. Markets are found before the development of merchants, and before their most important innovation, currency as we know it. They functioned before they took the modern forms (Semitic, Hellenic, Hellenistic, and Roman) of contract and sale and capital. We shall take note of the moral and economic features of these institutions.

We contend that the same morality and economy are at work, albeit less noticeably, in our own societies, and we believe that in them we have discovered one of the bases of social life; and thus we may draw conclusions of a moral nature about some of the problems confronting us in our present economic crisis. These pages of social history, theoretical sociology, political economy, and morality do no more than lead us to old problems which are constantly turning up under new guises. [...]

PRESTATION, GIFT, AND POTLATCH

This work is part of the wider research carried out by M. Davy and myself upon archaic forms of contract, so we may start by summarizing what we have found so far. It appears that there has never existed, either in the past or in modern primitive societies, anything like a "natural" economy. By a strange chance the type of that economy was taken to be the one described by Captain Cook when he wrote on exchange and barter among the Polynesians. In our study here of these same Polynesians we shall see how far removed they are from a state of nature in these matters.

In the systems of the past we do not find simple exchange of goods, wealth, and produce through markets established among individuals. For it is groups, and not individuals, which carry on exchange, make contracts, and are bound by obligations; the persons represented in the contracts are moral persons – clans, tribes, and families; the groups, or the chiefs as intermediaries for the groups, confront and oppose each other. Further, what they exchange is not exclusively goods and wealth, real and personal property, and things of economic value. They exchange rather courtesies, entertainments, ritual, military assistance, women, children, dances, and feasts; and fairs in which the market is but one element, and the circulation of wealth but one part of a wide and enduring contract. Finally, although the prestations and counter-prestations take place under a voluntary guise they are in essence strictly obligatory, and their sanction is private or open warfare. We propose to call this the system of *total prestations*. Such institutions seem to us to be best represented in the alliance of pairs and phratries in Australian and North American tribes, where ritual, marriages, succession to wealth, community of right and interest, military and religious rank, and even games all form part of one system and presuppose the collaboration of the two moieties of the tribe. The Tlingit and Haida of North-West America give a good expression of the nature of these practices when they say that they "show respect to each other."

But with the Tlingit and Haida, and in the whole of that region, total prestations appear in a form which, although quite typical, is yet evolved and relatively rare. We propose, following American authors, to call it the *potlatch*. This Chinook word has passed into the current language of Whites and Indians from Vancouver to Alaska. Potlatch meant originally "to nourish" or "to consume." The Tlingit and Haida inhabit the islands, the coast, and the land between the coast and the Rockies; they are very rich, and pass their winters in continuous festival, in banquets, fairs, and markets which at the same time are solemn tribal gatherings. The tribes place themselves hierarchically in their fraternities and secret societies. On these occasions are practiced marriages, initiations, and shamanic seances, and the cults of the great gods, totems, and group or individual ancestors. These are all accompanied by ritual and by prestations by whose means political rank within sub-groups, tribes, tribal confederations, and nations is settled. But the remarkable thing about these tribes is the spirit of rivalry and antagonism which dominates all their activities. A man is not afraid to challenge an opposing chief or nobleman. Nor does one stop at the purely sumptuous destruction of accumulated wealth in order to eclipse a rival chief (who may be a close relative). We are here confronted with total prestation in the sense that the whole clan, through the intermediacy of its chiefs, makes contracts involving all its members and everything it possesses. But the agonistic character of the prestation is pronounced. Essentially usurious and extravagant, it is above all a struggle among nobles to determine their position in the hierarchy to the ultimate benefit, if they are successful, of their own clans. This agonistic type of total prestation we propose to call the "potlatch."

So far in our study Davy and I had found few examples of this institution outside North-West America, Melanesia, and Papua. Everywhere else – in Africa, Polynesia, and Malaya, in South America and the rest of North America – the basis of exchange seemed to us to be a simpler type of total prestation. However, further research brings to light a number of forms intermediate between exchanges marked by exaggerated rivalry like those of the American north-west and Melanesia, and others more moderate where the contracting parties rival each other with gifts: for instance, the French compete with each other in their ceremonial gifts, parties, weddings, and invitations, and feel bound, as the Germans say, to *revanchieren* themselves. We find some of these intermediate forms in the Indo-European world, notably in Thrace.

Many ideas and principles are to be noted in systems of this type. The most important of these spiritual mechanisms is clearly the one which obliges us to make a return gift for a gift received. The moral and religious reasons for this constraint are nowhere more obvious than in Polynesia; and in approaching the Polynesian data in the following chapter we shall see clearly the power which enforces the repayment of a gift and the fulfillment of contracts of this kind.

3.3. The Science of Custom (1935)

Ruth Benedict

Anthropology is the study of human beings as creatures of society. It fastens its attention upon those physical characteristics and industrial techniques, those conventions and values, which distinguish one community from all others that belong to a different tradition.

The distinguishing mark of anthropology among the social sciences is that it includes for serious study other societies than our own. For its purposes any social regulation of mating and reproduction is as significant as our own, though it may be that of the Sea Dyaks, and have no possible historical relation to that of our civilization. To the anthropologist, our customs and those of a New Guinea tribe are two possible social schemes for dealing with a common problem, and in so far as he remains an anthropologist he is bound to avoid any weighting of one in favor of the other. He is interested in human behavior, not as it is shaped by one tradition, our own, but as it has been shaped by any tradition whatsoever. He is interested in the great gamut of custom that is found in various cultures, and his object is to understand the way in which these cultures change and differentiate, the different forms through which they express themselves, and the manner in which the customs of any peoples function in the lives of the individuals who compose them.

Now custom has not been commonly regarded as a subject of any great moment. The inner workings of our own brains we feel to be uniquely worthy of investigation, but custom, we have a way of thinking, is behavior at its most commonplace. As a matter of fact, it is the other way around. Traditional custom, taken the world over, is a mass of detailed behavior more astonishing than what any one person could ever evolve in individual actions no matter how aberrant. Yet that is a rather trivial aspect of the matter. The fact of first-rate importance is the predominant role that custom plays in experience and in belief, and the very great varieties it may manifest.

No man ever looks at the world with pristine eyes. He sees it edited by a definite set of customs and institutions and ways of thinking. Even in his philosophical probings he cannot go behind these stereotypes; his very concepts of the true and the false will still have reference to his particular traditional customs. [...] The life-history of the individual is first-and-foremost an accommodation to the patterns and standards traditionally handed down in his community. From the moment of his birth the customs into which he is born shape his experience and behavior. By the time he can talk, he is the little creature of his culture, and by the time he has grown and able to take part in its activities, its habits are his habits, its beliefs his beliefs, its impossibilities his impossibilities. Every child that is born into his group will share them with him, and no child born into one on the opposite side of the globe can ever achieve the thousandth part. There is no social problem it is more incumbent upon us to understand than this of the role of custom. Until we are intelligent as to its laws and varieties, the main complicating facts of human life must remain unintelligible.

The study of custom can be profitable only after certain preliminary propositions have been accepted, and some of these propositions have been violently opposed. In the first place, any scientific study requires that there be no preferential weighting of one or another of the items it selects for its consideration. In all the less controversial fields like the study of cacti or termites or the nature of nebulae, the necessary method of study is to group the relevant material and to take note of all possible variant forms and conditions. In this way we have learned all that we know of the laws of astronomy, or the habits of the social insects, let us say. It is only in the study of man himself that the major social sciences have substituted the study of one local variation, that of Western civilization.

Anthropology was by definition impossible as long as these distinctions between ourselves and the primitive, ourselves and the barbarian, ourselves and the pagan, held sway over people's minds. It was necessary first to arrive at that degree of sophistication where we no longer set our own belief over against our neighbor's superstition. It was necessary to recognize that those institutions which are based on the same premises, let us say the supernatural, must be considered together, our own among the rest.

In the first half of the nineteenth century this elementary postulate of anthropology could not occur to the most enlightened person of Western civilization. Man, all down his history, has defended his uniqueness like a point of honor. In Copernicus's time this claim to supremacy was so inclusive that it took in even the earth on which we live, and the fourteenth century refused with passion to have this planet subordinated to a place in the solar scheme. By Darwin's time, having granted the solar system to the enemy, man fought with all the weapons at his command for the uniqueness of the soul, an unknowable attribute given by God to man in such a manner that it disproved man's ancestry in the animal kingdom. No lack of continuity in the argument, no doubts of the nature of this "soul," not even the fact that the nineteenth century did not care in the least to defend its brotherhood with any group of aliens – none of these facts counted against the first-rate excitement that raged on account of the indignity evolution proposed against the notion of man's uniqueness.

Both these battles we may fairly count as won – if not yet, then soon; but the fighting has only massed itself upon another front. We are quite willing to admit now that the revolution of the earth about the sun or the animal ancestry has next to nothing to do with the uniqueness of our human achievements. If we inhabit another chance planet out of a myriad solar systems, so much the greater glory, and if all the ill-assorted human races are linked by evolution with the animal, the provable differences between ourselves and them are the more extreme and the uniqueness of our institutions the more remarkable. But *our* achievements, *our* institutions, are unique; they are of a different order than those of lesser races and must be protected at all costs. So that to-day, whether it is a question of imperialism, or of race prejudice, or a comparison between Christianity and paganism, we are still preoccupied with the uniqueness, not of the human institutions of the world at large, which no one has ever cared about anyway, but most of our own institutions and achievements, our own civilization.

Western civilization, because of fortuitous historical circumstances, has spread itself more widely than any other local group that has so far been known. It has standardized itself over most of the globe, and we have been led, therefore, to accept a belief in the uniformity of human behavior that under other circumstances would not have arisen. Even very primitive people are sometimes far more conscious of the role of cultural traits than we are, and for good reason. They have had intimate experience of different cultures. They have seen their religion, their economic system, their myriad prohibitions, go down before the white man's. They have laid down the one and accepted the other, often uncomprehendingly enough, but they are quite clear that there are variant arrangements of human life. They will sometimes attribute dominant characteristics of the white man to his commercial competition, or to his institution of warfare, very much in the fashion of the anthropologist.

The white man has had a different experience. He has never seen an outsider, perhaps, unless the outsider has been already Europeanized. If he has traveled, he has very likely been around the world without ever staying outside a cosmopolitan hotel. He knows little of any ways of life but his own. The uniformity of custom, of outlook, that he sees spread about him, seems convincing enough, and conceals from him the fact that it is after all an historical accident. He accepts without more ado the equivalence of human nature and his own cultural standards.

Yet the great spread of white civilization is not an isolated historical circumstance. The Polynesian group, in comparatively recent times, has spread itself from Ontong, Java, to Easter Island, from Hawaii to New Zealand, and the Bantu-speaking tributes spread from the Sahara to southern Africa. But in neither case do we regard these peoples are more than an overgrown local variation of the human species. Western civilization has had all its inventions in transportation and all its far-flung commercial arrangements to back up its great dispersion, and it is easy to understand historically how this came about.

The psychological consequences of this spread of white culture have been out of all proportion to the materialistic. This world-wide cultural diffusion has protected us as man had never been protected before from having to take seriously the civilizations of other peoples; it has given to our culture a massive universality that we have long ceased to account for historically, and which we read off rather as necessary and inevitable. We interpret our dependence, in our civilization, upon economic competition, as proof that this is the prime motivation that human nature can rely upon, or we read off the behavior of small children as it is molded in our civilization and recorded in child clinics, as child psychology or the way in which the young human animal is bound to behave. It is the same whether it is a question of our ethics or of our family organization. It is the inevitability of each familiar motivation that we defend, attempting always to identify our own local ways of behaving with Behavior, or our own socialized habits with Human Nature.

3.4. Facing Mt. Kenya (1938)

Jomo Kenyatta

PREFACE

The country of the Gikuyu, whose system of tribal organization will be described in this book, is in the central part of Kenya. It is divided into five administrative districts: Kiambu, Fort Hall (Murang'a), Nyeri, Embu, and Meru. The population is approximately one million. Owing to the alienation of agricultural and pastoral land, about 110,000 Gikuyu live mostly as squatters on farms on European land and in various districts of Kenya. The rest of the population inhabits the Gikuyu Reserve and the towns. The Gikuyu people are agriculturalists; they herd large flocks of sheep and goats, and, to a less extent, cattle, since their social organization requires a constant supply of stock for such varied purposes as "marriage insurance," payments, sacrifices, meat feasts, magical rites, purification ceremonies, and as a means of supplying clothing to the community.

The cultural and historical traditions of the Gikuyu people have been verbally handed down from generation to generation. As a Gikuyu myself, I have carried them in my head for many years, since people who have no written records to rely on learn to make a retentive memory do the work of libraries. Without note-book or diary, the African learns to make an impression on his own mind which he can recall whenever it is wanted. Throughout his life he has much to commit to memory, and the vivid way in which stories are told to him and their incidents acted out before his eyes helps the child to form an indelible mental picture from his early teaching. [...]

THE GIKUYU SYSTEM OF LAND TENURE

[...] The relation between the Gikuyu and the Europeans can well be illustrated by a Gikuyu story which says: That once upon a time an elephant made a friendship with a man. One day a heavy thunderstorm broke out, the elephant went to his friend, who had a little hut at the edge of the forest, and said to him: "My dear good man, will you please let me put my trunk inside your hut to keep it out of this torrential rain?" The man, seeing what situation his friend was in, replied: "My dear good elephant, my hut is very small, but there is room for your trunk and myself. Please put your trunk in gently." The elephant thanked his friend, saying: "You have done me a good deed and one day I shall return your kindness." But what followed? As soon as the elephant put his trunk inside the hut, slowly he pushed his head inside, and finally flung the man out in the rain, and then lay down comfortably inside his friend's hut, saying: "My dear good friend, your skin is harder than mine, and as there is not enough room for both of us, you can afford to remain in the rain while I am protecting my delicate skin from the hailstorm."

The man, seeing what his friend had done to him started to grumble, the animals in the nearby forest heard the noise and came to see what was the matter. All stood around listening to the heated argument between the man and his friend the elephant. In this turmoil the lion came along roaring and said in a loud voice: "Don't you all know that I am the King of the Jungle! How dare anyone disturb the peace of my kingdom?" On hearing this the elephant, who was one of the high ministers in the jungle kingdom, replied in a soothing voice, and said: "My Lord, there is no disturbance of the peace in your kingdom. I have only been having a little discussion with my friend here as to the possession of this little hut which your lordship sees me occupying." The lion, who wanted to have "peace and tranquility" in his kingdom, replied in a noble voice, saying: "I command my ministers to appoint a Commission of Enquiry to go thoroughly into this matter and report accordingly." He then turned to the man and said: "You have done well by establishing friendship with my people, especially with the elephant who is one of my honorable ministers of state. Do not grumble any more, your hut is not lost to you. Wait until the sitting of my Imperial Commission, and there you will be given plenty of opportunity to state your case. I am sure that you will be pleased with the findings of the Commission." The man was very pleased by these sweet words from the King of the Jungle, and innocently waited for his opportunity, in the belief that, naturally, the hut would be returned to him.

The elephant, obeying the command of his master, got busy with other ministers to appoint the Commission of Enquiry. The following elders of the jungle were appointed to sit in the Commission: (1) Mr. Rhinoceros; (2) Mr. Buffalo; (3); Mr. Alligator; (4) The Rt. Hon. Mr. Fox to act as chairman; and (5) Mr. Leopard to act as Secretary to the Commission. On seeing the personnel, the man protested and asked if it was not necessary to include in this Commission a member from his side. But he was told that it was impossible, since no one from his side was well enough educated to understand the intricacy of jungle law. Further, that there was nothing to fear, for the members of the Commission were all men of repute for their impartiality in justice, and as they were gentlemen chosen by God to look after the interests of races less adequately endowed with teeth and claws, he might rest assured that they would investigate the matter with the greatest care and report impartially.

The Commission sat to take the evidence. The Rt. Hon. Mr. Elephant was first called. He came along with a superior air, brushing his tusks with a sapling which Mrs. Elephant had provided, and in an authoritative voice said: "Gentlemen of the Jungle, there is no need for me to waste your valuable time in relating a story which I am sure you all know. I have always regarded it as my duty to protect the interests of my friends, and this appears to have caused the misunderstanding between myself and my friend here. He invited me to save his hut from being blown away by a hurricane. As the hurricane had gained access, owing to the unoccupied space in the hut, I considered it necessary, in my friend's own interests, to turn the undeveloped space to a more economic use by sitting in it myself; a duty which any of you would undoubtedly have performed with equal readiness in similar circumstances."

After hearing the Rt. Hon. Mr. Elephant's conclusive evidence, the Commission called Mr. Hyena and other elders of the jungle, who all supported what Mr. Elephant had said. Then they called the man, who began to give his own account of the dispute. But the Commission cut him short, saying: "My good man, please confine yourself to relevant issues. We have already heard the circumstances from various unbiased sources; all we wish you to tell us is whether the undeveloped space in your hut was occupied by anyone else before Mr. Elephant assumed his position?" The man began to say: "No, but – " But at this point the Commission declared that they had heard sufficient evidence from both sides and retired to consider their decision. After enjoying a delicious meal at the expense of Rt. Hon. Mr. Elephant, they reached their verdict, called the man, and declared as follows: "In our opinion this dispute has arisen through a regrettable misunderstanding due to the backwardness of your ideas. We consider that Mr. Elephant has fulfilled his sacred duty of protecting your interests. As it is clearly for your good that the space should be put to its most economic use, and as you yourself have not yet reached the stage of expansion which would enable you to fill it, we consider it necessary to arrange a compromise to suit both parties. Mr. Elephant shall continue his occupation of your hut, but we give you permission to look for a site where you can build another hut more suited to your needs, and we will see that you are well protected."

The man, having no alternative, and fearing that his refusal might expose him to the teeth and claws of members of the Commission, did as they suggested. But no sooner had he built another hut than Mr. Rhinoceros charged in with his horn lowered and ordered the man to quit. A Royal Commission was again appointed to look into the matter, and the same finding was given. This procedure was repeated until Mr. Buffalo, Mr. Leopard, Mr. Hyena and the rest were all accommodated with new huts. Then the man decided that he must adopt an effective method of protection, since Commissions of Enquiry did not seem to be of any use to him. He sat down and said: "*Ng'enda thi ndeagaga motegi*" which literally means "there is nothing that treads on the earth that cannot be trapped," or in other words, you can fool people for a time, but not for ever.

Early one morning, when the huts already occupied by the jungle lords were all beginning to decay and fall to pieces, he went out and built a bigger and better hut a little distance away. No sooner had Mr. Rhinoceros seen it than he came rushing in, only to find that Mr. Elephant was already inside, sound asleep. Mr. Leopard next came in at the window,

Mr. Lion, Mr. Fox, and Mr. Buffalo entered the doors, while Mr. Hyena howled for a place in the shade and Mr. Alligator basked on the roof. Presently they all began disputing about their rights of penetration, and from disputing they came to fighting, and while they were all embroiled together the man set the hut on fire and burned it to the ground, jungle lords and all. Then he went home, saying: "Peace is costly, but it's worth the expense," and lived happily ever after.

3.5. Language and the Analysis of Social Laws (1951)

Claude Lévi-Strauss

Language is a social phenomenon; and, of all social phenomena, it is the one which manifests to the greatest degree two fundamental characteristics which make it susceptible of scientific study. In the first place, much of linguistic behavior lies on the level of unconscious thought. When we speak, we are not conscious of the syntactic and morphological laws of our language. Moreover, we are not ordinarily conscious of the phonemes that we employ to convey different meanings; and we are rarely, if ever, conscious of the phonological oppositions which reduce each phoneme to a bundle of differential features. This absence of consciousness, moreover, still holds when we do become aware of the grammar or the phonemics of our language. For, while this awareness is but the privilege of the scholar, language, as a matter of fact, lives and develops only as a collective construct; and even the scholar's linguistic knowledge always remains dissociated from his experience as a speaking agent, for his mode of speech is not affected by his ability to interpret his language on a higher level. We may say, then, that as concerns language, we need not fear the influence of the observer on the observed phenomenon, because the observer cannot modify the phenomenon merely by becoming conscious of it. [...]

Among all social phenomena, language alone has thus far been studied in a manner which permits it to serve as the object of truly scientific analysis, allowing us to understand its formative process and to predict its mode of change. This results from modern researches into the problems of phonemics, which have reached beyond the superficial conscious and historical expression of linguistic phenomena to attain fundamental and objective realities consisting of systems of relations which are the products of unconscious thought processes. The question which now arises is this: is it possible to effect a similar reduction in the analysis of other forms of social phenomena? If so, would this analysis lead to the same result? And if the answer to this last question is in the affirmative, can we conclude that all forms of social life are substantially of the same nature – that is, do they consist of systems of behavior that represent the projection, on the level of conscious and socialized thought, of universal laws which regulate the unconscious activities of the mind? Obviously, no attempt can be made here to do more than to sketch this problem by indicating certain points of reference and projecting the principal lines along which its orientation might be effective.

Some of the researches of Kroeber appear to be of the greatest importance in suggesting approaches to our problem, particularly his work on changes in the styles of women's dress. Fashion actually is, in the highest degree, a phenomenon which depends on the unconscious activity of the mind. We rarely take note of why a particular style pleases us, or falls into disuse. Kroeber has demonstrated that this seemingly arbitrary evolution follows definite laws. These laws cannot be reached by purely empirical observation, or by intuitive consideration of phenomena, but result from measuring some basic relationships between the various elements of costume. The relationship thus obtained can be expressed in terms of mathematical functions, whose values, calculated at a given moment, make prediction possible. [...]

An analogous method has been followed in studying certain features of social organization, particularly marriage rules and kinship systems. It has been shown that the complete set of marriage regulations operating in human societies, and usually classified under different headings such as incest prohibitions, preferential forms of marriage, and the like, can be interpreted as being so many different ways of insuring the circulation of women within the social group, or, of substituting the mechanism of a sociologically determined affinity for that of a biologically determined consanguinity. Proceeding from this hypothesis, it would only be necessary to make a mathematical study of every possible type of exchange between partners to enable one almost automatically to arrive at every type of marriage rule actually operating in living societies and, eventually, to discover others which are merely possible; one would also understand their function and the relationships between each type and the others.

This approach was fully validated by the demonstration, reached by pure deduction, that the mechanisms of reciprocity known to classical anthropology – namely, those based on dual organization and exchange-marriage between two partners or whose number is a multiple of two – are but a special instance of a wider kind of reciprocity between any number of partners. This fact has tended to remain unnoticed, because the partners in those matings, instead of giving and receiving from one another, do not give to those from whom they receive, and do not receive from those to whom they give. They give to and receive from different partners to whom they are bound by a relationship that operates only in one direction.

This type of organization, no less important than the moiety system, has thus far been observed and described only imperfectly and incidentally. Starting with the results of mathematical study, data had to be compiled; thus, the real extension of the system was shown and its first theoretical analysis offered. At the same time, it became possible to explain the more general features of marriage rules such as preferential marriage between bilateral cross-cousins or with only one kind of cross-cousin, on the father's side (patrilateral), or on that of the mother (matrilateral). Thus, for example, though such customs had been unintelligible to anthropologists, they were perfectly clear when regarded as illustrating different modalities of the laws of exchange. In turn, these were reduced to a still more basic relationship between the rules of residence and the rules of descent.

Now, these results have only been achieved by treating marriage regulations and kinship systems as a kind of language, a set of processes permitting the establishment, between individuals and groups, of a certain type of communication. That the mediating factor, in this case, should be the women of the group, who are circulated between clans, lineages, or families, in place of the words of the group, which are circulated between individuals, does not at all change the fact that the essential aspect of the phenomenon is identical in both cases.

We may now ask whether, in extending the concept of communication so as to make it include exogamy and the rules flowing from the prohibition of incest, we may not, reciprocally, achieve insight into a problem that is still very obscure, that of the origin of language. For marriage regulations, in relation to language, represent a complex much more rough and archaic than the latter. It is generally recognized that words are signs: but poets are practically the only ones who know that words have also been values. As against this, women are held by the social group to be values of the most essential kind, though we have difficulty in understanding how these values become integrated in systems endowed with a significant function. This ambiguity is clearly manifested in the reactions of persons who, on the basis of the analysis of social structures referred to, have laid against it the charge of "anti-feminism," because women are referred to as objects. Of course, it may be disturbing to some to have women conceived as mere parts of a meaningful system. However, one should keep in mind that the processes by which phonemes and words have lost – even though in an illusory manner – their character of value, to become reduced to pure signs, will never lead to the same results in matters concerning women. For words do not speak, while women do; as producers of signs, they can never be reduced to the status of symbols or tokens. But it is for this very reason that the position of women, as actually found in this system of communication between men that is made up of marriage regulations and kinship nomenclature, may afford us a workable image of the type of relationships that could have existed at a very early period in the development of language, between human beings and their words. As in the case of women, the original impulse which compelled men to exchange words must be sought for in that split-representation which pertains to the symbolic function. For, since certain terms are simultaneously perceived as having a value both for the speaker and the listener, the only way to resolve this contradiction is in the exchange of complementary values, to which all social existence reduces itself. [...]

How can this hypothesis be verified? It will be necessary to develop the analysis of the different features of social life, either for a given society or for a complex of societies, so that a deep enough level can be reached to make it possible to cross from one to the other; or to express the specific structure of each in terms of a sort of general language, valid for each system separately and for all of them taken together. It would thus be possible to ascertain if one had reached their inner nature, and to determine if this pertained to the same kind of reality. In order to develop this point, an experiment can be attempted. It will consist, on the part of the anthropologist, in translating the basic features of the kinship systems from different parts of the world in terms general enough to be meaningful to the linguist, and thus be equally applicable by the latter to the description of the languages from the same regions. Both could thus ascertain whether or not different types of communication systems in the same societies – that is, kinship and language – are or are not caused by identical unconscious structures. Should this be the case, we would be assured of having reached a truly fundamental formulation.

Indo-European: As concerns the kinship systems, we find that the marriage regulations of our contemporary civilization are entirely based on the principle that, a few negative prescriptions being granted, the density and fluidity of the population will achieve by itself the same results which other societies have sought in more complicated sets of rules; i.e. social cohesion obtained by marriage in degrees far removed or even impossible to trace. This statistical solution has its origin in a typical feature of most ancient IndoEuropean systems. These belong, in the author's terminology, to a simple formula of generalized reciprocity (*Formule simple de l'echange generalise*). However, instead of prevailing between lineages, this formula operates between more complex units of the brastsvo type, which actually are clusters of lineages, each of which enjoys a certain freedom within the rigid framework of general reciprocity in effect at the level of the cluster. Therefore, it can be said that a characteristic feature of Indo-European kinship structure lies in the fact that a problem set in simple terms always admits of many solutions.

Should the linguistic structure be homologous with the kinship structure it would thus be possible to express the basic feature of Indo-European languages as follows: The languages have simple structures, utilizing numerous elements. The opposition between the simplicity of the structure and the multiplicity of elements is expressed in the fact that several elements compete to occupy the same positions in the structure.

1 Sino-Thibetan kinship systems exhibit quite a different type of complexity. They belong to or derive directly from the simplest form of general reciprocity, namely mother's brother's daughter marriage, so that, as has been shown, while this type of marriage insures social cohesion in the simplest way, at the same time it permits this to be indefinitely extended so as to include any number of participants.

Translated into more general terms applicable to language that would correspond to the following linguistic pattern, we may say that the structure is complex, while the elements are few, a feature that may be related to the tonal structure of these languages.

2 The typical feature of African kinship systems is the extension of the bride-wealth system, coupled with a rather frequent prohibition on marriage with the wife's brother's wife. The joint result is a system of general reciprocity already more complex than the one with the mother's brother's daughter, while the types of unions resulting from the circulation of the marriage-price approaches, to some extent, the statistical mechanism operating in our own society.

Therefore one could say that African languages have several modalities corresponding in general to a position intermediate between 1) and 2).

3 The widely recognized features of Oceanic kinship systems seem to lead to the following formulation of the basic characteristics of the linguistic pattern: simple structure and few elements.

[...] If the general characteristics of the kinship systems of given geographical areas, which we have tried to bring into juxtaposition with equally general characteristics of the linguistic structures of those areas, are recognized by linguists as an approach to equivalences of their own observations, then it will be apparent, in terms of our preceding discussion, that we are much closer to the understanding of the fundamental characteristics of social life than we have been accustomed to think.

The road will then be open for a comparative structural analysis of customs, institutions, and accepted patterns of behavior. We will be in a position to understand basic similarities between forms of social life, such as language, art, law, religion, that, on the surface, seem to differ greatly. At the same time, we will have the hope of overcoming the opposition between the collective nature of culture and its manifestations in the individual, since the so-called "collective consciousness" would, in the final analysis, be no more than the expression, on the plane of individual thought and behavior, of certain time and space modalities of these universal laws which make up the unconscious activity of the mind.

Section Three Glossary

culture and personality school   A body of social science scholarship that emphasized the role of cultural socialization in the formation of individual personality. The culture and personality school is most famously associated with the work of Margaret Mead, Ruth Benedict, and Gregory Bateson and was influential in psychology, as well.

French structuralism   The theory that there are universal structures of the human mind that are manifested in cultural traits such as myths, language, religion, kinship patterns, residence patterns, and art, among other things.

native anthropology   "Native" anthropology typically refers to an ethnographic situation in which the anthropologist and the people the anthropologist is studying or working with identify as members of the same community. Kenyatta, for example, identifies as Gikuyu and is presenting ethnographic information about the Gikuyu. For most of anthropology's disciplinary history, the "outsider" status of the anthropologist was thought to yield more objective or analytical insights (Malinowski championed this notion); even today some anthropology textbooks caution anthropologists against "going native." What are the implications of denying ethnographic authority to people working within their "own" societies?

psychological functionalism   The theory that cultural practices are interrelated and comprise an interdependent whole, like an organism. In this frame, social institutions exist to satisfy human needs such as sex, food, and shelter.

On History, Power, and Inequality

THE SOCIAL CONTEXT

The horrors of Nazism during World War II publicized the destructive effects of scientific racism, leading to a political distancing from eugenics programs in the United States and Europe. Outside of Europe, wars for national independence in Asia, Africa, and the Caribbean eroded widespread European imperialism by the mid-twentieth century. Yet globalized conflicts proliferated in the second half of the century, in particular the geopolitical rivalry between Western and Eastern blocs known as the "Cold War," as well as violent armed struggles in Vietnam, Cambodia, Korea, Guatemala, Nicaragua, El Salvador, Nigeria, Bangladesh, Sudan, Somalia, Ethiopia, Iraq, Iran, and many other places.

In the post–World War II context, global financial institutions and government bodies were established for the ostensible purpose of rebuilding, modernizing, and stabilizing societies in war-ravaged zones. Over time, these institutions, the World Bank and International Monetary Fund (IMF) in particular, turned their attention to conferring loans on recently independent nations to "develop" their economies. These twin pursuits of modernization and development, financed by wealthy nations, helped to spread capitalism across the globe and reinforced colonial inequalities in the postcolonial period. The theorists in this section largely draw on analyses grounded in **historical materialism** – an approach that contextualizes social history in political economy – to explain globalized inequalities.

THE CONVERSATION

The scholars in this section largely eschew cultural analyses grounded in evolution, historical particularism, or attention to hidden logics in favor of contextualizing societies in global histories. These scholars show how intergroup interactions have been deeply embedded in unequal relations of power that continue to shape political economy, cultural formation, and even identities. This attention to power, history, and inequality forms the theoretical thread that ties the articles in this section together.

Our first piece by W.E.B. Du Bois is an early theorization of whiteness in the United States. In Reading 4.1, Du Bois examines how successive waves of European immigrants learned to ally themselves with white elites rather than Black slaves or freemen as they sought upward mobility in a deeply racist society. Thus, rather than treat racial identity as a given feature of culture, Du Bois shows how burgeoning class affiliation was eclipsed by the adoption of a white identity among nineteenth-century European farmers-turned-industrial laborers, leading to an ambivalence about, or even support of, the enslavement of Black Americans among working-class whites.

Du Bois is followed by an essay from Cuban scholar Fernando Ortiz, who introduces the concept of transculturation. In this excerpt from his book, *Cuban Counterpoint: Tobacco and Sugar*, Ortiz shows how waves of newcomers to the island – from Tainos to Spaniards to African slaves – together created a Cuban "culture" unlike anything that exists elsewhere in the world. Unlike acculturation, Ortiz's concept of transculturation emphasizes the dynamic and complex nature of cultural exchange and hybridity that emerges from unequal social interactions.

Reading 4.3 by Eric Wolf pushes examinations of global interaction back in time, prior to the period of European expansion. Wolf's attention to the dynamic interconnectedness of people across the "Old World" demonstrates the embedded historicity of non-Europeans, who are often treated as living remnants of a European past, or as a "people without history" of their own (looking at you, social evolutionists!).

The fourth essay in this section by Ann L. Stoler considers the role of gender politics in the formation and maintenance of European imperial cultures in the early twentieth century. Stoler argues that sexual and social repression of European women and colonized men helped to consolidate colonial authority through the establishment of racialized sexual convention. The policing of sexual "transgressions" in colonial societies, Stoler shows, was used to heighten surveillance of white women and non-white men, foment a white identity in imperial societies, and confer upon European women a cultural role of moral guardians of white respectability.

Our final selection by medical anthropologist Paul Farmer delivers a scathing critique of the effects of global capitalism in Haiti. Farmer shows how global powers, France and the United States in particular, have sought to manipulate Haiti's political economy to their benefit since Haiti's war for independence from France (1791–1804). One profound effect of this manipulation is **structural violence**, a ubiquitous but oblique deprioritization of the health and well-being of Haitians that renders them especially vulnerable to injury, sickness, and early death.

THREE QUESTIONS FOR THE READINGS

1 What does attention to a globalized history contribute to an understanding of culture? Are notions of "local culture" or "historical particularism" tenable in light of these readings?

2 According to these selections, what factors tend to reproduce political economic inequalities in a "postcolonial" world?

3 Modernization and development are often unproblematically treated as desirable. What are the implications of these selections for our understandings of modernization in subordinated societies?

ON THE COMPANION WEBSITE

The film *Big Sugar*, intersectionality and Marxism, additional readings, and more.

www.anthropologicaltheory.com

4.1. The White Worker (1935)

W.E.B. Du Bois

The new [European immigrant] labor that came to the United States, while it was poor, used to oppression and accustomed to a low standard of living, was not willing, after it reached America, to regard itself as a permanent laboring class and it is in the light of this fact that the labor movement among white Americans must be studied. The successful, well-paid American laboring class formed, because of its property and ideals, a petty bourgeoisie ready always to join capital in exploiting common labor, white and black, foreign and native. The more energetic and thrifty among the immigrants caught the prevalent American idea that here labor could become emancipated from the necessity of continuous toil and that an increasing proportion could join the class of exploiters, that is of those who made their income chiefly by profit derived through the hiring of labor. [...]

These workers came to oppose slavery not so much from moral as from the economic fear of being reduced by competition to the level of slaves. They wanted a chance to become capitalists; and they found that chance threatened by the competition of a working class whose status at the bottom of the economic structure seemed permanent and inescapable. At first, black slavery jarred upon them, and as early as the seventeenth century German immigrants to Pennsylvania asked the Quakers innocently if slavery was in accord with the Golden Rule. Then, gradually, as succeeding immigrants were thrown in difficult and exasperating competition with black workers, their attitude changed. These were the very years when the white worker was beginning to understand the early American doctrine of wealth and property; to escape the liability of imprisonment for debt, and even to gain the right of universal suffrage. He found pouring into cities like New York and Philadelphia emancipated Negroes with low standards of living, competing for the jobs which the lower class of unskilled white laborers wanted.

For the immediate available jobs, the Irish particularly competed and the employers because of race antipathy and sympathy with the South did not wish to increase the number of Negro workers, so long as the foreigners worked just as cheaply. The foreigners in turn blamed blacks for the cheap price of labor. The result was race war; riots took place which were at first simply the flaming hostility of groups of laborers fighting for bread and butter; then they turned into race riots. [...]

In the [eighteen] forties came quite a different class, the English and German workers, who had tried by organization to fight the machine and in the end had to some degree envisaged the Marxian reorganization of industry through trade unions and class struggle. The attitude of these people toward the Negro was varied and contradictory. At first, they blurted out their disapprobation of slavery on principle. It was a phase of all wage slavery. Then they began to see a way out for the worker in America through the free land of the West. Here was a solution such as was impossible in Europe: plenty of land, rich land, land coming daily nearer its own markets, to which the worker could retreat and restore the industrial balance ruined in Europe by the expropriation of the worker from the soil. [...] This though, curiously enough, instead of increasing the sympathy for the slave turned it directly into rivalry and enmity. [...]

The new immigrants in their competition with this group reflected not simply the general attitude of America toward colored people, but particularly they felt a threat of slave competition which these Negroes foreshadowed. The Negroes worked cheaply, partly from custom, partly as their only defense against competition. The white laborers realized that Negroes were part of a group of millions of workers who were slaves by law, and whose competition kept white labor out of the work of the South and threatened its wages and stability in the North. [...]

[T]wo labor movements [eventually emerged]: the movement to give the black worker a minimum legal status which would enable him to sell his own labor, another movement which proposed to increase the wage and better the condition of the working class in America now largely composed of foreign immigrants, and dispute with the new American capitalist the basis upon which the new wealth was to be divided. [...]

[...] These two movements might easily have cooperated and differed only in matters of emphasis; but the trouble was that black and white laborers were competing for the same jobs just of course as all laborers always are. The immediate competition became open and visible because of racial lines and racial philosophy and particularly in Northern states where free negroes and fugitive slaves had established themselves as workers, while the ultimate and overshadowing competition of free and slave labor was obscured and pushed into the background. This situation, too, made extraordinary reaction, led by the ignorant mob and fomented by authority and privilege; abolitionists were attacked and their meeting places burned; women suffragists were hooted; laws were proposed making the kidnaping of Negroes easier and disfranchising Negro voters in conventions called for purposes of "reform." [...]

[...] Labor in eastern cities refused to touch the slavery controversy, and the control which the Democrats had over the labor vote in New York and elsewhere increased this tendency to ignore the Negro, and increased the division between white and colored labor. In 1850, a Congress of Trade Unions was held with 110 delegates. They stressed land reform but said nothing about slavery and the organization eventually was captured by Tammany

Hall. After 1850 unions composed of skilled laborers began to separate from common laborers and adopt a policy of closed shops and a minimum wage and excluded farmers and Negroes. Although this movement was killed by the panic of 1857, it eventually became triumphant in the eighties and culminated in the American Federation of Labor which today allows any local or national union to exclude Negroes on any pretext. [...]

In all this consideration, we have so far ignored the white workers of the South and we have done this because the labor movement ignored them and the abolitionists ignored them; and above all, they were ignored by Northern capitalists and Southern planters. They were in many respects almost a forgotten mass of men. Cairnes describes the slave South, the period just before the war:

> It resolves itself into three classes, broadly distinguished from each other, and connected by no common interest – the slaves on whom devolves all the regular industry, the slaveholders who reap all fruits, and an idle and lawless rabble who live dispersed over vast plains in a condition little removed from absolute barbarism.

From all that has been written and said about the antebellum South, one almost loses sight of about 5,000,000 people in 1860 who lived in the South and held no slaves. Even among the two million slave-holders, an oligarchy of 8,000 really ruled the South, while as an observer said: "For twenty years, I do not recollect ever to have seen or heard these non-slaveholding whites referred to by the Southern gentleman as constituting any part of what they called the South" (Schluter 1913: 86). They were largely ignorant and degraded; only 25% could read and write. [...]

Two classes of poor whites have been differentiated: the mountain whites and the poor whites of the lowlands. [...] The so-called "mountain boomer," says an observer, "has little self-respect and no self-reliance. [...] So long as his corn pile lasts the "cracker" lives in contentment, feasting on a sort of hoc cake made of grated corn meal mixed with salt and water and baked before the hot coals, with addition of what game the forest furnishes him when he can get up the energy to go out and shoot or trap it" (Hart 1910: 34–5). [...] Above this lowest mass rose a middle class of poor whites in the making. There were some small farmers who had more than a mere sustenance and yet were not large planters. There were overseers. There was a growing class of merchants who traded with the slaves and free Negroes and became in many cases larger traders, dealing with the planters for the staple crops. Some poor whites rose to the professional class, so that the rift between the planters and the mass of the whites was partially bridged by this smaller intermediate class.

While revolt against the domination of the planters over the poor whites was voiced by men like Helper, who called for a class struggle to destroy the planters, this was nullified by deep-rooted antagonism to the Negro, whether slave or free. If black labor could be expelled from the United States or eventually exterminated, then the fight against the planter could take place. But the poor whites and their leaders could not for a moment contemplate a fight of united white and black labor against the exploiters. Indeed, the natural leaders of the poor whites, the small farmer, the merchant, the professional man, the white mechanic and slave overseer, were bound to the planters and repelled from the slaves and even from the mass of the white laborers in two ways: first, they constituted the police patrol who could ride with planters and now and then exercise unlimited force upon recalcitrant or runaway slaves; and then, too, there was always a chance that they themselves might also become planters by saving money, by investment, by the power of good luck; and the only heaven that attracted them was the life of the great Southern planter. [...]

The resultant revolt of the poor whites, just as the revolt of the slaves, came through migration. And their migration, instead of being restricted, was freely encouraged. As a result, the poor whites left the South in large numbers. In 1860, 399,700 Virginians were living out of their native state. From Tennessee, 344,765 emigrated; from North Carolina, 272,606, and from South Carolina, 256,868. The majority of these had come to the Middle West and it is quite possible that the Southern states sent as many settlers to the West as the Northeastern states, and while the Northeast demanded free soil, the Southerners demanded not only free soil but the exclusion of Negroes from work and the franchise. They had a very vivid fear of the Negro as a competitor in labor, whether slave or free. [...]

This brings us down to the period of the Civil War. Up to the time that the war actually broke out, American labor simply refused, in the main, to envisage black labor as a part of its problem. Right up to the edge of the war, it was talking about the emancipation of white labor and the organization of stronger unions without saying a word, or apparently giving a thought, to four million black slaves. During the war, labor was resentful. Workers were forced to fight in a strife between capitalists in which they had no interest and they showed their resentment in the peculiarly human way of beating and murdering the innocent victims of it all, the black free Negros of New York and other Northern cities; while in the South, five million non-slaveholding poor white farmers and laborers sent their manhood by the thousands to fight and die for a system that had degraded them equally with the black slave. Could one imagine anything more paradoxical than this whole situation? [...]

Indeed, the plight of the white working class throughout the world today is directly traceable to Negro slavery in America, on which modern commerce and industry was founded, and which persisted to threaten free labor until it was partially overthrown in 1863. The resulting color caste founded and retained by capitalism was adopted, forwarded and approved by white labor and resulted in subordination of colored labor to white profits the world over. Thus, the majority of the world's laborers, by the insistence of white labor, became the basis of a system of industry which ruined democracy and showed its perfect fruit in World War and Depression.

REFERENCES

Hart, Albert Bushnell. 1910. *The Southern South*. New York: D. Appleton and Company.
Schluter, Hermann. 1913. *Lincoln, Labor, and Slavery*. New York: Socialist Literature Company.

4.2. On the Social Phenomenon of "Transculturation" and Its Importance in Cuba (1940)

Fernando Ortiz

With the reader's permission, especially if he happens to be interested in ethnographic and sociological questions, I am going to take the liberty of employing for the first time the term *transculturation*, fully aware of the fact that it is a neologism. And I venture to suggest that it might be adopted in sociological terminology, to a great extent at least, as a substitute for the term *acculturation*, whose use is now spreading.

Acculturation is used to describe the process of transition from one culture to another, and its manifold social repercussions. But *transculturation* is a more fitting term.

I have chosen the word *transculturation* to express the highly varied phenomena that have come about in Cuba as a result of the extremely complex transmutations of culture that have taken place here, and without a knowledge of which it is impossible to understand the evolution of the Cuban folk, either in the economic or in the institutional, legal, ethical, religious, artistic, linguistic, psychological, sexual, or other aspects of its life.

The real history of Cuba is the history of its intermeshed transculturations. First came the transculturation of the paleolithic Indian to the Neolithic, and the disappearance of the latter because of his inability to adjust himself to the culture brought in by the Spaniards. Then the transculturation of an unbroken stream of white immigrants. They were Spaniards, but representatives of different cultures and themselves torn loose, to use the phrase of the time, from the Iberian Peninsula groups and transplanted to a New World, where everything was new to them, nature and people, and where they had to readjust themselves to a new syncretism of cultures. At the same time there was going on the transculturation of a steady human stream of African Negroes coming from all the coastal regions of Africa along the Atlantic, from Senegal, Guinea, the Congo, and Angola and as far away as Mozambique on the opposite shore of that continent. All of them snatched from their original social groups, their own cultures destroyed and crushed under the weight of the cultures in existence here, like sugar cane ground in the rollers of the mill. And still other immigrant cultures of the most varying origins arrived, either in sporadic waves or a continuous flow, always exerting an influence and being influenced in turn: Indians from the mainland, Jews, Portuguese, Anglo-Saxons, French, North Americans, even yellow Mongoloids from Macao, Canton, and other regions of the sometime Celestial Kingdom. And each of them torn from his native moorings, faced with the problem of disadjustment and readjustment, of deculturation and acculturation – in a word, of transculturation.

Among all peoples, historical evolution has always meant a vital change from one culture to another at tempos varying from gradual to sudden. But in Cuba the cultures that have influenced the formation of its folk have been so many and so diverse in their spatial position and their structural composition that this vast blend of races and cultures overshadows in importance every other historical phenomenon. Even economic phenomena, the most basic factors of social existence, in Cuba are almost always conditioned by the different cultures. In Cuba the terms Ciboney, Taino, Spaniard, Jew, English, French, Anglo-American Negro, Yucatec, Chinese, and Creole do not mean merely the different elements that go into the make-up of the Cuban nation, as expressed by their different indications of origin. Each of these has come to mean in addition the synthetic and historic appellation of one of the various economies and cultures that have existed in Cuba successively and even simultaneously, at times giving rise to the most terrible clashes. We have only to recall that described by Bartolomé de las Casas as the "destruction of the Indies."

[…] First there was the culture of the Ciboneys and the Guanajabibes, the paleolithic culture, our stone age. […]

After this came the culture of the Taino Indians, which was Neolithic. […] Then came a hurricane of culture: Europe. There arrived together, and in mass, iron, gunpowder, the horse, the wheel, the printing-press, books, the master, the King, the Church, the banker…. A revolutionary upheaval shook the Indian peoples of Cuba, tearing up their institutions by the roots and destroying their lives. […] In a single day various of the intervening ages were crossed in Cuba; one might say thousands of "culture-years," if such measurement were admissible in the chronology of peoples. If the Indies of America were a New World for the Europeans, Europe was a far newer world for the people of America. They were two worlds that discovered each other and collided head-on. […]

There was no more important human factor in the evolution of Cuba than these continuous, radical, contrasting geographic transmigrations, economic and social, of the first settlers, this perennial transitory nature of their objectives, and their unstable life in the land where they were living, in perpetual disharmony with the society from which they drew their living. Men, economies, cultures, ambitions were all foreigners here, provisional, changing, "birds of passage" over the country, at its cost, against its wishes, and without its approval.

With the whites came the Negroes, first from Spain, at that time full of slaves from Guinea and the Congo, and then directly from all the Dark Continent. They brought with them their diverse cultures, some as primitive as that of the Ciboneys, others in a state of advanced barbarism like that of the Tainos, and others more economically and socially developed, like the Mandingas, Yolofes (Wolofs), Hausas, Dahomeyans, and centralized governments ruling territories and populations as large as Cuba; intermediate cultures between the Taino and the Aztec, with metals, but as yet without writing.

The Negroes brought with their bodies their souls, but not their institutions nor their implements. They were of different regions, races, languages, cultures, classes, ages, sexes, thrown promiscuously into the slave ships, and socially equalized by the same system of slavery. They arrived deracinated, sounded, shattered, like the cane of the fields, and like it they were ground and crushed to extract the juice of their labor. No other human element has had to suffer such a profound and repeated change of surroundings, cultures, class, and conscience. […] Under these conditions of mutilation and social amputation, thousands and thousands of human beings were brought to Cuba year after year and century after century from continents beyond the sea. To a greater or lesser degree whites and Negroes were in the same state of dissociation in Cuba. All, those above and those below, living together in the same atmosphere of terror and oppression, the oppressed in terror of punishment, the oppressor in terror of reprisals, all beside justice, beside adjustment, beside themselves. And all in the pain process of transculturation.

After the Negroes began the influx of Jews, French, Anglo-Saxons, Chinese, and peoples from the four quarters of the globe. They were all coming to a new world, all on the way to a more or less rapid process of transculturation.

I am of the opinion that the word *transculturation* better expresses the different phases of the process of transition from one culture to another because this does not consist merely in acquiring another culture, which is what the English word acculturation really implies, but the process also necessarily involves the loss or uprooting of a previous culture, which could be defined as a deculturation. In addition, it carries the idea of the consequent creation of new cultural phenomena, which could be called neoculturation. In the end, as the school of Malinowski's followers maintains, the result of every union of cultures is similar to that of the reproductive process between individuals: the offspring always has something of both parents but is always different from each of them.

These questions of sociological nomenclature are not to be disregarded in the interests of a better understanding of social phenomena, especially in Cuba, whose history, more than that of any other country of America, is an intense, complex, unbroken process of transculturation of human groups, all in a state of transition. The concept of transculturation is fundamental and indispensable for an understanding of the history of Cuba, and, for analogous reasons, of that of America in general. But this is not the moment to go into this theme at length, which will be considered in another work in progress dealing with the effects on Cuba of the transculturations of Indians, whites, Negroes, and Mongols. […]

4.3. The World in 1400 (1982)

Eric Wolf

In the year 1271 the Venetian merchants Niccolo and Maffeo Polo, together with Niccolo's son Marco, left the eastern shore of the Mediterranean and traveled through Iran to Hormuz on the Persian Gulf. From there they set off northeastward to Kashgar, where they took the old Silk Road and went on to Peking. After long travels through China and South Asia, the Polos set sail for Europe, arriving in Venice in 1295. Some forty years later, Ibn Battutah, a scholar-official from Morocco, embarked on a pilgrimage to Mecca, and went on through Iran, Anatolia, and the Crimea to Constantinople. From there he traveled to Central Asia and India, spending some years in government positions in Delhi and the Maldive Islands. After visiting southern China and Sumatra, he went home to Morocco in 1349. Three years later he accompanied Moroccan merchants across the Sahara to the kingdom of Mali in the Western Sudan and returned to Fez to dictate his travel story to a scribe. Between 1405 and 1433 the Chinese admiral Cheng-ho sailed seven times to southern Asia, reaching as far as the Red Sea and the East African coast. In 1492 a Genoese sea captain in the employ of the Queen of Aragon got his first glimpse of the New World, where he sighted the Bahamas and thought he had arrived in Japan.

These voyages were not isolated adventures but manifestations of forces that were drawing the continents into more encompassing relationships and would soon make the world a unified stage for human action. In order to understand what the world would become, we must first know what it was. I shall therefore follow an imaginary voyager in the year 1400 and depict the world that he might have seen.

In this effort at global anthropology, I will go beyond the portrayal of distinctive tribes, culture areas, and civilizations to delineate the interlocking networks of human interaction that extended across each of the two still separate hemispheres – the "Old World" of Europe, Asia, and Africa, and the "New World" of the Americas. These networks grew up and spread out in time as well as space. To account for them – to follow their growth and spread – means also to trace the historical itineraries of populations that history written from a Western point of view has tended to ignore or to caricature. Like the anthropologist's "primitive contemporaries," they have been treated as people without a history of their own.

These wide-ranging linkages among populations before European expansion were outcomes of identifiable material processes. One of these processes was the build-up of contentious hegemonic political and military systems. Each of the two hemispheres witnessed, separately, the rise of empires, which drew toward themselves the surpluses produced by varied and manifold groups. A second process at work was the growth of long-distance trade, which everywhere connected zones of supply with centers of concentrated demand, and which opened up specialized roles for the peoples who sat astride the routes of commerce. Empire building and trade, in turn, created extensive grids of communication, which bound together different populations under the aegis of dominant religious or political ideologies. Together these processes shaped the world that Europe would soon reorganize to answer to requirements of its own.

POLITICAL GEOGRAPHY OF THE OLD WORLD

To understand this world of 1400, we must begin with geography. A map of the Old World reveals certain physical constants. One of these is the great chain of mountains running in an east-west direction across the Eurasian landmass. Rising up from the rugged ranges of southern and western China, the chain ascends to the heights of the Kunlun, Himalayas and Pamir, "roof of the world," and reaches across the Elburz Range to the Caucasus, the Carpathians, the Alps, and finally the Pyrenees. Sometimes these mountains retarded contact between north and south. At other times, gaps in the chain encouraged population movement and attacks. In northern China, the Han had to build their big wall to keep the Chinese in and the Mongols and Turks out. In Turkestan, roads led southward into Iran and India. In the west, raiders could move up the valley of the Danube into the heart of Europe.

An endpaper map shows us a second constant, the distribution of major climatic zones. These encourage different covers of natural vegetation and, hence, favor different kinds of human habitation. The map immediately shows us a major belt of dry country running east and west from the Sahara and the Arabian deserts across the plateau of Iran into Turkestan and Mongolia. This is the country of pastoral populations, driving their herds over the pasture available along desert margins and on the steppe. Cultivation is possible only around permanent water sources in oases. South of the dry zone of desert and steppe lie warm and moist tropical and subtropical forest and savanna, often favorable to cultivation, as in West Africa, the Gangetic Plain, the peninsulas and islands of Southeast Asia, and southern China. To the north of the dry zone extends the forest. West of the Ural Mountains, the forest country is rainy and experiences a longer growing season; hence, when cleared, it makes good farming country. To the east of the Urals, the forest is drier and colder. It becomes taiga, cold-weather coniferous forest, and – together with the treeless, lichen-covered belt of circumpolar tundra – the predilect habitat of forest hunters. Here cultivators ventured only rarely, and herders found it difficult to keep their animals alive.

When we compare the distribution of cultivable and improvable agricultural land with that of desert and steppe, a significant contrast emerges. The distribution of the dry belt is continuous; that of the cultivable landscape is spotty and archipelagic. The pastoral corridor facilitated centrifugal movement; the compartmentalized arable zones oriented people centripetally toward the grounds of their home village. This dichotomy between steppe and sown shaped much of the course of human action in the Old World, sometimes dividing pastoralist and villager, at other times prompting them into interaction.

Cultivation in northwestern Africa is confined mainly to the Mediterranean vertient north of the Atlas, and is impeded to the south and east by steppe and desert. Wheat raised in the Sus Valley and the Rharb of Morocco, in the plains of Shelif and Mitidja in Algeria, and in the Medjerda Plain of Tunis was important in sustaining local courts and elites. East of Tunis lies the oasis of Tripoli, and beyond that Egypt, the great oasis formed by the Nile. Its grain had fed Rome during the days of the Roman Empire, and thereafter it played the same role for Byzantium, for the Arabs at Damascus, and – after 1453 – for the Ottomans.

Byzantium and the Ottoman Empire also drew increasingly on the lands of the lower Danube and the shores of the Black Sea for their grain supply. [...] Small islands of cultivation could be sustained on terraced hillsides in Palestine, and there were major agricultural oases at Antioch (now Antakya) and Damascus. The Syrian steppe, farmed in Roman times and again in the twentieth century, is ecologically marginal and long lay abandoned to occupation by pastoral nomads. In Anatolia agriculture is possible along the shores of the Mediterranean and the Black Sea and in occasional patches on the mountainous plateau, but the rest is steppe, and to the southeast the desert again supervenes. Iraq – the land between the Tigris and the Euphrates – was once enormously productive. Surplus production, aided by hydraulic works, had underwritten state formation since Akkadian times; construction of waterworks of all kinds reached a climax here under the Sassanid dynasty of Iran (A.O. 226–637). But with the Islamic conquest of the area and the concomitant growth of Baghdad into a capital with over 300,000 inhabitants, agricultural wealth and human resources were increasingly sacrificed to the city. This led to a decline in agricultural output and a steady decrease in the amount of tribute obtained (Adams 1965: 84 ff.). A final blow to productivity was delivered by the Mongol invasion in the mid-thirteenth century, when the Mongol khan Hulagu destroyed the irrigation works of the lower valley.

Beyond the mountain chain of the Zagros lies the Iranian plateau. Most of it is covered by steppe and desert, with cultivation possible only in favored spots along a belt of alluvial fans extending around the inside rim of the mountain chain. On occasion cultivation has been extended into the drier zone by means of underground tunnels (qanats), which carry water by gravity flow along the water table to outlying fields. Waste and desert again restrict cultivation in Afghanistan and Baluchistan to the east.

Despite the prevalence of inhospitable desert and steppe throughout this area, a string of urbanized oases based on irrigation agriculture furnished rest stops and supply stations for caravans moving east and west. The most important of these caravan routes was the Silk Road. It began at Antioch in northern Syria, ran through Rai (near Teheran), then passed through Merv and Balich (Bactria) to Kashgar. At Kashgar the road forked, conducting travelers both north and south of the Taklamakan (southern Gobi) Desert. The northern fork led to Kucha and Karashahr, the southern one through Yarkand and Khotan. Both forks met again at Tunhwang in Chinese Kansu, whence roads led on into China. Kashgar – which Marco Polo praised for its gardens and vineyards – was thus a major hub of long-distance commerce, inhabited, in Polo's words, by people "who travel and trade all over the world." From Kashgar another route led northward to Samarkand and on to Sarai on the lower Volga, from which point one could reach Azov and the Black Sea. All along the northern escarpment of the great Eurasian mountain chain, too, there were pockets of arable land that could be cultivated if the herders, with their demand for pasture and water, could be kept at bay. [...]

North of the Eurasian mountain chain lay the steppe, forming a vast corridor from the Mongolian steppe in the east, through the Kirghiz and Russian steppes, to the Hungarian steppe close to the heart of Central Europe. These were the predilect traveling grounds of pastoral nomads. The conversion of the southern Russian prairie to permanent cultivation had to await the defeat of the pastoralists and their khans by the Russians in the seventeenth century A.O. [...]

Everywhere in this world of 1400, populations existed in inter-connections. Groups that defined themselves as culturally distinct we linked by kinship or ceremonial allegiance; states expanded, incorporating other peoples into more encompassing political structures; elite groups succeeded one another, seizing control of agricultural populations and establishing new political and symbolic orders. Trade formed networks from East Asia to the Levant, across the Sahara, from East Africa through the Indian Ocean to the Southeast Asian archipelago. Conquest, incorporation, recombination, and commerce also marked the New World. In both hemispheres, populations impinged upon other populations through permeable social boundaries, creating intergrading, interwoven social and cultural entities. If there were any isolated societies these were but temporary phenomena – a group pushed to the edge of a zone of interaction and left to itself for a brief moment in time. Thus, the social scientist's model of distinct and separate systems, and of a timeless "precontact" ethnographic present, does not adequately depict the situation before European expansion; much less can it comprehend the worldwide system of links that would be created by that expansion.

REFERENCE

Adams, Robert M. 1965. *Land Behind Baghdad: A History of Settlement on the Diyala Plain.* Chicago: University of Chicago Press.

4.4. Making Empire Respectable: The Politics of Race and Sexual Morality in Twentieth-Century Colonial Cultures (1989)

Ann L. Stoler

Feminist attempts to engage the gender politics of Dutch, French and British imperial cultures converge on some strikingly similar observations; namely that European women in these colonies experienced the cleavages of racial dominance and internal social distinctions very differently than men precisely because of their ambiguous positions, as both subordinates in colonial hierarchies and as active agents of imperial culture in their own right. Concomitantly, the majority of European women who left for the colonies in the late 19th and early 20th centuries confronted profoundly rigid restrictions on their domestic, economic and political options, more limiting than those of metropolitan Europe at the time and sharply contrasting the opportunities open to colonial men.

In one form or another these studies raise a basic question: in what ways were gender inequalities essential to the structure of colonial racism and imperial authority? Was the strident misogyny of imperial thinkers and colonial agents a byproduct of received metropolitan values ("they just brought it with them"), a reaction to contemporary feminist demands in Europe ("women need to be put back in their breeding place"), or a novel and pragmatic response to the conditions of conquest? Was the assertion of European supremacy in terms of patriotic man hood and racial virility an expression of imperial domination or a defining feature of it?

In this paper I examine some of the ways in which colonial authority and racial distinctions were fundamentally structured in gendered terms. I look specifically at the administrative and medical discourse and management of European sexual activity, reproduction and marriage as it articulated with the racial politics of colonial rule. Focusing on French Indochina and the Dutch East Indies in the early 20th century, but drawing on other contexts, I suggest that the very categories of "colonizer" and "colonized" were secured through forms of sexual control which defined the domestic arrangements of Europeans and the cultural investments by which they identified themselves. Gender specific sexual sanctions demarcated positions of power by refashioning middle-class conventions of respectability, which, in turn, prescribed the personal and public boundaries of race. [...]

DEALING WITH TRANSGRESSIONS: POLICING THE PERIL

The gender-specific requirements for colonial living, referred to above, were constructed on heavily racist evaluations which pivoted on the heightened sexuality of colonized men (Tiffany and Adams 1985). Although European women were absent from men's sexual reveries in colonial literature, men of color were considered to see them as desired and seductive figures. European women needed protection because men of color had "primitive" sexual urges and uncontrollable lust, aroused by the sight of white women (Strobel 1987:379; Schmidt 1987:411). In some colonies, that sexual threat was latent; in others it was given a specific name.

In southern Rhodesia and Kenya in the 1920s and 1930s, preoccupations with the "Black Peril" (referring to the professed dangers of sexual assault on white women by black men) gave rise to the creation of citizens' militias, ladies' riflery clubs and investigations as to whether African female domestic servants would not be safer to employ than men (Kirkwood 1984:158; Schmidt 1987:412; Kennedy 1987:128–47). In New Guinea the White Women's Protection Ordinance of 1926 provided "the death penalty for any person convicted for the crime of rape or attempted rape upon a European woman or girl" (Inglis 1975:vi). And as late as 1934, Solomon Islands authorities introduced public flogging as punishment for "criminal assaults on [white] females" (Boutilier 1984:197).

What do these cases have in common? The rhetoric of sexual assault and the measures used to prevent it had virtually no correlation with the incidence of rape of European women by men of color. Just the contrary: there was often no evidence, *ex post facto* or at the time, that rapes were committed or that rape attempts were made (Schmidt 1987; Inglis 1975; Kirkwood 1984; Kennedy 1987; Boutilier 1984). This is not to suggest that sexual assaults never occurred, but that their incidence had little to do with the fluctuations in anxiety about them. Secondly, the rape laws were race-specific; sexual abuse of black women was not classified as rape and therefore was not legally actionable, nor did rapes committed by white men lead to prosecution (Mason 1958:246–7). If these accusations of sexual threat were not prompted by the fact of rape, what did they signal and to what were they tied?

Allusions to political and sexual subversion of the colonial system went hand in hand. Concern over protection of white women intensified during real and perceived crises of control – provoked by threats to the internal cohesion of the European communities or by infringements on their borders. While the chronologies differ, we can identify a patterned sequence of events in which Papuan, Algerian, and South African men heightened their demands for civil rights and refused the constraints imposed upon their education, movements, or dress (Inglis 1975:8, 11; Sivan 1983:178). Rape charges were thus based on perceived transgressions of political and social space. "Attempted rapes" turned out to be "incidents" of a Papuan man "discovered" in the vicinity of a white residence, a Fijian man who entered a European patient's room, a male servant poised at the bedroom door of a European woman asleep or in half-dress (Boutilier 1984:197; Inglis 1975:11; Schmidt 1987:413). With such a broad definition of danger, all colonized men of color were potential aggressors.

Accusations of sexual assault frequently followed upon heightened tensions within European communities – and renewed efforts to find consensus within them. In South Africa and Rhodesia, the relationship between reports of sexual assault and strikes among white miners and railway workers is well documented (van Onselen 1982:51; Kennedy 1987:138). Similarly, in the late 1920s when labor protests by Indonesian workers and European employees were most intense, Sumatra's corporate elite expanded their vigilante organizations, intelligence networks and demands for police protection to ensure their women were safe and their workers "in hand" (Stoler 1985). In this particular context where the European community had been blatantly divided between low-ranking estate employees and the company elite, common interests were emphasized and domestic situations were rearranged.

In Sumatra's plantation belt, subsidized sponsorship of married couples replaced the recruitment of single Indonesian workers and European staff, with new incentives provided for family formation in both groups. This recomposed labor force of family men in "stable households" explicitly weeded out the politically malcontent. With the marriage restriction finally lifted for European staff in the 1920s, young men sought marriages with Dutch women. Higher salaries, upgraded housing, elevated bonuses, and a more mediated chain of command between colonized fieldworker and colonial managers clarified economic and political interests. With this shift, the vocal opposition to corporate and government directives, sustained by an independent union of European subordinates for nearly two decades, was effectively dissolved (Stoler 1989:152–3).

The remedies intended to alleviate sexual danger embraced a common set of prescriptions for securing white control: increased surveillance of native men, new laws stipulating severe corporal punishment for the transgression of sexual and social boundaries, and the creation of areas made racially off limits. This moral rearmament of the European community and reassertion of its cultural identity charged European women with guarding new norms. While instrumental in promoting white solidarity, it was partly at their own expense. As we shall see, they were nearly as closely surveilled as colonized men (Strobel 1987).

While native men were legally punished for alleged sexual assaults, European women were frequently blamed for provoking those desires. New arrivals from Europe were accused of being too familiar with their servants, lax in their commands, indecorous in speech and dress (Vellut 1982:100; Kennedy 1987:141; Schmidt 1987:413). The Rhodesian immorality act of 1916 "made it an offence for a white woman to make an indecent suggestion to a male native" (Mason 1958:247). In Papua New Guinea "everyone" in the Australian community agreed that rape assaults were caused by a "younger generation of white women" who simply did not know how to treat servants (Inglis 1975:80). In Rhodesia as in Uganda, women were restricted to activities within the European enclaves and dissuaded from taking up farming on their own (Gartrell 1984:169; Kennedy 1987:141). As in the American South, "etiquettes of chivalry controlled white women's behavior even as [it] guarded caste lines" (Dowd Hall 1984:64). A defense of community, morality and white male power affirmed the vulnerability of white women and the sexual threat posed by native men, and created new sanctions to limit the liberties of both.

Although European colonial communities in the early 20th century assiduously monitored the movements of European women, some European women did work. French women in the settler communities of Algeria and Senegal ran farms, rooming houses, and shops along with their men (Baroli 1967:159; O'Brien 1972). Elsewhere, married European women "supplemented" their husbands' incomes, helping to maintain the "white standard" (Tirefort 1979; Mercier 1965:292). Women were posted throughout the colonial empires as missionaries, nurses, and teachers; while some women openly questioned the sexist policies of their male superiors, by and large their tasks buttressed rather than contested the established cultural order (Knibiehler and Goutalier 1985; Callaway 1987:111).

French feminists urged women with skills (and a desire for marriage) to settle in Indochina at the turn of the century, but colonial administrators were adamantly against their immigration. Not only was there a surfeit of widows without resources, but European seamstresses, florists and children's outfitters could not compete with the cheap and skilled labor provided by well established Chinese firms (Corneau 1900:10, 12). In Tonkin in the 1930s there was still "little room for single women, be they unmarried, widowed or divorced"; most were shipped out of the colony at the government's charge (Gantes 1981:45). Firmly rejecting expansion based on "poor white" (*petit blanc*) settlement as in Algeria, French officials in Indochina dissuaded *colons* with insufficient capital from entry and promptly repatriated those who tried to remain. Single women were seen as the quintessential *petit blanc,* with limited resources and shopkeeper aspirations. Moreover, they presented the dangerous possibility that straitened circumstances would lead them to prostitution, thereby degrading European prestige at large.

In the Dutch East Indies, state officials identified European widows as one of the most economically vulnerable and impoverished segments of the European community (Het Pauperisme onder de Europeanen 1901:28). Professional competence did not leave European women immune from marginalization. Single professional women were held in contempt as were European prostitutes, with surprisingly similar objections. The important point is that numerous categories of women fell outside the social space to which European colonial women were assigned; namely, as custodians of family welfare and respectability, and as dedicated and willing subordinates to, and supporters of, colonial men. The rigor with which these norms were applied becomes more comprehensible when we see how a European family life and bourgeois respectability became increasingly tied to notions of racial survival, imperial patriotism and the political strategies of the colonial state. [...]

I have focused here on the multiple levels at which sexual control figured in the substance, as well as the iconography, of racial policy and imperial rule. But colonial politics was obviously not just about sex; nor did sexual relations reduce to colonial politics. On the contrary, sex in the colonies was about sexual access and reproduction, class distinctions and racial privileges, nationalism and European identity in different measure and not all at the same time. These major shifts in the positioning of women were not signaled by the penetration of capitalism per se but by more subtle changes in class politics, imperial morality and as responses to the vulnerabilities of colonial control. As we attempt broader ethnographies of empire, we may begin to capture how European culture and class politics resonated in colonial settings, how class and gender discriminations not only were translated into racial attitudes, but themselves reverberated in the metropole as they were fortified on colonial ground. Such investigations should help show that sexual control was both an instrumental image for the body politic, a salient part standing for the whole, and itself fundamental to how racial policies were secured and how colonial projects were carried out.

REFERENCES

Baroli, Marc. 1967. *La vie quotidienne des Français en Algerie*. Paris: Hachette.

Boutilier, James. 1984. "European Women in the Solomon Islands, 1900–1942." In *Rethinking Women's Roles: Perspectives from the Pacific*, edited by Denise O'Brien and Sharon Tiffany, 173–99. Berkeley: University of California Press.

Callaway, Helen. 1987. *Gender, Culture and Empire: European Women in Colonial Nigeria*. London: Macmillan Press.

Corneau, Grace. 1900. *La femme aux colonies*. Paris: Librairie Nilsson.

Dowd Hall, Jacquelyn. 1984. "'The Mind that Burns in Each Body': Women, Rape, and Racial Violence." *Southern Exposure* 12 (6): 61–71.

Gantes, Gilles de. 1981. *La population francaise au Tonkin entre 1931 et 1938*. Memoire. Aix-en-Provence: Institut d'Histoire des Pays d'Outre Mer.

Gartrell, Beverley. 1984. "Colonial Wives: Villains or Victims?" In *The Incorporated Wife*, edited by H. Callan and S. Ardener, 165–85. London: Croom Helm.

Het Pauperisme Commissie. 1901. Het Pauperisme onder de Europeanen. Batavia: Landsdrukkerij

Het Pauperisme Commissie. 1903. Rapport der Pauperisme-Commissie. Batavia: Landsdrukkerij.

Inglis, Amirah. 1975. *The White Women's Protection Ordinance: Sexual Anxiety and Politics in Papua*. London: Sussex University Press.

Kennedy, Dane. 1987. *Islands of White*. Durham: Duke University Press.

Kirkwood, Deborah. 1984. "Settler Wives in Southern Rhodesia: A Case Study." In *The Incorporated Wife*, edited by H. Callan and S. Ardener. London: Croom Helm.

Knibiehler, Y., and R. Goutalier. 1985. *La femme au temps des colonies*. Paris: Stock.

Mason, Philip. 1958. *The Birth of a Dilemma: The Conquest and Settlement of Rhodesia*. New York: Oxford University Press.

Mercier, Paul. 1965. "The European Community of Dakar." In *Africa: Social Problems of Change and Conflict,* edited by Pierre van den Berghe, 284–304. San Francisco: Chandler.

O'Brien, Rita Cruise. 1972. *White Society in Black Africa: The French in Senegal*. London: Faber & Faber.

Schmidt, Elizabeth. 1987. Ideology, Economics and the Role of Shona Women in Southern Rhodesia, 1850–1939. Ph.D. dissertation, University of Wisconsin.

Sivan, Emmanuel. 1983. *Interpretations of Islam*. Princeton: Darwin Press.

Stoler, Ann. 1985. "Perceptions of Protest." *American Ethnologist* 12 (4): 642–58. https://doi.org/10.1525/ae.1985.12.4.02a00030.

Stoler, Ann. 1989. "Rethinking Colonial Categories: European Communities and the Boundaries of Rule." *Comp. Studies in Society and History* 13 (1): 134–61. https://doi.org/10.1017/S0010417500015693.

Strobel, Margaret. 1987. "Gender and Race in the 19th and 20th Century British Empire." In *Becoming Visible: Women in European History*, edited by R. Bridenthal et al., 375–96. Boston: Houghton Mifflin.

Tiffany, Sharon, and Kathleen Adams. 1985. *The Wild Woman: An Inquiry into the Anthropology of an Idea*. Cambridge, MA: Schenkman Publishing Co.

Tirefort, A. 1979. Le Bon Temps: La Communaute Francaise en Basse Cote d'Ivoire Pendant l'Entre-Deux Guerres, 1920–1940. Troiseme Cycle, Centre d'Etudes Africaines, Paris.

Van Onselen, Charles. 1982. *Studies in the Social and Economic History of the Witwatersrand 1886–1914*. Vol. I. New York: Longman.

Vellut, Jean-Luc. 1982. "Materiaux pour une image du Blanc dans la societe coloniale du Congo Beige." In *Stereotypes Nationaux et Prejuqes Raciaux aux XIXe et XXe Siecles*, edited by Jean Pirotte. Leuven: Editions Nauwelaerts.

4.5. An Anthropology of Structural Violence (2004)

Paul Farmer

To foreign eyes, the Haitian story has become a confused skein of tragedies, most of them seen as local. Poverty, crime, accidents, disease, death – and more often than not their causes – are also seen as problems locally derived. The transnational tale of slavery and debt and turmoil is lost in the vivid poverty, the understanding of which seems to defeat the analyses of journalists and even many anthropologists, focused as we are on the ethnographically visible – what is there in front of us. [...]

[...] Standing on the shoulders of those who have studied slavery, racism, and other forms of institutionalized violence, a growing number of anthropologists now devote their attention to structural violence. [...] Structural violence is violence exerted systematically – that is, indirectly – by everyone who belongs to a certain social order: hence the discomfort these ideas provoke in a moral economy still geared to pinning praise or blame on individual actors. In short, the concept of structural violence is intended to inform the study of the social machinery of oppression. Oppression is a result of many conditions, not the least of which reside in consciousness. We will therefore need to examine, as well, the roles played by the erasure of historical memory and other forms of desocialization as enabling conditions of structures that are both "sinful" [Galtung 1969] and ostensibly "nobody's fault." [...]

An ethnographic study of modern Haiti may or may not discuss the ways in which West Africans were moved to Haiti [as slaves of the French]. It may or may not discuss tuberculosis, small-pox, measles, or yellow fever. A modern ethnographer may not mention the former colony's having been forced to repay a "debt" to the French supposedly incurred by the loss of the world's most profitable slave colony. But these facts need to be included and their sequelae addressed: their absence makes a fully socialized accounting of the present nearly unthinkable. Allow me to sum up the post-independence history of Haiti:

The Haitian revolution began in 1791. France's refusal to accept the loss of so "efficient" and profitable a colony led, ultimately, to the expedition of the largest armada ever to cross the Atlantic. After the 1803 Battle of Vertières, in which Napoleon's troops were defeated, Haiti was declared an independent nation. But its infrastructure lay in ruins: some estimate that more than half of the island's population perished in the war. The land was still fertile, if less so than when the Europeans began monocropping it, and so the new republic's leadership, desperate to revive the economy, fought to restore the plantations without overt slavery. [...]

Even if there were other ways of growing these products – and coffee, unlike sugar, was clearly a product that could be grown on small homesteads – who would buy them? The Europeans and the only other republic in the Western Hemisphere, the United States, were the only likely customers, and they mostly followed a French-led embargo on Haiti. How many people in France remember that, in order to obtain diplomatic recognition, Haiti was required to indemnify France to the tune of 150 million francs, with payments to the government of Charles X beginning in 1825? One hundred fifty million francs in reparations *to the slave owners* – a social and economic fact redolent with meaning then and today and one with grave material consequences for the Haitians. [...]

This set the tone for the new century: trade concessions for European and U.S. partners and indirect taxes for the peasants who grew the produce, their backs bent under the weight of a hostile world. Especially hostile was the United States, the slave-owning republic to the north (Lawless 1992:56):

> The United States blocked Haiti's invitation to the famous Western Hemisphere Panama Conference of 1825 and refused to recognize Haitian independence until 1862. This isolation was imposed on Haiti by a frightened white world, and Haiti became a test case, first for those arguing about emancipation and then, after the end of slavery, for those arguing about the capacity of blacks for self-government.

In the years following independence, the United States and allied European powers helped France orchestrate a diplomatic quarantine of Haiti, and the new republic soon became the outcast of the international community. In 1824 Senator Robert Hayne of South Carolina declared, "Our policy with regard to Hayti is plain. We never can acknowledge her independence. The peace and safety of a large portion of our union forbids us even to discuss [it]" (quoted in Schmidt 1995:28).

But the isolation was largely diplomatic and rhetorical, as those who remember the broad outlines of gunboat diplomacy recall. The United States was increasingly present as a trading partner and policeman, leading to a number of famous run-ins with the Haitians – famous, I mean, in Haiti, though largely forgotten, of course, in the United States (for details, see Farmer 2003). Continuous U.S. naval presence led, eventually, to an armed occupation of Haiti in 1915. This occupation, another chapter of U.S. history now almost completely forgotten by the occupiers, was to last 20 years. Although the rationale for our military occupation is debated, "control of the customs houses," observed President Woodrow Wilson, "constituted the essence of this whole affair."

Since 1915, at the latest, the United States has been the dominant force in Haitian politics. The modern Haitian army was created, in 1916, by an act of the U.S. Congress. From the time of troop withdrawal in 1934 until 1990, no Haitian administration has risen to power without the blessing of the U.S. government. This gave us a string of military and paramilitary governments leading in 1957 to the Duvalier regime, which was, in terms of dollar support, a leading recipient of U.S. largesse. Indeed, there have been no major political discontinuities until perhaps 1990, with the result that the template of colony – a slave colony – continued to shape life in Haiti. Just as the wealthy were socialized for excess, the Haitian poor were socialized for scarcity. Management of time, affection, food, water, and family crises (including illness) all fit into this ancient framework of too much and too little.

This is the framework I had in mind when I began studying specific infectious diseases – one old, one new – in rural Haiti. In anthropology a version of this framework has been called "world-systems theory" (Wallerstein 1974), but it is not really theory-driven. It is an approach that is committed to ethnographically embedding evidence within the historically given social and economic structures that shape life so dramatically on the edge of life and death. These structures are transnational, and therefore not even their modern vestiges are really ethnographically visible. Many anthropologists have used this framework in an attempt to depict the social machinery of oppression by bringing connections into relief (Mintz 1977; Roseberry 1988).

Regardless of our specific research questions, we have struggled to define these social and economic structures, to understand how they work. For want of a better word, I have often used the term "neoliberal economics" to refer to the prevailing (at times contradictory) constellation of ideas about trade and development and governance that has been internalized by many in the affluent market societies. Neoliberalism is the ideology promoted by the victors of the struggles mentioned above. The dominance of a competition-driven market is said to be at the heart of this model, but in truth this ideology is indebted to and helps to replicate inequalities of power. It is an ideology that has little to say about the social and economic inequalities that distort *real* economies and instead, reveals yet another means by which these economies can be further exploited. Neoliberal thought is central to modern development efforts, the goal of which is less to repair poverty and social inequalities than to manage them. Its opponents include some of those left behind by development, whose deep disaffection is rooted in the erased experience I have tried to summarize. Work throughout Latin America has convinced me that the disaffection is also associated with a set of ideas not too different, interestingly, from that expressed by the late Pierre Bourdieu (1998:25):

> Scientific rationalism – the rationalism of the mathematical models which inspire the policy of the IMF or the World Bank, that of the great law firms, great juridical multinationals which impose the traditions of American law on the whole planet, that of rational-action theories, etc. – is both the expression and the justification of a Western arrogance, which leads [some] people to act as if they had the monopoly of reason and could set themselves up as world policemen, in other words as self-appointed holders of the monopoly of legitimate violence, capable of applying the force of arms in the service of universal justice.

As someone who believes deeply in the promise and progress of science, I would point out that it is the ideology springing from market economies that is critiqued by most opponents of neoliberal thought. It is not affluence or modernity itself, still less a certain "way of life," that is under attack. Haitians living in poverty have ample reason to be wary of neoliberal nostrums, for theirs is an embodied understanding of modern inequality. Over the past decade, Haiti has undergone something of an economic devolution. Gross national product has declined; so has life expectancy. What are the causes of all of this present-day misery? There is slavery, of course, and racism is central to slavery and this is one reason that recent meetings in Durban, South Africa, focused on both. Allow me to quote from the document signed there by representatives of over 150 countries:

> The world conference acknowledges and profoundly regrets the massive human sufferings and the tragic plight of millions of men, women and children caused by slavery, slave trade, trans-Atlantic slave trade, apartheid, colonialism and genocide and calls upon states concerned to honor the memory of the victims of past tragedies and affirms that wherever and whenever these occurred they must be condemned and their reoccurrence prevented.
>
> The world conference regrets that these practices and structures, political, socioeconomic and cultural, have led to racism, racial discrimination, xenophobia and related intolerance.
>
> The world conference recognizes that these historical injustices have undeniably contributed to poverty, underdevelopment, marginalization, social exclusion, economic disparities, instability and insecurity that affect many people in different parts of the world, in particular in developing countries.
>
> The world conference recognizes the need to develop programs for the social and economic development of these societies and the diaspora within the framework of a new partnership based on the spirit of solidarity and mutual respect in the following areas: debt relief, poverty eradication, building or strengthening democratic institutions, promotion of foreign direct investment, market access.

Imagine what it is like for poor villagers to hear (I say "hear," because most cannot read) these words in Haiti, a country stinging, still, not only from the reparations paid to their former masters but from a series of sanctions that continue to this day. [...]

[...] Take as an example Inter-American Development Bank (IDB) Loan No. 1009/SF-HA, "Reorganization of the National Health System." On July 21, 1998, the Haitian government and the IDB signed a $22.5-million loan for phase 1 of a project to decentralize and reorganize the Haitian health care system. The need to improve the health care system was and remains urgent: there are 1.2 doctors, 1.3 nurses, and 0.04 dentists per 10,000 Haitians; 40% of the population is without access to any form of primary health care. HIV and tuberculosis rates are by far the highest in the hemisphere, as are infant, juvenile, and maternal mortality. To use the bank's jargon, the project was to target 80% of the population for access to primary health care through the construction of low-cost clinics and local health dispensaries, the training of community health agents, and the purchase of medical equipment and essential medicines. To be judged successful by its own criteria, the project would need to produce a drop in the infant mortality rate from 74 to 50 deaths per 1,000 live births, a drop in the juvenile mortality rate from 131 to 110 deaths per 1,000 births, a drop in the birth rate from 4.6 to 4, and a drop in the general mortality rate attributable to the lack of proper health care from 10.7 to 9.7 per 1,000. These were not overly ambitious goals. Most who evaluated the project thought it feasible and well designed. The signing took place several years ago. [...]

[...] Nevertheless, by early March 2001, the IDB had not yet disbursed the loan but announced that it fully intended to work with the new Aristide government and to finance projects already in the pipeline. It demanded, however, that a number of conditions be met, requiring the poorest nation in the hemisphere to pay back millions of dollars of outstanding debts racked up by the previous U.S.-supported dictatorships, as well as "credit commissions" and interest on undisbursed funds. For example, as of March 31, 2001, Haiti already owed the IDB $185,239.75 as a "commission fee" on a loan it had never received. The total amount of fees owed on five development loans from the IDB was $2,311,422. Whereas in the nineteenth century Haiti had had to pay "reparations" to slave owners, at the start of the twenty-first century a different sort of extortion was being practiced to ensure that Haiti not become too independent. The health loan has still not been disbursed and thus the embargo on international aid to Haiti continues, despite the fact that the Haitian government has followed all the stipulations set down for resolving the disputed elections. In the meantime, the courtyard around our hospital remains overflowing – that is the ethnographically visible part.

REFERENCES

Bourdieu, Pierre. 1998. *Contre-feux: Propos pour servir à la résistance contre l'invasion néo-libérale*. Paris: Raisons d'Agir.

Farmer, Paul. 2003. *The Uses of Haiti*. 2nd edition. Monroe: Common Courage Press.

Galtung, Johan. 1969. "Violence, Peace, and Peace Research." *Journal of Peace Research* 6: 167–91. https://doi.org/10.1177%2F002234336900600301.

Lawless, Robert. 1992. *Haiti's Bad Press*. Rochester: Schenkman Books.

Mintz, Sidney. 1977. "The So-Called World System: Local Initiative and Local Response." *Dialectical Anthropology* 2: 253–70. https://doi.org/10.1007/BF00249489.

Roseberry, William. 1988. "Political Economy." *Annual Review of Anthropology* 17: 161–85. https://doi.org/10.1146/annurev.an.17.100188.001113.

Schmidt, Hans. 1995. *The United States Occupation of Haiti, 1915–1934*. New Brunswick: Rutgers University Press.

Wallerstein, Immanuel. 1974. *The Modern World-System: Capitalist Agriculture and the Origins of the European World-Economy in the Sixteenth Century*. San Diego: Academic Press.

Section Four Glossary

historical materialism   An approach to cultural analysis grounded in Marxism that emphasizes the role of political economy in a society's historical and institutional development.

structural violence   An approach to understanding harm that focuses on structural factors that create disproportionate vulnerabilities, such as racism, poverty, and colonialism, among others.

On Writing Cultures

THE SOCIAL CONTEXT

The United States emerged from World War II as one of the wealthiest and most powerful nations in the world. In pursuit of global influence and wealth, the United States sought to expand capitalist hegemony through military incursions in South Korea and Vietnam, then Guatemala, El Salvador, and Honduras among other places. Back home, members of racialized communities remained largely excluded from the spoils of imperial domination. By the 1960s, frustrations with ongoing structural racism, imperialism, and heterosexism led to the emergence of several related social movements, including the Civil Rights Movement, Gay Rights Movement, American Indian Movement, anti-war protests, and second wave feminism. These movements not only challenged neocolonialist power structures, police brutality, and inequality, they also sought to broaden the participation of members of oppressed communities in positions of power and influence. This included the academy.

In academia, movement insights challenged hegemonic sources of academic authority – authority that had accrued to certain types of people and to certain forms of knowledge production – and pointed to its complicity with power. Movement organizers introduced alternative histories by and for marginalized communities that contextualized contemporary inequality in histories of colonialism and white supremacy long cemented in US law.

In anthropology, increasing rejection of colonialist and "othering" approaches helped give rise to what is often called the **postmodern** turn, when scholars within the discipline began writing and thinking more explicitly about researcher subjectivity, ethnographic authority, and the art of writing. The postmodern movement in anthropology emphasized text deconstruction, subjectivity of experience, and a recognition that ethnographic "truths" are always "partial truths" (Clifford and Marcus 1986; see also Behar and Gordon 1995). Presentation of ethnographic information as objective and omniscient, then, reflects not so much an absence of partiality and subjectivity as a denial of them (the contents of Malinowski's personal diary, for example, posthumously undermined his claims to outsider objectivity). If ethnography is but a partial truth, and a subjective one at that, these anthropologists reasoned, then ethnographic texts are more akin to stories than scientific doctrine. And the ethnographer's **positionality** – their standpoint or situatedness (see Reading 9.1 by Donna Haraway) – always shapes the truths they discover and the stories they tell.

Eschewing positivist scientific methods, attention to reflexivity and writing became central to postmodern anthropology, an approach that built on **interpretive anthropology**, most associated with Clifford Geertz, which emphasized the interpretive nature of anthropological work. Postmodernism is also in conversation with **poststructuralism**, heavily influenced by the work of Pierre Bourdieu and Michel Foucault, which rejects the notion that there is an underlying and systematic explanation for culture (i.e., a "structure"), and instead approaches culture as dynamic and influenced by discourses and relations of power.

THE CONVERSATION

The pieces in this section all draw attention to the ethnographer as a particular actor in the ethnographic landscape (contrast this to earlier pieces in which the ethnographer is all but absent from the text) who is privy to some sources of information and not others. They also challenge positivist methodologies in which the ethnographer is expected to be a neutral scientist whose job is to discover and make sense of "culture." Instead, these pieces embrace reflexivity and introduce **phenomenological**, deeply personal, and embodied forms of learning and sharing cultural insight.

This section opens with a chapter from Katherine Dunham's book *Journey to Accompong* entitled "Twenty-Seventh Day." Reading 5.1 is an excerpt from her notes during her 1935 stay in the community of Accompong, Jamaica, where she traveled to research African war dances that were rumored to still be performed in this Maroon community. In the piece, Dunham documents the suspicions and evasions she encountered along her journey to witness and dance the legendary Koromantee war dance. Not only was Dunham one of the first Black women to earn an advanced degree in anthropology, but her research-to-performance method was also a radical intervention into conceptualizing the ethnographic process. Dunham defended her dissertation with a dance performance, illustrating how her theory and method of "writing culture" "works on its feet rather than moves across the page" (Chin 2014, xxi). Written in the first person, "Twenty-Seventh Day" grabs the reader in its artistic prose and reflexivity decades before the postmodern turn.

The second piece in this section represents the turn toward meaning and interpretation that characterized cultural anthropology in the late twentieth century. In "Deep Play," Clifford Geertz's writing style reflects his ethnographic method of **thick description**, a process whereby the anthropologist interprets culture as text. In the piece, Geertz analyzes the Balinese cockfight as symbolic ritual that, when read as text, tells the story of Balinese social relations, which are characterized by status competition and hierarchical rankings. Geertz's approach to doing and writing ethnography is one that seeks to unravel the "webs" of intertwined layers of cultural meaning. This essay is also famous for the opening vignette, in which Geertz describes running from a police crackdown at a cockfight and accidentally building rapport with his Balinese study subjects.

Reckoning with one's own subjective position in understanding cultural phenomena is also the central theme of Reading 5.3, "Grief and a Headhunter's Rage." Here Renato Rosaldo describes his search for deeper meanings and anthropological interpretations of Ilongot headhunting in the Philippines. It was not until Rosaldo suffered the sudden loss of his wife, Michelle, that he began to comprehend the rage and grief that catalyzed headhunting – which was what the Ilongot had been telling him all along. This is a shattering observation for anthropology: What if, Rosaldo asks, there is no hidden cultural meaning for anthropologists to discover? What if things just are what people say they are?

In Reading 5.4, "Writing against Culture," Lila Abu-Lughod explores the ways in which feminists and "halfies" (ethnographers who are meaningfully part of more than one cultural world) are uniquely positioned to challenge conceptions of culture that speciously invent timeless, homogenous anthropological "others." What is true for women and halfies, Abu-Lughod continues, is also true but less apparent for ethnographers who position themselves outside of the culture they study. "The outsider self never simply stands outside," she cautions. "What we call the outside is a position within a larger political-historical complex. No less than the halfie, the 'wholie' is in a specific position vis-à-vis the community being studied." Refusing the discourse of ethnographic "objectivity," then, Abu-Lughod instead favors an ethnographic approach that tells stories of particular people engaging in particular activities that ethnographers encounter during fieldwork.

In "Sensuous Stories in the Indian Ocean Islands," Rosabelle Boswell advances a sensory scholarship that activates listening as sense-work. Her theory and writing method render the colonial encounter and experience audible through an approach where a sense-embedded and self-reflexive anthropologist attends to the sensuous quality of stories. In the piece, she presents stories from the Indian Ocean region "in the raw" alongside her reflexive sensory analysis of listening to sense. Boswell's piece bookends nicely with Dunham, bringing us back to the importance of multisensory approaches to fieldwork.

THREE QUESTIONS FOR THE READINGS

1 What embodied forms of knowledge do you hold? What insights does that embodiment give you that you would not otherwise be able to access?
2 These pieces share with the essays in Section Two an emphasis on the particular, but diverge in their conceptualization of methodology. How do these pieces build on and depart from Boasian-style ethnography?
3 What are the political implications of this approach to anthropology? If "truth" is always partial and subjective, can we say anything definitive about the world that we live in? How can we act to change it?

ON THE COMPANION WEBSITE

The Dunham Technique Dance Lab, additional readings, and more.

www.anthropologicaltheory.com

REFERENCES

Behar, Ruth, and Deborah A. Gorden (eds.). 1995. *Women Writing Culture.* Berkeley: University of California Press.

Chin, Elizabeth (ed.). 2014. *Katherine Dunham: Recovering an Anthropological Legacy, Choreographing Ethnographic Futures.* Santa Fe: School for Advanced Research Press.

Clifford, James, and George E. Marcus (eds.). 1986. *Writing Culture: The Poetics and Politics of Ethnography.* Santa Fe: School of American Research Press.

5.1. Twenty-Seventh Day: Journey to Accompong (1946)

Katherine Dunham

I looked at Ba' Weeyums. He was first on one foot and then on the other, twisting his little felt hat around his forefinger and looking anxiously at me the while. Then suddenly I realized that this was the long hoped-for opportunity – that here were the dances I had waited so many weeks to see, and that it was not for the fieldworker to bear personal grudges and carry personal grievances, but to get what the field has to offer in as graceful a manner as possible. Now it was my turn to look anxiously at Ba' Weeyums.

"But everyone's going!" I said. And to be sure, of the score of old and young who had circled the dancers when I arrived, there were now less than half.

"De' goombay eem good 'nuf," said Ba' Weeyums slowly, "but eem need *rum*. Don't no goombay talk like eem *should* talk *eef* eem no had de *rum*."

The rum! The rum! Of course. I loudly asked Ral if he would go up to my cottage and bring down the jug of rum from under Mai's bunk in the kitchen. He was off with unusual alacrity, whether because of the rum or because of the chance that Mai might by this hour have retired to the bunk, I do not know.

While we waited Ba' Weeyums explained that of course he could have beat the drum for me any day, but that there had been no drum to beat. Ba' Teddy explained further that all this was strictly forbidden by the Colonel, that he had cautioned them against doing these dances while I was there (my suspicions of hypocrisy were well founded), that Ba' Foster's story was true that nothing had been planned but only by the accident of Ba' Weeyums drum beating had these passers-by gathered, and that were the Colonel not at Balaclava even this would have been out of the question. Of course I must not mention these dances to anyone, and tomorrow it would be best if I would have forgotten all about them. Further, we must be very brief tonight, because while the thicket and the seclusion of the spot and the direction of the wind prevented the sound of the drum from traveling far, it wouldn't be long before all Accompong would be aroused by these almost forgotten drum rhythms which stripped them of the veneer of the Scotch minister and cricket games at the parade and set dances, and the sleeping Koromantee and Eboe and Nago would come to the fore and things would happen that the Colonel would be certain to hear about, even at Balaclava. Just a little while, I pleaded to break in the goombay and so that I might partake once of the things that belonged to the Maroons in the old days.

Ral returned, and Ba' Weeyums took drum and bottle off to one side. There he poured rum on the goatskin head, rubbed it in, took a long drink himself, then spat a mouthful at the drum again. Between times he mumbled in a tongue which I gathered was Koromantee. Then he poured a few drops of rum on the ground, and the baptism was over. This was for the spirit of the drum, he explained. Then he squatted over the drum again, and indeed it seemed to me that it was suddenly alive.

Though the body of the drum was shallow, and it more reassembled a square stool than any drum I had previously seen, the tone was full and less staccato than before, and I was almost inclined to believe that it was alive, and that it was the spirit of some Gold Coast god come to life to grumble a protest against the long silence.

Gradually they returned, slipping from behind the coconut palms and up from the ravines and down from the mountains. I don't know how many, because I was in the midst, and there was now only one kerosene torch, and the rum was going the rounds and it had all become unreal, though it all happened because the dances are still very clear to me.

I might not have come at all, for the difference that it has made. I was accepted and one of them.

The dance I had interrupted was a myal dance. Ba' Teddy explained it, as, fascinated, I watched Mis' Mary and the old man. They were facing each other. The old man took the part of the myal "doctor" and the dance was to entice into his power an evil spirit, the "duppy" of some dead worker of black magic. Ba' Weeyums led a chant in Koromantee, and the women answered. The dance interested me too much for me to try and remember the sound of the words. The evil spirit circled around the doctor hesitant, advancing and retreating, her eyes fixed, mouth clamped shut tightly, body rigid. The doctor squatted in front of her, arms wide as though to embrace her, fingers wide open and hands trembling violently. As he advanced slowly toward her, his pelvis began to move with an unmistakable sexual purpose, and the duppy responded in like manner. They hesitated in front of each other, swaying. Then she eluded his embrace with a sharp convulsive bend, and was on the other side of the circle, taunting, enticing features still hard and set but body liquid and so full of desire that I could scarcely believe that it was old Mis' Mary, grandmother of goodness knows how many.

The doctor reached out for her, gesticulating, grimacing, insinuating. Then she came to life suddenly and the pursuit was reversed. The doctor was afraid of this thing which he had done, of this woman whom he had raised from the dead with these fleshly promises. They were face to face, bodies touching, both of them squatting now with arms pressed close to their sides, elbows bent, and widespread fingers quivering violently. Ba' Teddy had stopped explaining and among the onlookers there was no sound except heavy breathing, but the chant continued and the drum, and it seemed that the air was heavy with some other heat and sound. The duppy leaned over the man, who cowered in fear from her, though their bodies were pressed tightly together. As I decided that I must close my eyes for a moment, Ba' Teddy raised his hand, and the drum and chant stopped on a single note: there was a blank silence that left both dancers and spectators dangling helplessly in mid-air.

"Dat dance bad dance," Ba' Teddy muttered, trying to calm his voice and appear merely annoyed in spite of his quick breathing. I opened my mouth to speak, but he anticipated my question and answered sharply. "Bes don' ax no furder questions, missus. Me don' see dat fer long time, en hit bad. Dat mix up wid bad biznuss. Better fer missus ef she fergit."

I was almost relieved to be thus reprimanded. But the mood of the dance had already changed, and to a far livelier rhythm. Two men were hopping about in the circle mimicking two cocks in the thick of a fight. They switched their middles, bobbed their heads, wrinkled their faces, and stuck their necks far out crowing a challenge. The audience, tense a moment before, was now in a hysteria of laughter. One of the dancers picked up his foot high and hopped around in a circle, the other following at a gallop, hand thrust in coat pocket and flapping widely for wings. Finally one was vanquished and with a feeble squawk rolled over sadly, feet in the air. The other strutted over to him, looked disdainfully around, and flapped his wings in victory as he trotted around the circle.

I plead with Ba' Weeyums for a Koromantee war dance, and find that it is no other than the wild dance which I saw only a suggestion of at Ol' Mis' Cross's gravedigging. In this I join, along with Simon Rowe and others who have only watched so far. The few young people who are here, however, do not join in these traditional dances. They are ashamed, and I am sure that I shock them greatly; on the other hand, I feel that they watch us rather wistfully, wishing that they had the courage to give themselves up for a moment to their traditions and forget that there is a market at Maggotty and cricket games on the outside, and store-bought shoes.

The war dances are danced by both men and women. The introduction seemed to be a disjointed walking around in a loose circle, much like the warming up of an athlete. There Henry Rowe and I are facing each other doing a step which could easily be compared to an Irish reel. Hands on hips, we hop from one foot to the other, feet turned out at right angle to the body or well "turned out," in ballet vernacular. This hopping brought us close together, and I had to watch the other closely to keep up with Henry. We turned our backs and walked away, then turned suddenly again and hopped together. The songs are in lusty Koromantee, and from somewhere a woman procured a rattle and is shaking it in accompaniment to Ba' Weeyums. Some of the men wave sticks in the air, and the women tear off their handkerchiefs and wave them on high as they dance. Henry and I grabbed each other around the waist and ran circles around each other, first one way, then the other. A few of these turns and we separate in a melee of leaping, shouting warriors; a moment later we are "bush fightin'," crouching down and advancing in line to attack an imaginary enemy with many feints, swerves, and much pantomime. At one stage of the dance Mis' Mary and I are face to face, she no longer a duppy but a Maroon woman of the old days working the men up to a pitch where they will descend into the cockpit and exterminate one of his Majesty's red-coated platoons. She grabbed me by the shoulders and shook me violently, then we were again hopping around each other with knees high in the air, handkerchiefs and skirts flying.

When this was over we were all exhausted. The Maroons have not been accustomed to this sort of thing for a long time; nor am I who until now have known only the conventional techniques, and the far less strenuous set dances. We dispersed and I was in possession of the goombay. Ba' Teddy and Ba' Weeyums and I labored up the mountainside, and behind us shutters closed and candles were extinguished and I knew that they were all talking about the escapade of the evening, and how angry Colonel would be if he knew, and that the "missus" must have known things that she hadn't so far divulged, about myal and obi and the old Koromantee traditions, maybe even the language. [...]

At my cottage door, I could hear Mai snoring peacefully within, and this was very comforting after the orgy in the ravine. I remembered vaguely that Ral had left the dancing soon after he returned with the rum, and was certain that he was responsible for Mai's not having come to the dance, and perhaps for her peaceful snoring.

I pulled off my muddy shoes and crawled on top of the marosh, ignoring the bowl of rice and gourd of fresh coconut water that Mai had thoughtfully left on the kitchen table for me. I felt extremely tired and extremely comfortable. My notebook still lay open on the table. Earlier in the day I had harbored a strong resentment against the Maroons and a strong disappointment in myself. Now I had the delicious thrill of accomplishment, of having conquered an unseen enemy (the Colonel, no doubt), and of belonging completely. I only regretted as I pulled the sheet up around my chin that it had all happened so late. Well, if I ever return – I sincerely hope that I shall – at least I shall know where to begin.

5.2. Deep Play: Notes on the Balinese Cockfight (1973)

Clifford Geertz

THE RAID

Early in April of 1958, my wife and I arrived, malarial and diffident, in a Balinese village we intended, as anthropologists, to study. [...] We were intruders, professional ones, and the villagers dealt with us [...] as though we were not there. [...]

The indifference, of course, was studied; the villagers were watching every move we made, and they had an enormous amount of quite accurate information about who we were and what we were going to be doing. But they acted as if we simply did not exist, which, in fact, as this behavior was designed to inform us, we did not, or anyway not yet. [...]

[...] In Balinese villages, at least those away from the tourist circuit, nothing happens at all. People go on pounding, chatting, making offerings, staring into space, carrying baskets about while one drifts around feeling vaguely disembodied. And the same thing is true on the individual level. When you first meet a Balinese, he seems virtually not to relate to you at all; he is, in the term Gregory Bateson and Margaret Mead made famous, "away." Then – in a day, a week, a month [he decides] that you are real, and then he becomes a warm, gay, sensitive, sympathetic, though, being Balinese, always precisely controlled, person. You have crossed, somehow, some moral or metaphysical shadow line. Though you are not exactly taken as a Balinese (one has to be born to that), you are at least regarded as a human being rather than a cloud or a gust of wind. The whole complexion of your relationship dramatically changes to, in the majority of cases, a gentle, almost affectionate one – a low-keyed, rather playful, rather mannered, rather bemused geniality.

My wife and I were still very much in the gust-of-wind stage [...] when, ten days or so after our arrival, a large cockfight was held in the public square to raise money for a new school.

Now, a few special occasions aside, cockfights are illegal in Bali under the Republic. [...] Of course, like drinking during Prohibition or, today, smoking marihuana, cockfights, being a part of "The Balinese Way of Life," nonetheless go on happening, and with extraordinary frequency. And [...] from time to time the police [...] feel called upon to make a raid, confiscate the cocks and spurs, fine a few people, and even now and then expose some of them in the tropical sun for a day as object lessons which never, somehow, get learned, even though occasionally, quite occasionally, the object dies.

As a result, the fights are usually held in a secluded corner of a village in semisecrecy. [...] In this case, however, perhaps because they were raising money for a school [...] they thought they could take a chance on the central square and draw a larger and more enthusiastic crowd without attracting the attention of the law.

They were wrong. In the midst of the third match, with hundreds of people, including, still transparent, myself and my wife, fused into a single body around the ring, a superorganism in the literal sense, a truck full of policemen armed with machine guns roared up. Amid great screeching cries of "pulisi! pulisi!" from the crowd, the policemen jumped out, and, springing into the center of the ring, began to swing their guns around like gangsters in a motion picture, though not going so far as actually to fire them. The superorganism came instantly apart as its components scattered in all directions. People raced down the road, disappeared headfirst over walls, scrambled under platforms, folded themselves behind wicker screens, scuttled up coconut trees. Cocks armed with steel spurs sharp enough to cut off a finger or run a hole through a foot were running wildly around. Everything was dust and panic.

On the established anthropological principle, "When in Rome," my wife and I decided [...] that the thing to do was run too. We ran down the main village street, northward, away from where we were living, for we were on that side of the ring. About halfway down another fugitive ducked suddenly into a compound – his own, it turned out – and we, seeing nothing ahead of us but rice fields, open country, and a very high volcano, followed him. As the three of us came tumbling into the courtyard, his wife, who had apparently been through this sort of thing before, whipped out a table, a tablecloth, three chairs, and three cups of tea, and we all, without any explicit communication whatsoever, sat down, commenced to sip tea, and sought to compose ourselves.

A few moments later, one of the policemen marched importantly into the yard, looking for the village chief. (The chief had not only been at the fight, he had arranged it. When the truck drove up he ran to the river, stripped off his sarong, and plunged in so he could say, when at length they found him sitting there pouring water over his head, that he had been away bathing when the whole affair had occurred and was ignorant of it. [...]) Seeing me and my wife, "White Men," there in the yard, the policeman performed a classic double take. When he found his voice again he asked, approximately, what in the devil did we think we were doing there. Our host of five minutes leaped instantly to our defense, producing an impassioned description of who and what we were, so detailed and so accurate that [I was] astonished. We had a perfect right to be there, he said. [...] We were American professors; the government had cleared us; we were there to study culture; we were going to write a book to tell Americans about Bali. And we had all been there drinking tea and talking about cultural matters all afternoon and did not know anything about any cockfight. Moreover, we had not seen the village chief all day; he must have gone to town. The policeman retreated in rather total disarray. And, after a decent interval, bewildered but relieved to have survived and stayed out of jail, so did we.

The next morning the village was a completely different world for us. Not only were we no longer invisible, we were suddenly the center of all attention, the object of a great out-pouring of warmth, interest, and most especially, amusement. Everyone in the village knew we had fled like everyone else. They asked us about it again and again […] gently, affection-ately, but quite insistently teasing us: "Why didn't you just stand there and tell the police who you were?" "Why didn't you just say you were only watching and not betting?" "Were you really afraid of those little guns?" As always, kinesthetically minded and […] the world's most poised people, they gleefully mimicked, also over and over again, our graceless style of running and what they claimed were our panic-stricken facial expressions. But above all, everyone was extremely pleased and even more surprised that we had not simply "pulled out our papers" (they knew about those too) and asserted our Distinguished Visitor status, but had instead demonstrated our solidarity with what were now our covillagers. […]

In Bali, to be teased is to be accepted. It was the turning point so far as our relationship to the community was concerned, and we were quite literally "in." The whole village opened up to us, probably more than it ever would have otherwise. […]

OF COCKS AND MEN

[…] As much as America surfaces in a ball park, on a golf links, at a race track, or around a poker table, much of Bali surfaces in a cock ring. For it is only apparently cocks that are fighting there. Actually, it is men.

To anyone who has been in Bali any length of time, the deep psychological identification of Balinese men with their cocks is unmistakable. The double entendre here is deliberate. It works in exactly the same way in Balinese as it does in English, even to producing the same tired jokes, strained puns, and uninventive obscenities. […]

The language of everyday moralism is shot through, on the male side of it, with rooster-ish imagery. *Sabung*, the word for cock […] is used metaphorically to mean "hero," "war-rior," "champion," "man of parts," "political candidate," "bachelor," "dandy," "lady-killer," or "tough guy." A pompous man whose behavior presumes above his station is compared to a tailless cock who struts about as though he had a large, spectacular one. A desperate man who makes a last, irrational effort to extricate himself from an impossible situation is likened to a dying cock who makes one final lunge at his tormentor to drag him along to a common destruction. A stingy man, who promises much, gives little, and begrudges that, is compared to a cock which, held by the tail, leaps at another without in fact engaging him. A marriage-able young man still shy with the opposite sex or someone in a new job anxious to make a good impression is called "a fighting cock caged for the first time." Court trials, wars, polit-ical contests, inheritance disputes, and street arguments are all compared to cockfights. […]

But the intimacy of men with their cocks is more than metaphorical. Balinese men, or anyway a large majority of Balinese men, spend an enormous amount of time with their favorites, grooming them, feeding them, discussing them, trying them out against one another, or just gazing at them with a mixture of rapt admiration and dreamy self-absorption. Whenever you see a group of Balinese men squatting idly in the council shed or along the road in their hips down, shoulders forward, knees up fashion, half or more will have a rooster in his hands, holding it between his thighs, bouncing it gently up and down to strengthen its legs, ruffling its feathers with abstract sensuality, pushing it out against a neighbor's rooster to rouse its spirit, withdrawing it toward his loins to calm it again. Now and then, to get a feel for another bird, a man will fiddle this way with someone else's cock for a while […].

[… F]ighting cocks are kept in wicker cages, moved frequently about so as to maintain the optimum balance of sun and shade[,] fed a special diet […] bathed in the same ceremonial preparation of tepid water, medicinal herbs, flowers, and onions in which infants are bathed. […] Their combs are cropped, their plumage dressed, their spurs trimmed, and their legs massaged, and they are inspected for flaws with the squinted concentration of a diamond merchant. A man who has a passion for cocks […] can spend most of his life with them. […] "I am cock crazy," my landlord […] used to moan as he went to move another cage, give another bath, or conduct another feeding. "We're all cock crazy."

The madness has some less visible dimensions, however, because although it is true that cocks are symbolic expressions or magnifications of their owner's self […] they are also expressions […] of what the Balinese regard as the direct inversion, aesthetically, morally, and metaphysically, of human status: animality.

The Balinese revulsion against any behavior regarded as animal-like can hardly be overstressed. Babies are not allowed to crawl for that reason. Incest […] is a much less horrifying crime than bestiality. […] Most demons are represented [in] animal form. The main puberty rite consists in filing the child's teeth so they will not look like animal fangs. Not only defecation but eating is regarded as a disgusting, almost obscene activity, to be conducted hurriedly and privately, because of its association with animality. […] In identifying with his cock, the Balinese man is identifying not just with his ideal self, or even his penis, but also, and at the same time, with what he most fears, hates, and ambivalence being what it is, is fascinated by – "The Powers of Darkness." […]

In the cockfight, man and beast, good and evil, ego and id, the creative power of aroused masculinity and the destructive power of loosened animality fuse in a bloody drama of hatred, cruelty, violence, and death. […]

PLAYING WITH FIRE

Bentham's concept of "deep play" […] means play in which the stakes are so high that it is, from his utilitarian standpoint, irrational for men to engage in it at all. […] In genuine deep play [both are] in over their heads. Having come together in search of pleasure they have entered into a relationship which will bring the participants, considered collectively, net pain rather than net pleasure. […]

[F]or the Balinese […] money is less a measure of utility, had or expected, than it is a symbol of moral import, perceived or imposed. […] This […] is *not* to say that the money does not matter. [M]oney *does,* in this hardly unmaterialistic society, matter and matter very much that the more of it one risks, the more of a lot of other things, such as one's pride, one's poise, one's dispassion, one's masculinity, one also risks, again only momentarily but again very publicly as well. In deep cockfights an owner and his collaborators […] put their money where their status is. […]

FEATHERS, BLOOD, CROWDS, AND MONEY

[…] The cockfight [in the] colloquial sense, makes nothing happen. Men go on allegorically humiliating one another and being allegorically humiliated by one another, day after day, glorying quietly in the experience if they have triumphed, crushed only slightly more openly by it if they have not. But no one's status really changes. You cannot ascend the status ladder by winning cockfights; you cannot, as an individual, really ascend it at all. Nor can you descend it. […]

[T]he cockfight renders ordinary, everyday experience comprehensible by presenting it in terms of acts and objects which have had their practical consequences removed and been reduced (or, if you prefer, raised) to the level of sheer appearances, where their meaning can be more powerfully articulated and more exactly perceived. The cockfight is "really real" only to the cocks – it does not kill anyone, castrate anyone, reduce anyone to animal status, alter the hierarchical relations among people, or refashion the hierarchy; it does not even redistribute income in any significant way.[1] What it does is what, for other peoples with other temperaments and other conventions […] catches up these themes – death, masculinity, rage, pride, loss, beneficence, chance – and, ordering them into an encompassing structure, presents them in such a way as to throw into relief a particular view of their essential nature. It puts a construction on them, makes them, to those historically positioned to appreciate the construction, meaningful – visible, tangible, graspable – "real," in an ideational sense. An image, fiction, a model, a metaphor, the cockfight is a means of expression; its function is neither to assuage social passions nor to heighten them […] but, in a medium of feathers, blood, crowds, and money, to display them. […]

SAYING SOMETHING OF SOMETHING

[…] In the case at hand, to treat the cockfight as a text is to bring out a feature of it […] that treating it as a rite or a pastime, the two most obvious alternatives, would tend to obscure: its use of emotion for cognitive ends. What the cockfight says it says in a vocabulary of

---

1 Here, Geertz is rejecting a materialist interpretation of the cockfight.

sentiment – the thrill of risk, the despair of loss, the pleasure of triumph. Yet what it says is not merely that risk is exciting, loss depressing, or triumph gratifying, banal tautologies of affect, but that it is of these emotions, thus exampled, that society is built and individuals are put together. [...]

The culture of a people is an ensemble of texts, themselves ensembles, which the anthropologist strains to read over the shoulders of those to whom they properly belong. [...]

As in more familiar exercises in close reading, one can start anywhere in a culture's repertoire of forms and end up anywhere else. One can stay, as I have here, within a single, more or less bounded form, and circle steadily within it. One can move between forms in search of broader unities or informing contrasts. One can even compare forms from different cultures to define their character in reciprocal relief. But whatever the level at which one operates, and however intricately, the guiding principle is the same: societies, like lives, contain their own interpretations. One has only to learn how to gain access to them.

5.3. Grief and a Headhunter's Rage (1989)

Renato Rosaldo

If you ask an older Ilongot man of northern Luzon, Philippines, why he cuts off human heads, his answer is brief, and one on which no anthropologist can readily elaborate: He says that rage, born of grief, impels him to kill his fellow human beings. He claims that he needs a place "to carry his anger." The act of severing and tossing away the victim's head enables him, he says, to vent and, he hopes, throw away the anger of his bereavement. Although the anthropologist's job is to make other cultures intelligible, more questions fail to reveal any further explanation of this man's pithy statement. To him, grief, rage, and headhunting go together in a self-evident manner. Either you understand it or you don't. And, in fact, for the longest time I simply did not.

In what follows, I want to talk about how to talk about the cultural force of emotions. The *emotional force* of a death, for example, derives less from an abstract brute fact than from a particular intimate relation's permanent rupture. It refers to the kinds of feelings one experiences on learning, for example, that the child just run over by a car is one's own and not a stranger's. Rather than speaking of death in general, one must consider the subject's position within a field of social relations in order to grasp one's emotional experience.

My effort to show the force of a simple statement taken literally goes against anthropology's classic norms, which prefer to explicate culture through the gradual thickening of symbolic webs of meaning. By and large, cultural analysts use not *force* but such terms as *thick description, multivocality, polysemy, richness,* and *texture.* The notion of force, among other things, opens to question the common anthropological assumption that the greatest human import resides in the densest forest of symbols and that analytical detail, or "cultural depth," equals enhanced explanation of a culture, or "cultural elaboration." Do people always in fact describe most thickly what matters most to them?

THE RAGE IN ILONGOT GRIEF

Let me pause a moment to introduce the Ilongots, among whom my wife, Michelle Rosaldo, and I lived and conducted field research for thirty months (1967–69, 1974). They number about 3,500 and reside […] northeast of Manila, Philippines. They subsist by hunting […] and by cultivating rain-fed gardens. […] Their (bilateral) kin relations are reckoned through men and women. After marriage, parents and their married daughters live in the same or adjacent households. The largest unit within the society, a largely territorial descent group called the *bertan,* becomes manifest primarily in the context of feuding. For themselves, their neighbors, and their ethnographers, headhunting stands out as the Ilongots' most salient cultural practice.

When Ilongots told me, as they often did, how the rage in bereavement could impel men to headhunt, I brushed aside their one-line accounts as too simple, thin, opaque, implausible, stereotypical, or otherwise unsatisfying. […] My own inability to conceive the force of anger in grief led me to seek out another level of analysis that could provide a deeper explanation for older men's desire to headhunt.

Not until some fourteen years after first recording the terse Ilongot statement about grief and a headhunter's rage did I begin to grasp its overwhelming force. For years I thought that more verbal elaboration (which was not forthcoming) or another analytical level (which remained elusive) could better explain older men's motives for headhunting. Only after being repositioned through a devastating loss of my own could I better grasp that Ilongot older men mean precisely what they say when they describe the anger in bereavement as the source of their desire to cut off human heads. […]

HOW I FOUND THE RAGE IN GRIEF

One burden of this introduction concerns the claim that it took some fourteen years for me to grasp what Ilongots had told me about grief, rage, and headhunting. During all those years I was not yet in a position to comprehend the force of anger possible in bereavement, and now I am. Introducing myself into this account requires a certain hesitation both because of the discipline's taboo and because of its increasingly frequent violation by essays laced with trendy amalgams of continental philosophy and autobiographical snippets. If classic ethnography's vice was the slippage from the ideal of detachment to actual indifference, that of present-day reflexivity is the tendency for the self-absorbed Self to lose sight altogether of the culturally different Other. Despite the risks involved, as the ethnographer I must enter the discussion at this point to elucidate certain issues of method.

The key concept in what follows is that of the positioned (and repositioned) subject. In routine interpretive procedure, according to the methodology of hermeneutics, one can say that ethnographers reposition themselves as they go about understanding other cultures. Ethnographers begin research with a set of questions, revise them throughout the course of inquiry, and in the end emerge with different questions than they started with. One's surprise at the answer to a question, in other words, requires one to revise the question until lessening surprises or diminishing returns indicate a stopping point. This interpretive approach has been most influentially articulated within anthropology by Clifford Geertz.

Interpretive method usually rests on the axiom that gifted ethnographers learn their trade by preparing themselves as broadly as possible. To follow the meandering course of ethnographic inquiry, field-workers require wide-ranging theoretical capacities and finely tuned sensibilities. After all, one cannot predict beforehand what one will encounter in the field. [...]

Although the doctrine of preparation, knowledge, and sensibility contains much to admire, one should work to undermine the false comfort that it can convey. [...] The problem with taking this mode of preparing the ethnographer too much to heart is that it can lend a false air of security, an authoritative claim to certitude and finality that our analyses cannot have. All interpretations are provisional; they are made by positioned subjects who are prepared to know certain things and not others. Even when knowledgeable, sensitive, fluent in the language, and able to move easily in an alien cultural world, good ethnographers still have their limits, and their analyses always are incomplete. Thus, I began to fathom the force of what Ilongots had been telling me about their losses through my own loss, and not through any systematic preparation for field research.

My preparation for understanding serious loss began in 1970 with the death of my brother, shortly after his twenty-seventh birthday. By experiencing this ordeal with my mother and father, I gained a measure of insight into the trauma of a parent's losing a child. [...] At the same time, my bereavement was so much less than that of my parents that I could not then imagine the overwhelming force of rage possible in such grief. My former position is probably similar to that of many in the discipline. One should recognize that ethnographic knowledge tends to have the strengths and limitations given by the relative youth of field-workers who, for the most part, have not suffered serious losses and could have, for example, no personal knowledge of how devastating the loss of a long-term partner can be for the survivor.

In 1981 Michelle Rosaldo and I began field research among the Ifugaos of northern Luzon, Philippines. On October 11 of that year, she was walking along a trail with two Ifugao companions when she lost her footing and fell to her death some 65 feet down a sheer precipice into a swollen river below. Immediately on finding her body I became enraged. How could she abandon me? How could she have been so stupid as to fall? I tried to cry. I sobbed, but rage blocked the tears. Less than a month later I described this moment in my journal: "I felt like in a nightmare, the whole world around me expanding and contracting, visually and viscerally heaving. Going down I find a group of men, maybe seven or eight, standing still, silent, and I heave and sob, but no tears." An earlier experience, on the fourth anniversary of my brother's death, had taught me to recognize heaving sobs without tears as a form of anger. This anger, in a number of forms, has swept over me on many occasions since then, lasting hours and even days at a time. Such feelings can be aroused by rituals, but more often they emerge from unexpected reminders (not unlike the Ilongots' unnerving encounter with their dead uncle's voice on the tape recorder).

Lest there be any misunderstanding, bereavement should not be reduced to anger, neither for myself nor for anyone else. Powerful visceral emotional states swept over me, at times separately and at other times together. I experienced the deep cutting pain of sorrow almost beyond endurance, the cadaverous cold of realizing the finality of death, the trembling beginning in my abdomen and spreading through my body, the mournful keening that started without my willing, and frequent tearful sobbing. My present purpose of revising earlier understandings of Ilongot headhunting, and not a general view of bereavement, thus focuses on anger rather than on other emotions in grief.

Writings in English especially need to emphasize the rage in grief. Although grief therapists routinely encourage awareness of anger among the bereaved, upper-middle-class Anglo-American culture tends to ignore the rage devastating losses can bring. Paradoxically, this culture's conventional wisdom usually denies the anger in grief at the same time that therapists encourage members of the invisible community of the bereaved to talk in detail about how angry their losses make them feel. My brother's death in combination with what I learned about anger from Ilongots (for them, an emotional state more publicly celebrated than denied) allowed me immediately to recognize the experience of rage.

Ilongot anger and my own overlap, rather like two circles, partially overlaid and partially separate. They are not identical. Alongside striking similarities, significant differences in tone, cultural form, and human consequences distinguish the "anger" animating our respective ways of grieving. My vivid fantasies, for example, about a life insurance agent who refused to recognize Michelle's death as job-related did not lead me to kill him, cut off his head, and celebrate afterward. In so speaking, I am illustrating the discipline's methodological caution against the reckless attribution of one's own categories and experiences to members of another culture. Such warnings against facile notions of universal human nature can, however, be carried too far and harden into the equally pernicious doctrine that, my own group aside, everything human is alien to me. One hopes to achieve a balance between recognizing wide-ranging human differences and the modest truism that any two human groups must have certain things in common.

Only a week before completing the initial draft of an earlier version of this introduction, I rediscovered my journal entry, written some six weeks after Michelle's death, in which I made a vow to myself about how I would return to writing anthropology, if I ever did so, "by writing Grief and a Headhunter's Rage ..." My journal went on to reflect more broadly on death, rage, and headhunting by speaking of my "wish for the Ilongot solution; they are much more in touch with reality than Christians. So, I need a place to carry my anger – and can we say a solution of the imagination is better than theirs? And can we condemn them when we napalm villages? Is our rationale so much sounder than theirs?" All this was written in despair and rage.

Not until some fifteen months after Michelle's death was I again able to begin writing anthropology. Writing the initial version of "Grief and a Headhunter's Rage" was in fact cathartic, though perhaps not in the way one would imagine. Rather than following after the completed composition, the catharsis occurred beforehand. When the initial version of this introduction was most acutely on my mind, during the month before actually beginning to write, I felt diffusely depressed and ill with a fever. Then one day an almost literal fog lifted and words began to flow. It seemed less as if I were doing the writing than that the words were writing themselves through me.

My use of personal experience serves as a vehicle for making the quality and intensity of the rage in Ilongot grief more readily accessible to readers than certain more detached modes of composition. At the same time, by invoking personal experience as an analytical category one risks easy dismissal. Unsympathetic readers could reduce this introduction to an act of mourning or a mere report on my discovery of the anger possible in bereavement. Frankly, this introduction is both and more. An act of mourning, a personal report, *and* a critical analysis of anthropological method, it simultaneously encompasses a number of distinguishable processes, no one of which cancels out the others. [...] Aside from revising the ethnographic record, the paramount claim made here concerns how my own mourning and consequent reflection on Ilongot bereavement, rage, and headhunting raise methodological issues of general concern in anthropology and the human sciences. [...]

SUMMARY

The ethnographer, as a positioned subject, grasps certain human phenomena better than others. He or she occupies a position or structural location and observes with a particular angle of vision. Consider, for example, how age, gender, being an outsider, and association with a neocolonial regime influence what the ethnographer learns. The notion of position also refers to how life experiences both enable and inhibit particular kinds of insight. In the case at hand, nothing in my own experience equipped me even to imagine the anger possible in bereavement until after Michelle Rosaldo's death in 1981. Only then was I in a position to grasp the force of what Ilongots had repeatedly told me about grief, rage, and headhunting. By the same token, so-called natives are also positioned subjects who have a distinctive mix of insight and blindness. Consider the structural positions of older versus younger Ilongot men, or the differing positions of chief mourners versus those less involved during a funeral. My discussion of anthropological writings on death often achieved its effects simply by shifting from the position of those least involved to that of the chief mourners. [...]

This book argues that a sea change in cultural studies has eroded once-dominant conceptions of truth and objectivity. The truth of objectivism – absolute, universal, and timeless – has lost its monopoly status. It now competes, on more nearly equal terms, with the truths of case studies that are embedded in local contexts, shaped by local interests, and colored by local perceptions. The agenda for social analysis has shifted to include not only eternal verities and lawlike generalizations but also political processes, social changes, and human differences. Such terms as *objectivity, neutrality,* and *impartiality* refer to subject positions once endowed with great institutional authority, but they are arguably neither more nor less valid than those of more engaged, yet equally perceptive, knowledgeable social actors. Social analysis must now grapple with the realization that its objects of analysis are also analyzing subjects who critically interrogate ethnographers – their writings, their ethics, and their politics.

5.4. Writing against Culture (1991)

Lila Abu-Lughod

Writing Culture, the [1986] collection that marked a major new form of critique of cultural anthropology's premises, more or less excluded *two* critical groups whose situations neatly expose and challenge the most basic of those premises: feminists and "halfies" – (people whose national or cultural identity is mixed by virtue of migration, overseas education, or parentage). In his introduction, [James] Clifford apologizes for the feminist absence; no one mentions halfies or the indigenous anthropologists to whom they are related. [...] The importance of these two groups lies not in any superior moral claim or advantage they might have in doing anthropology, but in the special dilemmas they face, dilemmas that reveal starkly the problems with cultural anthropology's assumption of a fundamental distinction between self and other. [...]

SELVES AND OTHERS

[... An] interesting aspect of the feminist's situation [...] is what she shares with the halfie: a blocked ability to comfortably assume the self of anthropology. For both, although in different ways, the self is split, caught at the intersection of systems of difference. I am less concerned with the existential consequences of this split ... than with the awareness such splits generate about three crucial issues: positionality, audience, and the power inherent in distinctions of self and other. What happens when the "other" that the anthropologist is studying is simultaneously constructed as, at least partially, a self? [...]

Two common, intertwined objections to the work of feminist or native or semi-native anthropologists, both related to partiality, betray the persistence of ideals of objectivity. The first has to do with the partiality (as bias or position) of the observer. The second has to do with the partial (incomplete) nature of the picture presented. Halfies are more associated with the first problem, feminists the second. The problem with studying one's own society is alleged to be the problem of gaining enough distance. Since, for halfies, the Other is in certain ways the self, there is said to be the danger shared with indigenous anthropologists of identification and the easy slide into subjectivity. These worries suggest that the anthropologist is still defined as a being who must stand apart from the Other, even when he or she seeks explicitly to bridge the gap. Even Bourdieu, who perceptively analyzed the effects this outsider stance has on the anthropologist's (mis)understanding of social life, fails to break with this doxa. The obvious point he misses is that the outsider self never simply stands outside. He or she stands in a definite relation with the Other of the study. [...] What we call the outside is a position within a larger political-historical complex. No less than the halfie, the "wholie" is in a specific position vis-à-vis the community being studied.

[...] James Clifford, among others, has convincingly argued that ethnographic representations are always "partial truths." What is needed is a recognition that they are also positioned truths. [...]

[... F]eminist and halfie anthropologists [force us to confront] the dubiousness of maintaining that relationships between self and other are innocent of power. Because of sexism and racial or ethnic discrimination, they may have experienced – as women, as individuals of mixed parentage, or as foreigners – being other to a dominant self, whether in everyday life in the U.S., Britain, or France, or in the Western academy. [...]

CULTURE AND DIFFERENCE

[...] Most American anthropologists believe or act as if "culture," notoriously resistant to definition and ambiguous of referent, is nevertheless the true object of anthropological inquiry. Yet it could also be argued that culture is important to anthropology because the anthropological distinction between self and other rests on it. Culture is the essential tool for making other. As a professional discourse that elaborates on the meaning of culture in order to account for, explain, and understand cultural difference, anthropology also helps construct, produce, and maintain it. [...]

[...] The most important of culture's advantages [...] is that it removes difference from the realm of the natural and the innate. Whether conceived of as a set of behaviors, customs, traditions, rules, plans, recipes, instructions, or programs ... culture is learned and can change.

Despite its anti-essentialist intent, however, the culture concept retains some of the tendencies to freeze difference possessed by concepts like race. [...]

THREE MODES OF WRITING AGAINST CULTURE

If "culture," shadowed by coherence, timelessness, and discreteness, is the prime anthropological tool for making "other," and difference, as feminists and halfies reveal, tends to be a relationship of power, then perhaps anthropologists should consider strategies for writing against culture. [...]

[1] Discourse and Practice

Theoretical discussion, because it is one of the modes in which anthropologists engage each other, provides an important site for contesting culture. It seems to me that current discussions and deployments of two increasingly popular terms – practice and discourse – do signal a shift away from culture. [...]

Practice is associated, in anthropology, with Bourdieu, whose theoretical approach is built around problems of contradiction, misunderstanding, and misrecognition, and favors strategies, interests, and improvisations over the more static and homogenizing cultural tropes of rules, models, and texts. Discourse has more diverse sources and meanings in anthropology. In its Foucauldian derivation, as it relates to notions of discursive formations, apparatuses, and technologies, it is meant to refuse the distinction between ideas and practices or text and world that the culture concept too readily encourages. In its more sociolinguistic sense, it draws attention to the social uses by individuals of verbal resources. In either case, it allows for the possibility of recognizing within a social group the play of multiple, shifting, and competing statements with practical effects. Both practice and discourse are useful because they work against the assumption of boundedness, not to mention the idealism, of the culture concept.

[2] Connections

Another strategy [...] is to reorient the problems or subject matter anthropologists address. An important focus should be the various connections and interconnections, historical and contemporary, between a community and the anthropologist working there and writing about it, not to mention the world to which he or she belongs and which enables him or her to be in that particular place studying that group. This is more of a political project than an existential one, although the reflexive anthropologists who have taught us to focus on the fieldwork encounter as a site for the construction of the ethnographic facts have alerted us to one important dimension of the connection. Other significant sorts of connections have received less attention. [...] We need to ask questions about the historical processes by which it came to pass that people like ourselves could be engaged in anthropological studies of people like those, about the current world situation that enables us to engage in this sort of work in this particular place, and about who has preceded us and is even now there with us (tourists, travelers, missionaries, AID consultants, Peace Corps workers). We need to ask what this "will to knowledge" about the Other is connected to in the world.

These questions cannot be asked in general; they should be asked about and answered by tracing through specific situations, configurations, and histories. Even though they do not address directly the place of the ethnographer, and even though they engage in an over systemization that threatens to erase local interactions, studies like those of Wolf [*Europe and the People without History*] on the long history of interaction between particular Western societies and communities in what is now called the Third World represent important means of answering such questions. [...]

Not all projects about connections need be historical. Anthropologists are increasingly concerned with national and transnational connections of people, cultural forms, media, techniques, and commodities. They study the articulation of world capitalism and international politics with the situations of people living in particular communities. All these projects, which involve a shift in gaze to include phenomena of connection, expose the inadequacies of the concept of culture and the elusiveness of the entities designated by the term cultures. [...]

[3] Ethnographies of the Particular

[...] Insofar as anthropologists are in the business of representing others through their ethnographic writing, then surely the degree to which people in the communities they study appear "other" must also be partly a function of how anthropologists write about them. Are there ways to write about lives so as to constitute others as less other?

I would argue that one powerful tool for unsettling the culture concept and subverting the process of "othering" it entails is to write "ethnographies of the particular." Generalization, the characteristic mode of operation and style of writing of the social sciences, can no longer be regarded as neutral description. [...]

There are two reasons for anthropologists to be wary of generalization. The first is that, as part of a professional discourse of "objectivity" and expertise, it is inevitably a language of power. On the one hand, it is the language of those who seem to stand apart from and outside of what they are describing. [...] On the other hand, even if we withhold judgment on how closely the social sciences can be associated with the apparatuses of management, we have to recognize how all professionalized discourses by nature assert hierarchy. The very gap between the professional and authoritative discourses of generalization and the languages of everyday life (our own and others') establishes a fundamental separation between the anthropologist and the people being written about that facilitates the construction of anthropological objects as simultaneously different and inferior. [...]

The second problem with generalization derives not from its participation in the authoritative discourses of professionalism but from the effects of homogeneity, coherence, and timelessness it tends to produce. When one generalizes from experiences and conversations with a number of specific people in a community, one tends to flatten out differences among them and to homogenize them. The appearance of an absence of internal differentiation makes it easier to conceive of a group of people as a discrete, bounded entity, like the "the Nuer," "the Balinese," and "the Awlad 'Ali Bedouin" who do this or that and believe such-and-such. The effort to produce general ethnographic descriptions of people's beliefs or actions tends to smooth over contradictions, conflicts of interest, and doubts and arguments, not to mention changing motivations and circumstances. The erasure of time and conflict make what is inside the boundary set up by homogenization something essential and fixed. [...]

By focusing closely on particular individuals and their changing relationships, one would necessarily subvert the most problematic connotations of culture: homogeneity, coherence, and timelessness. Individuals are confronted with choices, struggle with others, make conflicting statements, argue about points of view on the same events, undergo ups and downs in various relationships and changes in their circumstances and desires, face new pressures, and fail to predict what will happen to them or those around them. So, for example, it becomes difficult to think that the term "Bedouin culture" makes sense when one tries to piece together and convey what life is like for one old Bedouin matriarch.

When you ask her to tell the story of her life, she responds that one should only think about God. Yet she tells vivid stories, fixed in memory in particular ways, about her resistances to arranged marriages, her deliveries of children, her worries about sick daughters. She also tells about weddings she has attended, dirty songs sung by certain young men as they sheared the elders' sheep herds, and trips in crowded taxis where she pinched a man's bottom to get him off her lap.

The most regular aspect of her daily life is her wait for prayer times. Is it noon yet? Not yet. Is it afternoon yet? Not yet. Is it sunset yet? Grandmother, you haven't prayed yet? It's already past sunset. She spreads her prayer rug in front of her and prays out loud. At the end, as she folds up her prayer rug, she beseeches God to protect all Muslims. She recites God's names as she goes through her string of prayer beads. The only decoration in her room is a photograph on the wall of herself and her son as pilgrims in Mecca.

Her back so hunched she can hardly stand, she spends her days sitting or lying down on her mattress. She is practically blind and she complains about her many pains. People come and go, her sons, her nephews, her daughter, her nieces, her granddaughters, her great-grandson. They chat, they confer with her about connections between people, marriages, kinship. She gives advice; she scolds them for not doing things properly. And she plays with her great grandson, who is three, by teasing, "Hey, I've run out of snuff. Come here so I can sniff your little tuber."

Being pious and fiercely preserving protocol in the hosting of guests and the exchanging of visits and greetings does not seem to stop her from relishing the outrageous story and the immoral tale. A new favorite when I saw her in 1987 was one she had just picked up from her daughter, herself a married mother of five living near Alamein. It was a tale about an old husband and wife who decide to go visit their daughters, and it was funny for the upside-down world it evoked.

This tale depicted a world where people did the unthinkable. Instead of the usual candy and biscuits, the couple brought their daughters sacks of dung for gifts. When the first daughter they stayed with went off to draw water from the well, they started dumping out all the large containers of honey and oil in her merchant husband's house. She returned to find them spilling everything and threw them out. So they headed off to visit the second daughter. When she left them minding her baby for a while, the old man killed it just to stop it from crying. She came back, discovered this and threw them out. Next they came across a house with a slaughtered sheep in it. They made belts out of the intestines and caps out of the stomachs and tried them on, admiring each other in their new finery. But when the old woman asked her husband if she didn't look pretty in her new belt he answered, "You'd be really pretty, except for that fly sitting on your nose." With that he smacked the fly, killing his wife. As he wailed in grief he began to fart. Furious at his anus for farting over his dead wife, he heated up a stake and shoved it in, killing himself.

The old woman chuckles as she tells this story, just as she laughs hard over stories about the excessive sexuality of old women. How does this sense of humor, this appreciation of the bawdy, go with devotion to prayer and protocols of honor? How does her nostalgia for the past – when the area was empty and she could see for miles around when she used to play as a little girl digging up the occasional potsherd or glass bottle in the area now fenced and guarded by the government Antiquities Organization; when her family migrated with the sheep herds and milked and made butter in desert pastures – go with her fierce defense of her favorite grandson, whose father was furious with him because the young man was rumored to have drunk liquor at a local wedding? People do not drink in the community, and drinking is, of course, religiously proscribed. What can "culture" mean given this old woman's complex responses?

5.5. Sensuous Stories in the Indian Ocean Islands (2017)

Rosabelle Boswell

THE SENSE-WORK OF LISTENING

[...] White, male anthropologists (especially in southern Africa) have tended to look "north" for theoretical inspiration and guidance on practice. [...] They have engaged, like their forebears with a good measure of scholarly conviction, authority and power when researching the situation of their mostly colonized black research subjects. Subjects are routinely distanced via the "anthropological lens" (Peacock 1987), their words filtered, and their stories reformulated for consumption in places far removed from local realities. This is why a theory of the local listener [...] is so important. It matters whether one is a black woman anthropologist, like myself, or a white, male anthropologist. It matters both to how one listens and how one writes. [...]

LISTENING TO SMELL, FEEL, TASTE, SEE AND BALANCE RELATIONS IN THE IOR

[...] I offer a few stories as they were told (i.e. in the raw, as Bourdieu would say) and alongside each, I offer an alternative sensory perspective, my own introspective embodied analysis of what I heard and experienced. [...] A brief, embodied experience of listening to the story being told is offered for each, to provide a reflexive sensory analysis of listening to sense. [...]

In the Seychelles in 2005, during a particularly rainy season, I learned that listening requires emotional dissociation. I knew that what whites suffered in the islands paled in comparison to what blacks experienced. Listening to white people discussing their suffering after the institution of socialist rule in Seychelles taught me that the fieldwork process may require emotional sublimation, a sort of listening without hearing for white suffering in

Seychelles (or so it seemed to me at the time) was about the indignity of being reduced to the black experience.

The breadfruit eaters. Seychelles 2005.

It is very true that we are settlers. When we left England in 1980, we were poor but we were determined not to stay that way. Mahé [Seychelles] just felt like the right place to be and with the socialist government we knew that things were going to be difficult but at the same time, we wanted a different way of being. After all, Thatcher was destroying England and we did not want to live under an oppressive regime.

The socialist years were really tough, so much so that everyone was "reduced" to breadfruit. You can see them dangling from the trees across the island and that is what everyone ate, breadfruit soup, breadfruit stew, breadfruit salad, every day, all day. It was also about that time that I became interested in sculpture, especially the use of bronze to produce the human form. You can see my work online these days but for the longest time, I worked here, alone [points to a shed] close to the forest. We still don't have much. Not many artists are rich but to be here in this verdant forest and looking out over the greenest sea, that is just fine for me. I don't need to have anything else but this.

Of course, things are not always easy. Lately, you can go to the shop and expect a bit of sugar or tea or something else special. It is not there. I've eaten cake without sugar and had to make do without tea! Would I change it for something else? Not likely.

In Seychelles and Mauritius, many black descendants experience lack, monotony, hardship, discrimination and indifference. The day I heard the story of the breadfruit eaters, I had already tasted indifference. Five months pregnant and craving a sweet treat, I walked up a fairly steep hill in Victoria, Mahé to buy cakes from a local patisserie. I carefully chose a gaudy pink *napolitaine* (two round shortbread biscuits wedged together with strawberry jam and covered in pink fondant icing), a *millefeuille* (many layers of pastry laced with homemade custard filling) and several crispy biscuits known as *langue-de-chat*. Eager to devour the sweetness and jaunty with the knowledge that at least I had some money, I bit into the *napolitaine*. A tasteless crumbly mixture of pink nothingness filled my mouth. There was no sugar in it. Angry that I had been sold a simulated dessert, I walked past some people picking through the remaining vegetables and fish stacked in little stinking piles for the last hour of the market. I also passed a man fishing in what looked like a very clean canal, but there was to be no reprieve, the main supermarket had no sugar either, the latest consignment from Mauritius had not arrived.

The next day, hiding from a sudden torrential downpour in the southern village of Takamaka, I watched, as black Seychellois clambered up a steep hill to reach their homes. Looking more closely I saw that some of them had breadfruit in each hand. Black African descendants, I found, ate breadfruit almost every day. They ate what they could forage (at sea and in the forests) and sometimes buy. Their diet consisted largely of rice and fish or shellfish. The very poor bought clothing only a few times a year. It was for celebratory times when dignity had to be publicly displayed and suffering obscured.

The story of the breadfruit eaters revealed two things. One, the stoicism required to live in an isolated and often unpredictable paradise. Two, the sheer emotional resilience it required of a local, black listener to listen to whites (and those similarly privileged) in the midst of the immense suffering of black Africans. Listening to white descendants, their ambitions and preoccupations, their deft avoidance of the dread-fullness of racism around them, their complaints about being "reduced" to breadfruit (i.e. black experience), forced me to swallow the heaviness of anger, to adjust my posture and tone to reach for a professional, unaffected, objective and analytical stance.

The business of maintaining face and indeed maintaining body, is however, deeply complicated and often contradictory. Such a story appeared in Zanzibar in 2006, where I found that sustaining love is a profoundly sensual business ultimately (perhaps) concerned with sustaining socially embedded norms.

Aroma. Zanzibar 2006.

For us women, this [pointing to a little vial] is what makes us sing. Everything here is fragrance since we know, Allah (Peace be Upon Him), is as fragrant as the gardens of paradise. We look to Him then to make ourselves and for us, nothing is more important than to please Him. Any woman seeking happiness must surround herself with fragrance. The fragrance of innocence, peace, love and faithfulness. For seven days before I married, I was made fragrant just for him [husband]. My *somo* used *liwa* (sandalwood) to polish my skin. Then, she and others massaged for seven nights making my skin as smooth as the moon. Our people and our city was once as fragrant as the holy ones among us. Sadly, this is no longer so. There is no longer the smoke of believers rising from the rooftops. In the old days, as my grandma used to tell us, incense rising from the city at prayers, filled each person with goodness. Any young woman seeking noble love should place her *kanga* [two piece fabric] on the *mrashi ya moshi* [incense dispenser] every morning, the scent, made up of our *ylang ylang*, patchouli or jasmine leaves will rise like the spirit to purify her. A woman need not be afraid of being so. She is unclean and she needs to comb her hair and infuse it with lemongrass, her skin, like her soul must be free of blemish. So you have heard, that our *kangas* speak for us? Any woman who wants to be heard does not need to speak out loud. See, the *kanga* I am wearing today sends a message to my husband without me opening my mouth, it says, "you can eat all the meat in the butchery but it will all taste the same" [...]

Preoccupied with getting "valuable" or "hard" data, I was surprised by the omnipresence of scent, its varied contribution to my personal wellbeing and its particular framing of a little known world. I had come to the field and left behind a one-year-old son, forcibly weaned. Weaning and the process of healing after childbirth takes time. However, women often mask this healing process so that they can be "reintegrated" in a masculinized society. The cesarean wound incurred the year before still itched and pulled. My breasts leaked at night. I padded them in the day so that I would not reveal my "state" in the research process. Still, each time they leaked, a weepiness overwhelmed me which I pressed down by focusing on the obligation to obtain data. I searched for ostensibly cultural experiences that could be documented. It was as my interpreter and friend stepped off her porch that she turned to me, touching a fragile leaf of *ylang ylang* and said, "now there is something worth studying" that I did a "double take," but only after I inhaled the scent of the long, pale green leaves. The scent was so intoxicating that it left me lightheaded and euphoric. Ashamed that I was somehow "high," I did not reveal this to my friend. But it was long since I had felt euphoric, for love, like childbirth had drained and exhausted me. Days later, her friend told me the story of *ylang ylang*.

We were seated in a small room, lit by the piercing sun pouring through a narrow window. For a moment I was transported back to my own grandmother's shack in Port Louis, Mauritius. I remembered how eventually the discomfort of shabby surroundings melts away, it is only the voice of the story-teller that remains, a grounding voice that brings comfort and familiarity. There is no hiding here, for the listener finds herself among people who look like her, people who know that love is difficult, that love involves public display for the satisfaction of society. As the story of "aroma" unfolded, I found myself reflecting on the fleshliness and ethereality of women's bodies. A woman's body was many things, a changing canvas, once smooth unblemished and proportioned to being something possibly ungainly, unpredictable and full of inexplicable aches. Feeling the imperfection of the canvas changed by birth that is my body, I listened to the story-teller describe the perfection of the smoothness of her skin, the opulence of the bed linen, the fragrance in the room and then, the diminishment of flawlessness, as she offers her unblemished and fragranced self, almost as love itself, to her husband and society.

I came to learn, as I did through the story of fragrance, that the local listener is often drawn into not only the sublime but also the banal. As the sublime brings comfort and familiarity, the banal elicits feelings of violation, requiring the listener to recoil into themselves, as if to protect their core from taint and disrepute. In the [next] story of Cocktail Hour [...], I found that story-telling is very much a time specific process. Cocktail Hour is that time of the day when all is permissible, banality, crassness, advances, bragging and largesse. It is a time when the local listener may not have the necessary tools to respond, for the existing social mores and restraints do not apply. Plus and often in anthropology, we interview those who are either equal to or less powerful than ourselves. In the presence of the hotelier, I found myself unsettled by a powerful interviewee, trying to lure me to have sex with him, whilst I pretended not to notice his sexual advances. In this instance, maintaining face and body involved adjusting self and pretending to be oblivious to the overtly sexual innuendoes, pretending not to feel vulnerable lest it became apparent that I was.

Cocktail Hour. Zanzibar 2007.
[...] Before I had a chance to show him my research permit on which it was clearly stated that my research [...] had now been "properly passed" by the Revolutionary Government of Zanzibar, [the hotelier] whisked me into the lobby of his two storey establishment and began to tell me a tale to which I had to listen. He said,

You know, we seize every chance we can to show our hotel. It is not much but it is better than what it was before, all broken down and dilapidated. We carefully restored this place you know, without us, well, I don't know where this place would be today. You say you are Mauritian? Or is it South African? Never mind, never mind, we can manage in both English and French. My wife is not here so not to worry, she cannot interrupt us. Not on anything! I can show each room and you will see just how different they are. We have tried, yes, tried not to spare a penny. We were lucky to get all the furniture from one outlet. You know him? The man who also runs a shop, photography business and tourist company? Yes it was him. It seems that a lot of the furniture came from the old houses. We just cleaned them up a little and they keep that charm you know? They just look so beautiful, who cares where they come from? Ah, here is the room of the princess, like princess Salme. Slaves were so important to the economy that beds were built to stand high off the floor, so that there was enough space for the slave servant to guard their owner by sleeping underneath. Imagine that, your own slave sleeping under your bed to make sure that you're ok! The doors back in those days, what magnificence! Huge ornate doors to repel ferocious elephants. Not that there were any on this island you know but they took precautions. The bathrooms well, they are not quite like they were back then but, we try. Try to make it like it was back then. People like that stuff you know, all these fantasies.

Here you can go back to the past. Look, the silk sheets, the colours, the embroidery ... when you lie in that bed you will feel like a real princess. Ok, never mind, never mind you don't have to try it but come! Right to the top, you have to see my sunset. It's the best view up here. Only I can be up here, no servants, no wife, no-one but me and ... [laughs] you of course! Drink up [hands me a glass of wine], chin-chin, you will never have this experience again. And look, I even have my own shower up here. I can see the whole city and it cannot see me. Take a photo, you have to take a photo of that. A view like none other. My sun setting, my wine, this table and me.

The fact that informants may advance hegemonic and violent forms of masculinity and that interactions with hegemonic males affects the research process requires further exposition. I experienced this not only in Zanzibar but also Madagascar and it definitely produced negative sensorial experiences of research. As noted previously, the sexual advances of the hotelier rendered me vulnerable and made me recoil into myself. I had to pretend that I did not feel vulnerable, that I was still conducting an ethnographic interview. I had to maintain both a disciplinary face and analytical posture. [...]

LISTENING TO SENSE

[...] The side stories reveal that it is not only the storytellers who are positioned, so is the listener – encouraged to wean and to conceal wounds in the pursuit of data. Anthropological stories generally go to a cool world of analysis, a place where the heat of belief and the cold of loss are tempered for analytical purposes. In the "analysis-scape" inequality, violence and discrimination are deconstructed and rendered palatable. Local listeners find it difficult to distance themselves from the grief and horror of dispossession or colonial fantasies of control. The sweetly idealized past lingers, as does the bitterness of dispossession. By releasing stories raw, anthropologists can convey and entice some of the sensorial experiences they have had in the field. Sensuous stories well told should elicit sensuous listening.

REFERENCE

Peacock, J.L. 1987. *The Anthropological Lens: Harsh Light, Soft Focus*. Cambridge: University Press.

Section Five Glossary

interpretive anthropology   Developed most fully by Clifford Geertz, this approach to anthropology treats cultures as ensembles of texts. The job of the anthropologist is akin to the job of a literary critic to interpret the text. In particular, the anthropologist should draw out the meanings of cultural practices – not just describe them, but seek to explain what they mean to the people who practice them. Interpretive anthropology was proposed by Geertz as a corrective to structuralism.

phenomenological anthropology   An approach to anthropological study that prioritizes people's lived experiences, particularly bodily experiences and their interactions with consciousness and cognition.

positionality   Attention to the ways in which our social positions (especially vis á vis racial, class, gendered, and sexual categories) influence what we know and how we understand it.

postmodernism   Broadly, postmodernism describes intellectual and artistic trends from the mid- to late twentieth-century Western world that eschew grand theories associated with modernism. In anthropology, postmodernism typically refers to a focus on subjectivity, positionality, and interpretation (as opposed to objectivity, neutrality, and universally applicable theory) in ethnographic research and writing.

poststructuralism   The theoretical orientation that emerged in critical response to the apolitical, uncontextualized, and overly rigid nature of structuralism. Poststructuralists, influenced by the work of Pierre Bourdieu and Michel Foucault, reject the notion that there is an underlying and systematic explanation for culture and instead approach culture as dynamic and influenced by flows of power.

thick description   A term coined by Clifford Geertz to describe an interpretive approach to writing that incorporates cultural meanings and not just descriptive narratives into ethnographic texts. In one well-known passage, Geertz points out that a description of a person winking and blinking might be the same: a rapid contraction of the eyelid. But the cultural meanings of winks and blinks are vastly different, and it is up to the anthropologist to convey those meanings.

On Colonialism and Anthropological "Others"

THE SOCIAL CONTEXT

For centuries, colonial domination had been enforced by horrific violence and legitimized by colonialist ideologies that portrayed colonized people as infantile, incapable of self-rule, benefiting from subjugation, and, above all, as inherently inferior to their European colonizers. During wars for independence in the mid-twentieth century, people in colonized places spoke powerfully against their subjugation, challenging such portrayals in the Western world. We have already seen instances of anti-colonialist scholarship in essays by William Apess and Fernando Ortiz. The essays in this section further develop anti-colonial critiques, and they challenge the role of Western academia, and anthropology in particular, in propagating colonialist hegemony.

Anthropology has famously been called "**the child and handmaiden of colonialism**" (Gough 1968). While the accuracy of this characterization is disputed among anthropologists, early ethnologists such as Powell, Brinton, and Morton were key figures in the development of scientific racism who not only fostered theories of racial hierarchy but who also put colonized people on public display like zoo animals. Bronislaw Malinowski openly advocated anthropology's utility for colonial administration. And even anti-racist anthropologists such as Franz Boas participated in "**salvage anthropology**" under the assumption that Indigenous people of the Americas were irreversibly careening toward extinction. More broadly, anthropology's preoccupation with researching non-Western, "exotic," and "isolated" people cemented its place as a discipline that, in spite of its dependence on global inequality, often elided the role that colonialism has played in creating the vastly unequal landscapes in which anthropologists work.

This history helped to fuel postmodern critique, discussed in Section Five, which challenged the putative neutrality and objectivity of anthropological analysis. Postmodern scholarship levied important and highly critical charges against anthropology that have shaped our discipline ever since. Yet, once the dust settled, anti-colonialist anthropologists and other critical thinkers struggled with how to move forward from the depoliticized "texts" that comprised a lot of postmodernist work (think of Geertz's colonialist characterization of Balinese men as obsessed with their small brown cocks instead of as actors in anti-colonial struggles). This is where the essays in this section make their critical contributions.

THE CONVERSATION

The pieces in this section share a concern with turning anthropological analyses onto colonial "culture" and its legacies. They consider not only how colonial power relations produce certain forms of knowing colonized "others," but also how experiences of colonization differently shape the cultivation of intellectual expertise and the goals of anthropological research in colonial and formerly colonial contexts.

Beatrice Medicine is the author of Reading 6.1, which brings an **applied anthropological** perspective to bear on research with colonized and formerly colonized people. This is our first piece that is explicitly "applied," and it introduces methods of anthropological research that are meant to address social problems, including treating study "subjects" as partners in the research process, prioritizing research that addresses community concerns, and making research outputs accessible in the study community. These practices, Medicine writes, have developed as part of her own journey navigating twin responsibilities as a Native anthropologist.

Our second piece is an excerpt from Edward Said's book *Orientalism*. In it, Said argues that "knowledge" of colonized people is an important tool of British imperialism in Egypt. Such knowledge, Said argues, is cultivated by "the developing sciences of ethnology, comparative anatomy, philology, and history" and comes to stand in for the reality of colonized people in English law and society. Thus, hegemonic British conceptions of the "Orient" and "Oriental" – what Said terms "Orientalism" – form the basis for imperial rule, making imperialism possible.

Our third selection is written by anthropologist Esteban Krotz, and it delineates three key features of an "anthropology of the South," or anthropology produced in "developing" countries of the Global South. Anthropologists working from and in "Southern" contexts – the typical dominion of anthropological subjects but not anthropological theorists – Krotz argues, are creating a form of anthropological study shaped by relationships, realities, and subjectivities that distinguish it from "Northern" ones. Anthropology in the South, Krotz says, has "acquired its own life."

Our fourth piece by Michel-Rolph Trouillot presents his theorization of anthropology as occupying the "Savage slot" in Western knowledge production. The problem with Savages in modernity, Trouillot argues, is not that they no longer exist, for they never really existed. The problem is that postmodernism has exposed this fiction, leaving anthropology as "the specialist in savagery [in] dire straits." Further, Trouillot continues, moving beyond anthropology's postmodern "exercise in reflexivity" requires engaging with real people in all of their history and complexity. Such a move will destroy the illusion of the Other, compel recognition that "there is no Savage slot," and only then allow us to "reenter" anthropology as a project of significance in the world.

Reading 6.5 is an essay by Epeli Hau'ofa that grapples with hegemonic characterizations of Pacific Island peoples. Such characterizations depict the Pacific Islands as too isolated, too small, and too far away to achieve politico-economic independence from wealthy nations (consider Malinowski's depiction of the Trobriand Islands in Section Three). But these characterizations, Hau'ofa argues, are the product and not the cause of colonial control. In contrast, Hau'ofa proposes a conception of Oceania as "a sea of islands" rather than "islands in a far sea." This shift allows us to perceive the people of Oceania as interconnected residents of a vast ocean terrain with rich and expansive cultural, social, and economic practices.

THREE QUESTIONS FOR THE READINGS

1 What is the context or problem that these selections are responding to? What argument is common to all of these essays?
2 How might the subject position of these scholars shape their historicizing and critique of anthropology?
3 Where do these critiques take us? If anthropology is "salvageable" as a discipline, what kinds of anthropological research might these scholars support?

ON THE COMPANION WEBSITE

"Here Come the Anthros" song, "Anthropology on Trial," additional readings, and more.

www.anthropologicaltheory.com

REFERENCE

Gough, Kathleen. 1968. "Anthropology and Imperialism." *Monthly Review* 19 (11): 12–27.

6.1. Learning to Be an Anthropologist and Remaining "Native" (1978)

Beatrice Medicine

Recently, many students – particularly Native Americans – have been dazzled by Vine Deloria, Jr.'s scathing attack on "anthros," as we are called by most Native Americans. His article, which first appeared in *Playboy* (Deloria 1969a), has since been reprinted in many anthropological works. Besides serving as a "sweat bath" to purge anthropologists of their guilt feelings, it has become a rallying cry for Indian militants and tribal people alike. Many Native people have articulated their discontent with the exploitative adventures of anthros in the American Indian field. (See, for example, the proceedings of a symposium entitled "Anthropology and the American Indian," held in San Diego at the 1970 annual meeting of the American Anthropological Association and published by the Indian Historian Press in 1973.) However, Native readers seemingly do not go beyond page 100 of Deloria's manifesto entitled *Custer Died for Your Sins*. Later, he states: "This book has been the hardest on those people in whom I place the greatest amount of hope for the future – Congress, the anthropologists, and the churches" ([Deloria] 1969b:275). Because the churches and Congress have eroded my faith in the institutions of the dominant society, I shall focus on anthropology. It is, after all, the source of my livelihood.

"Anthropologist" as a role designation has been traditionally meaningful to American Indians or, as we have recently been glossed, "Native Americans." In the early days of American anthropology, we were seen as "vanishing Americans." Thus, students of Boas collected data on Plains Indian reservations and Northwest Coast villages in order to recapture "memory cultures" that reflected the "golden days" of Natives whose aboriginal culture was denigrated and whose future was seen as oblivion or civilization. Many felt that American anthropology was built upon the backs of Natives (DeLaguna 1960:792), but the contributions of American Indians to the discipline has never been fully assessed. Panday (1972), however, has detailed the interactions of anthros and Natives at Zuni pueblo.

Initially, it was Franz Boas's interest in folklore, linguistics, and other aspects of culture that led him to seek and train indigenous persons who seemed especially responsive to viewing their own cultures. Among the tribes of the American Midwest, there were persons such as Francis LaFlesche, an Omaha, and William Jones, a Mesquakie (Fox), who worked in the discipline. The latter died on a field trip to the Philippines while working among the Ilongots.

Nevertheless, the role of informant as anthropological reporter creates qualms among Natives who contemplate becoming anthropologists, and it is not surprising that early contributions by Native Americans were primarily in texts on the Native languages and in folklore and mythology. A pertinent observation was made by a black anthropologist:

> In the same spirit that Boas encouraged Natives to become anthropologists, he also encouraged women because they could collect information on female behavior more easily than a male anthropologist. This attitude strongly implied that native and female anthropologists are seen as potential "tools" to be used to provide important information to the "real" white male anthropologist (Jones 1970:252). [...]

Being a Native female delineated areas of investigation that were closed to me. This was aggravated by my prolonged infertility. Conversation or gossip about such matters as deviant sexual practices, abortions, and pregnancy taboos was immediately terminated when I appeared at female gatherings. It was only after ten years of marriage and producing a male child that I was included in "womanly" spheres. Until then, I was referred to as "Little Bea." The cultural constrictions of working within my own group caused me to reexamine value configurations, sex roles, Indian-white relationships, and socialization practices by spending most of my time with the children. Some persons in my *tiospaye* (extended kin group) said I "spoiled" (i.e., "catered to") children. But by treating children as people, I was only acting in the way I myself had been socialized.

In the contemporary era, the concepts of acculturation or culture change, cultural transmission, role-modeling, bicultural and bilingual education, cultural brokerage, and others are highlighted in anthropological research. For me, these concepts have become personal and concrete during the years of learning to be an anthropologist while remaining a native. My learning began in childhood and continues in the present.

EARLY LEARNING

Of significance to many of us Lakota people was Ella Deloria, a daughter of a Santee Dakota Episcopal missionary who worked among the Hunkpapa and Sihasapa (Blackfeet) bands of the Teton (Western) Sioux who were placed on the Standing Rock Reservation. She and other Native Americans and Canadians came within the orbit of Boas, with whom she coauthored a book on Dakota grammar (Boas and Deloria 1941). Her other work included linguistic, folklore, and kinship studies (Deloria 1944). [...]

Aunt Ella's participation in a world far removed from Standing Rock Reservation where she lectured "about Lakota" presented a model that I found attractive. Much later, I attended a lecture by a physical anthropologist (now deceased) who asked, "Will all the persons in the room who have shovel-shaped incisors please indicate?" This experience and being used as an informant (together with a Swedish student) in a "Personality and Culture" course raised many questions in my mind about becoming an anthropologist. Would it be possible to retain dignity as a Native while operating in roles other than informant? Would anthropological training alienate me from my people? Would it affect marriage? Aunt Ella had never married. Lakota ideals for women included marriage and children. I knew my father did not believe in what he later termed "cross-cultural" marriages. [...]

THE TEACHER ROLE

[... Among the work that is expected of me by Native communities, one major request] is the distribution of anthropological sources to various tribes or Native organizations for specific, usually legal, cases. This is a continuing process, as is the dissemination of knowledge about private and governmental sources of funding that can be utilized by these groups. Monitoring proposals without jeopardizing one's position as a reader of them entails a constant weighing of benefits to both tribal groups and educational agencies. Extremely delicate situations are created when cousins and other relatives call for special considerations. Reliance on "old Lakota values" such as integrity is a healthy and understandable resolution for all concerned. [...]

Work among Natives, however, is difficult when they view anthropological reports about their tribes as unreliable. Susie Yellow Tail (Crow) defines ethnographies as "Indian joke books." There is no noticeable reliance or reference to many of the earlier ethnographic sources, especially linguistics and ethnohistorical studies. Many tribes are writing their own tribal histories in an attempt to present their experiences from their own unique point of view. Native Americans often believe that most anthropologists already have a theoretical framework when they enter an indigenous social system and collect and report data in support of this prior formulation.

I have attempted a concerted effort to let people know the focus of my own investigations. Among the Lakota on Standing Rock, it is customary for "powwow committees" from various communities to ask visiting returnees to the reservation to address such gatherings of people. I have found this an ideal way to present interpretations of research in an acceptable manner. There is response and reaction to the speech-maker and members of my *tiospaye* (extended family). It is also an accepted means of conforming to tribal expectations. Many of us have been criticized by persons in governmental agencies, such as the United States Public Health Service and Bureau of Indian Affairs, who see our statements as ego-centered accounts of our activities in the "outside world." They fail to understand that this modern form of "coup-counting" is viewed by most community members as a means of modeling and enhancing Lakota values and conforming to expected behavior in contemporary reservation culture. It is a valuable outlet for letting the people know what will be written and for obtaining their assessment of it. [...]

The translation of research terminology into an English vernacular that Native parents and students can comprehend is a formidable task that "target populations" take for granted.

This is not to disparage the intellect of tribal people, but rather to acknowledge their estimate of anthropological research and indicate their preoccupation with the many daily tasks of reservation life. It speaks to the need for less jargon in anthropological reporting. The increasing number of Native college graduates who return to reservations or urban Indian centers and survival schools seldom utilize these studies at all. Their concern is the development of curricular materials that are more pertinent to their own and their students' needs. [...]

[...] Native pressure to take fellowships and jobs to ensure continued occupancy by Native people is great. Although I have, since 1969, spent two years in "my own area" of Montana and South Dakota, I have frequently moved to areas where Indian students have expressed interest or initiated action in hiring me. A common accusation, especially in California, is, "Why aren't you working with your own people?" This is an indication, it seems to me, of a growing tribalism with incipient and, in some cases, strong ethnocentrism. As far as moving so often is concerned, I jokingly refer to the former nomadism of my people. More recently, I have utilized a pan-Indian joke: "Sioux are just like empty beer cans, you find them everywhere." [...]

Even more challenging dilemmas result from requests Native intellectuals make upon anthropologists. One example came from an Oglala (Sioux) law graduate who requested that I present evidence that Native Americans had originated in the New World. (What temptation for a Native American Piltdown "plant.") Concerns of this nature have even greater future repercussions because of the current rejection of the Bering Straits migration theory advocated by some tribal leaders. Many tribal people are as committed to their origin and creation statements as any other people. "What do you think of the story told by anthropologists that we all came across the Bering Straits?" was the question asked of me by a Navajo teenager in 1960.

Issues based on Indians' tribal sovereignty, water, and treaty rights will make the future interface of anthropologists and Natives a vital concern for those of us committed to a changing profession. This is especially evident in the use of the latter in the "contrived cultures" of Native militants. [...]

More importantly, our sheer survival has hinged upon a flexible ability to segment, synthesize, and act in changing situations. Although this should be understood and respected by anthropologists and others, a lack of sensitivity and perception has been a main tragedy of comprehending Native life. There is often a unidimensional aspect of power. The indigenous society is seen as a target population for manipulation and change, with little or no attempt to understand the textured and realigning configurations of persons and ideas, through time, that have allowed for Native persistence. For me, the categories of constituency are meaningless because my identity rests as a constituent of a viable Native group. Advocacy is constant and resides with powerless people. Involvement is ongoing, demanding, and debilitating emotionally, economically, and educationally.

To me, the most important aspect of applied work is the delineation of social forces that impinge upon indigenous societies and the ways that these affect each distinctive group. Social change, and how it is understood and acted upon by Native Americans, is the crux of anthropological understanding. It is through the role of cultural broker that the lack of insight and understanding of a more powerful social order may be mediated. The fact of living in social situations of administered human relations, where decisions affecting the present and future of Native Americans are controlled by external power components, is understandable and workable with anthropological concepts. In educational aspects especially, it has been imperative to reinterpret and flesh out the parameters of methods and techniques of change in terms that are meaningful to Native aggregates. Moreover, it is important that persons on both the receiving and applying levels understand the nature of factions in these societies. For Native societies, the labels "progressive" and "traditionalist" have many different meanings. [...]

The politics of social capital and power are elements that are forever present in Native social systems. They have served as vehicles for differential adjustment to the dominant culture. To an anthropologist from the Native enclave, kin affiliation is often within both spheres of social structure, necessitating a constant reassessment of power and emotional alliances. Surges of disaffection and disenchantment have to be isolated and put in proper perspective as a prelude to action.

Some events involve simple and fulfilling moments, such as sitting around a campfire and visiting with friends and kin, "waiting for the coffee to boil," or watching Lakota children "playing cowboy" in the bright moonlight. Listening to the Sioux National Anthem and then "dancing the drum out" in the cold dawn of a Northern Plains summer have become memories that sustain me in university settings, at meetings of governmental advisory boards, and during anthropological "tribal rites" (annual meetings) where we hear new interpretations and speculations about our Native life-styles. Being home and doing fieldwork recall Al Ortiz's significant statement: "I initially went into anthropology because it was one field in which I could read about and deal with Indians all of the time and still make a living" (1973:86).

I know I went into anthropology to try and make living more fulfilling for Indians and to deal with others in attempts of anthropological application meaningful to Indians and others.

REFERENCES

Boas, Franz, and Ella Deloria. 1941. *Dakota Grammar: Memoirs of the National Academy of Sciences*, vol. 23. Washington: Government Printing Office.

DeLaguna, Frederica. 1960. "Method and Theory of Ethnology." In *Selected Papers from the American Anthropologist (1888–1920)*, edited by Frederica DeLaguna, 792. Evanston: Row, Peterson.

Deloria, Ella. 1944. *Speaking of Indians*. New York: Friendship Press.

Deloria, Vine, Jr. 1969a. "Custer Died for Your Sins." *Playboy* 16 (8): 131–2, 172–5.

Deloria, Vine, Jr. 1969b. *Custer Died for Your Sins*. New York: Macmillan.

Jones, Delmos J. 1970. "Towards a Native Anthropology." *Human Organization* 29 (4): 251–9. https://doi.org/10.17730/humo.29.4.717764244331m4qv.

Ortiz, Alfonso [discussant]. 1973. In *Anthropology and the American Indian,* 86. San Francisco: Indian Historian Press.

Panday, Triloki Nath. 1972. "Anthropologists at Zuni." *Proceedings of the American Philosophical Society* 116 (4): 321–36. https://doi.org/10.1093/OBO/9780199766567-0204.

6.2. Knowing the Oriental (1979)

Edward W. Said

On June 13, 1910, Arthur James Balfour lectured the [English] House of Commons on "the problems with which we have to deal in Egypt." [...]

As Balfour justifies the necessity for British occupation of Egypt, supremacy in his mind is associated with "our" [British] knowledge of Egypt and not principally with military or economic power. Knowledge to Balfour means surveying a civilization from its origins to its prime to its decline – and of course, it means *being able to do that*. Knowledge means rising above immediacy, beyond self, into the foreign and distant. The object of such knowledge is inherently vulnerable to scrutiny; this object is a "fact" which, if it develops, changes, or otherwise transforms itself in the way that civilizations frequently do, nevertheless is fundamentally, even ontologically stable. To have such knowledge of such a thing is to dominate it, to have authority over it. And authority here means for "us" to deny autonomy to "it" – the Oriental country – since we know it and it exists, in a sense, *as* we know it. British knowledge of Egypt is Egypt for Balfour, and the burdens of knowledge make such questions as inferiority and superiority seem petty ones. Balfour nowhere denies British superiority and Egyptian inferiority; he takes them for granted as he describes the consequences of knowledge.

> First of all, look at the facts of the case. Western nations as soon as they emerge into history show the beginnings of those capacities for self-government. [Y]ou may look through the whole history of the Orientals in what is called, broadly speaking, the East, and you never find traces of self-government. All their great centuries – and they have been very great – have been passed under despotisms, under absolute government. All their great contributions to civilisation – and they have been great – have been made under that form of government. Conqueror has succeeded conqueror; one domination has followed another; but never in all the revolutions of fate and fortune have you seen one of those nations of its own motion establish what we from a Western point of view, call self-government. That is the fact. It is not a question of superiority

and inferiority. I suppose a true Eastern sage would say that the working government which we have taken upon ourselves in Egypt and elsewhere is not a work worthy of a philosopher – that it is the dirty work, the inferior work, of carrying on the necessary labour.

Since these facts are facts, Balfour must then go on to the next part of his argument.

> Is it a good thing for these great nations – I admit their greatness – that this absolute government should be exercised by us? I think it is a good thing. I think that experience shows that they have got under it far better government than in the whole history of the world they ever had before, and which not only is a benefit to them, but is undoubtedly a benefit to the whole of the civilised east. [W]e are in Egypt not merely for the sake of the Egyptians, though we are there for their sake; we are there also for the sake of Europe at large.

Balfour produces no evidence that Egyptians and "the races with whom we deal" appreciate or even understand the good that is being done them by colonial occupation. It does not occur to Balfour, however, to let the Egyptian speak for himself, since presumably any Egyptian who would speak out is more likely to be "the agitator [who] wishes to raise difficulties" than the good native who overlooks the "difficulties" of foreign domination. And so, having settled the ethical problems, Balfour turns at last to the practical ones. "If it is our business to govern, with or without gratitude, with or without the real and genuine memory of all the loss of which we have relieved the population [Balfour by no means implies, as part of that loss, the loss or at least the indefinite postponement of Egyptian independence] and no vivid imagination of all the benefits which we have given to them; if that is our duty, how is it to be performed?" England exports "our very best to these countries." These selfless administrators do their work "amidst tens of thousands of persons belonging to a different creed, a different race, a different discipline, different conditions of life." What makes their work of governing possible is their sense of being supported at home by a government that endorses what they do. Yet

> directly the native populations have that instinctive feeling that those with whom they have got to deal have not behind them the might, the authority, the sympathy, the full and ungrudging support of the country which sent them there, those populations lose all that sense of order which is the very basis of their civilisation, just as our officers lose all that sense of power and authority, which is the very basis of everything they can do for the benefit of those among whom they have been sent.

Balfour's logic here is interesting, not least for being completely consistent with the premises of his entire speech. England knows Egypt; Egypt is what England knows; England knows that Egypt cannot have self-government; England confirms that by occupying Egypt; for the Egyptians, Egypt is what England has occupied and now governs; foreign occupation therefore becomes "the very basis" of contemporary Egyptian civilization; Egypt requires, indeed insists upon, British occupation. [...]

If British success in Egypt was as exceptional as Balfour said, it was by no means an inexplicable or irrational success. Egyptian affairs had been controlled according to a general theory expressed both by Balfour in his notions about Oriental civilization and by Cromer in his management of everyday business in Egypt. The most important thing about the theory during the first decade of the twentieth century was that it worked, and worked staggeringly well. The argument, when reduced to its simplest form, was clear, it was precise, it was easy to grasp. There are Westerners, and there are Orientals. The former dominate; the latter must be dominated, which usually means having their land occupied, their internal affairs rigidly controlled, their blood and treasure put at the disposal of one or another Western power. That Balfour and Cromer, as we shall soon see, could strip humanity down to such ruthless cultural and racial essences was not at all an indication of their particular viciousness. Rather it was an indication of how streamlined a general doctrine had become by the time they put it to use – how streamlined and effective. [...]

We would be wrong, I think, to underestimate the reservoir of accredited knowledge, the codes of Orientalist orthodoxy, to which Cromer and Balfour refer everywhere in their writing and in their public policy. To say simply that Orientalism was a rationalization of colonial rule is to ignore the extent to which colonial rule was justified in advance by Orientalism, rather than after the fact. Men have always divided the world up into regions having either real or imagined distinction from each other. The absolute demarcation between East and West, which Balfour and Cromer accept with such complacency, had been years, even centuries, in the making. There were of course innumerable voyages of discovery; there were contacts through trade and war. But more than this, since the middle of the eighteenth century there had been two principal elements in the relation between East and West. One was a growing systematic knowledge in Europe about the Orient, knowledge reinforced by the colonial encounter as well as by the widespread interest in the alien and unusual, exploited by the developing sciences of ethnology, comparative anatomy, philology, and history; furthermore, to this systematic knowledge was added a sizable body of literature produced by novelists, poets, translators, and gifted travelers. [...]

Many terms were used to express the relation: Balfour and Cromer, typically, used several. The Oriental is irrational, depraved (fallen), childlike, "different"; thus the European is rational, virtuous, mature, "normal." But the way of enlivening the relationship was everywhere to stress the fact that the Oriental lived in a different but thoroughly organized world of his own, a world with its own national, cultural, and epistemological boundaries and principles of internal coherence. Yet what gave the Oriental's world its intelligibility and identity was not the result of his own efforts but rather the whole complex series of knowledgeable manipulations by which the Orient was identified by the West. Thus the two features of cultural relationship I have been discussing come together. Knowledge of the Orient, because generated out of strength, in a sense *creates* the Orient, the Oriental, and his world. In Cromer's and Balfour's language the Oriental is depicted as something one judges (as in a court of law), something one studies and depicts (as in a curriculum), something one disciplines (as in a school or prison), something one illustrates (as in a zoological manual). The point is that in each of these cases the Oriental is *contained* and *represented* by dominating frameworks. [...]

[...] Orientalism can also express the strength of the West and the Orient's weakness – as seen by the West. Such strength and such weakness are as intrinsic to Orientalism as they are to any view that divides the world into large general divisions, entities that coexist in a state of tension produced by what is believed to be radical difference.

For that is the main intellectual issue raised by Orientalism. Can one divide human reality, as indeed human reality seems to be genuinely divided, into clearly different cultures, histories, traditions, societies, even races, and survive the consequences humanly? By surviving the consequences humanly, I mean to ask whether there is any way of avoiding the hostility expressed by the division, say, of men into "us" (Westerners) and "they" (Orientals). For such divisions are generalities whose use historically and actually has been to press the importance of the distinction between some men and some other men, usually toward not especially admirable ends. When one uses categories like Oriental and Western as both the starting and the end points of analysis, research, public policy (as the categories were used by Balfour and Cromer), the result is usually to polarize the distinction – the Oriental becomes more Oriental, the Westerner more Western – and limit the human encounter between different cultures, traditions, and societies. In short, from its earliest modern history to the present, Orientalism as a form of thought for dealing with the foreign has typically shown the altogether regrettable tendency of any knowledge based on such hard-and-fast distinctions as "East" and "West": to channel thought into a West or an East compartment. Because this tendency is right at the center of Orientalist theory, practice, and values found in the West, the sense of Western power over the Orient is taken for granted as having the status of scientific truth.

6.3. Anthropologies of the South: Their Rise, Their Silencing, Their Characteristics (1997)

Esteban Krotz

THE RISE OF ANTHROPOLOGIES IN THE SOUTH

Cultural contacts are as old as cultures themselves and, as far as we know, just as ancient is human reflection on the different aspects of cultural contact and cultural diversity. Thus understood, anthropological sciences constitute only one particular (and quite recent) form of knowledge that developed within a certain civilization and during a specific period: in 19th-century Europe and its western (North America) and eastern (the Tsarist empire) "annexes," and which was definitely consolidated as such during the last third of last century. [...]

The establishment of anthropology as a scientific discipline took place at the crossroads between two previously unseen processes. One was the expansion at a planetary scale of one single civilization, a movement among whose motives we find nationalism and militarism, Christian mission and racism, the capitalist-industrialist search for markets and raw materials and the intellectual eagerness to take an inventory of all the phenomena in the world. The other was the hegemonization of a specific, recently created type of knowledge, characterized by a certain social organization of those who practice it and by consensus among them about certain procedures for generating and validating propositions about empirical reality and for accepting determinate results of research. Anthropology arose as a particular field within the social sciences, showing variations derived from the somewhat different political and academic traditions of the northern nations who divided up the world among themselves at that time. It began its existence undertaking the task of ordering the huge amount of data on other cultures – overseas, in the interior of Europe, in the past – accumulated for centuries through collections and report, libraries and museums, which were being enlarged from the 18th century onwards with ever faster growing amounts of new information. [...]

[...] One of the changes resulting from over a century of world domination by the North Atlantic model of civilization, which has hardly been studied, is precisely this article's subject matter: the fact that anthropology rooted itself and acquired its own life in the South itself, which traditionally had been only the main habitat of the objects of study of anthropological science. Although in some countries there were earlier beginnings, it is particularly during the last three or four decades that in many parts of the South all sorts of academic institutions have been established, as well as periodic congresses and museums, specialist journals and professional associations, long-term publishing projects and research programs. Most recently, a good number of the traditional undergraduate programs have been complemented by masters and doctoral studies courses in anthropology.

All this has made commonplace a previously almost non-existent situation: anthropology practitioners coming from the cultures of the North meet in "their" traditional places of study not only informants, but also native colleagues and students. At the same time, there is in the growing anthropological communities of the South an increasing awareness that certain scientific difficulties which are ignored by the traditional bibliography of their discipline are not passing or marginal, but might have to do with the "use" of anthropology in situations where the socio-cultural phenomena dealt with are not "others" in the same way as they are in the anthropology originated in the North, and where researchers are in another way part of what they study. [...]

FOUR "CRITICAL ISSUES" FOR THE CHARACTERIZATION OF THE ANTHROPOLOGIES OF THE SOUTH

[... T]he anthropologies of the South can no longer be reduced to mere "extensions" or "replicas" (somewhat imperfect ones) of one original anthropological model. Rather, we find ourselves looking at different forms of producing and using anthropological knowledge which have particular characteristics. [F]or instance, the centuries of similar colonial experience of most Latin American countries, the anticolonial struggle of many African countries during the 1950s and 1960s, and their post-independence problems with establishing nation-state institutions, the involvement of several Asiatic countries in the Vietnam War and the recent fast economic development of others in the same continent, have all marked in different ways the anthropologies created in these regions. But in spite of these diversities, some common characteristics can be recognized in the whole South. [...]

The following four "critical issues" for an incipient, tentative and fragmentary characterization of the anthropology of the South are formulated principally, as already indicated, from a Latin American perspective. Regardless of the national and regional peculiarities present throughout the so-called "subcontinent," it seems not too difficult to recognize a certain group of common traits that could be found also in other regions of the South. Therefore they can also be seen as part of a future agenda for anthropological research on anthropological science and, especially, on the anthropology of the South. [...]

Those Studying and Those Being Studied Are Citizens of the Same Country

One of the characteristics which, at first glance, distinguishes "classical" anthropology from the one practiced at the present time in the South is that, in the latter, those studying and those being studied are citizens of the same country. This is obviously not a matter of geography, although often the physical closeness between the places where the empirical information is being collected and the places where these materials are being analyzed, discussed and the results of the research published, is important. It is more fundamentally important that, today, even relatively distant indigenous and peasant communities can have access to the results of anthropological studies generated about them in another part of the country, and that they can establish several types of interaction with the authors of those studies. [H]ere also are we dealing with a situation that is very different from the relationship that a visiting researcher may establish with a group of persons he or she studies during a certain number of months. Finally, when we assume that the socio-cultural origin (socioeconomic stratum, religion, region, ethnic group, and even gender and age group, etc.) of the authors of anthropological studies influences the study's point of departure, development and results, this influence will vary when the researchers are part of the same national (socioeconomic, religious, regional imbalance, ethnic, gender and age group, etc.) system as those they study, or when they usually live in individual and sociocultural conditions totally different from those of the people that they are temporarily observing or even living with.

Conceptualizations and Valuations of Science and Social Science

A crucial aspect which distinguishes most countries of the South from the countries where anthropology once originated is the social appraisal of scientific knowledge in general and of scientific anthropological knowledge in particular. […] Although [a] lack of appreciation for the science produced in the countries of the South is seldom expressed explicitly, the [relatively low] social status of scientific researchers and the fact that so few university workers in the South can dedicate themselves full time to academic activities are eloquent enough indicators. Another is the lack of effective diffusion mechanisms for the results of research. Also, observing the classrooms in most of the universities in Latin American countries, where a lot of academic programs in archaeology and linguistics lack laboratories and where postgraduate studies in ethnology continue to be introduced without any thought for the provision of books and journals, grants and organized training in the field, so that students are sometimes limited to learning from the notes they take in class, anyone who has been able to visit universities in Europe and North America may wonder if the word "university" has the same meaning in the North and in the South. Thus, the specific academic and intellectual context of academic teachers and researchers – and, of course, of the students – is also rather different from that of their colleagues in the North.

Different Alterities

[… There is an idea that], except for some rather insignificant relics in some distant corners of the countries, there does not exist any real sociocultural alterity [in anthropology] within Latin America. Moreover, as in other parts of the South, these "premodern relics" are usually considered causes of the "underdevelopment" of the indigenous population and of the whole country. This is why it is highly significant that it is precisely some of the so-called "survivals" of several indigenous cultures (for example, in the areas of medicine, agriculture and housing but also in world view and organization of social relations) and the demands by certain American indigenous groups which have lately become more audible that have contributed to the recovery of a perception of the existence of a cultural alterity *within* all Latin American countries. Obviously this alterity does not restrict itself to the actually living indigenous peoples – its presence can also be observed in wide segments of the "*mestizo*" population. Therefore it is not surprising that the anthropological study of political processes and social movements, of urban culture and of popular religion, reveals that there are problems when conceptual molds and methodological tools inherited from the dominant anthropological traditions are simply and plainly "applied" instead of "recreated." And, of course, it is different to study cultural alterity from a position of neutrality or general respect for indigenous peoples in a faraway country and to be involved by these studies in the claims for rights of human groups of one's own country, whose legal recognition may affect the anthropologist's own social, political or even economic interests.

Rediscovering the Own Antecedents

The three aspects we have already mentioned are intrinsically related to the problem of the local "antecedents" of the present anthropologies of the South. When the biographies of the first persons, dedicated since the late 18th century to the study of the cognitive and practical problems of cultural diversity, are narrated, when their works are analyzed and when their efforts to create communication circuits with the other emerging specialists are described, the citizens of the powerful countries of those days and of today are usually considered "forerunners" of the discipline, while those of the countries of the South are no more than simple "amateurs."

Is belonging or not belonging to the societies where anthropology was born as a scientific discipline enough to justify these classifications? Up to a certain degree it is, because anthropology initially developed in North Atlantic civilization and not in the South. The danger lies in the concealment brought about by the un-reflexive use of this kind of classification. For in consequence, the very existence of the anthropologies of the South is once again ignored. And as long as the value of their own antecedents is diminished, it is harder for them to recognize themselves as traditions with a proper profile. On the other hand, the deep transformation which anthropology has undergone since it started is hidden. Repeating the point very schematically: during the 19th century and the first half of the 20th century, anthropology only had one center. Any scientific anthropological practice was, above all, albeit to different degrees, an extension and ramification of the impulses generated in the center. But during the second half of this century, many of these transplants have started revealing themselves as roots, as forms of anthropological life which in different ways combine the influences from a long North Atlantic anthropological discussion with their own efforts, made in the past and the present, to understand the cultural diversity within different civilizations and among all of them.

CONCLUSION: THE NEED FOR AN ANTHROPOLOGY OF THE ANTHROPOLOGIES OF THE SOUTH

It is not difficult to formulate the conclusions from all of this. In the first place it is obvious that every time we speak of "the anthropology of the South," we are talking, in fact, in the plural: the anthropologies of the South are as manifold as the different "schools" or "currents" which are acknowledged within the anthropology of the North, or even more so. However, just like the latter, they share certain characteristics. These are not very clear yet, but naturally they have to do with the situation of having been traditionally the place of the "object" of the original anthropology and with the principal worldwide inter-civilizational conflict that in our day divides the planet into two different and in a certain sense opposing spheres: the North and the South.

6.4. Anthropology and the Savage Slot: Poetics and Politics of Otherness (2003)

Michel-Rolph Trouillot

PORTRAIT OF THE ARTIST AS A BUBBLE

[I] have argued that to historicize the West is to historicize anthropology and vice versa. I have also suggested that ongoing changes in the world within and outside of academe make that two-pronged historicization both urgent and necessary. If these two arguments are correct, together they expose the seriousness of the challenges we face. Yet they also expose the limitations of some of the solutions proposed. The portrait of the postmodernist anthropologist that emerges from this dual exercise is not a happy one indeed. Camera and notebooks in hand, he is looking for the Savage, but the Savage has vanished. The problem starts with the fated inheritance of the moderns themselves. The world that the anthropologist inherits has wiped out the empirical trace of the Savage-object: Coke bottles and cartridges now obscure the familiar tracks. To be sure, one could reinvent the Savage, or create new Savages within the West itself. Solutions of this kind are increasingly appealing. [T]he very notion of savagery is increasingly redundant on empirical grounds, irrespective of the Savage-object. Lingering conditions of modernity make the notion a hard one to evoke in imagination, now that hordes of Savages have joined the slums of the Third World or touched the shores of the North Atlantic. We are far from the days when five Eskimos caused an uproar in London. The primitive has become terrorist, refugee, freedom fighter, opium or coca grower, or parasite. He can even play anthropologist, at times. Televised documentaries show his "real" conditions of existence; underground newspapers expose his dreams of modernity. Thanks to modernity and modernization, the savage has changed, the West has changed, and the West knows that both have changed empirically.

But modernity is only part of the anthropologist's difficulty. Modern obstacles have modern (technical) answers, or so we used to think. The more serious issue is that technical solutions do not suffice anymore. At best, they can solve the problem of the empirical object by removing the Cokes and cartridges. At worst, they can fabricate an entire new face for savagery. But they cannot remedy changes in the larger thematic field, especially since the Savage never dominated this field. He was only one of the requisite parts of a tripartite relation, the mask of a mask. [...]

This is altogether a *postmodern* quandary. It is part of the world of constructs and relations revealed by our juxtaposed snapshots, and it is an intrinsic dilemma of postmodern anthropology. For if indeed foundational thoughts are seen as collapsing, if indeed utopias are arguments about order and foundational thoughts, and if indeed the Savage exists primarily within an implicit correspondence with utopia, the specialist in savagery is in dire straits. He does not know what to aim at. His favorite model has disappeared or, when found, refuses to pose as expected. The fieldworker examines his tools and finds his camera inadequate. Most importantly, his very field of vision now seems blurred. Yet he needs to come back home with a picture. It's pouring rain out there, and the mosquitoes are starting to bite. In desperation, the baffled anthropologist burns his notes to create a moment of light, moves his face against the flame, closes his eyes and, hands grasping the camera, takes a picture of himself. [...]

METAPHORS IN ETHNOGRAPHY AND ETHNOGRAPHY AS METAPHOR

[...] Not surprisingly, the archaeological exploration that underpins the North American exercise in reflexivity tends to stop at the institutionalization of anthropology as a discipline in the Anglophone world, or at best to the delineation of a specialized anthropological discourse in the Europe of the Enlightenment. In spite of the professed renunciation of labels, boundaries are set in modern terms to produce a history of the discipline, albeit one with different emphases. The construction exposed is a discursive order *within* anthropology, not the discursive order within which anthropology operates and makes sense – even though, here again, this larger field seems to warrant passing mention. The representational aspect of ethnographic discourse is attacked with a vigor quite disproportionate to the referential value of ethnographies in the wider field within which anthropology finds its significance. To use a language that still has its validity, the object of inquiry is the "simple" rather than the "enlarged" reproduction of anthropological discourse. Terminology and citations notwithstanding, the larger thematic field on which anthropology is premised is barely scratched.

If we take seriously the proposition to look at anthropology as metaphor – as I think we can, given the thematic field outlined – we cannot just look at metaphors in anthropology. The study of "ethnographic allegory" (Clifford 1986b; Tyler 1986) cannot be taken to refer primarily to allegorical forms *in* ethnography without losing sight of the larger picture. Our starting point cannot be "a crisis in anthropology" (Clifford l986a:3), but the histories of the world. We need to go out of anthropology to see the construction of "ethnographic authority" not as a late requirement of anthropological discourse (Clifford 1983) but as an early component of this wider field that is itself constitutive of anthropology (see chapter 6). Would that the power of anthropology hinged upon the academic success of genial immigrants such as Franz Boas and Bronislaw Malinowski! It would allow us to find new scapegoats without ever looking back at the Renaissance. But the exercise in reflexivity must go all the way and examine fully the enlarged reproduction of anthropological discourse.

Observers may wonder why the postmodernist experiment in U.S. anthropology has not encouraged a surge of substantive models. The difficulty of passing from criticism to substance is not simply due to a theoretical aversion to content or an instinctive suspicion toward exemplars. After all, the postmodernist wave revitalized substantive production in other academic fields. It stimulated architects and political theorists alike. At the very least, it has provoked debates on and of substance. Further, some political radicals advocate the possibility of militant practices rooted in postmodernism – although not without controversies (Arac 1986; Laclau and Mouffe 1985; Ross 1986). More important, the implicit awareness of an expanding situation of postmodernity continues to motivate grassroots movements all over the world with their partial truths and partial results. In fact, an anthropologist could well read postmodernism, or at the very least the postmodern situation, as a case for the specificity of otherness, for the destruction of the Savage slot.

To claim the specificity of otherness is to suggest a residual of historical experience that always escapes universalisms exactly because history itself always involves irreducible objects. It is to reserve a space for the subject – not the existential subject favored by the early Sartre and who keeps creeping back into the mea culpa anthropology, but the men and women who are the subjects of history. It is to acknowledge that this space of the historical subject is out of reach of all metanarratives, not because all metanarratives are created equal and are equally wrong – which is the claim of nihilism and always ends up favoring *some* subjects and *some* narratives – but because those claims to universality necessarily imply the muting of first persons, singular or plural, that are deemed marginal. To say that otherness is always specific and historical is to reject this marginality. The Other cannot be encompassed by a residual category: there is no Savage slot. The "us and all of them" binary, implicit in the symbolic order that creates the West, is an ideological construct and the many forms of Third-World-ism that reverse its terms are its mirror images. There is no Other, but multitudes of others who are all others for different reasons, in spite of totalizing narratives, including that of capital.

Many propositions follow from this statement, not the least of which may be that a discipline whose object is the Other may in fact have no object – which may lead us to take a much needed look at the methodological specificity of anthropology. It also follows that the authenticity of the historical subject may not be fully captured from the outside even by way of direct quotes; there may be something irreducible in the first person singular. This, in turn, raises two related issues: that of the epistemological status of native discourse; and that of the theoretical status of ethnography. I will turn to these issues in chapter 6, but some preliminary conclusions are worth posting now.

First, anthropology needs to evaluate its gains and losses with a fair tally of the knowledge anthropologists have produced in the past, sometimes in spite of themselves and almost always in spite of the Savage slot. We owe it to ourselves to ask what remains of anthropology and specific monographs when we remove this slot – not to revitalize disciplinary tradition through cosmetic surgery, but to build both an epistemology and a semiology of what anthropologists have done and can do. We cannot simply assume that modernism has exhausted all its potential projects. Nor can we assume that "realist ethnography" has produced nothing but empty figures of speech and shallow claims to authority.

Second, armed with this renewed arsenal, we can recapture domains of significance by creating strategic points of "reentry" into the discourse on otherness: areas within the discourse where the production of new voices or new combinations of meaning perturbate the entire field and open the way to its (partial) recapture. [...] I can only tease the reader by pointing to a few tasks that seem urgent in this new context: an epistemological reassessment of the historical subject (the first person singular that has been overwhelmed by the voice of objectivity or by that of the narrator and that is so important to many feminists, especially African American feminists); a similar reassessment of nativeness and native discourse, now barely conceptualized; and a theory of ethnography, now repudiated as the new "false consciousness." And for the time being, at least, we need more ethnographies that raise these issues through concrete cases. Not so much ethnographies that question the author/native dichotomy by exposing the nude as nakedness, but ethnographies (ethno-historio-semiologies?) that offer new points of reentry by questioning the symbolic world upon which "nativeness" is premised. At the very least, anthropologists can show that the Other, here and elsewhere, is indeed a product – symbolic and material – of the same process that created the West. In short, the time is ripe for substantive propositions that aim explicitly at the destabilization and eventual destruction of the Savage slot.

That it has not been so in North American anthropology is thus a matter of choice. In spite of a terminology that intimates a decoding of "anthropology as metaphor," we are barely reading anthropology itself. Rather, we are reading anthropological pages, and attention remains focused primarily on the metaphors in anthropology. This recurring refusal to pursue further the archaeological exercise obscures the asymmetrical position of the savage-other in the thematic field upon which anthropology was premised. It negates the specificity of otherness, subsuming the Other in the sameness of the text perceived as liberating cooperation. "We are the world"?

Anthropology did not create the Savage. Rather, the Savage was the raison d'etre of anthropology. Anthropology came to fill the Savage slot in the trilogy order-utopia-savagery, a trilogy that preceded anthropology's institutionalization and gave it continuing coherence in spite of intradisciplinary shifts. This trilogy is now in jeopardy. The time is ripe to attack frontally the visions that shaped this trilogy, to uncover its ethical roots and its consequences, and to find a better anchor for an anthropology of the present, an anthropology of the changing world and its irreducible histories. But many anthropologists only pass near this opportunity while looking for the Savage in the text. They want us to read the internal tropes of the Savage slot, no doubt a useful exercise in spite of its potential for self-indulgence, but they refuse to directly address the thematic field (and thus the larger world) that made (makes) this slot possible, morosely preserving the empty slot itself.

REFERENCES

Arac, Jonathan. 1986. *Post-Modernism and Politics*. Minneapolis and London: University of Minnesota Press.

Clifford, James. 1983. "On Ethnographic Authority." *Representations* 1 (2): 118–46.

Clifford, James. 1986a. "Introduction: Partial Truths." In *Writing Culture: The Poetics and Politics of Ethnography*, edited by James Clifford and George E. Marcus, 1–26. Berkeley: University of California Press.

Clifford, James. 1986b. "On Ethnographic Allegory." In *Writing Culture: The Poetics and Politics of Ethnography*, edited by James Clifford and George E. Marcus, 98–121. Berkeley: University of California Press.

Laclau, Ernesto, and Chantal Mouffe. 1985. *Hegemony and Socialist Strategy: Towards a Radical Democratic Politics*. London: Verso.

Ross, Andrew. 1988. *Universal Abandon? The Politics of Post-Modernism*. Minneapolis and London: University of Minnesota Press.

Tyler, Stephen. 1986. "Post-Modern Ethnography: From Document of the Occult to Occult Document." In *Writing Culture: The Poetics and Politics of Ethnography*, edited by James Clifford and George E. Marcus, 122–40. Berkeley: University of California Press.

6.5. Our Sea of Islands (2008)

Epeli Hau'ofa

[There is a prevailing view that] the small island states and territories of the Pacific, that is, all of Polynesia and Micronesia, are too small, too poorly endowed with resources, and too isolated from the centers of economic growth for their inhabitants ever to be able to rise above their present condition of dependence on the largesse of wealthy nations.

Initially I not only agreed wholeheartedly with this perspective but participated actively in its propagation. [...] Then two years ago I began noticing the reactions of my students when I explained our situation of dependence. Their faces crumbled visibly, they asked for solutions, I could offer none. I was so bound to the notion of smallness that even if we improved our approaches to production, for example, the absolute size of our islands would still impose such severe limitations that we would be defeated in the end.

But the faces of my students continued to haunt me mercilessly. I began asking questions of myself. What kind of teaching is it to stand in front of young people from your own region, people you claim as your own, who have come to university with high hopes for the future, and you tell them that our countries are hopeless? Is this not what neocolonialism is all about? To make people believe that they have no choice but to depend?

Soon the realization dawned on me. In propagating a view of hopelessness, I was actively participating in our own belittlement. [...]

The idea that the countries of Polynesia and Micronesia are too small, too poor, and too isolated to develop any meaningful degree of autonomy is an economistic and geographic deterministic view of a very narrow kind that overlooks culture history and the contemporary process of what may be called world enlargement that is carried out by tens of thousands of ordinary Pacific Islanders right across the ocean – from east to west and north to south, under the very noses of academic and consultancy experts, regional and international development agencies, bureaucratic planners and their advisers, and customs and immigration officials – making nonsense of all national and economic boundaries, borders that have been defined only recently, crisscrossing an ocean that had been boundless for ages before Captain Cook's apotheosis.

If this very narrow, deterministic perspective is not questioned and checked, it could contribute importantly to an eventual consignment of whole groups of human beings to a perpetual state of wardship wherein they and their surrounding lands and seas would be at the mercy of the manipulators of the global economy and "world orders" of one kind or another. [...]

There is a world of difference between viewing the Pacific as "islands in a far sea" and as "a sea of islands." The first emphasizes dry surfaces in a vast ocean far from the centers of power. Focusing in this way stresses the smallness and remoteness of the islands. The second is a more holistic perspective in which things are seen in the totality of their relationships. I return to this point later. Continental men, namely Europeans, on entering the Pacific after crossing huge expanses of ocean, introduced the view of "islands in a far sea." From this perspective the islands are tiny, isolated dots in a vast ocean. Later on, continental men – Europeans and Americans – drew imaginary lines across the sea, making the colonial boundaries that confined ocean peoples to tiny spaces for the first time. These boundaries today define the island states and territories of the Pacific. I have just used the term "ocean peoples" because our ancestors, who had lived in the Pacific for over two thousand years, viewed their world as "a sea of islands" rather than "islands in the sea." This may be seen in a common categorization of people, as exemplified in Tonga by the inhabitants of the main, capital island, who used to refer to their compatriots from the rest of the archipelago not so much as "people from the outer islands," as social scientists would say, but as *kakai mei tahi* or just *tahi*: "people from the sea." This characterization reveals the underlying assumption that the sea is home to such people.

The difference between the two perspectives is reflected in the two terms used for our region: Pacific Islands and Oceania. The first term, "Pacific Islands," is the prevailing one used everywhere; it denotes small areas of land sitting atop submerged reefs or seamounts. Hardly any anglophone economist, consultancy expert, government planner, or development banker in the region uses the term "Oceania," perhaps because it sounds grand and somewhat romantic and may denote something so fast that it would compel them to a drastic review of their perspectives and policies. [...]

"Oceania" denotes a sea of islands with their inhabitants. The world of our ancestors was a large sea full of places to explore, to make their homes in, to breed generations of seafarers like themselves. People raised in this environment were at home with the sea. They played in it as soon as they could walk steadily, they worked in it, they fought on it. They developed great skills for navigating their waters – as well as the spirit to traverse even the few large gaps that separated their island groups.

Theirs was a large world in which peoples and cultures moved and mingled, unhindered by boundaries of the kind erected much later by imperial powers. From one island to another they sailed to trade and to marry, thereby expanding social networks for greater flows of wealth. They traveled to visit relatives in a wide variety of natural and cultural surroundings, to quench their thirst for adventure, and even to fight and dominate.

Fiji, Samoa, Tonga, Niue, Rotuma, Tokelau, Tuvalu, Futuna, and Uvea formed a large exchange community in which wealth and people with their skills and arts circulated endlessly. From this community people ventured to the north and west, into Kiribati, the Solomon Islands, Vanuatu, and New Caledonia, which formed an outer arc of less intensive exchange.

Evidence of this voyaging is provided by present-day settlements within Melanesia of descendants of these seafarers. (Only blind landlubbers would say that settlements like these, as well as those in New Zealand and Hawai'i, were made through accidental voyages by people who got blown off course – presumably while they were out fishing with their wives, children, pigs, dogs, and food-plant seedlings during a hurricane.) The Cook Islands and French Polynesia formed a community similar to that of their cousins to the west; hardy spirits from this community ventured southward and founded settlements in Aotearoa, while others went in the opposite direction to discover and inhabit the islands of Hawai'i. Also north of the equator is the community that was centered on Yap.

Melanesia is supposedly the most fragmented world of all: tiny communities isolated by terrain and at least one thousand languages. The truth is that large regions of Melanesia were integrated by trading and cultural exchange systems that were even more complex than those of Polynesia and Micronesia. Lingua francas and the fact that most Melanesians have always been multilingual (which is more than one can say about most Pacific Rim countries) make utter nonsense of the notion that they were (and still are) babblers of Babel. It was in the interest of imperialism – and is in the interest of neocolonialism – to promote this blatant misconception of Melanesia.

Evidence of the conglomerations of islands with their economies and cultures is readily available in the oral traditions of the islands and, too, in blood ties that are retained today. The highest chiefs of Fiji, Samoa, and Tonga, for example, still maintain kin connections, forged centuries before Europeans entered the Pacific, in the days when boundaries were not imaginary lines in the ocean but points of entry that were constantly negotiated and even contested. The sea was open to anyone who could navigate a way through.

This was the kind of world that bred men and women with skills and courage that took them into the unknown, to discover and populate all the habitable islands east of the 130th meridian. The great fame that they have earned posthumously may have been romanticized, but it is solidly based on real feats that could have been performed only by those born and raised with an open sea as their home.

Nineteenth-century imperialism erected boundaries that led to the contraction of Oceania, transforming a once boundless world into the Pacific Island states and territories that we know today. People were confined to their tiny spaces, isolated from each other. They were cut off from their relatives abroad, from their far-flung sources of wealth and cultural enrichment. This is the historical basis of the view that our countries are small, poor, and isolated. It is true only insofar as people are still fenced in and quarantined.

This assumption is no longer tenable as far as the countries of central and western Polynesia are concerned; it may be untenable also of Micronesia. The rapid expansion of the world economy in the years since World War II may have intensified third-world dependency, as has been noted from certain vantage points at high-level academia, but it also had a liberating effect on the lives of ordinary people in Oceania, as it did in the Caribbean islands. The new economic reality made nonsense of artificial boundaries, enabling the people to shake off their confinement. They have since moved, by the tens of thousands, doing what their ancestors did in earlier times: enlarging their world, as they go, on a scale not possible before. Everywhere they go – to Australia, New Zealand, Hawai'i, the mainland United States, Canada, Europe, and elsewhere – they strike roots in new resource areas, securing employment and overseas family property, expanding kinship networks through which they circulate themselves, their relatives, their material goods, and their stories all across their ocean, and the ocean is theirs because it has always been their home. Social scientists may write of Oceania as a Spanish Lake, a British Lake, an American Lake, even a Japanese Lake. But we all know that only those who make the ocean their home, and love it, can really claim it as their own. Conquerors come, conquerors go, the ocean remains, mother only to her children. This mother has a big heart though; she adopts anyone who loves her.

The resources of Samoans, Cook Islanders, Niueans, Tokelauans, Tuvaluans, I-Kiribati, Fijians, Indo-Fijians, and Tongans are no longer confined to their national boundaries. They are located wherever these people are living, permanently or otherwise, as they were before the age of Western imperialism. One can see this any day at seaports and airports throughout the Central Pacific, where consignments of goods from homes abroad are unloaded as those of the homelands are loaded. Construction materials, agricultural machinery, motor vehicles, other heavy goods, and a myriad other things are sent from relatives abroad, while handicrafts, tropical fruits and root crops, dried marine creatures, kava, and other delectables are dispatched from the homelands. Although this flow of goods is generally not included in official statistics, much of the welfare of ordinary people of Oceania depends on an informal movement along ancient routes drawn in bloodlines invisible to the enforcers of the laws of confinement and regulated mobility.

The world of Oceania is neither tiny nor deficient in resources. It was so only as a condition of the colonial confinement that lasted less than a century in a history of millennia. Human nature demands space for free movement – and the larger the space the better it is for people. Islanders have broken out of their confinement, are moving around and away from their homelands, not so much because their countries are poor, but because they were unnaturally confined and severed from many of their traditional sources of wealth, and because it is in their blood to be mobile. They are once again enlarging their world, establishing new resource bases and expanding networks for circulation. […] They have already made their presence felt in these homelands and have stamped indelible imprints on the cultural landscapes.

Section Six Glossary

anthropology as "the child and handmaiden of colonialism"   This characterization by Kathleen Gough (1968) focuses on anthropology's emergence and utility in association with colonial governance. The accuracy of this assertion is disputed in the discipline.

applied anthropology   The application of anthropological principles and methodologies to real-world problems (often opposed to anthropology that is done for the purpose of theory-building).

salvage anthropology   The impetus to collect, record, and disseminate cultural and biological materials from people who are thought to be nearing extinction. In assuming the inevitability of a community's disappearance, rather than calling attention to and supporting their struggles to survive, salvage anthropology facilitates cultural genocide. See Audra Simpson's 2018 chapter, "Why White People Love Franz Boas," in *Indigenous Visions: Rediscovering the World of Franz Boas*, edited by Ned Blackhawk and Isaiah Lorado Wilner.

SECTION SEVEN

On Anthropology and Gender

THE SOCIAL CONTEXT

The "first wave" of feminism (roughly 1850 to 1940) had won important rights for many women in the "West," including the right to vote. During World War II in the United States, middle-class women were recruited into the industrial labor force in large numbers, allowing a generation of women access to pathways toward financial autonomy. Yet by the mid-twentieth century, most women remained in positions of subjugation in relation to men: both in the home and the workplace. Further, as a movement led largely by middle-class white women, first wave feminism had failed to productively account for the ways in which race, class, and sexuality differentiated the experiences of "women" in highly unequal ways.

In academia, feminists had pushed for the inclusion of women in intellectual spaces – both as producers and subjects of analysis. This helped pave the way for the success of early women anthropologists such as Ruth Benedict, Zora Neale Hurston, and Margaret Mead – the last of whom was a household name in the United States by mid-century. Still, while emergent "women's studies" programs recognized women as important social actors – a significant and necessary step – they often took "womanhood" (and "manhood") as assumed and fixed categories rooted in biology. This limited their ability to perceive gender roles as sociocultural productions worthy of analytical attention.

By the 1980s and 1990s, postcolonial and poststructural theorists began shifting away from a focus on women and toward a focus on gender. This shift isolated gender as an analytical category, leading to studies showing that gendered roles and ideologies deeply shape social life, are highly culturally variable, and are not attributable to biological sex differences. This move also opened analytical spaces for the study of masculinity and diverse forms of gender expression and gender roles. Ethnographic projects today view gender classifications as highly variable and fluid, as well as deeply embedded in social, political, and economic contexts.

Much of the subsequent critique and expansion of feminist anthropology came from Black feminists, Latina scholars, Indigenous theorists, and scholars from the Global South who maintained that understandings of gendered oppression must be elucidated via **intersectionality** – that is, by paying attention to the ways in which intersecting social categories (e.g., race, class, gender, sexuality, ability) combine to create a person's particular lived experiences. The essays in this section trace the development of anthropological scholarship on gender from early considerations of the emergence of gender roles to analyses of gender's complex interactions with other social categories related to race, class, and colonialism.

THE CONVERSATION

The section begins with an essay by Marxist feminist anthropologist Eleanor "Happy" Leacock, which she wrote as an introduction to Friedrich Engels's *On the Origin of the Family, Private Property and the State* – a text itself informed by the research of Lewis Henry Morgan. In this essay, Leacock traces the apparently universal subordination of women to historical shifts in production that made nuclear family households centers of social and economic life and which rendered women dependents of their husbands. By contextualizing gender inequality in the historical emergence of capitalist relations of production, Leacock helps to denaturalize gendered roles within families, as well as normative kinship configurations and scholarly assumptions about the universality – and presumed biological basis – of women's subjugation. Leacock closes the essay with a call to attend more closely to the experiences of working-class, Black, and Latina women within both anthropological scholarship and feminist social movements.

In "Toward a Unified Analysis of Gender and Kinship" (Reading 7.2), Sylvia Yanagisako and Jane Collier build on the conceptual decoupling of sex and gender to ask how and why biological notions of gender come to be culturally produced along with **biodeterministic** configurations of descent and kinship. Rather than take biological "facts" about sexual difference, coitus, birth, blood, and semen for granted, then, Yanagisako and Collier ask what cultural work the biologicalization of gender and kinship does in unequal, patriarchal social systems.

Reading 7.3, by Ifi Amadiume, builds on the conceptual decoupling of sex and gender to show how Igbo women use gender flexibility to inhabit positions in ritual, land tenure, and political systems that are reserved for males. In particular, Igbo women can become their father's sons to inherit land and can be husbands to their wives. These moves do not require any performances of masculinity – that is, Igbo women do not become "men," but males. Such gender shifts, Amadiume argues, are made possible by the fluid gender ideologies central to Igbo society.

Gloria Anzaldúa's "La conciencia de la mestiza" [The Mestiza Consciousness] (Reading 7.4) both bridges and advances feminist and borderlands theories. Drawing on her personal experiences as a Chicana feminist and lesbian, Anzaldúa argues that as *mestizas* navigate their social and cultural (not to mention geopolitical) positioning at the convergence of ethnic, racial, gendered, and sexed borderlands, their consciousness develops a multidimensional, flexible, pluralistic, and amorphous quality. This dynamism at once takes shape in opposition to the dominant, Anglo culture and has the potential to bypass and ultimately deconstruct it. Note that the style in which this piece is written – integrating Spanish, English, and Nahuatl words, as well as poetry, personal narrative, and scholarly analysis – is itself an example of this borderlands aesthetic.

The final selection, "In Search of Masculinity" by Philippe Bourgois, offers a case study of second and third generation Puerto Rican men in East Harlem. As a result of global restructuring in the 1980s, demand for industrial labor in New York plummeted, leading to high rates of unemployment and underemployment among Puerto Ricans who had been recruited to work in industry. These changes, Bourgois argues, blocked many young Puerto Rican men from attaining norms of masculinity, such as financial provisioning, practiced by their rural Puerto Rican forefathers. Instead, the marginalized men in Bourgois's study became active in a drug economy that normalizes misogyny, sexual violence, and paternal abandonment. This form of masculinity, Bourgois shows, is neither the product of Puerto Rican "culture" nor independent of men's material realities in New York: it is, rather, a result of foreclosed pathways to social esteem and financial stability.

THREE QUESTIONS FOR THE READINGS

1 What is the underlying explanation for gender inequality in each piece? What is the role of power in the construction of gendered identities?
2 Most of these pieces privilege **etic** understandings of gender and do not closely attend to how people in a community understand their gendered experiences. How does considering **emic** understandings of gender enrich and/or trouble these analyses?
3 How are these pieces in conversation with each other? What assumptions do they hold in common, and where do they diverge?

ON THE COMPANION WEBSITE

"Left of Black" with Johnetta B. Cole, "This Girl Has Balls," additional readings, and more.

www.anthropologicaltheory.com

7.1. Introduction to *The Origin of the Family, Private Property and the State: In the Light of the Researches of Lewis H. Morgan,* by Friedrich Engels (1972)

Eleanor Burke Leacock

THE EMERGENCE OF MONOGAMY AND THE SUBJUGATION OF WOMEN

The significant characteristic of monogamous marriage was its transformation of the nuclear family into the basic economic unit of society, within which a woman and her children became dependent upon an individual man. Arising in conjunction with exploitative class relations, this transformation resulted in the oppression of women that has persisted to the present day. [...]

The significant point for women's status is that the [horticultural, non-capitalist] household was communal and the division of labor between the sexes reciprocal; the economy did not involve the dependence of the wife and children on the husband. All major food supplies, large game and produce from the fields, were shared among a group of families. These families lived together in large dwellings among most village agriculturalists, and in hunting-gathering societies either shared large tepees or other such shelters in adverse climates, or might simply group together in separate wickiups or lean-tos in tropical or desert areas. The children in a real sense belonged to the group as a whole; an orphaned child suffered a personal loss, but was never without a family. Women did not have to put up with personal injuries from men in outbursts of violent anger for fear of economic privation for themselves or their children. By comparison with more "advanced" societies where wife-beating became accepted, even to the point of death, a mistreated wife could call on her relatives for redress or leave if it was not forthcoming. Nor can "household management" be construed as it would be today. Whether a "public" industry or not, "managing the household" as the "task entrusted to the women" might be viewed dubiously as hardly very satisfactory. However, in primitive communal society, the distinction did not exist between a public world of men's work and a private world of women's household service. The large collective household *was* the community, and within it both sexes worked to produce the goods necessary for livelihood. Goods were as yet directly produced and consumed; they had not become transformed into "commodities" for exchange, the transformation upon which the exploitation of man by man, and the special oppression of women, was built.

In fact, women usually furnished a large share – often the major share – of the food. Many hunter-gatherers depended on the vegetable foods gathered by women as the staples to be augmented by meat (the Bushmen of the Kalahari Desert area, case in point), and in horticultural societies women, as the former gatherers of vegetable foods and in all likelihood, therefore, responsible for the domestication of crops, generally did most of the farming. Since in primitive communal society decisions were made by those who would be carrying them out, the participation of women in a major share of socially necessary labor did not reduce them to virtual slavery, as is the case in class society, but accorded them decision-making powers commensurate with their contribution.

There has been little understanding of this point in anthropological literature. Instead, the fact that men typically made decisions about hunting and warfare in primitive society is used to support the argument that they were the "rulers" in the Western sense. Men did indeed acquire power under the conditions of colonial rule within which the lifeways of hitherto primitive peoples have been recorded. Nonetheless, the literature again and again reveals the autonomy of women and their role in decision making; albeit such data are as often as not sloughed off with supposedly humorous innuendos about "henpecked husbands" or the like, rather than treated seriously as illustrative of social structure and dynamics. [...]

There is a real need for studies that reconstruct from extant materials on primitive communal and transitional societies something of women's functioning before the development of the male dominance that accompanied European economic and colonial exploitation. For example, how were goods distributed in horticultural societies where garden produce still lay in the women's domain? How did older women function in the settling of disputes, a role often referred to but little documented? What were the paths of influence women held in relation to the men's sphere of war and the hunt? Conversely, what was the role of men in socializing young children? [...]

An interesting subject for reassessment is the mystique that surrounds the hunt and, in comparison, that surrounding childbirth. A common formulation of status among hunter-gatherers overlooks the latter and stresses the importance and excitement of the hunt. Albeit the primary staple foods may be the vegetable products supplied by the women, they afford no prestige, it is pointed out, so that while not precisely subservient women are still of lower status than men. However, women's power of child-bearing has been a focus for awe and even fear as long ago as the Upper Paleolithic, judging from the fertility figurines that date from that period. This point is easy to overlook, for the ability to bear children has led in our society not to respect but to women's oppressed status. [...]

In some ways it is the ultimate alienation in our society that the ability to give birth has been transformed into a liability. The reason is not simply that, since women bear children, they are more limited in their movements and activities. As the foregoing discussion indicates, this was not a handicap even under the limited technology of hunting-gathering life; it certainly has no relevance today. Nor did women's low status simply follow their declining importance in food production when men moved into agriculture; nor automatically follow the growth in importance of domestic animals, the province of the men, although herding did relate to lowered status for women. However, what was basic was that these transitions occurred in the context of developing exploitative relations whereby communal ownership was being undermined, the communal kin group broken up, and the individual family separated out as an isolated and vulnerable unit, economically responsible for the maintenance of its members and for the rearing of the new generation. The subjugation of the female sex was based on the transformation of their socially necessary labor into a private service through the separation of the family from the clan. It was in this context that women's domestic and other work came to be performed under conditions of virtual slavery.

The separation of the family from the clan and the institution of monogamous marriage were the social expressions of developing private property; so-called monogamy afforded the means through which property could be individually inherited. And private property for some meant no property for others, or the emerging of differing relations to production on the part of different social groups. [...]

POLITICAL RAMIFICATIONS OF ENGELS'S ARGUMENT ON THE STATUS OF WOMEN

[...] There has recently been much discussion about the extent to which women can achieve a measure of personal "liberation" by rejecting the sex-role definitions of the contemporary "monogamous" family, and about the relevance such rejection can have to the furthering of revolutionary aims and consciousness. There has also been considerable argument about the basis for women's inferior position, ranging from the extreme psychobiological view that it results from an innate masculine drive for domination and can be changed only through a single-minded "battle of the sexes," to the extreme economic determinist – and generally masculine – view that since all basic changes ultimately depend on the revolutionary restricting of society, it is both illusory and diversionary to focus on ameliorating the special problems of women.

While there is still a great deal of abstract argument about the correct position on women's liberation, there is also a growing recognition that it is fruitless to debate the extent to which various parts of the women's movement can or cannot be linked with revolutionary goals, and there is a growing commitment to developing concrete tactics of program and organization around situations where women are in motion on basic issues. It might seem that [Friedrich] Engels's discussion of family arrangements that have long ceased to exist in their pristine forms is somewhat esoteric and of little relevance today. However, it is crucial to the organization of women for their liberation to understand that it is the monogamous family as an economic unit, at the heart of class society, that is basic to their subjugation. Such understanding makes clear that child-bearing itself is not responsible for the low status of women, as has been the contention of some radical women's groups. And more important, it indicates the way in which working-class women, not only in their obviously basic fight on the job but also in their seemingly more conservative battles for their families around schools, housing and welfare, are actually posing a more basic challenge than that of the radicals. By demanding that society assume responsibility for their children, they are attacking the nature of the family as an economic unit, the basis of their own oppression and a central buttress of class exploitation. Therefore, while some of the activities of middle-class radical women's groups can be linked with the struggles of working-class women, such as the fight for free legalized abortion, others are so psychologically oriented as to be confusing and diversionary.

The self-declared women's movement in this country has historically been middle class and largely oriented toward a fight for the same options as middle-class men within the system, while the struggles of working-class women have not been conceived as fights for women's liberation as such. This has been true since the close of the Civil War, when the women's movement that had been closely concerned with the fight against slavery and for the rights of women factory workers broke away on its "feminist" course. Today there is more widespread awareness that all oppressive relations are interconnected and embedded in our system as a whole, and that only united effort can effect fundamental change. However, there has been little clear and consistent effort made to achieve such unity. For example, the committees formed by professional women to fight job discrimination are generally prepared to admit forthrightly that their battle is ultimately inseparable from that of working-class and especially Black working-class women, but they have done virtually nothing to find ways of linking the two. And it is commonplace to point out that, despite basic differences between the oppression of women and the oppression of Blacks, there are marked parallels of both an economic and a social-psychological nature – not to mention the fact that half of Black people are women. But again, there has been no solid commitment to building organizational ties between the two movements around specific issues. The theoretical differentiation between the symptoms and the causes of women's oppression can help clarify the issues around which united organization must be built, and can help remove the blocks hampering the enormous potential a women's movement could have for unifying sections of the middle and working classes and bridging some of the disastrous gap between white workers and Black, Puerto Rican, and Mexican American workers. However, in this effort it is important to be wary of a certain suspect quality of many white middle-class women (akin to that of their male counterparts) to be attracted and exhilarated by the assertiveness of the struggle for Black liberation, and to neglect their responsibility to find ways of also building an alliance with white working-class women and men.

Theoretical understanding is sorely needed to help combat the difficulties that will continue to beset the women's movement. Male supremacy, the enormous difficulty men have in facing up to their pathetic feelings of superiority and display of petty power over women, even when theoretically dedicated to revolutionary change, will continue to feed what is often a narrowly anti-men orientation among "movement women;" and the media will continue to exploit this as a gimmick that serves at the same time to sell cigarettes and shampoo, dissipate energies, and divide women from each other and from what should be allied struggles. As with the black-power movement, the sheer possibility of open confrontation will for some serve the need to express a great pent-up anger, and token victories will temporarily serve to give the illusion of some success. The overwhelming need is to keep this powerful anger from being dissipated – to find ways of building upon it through taking organizationally meaningful steps.

7.2. Toward a Unified Analysis of Gender and Kinship (1987)

Sylvia Junko Yanagisako and Jane Fishburne Collier

We do not assume the existence of a gender system based on natural differences in sexual reproduction, a kinship system based on the genealogical grid, a polity based on force, or an economy based on the production and distribution of needed resources. Rather than take for granted that societies are constituted of functionally based institutional domains, we propose to investigate the social and symbolic processes by which human actions within particular social worlds come to have consequences and meanings, including their apparent organization into seemingly "natural" social domains.

We begin with the premise that social systems are, by definition, systems of inequality. This premise has three immediate advantages. First, it conforms to common usage. By most definitions, a society is a system of social relationships and values. Values entail evaluation. [...] [V]alues inevitably create inequalities by ensuring rewards for those who live up to valued ideals and punishments for those who, for one reason or another, fail to do so. [...]

Second, [b]y presuming that all societies are systems of inequality, we are forced to separate the study of our own and other people's cultural systems of evaluation from considerations of whether or not such systems meet our standards of honor and fairness.

Finally, the premise that all societies are systems of inequality frees us from having to imagine a world without socially created inequities. [...] If we assume that all societies are systems of inequality, then we [...] are forced to explain not the existence of inequality itself but rather why it takes the qualitatively different forms it does. [...]

Given our premise that social systems are systems of inequality, we propose an analytical program with three facets[:] the explication of cultural meanings, the construction of models specifying the dialectical relationship between practice and ideas in the constitution of social inequalities, and the historical analysis of continuities and changes. [...]

THE CULTURAL ANALYSIS OF MEANING

[... W]e must begin by explicating the cultural meanings people realize through their practice of social relationships. Rather than assume that the fundamental units of gender and kinship in every society are defined by the difference between males and females in sexual reproduction, we ask what are the socially meaningful categories people employ and encounter in specific social contexts and what symbols and meanings underlie them. [R]ather than [take for granted] the meanings of blood, love, and sexual intercourse in American kinship and their influence on the construction of categories of relatives, so we have to question the meanings of genes, love, sexual intercourse, power, independence, and whatever else plays into the symbolic construction of categories of people in any particular society. [...] By attending to the public discourses through which people describe, interpret, evaluate, make claims about, and attempt to influence relationships and events, we can extract the relatively stable symbols and meanings people employ in everyday life.

These symbols and meanings [...] are always evaluative. As such, they encode particular distributions of prestige, power, and privilege. However, because they are realized through social practice, they are not static. [W]e do not assume cultural systems of meaning to be timeless, self-perpetuating structures of "tradition." Yet, even when the meanings of core symbols are changing, we can tease apart their different meanings in particular contexts and, thereby, better understand the symbolic processes involved in social change (Yanagisako 1985; Yanagisako 1987).

Once we have investigated the various ways in which difference is conceptualized in other societies – including whether and how sex and reproduction play into the construction of differences that make a difference – we can return to examine the biological model that defines gender in our own society. [W]e can ask what a conception of gender as rooted in biological difference does and does not explain about relations between men and women in our society. Having recognized our model of biological difference as a particular cultural mode of thinking about relations between people, we should be able to question the "biological facts" of sex themselves. We expect that our questioning of the presumably biological core of gender will eventually lead to the rejection of any dichotomy between sex and gender as biological and cultural facts and will open up the way for an analysis of the symbolic and social processes by which both are constructed in relation to each other. [...]

SYSTEMIC MODELS OF INEQUALITY

[...] Following Bourdieu (1977), we analyze a social system not by positing an unseen, timeless structure but rather by asking how ordinary people, pursuing their own subjective ends, realize the structures of inequality that constrain their possibilities. This is why the first facet of our strategy requires an analysis of the commonsense meanings available to people for monitoring and interpreting their own and others' actions. But this analysis of meaning must be followed by an analysis of the structures that people realize through their actions. Because we understand the commonsense meanings available to people not by positing an unseen, timeless culture but rather by exploring how people's understandings of the world are shaped by their structured experiences, we must move back and forth between an analysis of how structures shape people's experience and an analysis of how people, through their actions, realize structures.

Although a systemic model of inequality may be constructed for any society, developing a typology of models aids in the analysis of particular cases. In the end [...] each society must be analyzed in its own, historically specific terms, but a set of ideal typic models helps us to see connections we might otherwise miss. All attempts to understand other cultures are, by their nature, comparative. It is impossible to describe a particular, unique way of life without explicitly or implicitly comparing it to another – usually the analyst's own society or the society of the language the analyst is using. [...]

An example of the kind of model of inequality we are proposing is Jane Collier and Michelle Rosaldo's ideal typic model of "brideservice" societies (1981). [This model] uses marriage transaction terms – brideservice, equal or standard bridewealth, and unequal or variable bridewealth – as labels for systemic models, treating marriage transactions not as determinants of social organization or ideas but rather as moments when practice and meaning are negotiated together. Marriage negotiations are moments of "systemic reproduction" (see Comaroff 1987) in those societies in which "kinship" appears to organize people's rights and obligations relative to others. Societies with different bases of organization will have different moments of "systemic reproduction."

Just as we do not posit determining traits, so the kind of understanding we seek is not linear. Rather, the type of model we propose traces complex relationships between aspects of what – using conventional analytical categories – we might call gender, kinship, economy, polity, and religion. The principal virtue of such models is that they provide insights into the cultural meanings and social consequences of actions, events, and people's attributes by tracing the processes by which these elements are realized. Such systemic models privilege no domains over others. Unlike Ortner and Whitehead, who advocate a focus on "male prestige-oriented action" as the key to understanding gender relations in any society (1981: 20), we suggest that "prestige systems" also need explanation. When men, for example, talk as if male prestige is generated through activities that do not involve relations with women, such as hunting and warfare, we ask why men make such statements and what social processes make them appear reasonable. A "brideservice" model suggests that – at least in societies of foragers and hunter-horticulturalists – people celebrate "Man the Hunter" not because male prestige is actually based on hunting, but rather because hunting is a principal idiom in which men talk about their claims to the wives whose daily services allow them to enjoy the freedom of never having to ask anyone for anything (Collier and Rosaldo 1981).

Because systemic models specify the contexts in which people articulate particular concerns, such models can help us to understand the apparently inconsistent meanings we discover through cultural analysis. In their analysis of "bride service societies," for example, Collier and Rosaldo (1981) suggest why male violence is feared even as it is celebrated, why women who contribute as much or more than men to the diet do not emphasize their economic contribution but rather stress their sexuality, why bachelors are lazy hunters when sex is portrayed as the hunter's reward, and why notions of direct-exchange marriage coexist with the belief that men earn their wives through feats of prowess. Systemic models, by allowing us to understand such apparent inconsistencies, provide the analytic tools necessary for overcoming our own cultural bias toward consistency. Once we understand that force is both feared and celebrated, for example, then we are no longer tempted to ignore one aspect or choose which one is more empirically valid. [...]

HISTORICAL ANALYSIS

The third facet of our analytical strategy [is] to counterbalance the emphasis on social reproduction in our systemic models, so that we can see how social systems change and, at the same time, better understand the processes that enable them to remain relatively stable over time. A historical analysis that interprets current ideas and practices within the context of the unfolding sequence of action and meaning that has led to them provides this balance. Such an analysis broadens the temporal range of our analysis of social wholes by asking how their connection with the past constrains and shapes their dynamics in the present, whether that connection is one of relative continuity or of radical disjunction. [...]

[...] Our proposal to link historical analysis with symbolic analysis rests on the premise that we cannot comprehend present discourse and action without understanding their relation to past discourse and action (Yanagisako 1985). The relevant context of specific cultural elements, such as "marriage," "mother," "blood " or "semen," is not limited to current practices and meanings, but includes past practices and their symbolic meanings. [W]e must know the dialectical, historical processes through which practices and meanings have unfolded if we are to understand how they operate in the present.

Similarly, grounding our analysis of social wholes and fashioning our systemic models of inequality within particular historical sequences will enable us to see how the dynamics of past actions and ideas have created structures in the present. [...] By taking such a historical perspective on the constitution of social wholes, we avoid assuming that present systems of inequality are the timeless products of identical pasts; instead, we question whether and how these systems developed out of dissimilar pasts (Lindenbaum [1987]; Smith [1987]). We can see how aspects of ideas and practices, which in our systemic models seem to reinforce and reproduce each other, also undermine and destabilize each other.

A historical perspective also highlights the interaction of ideas and practices as dialectical, ongoing processes and so avoids the teleological bent of those models that seek a single determinant, whether material or ideational, for social reproduction. [...]

CONCLUSION

[...] We do not doubt that men and women are different, just as individuals differ, generations differ, races differ. [...] Rather, we question whether the particular biological difference in reproductive function that our culture defines as the basis of difference between males and females, and so treats as the basis of their relationship, is used by other societies to constitute the cultural categories of male and female.

[...] By doubting the common assumption that sex and age are "natural" bases for the differential allocation of social rights and duties, feminist scholars paved the way for studies of the social processes that granted men prestige and authority over women and children. Yet feminists' attempts to provide social explanations for perceived universal sexual asymmetry used the analytic dichotomies of domestic/public and nature/culture that themselves became problematic.

[...] Both gender and kinship studies, we suggest, have foundered on the unquestioned assumption that the biologically given difference in the roles of men and women in sexual reproduction lies at the core of the cultural organization of gender, even as it constitutes the genealogical grid at the core of kinship studies. Only by calling this assumption into question can we begin to ask how other cultures might understand the difference between women and men, and simultaneously make possible studies of how our own culture comes to focus on coitus and parturition as the moments constituting masculinity and femininity. [...]

REFERENCES

Bourdieu, Pierre. 1977. *Outline of a Theory of Practice*. Cambridge: Cambridge University Press.

Collier, Jane Fishburne, and Michelle Z. Rosaldo. 1981. "Politics and Gender in Simple Societies." In *Sexual Meanings: The Cultural Construction of Gender and Sexuality*, edited by Sherry B. Ortner and Harriet Whitehead, 275–329. Cambridge: Cambridge University Press.

Comaroff, John. 1987. "Sui generis: Feminism, Kinship Theory, and Structural 'Domains.'" In *Gender and Kinship: Essays Toward a Unified Analysis*, edited by Jane Fishburne Collier and Sylvia Junko Yanagisako, 53–85. Stanford: Stanford University Press.

Lindenbaum, Shirley. 1987. "The Mystification of Female Labors." In *Gender and Kinship: Essays Toward a Unified Analysis*, edited by Jane Fishburne Collier and Sylvia Junko Yanagisako, 221–43. Stanford: Stanford University Press.

Ortner, Sherry, and Harriett Whitehead. 1981. "Introduction: Accounting for Sexual Meanings." In *Sexual Meanings: The Cultural Construction of Gender and Sexuality*, edited by Sherry B. Ortner and Harriet Whitehead, 1–28. Cambridge: Cambridge University Press.

Smith, Raymond T. 1987. "Hierarchy and the Dual Marriage System in West Indian Society." In *Gender and Kinship: Essays Toward a Unified Analysis*, edited by Jane Fishburne Collier and Sylvia Junko Yanagisako, 163–96. Stanford: Stanford University Press.

Yanagisako, Sylvia Junko. 1985. *Transforming the Past: Tradition and Kinship Among Japanese Americans*. Stanford: Stanford University Press.

———. 1987. "Mixed Metaphors: Native and Anthropological Models of Gender and Kinship Domains." In *Gender and Kinship: Essays Toward a Unified Analysis*, edited by Jane Fishburne Collier and Sylvia Junko Yanagisako, 86–118. Stanford: Stanford University Press.

7.3. Male Daughters, Female Husbands: Gender and Sex in an African Society (1987)

Ifi Amadiume

Igbo women of eastern Nigeria were among the first to gain the attention of researchers as a group distinct from Igbo men. This recognition came only after both peaceful and violent mass demonstrations, riots, and finally open war with the British colonial government in 1929. From then onwards, Igbo women were universally recognized as the most militant of women. [...]

By 1929, the British colonial government finally admitted that it was facing two problems in Igboland: 1) the people as a whole were proving impossible to rule; and 2) the women were rebellious and rioting all over the place, with a militancy unfamiliar to White men. The colonial government consequently sent colonial officials and ethnographers into the field to study indigenous Igbo political systems. Inevitably, the experienced ethnographers were men and studied their fellow men. Early publications were therefore male-biased. [...]

[...] Much could have been learned from the two British women who were sent to conduct studies in the southern Igbo provinces, following the 1929 Women's War. Mrs. Leith-Ross's study, solely on women, is an account by an inexperienced and untrained wife of a colonial official who describes herself as "having more experience of the native than scientific training" (1939:44). Her experiences and impressions in a limited Igbo area were published under the ambitious and broad title, *African Women*. It reads more like a diary, full of contradictory statements as a result of her racism. [...]

Igbo women were clearly unlike European women. One less prejudiced would have viewed with an open mind differences in gender systems and consequently gender relations. Leith-Ross had, for example, observed that in the concept of reincarnation in one of the villages, a woman might be reincarnated as a man, but not vice versa (1939:101). A middle-aged woman had remarked that it would be foolish for a man to wish to become a woman and some of the women present had declared that they would like to become men. These statements of obvious identification with authority, privilege and power were completely misunderstood by Mrs. Leith-Ross, who was socialized in rigid Victorian gender ideology in which gender corresponded to sex. In their system, male attributes and male status referred to the biologically male sex – man – as female attributes and female status referred to the biologically female sex – woman. To break this rigid gender construction carried a stigma. Consequently, it was not usual to separate sex from gender, as there was no status ambiguity in relation to gender.

The flexibility of Igbo gender construction meant that gender was separate from biological sex. Daughters could become sons and consequently male. Daughters and women in general could be husbands to wives and consequently males in relation to their wives, etc. Leith-Ross was familiar with Igbo women's feminism and ambition for power. That the women she studied did not wish to become men, but males, was beyond Leith-Ross's imagination. As a result, she wrote such ethnocentric remarks as:

> I had occasionally caught glimpses of some peculiar conception of sex or of a thread of bisexuality running through everything (yet I think hermaphrodites are "abomination") – or of a lack of differentiation between the sexes – or of an acceptance of the possibility of the transposition of sex – which it would have been interesting to study.

An insight into this remarkable gender system is crucial to the understanding and appreciation of the political status women had in traditional Igbo societies and the political choices open to them. […]

[… T]he traditional Igbo dual-sex social systems were mediated by the flexibility of gender constructions in the Igbo language and culture. The conceptualization of daughters as males in ritual matters, and politically in relation to wives, is a good example of this gender flexibility and did not imply that daughters should be seen as "man-like." Another example of the looseness of gender association is the fact that in Igbo grammatical construction of gender, a neuter particle is used in Igbo subject or object pronouns, so that no gender distinction is made in reference to males and females in writing or in speech. There is, therefore, no language or mental adjustment or confusion in references to a woman performing a typical male role. […]

The Igbo in general and Nnobi people in particular trace the gender ideologies behind their sexual division of labor, and those governing the relations of production, to their myths of origin. […] As a result of ecological factors, agricultural production was not profitable in Nnobi, hence the development of a sexual division of labor and gender ideology which gave women a central place in the subsistence economy, while men sought authority through ritual specialization and ritual control.

The gender ideology governing economic production was that of female industriousness, *Idi uchu*, perseverance and industriousness, and *ite uba*, the pot of prosperity, were gifts women were said to have inherited from the goddess Idemili. Associated with this were strong matrifocality and female orientation in this supposedly "patrilineal" society. The culture prescribing industriousness is derived from the goddess Idemili – the central religious deity. […]

There was, therefore, a dual-sex organizational principle behind the structure of the economy, which was supported by various gender ideologies. These principles and ideologies governed the economic activities of men and women. They also governed access to wealth, and prescribed achievement-based statuses and roles, such as titles and the accumulation of wives, which, in the indigenous society, brought power, prestige and more wealth. However, a flexible gender system mediated the dual-sex organizational principle. [...]

Both Nnobi and Nri men have manipulated certain gender ideologies implicit in their myths of origin in an effort to deal with the constraints imposed upon them by ecological factors. [...] In the explanation of the invention of agriculture and the sexual division of labor, yam, the prestige crop which requires expert knowledge for its production, both in the ritual and technical senses, sprang from the male head, and [...] was grown and distributed by men. Only ritual heads and male heads of families distributed yam medicine and performed the ritual which permitted the eating of yam. Yet, in reality, the role played by men in yam production in the Igbo areas where less food was produced was minimal.

Cocoyam, according to the Nri myth, grew out of the female head. This crop, grown by women, required less specialized knowledge than did the yam. To ensure a good yield of sizeable yam tubers a lot of work was necessary, first to thoroughly dig the soil with a large hoe. Then the soil dug out had to be heaped into huge mounds, both to survive erosion by the rains and to hold the growing tubers, some of which have been known to grow as large as a human being. Cocoyam is grown in small mounds or ridges which can easily be worked by women, and no special ritual secrets were associated with them.

Similarly, cassava, when introduced into Igboland, was regarded as an inferior crop, grown by women. Although it demanded a lot of time and hard labor to harvest and process into food, the actual cultivation required little specialized knowledge, as it can grow wild. [...]

There is, then, a clear interrelationship between ecological factors, economic production and gender ideas. [...]

In Nnobi myth of origin, Edo inherits industriousness from her mother, the goddess Idemili. Here, female crops such as cocoyam, plantain and cassava compensated for the shortage of yam for staple food. Nnobi, therefore, depended very heavily on female labor in agriculture.

One begins to see a system of prescribed achievements and rewards. From it women in Nnobi might be expected to derive prestige and power from their control and successful management of, and effective organization around, this subsistence economy. [...]

Nnobi people were, traditionally, subsistence farmers and traders. Land was therefore a major economic resource; ownership of land was both communal and individual. [...]

[...] The principle of individual ownership of land applied in the family as long as the owner was alive and had male descendants or "male daughters" to inherit the land. Where there was no one to inherit land, right of ownership returned to the extended family, the deceased man's brothers.

As a result of Nnobi's flexible gender system, the institution of "male daughters" was manipulated in the conflicts which arose as a result of the coexistence of principles of individual and collective ownership of land. I shall illustrate this point by the case of Nwajiuba Ojukwu, the 70-year-old "male daughter." [...] According to Nwajiuba, because of this absence of close relatives, when her father became ill, he decided to recall her from her marital home and allow her to remain in his house as a male. She would then have the status of a son, and be able to inherit her father's property. This practice was known as *nhayikwa* or *nhanye*, a kind of replacement, in Nnobi, a custom. [...]

The formalist approach in anthropology to the patrilineal system of inheritance is that sons inherit their father's land and daughters do not; therefore women do not own land. As we have seen in the case of Nnobi, the institution of "male daughters" disproves this theory. [...]

As women took control of the subsistence economy, men sought authority through the control of ritual specialization. Even though women were economically self-sufficient, men monopolized the right to tell them when, for example, they could begin to eat yam every year. Various patriarchal and matriarchal ideologies embedded in myths of origin were used to justify this sexual division of labor. At the same time, the presence of strong matrifocality and female orientation in the culture gave women in general a favorable position in both the domestic and public sectors of the traditional society. Female industriousness was, for example, rewarded with both prestigious and political titles *ogbuefi* and Ekwe. But, more importantly, we find that a flexible gender system encouraged the institutions of "female husband" and "male daughter." This meant that certain women could occupy roles and positions usually monopolized by men, and thereby exercise considerable power and authority over both men and women. [...]

REFERENCE

Leith-Ross, S. 1939. *African Women (London)*. (Reissued by Routledge & Kegan Paul, London, 1965.)

7.4. La conciencia de la mestiza / Towards a New Consciousness (1987)

Gloria Anzaldúa

> *Por la mujer de mi raza*
> *hablará el espíritu.*

José Vasconcelos, Mexican philosopher, envisaged *una raza mestiza, una mezcla de razas afines, una raza de color – la primera raza síntesis del globo*. He called it a cosmic race, la raza cósmica, a fifth race embracing the four major races of the world. Opposite to the theory of the pure Aryan, and to the policy of racial purity that white America practices, his theory is one of inclusivity. At the confluence of two or more genetic streams, with chromosomes constantly "crossing over," this mixture of races, rather than resulting in an inferior being, provides hybrid progeny, a mutable, more malleable species with a rich gene pool. From this racial, ideological, cultural and biological cross-pollinization, an "alien" consciousness is presently in the making – a new *mestiza* consciousness, *una conciencia de mujer*. It is a consciousness of the Borderlands.

UNA LUCHA DE FRONTERAS / A STRUGGLE OF BORDERS

> Because I, a *mestiza*,
> Continually walk out of one culture
> and into another,
> because I am in all cultures at the same time,
> *alma entre dos mundos, tres, cuatro,*
> *me zumba la cabeza con lo contradictorio.*
> *Estoy norteada por todas las voces que me hablan*
> *simultáneamente.*

The ambivalence from the clash of voices results in mental and emotional states of perplexity. Internal strife results in insecurity and indecisiveness. The *mestiza*'s dual or multiple personality is plagued by psychic restlessness.

In a constant state of mental nepantilism, an Aztec word meaning torn between ways, *la mestiza* is a product of the transfer of the cultural and spiritual values of one group to another. Being tricultural, monolingual, bilingual, or multilingual, speaking a patois, and in a state of perpetual transition, the *mestiza* faces the dilemma of the mixed breed: which collectivity does the daughter of a darkskinned mother listen to?

El choque de una alma atrapado entre el mundo del espíritu y el mundo de la técnica a veces la deja entullada. Cradled in one culture, sandwiched between two cultures, straddling all three cultures and their value systems, *la mestiza* undergoes a struggle of flesh, a struggle of borders, an inner war. Like all people, we perceive the version of reality that our culture communicates. Like others having or living in more than one culture, we get multiple, often opposing messages. The coming together of two self-consistent but habitually incompatible frames of references causes *un choque*, a cultural collision.

Within us and within *la cultural chicana*, commonly held beliefs of the white culture attack commonly held beliefs of the Mexican culture, and both attack commonly held beliefs of the indigenous culture. Subconsciously, we see an attack on ourselves and our beliefs as a threat and we attempt to block with a counterstance.

But it is not enough to stand on the opposite river bank, shouting questions, challenging patriarchal, white conventions. A counterstance locks one into a duel of oppressor and oppressed; locked in mortal combat, like the cop and the criminal, both are reduced to a common denominator of violence. The counterstance refutes the dominant culture's views and beliefs, and, for this, it is proudly defiant. All reaction is limited by, and dependent on, what it is reacting against. Because the counterstance stems from a problem with authority – outer as well as inner – it's a step toward liberation from cultural domination. But it is not a way of life. At some point, on our way to a new consciousness, we will have to leave the opposite bank, the split between the two mortal combatants somehow healed so that we are on both shores at once and, at once, see through serpent and eagle eyes. Or perhaps we will decide to disengage from the dominant culture, write it off altogether as a lost cause, and cross the border into a wholly new and separate territory. Or we might go another route. The possibilities are numerous once we decide to act and not react.

A TOLERANCE FOR AMBIGUITY

These numerous possibilities leave *la mestiza* floundering in uncharted seas. In perceiving conflicting information and points of view, she is subjected to a swamping of her psychological borders. She has discovered that she can't hold concepts or ideas in rigid boundaries. The borders and walls that are supposed to keep the undesirable ideas out are entrenched habits and patterns of behavior; these habits and patterns are the enemy within. Rigidity means death. Only by remaining flexible is she able to stretch the psyche horizontally and vertically. *La mestiza* constantly has to shift out of habitual formations; from convergent thinking, analytical reasoning that tends to use rationality to move toward a single goal (a Western mode), to divergent thinking, characterized by movement away from set patterns and goals and toward a more whole perspective, one that includes rather than excludes.

The new *mestiza* copes by developing a tolerance for contradictions, a tolerance for ambiguity. She learns to be an Indian in Mexican culture, to be Mexican from an Anglo point of view. She learns to juggle cultures. She has a plural personality, she operates in a pluralistic mode – nothing is thrust out, the good the bad and the ugly, nothing rejected, nothing abandoned. Not only does she sustain contradictions, she turns the ambivalence into something else.

She can be jarred out of ambivalence by an intense, and often painful, emotional event which inverts or resolves the ambivalence. I'm not sure exactly how. The work takes place underground – subconsciously. It is work that the soul performs. That focal point or fulcrum, that juncture where the *mestiza* stands, is where phenomena tend to collide. It is where the possibility of uniting all that is separate occurs. This assembly is not one where severed or separated pieces merely come together. Nor is it a balancing of opposing powers. In attempting to work out a synthesis, the self has added a third element which is greater than the sum of its severed parts. That third element is a new consciousness – a *mestiza* consciousness – and though it is a source of intense pain, its energy comes from continual creative motion that keeps breaking down the unitary aspect of each new paradigm.

En unas pocas centurias, the future will belong to the *mestiza*. Because the future depends on the breaking down of paradigms, it depends on the straddling of two or more cultures. By creating a new mythos – that is, a change in the way we perceive reality, the way we see ourselves, and the ways we behave – *la mestiza* creates a new consciousness.

The work of *mestiza consciousness* is to break down the subject-object duality that keeps her a prisoner and to show in the flesh and through the images in her work how duality is transcended. The answer to the problem between the white race and the colored, between males and females, lies in healing the split that originates in the very foundation of our lives, our culture, our languages, our thoughts. A massive uprooting of dualistic thinking in the individual and collective consciousness is the beginning of a long struggle, but one that could, in our best hopes, bring us to the end of rape, of violence, of war.

LA ENCRUCIJADA / THE CROSSROADS

A chicken is being sacrificed
    at a crossroads, a simple mound of earth
a mud shrine for *Eshu*,
    Yoruba god of indeterminacy,
who blesses her choice of path.
    She begins her journey.

Su cuerpo es una bocacalle. La mestiza has gone from being the sacrificial goat to becoming the officiating priestess at the crossroads.

As a *mestiza* I have no country, my homeland cast me out; yet all countries are mine because I am every woman's sister or potential lover. (As a lesbian I have no race, my own people disclaim me; but I am all races because there is the queer of me in all races.) I am cultureless because, as a feminist, I challenge the collective cultural/religious male-derived beliefs of Indo-Hispanics and Anglos; yet I am cultured because I am participating in the creation of yet another culture, a new story to explain the world and our participation in it, a new value system with images and symbols that connect us to each other and to the planet. *Soy un amasamiento*, I am an act of kneading, of uniting and joining that not only has produced both a creature of darkness and a creature of light, but also a creature that questions the definitions of light and dark and gives them new meanings.

We are the people who leap in the dark, we are the people on the knees of the gods. In our very flesh, (r)evolution works out the clash of cultures. It makes us crazy constantly, but if the center holds, we've made some kind of evolutionary step forward. *Nuestra alma el trabajo*, the opus, the great alchemical work; spiritual *mestijae*, a "morphogenesis," an inevitable unfolding. We have become the quickening serpent movement.

Indigenous like corn, like corn, the *mestiza* is a product of crossbreeding, designed for preservation under a variety of conditions. Like an ear of corn – a female seed-bearing organ – the *mestiza* is tenacious, tightly wrapped in the husks of her culture. Like kernels she clings to the cob; with thick stalks and strong brace roots, she holds tight to the earth – she will survive the crossroads.

Lavando y remojando el maíz en agua de cal, despojando el pellejo. Moliendo, mixteando, amasando, hacienda tortillas de masa. She steeps the corn in lime, it swells, softens. With stone roller on *metate*, she grinds the corn, then grinds again. She kneads and molds the dough, pats the round balls into tortillas.

> We are the porous rock in the stone metate
> squatting on the ground
> We are the rolling pin, *el maíz y agua*,
> *la masa harina. Somos el amasijo.*
> *Somos lo molido en el metate.*
> We are the *comal* sizzling hot,
> the hot *tortilla*, the hungry mouth.
> We are the coarse rock.
> We are the grinding motion,
> the mixed potion, *somos el molcajete*,
> We are the pestle, the *comino, ajo, pimiento*,
> We are the *chile colorado*,
> the green shoot that cracks the rock.
> We will abide.

EL CAMINO DE LA MESTIZA / THE MESTIZA WAY

Caught between the sudden contraction, the breath sucked in and the endless space, the brown woman stands still, looks at the sky. She decides to go down, digging her way along the roots of tree. Sifting through the bones, she shakes them to see if there is any marrow in them. Then, touching the dirt to her forehead, to her tongue, she takes a few bones, leaves the rest in their burial place.

She goes through her backpack, keeps her journal and address book, throws away the muni-bart metromaps. The coins are heavy and they go next, then the greenbacks fluttering through the air. She keeps her knife, can opener, and eyebrow pencil. She puts bone, pieces of bark, *hierbas*, eagle feather, snakeskin, tape recorder, the rattle and drum in her pack and she sets out to become the complete *tolteca*.

Her first step is to take inventory. *Despojando, desgranando, quitando paja.* Just what did she inherit from her ancestors? This weight on her back – which is the baggage from the Indian mother, which the baggage from the Spanish father, which the baggage from the Anglo?

Pero es difícil differentiating between *lo heredado, lo adquiridi, lo impuesto.* She puts history through a sieve, winnows out the lies, looks at the forces that we as a race, as woman, have been a part of. *Luego bota lo que no vale, los desmientos, los desencuentros, el embrutecimiento. Aguarda el juicio, hondo y enraízado, de la gente antigua.* This step is a conscious rupture with all oppressive traditions of all cultures and religions. She communicates that rupture, documents the struggle. She reinterprets history and, using new symbols, she shapes new myths. She adopts new perspectives toward the darkskinned, women and queers. She strengthens her tolerance (and intolerance) for ambiguity. She is willing to share, to make herself vulnerable to foreign ways of seeing and thinking. She surrenders all notions of safety, of the familiar. Deconstruct, construct. She becomes a *nahual*, able to transform herself into a tree, a coyote, into another person. She learns to transform the small "I" into the total self. *Se hace moldeadora de su alma. Según la concepción que tiene de sí mísma, así será.*

7.5. In Search of Masculinity: Violence, Respect, and Sexuality among Puerto Rican Crack Dealers in East Harlem (1996)

Philippe Bourgois

In the decades following World War II between one third and one half of Puerto Rico's population migrated to New York City in search of employment in factory sweatshops (Bonilla and Campos 1986; Bose 1986). They arrived at precisely the historical moment when these kinds of manufacturing jobs were leaving the industrialized countries. [...] This sets the stage for the dramatic changes in family structure and male power roles among second- and third-generation East Harlem residents. Coming primarily from the poorest sectors of society, and often arriving directly from sugar plantations, marginal family farms, or decaying coffee haciendas, definitions of masculinity among Puerto Rican immigrants are embedded in interpersonal webs of *"respeto* [respect]" defined around gender, age, kinship, and community status. [...] In the classic "traditional" setting of the family farm, the worth of the autocratic paterfamilias hinged most immediately on the larger community's perception of the respect accorded to him by his wife and her abundant children. Several generations later on the inner-city street, the idealized legacies of the hierarchies and prestiges that were formerly rooted in the rural family and in the personal hierarchies of small farming or plantation communities have been redefined into an explicitly misogynist and sexually violent street culture. The traditional search for respect has been radically transformed into a fear of disrespect. [...]

Vivid memories of a rural patriarchy repeatedly surface in the idealized childhood reminiscences of the mothers of the crack dealers I befriended:

> MRS. ORTIZ: [...] In those days children were respectful. [...] When a visitor came, my father only spoke to us with his eyes, because children were not supposed to be in the room. He would just look at us, and that meant we had to disappear. [...]
>
> I tried to teach my children a little of what my father had taught me.

Mrs. Ortiz's son, Primo, the manager of the crackhouse where I spent much of my [research] time, can no longer "speak" to his children "with his eyes" and expect to have his commands immediately obeyed. A man's oppressive power in his home in rural Puerto Rico was predicated upon his being able to work hard and provide materially for his wife and children. He was supposed to coordinate the labor power of his wife and children around the agricultural cycles and intermittent wage labor opportunities of the precarious semi-subsistence rural economy. In inner-city New York, the increasingly large cohort of male high school dropouts who are excluded from the new service sector jobs that require a minimal education and which entail public subservience to anglo-dominated professional office culture has lost the material basis for the patriarchal family prerogative of rural Puerto Rico. Former modalities of male respect can no longer be achieved. [...] Instead, the unemployed or drug dealing man lashes out at the women and children he can no longer support or control effectively. The memory of his grandfather's former power hangs heavily upon him as he harks back to a patriarchal "jibaro" past he can no longer reproduce.

THE POLARIZATION OF DOMESTIC VIOLENCE

This was the case for Primo's father when he lost his job at a garment factory and became "a nasty alcoholic (borrachón sucio)." Primo's earliest memories of his father are of him beating up his mother. Worse yet, all the subsequent men in Primo's mother's life offered the growing boy a similarly brutal masculine model defined around physically victimizing women. [...]

Primo reproduced this cycle of brutality 15 years later when he too beat up his girlfriend in front of her children. Powerlessly struggling with his inability to hold a steady job and earn respect through economic faithfulness to his household, he had pursued the street male role of gigolo, and was living off a woman named Candy, who was one of the few female sellers in the crack dealing network. [...] Primo pretended publicly to enjoy "free loading (*cacheteando*)" on Candy's generosity and love for him. [...] After several months of the patriarchal role reversal of being economically supported by a woman and forced to satisfy her sexual desires upon demand, however, he attempted to recoup his personal sense of male respect by the only means immediately at his disposal: public physical violence. [...]

[... T]he final fight that ended his economically and sexually dependent relationship with Candy [...] began when Primo refused to make love to Candy. This prompted her to accuse him of having outside girlfriends. [...] His description climaxed with how he managed to disarm Candy, in order to beat her more severely in front of her children:

> PRIMO: As soon as she put the gun down [...] I went, "Fucking Bitch!" (swinging both fists). And I mushed her. I was pissed man. I shouted, "Come on, Bitch! I'm not playing with you anymore."
>
> PHILIPPE: What about the kids?
>
> PRIMO: The kids were there in the room all nervous, I guess they were crying ... Put it this way: the children knew their mother was wrong, but I was hitting their mother. [...]

VULNERABLE MALES

In contrast to the legitimation that Primo constructs for his violence against Candy, Primo condemns his own father's violence toward his mother and sisters. He explicitly sees his father as a failure; he was never able to respect him as a patriarchally socialized child should:

> PRIMO: My father's [...] a chronic drinker; and when he gets drunk he gets violent. So it's like he's no fucking good, so why be with him? [...] And every time I would see my father, once they were separated [...] Always drunk and crying. We were kids [...] he used to come to me, and ask, "Is your mother with anybody?" [...] I probably used to say "yes," or whatever. He was drunk and stupid. [...] Maybe he regretted the things that he did. [...] And then he collapses, shakes. I used to hate that.

[...] Primo's father collapsing in a shaking fit [is an example of] "nervous attacks" [that] usually afflict women, and are associated with jealousy, abuse, and/or failure in love. The fact that Primo's father might engage in such a feminine expression of angry vulnerability in front of his children and close friends illustrates the sense of male impotence he must have felt as a failed labor migrant in the United States. He would respond by beating up the nearest vulnerable female, whose respect he was no longer capable of commanding. [...]

CONJUGAL STABILITY AND LEGAL EMPLOYMENT

In contrast to their often bravado behavior and explicitly misogynist diatribes, most [crack dealers] admitted to aspiring to an ideal-type, middle-class, nuclear family. [...] The following account [...] illustrates the interaction between personality and social structure in the construction of masculine subjectivities.

> PRIMO: I was 19 [...] We were teenagers going steady – me and Sandra. I had found a job and stayed steady with her [...] She got pregnant. We didn't really want it. But then I told her, "I'm just as responsible as you are, so if you keep it, I'll take the consequences." So she kept it. [...] And I wasn't selling drugs or doing nothing. I was a goodie, goodie. I had money in the bank, I had money in the house. Sandra never suffered [...] When Papito was born I was working at US Litho [...] I had good hours. I was working from 4:00 to 12:00 at nights ... I was a hard worker, I was into that overtime. Whatever they give me, I gonna work. I want to bring money to the house ... This is how I stopped sniffing (cocaine) [...] I used to sit in a rocking chair, reading him his ABCs and numbers, just to keep his mind busy. You got to read to your kids when they're little, like even when they're only months old, so that they always got things in their brain ... Then at work they changed my hours to 2:00 a.m. to 10:00 a.m. I said, "I can't handle them hours; I have a family." ... I used to fall asleep on the job; 'cause I had my son. And this girl, Sandra, my son's mother, had found work off the books. And as she was leaving, I was coming in, and my son was on top of me. He wanted

to play. He already slept, you know, so I couldn't sleep ... And that's when I started fucking up. That's when I started smoking "woollies" (marijuana cigarettes laced with crack), and I was drinking a little. I was staying up all day ... I used to come from work; I didn't know whether to go to sleep, or hang out and sleep later. And my son was there, wide awake; he was two, and wanted to play with me. So they fired me because I was falling asleep on the job. [...] After that I went AWOL smoking crack.

Primo acutely felt his failure as a father – and as a man:

You know, Felipe? Now my son is 6 years old. It gets me sad when I think about shit like that ... It's like, I'm not there for 'im. Just like my father was never there for me ... And my son loved being with me. [...] That's why I used to cry a lot when I first left my son. It was only a couple months after they fired me at US Litho [...] I believe that when you're with someone, and you have a child, you should make the fucking best of it. [...] You gotta make a commitment; like a family thing, like old-fashioned. [...]

Stable legal employment for both spouses is crucial for enabling young men to begin defining masculinity around sharing in the material and emotional reproduction of children. The problem is that most of the legal jobs available to high school drop-outs in New York City are not only poorly remunerated but are also considered to be feminizing. [...] Most of the supervisors at the lowest levels of the service sector are women, and street culture castigates males who are publicly subordinated across gender lines. Typically, in their angrier memories of disrespect at work, many of the male crack dealers refer to their female bosses in explicitly sexist language, often insulting their body parts, and dismissing them with street slang and sexualized curses. [...]

Not only do young men have difficulty politely taking orders from women, but they often consider it to be downright emasculating to have to run and fetch coffee for their work-place superiors and, worse yet, to have to deliver their services with a cheerful smile. [...]

INVESTING IN PROMISCUITY [AND GANG RAPE]

Sexual conquest and promiscuity represent another important forum for redefining masculine dignity in street culture. [...] Unable to reproduce the patriarchal aspirations of [one's] grandfather's generation within the context of a nuclear family and an extended kin-based community, [crack dealers concentrated] male energies into macho one-upmanship and sexual belt-notching. [...]

[As well, several] admitted to having been gang rapists in their adolescence. [...]

In addition to emphasizing the ritual dimension to adolescent gang rape and its particular frequency in the youth gang context, it is important to understand public rape within the same context that I have presented domestic violence. Gang rape is an extension into the public domain of males trying to reassert the anachronistic patriarchal power relations of previous generations that have been undermined by shifts in gender power relations. As girls increasingly carve out more autonomous roles in public male-dominated settings, boys lash out violently. They legitimatize their sexual violence against young teenage girls, claiming that they are "teaching them a lesson." [...]

INDIVIDUAL RESPONSIBILITY AND SOCIAL STRUCTURAL VICTIMIZATION

[...] Chicano cultural critics have long since noted how anglo perceptions of latino machismo reflect deep-seated historical prejudices (Paredes 1971). This is exacerbated by the fact that ethnocentric assumptions are so unconsciously ingrained in the public "common sense" that descriptions of extreme social misery and brutality such as those presented in these pages are interpreted as a cultural reflection of a particular ethnic community – in this case Puerto Rican immigrants in the United States. [T]he theoretical and political arguments of this article [...] are opposed to cultural essentialist explanations for human action. [...]

[...] The men in these pages often behave in cruel and violent ways, not only against the women and children in their lives but also against themselves. [...] I feel that if I failed to confront it – especially the most painful dimensions of misogyny and sexual violence in street culture and in individual action – I would be colluding in the sexist status quo. While all of the crack dealers are victims from a social structural perspective, they are also agents of destruction in their daily lives. They wreak havoc on their loved ones and on their larger community. [...] The polarization of formerly rural-based patriarchal masculine subjectivities toward greater public violence, widespread sexual abuse, and overt economic parasitism on inner-city streets are merely symptomatic expressions of these basic political and cultural inequities. [...]

REFERENCES

Bonilla, A.F., and Campos, R. 1986. *Industry and Idleness*. New York: Centro de Estudios Puertoriqueños, Hunter College.

Bose, C.E. 1986. "Puerto Rican Women in the United States: An Overview." In E. Acosta-Belén, ed., *The Puerto Rican Woman: Perspectives on Culture, History, and Society*, 2nd ed., 147–69. New York: Praeger.

Paredes, A. 1971. "The United States, Mexico, and Machismo." *Journal of the Folklore Institute* 8 (1): 17–37.

Section Seven Glossary

biodeterminism   The belief that sociocultural roles are determined by biology. Biodeterminist theories of race, class, and gender tend to see social inequalities as outgrowths of biological differences, but biodeterministic norms are also applied more widely to ideas about family, descent, "intelligence," and so on.

emic   An understanding of human societies that privileges understandings "from within" the society, usually derived from internal meanings and workings.

etic   An understanding of human societies that privileges understandings "from outside" the society, usually derived from theoretical frameworks.

intersectionality   Most widely associated with the writings of Kimberlé Crenshaw, intersectionality is an approach to understanding lived experiences of categorical inequalities by attending to more than one social category at a time. A legal scholar, Crenshaw observed that the disadvantages experienced by Black women, for example, cannot be adequately addressed with measures designed for Black men nor for white women; the intersection of race and gender yields experiences with racism and sexism that are particular to Black women (and additionally shaped by class position, skin color, sexuality, and other factors).

SECTION EIGHT

On Queering Anthropological Knowledge Production

THE SOCIAL CONTEXT

Throughout the 1960s, gay rights activists in cities including San Francisco, Los Angeles, Philadelphia, and New York engaged in public demonstrations to protest police violence and criminalization and to advance gay rights in the United States. These uprisings gradually resulted in federal decriminalization of non-heterosexual practices (although several states still have anti-sodomy laws on their books) and the repeal of legal prohibitions on gay marriage in 2015 and the legalization of adoption by same-sex couples in 2017. Still, even "progressive" discourse on sexuality has tended to reproduce dichotomous categories of men/women, heterosexual/homosexual, and gay/lesbian to advance a depoliticized "gay culture" compatible with capitalist middle-class values. Resulting hegemonic **homonormativity** tolerated narrow forms of white, middle-class, and cisgender same-sex relationships. Questioning the legitimacy of gendered and sexual categories altogether would become centered by the work of queer activists and theorists by the 1990s.

Queer theory conceptualizes gender and sexuality as performative and fluid, decouples sexuality from gender expression, and challenges rigid categorizations of gender, sex, and sexuality. Queer anthropology, as a body of scholarship, draws on queer theory and lesbian and gay anthropology to attend closely to the role of power in shaping relations among people and expressions of desire. By reclaiming the label "queer," once deployed as a slur, queer studies recast theories of sex and gender from restrictive and universalizing to fluid and variable, showing the multitude of ways in which queer existence unfolds. That is where the pieces in this section make their critical interventions.

THE CONVERSATION

The first selection is the opening of Michel Foucault's *The History of Sexuality,* which argues that the emergence of capitalism in the eighteenth century was accompanied by increasing repression of sexual behaviors: Foucault's "repressive hypothesis" of sexuality. In the multi-volume work where this brief introduction appears, Foucault, a poststructuralist, follows the development of the dominant narrative that sexuality belongs in the private home and solely for procreative purposes in marital sex. Such sexual repression emerged during the Victorian era, Foucault argues, when it was carefully crafted by a bourgeoisie deeply concerned that workers' energy was wasted on non-procreative sexual pursuits that slowed their productivity. From the seventeenth century forward, in an attempt to control sexuality and increase "productive" citizenship, the bourgeoisie deployed a repressive discourse, squashing the sexual freedom of the Middle Ages and the Renaissance. As a result, any form of sexuality that did not fit within the mold of procreative, marital sex was pushed to the margins and considered "illegitimate."

Well before Foucault's intervention into the study of sexuality, twentieth-century anthropologists had long been documenting cross-cultural gender variance, first developing and later confounding the sex/gender distinction, making clear that anatomical sex, gender, and sexuality are all socially constructed. These studies also described diverse genders cross-culturally, showing cultural acceptance and value for gender variance. Many studies, however, collapsed members of the transgender community under the singular label "third gender," limiting conceptual exploration of gender diversity.

Reading 8.2, "Romancing the Transgender Native," is a critical intervention into the use of "third gender" in writings by and about transgender people. Evan Towle and Lynn Morgan argue that while anthropological accounts of the "third gender" variation have benefited Western activist interventions to upend binary gender systems and reveal that gender is neither innate nor universal, the rise in popularity of these accounts has emerged at the same time that transgender anthropologists have found serious fault with the "third gender" concept, especially as it relies on a romanticized stereotype of the transgender native.

In the next selection, transgender historian Susan Stryker considers the erasure of queerness and gender diversity in homonormative depictions of the Gay Rights Movement in the United States. This erasure, Stryker argues, is perpetuated in academic spaces that too often relegate the scholarship of transgender researchers to "subjective" or personal perspectives, delegitimizing the authority of both their research and their lived experiences. This devaluation, Stryker continues, upholds epistemological hierarchies that imbue certain forms of (raced, gendered, classed) knowledge with authority and discount others, particularly knowledge produced within and by marginalized communities, as subjective. The work of radical intellectuals, then, must include "disturb[ing] the normative" categories that not only circumscribe gender expressions but delimit our own disciplinary practices as well.

The final two selections were written by anthropologists working at the nexus of Black/queer/diaspora studies. In "One Way or Another" (Reading 8.4), Jafari Allen considers the possibilities and limitations of "erotic subjectivity" under Cuba's Special Period, a time of economic crisis as well as social and political possibility for Black and queer Cubans. Through an ethnographic account of Octavio-Lili, Allen shows how non-heteronormative Black Cubans both reproduce and challenge racial and gendered social expectations. Allen's focus on experience and embodiment operationalizes Stryker's observations in Reading 8.3, as it builds on Black feminist **standpoint epistemology**, which argues that a shared subject position – and thus knowledge or "standpoint" – emerges out of categorical disempowerment within a given power structure. The piece also introduces the concept of "color drag" to capture gender–race performance in discourse and practice.

Savannah Shange's "Play Aunties and Dyke Bitches" (Reading 8.5) explores the lived experiences of gendered and raced disciplinary practices in a California school. Placing herself reflexively within a physical confrontation between two students, La'Nea and Kairo, whose gender performances are of Black girlhood and Black masculinity, respectively, Shange analyzes their interaction as a "queered scene of Black gender socialization." As Shange considers her role as femme auntie to Black queer students at the school, she theorizes masculinity through queer theory and lived forms of Blackness, drawing on ethnographic detail to show how queerness is a communal and fluid, not solitary or fixed, experience.

THREE QUESTIONS FOR THE READINGS

1 How are these pieces in conversation with those offered in Section Seven? What assumptions do they hold in common, and where do they diverge?
2 Where are the intersections of race, gender, sexuality, and power in each of these pieces? How does one tease out these distinctions ethnographically?
3 How does the social position or categorization of the scholar inform their analysis in the piece?

ON THE COMPANION WEBSITE

"Screaming Queens," AnthroBites, additional readings, and more.

www.anthropologicaltheory.com

8.1. The History of Sexuality (1976)

Michel Foucault

For a long time, the story goes, we supported a Victorian regime, and we continue to be dominated by it even today. Thus the image of the imperial prude is emblazoned on our restrained, mute, and hypocritical sexuality.

At the beginning of the seventeenth century a certain frankness was still common, it would seem. Sexual practices had little need of secrecy; words were said without undue reticence, and things were done without too much concealment; one had a tolerant familiarity with the illicit. Codes regulating the coarse, the obscene, and the indecent were quite lax compared to those of the nineteenth century. It was a time of direct gestures, shameless discourse, and open transgressions, when anatomies were shown and intermingled at will, and knowing children hung about amid the laughter of adults: it was a period when bodies "made a display of themselves."

But twilight soon fell upon this bright day, followed by the monotonous nights of the Victorian bourgeoisie. Sexuality was carefully confined; it moved into the home. The conjugal family took custody of it and absorbed it into the serious function of reproduction. On the subject of sex, silence became the rule. The legitimate and procreative couple laid down the law. The couple imposed itself as model, enforced the norm, safeguarded the truth, and reserved the right to speak while retaining the principle of secrecy. A single locus of sexuality was acknowledged in social space as well as at the heart of every household, but it was a utilitarian and fertile one: the parents' bedroom. The rest had only to remain vague; proper demeanor avoided contact with other bodies, and verbal decency sanitized one's speech. And sterile behavior carried the taint of abnormality; if it insisted on making itself too visible, it would be designated accordingly and would have to pay the penalty.

[...] Not only did it not exist, it had no right to exist and would be made to disappear upon its least manifestation – whether in acts or in words. Everyone knew, for example, that children had no sex, which was why they were forbidden to talk about it, why one closed one's eyes and stopped one's ears whenever they came to show evidence to the contrary, and why a general and studied silence was imposed. These are the characteristic features attributed to repression, which serve to distinguish it from the prohibitions maintained by penal law: repression operated as a sentence to disappear, but also as an injunction to silence, an affirmation of nonexistence, and, by implication, an admission that there was nothing to say about such things, nothing to see, and nothing to know. Such was the hypocrisy of our bourgeois societies with its halting logic. It was forced to make a few concessions, however. If it was truly necessary to make room for illegitimate sexualities, it was reasoned, let them take their infernal mischief elsewhere: to a place where they could be reintegrated, if not in the circuits of production, at least in those of profit. The brothel and the mental hospital would be those places of tolerance: the prostitute, the client, and the pimp, together with the psychiatrist and his hysteric [...] seem to have surreptitiously transferred the pleasures that are unspoken into the order of things that are counted. Words and gestures, quietly authorized, could be exchanged there at the going rate. Only in those places would untrammeled sex have a right to (safely insularized) forms of reality, and only to clandestine, circumscribed, and coded types of discourse. Everywhere else, modern puritanism imposed its triple edict of taboo, nonexistence, and silence. [...]

[...] By placing the advent of the age of repression in the seventeenth century, after hundreds of years of open spaces and free expression, one adjusts it to coincide with the development of capitalism: it becomes an integral part of the bourgeois order. The minor chronicle of sex and its trials is transposed into the ceremonious history of the modes of production; its trifling aspect fades from view. A principle of explanation emerges after the fact: if sex is so rigorously repressed, this is because it is incompatible with a general and intensive work imperative. At a time when labor capacity was being systematically exploited, how could this capacity be allowed to dissipate itself in pleasurable pursuits, except in those – reduced to a minimum – that enabled it to reproduce itself? [...]

But there may be another reason that makes it so gratifying for us to define the relationship between sex and power in terms of repression: something that one might call the speaker's benefit. If sex is repressed, that is, condemned to prohibition, nonexistence, and silence, then the mere fact that one is speaking about it has the appearance of a deliberate transgression. A person who holds forth in such language places himself to a certain extent outside the reach of power; he upsets established law; he somehow anticipates the coming freedom. This explains the solemnity with which one speaks of sex nowadays. When they had to allude to it, the first demographers and psychiatrists of the nineteenth century thought it advisable to excuse themselves for asking their readers to dwell on matters so trivial and base. But for decades now, we have found it difficult to speak on the subject without striking a different pose: we are conscious of defying established power, our tone of voice shows that we know we are being subversive, and we ardently conjure away the present and appeal to the future, whose day will be hastened by the contribution we believe we are making. Something that smacks of revolt, of promised freedom, of the coming age of a different law, slips easily into this discourse on sexual oppression. Some of the ancient functions of prophecy are reactivated therein. Tomorrow sex will be good again. Because this repression is affirmed, one can discreetly bring into coexistence concepts which the fear of ridicule or the bitterness of history prevents most of us from putting side by side: revolution and happiness; or revolution and a different body, one that is newer and more beautiful; or indeed, revolution and pleasure. What sustains our eagerness to speak of sex in terms of repression is doubtless this opportunity to speak out against the powers that be, to utter truths and promise bliss, to link together enlightenment, liberation, and manifold pleasures; to pronounce a discourse that combines the fervor of knowledge, the determination to change the laws, and the longing for the garden of earthly delights. This is perhaps what also explains the market value attributed not only to what is said about sexual repression, but also to the mere fact of lending an ear to those who would eliminate the effects of repression. Ours is, after all, the only civilization in which officials are paid to listen to all and sundry impart the secrets of their sex: as if the urge to talk about it, and the interest one hopes to arouse by doing so, have far surpassed the possibilities of being heard, so that some individuals have even offered their ears for hire.

[...] My aim is to examine the case of a society which has been loudly castigating itself for its hypocrisy for more than a century, which speaks verbosely of its own silence, takes great pains to relate in detail the things it does not say, denounces the powers it exercises, and promises to liberate itself from the very laws that have made it function. I would like to explore not only these discourses but also the will that sustains them and the strategic intention that supports them. The question I would like to pose is not, Why are we repressed? but rather, Why do we say, with so much passion and so much resentment against our most recent past, against our present, and against ourselves, that we are repressed? By what spiral did we come to affirm that sex is negated? What led us to show, ostentatiously, that sex is something we hide, to say it is something we silence? And we do all this by formulating the matter in the most explicit terms, by trying to reveal it in its most naked reality, by affirming it in the positivity of its power and its effects. It is certainly legitimate to ask why sex was associated with sin for such a long time – although it would remain to be discovered how this association was formed, and one would have to be careful not to state in a summary and hasty fashion that sex was "condemned" – but we must also ask why we burden ourselves today with so much guilt for having once made sex a sin. What paths have brought us to the point where we are "at fault" with respect to our own sex? And how have we come to be a civilization so peculiar as to tell itself that, through an abuse of power which has not ended, it has long "sinned" against sex? [...]

[...] Why has sexuality been so widely discussed, and what has been said about it? What were the effects of power generated by what was said? What are the links between these discourses, these effects of power, and the pleasures that were invested by them? What knowledge (savoir) was formed as a result of this linkage? The object, in short, is to define the regime of power-knowledge-pleasure that sustains the discourse on human sexuality in our part of the world. The central issue, then (at least in the first instance), is not to determine whether one says yes or no to sex, whether one formulates prohibitions or permissions, whether one asserts its importance or denies its effects, or whether one refines the words one uses to designate it; but to account for the fact that it is spoken about, to discover who does the speaking, the positions and viewpoints from which they speak, the institutions which prompt people to speak about it and which store and distribute the things that are said. What is at issue, briefly, is the overall "discursive fact," the way in which sex is "put into discourse." Hence, too, my main concern will be to locate the forms of power, the channels it takes, and the discourses it permeates in order to reach the most tenuous and individual modes of behavior, the paths that give it access to the rare or scarcely perceivable forms of desire, how it penetrates and controls everyday pleasure – all this entailing effects that may be those of refusal, blockage, and invalidation, but also incitement and intensification: in short, the "polymorphous techniques of power." [The] essential aim [is not] to determine whether these discursive productions and these effects of power lead one to formulate the truth about sex, or on the contrary falsehoods designed to conceal that truth, but rather to bring out the "will to knowledge" that serves as both their support and their instrument.

Let there be no misunderstanding: I do not claim that sex has not been prohibited or barred or masked or misapprehended since the classical age; nor do I even assert that it has suffered these things any less from that period on than before. I do not maintain that the prohibition of sex is a ruse; but it is a ruse to make prohibition into the basic and constitutive element from which one would be able to write the history of what has been said concerning sex starting from the modern epoch. All these negative elements – defenses, censorships, denials – which the repressive hypothesis groups together in one great central mechanism destined to say no, are doubtless only component parts that have a local and tactical role to play in a transformation into discourse, a technology of power, and a will to knowledge that are far from being reducible to the former.

In short, I [search] for instances of discursive production (which also administer silences, to be sure), of the production of power (which sometimes have the function of prohibiting), of the propagation of knowledge (which often cause mistaken beliefs or systematic misconceptions to circulate). [...] A first survey made from this viewpoint seems to indicate that since the end of the sixteenth century, the "putting into discourse of sex," far from undergoing a process of restriction, on the contrary has been subjected to a mechanism of increasing incitement; that the techniques of power exercised over sex have not obeyed a principle of rigorous selection, but rather one of dissemination and implantation of polymorphous sexualities; and that the will to knowledge has not come to a halt in the face of a taboo that must not be lifted, but has persisted in constituting – despite many mistakes, of course – a science of sexuality. [...]

8.2. Romancing the Transgender Native: Rethinking the Use of the "Third Gender" Concept (2002)

Evan B. Towle and Lynn M. Morgan

This essay offers a critical examination of how "third gender" concepts are used in popular American writing by and about transgendered people. Over the past decade there has been an increase in the popular use of cross-cultural examples to provide legitimacy to transgender movements in the United States. Descriptions of the "transgender native" are often drawn from ethnographic portrayals of gender variation written by anthropologists for American audiences. Introductory anthropology textbooks commonly cite the *hijra* of India, the *berdache* of native North America, the *xanith* of the Arabian peninsula, the female husbands of western Africa, and the Sambia (a pseudonym) boys of Papua New Guinea who engage in "semen transactions." Such examples are often glossed together under the "third gender" rubric.

"Third gender" roles and practices were once regarded by most Western readers as exotica, with little relevance to our "modern" societies. These days, however, anthropological accounts of "third gender" variation are used [...] to buttress the argument that Western binary gender systems are neither universal nor innate. Paradoxically, this rise in popularity comes just when some anthropologists are finding serious fault with the "third gender" concept. [...]

We come to this discussion from anthropological experience as well as from personal transsexual experience. As the self-conscious subjects of our own inquiry into how anthropologists and trans-identified individuals alike use transgender-native models, we are ultimately invested in ensuring careful, responsible representation of individuals outside our culture. We are simultaneously committed to supporting transgender/transsexual scholarship, representation, and activism. If a common complaint among trans individuals is that their lives and identities are violated and misrepresented for the goals of scholarship, then it behooves us to make sure that we do not commit the same offense against others for the goal of political advancement. [...]

A BRIEF HISTORY OF "THIRD GENDER" CONCEPTS IN ANTHROPOLOGY

[...] Well before Michel Foucault restored historicity to the study of sexuality, anthropologists had provided ethnographic accounts of gender practices in various cultures. One of the most important analytic contributions was the sex/gender distinction, which made it possible to argue that biological features did not "naturally" correspond to sexual practice, sexual orientation, gender identity, or sexual desire. The sex/gender distinction itself has been confounded and criticized over the years, with critics arguing that anatomical sex as well as sexuality and gender can be socially constructed. Subsequent theories have resulted in an increasingly complex understanding of the intersections among biology, identity, performance, power, and practice. [...]

The term *third gender* was apparently introduced in 1975 by M. Kay Martin and Barbara Voorhies, who employed it to draw attention to the ethnographic evidence that gender categories in some cultures could not be adequately explained with a two-gender framework. This revelation had profound implications for feminist and gender theory as well as for social movements and political activists in the United States, because it allowed them to think outside a dichotomous gender system. Third gender began to be applied to behaviors that transcended or challenged dyadic male-female codes or norms. It was also applied to societies (most of them non-Western) that seemed to provide institutionalized "intermediate" gender concepts and practices.

Gilbert H. Herdt, one of anthropology's most ardent and widely read proponents of the "third gender" concept, has used the term [...] to open the discursive space for analyzing nondichotomous gender categories. But a close reading of Herdt's work suggests that he is motivated to use third gender more by his own dissatisfaction with dualistic theories than by any conviction that the term is ethnographically accurate or adequate. In short, he uses it as a heuristic device, for illustrative purposes. In his preface to *Third Sex, Third Gender* Herdt cautions the reader that the word third should not be taken too literally. [...] Herdt has been influential in introducing non-Western perspectives into the gay rights and transgender movements in the United States. Articles written by Herdt [...] allow transgender activists to argue, loaded with ethnographic ammunition, that they were "born [not into the wrong body but] into the wrong culture."

[...] For many transgender activists and their allies, the cross-cultural perspective provides a welcome alternative to the heavily psychologized, medicalized, and moralistic analyses previously invoked in the West to explain gender variation. [...]

In recent years, the term *transgender* has sometimes replaced *third gender* to designate "gender roles and practices which are not definable in terms of local understandings of gender normativity," but the substitution has not necessarily rectified the attendant epistemological problems. David Valentine argues that the concept of "transgenderism," and the corresponding social movements, arose recently and rapidly in the United States out of specific, identifiable developments in the cultural politics of sexuality. The birth of transgenderism responded to the sentiment among gay and lesbian rights advocates that one's sexual orientation does not reflect on one's gender; that is, "you can be a man and desire a man [...] without any implications for your gender identity as a man," and the same is true if you are a woman (190). This envisioning of gays and lesbians, who are to be seen as identical to heterosexuals in all ways but private sexual practices, removed many individuals – drag queens, butch lesbians, cross-dressers, and others – from the categories "gay" and "lesbian." These individuals, who are different from heterosexual and gender-normative people in other, possibly more conspicuous ways, are left to assume the category "transgender(ed)" (191–3).

The word *transgender* is a trendy signifier. But Valentine argues that it should not be applied incautiously to nonnormative gender practices elsewhere:

> If […] "transgender" has a specific history and set of meanings which implicitly mark it in terms of its difference from US American understandings of "gay," then labeling *bantut* [Philippines] or *travesti* [Brazil] as "transgender" is just as problematic. That is, despite the sensitivity to local practices and beliefs, the use of "transgender" in these ethnographic texts actually relies on the same ontologies of gender and sexuality presupposed by the category "gay" which these authors [Mark Johnson and Don Kulick] so assiduously avoid.

Anthropologists are not immune from the temptation to use the word transgender as a shorthand gloss. […] Valentine points out that they sometimes sweep a variety of nonnormative gender identities under the heading of "transgender" (91). […]

EMANCIPATORY POSSIBILITY MEETS ANALYTIC PARADOX

[…] "Third gender" ideas build on our long-standing cultural fascination with societies that are allegedly less inhibited than our own. "A common and more or less clearly articulated motivation in this corpus of work," Niko Besnier writes, "is to demonstrate that preindustrial societies are more 'tolerant,' 'accepting,' 'approving,' or 'accommodating' of erotic diversity and gender variation than 'the West.'" Thus the "third gender" concept set the stage for celebrating non-Western societies while disparaging Western ones. […]

The "third gender" is a uniquely Western concept produced by a society just beginning to grapple with the theoretical, social, political, and personal consequences of nondichotomous gender variability. It is thus an apt rhetorical and analytic device for the current historical moment, because it can accommodate contradictory social impulses; it signals both tolerance for cultural diversity and adherence to Western categories. Rather than accept uncritically the need for a "third" gender category, though, we should ask how "our" narratives about "them" (cultural others) reflect our own society's contradictory agendas concerning sexuality, gender, and power.

In spite of the obvious imaginative and political potential created by the awareness of gender diversity across cultures, several flaws emerge in the utilization of "third gender" concepts […]:

1 The primordial location. "Third gender" societies are accorded a primordial, foundational location in our thinking, as though they underlay or predated Western gender formulations.

2 Reductionism and exclusionism. The "third gender" concept lumps all nonnormative gender variations into one category, limiting our understandings of the range and diversity of gender ideologies and practices.

3 Typological errors. By identifying "third gender" types, the concept ignores the diversity of experience within categories and glosses over the often contentious processes through which social formations, relations, and hierarchies are created, lived, negotiated, and changed.

4 Inconsistent use of the culture concept. Does culture facilitate or delimit social change?

5 The West versus the rest. "Third gender" concepts may isolate the West, for analytic purposes, from other societies, thereby reinforcing our ethnocentric assumptions; inhibiting us from forging alliances across national or cultural borders; and inducing us to focus on diversity between cultures while ignoring diversity, or the complexities of social change, within them.

[In popular writing the] reader will find the figure of the transgender native woven throughout the discussion. This figure is a literary trope often used in transgender testimonial writing to invoke longing for the other. It serves in several texts as a generic, seductive figure who lives an idealized existence in a utopian place and time. The transgender native is portrayed not as a normal, fallible human being living within the gender constraints of his or her own society but as an appealing, exalted, transcendent being (often a hero or healer). He or she can be imagined (e.g., as a transgender ancestor), discovered (e.g., on a trip to a foreign land), enacted (e.g., as one's own persona), or simply cited to justify one's own argument. [...]

CONCLUSION

We join an increasing number of anthropologists who caution against using caricatures of other cultures to advance locally situated arguments. The "third gender" concept encourages Westerners to make poorly informed assumptions about the meaning and significance of gender dynamics in non-Western societies. [...]

The issues we raise in this essay ask whose knowledge is authorized and legitimated in the struggle for greater freedom and knowledge. Debates over appropriate gender behavior have not always included the input of gay, lesbian, bisexual, and transgendered individuals and collectivities, but the rise of social movements has made space for these voices. [...]

Transgender and transsexual activists need not invoke mythical gender warriors to support the idea that individuals should be free to express and embody themselves as they see fit or to justify their existence. (If warriors are sought, they are here.) Nor do they need to look elsewhere for acceptance. (Acceptance comes through understanding and mutual respect.) The potential that trans bodies and trans lives have to shed light on normative gender relations is immense. Who else has the opportunity to live these questions: What is the difference between women and men? Through what acts are gender identities communicated? What does failing to communicate a gender identity mean for social interactions?

Some use this potential to enable the study of gender "transgressions" in the United States to help illuminate what it means for everyone to inhabit gendered bodies. [...] Research that positions the trans body and life as foundational to the study of gender allows for the possibility of our (transgender/transsexual) greater freedom and also for greater knowledge about how we, collectively, have come to this point in the social life of bodies.

Rather than reify or romanticize presumed gender variability in non-Western societies, we would prefer to see greater attention given to the historical and social contexts in which gendered and sexualized bodies and relationships are produced, reproduced, and transformed. The examination of context should include a critical interrogation of the circumstances under which other cultural examples are brought into American gender discourse. Why are such examples salient now? To what end have they become so? When we look at gender variability in other cultures, whom do we see and not see, and why? What are those individuals doing, and how are their actions constrained or facilitated by their social, political, and religious milieus? How much wishful thinking is evident in the way that cross-cultural evidence is mobilized and popularized in the United States? Is such evidence used to legitimate certain gender agendas (e.g., bodily reconfiguration through hormones or surgery) over others (e.g., symbolic or spiritually based gender reassignment)? These contexts will increasingly be transnational because of the heavy traffic across borders in images, bodies, ideas, technologies, and transgender political activism. What new social movements are created by connections made across cultural and national borders? What new possibilities for social and political solidarity might be fostered? The sensitivity with which we address these questions will depend on our ability to understand the limits of "third gender" thinking.

REFERENCES

Besnier, Niko. 1996. "Polynesian Gender Liminality through Time and Space." In *Third Sex, Third Gender: Beyond Sexual Dimorphism in Culture and History*, edited by Gilbert H. Herdt, 285–328. New York: Zone.

Herdt, Gilbert H. 1981. *Guardians of the Flutes: Idioms of Masculinity*. New York: McGraw-Hill.

———. 1987. *The Sambia: Ritual and Gender in New Guinea*. New York: Holt, Rinehart and Winston.

———. 1996. "Introduction: Third Sexes and Third Genders," In *Third Sex, Third Gender: Beyond Sexual Dimorphism in Culture and History*, edited by Gilbert H. Herdt. New York: Zone.

Martin, M. Kay, and Barbara Voorhies. 1975. "Supernumerary Sexes." In *Female of the Species*. New York: Columbia University Press.

Valentine, David. 2000. "'I Know What I Am': The Category 'Transgender' in the Construction of Contemporary U.S. American Conceptions of Gender and Sexuality." Ph.D. diss., New York University, 90.

8.3. Transgender History, Homonormativity, and Disciplinarity (2008)

Susan Stryker

ANTIHOMONORMATIVE TRANSGENDER HISTORY

As important as queer identitarian disputes have been for present and future transgender politics, they have been equally important for reinterpreting the queer past. I first started researching the transgender history of San Francisco, particularly in relation to the city's gay and lesbian community, while participating in the Bay Area's broader queer culture during the early 1990s. In 1991, during my final year as a PhD student in U.S. history at the University of California at Berkeley, the same year I began transitioning from male to female, I became deeply involved with an organization then known as the Gay and Lesbian Historical Society of Northern California. That organization, now the GLBT Historical Society, houses the preeminent collection of primary source materials on San Francisco Bay Area gay, lesbian, bisexual, and transgender communities, and one of the best collections of sexuality-related materials anywhere in the world. I started there as a volunteer in the archives, joined the board of directors in 1992, and later became the first executive director of the organization, from 1999 to 2003.

Through my long and intimate association with the GLBT Historical Society, as well as through two years of postdoctoral funding from the Sexuality Research Fellowship Program of the Social Science Research Council, I had ample opportunity to exhaustively research the status of transgender issues within gay and lesbian organizations and communities in post–World War II San Francisco. I was able to scan all the periodical literature, community newspapers, collections of personal papers, organizational records, ephemera, and visual materials – tens of thousands of items – for transgender-related content. [...]

In the centerfold of the program for the first Gay Pride Parade in San Francisco, held in 1972, I found a description of a 1966 riot in San Francisco's Tenderloin District, in which drag queens and gay hustlers banded together at a popular late-night hangout called Gene

Compton's Cafeteria to fight back against police harassment and social oppression. The key text [from Broshears 1972] reads as follows:

In the streets of the Tenderloin, at Turk and Taylor on a hot August night in 1966, Gays rose up angry at the constant police harassment of the drag-queens by the police. It had to be the first ever recorded violence by Gays against police anywhere. For on that evening when the SFPD paddy wagon drove up to make their "usual" sweeps of the streets, Gays this time did not go willingly. It began when the police came into a cafeteria, still located there at Turk and Taylor, Compton's, to do their usual job of hassling the drag-queens and hair-fairies and hustlers sitting at the table. This was with the permission of management, of course. But when the police grabbed the arm of one of the transvestites, he threw his cup of coffee in the cop's face, and with that, cups, saucers, and trays began flying around the place, and all directed at the police. They retreated outside until reinforcements arrived, and the Compton's management ordered the place closed, and with that, the Gays began breaking out every window in the place, and as they ran outside to escape the breaking glass, the police tried to grab them and throw them into the paddy wagon, but they found this no easy task for Gays began hitting them "below the belt" and drag-queens smashing them in the face with their extremely heavy purses. A police car had every window broken, a newspaper shack outside the cafeteria was burned to the ground, and general havoc was raised that night in the Tenderloin. The next night drag-queens, hair-fairies, conservative Gays, and hustlers joined in a picket of the cafeteria, which would not allow drags back in again. It ended with the newly installed plate glass windows once more being smashed. The Police Community Relations Unit began mediating the conflict, which was never fully resolved, which ended in a group called VANGUARD being formed of the street peoples and a lesbian group of street people being formed called the STREET ORPHANS, both of which later became the old GAY LIBERATION FRONT in San Francisco, and is today called the GAY ACTIVISTS ALLIANCE.

The story seemed important in several respects. First, what reportedly happened at Compton's Cafeteria bore obvious similarities to the famous Stonewall uprising in New York in 1969, where the militant phase of gay liberation is commonly supposed to have begun, but reputedly preceded it by three years. How the San Francisco gay activist community positioned the Compton's story vis-à-vis Stonewall in their first commemorative Gay Pride Parade was clearly intended as an early revisionist account of gay liberation history. Furthermore, the inciting incident of the riot was described as an act of antitransgender discrimination, rather than an act of discrimination against sexual orientation. At the time I came across this source in 1995, the role of drag queens in the Stonewall riots had become a site of conflict between transgender and normative gay/lesbian histories – transgender activists pointed to the act of mythologizing Stonewall as the "birth" of gay liberation as a homonormative co-optation of gender queer resistance, while homonormative gay and lesbian commentators tended to downplay the significance of antidrag oppression at Stonewall – and whatever I could learn about the Compton's incident would certainly inform that debate. The 1972 document also related a genealogy of gay liberation activism at odds with the normative accounts – one rooted in the socioeconomics of the multiethnic Tenderloin sex-work ghetto rather than in campus-based activism oriented toward counter-cultural white youth of middle-class origin. For all these reasons, the Compton's Cafeteria riot became a central focus of my research into San Francisco's transgender history and its intersectional relationship to the history of gay and lesbian communities.

Although the 1972 document proved factually inaccurate in several particulars (the picketing happened before the riot, for example), I was ultimately able to verify its basic account of the Compton's Cafeteria riot, and to situate that event in a history of transgender community formation and politicization that both complemented and contested homonormative gay and lesbian history. Most important, I was able to connect the location and timing of the riot to social, political, geographical, and historical circumstances in San Francisco in ways that the Stonewall story had never connected gay liberation discourse to similar circumstances in New York – thereby opening up new ways to think about the relationship between identity politics and broader material conditions. The 1966 riot at Compton's Cafeteria took place at the intersection of several broad social issues that continue to be of concern today, such as discriminatory policing practices in minority communities, the lack of minority access to appropriate health care, elitist urban land-use policies, the unsettling domestic consequences of foreign wars, and civil rights campaigns that aim to expand individual liberties and social tolerance on matters of sexuality and gender. [...]

HOMONORMATIVE DISCIPLINARITY

Although the history of the Compton's Cafeteria riot provides a productive point of critique and revision for homonormative accounts of the recent history of sexual identity communities and movements, most knowledge of this event has circulated through works of public history (most notably the 2005 public television documentary *Screaming Queens: The Riot at Compton's Cafeteria*), work by nonacademic writers, and in community-based publications, rather than through professional academic channels. In those few instances in which this history has been examined in peer-reviewed journals, the articles have been placed, as this one has been, in sections of the journals set aside for uses other than feature articles. In the one instance where this has not been the case, the article was written by another (non-transgendered) scholar who interviewed me and made use of primary source documents I directed her to, in order to relate the Compton's Cafeteria riot to her own research interest in the sociology of historical memory. I point this out not as a complaint – it was my own decision to pursue the public history dissemination of my research findings; I actually guest-edited a journal issue that put my own research into the back matter and anonymized my authorship, and I have eagerly collaborated with other scholars who have never failed to accurately and appropriately cite the use of my research in their own projects. My aim, rather, is to call needed attention to the micropolitical practices through which the radical implications of transgender knowledges can become marginalized. Even in contexts such as this special homonormativities issue of *Radical History Review*, which explicitly called for transgender scholarship that could generate "new analytical frameworks for talking about lesbian, gay, bisexual, transgender, and queer history that expand and challenge current models of identity and community formation as well as models of political and cultural resistance," transgender knowledges are far too easily subjugated to what Michel Foucault [2003] once called "the hierarchies of erudition."

In my original abstract for this issue, I proposed not only to recount the little-known history of the Compton's Cafeteria riot but also to call attention to the multiple normativizing frames of reference that kept the Compton's story "hidden in plain sight" for so long – the confluence of class, race, and gender considerations, as well as the homonormative gaze that did not construct transgender subjects, actions, embodiments, or intentions as the objects of its desire. I wanted, too, to make methodologically explicit the critical role of embodied difference in the practice of archival research. As a range of new scholarship on the recent so-called archival turn in the humanities begins to make evident, embodiment – that contingent accomplishment through which the histories of our identities become invested in our corporeal space – not only animates the research query but modulates access to the archive, in both its physical and its intellectual arrangement. Discussing how my transsexual embodiment figured into reading a gay and lesbian archive against the grain served the larger purpose of calling critical attention to homonormative constructions of knowledge embedded in the content and organization of the archive itself. My goal was to offer a radical critique not just of historiography but of the political epistemology of historical knowledge production.

Because the tone of what I proposed was deemed "personal," however, due to how I situated my own research activities as part of the narrative, and because, I suspect, I tend to work outside the academy, I was invited to contribute an essay to either the "Reflections" or "Public History" section of *Radical History Review*, rather than a feature article. I felt some reservations in doing so because my intent had been to do something else. "Reflections" are not as intellectually rigorous as the documented arguments expected in feature articles, and "Public History," as distinguished from what academic historians do, can come off as a form of popularization in which knowledge produced by specialists is transmitted to the consuming masses through less intellectually accomplished intermediaries. The journal's own division of knowledge into "less formal" and "more formal" categories, and the positioning of my work within this two-tiered economy, would replicate the very hierarchies I had set out to critique by containing what I had to say within a structurally less legitimated space.

The most basic act of normativizing disciplinarity at work here is not directly related to the increasingly comfortable fit between gender-normative homosexuality and neoliberal policy. It is rooted in a more fundamental and culturally pervasive disavowal of intrinsically diverse modes of bodily being as the lived ground of all knowing and of all knowledge production. In an epistemological regime structured by the subject-object split, the bodily situatedness of knowing becomes divorced from the status of formally legitimated objective knowledge; experiential knowledge of the material effects of one's own antinormative bodily difference on the production and reception of what one knows consequently becomes delegitimated as merely subjective. This in turn circumscribes the radical potential of that knowledge to critique other knowledge produced from other bodily locations, equally partial and contingent, which have been vested with the prerogatives of a normativity variously figured as white, masculinist, heterosexist, or Eurocentric – as feminism, communities of color, and third world voices have long maintained, and as the disabled, intersexed, and transgendered increasingly contend.

The peculiar excitement of academic humanities work at this moment in time lies, in my estimation, in the potential of interdisciplinary critical work to produce new strategies through which disruptive knowledges can dislodge the privileges of normativity. Breaking "personal voice" away from the taint of "mere" subjective reflection, and recuperating embodied knowing as a formally legitimated basis of knowledge production, is one such disruptive strategy. Deploying disciplinary distinctions that foreclose this possibility is not. [...]

Homonormativity, I conclude, is more than an accommodation to neoliberalism in its macropolitical manifestations. It is also an operation at the micropolitical level, one that aligns gay interests with dominant constructions of knowledge and power that disqualify the very modes of knowing threatening to disrupt the smooth functioning of normative space and that displace modes of embodiment calling into question the basis of authority from which normative voices speak. Because transgender phenomena unsettle the categories on which the normative sexualities depend, their articulation can offer compelling opportunities for contesting the expansion of neoliberalism's purview through homonormative strategies of minority assimilation. And yet, even well-intentioned antihomonormative critical practices that take aim at neoliberalism can fall short of their goal when they fail to adequately account for the destabilizing, cross-cutting differences within sexual categories that transgender issues represent. Such critical practices can function in unintentionally homonormative ways that circumvent and circumscribe, rather than amplify, the radical potential of transgender phenomena to profoundly disturb the normative – even in so seemingly small a thing as where an article gets placed in a journal. Creating a proper space for radical transgender scholarship, in the double sense of scholarship on transgender issues and of work by transgender scholars, should be a vital part of any radically antinormative intellectual and political agenda.

REFERENCES

Broshears, Raymond. 1972. "History of Christopher Street WestSF." Gay Pride: The Official Voice of the Christopher Street West Parade '72 Committee of San Francisco, California, June 25, 8.
Foucault, Michel. 2003. *Society Must Be Defended: Lectures at the College de France, 1975–1976*, trans. by David Macey, 7–8. New York: Picador, 2003.

8.4. One Way or Another: Erotic Subjectivity in Cuba (2012)

Jafari Allen

One afternoon in Central Havana [...] Lili, a 25-year-old *mulata*, was walking out of her apartment wearing bright orange Capri pants, flat sandals, and a floral shirt tied just below her breasts. Those of us on the street that afternoon were witnessing a rare occasion. Lili was leaving home in the brightest part of the day to attend a party for a friend, La India, who had returned on a visit from North America. A few neighbors had already suspected Lili's avocation. Brightly colored spandex, Lycra dresses, and fancy hose hanging on the apartment balcony at the back of the building suggested to them that the young man they knew as 33-year-old Octavio, whom they suspected of being a *pájaro* (sissy; lit. bird) because of his effeminate gait and public shyness, was actually a transformista (transvestite, or drag queen). Instead of cowering in darkened doorways, as I had witnessed her do on a few occasions, or quickly getting into a tourist taxi, Lili sauntered down Calle Romay to the Malecón (Havana's famous seawall boulevard), where she flagged a *colectivo* (jitney cab). The moment Lili appeared, she was greeted by stunned silence, then laughter, sucking of teeth, and other gestures of disdain. Some of the men around me commented that Octavio was a "sick faggot who ought to be put away" as a disgrace. [...]

Then, an old woman from my apartment building two doors away from Octavio's threw a mango peel toward Lili from her window. A litany of epithets was thrown as well: *maricón* (faggot), *puta* (whore, fem. form), *sucio* (dirty, masc. form), and *loca* (crazy, also sissy, fem. form). At first, Lili seemed slightly bemused, but she ignored the comments, as any woman would do in the street. Finally, before reaching the corner to cross the Malecón to catch the *colectivo*, and as the comments grew uglier, Lili replied loudly to one of the insulters, "Go ask your father how good a whore I am ... I still have bigger balls than you!"

Later on, I asked a few of the neighborhood dominoes players what they thought of the scene. [...] Although no one personally knew of a case in which a homosexual or *transformista* had been abused by anyone "other than their own family, a *bugarrón* (insertive sex partner), or the police," they agreed that Lili's midday walk had been a dangerous gauntlet.

But Octavio asserts that Cubans owe him respect because of his contributions to mass organizations and his job in one of the regulatory agencies. [...] For Octavio–Lili, no one is more embattled and struggling for full expression of humanity – as Cuba portrays itself – than the black transformista worker. Thus, Octavio–Lili is undeterred by the street-corner detractors. When I asked Lili why she did not merely travel with clothing to change into at the party, she told me that she was "just so tired." [Her friend] La India's visit after many years in North America reminded Octavio how he had allowed custom to inhibit self-expression *en la calle* (in the street) and in the daylight. When I probed the motivation for Lili's bold walk, Octavio insisted, "I too can walk the streets of my country." [...]

The central ethnographic scene here is set during Cuba's Special Period, which highlighted fissures in Cuba's gender, sexual, class, and racial terrain. The Special Period was brought on by the dissolution of the Soviet Union and Cuban state inefficiency and was worsened by a tightening of the U.S. blockade. It reached its height in 1993 as the island's economic crisis broadened. [...] During the Special Period, Cubans – especially blacks and queers, who had been shut out of other avenues of economic and wider social participation – were opened up to greater varieties of representational practices and cultural expression because of a conjuncture of a greater array of choices, changes in the capacity of the impaired state to repress those expressions, and powerful global forces exerting their own hegemonies on local ones – making the position and potential "politics of deviance" (Cohen 2004) of black (and) queer subjects especially problematic and promising. [...]

THE RADICAL POTENTIAL OF EROTIC SUBJECTIVITY

[...] The first points in the architecture of resistance are found in the deployment of the erotic subjectivity of a thinking, desiring, decision-making subject, willing to transgress. Erotic subjectivity is an alternate way of knowing, looking to one's own lived experiences and one's own intentions and desires, which are certainly complexly made but also more "authentic" than ways of knowing that are imposed or imbued by others. It can be used tactically or strategically. Out of this embodied experience, people may create a counterpublic in which new forms of affective and erotic relations and rules of public and private engagement not only inform choice [...] but also in fact condition new choices and new politics.

Octavio's experience attending boarding schools in the provinces, where he experienced greater freedom than in the city and where he metaphorically and literally "could breathe easier," informs his outlook on the Cuban Revolution. Octavio's parents hail from one of the most marginal sections of Havana and are grateful to the revolution for providing educational opportunities for their three children, all around the same age. [...] Octavio remembers how hard his parents worked to educate themselves later in life and how they encouraged him to continue with his technical studies and to pursue his love of the arts, with the support of state training. [...]

Octavio receives a share of his parents' household monthly allotment of sugar and tickets for fresh bread and a few cuts of meat. [...] Octavio brings his family's household things like cooking oil, imported cookies, and whiskey, which are only available in dollar stores. These are goods paid for by Lili's highly unofficial jobs as entertainer, party hostess, and occasional sex laborer. No one in the family asks the source of these goodies or questions how Octavio can afford to live apart from the family. [...] Despite the traffic in and out of his apartment, two of his friends described Octavio as someone who prefers to keep to himself. Although Octavio is well aware of the efforts of [...] the National Sex Education Center of Cuba to provide space for transgender individuals to gather and to encourage social recognition for lesbians and gays as well, participation in this new "vanguard" of Cuban revolutionary struggle holds little interest for Octavio–Lili. Octavio insists on remaining discreet, even with his friends, because the only collective he recognizes is "the Cuban people." [...]

COLOR DRAG

First, liquid foundation makeup and powder two or three shades lighter than Octavio's own skin color is applied. Though he and his mother share a rich brown skin color, Octavio cannot even imagine being a tobacco-colored woman. Lili draws lips covering only two-thirds of Octavio's actual lips. Eye shadow is used to further contour an already aquiline nose. Then, Octavio adds hip and buttock padding under a sort of leotard, being careful to tuck his penis between his legs. Finally, "wet and wild" hair extensions, braided from the base then combed out and spritzed with water for the appearance of natural curls, bring out the phenotypical features that suggest *mestizaje*. Lili's choice of songs to lip-synch – from Mariah Carey, Shakira, or Beyonce, for example – replete with hair tossing and shoulder shaking, is as essential to the illusion as high heels and feminine bravura. That Lili has begun taking this performance beyond the bounds of fiestas and carnivals [...] is a significant overstep. Lili has moved from the private sphere, under the cover of night, in which movements between liminal or illicit spaces is mitigated by the use of private taxis, to the sunlit streets of Cuba.

Perhaps, Octavio thought, Lili could do shows abroad like La India and save money to build a large extension on Octavio's parents' house. To do this, however, the transformation from man to woman would have to continue to be attenuated by color drag from negro to mulata. It is important for Lili to be desirable by the patrons who tip her for performances at parties. This suggests a form of passing or whitening that is not, of course, completely believable to all audiences but that is convincing enough to some individuals for it to have the effect of lessening perceived and real difficulties associated with blackness and increasing one's possibilities. The construction, or making, of the self has historicity – important racialized and gendered resonances with important material effects. [...] Octavio's erotic "transvestic" practices not only transgress the boundaries of gender but also pointedly question the potent symbolism and power associated with the trope of the mulata. [...]

Thus, to understand the racial formation of Cuba, and much of the Americas, one must grapple with complexities of *blanqueamiento*, or whitening, which at once seeks to disappear race and instantiates antiblack racism. The denial of race and uneven, conditional inclusion of people of color was one of the rhetorical lynchpins of the Cuba Libre (Cuban

Independence) movement (de la Fuente 2001; Ferrer 1999; Helg 1995). Denying race and racism through a celebration of "racial mixture" became the established ideology of nationalists because it could ascribe to black and other Cubans of color a measure of belonging – recognizing their crucial role in ending Spanish colonialism – while maintaining the status quo of European Creole (structurally white) control. [...] The material conditions of African-descendant Cubans have improved dramatically since the 1959 revolution. Still, there remains, on one hand, a vociferous denial of not only racism (Moore 1989, 2008) but also race, and, on the other hand, an acute awareness and anxiety about skin color and other phenotypical markers like hair texture and shapes of noses, lips, and eyes. [...] Even though the reproduction in which Octavio participates, through what I am calling "color drag," does not follow the usual cultural routes of whitening by "improving the race" or "cleansing blood lines" through sexual reproduction with a woman with lighter skin, straighter hair, and "sharper" features than his, it is no less conditioned by the Caribbean and Latin American cultural imperative of blanqueamiento. [...]

THE SIGN OF THE "HOMOSEXUAL"

Color drag is certainly about race, but it is no less complexly about gender and sexuality. Whereas to be black is to fail to be whitened into mestizo eligibility, to be homosexual is to fail the test of Cuban manhood altogether. Lesbians are effectively erased. Still, what makes Octavio identifiable in the street as homosexual is not how he prefers to have sex. In fact, because he nearly exclusively assumes the (anally and orally) insertive role with his lovers and clients, some scholars would bracket him out of the homosexual category entirely. Thus, by *homosexual*, I refer not to sexual behavior or identity exclusively but, rather, to a complex set of signifiers, which includes these but more centrally features, for example, a man's deportment, physicality, and vocal resonance. Octavio's life out of Lili drag – as a slightly effeminate, dark-skinned black gay man – exemplifies this. It is his gender performance, even out of drag – his swishy gait, expressive gesticulation, bright clothing, longish hair, and relatively high vocal range – that makes him identifiable as a *loca* (queen). Many men, of various sexual practices, are *entendido* – have sex with men who are "discreet" and typically masculine – and therefore often do not suffer all of the social consequences of homosexual identification. Male homosexuals, and those assumed to be so because of putatively effeminate gender performance, were objects of revolutionary government policies and campaigns to contain, reeducate, or eliminate their "unruliness" – most dramatically through forced-work camps. [...]

DRAWING FINER LINES OF AN ARCHITECTURE OF "RESISTANCE"

[... C]an the resistance of color drag be liberatory when the performance so clearly indexes black erasure? Octavio–Lili responds to cultural expectations and interpellations in two very distinct ways in one performance – first, resistance to norms of silence and invisibility surrounding non-heteronormative individuals and, second, accommodation to racial–gender beauty norms – which point to larger understandings of worth and personhood. At the same time that this racial performance troubles assumptions about gender, sexuality, and sexual behavior, it fits squarely within the dominative mode. Octavio's loyalty to old tropes of color and sexual hierarchy that he plays out – scripts, really – perhaps also shows him to be an agent of Octavio–Lili's oppression.

This story illustrates a subjectivity that cannot become an "identity" because of Octavio's commitment to remain politically isolated from other transformistas and transgender individuals who might have served as allies if not fellow travelers. His disidentification with revolutionary politics and color hierarchies ironically reflects both profound loyalty and ambivalence, and it also shows that the early black feminist conception of "standpoint" (Collins 1990) is in need of a supplement, which ethnography can provide. In standpoint epistemology, a shared position of disempowerment within a hierarchy of power – which can be understood as a perspective from which one both sees and can be seen – produces unique and often oppositional knowledges, and this positioning in the political economy constitutes individuals as certain types of subjects. [...] Still, this grounding in experience does not fully account for radical or revolutionary practices, because individual experience is especially susceptible to uninterrogated private standpoints when it is unconnected to a movement or community project. [...]

REFERENCES

Cohen, Cathy J. 2004. "Deviance as Resistance: A New Research Agenda for the Study of Black Politics." *Du Bois Review: Social Science Research on Race* 1 (1): 27–45. https://doi.org/10.1017/S1742058X21000217.

Collins, Patricia Hill. 1990. *Black Feminist Thought: Knowledge, Consciousness, and the Politics of Empowerment*. New York: Routledge.

de la Fuente, Alejandro. 2001. *A Nation for All: Race, Inequality, and Politics in Twentieth-Century Cuba*. Chapel Hill: University of North Carolina Press.

Ferrer, Ada. 1999. *Insurgent Cuba: Race, Nation, and Revolution, 1868–1898*. Chapel Hill: University of North Carolina Press.

Gilliam, Angela. 1991. "Women's Equality and National Liberation." In *Third World Women and the Politics of Feminism*, edited by Chandra Talpade Mohanty, Ann Russo, and Lourdes Torres, 215–36. Bloomington: Indiana University Press.

Helg, Aline. 1995. *Our Rightful Share: The Afro-Cuban Struggle for Equality, 1886–1912*. Chapel Hill: University of North Carolina Press.

Moore, Carlos. 1989. *Castro, the Blacks, and Africa*. Los Angeles: University of California, Center for Afro-American Studies.

8.5. Play Aunties and Dyke Bitches: Gender, Generation, and the Ethics of Black Queer Kinship (2019)

Savannah Shange

GENDER JUDO: DESIRE AS A WEAPON

Using the weight of my whole body, I pushed Kairo into the empty computer-lab-cum-library and shut the door behind me. Her gleaming red-and-white Jordans paced back and forth, baby dreads bouncing between her razor-sharp line up and the collar of her oversized white Polo. Having broken up my fair share of scuffles during a decade of youth work, I knew the drill: separate, de-escalate, reflect, repair. This one caught me by surprise, because La'Nea and Kairo were more likely to be seen cuddling than scrapping. […] I arrived just in time to see the rage on La'Nea's face and grabbed Kairo to separate them.

Down the hall, I could hear the thump-thump of La'Nea's sparkly Fuggs running toward us, her voice echoing epithets. I worked on the de-escalation phase, sitting down with her and reminding her of the stakes she faced while on probation. "Kairo – it don't matter what she said, you don't never put your hands on a woman. Plus you can't afford to be doing this shit – she is just … upset." I tried not to divulge my own suspicions about why La'Nea provoked a confrontation with Kairo in the hallway of San Francisco's Robeson Justice Academy minutes earlier, goading her into hitting her in the face.

La'Nea crammed her cocoa face into the tiny glass window of the computer lab. She punctuated her barrage of language with claps and head swivels so fierce that her high ponytail threatened to tumble off of its tightly brushed foundation.

"Dyke bitch! You wanna be a man, come out here and whoop my ass then! Always tryna look like a dude – you ain't no fuckin' dude!"

La'Nea's latter epithet almost lands heavier than the first: "bitch" is an attempt to melt away every meticulous inch Kairo had carved out between herself and the inherited image of womanhood. You ain't no fuckin' dude. La'Nea advertises her own learned equivalence between masculinity and violence when she tells Kairo, "you wanna be a man, come out here and whoop my ass then!" Here, to be a man is to beat a woman, laying bare the range of antagonisms that lie within the frame of The Black Family, and the constrained set of choices masquerading as the "agency" available to Black girls and women surviving the war at home. La'Nea renders masculinity – or perhaps more precisely, manhood – as a weapon always already formed against her. I knew well enough how La'Nea had to survive the men she loved; I was there when she came back to school crying and enraged one evening after her brother hit her with a hanger in her own home. Knowing that teachers were mandatory reporters, but not wanting to call the police on her own blood, she used the school bureaucracy as a self-defense tactic. Both La'Nea's invocation of intimate violence in the halls of her high school, and her ways of using that school as a strategy for protection, point to the flimsiness of the line between public and private space, particularly for Black women.

After being called a dyke, Kairo ran up on the door that I narrowly beat her to [...], bellowing and grabbing her crotch. "Oh, but you want the dick though! You want the dick though!" callously referencing La'Nea's long-time crush on her. Kairo fought back with gender judo, weaponizing the force of La'Nea's proto-femme desire against her while reasserting a sovereign form of masculinity.

By now I was out of breath, sandwiched between the two kids fighting to open the door I was leaning against to keep shut. Tears ambushed me as I shoved Kairo away from the door and shouted at my co-workers to get La'Nea back to her own space – this was too close, too raw, too much of our collective business in the street. As a baby gay, I too was outed by a peer as a form of retaliation, and the sense-memory of that social exposure overwhelmed me. I felt La'Nea's betrayal as my own in the midst of the fight, and probably pushed Kairo back with more force than necessary, a self-defense once removed. [...]

FRISCO GEOGRAPHIES: MAPPING A RESEARCH CONTEXT

Undergirding the tussle between La'Nea and Kairo over the boundaries of Black masculine practice are the broader penal technologies that work to confine and expunge unruly blackness in school settings. [...] Kairo, whose given name Juanita was ignored by peers and school staff alike, was one of several studs – or masculine-presenting people assigned female at birth – who had attended Robeson over the past decade. In reflection of the interlocking violences of gender normativity, toxic masculinity, and the carceral state, young studs of color in Frisco were hypercriminalized, and Kairo was no exception. At 16, she was on probation for the felony theft of an iPhone, and any formal write-up of the fight could mean her going back to jail. Even though Kairo was first to put hands on La'Nea, the staff specifically decided not to suspend Kairo or call her PO in an attempt to protect her from the tributaries of the school-to-prison pipeline. No such accommodation was made for La'Nea: her disciplinary file was too thin to merit an exception. The discrepancy between the disciplinary consequences for La'Nea and Kairo reveals the confluence of high risk and high reward that masculinity entails: the criminalization associated with Black boys and men stretched beyond those assigned male at birth to ensnare Kairo in the penal system, even as the hypervisibility of Black boys as victims of the system earned her protection within the anti-carceral logics of the progressive school. La'Nea's putatively unremarkable performance of Black girlhood afforded her no protection in the eyes of the state; no self to defend, indeed.

[…] Robeson is a small, in-district public high school serving about 250 students. It has an explicit social justice vision of "liberation," and yet is funded by the austerity-driven carceral state of California. […] For most of the past 10 years, Robeson was the Blackest high school in the least Black city in America, and functioned as one of the few remaining Black-serving institutions in the city. In this context, the school also served as a homeplace of sorts, its four hallways repurposed by Black students and staff alike as we stole away from class and meetings to create spaces of Black social life. […]

Because of its social justice theme, Robeson appears to be the complete inverse of the "paradigm of overt homophobic discourse and the removal of race" that one might find at a typical urban California high school. This is a school where the white administrator has asked police to park down the hill instead of in the parking lot whenever they have business in the building, so as not to create a militarized environment. Freshman Humanities classes analyze Huey Newton's speech about solidarity with gay struggle and are assigned Carla Trujillo's lesbian coming-of-age novel, *What Night Brings*, as required reading. Robeson is the best-case scenario for progressive state reform, and yet is still governed by the logics of anti-Blackness and heteronormativity, as revealed by its gender-biased and racially dispro-portionate disciplinary practices. […]

[… T]he majority people-of-color staff at Robeson was relatively gender- and sexuality-affirming. Trans-identified students were given a key to the teacher's bathroom if they felt uncomfortable in any of the student restrooms, and one year a Xicanx stud was crowned Prom King. I was one of several out gay teachers at Robeson – the visibility of queerness at Robeson is part of the matrix of sexual politics in neoliberal San Francisco. […] The context of Robeson allows us to examine schools as not just hostile territories to queer teachers or students in isolation, but also potentially as sites of the collaborative, contested production of queer communities of color.

AN INTIMACY AT WAR: CONFLICT AS MODE OF KINSHIP

[…] My relationship with La'Nea was in some ways reflective of what Mel Michelle Lewis found in her research on Black lesbian professors who embodied a "femme 'auntie' per-formance," in which "there is this familiarity, but at the same time, it's very authoritative." La'Nea and other students actually called me "play auntie" – I wasn't warm enough to be a "school mom," […] nor was I wise enough to be "everybody Grandma." […] As La'Nea's play auntie, I was the one who drove her to the public health clinic when she had a false STI alarm, and consoled her when Kairo started publicly dating a perfectly fine Xicanx girl, even though she and La'Nea had been lightweight talking. La'Nea (probably rightfully) felt wronged, and sitting on the couch in my classroom we sifted through layers of loyalty, col-orism, and […] good old-fashioned teenage ennui. It was on that same couch that La'Nea checked me for my failures as a femme auntie.

"How could you choose her over me?"

Steely-eyed and wet-faced, La'Nea demanded to know my answer. [...] Turns out that when I pulled Kairo out of the hall and away from her, La'Nea experienced my departure as a betrayal: I chose to prioritize Kairo's needs over hers. Despite my intentions to keep La'Nea safe, she was right, and I failed in the femme4femme imperative to destabilize heteropatriarchy by elevating the feminine-of-center – *hoes before bros.*

[...] When I chose to grab Kairo, some part of me was aware of her criminal record, and the stakes of getting in trouble for her. At best, it was care work, at worst it was coddling. At the same time, I had faith in La'Nea's maturity and ability to self-regulate, and trusted that she could handle this. I left La'Nea to fend for herself, as I was left so many times at that age, and that ain't right. Why do Black folks who are feminine-of-center have to always be handling business? [...] Black women and girls bear the brunt of the labor associated with state violence and captivity. From making sojourns to visit loved ones in prison to covering bills and working triple time to fill the financial pit left by mass incarceration. The activist hashtag #sayhername is a crucial intervention in this dynamic, calling upon Black organizers to address gendered violence against all Black women, trans and non-trans. La'Nea called me out when I let her down, and in doing so invited me to reflect on my own complicity in this uneven distribution of labor. As non-masc Black people, we are called upon to self-regulate and take up less space, use less resources, to make room for the crises of Black masculinity.

Ours was a queered scene of Black gender socialization – no Black male to fret about or blame, and yet the array of state and social resources were still oriented toward masculinity. Kairo's proximity to state violence warranted protection, and La'Nea called me on the ways my femme auntie self perpetuated the same hierarchy of care as the school that I critique. [...]

"I WAS A LIL' NIGGA": GIRLHOOD, STUD-FEMME & QUEER COALITION

A month or so after the fight, scabs were falling off of hearts and things were almost back to normal. La'Nea and Kairo were both part of a group of a dozen girls enrolled in "The Journey Within" yoga intersession that I co-taught with another Black Robeson teacher, Zahra. [...] Part of the course was an overnight retreat [...] and that evening we gathered: a cipher of 10 Black, Latina, and Filipina girls and two grown-ass women cuddled on a sectional couch on the first floor of an old Victorian boarding house overlooking the Pacific. We had a "sister circle" of advice and sharing, centered on anonymous questions that we each wrote on index cards like "Should age matter for going out with somebody?" or "Where do you go clear your head when shit gets to be too much?" Zahra unfolded and read aloud the last question – the only one that mentioned a name: "Ms. Shange – when did you first know you liked girls?"

I gave my usual spiel about playing doctor as a kid, being serially outed by my "friends," fucking other girls as a teenager in Philly but without a vision for a queer future; I settled for dudes until I moved to the Bay, where I found a robust queer community replete with mentorship and models of middle-aged lesbian women of color. After I spoke, I looked around tentatively: "Does anyone else wanna speak on this one?" Kairo laughed. "Why y'all all lookin at me tho'?! If you want me to speak, just say it's on me!" She shared:

> When I was younger, I still dressed like a boy, so girls would always think I was a boy, so, yeah. I mean like, they was likin me, so I liked the attention – I like that attention. So I was like aite, I just kept it going. But I don't like this attention, so stop it. ... I never seen nobody else gay except for my cousin. I grew up with hella boys – when I was younger I didn't mess with dolls, none of that. So I was like – aouno – I'm a boy. I was a lil' nigga.

Key here is the way Kairo narrates the development of her queerness as a communal, rather than a solitary, process. Kairo's intermeshing of desire and identity flummoxes Diversity 101 notions of sexuality and gender as both completely distinct and individual identities. [...]

The hyphen that links stud-femme is a bridge that carries more than a strap on its back – it is a weight-bearing social infrastructure that both destabilizes and jerry-rigs the gender binary. We who live in the house Black lesbians built make our lives in relation to the duality of stud-femme, even (or especially) when we create other formulas of gendered intimacy like femme4femme and stud4stud. Seen from this angle, stud-femme is not a rule to be followed or broken, but a cultural grammar that reveals the deviance encoded in every performance of queer Black gender, whether masculine, feminine, or gendered in ways that defy binarism. The gag is that instead of reveling in our fluid interrelation, we have been convinced that masc folks are somehow both more valiant and more vulnerable than their femme kin.

For Kairo, her "boy" gender was induced and stabilized by the desire of Black girls, one of whom was sitting right across the circle from her as she shared her story of growing up. Rather than transgressive gender as something that is centered on the defiantly masculine body, Kairo's studness was made coherent by the desire of ostensibly non-queer girls – they were why she "kept it going." This erotic potentiality, too, is femme labor, performed in ephemeral spaces like first-grade classrooms and middle school locker rooms. The sister circle is one such space – Kairo and I may have answered the question, but who asked it? It's possible that La'Nea wrote it; but she and I had had that conversation so many times over, it seemed unlikely. Among the crew of young women, there was another unnamed erotic subject peeking into the possibility of being In the Life. Her presence, and her desire to hear and be heard, was the impetus for the sharing of queer life stories.

She called me forth as "the genuine article," what Lewis calls "an embodied text that counters campus beliefs about 'what a feminist looks like.'" In the case of The Journey Within, the scales of power are reversed from what Lewis observed at white universities: I was a genuine article that provided a glimmer of what a grown, queer, colored life could be like for kids who live in the homonationalist capital of the United States, my body a countergeography to the white-on-white bourgeois men's space that the Castro has become. However, I was not the only genuine article to speak. Kairo and I both shared story, and in so doing we labored together against the absence of other lived models of queerness that linked our experiences across geography, gender, and generation. Boy or nah, this lil' nigga belonged in the circle. Lounging on those couches, there was space for each of us to speak as experts of our own experience, while also co-presencing girlhood as a queer coalitional space. [...] In the sister circle, and in the broader set of relations held by the school and The City, we queered kinship and forms of intimacy – we were the vessels of repetition with a difference, teaching each other how to be with and for ourselves. [...]

Section Eight Glossary

homonormativity   The normalization of particular forms of same-sex relationships, typically those most aligned with heteronormative family configurations privileging monogamy, marriage, parenthood, and middle-class consumptive practices.

queer theory   A broad and diverse body of theory that attends to sex, gender, and sexuality and challenges processes of categorization that label and restrict sexed and gendered roles and practices. Generally speaking, queer theory tends to focus on fluidity, diversity, and flexibility in relation to sex and gender, and it attends to the role of power in repressing such diversity. Queer theory thus more easily accounts for non-typical forms of sex and gender, such as intersex, gender ambiguity, and diverse genders, in social theory than lesbian and gay studies or women's studies do alone.

standpoint epistemology   A theory that privileges the advantaged standpoint of a knowledge-holder and producer, often through that person's experience or membership in a particular social group. However, Kimberlé Crenshaw questions the ability of any person to comprehensively understand experiences within a social category, since our worldviews depend on multiple, intersecting factors including race, class, sexuality, and ability.

On Social Position and Ethnographic Authority

THE SOCIAL CONTEXT

Growing acknowledgment of anthropology's disciplinary complicity with systems of oppression under the guise of scientific authority and objectivity helped pave the way for the postmodern turn, which we introduced in Section Five. And while postmodern critique was essential to advancing anthropological thinking about ethnographer positionality, reflexivity, and partiality, its epistemological relativism too often led to depoliticized texts written in impenetrable academic jargon. In the wake of the postmodern turn, many anthropologists and other social scientists found themselves grappling anew with questions of their position in relation to research "subjects," the goals of their life's work, and the politics of research in contexts of global inequality.

The essays in this section address these questions with an explicit focus on ethnographic authority and political responsibility. That is, if the essays in Section Five emphasized the need to acknowledge ethnographic positionality, the scholars in this section emphasize the need to move beyond acknowledging position and do something about it. But what? There is no simple answer, but as a collection, this section advances an interdisciplinary imperative for moral, political, reflexive, and engaged anthropology that unveils systems of domination and oppression and integrates multiple ways of knowing and representation. In so doing, anthropologists treat "ethnography as process" (Perley, this section) and not merely outcome.

THE CONVERSATION

The section opens with Donna Haraway's "Situated Knowledges: The Science Question in Feminism and the Privilege of Partial Perspective." Haraway introduces the notion of **situated knowledge,** or the idea that knowledge emerges from and reflects the social locations and positions in which it is produced (we saw this in Sections Five and Eight, as well). Haraway argues that objectivity pretends to be neutral, but in reality is a very specific position associated with power (an elite, white, masculine, heterosexual, human position). Developing the concept of situated knowledge through the metaphor of vision, Haraway pushes against relativism, totalization, and objectivity, arguing that they are "god tricks" that promise omniscience but deliver hegemony. For Haraway, the "god trick" has serious political and ethical consequences.

In "Anthropology and the Oppressed," Delmos Jones updates his seminal 1970 article "Towards a Native Anthropology." That classic piece challenged the assumption that ethnographic research must be conducted by an "outsider" who enters another society to document and describe, but never challenge nor address the social inequalities they observe (the position advanced by Malinowski in Section Three, for example). Instead, Jones theorizes research from an "insider" perspective, in which the ethnographer is a member of the community they are researching. In Reading 9.2, Jones grapples with his own position as an "insider" in a deeply divided community – when a group has opposing interests and goals, with whom should the native ethnographer side? Jones argues this fieldwork experience illuminated the importance of political principle, which led him to align with the most oppressed community members against the wishes of the project leaders. "Decolonizing" research with native ethnography, then, is not enough. Jones calls for an "anthropology of the oppressed," a critical social science focused on opposing systems of domination and exploitation.

In "What Did You Do Today?" (Reading 9.3), Dána-Ain Davis draws on a lineage of Black feminist epistemology to explore her political responsibilities to the working-class women at the center of her work. Using academic production to "give voice" to people whose participation in social and political spheres is suppressed is a worthy goal, Davis argues, but it is not enough. Instead, Davis advances an approach she calls "pracademics," which bridges theory and practice to mobilize anthropology in service to disempowered communities and their social movements. As an anthropologist, Davis routinely asks herself, "What did you today in the service of the women and girls who are the subjects of your research?" By holding herself accountable for advancing the interests and goals of marginalized community members, Davis ensures that her ethnographic research reaches beyond the silos of academia to inform policy and praxis.

Heike Becker, Emile Boonzaier, and Joy Owen build upon Haraway's and Davis's calls for a politically engaged anthropology that reckons with the situatedness of the anthropologist in Reading 9.4. Their essay "Fieldwork in Shared Spaces" draws upon the authors' fieldwork experiences "at home" in southern Africa to consider the ethical complexities and obligations of resident anthropologists. The authors adopt Cheater's (1987) notion of **"citizen anthropologist"** to analyze their own subjective and situated positions and power dynamics vis-à-vis the subjects of their research – as well as the political and ethical obligations that attend to it.

The final selection is an excerpt from one of our very own – Bernie Perley. In "Gone Anthropologist," Perley reflects on the "epistemic slippage" that occurs through the process of ethnographic writing and representation of "Others" as anthropologists slip into Other systems of knowing. Perley asks: What of the native who "goes anthropologist"? What epistemic slippage must be negotiated in these instances, and might there be alternative epistemic spaces that allow for emergent ethnographic representations? Perley, a member of the Tobique First Nation, shares one such alternative ethnographic space that he created: an assemblage of various "texts" – including a graphic novel, artistic productions that linked language and landscape, and articles and monographs – that invited anthropologists and "natives" alike to share and dialogue, integrating multiple ways of knowing and representation and paving the way for thinking of ethnography as process.

THREE QUESTIONS FOR THE READINGS

1 What is the role of situated knowledge in each of these pieces? How does the author's positionality shape their perspective on science, ethics, politics, and the ethnographic process?
2 How do the ideas of pracademics and citizen anthropologist engage with native and insider anthropology?
3 Put pracademics and Jones's alignment with political principle in conversation with the concept of cultural relativism. Is a politicized anthropology fully compatible with cultural relativism? And does the situated knowledge of "native-ness" shape an anthropologist's ability to offer sociopolitical critique?

ON THE COMPANION WEBSITE

"A Life of Learning," additional readings, and more.

www.anthropologicaltheory.com

REFERENCE

Cheater, A.P. 1987. "The Anthropologist as Citizen: The Diffracted Self?" In *Anthropology at Home*, edited by A. Jackson. London: Tavistock Publications.

9.1. Situated Knowledges: The Science Question in Feminism and the Privilege of Partial Perspective (1988)

Donna Haraway

THE PERSISTENCE OF VISION

I would like to proceed by placing metaphorical reliance on a much maligned sensory system in feminist discourse: vision. Vision can be good for avoiding binary oppositions. I would like to insist on the embodied nature of all vision and so reclaim the sensory system that has been used to signify a leap out of the marked body and into a conquering gaze from nowhere. This is the gaze that mythically inscribes all the marked bodies, that makes the unmarked category claim the power to see and not be seen, to represent while escaping representation. This gaze signifies the unmarked positions of Man and White, one of the many nasty tones of the word "objectivity" to feminist ears in scientific and technological, late-industrial, militarized, racist, and male-dominant societies, that is, here, in the belly of the monster, in the United States in the late 1980s. I would like a doctrine of embodied objectivity that accommodates paradoxical and critical feminist science projects: Feminist objectivity means quite simply *situated knowledges*.

The eyes have been used to signify a perverse capacity – honed to perfection in the history of science tied to militarism, capitalism, colonialism, and male supremacy – to distance the knowing subject from everybody and everything in the interests of unfettered power. The instruments of visualization in multinationalist, postmodernist culture have compounded these meanings of disembodiment. The visualizing technologies are without apparent limit. The eye of any ordinary primate like us can be endlessly enhanced by sonography systems, magnetic resonance imaging, artificial intelligence-linked graphic manipulation systems, scanning electron microscopes, computed tomography scanners, color-enhancement techniques, satellite surveillance systems, home and office video display terminals, cameras for every purpose from filming the mucous membrane lining the gut cavity of a marine worm living in the vent gases on a fault between continental plates to mapping a planetary hemisphere elsewhere in the solar system. Vision in this technological feast becomes unregulated gluttony; all seems not just mythically about the god trick of seeing everything from no-where, but to have put the myth into ordinary practice. And like the god trick, this eye fucks the world to make techno-monsters. [...]

But, of course, that view of infinite vision is an illusion, a god trick. [...] We need to learn in our bodies, endowed with primate color and stereoscopic vision, how to attach the objective to our theoretical and political scanners in order to name where we are and are not, in dimensions of mental and physical space we hardly know how to name. So, not so perversely, objectivity turns out to be about particular and specific embodiment and defi-nitely not about the false vision promising transcendence of all limits and responsibility. The moral is simple: only partial perspective promises objective vision. All Western cultural narratives about objectivity are allegories of the ideologies governing the relations of what we call mind and body, distance and responsibility. Feminist objectivity is about limited lo-cation and situated knowledge, not about transcendence and splitting of subject and object. It allows us to become answerable for what we learn how to see.

These are lessons that I learned in part walking with my dogs and wondering how the world looks without a fovea and very few retinal cells for color vision but with a huge neu-ral processing and sensory area for smells. It is a lesson available from photographs of how the world looks to the compound eyes of an insect or even from the camera eye of a spy sat-ellite or the digitally transmitted signals of space probe-perceived differences "near" Jupiter that have been transformed into coffee table color photographs. The "eyes" made available in modern technological sciences shatter any idea of passive vision; these prosthetic devices show us that all eyes, including our own organic ones, are active perceptual systems, build-ing on translations and specific *ways* of seeing, that is, ways of life. There is no unmediated photograph or passive camera obscura in scientific accounts of bodies and machines; there are only highly specific visual possibilities, each with a wonderfully detailed, active, partial way of organizing worlds. All these pictures of the world should not be allegories of infinite mobility and interchangeability but of elaborate specificity and difference and the loving care people might take to learn how to see faithfully from another's point of view, even when the other is our own machine. That's not alienating distance; that's a possible allegory for feminist versions of objectivity. Understanding how these visual systems work, techni-cally, socially, and psychically, ought to be a way of embodying feminist objectivity. [...]

[... T]his essay is an argument for situated and embodied knowledges and an argument against various forms of unlocatable, and so irresponsible, knowledge claims. Irresponsible means unable to be called into account. There is a premium on establishing the capacity to see from the peripheries and the depths. But here there also lies a serious danger of ro-manticizing and/or appropriating the vision of the less powerful while claiming to see from their positions. To see from below is neither easily learned nor unproblematic, even if "we" "naturally" inhabit the great underground terrain of subjugated knowledges. The position-ings of the subjugated are not exempt from critical reexamination, decoding, deconstruc-tion, and interpretation; that is, from both semiological and hermeneutic modes of critical inquiry. The standpoints of the subjugated are not "innocent" positions. On the contrary, they are preferred because in principle they are least likely to allow denial of the critical and interpretive core of all knowledge. They are knowledgeable of modes of denial through repression, forgetting, and disappearing acts. [...] The subjugated have a decent chance to be on to the god trick and all its dazzling – and, therefore, blinding – illuminations. "Subjugated" standpoints are preferred because they seem to promise more adequate, sustained, objective, transforming accounts of the world. [...]

Such preferred positioning is as hostile to various forms of relativism as to the most explicitly totalizing versions of claims to scientific authority. But the alternative to relativism is not totalization and single vision, which is always finally the unmarked category whose power depends on systematic narrowing and obscuring. The alternative to relativism is partial, locatable, critical knowledges sustaining the possibility of webs of connections called solidarity in politics and shared conversations in epistemology. Relativism is a way of being nowhere while claiming to be everywhere equally. The "equality" of positioning is a denial of responsibility and critical inquiry. Relativism is the perfect mirror twin of totalization in the ideologies of objectivity; both deny the stakes in location, embodiment, and partial perspective; both make it impossible to see well. Relativism and totalization are both "god tricks" promising vision from everywhere and nowhere equally and fully, common myths in rhetorics surrounding Science. But it is precisely in the politics and epistemology of partial perspectives that the possibility of sustained, rational, objective inquiry rests.

So, with many other feminists, I want to argue for a doctrine and practice of objectivity that privileges contestation, deconstruction, passionate construction, webbed connections, and hope for transformation of systems of knowledge and ways of seeing. But not just any partial perspective will do; we must be hostile to easy relativisms and holisms built out of summing and subsuming parts. "Passionate detachment" requires more than acknowledged and self-critical partiality. We are also bound to seek perspective from those points of view, which can never be known in advance, that promise something quite extraordinary, that is, knowledge potent for constructing worlds less organized by axes of domination. From such a viewpoint, the unmarked category would really disappear – quite a difference from simply repeating a disappearing act. The imaginary and the rational – the visionary and objective vision – hover close together. [...]

A commitment to mobile positioning and to passionate detachment is dependent on the impossibility of entertaining innocent "identity" politics and epistemologies as strategies for seeing from the standpoints of the subjugated in order to see well. One cannot "be" either a cell or molecule – or a woman, colonized person, laborer, and so on – if one intends to see and see from these positions critically. "Being" is much more problematic and contingent. Also, one cannot relocate in any possible vantage point without being accountable for that movement. Vision is *always* a question of the power to see – and perhaps of the violence implicit in our visualizing practices. With whose blood were my eyes crafted? These points also apply to testimony from the position of "oneself." We are not immediately present to ourselves. Self-knowledge requires a semiotic-material technology to link meanings and bodies. Self-identity is a bad visual system. [...]

The split and contradictory self is the one who can interrogate positionings and be accountable, the one who can construct and join rational conversations and fantastic imaginings that change history. Splitting, not being, is the privileged image for feminist epistemologies of scientific knowledge. "Splitting" in this context should be about heterogeneous multiplicities that are simultaneously salient and incapable of being squashed into isomorphic slots or cumulative lists. This geometry pertains within and among subjects. Subjectivity is multidimensional; so, therefore, is vision. The knowing self is partial in all its guises, never finished, whole, simply there and original; it is always constructed and stitched together imperfectly, and *therefore* able to join with another, to see together without claiming to be another. Here is the promise of objectivity: a scientific knower seeks the subject position, not of identity, but of objectivity, that is, partial connection. There is no way to "be" simultaneously in all, or wholly in any, of the privileged (i.e., subjugated) positions structured by gender, race, nation, and class. And that is a short list of critical positions. The search for such a "full" and total position is the search for the fetishized perfect subject of oppositional history, sometimes appearing in feminist theory as the essentialized Third World Woman. [...] Identity, including self-identity does not produce science; critical positioning does, that is, objectivity. [...]

Positioning is, therefore, the key practice in grounding knowledge organized around the imagery of vision, and much Western scientific and philosophic discourse is organized in this way. Positioning implies responsibility for our enabling practices. It follows that politics and ethics ground struggles for and contests over what may count as rational knowledge. That is, admitted or not, politics and ethics ground struggles over knowledge projects in the exact, natural, social, and human sciences. [...] Struggles over what will count as rational accounts of the world are struggles over *how* to see. [...]

I am arguing for politics and epistemologies of location, positioning, and situating, where partiality and not universality is the condition of being heard to make rational knowledge claims. These are claims on people's lives. I am arguing for the view from a body, always a complex, contradictory, structuring, and structured body, versus the view from above, from nowhere, from simplicity. Only the god trick is forbidden. [...]

Translation is always interpretive, critical, and partial. [... L]ocation is about vulnerability; location resists the politics of closure, finality, or to borrow from Althusser, feminist objectivity resists "simplification in the last instance." That is because feminist embodiment resists fixation and is insatiably curious about the webs of differential positioning. There is no single feminist standpoint because our maps require too many dimensions for that metaphor to ground our visions. But the feminist standpoint theorists' goal of an epistemology and politics of engaged, accountable positioning remains eminently potent. The goal is better accounts of the world, that is, "science."

Above all, rational knowledge does not pretend to disengagement: to be from everywhere and so nowhere, to be free from interpretation, from being represented, to be fully self contained or fully formalizable. Rational knowledge is a process of ongoing critical interpretation among "fields" of interpreters and decoders. Rational knowledge is power-sensitive conversation. Decoding and transcoding plus translation and criticism; all are necessary. So science becomes the paradigmatic model, not of closure, but of that which is contestable and contested. Science becomes the myth, not of what escapes human agency and responsibility in a realm above the fray, but, rather, of accountability and responsibility for translations and solidarities linking the cacophonous visions and visionary voices that characterize the knowledges of the subjugated. A splitting of senses, a confusion of voice and sight, rather than clear and distinct ideas, becomes the metaphor for the ground of the rational. We seek not the knowledges ruled by phallogocentrism (nostalgia for the presence of the one true Word) and disembodied vision. We seek those ruled by partial sight and limited voice – not partiality for its own sake but, rather, for the sake of the connections and unexpected openings situated knowledges make possible. Situated knowledges are about communities, not about isolated individuals. The only way to find a larger vision is to be somewhere in particular. The science question in feminism is about objectivity as positioned rationality. Its images are not the products of escape and transcendence of limits (the view from above) but the joining of partial views and halting voices into a collective subject position that promises a vision of the means of ongoing finite embodiment, of living within limits and contradictions – of views from somewhere. [...]

9.2. Anthropology and the Oppressed: A Reflection on "Native" Anthropology (1995)

Delmos J. Jones

In my article "Towards a Native Anthropology" (Jones 1970) I expressed my frustration and dissatisfaction with the social-class and racial bias of anthropology. What concerned me then, as now, is that anthropology is essentially a discipline that studies oppressed peoples, but the concepts and theories used to describe the lives of these groups do not adequately deal with the realities of their oppression. Thus I could just as well have called for an anthropology of the oppressed. [...]

My primary concern is neither anthropology nor native anthropology. Rather, it is social equality and social justice, and the manner in which anthropology and native anthropology relate to these concerns. I am referring here to the often stated idea that anthropology has provided justification for colonialism and oppression. With this principle in mind, native anthropology must be subjected to the same level of scrutiny as mainstream anthropology. The central question is whether a native anthropology advances the goals of social justice and social equality, or whether it merely mirrors mainstream anthropology. I will argue that some perspectives presented as critiques of mainstream anthropology are often no different from the point of view they are criticizing. Thus I agree with Narayan's recent argument (1993) against the fixity of a sharp distinction between "native" and "non-native" anthropology. However, I would go on to suggest that there should be a distinction. Narayan is critical of the idea that a "native anthropologist" can represent an unproblematic and authentic "insider's perspective" on social reality. I would suggest there are political implications to this claim. This claim tends to deny the multiple voices of the native population for whom the anthropologist purports to speak, and may serve to legitimize internal inequality.

[... A]ll relationships involving research are problematic, socially and politically complex, and require difficult choices. My argument is that if these choices are based on sentimentality as opposed to political considerations, they risk reinforcing inequality. The native anthropologist must be seen in relationship to a native population, but the native population must not be viewed as a homogeneous and cohesive entity. It is composed of diverse interests. [...]

In the following section I will describe a research situation in which I encountered the issues of multiple commitments and localities of a native anthropologist working with a native population. I will describe how my research agenda related to different segments of the group, and how each segment had different expectations. As a native anthropologist I had to make a choice. The nature of my choices was not based on my "nativeness," but on political and ideological grounds.

THE RESEARCH CASE

[...] It is primarily through organizations that an oppressed population attempts to bring about changes in its condition, but it is also through organizations that the state attempts to control urban populations. In a study conducted in 1968 on the origin and function of community organizations, I observed many aborted attempts at developing organizations, which rarely survived the incipient stage (see Jones 1972). Questions arose about the conditions that lead to failure or success in organizations. [...]

A second study, carried out between 1972 and 1973, focused on a "successful" organization, often touted as an example of what could be accomplished by local associations. According to my analysis, the group was successful because its goals, the development of low-income housing, coincided with the goals of the city's housing authority. To be successful, it appeared, an organization had to have a leadership that was acceptable to the community, and one that government agencies could do business with. Thus the leader of local organizations must respond to the demands and expectations of external agencies, and attempt to remain acceptable to the local community. The interest of these two groups, however, are often contradictory.

The study of the Community Action Group was designed to look in more detail inside an organization and to investigate the consequences of antagonistic elements – the interests of the state and the interests of the poor – locked into the same organizational structure. The patterns of social interaction between leaders and followers, and the relationship between the organization as a unit and the people of the larger community were the primary concerns of this research.

The Community Action Group operated a Head Start Center and emerged out of the atmosphere of the war on poverty and the Black Power ideology of the late 1960s (see Jones 1987). Like most organizations of this type, the group consisted of a board of directors, the governing and policymaking body of the organization; a working staff, including professionals and paraprofessionals; and clients, people from the community who received services offered by the organization.

While planning the study I appeared before the full board of directors. They carefully inspected my political views and asked specific questions about my proposed study. I was granted permission to do the study, partly because the board approved of my political concern about the position of black people, and because I am black. A white researcher would not have been allowed to do the study. As a condition of this approval, I was asked by the board to meet occasionally with them to report my findings. They explained that the organization was experiencing many internal problems and that my investigation might help them to solve them.

Being black was not enough in this all-black organization. The social class dimensions of my identity emerged immediately [...]. The manner in which I gained entry into the group was the source of my first problem. I had received permission from the board to conduct the research, but the research itself took place at the center among parents and a paraprofessional staff who had no voice in that decision. Thus when I started the research there was immediate suspicion by the parents and staff about who I was and what I was doing. Was I working for the central office, the city agency in charge of all city Head Start programs, as part of their monitoring team? Was I working for the board, collecting information they would use to fire the staff?

By the time I appeared on the scene the board had decided that the whole staff was inefficient and needed replacing; the staff, hiding behind the protection of community support and formal grievance procedures, was able to protect their jobs. Although most performed at a minimal level, most of them also reported a history of hard work and commitment to the job. They complained that their commitment and hard work went unrewarded. The board wanted to get rid of the staff, and the dominant sentiment of the parents was to get rid of the board.

Although I was asked at the beginning of the project to appear before the board to relate the findings of my research, I was not invited to do so until the study was completed and the analysis underway. When I did come before the board I gave an oral report in which I discussed the issues as outlined above. The report was politely received, and a written report was requested. When the written report was submitted to the board, the chairperson felt that the findings were all wrong and urged that it not be shown to anyone else in the organization. I was invited to reappear before the board to discuss the accuracy of the written report. I agreed.

I happened to mention the meeting to a board member. She was very surprised and said she had never heard of the meeting. When she looked into it, she discovered that the meeting was to involve me and the board's top leadership. This upset her, and when I understood that this was to be a meeting of a few select board members I refused to attend it. I was willing to discuss the accuracy of the report, but only before the full board.

News of the affair quickly spread. Everyone knew that a report had been written, and the staff and parents learned that they were not supposed to see it. I was now watched very closely. When I first came into the organization, I was suspected by the staff of working for the board. Would I now prove to be on the board's side? The report was seen by the board as an authoritarian document that would serve to support the position of the leadership against the parents and staff, but it was seen by the parents and staff as a statement that would discredit the board.

I decided to circulate the report in the organization over the objection of the leadership. This decision was not an easy one. It was based in part on my realization that parents and staff had a right to see my interpretation of their experience. As I struggled with the problem of what to do about the report, ideas associated with my role as a black anthropologist working in a black social situation were uppermost in my mind. I wish now to discuss some of these issues.

CONTRADICTIONS AND DILEMMAS

I started this line of research by raising political questions. I was concerned about the decline of politically viable organizations and their substitutions with organizations devoted to providing services. I was asking questions about the manipulation and control of black organizations and, indirectly, the control of leadership and political action. When the wider context of the problem is confronted, the relationship between leaders and followers among black Americans emerges as a core part of the problem. It was Marable who noted that "the Black petty bourgeoisie ... express tendencies toward political accommodation and class collaboration with the state" (1981:373). Marable went on to note that "part of the crisis in Black politics involves the breakdown in Black leadership" (1981:377 [...]). It is in this context that the role of the native anthropologist as ethnographer-critic and as a member of a minority group becomes problematic (see Mitchell 1982). Should the native researcher, in the name of group loyalty, fail to report socially destructive aspects of the native situation?

In my case I experienced a conflict between the political concerns that I was investigating and my personal sentiments about the idea of black unity. In my report to the board I made every effort to reveal the external roots of the internal conflict. However, I implicitly advocated unity. At the same time, the findings of the research suggested that the racial unity ideology was creating many of the interpersonal problems in the organization. This was because the idea of unity was often a device to suppress meaningful social, ideological, and political difference.

The Community Action Group case was a microcosm of a larger political and ideological scene in the United States during 1965–76. This was a period characterized by an ideology that stressed the organization of the black community as a precondition for wedging an attack on the oppressive conditions of society (Carmichael and Hamilton 1967:44–5). In the Community Action Group, for example, any discussion of social differences was viewed as inappropriate behavior resulting from "white brainwashing." Any suggestion that the leadership was anything but fully and totally committed to legitimate political goals and not out for their personal gain was called anti-black. Thus the situation lacked any kind of exchange between leaders and followers. Communications took the form of memorandums from the board to the rest of the organization. The group as a whole no longer mobilized to confront the policies of the central office and other outside institutions. Rather, the parents mobilized the community against the board [...] and the leadership spent a lot of effort trying to keep the parents in line.

The idea of unity in this situation meant that the parents would follow the dictates of the leadership without question. The more I examined the idea of unity the more it appeared that the notion that a black community could or should be built was more primordial than political, based more on principles of racial loyalty than on a specific political agenda, and functioned more to domesticate than to liberate.

In the oral report I implicitly advocated racial unity. In doing so I, along with central office personnel, did not acknowledge the parents' legitimacy as political actors who had characterized the leadership as the oppressors, and had decided that they no longer wanted to accept the structure as given. It is in the context of this realization that Paulo Freire's *Pedagogy of the Oppressed* (1970) became important to me. In his discussion of critical intervention he stressed "dialoguing with people about their actions" (1970:38–9) and noted that to substitute monologue, slogans, and communiques for dialogue is to attempt to liberate the oppressed with the instruments of domestication.

> Attempting to liberate the oppressed without their reflective participation in the act of liberation is to treat them as objects which must be saved from a burning building; it is to lead them into the populist pitfall and transform them into masses which can be manipulated. [Freire 1970:52]

Freire would give a voice to the oppressed and subject the relationship between the oppressed and their would-be liberators to critical analysis. It is not a relationship that is self-evident, but one that must be earned and revalidated over and over again (see Stavenhagen 1971). It is also in this context that the statement "urban ethnographers must agree readily to the boundaries of investigation as decided by ghetto nationalists" (Willis 1972:148) must be rejected.

CONCLUSION

[…] I have suggested that in the Community Action Group situation the notion of unity was used to suppress dissent. Additionally, there was the tendency to submerge internal social and individual differences. This emphasis on the group, defined largely in cultural terms, as opposed to the rights of the individual, is currently an important political and moral issue. […] Bromley points out that when the Universal Declaration of Human Rights was under discussion at the United Nations in the 1940s, a report was issued by the American Anthropological Association attempting to establish "on the basis of cultural relativism, that there could be no general human rights for all people" (1987:33). This idea that all ethnic cultures are relative leads to the conclusion that each culture has a permanent value and must be preserved for as long as possible in its "pure" form. The result, however well intended, is the perpetuation of the existing inequality within groups and between groups. From this perspective, groups are not only more important than individuals, but should and must limit individual freedom and action, and such restrictions are inherently justified. […]

[…] I ended "Towards a Native Anthropology" calling for the decolonization of anthropological knowledge. It should now be clear to everyone that decolonization is not always the same thing as liberation, especially if the process only replaces one system of domination with another. Schroyer (1973) noted that "contemporary establishment social science is essentially a science of managerial rationality." He called for a science capable of recognizing the ways in which existing structures exploit, alienate, and repress human possibilities. "We need a critical science whose primary focus is the critique of domination" (1973:27). This critique must not stop at the boundaries of minorities and oppressed populations, conceived as cohesive wholes, but must recognize that mechanisms of domination and exploitation operate at all levels of social reality. It is because of this that a critical native anthropology is now needed more than ever.

The idea that a native anthropology does not represent an "unproblematic perspective" on social reality does not diminish the potential of a transformative anthropology. Mitchell, for example, asks: "[H]ow does one objectively study a population considered 'deviant' when the researchers themselves, although considered exceptions, are members of that deviant population?" (1982:42). It is precisely by confronting, analyzing, and working through the multiple social realities, dilemmas, constraints, and choices that native anthropologists participate in as actors and observers that the potential rewards of the undertaking exist.

REFERENCES

Bromley, Yu V. 1987. "Anthropology, Ethnology and Ethnic and Racial Prejudice." *International Social Science Journal* 39: 31–43.

Carmichael, Stokely, and Charles Hamilton. 1967. *Black Power*. New York: Random House.

Freire, Paolo. 1970. *Pedagogy of the Oppressed*. New York: Seabury Press.

Jones, Delmos J. 1970. "Towards a Native Anthropology." *Human Organization* 29: 251–9.

———. 1972. "Incipient Organizations and Organizational Failures in an Urban Ghetto." *Urban Anthropology* 1: 51–67.

———. 1987. "The Community and Organizations in the Community." In *Anthropology in the United States*, edited by Leith Mullings, 115–36. New York: Columbia University Press.

Marable, Manning. 1981. "Reaganism, Racism, and Reaction: Black Political Realignment." *Black Scholar* 13: 215. https://doi.org/10.1080/00064246.1982.11414245.

Mitchell, Jacquelyn. 1982. "Reflections of a Black Social Scientist: Some Struggles, Some Doubts, Some Hopes." *Harvard Educational Review* 52: 27–44. https://doi.org/10.17763/haer.52.1.1p4h46u8gtu25382.

Narayan, Kirin. "How Native is a 'Native' Anthropologist?" *American Anthropologist* 95 (3): 671–86.

Schroyer, Trent. 1973. *The Critique of Domination: The Origins and Development of Critical Theory*. New York: George Braziller.

Stavenhagen, Rodolfo. 1971. "Decolonizing Applied Social Sciences." *Human Organization* 30: 333–58.

Willis, W.S. 1972. "Skeletons in the Anthropological Closet." In *Reinventing Anthropology*, edited by Dell Hymes, 121–52. New York: Random House.

9.3. What Did You Do Today? Notes from a Politically Engaged Anthropologist (2003)

Dána-Ain Davis

Thirty years after Dell Hymes articulated the dilemma anthropologists have concerning the discipline's commitment in, and to, the world, debates continue about politically engaged anthropology. The subject moves along a continuum that incorporates opposition to the discipline serving advocacy interests to those who view anthropology from an interventionist perspective capable of liberation (Harrison 1997). Of course there are some that employ anthropology to challenge the reproduction of structural inequality (Mullings 2000) and others whose anthropological work reaches beyond the boundaries of the intellectual endeavor influencing non-academic spheres (see, e.g., Sanjek 1987; Curtis n.d.). In the tradition of those anthropologists, particularly Black feminist anthropologists who view the discipline's potential to disrupt authoritative discourse and practice, I too, consider myself a politically engaged anthropologist because I conduct research that examines the lives of those who often have the most silenced voices in the public sphere, namely, battered women, low-income and poor women and young girls of color – especially those who are Black. They neither own nor control media outlets to challenge distorted representations; nor do they have the means to counter claims highlighting their deficits. And, although these groups live at the center of policy, their voices often go unheard. I purposefully investigate and document women's histories and views with the goal that their experiences will be strategically deployed in coalition and movement building. Therefore, I constantly ask myself, "What did you do today in the service of the women and girls who are the subjects of your research?" I also ask myself, "In what ways have you ensured that the principles of Black feminist theory and practice have been realized toward the goal of promoting social justice?"

It has not been difficult to arrive at the place of being a politically engaged anthropologist. As a Black feminist anthropologist, I have been influenced by a number of contemporary Black feminist scholar/activists, among them Zora Neale Hurston, A. Lynn Bolles, Leith Mullings, Angela M. Gilliam, Audre Lorde, and bell hooks. My intellectual genealogy lays claim to interrogating and problematizing inequity. Following the practitioners who have inspired me, I also seek to link thought, research and action in my work.

MOVING FROM MARGIN TO CENTER

In January 1998 I began my dissertation research in a small city in upstate New York. The project centered on the impact of welfare reform on battered Black women living in a shelter. The research began shortly after welfare reform was legislated in New York State in August 1997. Activists, policy analysts and the women with whom I did my work were reeling with concerns. The content of those concerns was shaped by the mandates of Personal Responsibility and Work Opportunity Reconciliation Act (PRWORA) of 1996 signed by President Clinton, which shredded the safety net of welfare. In large part this was achieved by devolving federal responsibility of providing for the poor to each state, and implementing policies placing five-year lifetime limits for the receipt of cash assistance. At the time of my research in 1998, welfare reform policies ushered in new requirements for recipients, including having to work in order to remain eligible for benefits, mandates to find employment regardless of the type of work, and draconian sanctions against those who did not meet the mandates of the law. I witnessed women's degradation and resilience as they crept through the Kafkaesque maze of new laws and requirements. They desperately worked within and against the controls of the state, whose only interest was to ensure their participation in the market economy (at almost any cost) even in the absence of opportunity and resources. They tried to find jobs, entered into training programs that were often meaningless or inappropriate, and were caught between a rock and a hard place as their desire to stay home with children was overruled by laws forcing them to work or be engaged in work-related activities (Davis et al., 2003).

That year, 1998, was also an election year for the Senate. In New York Charles S. Schumer and Geraldine Ferraro were running against incumbent New York State Senator, Alfonse D'Amato. On the national front anti-affirmative action initiatives gained momentum, as did anti-abortion measures. Within this context it was fascinating to note that in the Department of Social Service (DSS) office, where I spent innumerable hours with battered women as they attempted to secure social supports, there was a table set up to register people to vote. One day, after having waited an entire day at DSS with Leslie, a pregnant 18-year-old applying for benefits, I began to connect the ways in which the state co-opts civic participation. Over the next three weeks, Leslie spent approximately four days a week meeting social service mandates. At some point I asked her if she was going to vote and she did not respond. I thought to myself, "Why did I ask her that question? When will she get the chance to think about voting? When will she have the time to consider the candidates for office and their political perspectives?" I felt that the social services practices with regard to people needing assistance constituted a peculiar regulation of poor people, which prevented Leslie, as one example, from being an active citizen. The regulations are "meticulous rituals of power" (Staples 1997:3) that serve to discipline people into acting in certain ways.

Participating in these rituals can also limit the peripheral vision of the objects of control, in this case those on welfare, since so much energy is expended responding to the demands of social services while simultaneously meeting one's daily needs. The regimes of power that regulated activity led to Leslie's hyper-engagement with social services. This engagement included constantly reporting back to caseworkers, fear and actual denial of assistance, repeated attempts to reinstate suspended benefits, and being forced to live on what Susser (1992) has identified as "institutional time." These activities took up an inordinate amount of time, time lost to actually be an engaged citizen.

Was this one way to regulate the participation of those at the bottom of the social and economic ladder in electoral politics? Could the logical conclusion of this constriction circumscribe the ability of poor and working class peoples to challenge hegemonic structures through acts of resistance, community organizing and involvement in social movements?

While these questions may smell like conspiracy theory, and while we know that poor and working class people resist poverty-induced assaults on their integrity in a multitude of ways, being a poor Black woman who was battered and on welfare was certainly a roadblock to her engagement in any kind of civic participation. I knew this to be the case when one of the women, Sherita, asked me what was I going to do with all the information I collected. She made it very clear that she was only a "case file" at social services and that it was my responsibility to tell "people" how difficult life was and share the problems women faced while on welfare. Similarly, homeless women told Elliot Liebow (1993) the same thing when he conducted his research in Washington, D.C. What Sherita was asking of me was to move my work as an anthropologist from the margin of my own personal achievement, that of being awarded a degree and facilitating my employment as an academic, to a center of relevance, ostensibly in the realm of policy. In return for the "gift" of her life story and the stories of other women, I was asked to do something that might make a difference. My work as a politically engaged anthropologist began at that moment. My accountability was a moral and political issue, not so much because I am in academia, but rather because my responsibility as a moral agent is no different from the responsibilities of others, as Noam Chomsky (2001) points out. He also notes that intellectuals do enjoy a degree of privilege and power and should seek out an audience that matters, which is precisely what Sherita asked me to do as a gesture of reciprocity to accommodate her perceived (and real) lack of power in influencing policy.

Shortly after completing my dissertation research in 2000, I applied for a one-year appointment in anthropology at Purchase College. I was asked to comment on my teaching philosophy and quickly responded that I taught to "transgress." Teaching to transgress is of course the title of a book by bell hooks (1994) which I have unabashedly adopted as a strategy to motivate students to explore social issues. These issues include exploring the parameters of inequality and the persistence of structural barriers with an eye toward their becoming politically engaged students. Why? Because as hooks notes,

> The academy is not paradise … the classroom, with all its limitations, remains a location of possibility. In that field of possibility we have the opportunity to labor for freedom, to demand of

ourselves and our comrades, an openness of mind and heart that allows us to face reality even as we collectively imagine ways to move beyond boundaries, to transgress ... (hooks 1994: 207)

In this way, I reasoned, students could recognize the possibilities of anthropology not only as a discipline concerned with intellectual inquiry, nor only as "a field for those who believe that if we can better describe the world, decision makers will listen to our well-reasoned positions and act accordingly" as Kirk Dombrowski notes (Curtis n.d.). I embrace this perspective to encourage students to consider how intellectual work can serve in the interest of what I call "pracademics," that is, bridging theory and practice.

I lay the foundation for pracademics on the first day of class when I explain to my Anthropology of Poverty class that I live at the intersection of intellectual engagement and practice. I point out that the distinctions between research, service, and activism are not clearly defined if one is productively engaged in social justice work. And while each of those elements may constitute points against which tenure will be measured, I am, first and foremost, a person concerned about fairness and equity, concerned that the voices of those on the margins be centered. Anthropology can shift equations by incorporating not only "culture talk" but also "rights talk." There are research tools that facilitate this process, as Mullings (2000:20) points out. Anthropological research practices, she notes, including ethnography and community participation, can bring to the fore the voices of those who lie outside the centers of power. However, turning up the volume of underrepresented voices is not enough. There are other commitments that we as anthropologists have. We must link research practices to critical inquiry and ultimately to action that will dislodge power. Roger Sanjek (1987) argues that we need to be concerned about the outcome of our work, an issue also brought to the surface by Hymes (1972) who identified the relationship anthropologists can have to their work. He noted that the role of anthropologists is three-fold: (1) we are critics and scholars in the academic world, (2) we work for communities, movements, operational institutions, and (3) we are linked to direct action as members of a community or social movement. All three roles are necessary (Hymes 1972:56). In other words, we can all be pracademicians if we choose to make our connections to all of these worlds explicit in our work.

REFERENCES

Chomsky, Noam. 2001. "The Moral Role of Intellectuals," Public Anthropology: Engaging Ideas, Intellectuals, and the Responsibilities of Public Life: An Interview with Noam Chomsky. Public Anthropology Journals. Electronic document [URL no longer available].

Curtis, Ric. n.d. "Adventures in Engaged Anthropology, or Why 'Getting It Right' Isn't Enough." Electronic document [URL no longer available].

Davis, Dána, Ana Aparicio, Audrey Jacobs, Akemi Kochiyama, Leith Mullings, Andrea Queeley, and Beverly Thompson. 2003. "Working It Off: Welfare, Workfare and Work Experience Programs in New York City." *Souls: A Critical Journal of Black Politics, Culture and Society.*

Harrison, Faye.V. (ed.). 1997. *Decolonizing Anthropology: Moving Further Toward an Anthropology for Liberation*, 2nd ed. Arlington, VA: Association of Black Anthropologists and American Anthropological Association.

hooks, bell. 1994. *Teaching to Transgress: Education as the Practice of Freedom*. New York: Routledge.

Hymes, Dell (ed.). 1972. "The Uses of Anthropology: Critical, Political, Personal." In *Reinventing Anthropology*, edited by Dell Hymes, 3–79. New York: Vintage.

Liebow, Elliot. 1993. *Tell Them Who I Am: The Lives of Homeless Women*. New York: Penguin Books.

Mullings, Leith. 2000. "African-American Women Making Themselves: Notes on the Role of Black Feminist Research." *Souls: A Critical Journal of Black Politics, Culture, and Society* 2 (4): 18–29. https://doi.org/10.1080/10999940009362233.

Sanjek, Roger. 1987. "Work at a Gray Panther Health Clinic." In *Cities of the United States: Studies in Urban Anthropology*, edited by L. Mullings, 148–75. New York: Columbia University Press.

Staples, William G. 1997. *The Culture of Surveillance: Discipline and Social Control in the United States*. New York: St. Martin's Press.

Susser, Ida. 1992. *Norman Street: Poverty and Politics in an Urban Neighborhood*. New York: Oxford University Press.

9.4. Fieldwork in Shared Spaces: Positionality, Power, and Ethics of Citizen Anthropologists in Southern Africa (2005)

Heike Becker, Emile Boonzaier, and Joy Owen

The positionality of anthropologists who reside in, and share a long-term commitment to, the same society as the "subjects" of their research is one of the most conspicuous absences in the vast critical literature on fieldwork that has been published over the past 25 years or so. Very little has been published on the ethics, power and insider/outsider relations between anthropologists who do fieldwork "at home" and the people among whom they do their research. [...]

Most of the existing writings on "doing anthropology at home" strike us as particularly unhelpful as they tend to be of a generalizing and uncritical nature. [...] There appears to be a widely unquestioned assumption that anthropologists who do not pack their bags and leave for some "overseas" place at the end of a fieldwork period quasi-naturally engage in more equal and intersubjective relationships with the people studied.

[...] When we compared our extended notes, we realized that none of the present authors does fieldwork among people who, "one way or another, belong to the same *cultural* area as the anthropologist" (Hastrup 1987: 94; our emphasis). None of us studies our "own cultures from a position of intimate affinity" (Narayan 1993: 671), as "native" anthropologists are believed to do, even if our field site is physically a thoroughly familiar place, only a few minutes drive away from the anthropologist's parental home, as in Owen's case.

We differ in terms of "race," age, gender and country of birth, and so do the people among whom each of us works. Yet, the implications of us doing anthropology are inextricably linked to our shared constructive engagement in the trajectories of South Africa and the wider southern African region. Likewise, the "subjects" of our research, irrespective of *their* differences, are subjects of the southern African past and present. We came to recognize that the context of direct exchange in fieldwork is situated in a common geographical, but more importantly joint historical and political space that we share with one another and with the people among whom we work in the Richtersveld, in Owambo, or in Muizenberg/Cape Town. It is in these shared historical-political spaces, instead of in a "shared culture," that we need to locate the ethics and politics of our fieldwork.

Here, we found Angela Cheater's (1987) characterization of those who practice anthropology in their own societies as "citizen anthropologists" considerably more helpful as it transcends the paradigmatic dichotomy of "regular"/outsider and "native"/insider anthropologists which appears to be hinged on enduring notions of bounded cultures (cf. Narayan 1993). Cheater argues that citizen anthropologists face different subjective professional realities from those who work in societies other than their own. They are faced by issues of equality and, particularly, with the necessity to recognize the "conceptual frameworks of one's fellow-citizens ... [as] an equal and alternative reality that affects oneself" (p. 175). In other words, citizen anthropologists who do research and teach within their own societies are less able than their "visitor" colleagues to shelve local interpretations of reality in a safe compartment when being challenged by politicians, students and other fellow citizens.

Citizen anthropologists' interpretation of the shared lifeworld may, and often will, remain distant from those of politicians, students and other fellow-citizens. Yet, their ability to present them as a convincing interpretation relies to a large extent on what their fellow-citizens being studied define as the anthropologist's moral or ethical obligations; they do so because the citizen anthropologist is perceived in the first place as a fellow-citizen:

> The citizen anthropologist is "trackable" and accountable, where the visitor is not, precisely because his research subjects can assume that he is subjectively "one of us," an equal in terms of citizenship obligations, if not in terms of race, class or language. (Cheater 1987: 171)

Cheater alludes, thus, to the politics of being an anthropologist who lives and works in polyethnic, racially differentiated and class-structured societies. Her paper does not engage, however, with the ethnography of citizen anthropologists and their ethics and politics in the field. This is precisely what we would like to explore [...].

SHIFTING POWER DYNAMICS IN MUIZENBERG (JOY OWEN)

[...] As many anthropologists would admit, the field space is one's heart and life place at the time of its vivid experience. Not only are the field site and the people within it our "workplace." But this space is also the site where we cultivate rapport, where we seek information that will be of benefit to our particular projects; where we participate in the ebb and flow of people's lives and where we create friendships (Christman 1988). The anthropological enterprise is of such a nature that we are compelled to engage with research participants in a meaningful manner. A manner that not only elicits trust, but also personal information. We are thus encouraged to facilitate the creation of a relationship with feeling, thinking, conscious beings, like ourselves. Given the fragility of these relationships at various moments during the ethnographic process – negotiating access, gaining entry, cultural miscommunication etc. – it seems rational to have a set of standards or guidelines to assist us through this mutual sense making process with our research participants. The need for a set of ethical guidelines seems even more apparent when we understand that we are the authors of the final ethnographic product. However, while we attempt to protect our research participants from a number of unforeseen circumstances as a result of their participation in our research, the ethical guidelines ignore a very salient fact of research: what about the ethics of the research participants? Even a superficial consideration of this question raises the spectre of power, and its centrality within the research process. We are compelled to ask, who wields power *in* the field? [...]

AN INNOCENT ANTHROPOLOGIST IN THE RICHTERSVELD (EMILE BOONZAIER)

For anthropologists who work in their own societies and who try to foster long-term relationships with their research subjects, I would argue, there are intrinsic controls that promote appropriate and acceptable ethical conduct. In short, such anthropologists are held directly accountable for their behavior in the field and for the consequences of their research products.

When I embarked on my first fieldwork in the mid-1970s my primary concern was to establish that important ingredient of good research – "rapport." But looking back, I now emphasize that rapport and acceptance are the outcomes of power negotiations between researcher and subjects, and that such negotiations are a crucial aspect of ethics. [...]

SHIFTING POSITIONALITIES OF AN ANTHROPOLOGIST IN NORTHERN NAMIBIA (HEIKE BECKER)

Different ethnographic moments during 15 years of long-term, though rather intermittent fieldwork in Owambo, northern Namibia, have allowed me to reflect on the complexities of being a citizen anthropologist. Most importantly, these moments have urged me to rethink some received wisdoms, especially with respect to intersubjective power relations between the researcher and her "subjects" in the field. [...] In defiance of simplistic notions of "who wields power" in ethnographic research, at each turn, people perceived me and themselves differently within a complex web of power relations against the background of northern Namibian colonial and postcolonial history. [...]

Becoming a Citizen Anthropologist

When I first arrived in Namibia two months after the country's day of independence, I resolved that I would keep a respectful distance. I was just too wary to avoid getting too deeply "involved." Observing and learning from my informants was what I had been taught to be the position of the anthropologist in the field. My background as an activist in 1980s Germany in the then solidarity movement with the liberation struggles in southern Africa added its bit; as did the knowledge that Namibia's intellectual-activist circles were extremely small which heightened the "danger," as I saw it then, that I might actually influence the very postcolonial trajectories of gender activism in the newly-independent country that I was supposed to study.

This didn't quite work out. [...] A few weeks after my arrival, some of the younger gender activists roped me into a range of activities and social events. Those early guides into the "New Namibia" were my peers in many respects; they were confident, mostly university-educated [...] young women in their late twenties and early thirties; some had just returned to Namibia after years of exile; they, too, had to find their feet in a strange country. We talked politics and love interests, and on weekends partied until the early hours. What a relief that here were "locals" with whom I had no issues of power or guilt; I was seduced by a circle of friends who doubled as "key-informants" and who were at once "other" and "same."

On a more theoretical and methodological level, I soon enough realized that the non-involved stance contravened critical ideas about power in the field and the commitment to the values of dialogical anthropology [...].

The Fallacies of Applied Anthropology

[...] From 1993, I worked with a unit attached to the newly-established University of Namibia (UNAM). Over the next few years, I was constantly in and out of Owambo where I ran programs in applied research and adult education [...].

While relationships with much of the country's "official" society became more remote, as many of my friends moved into the higher echelons of politics and the civil service, moving around Owambo with a vehicle clearly marked "University of Namibia" opened the hearts and doors of people to whom the national university was a matter of immense pride and hope. On occasion, I found myself surrounded by older schoolchildren who asked endless questions about the University and the opportunities that it presented. Local dignitaries, such as pastors and teachers, turned out to be parents or grandparents of my students and insisted in friendly engagement with their children's teacher.

Yet, issues of power in the field were not absent; instead, they emerged – with increasing urgency – with people's expectations that "something come back" to them in exchange for their knowledge and insights that they so generously offered. People in Owambo came to realize, as did I, that the mushrooming enterprises of applied social, including anthropological, research hardly, if ever, resulted in improvements that benefited the local population. The knowledge on the part of both the researcher and her "subjects" that there is little hope for tangible benefits presents, perhaps, the greatest ethical challenge for the citizen anthropologist who engages in applied research with the aspiration "to make a difference" in her society. [...]

CONCLUSIONS

[... I]t would be a fallacy to assume that our relationships with the people studied were quasi naturally more equal and intersubjective, simply because we – as citizen anthropologists – share the same wider geographical and political-historical space with our "subjects." For the southern African context at least, this assumption can be safely thrown out along with the essentializing tag of the "native" anthropologist. Being "citizen anthropologist," instead, indicates a commitment to the broader social context and, most importantly, to issues of equality with the fellow-citizens among whom we work.

Citizenship, then, following Cheater's (1987: 165) understanding as ongoing constructive engagement in a society – in contrast to formal citizenship and the right to vote – transcends notions of bounded culture *and* of the nation state as yet another bounded entity. It includes those locally-based anthropologists who have adopted a long-term commitment to a society – which due to its past and present historical experience in the southern African context certainly extends beyond national boundaries into the wider southern and central African regions. Most importantly, it includes those anthropologists who strive toward an ethics of equality with their fellow-citizens whose lifeworlds they study. It follows that the citizenship of the anthropologist's "subjects" is an equally fluid category which transcends boundaries of "race," ethnicity or nationality.

Thus, essentialist categories of "race," ethnicity or even nationality prove to be of little relevance in the discussion of the ethics and politics of citizen anthropologists. Instead, we suggest viewing each anthropologist in terms of situated identifications. In this way the discussion of the positionality, power and ethics of citizen anthropologists leads the ethics debate to more historically and politically conscious considerations.

REFERENCES

Cheater, A.R. 1987. "The Anthropologist as Citizen: The Diffracted Self?" In *Anthropology at Home*, edited by A. Jackson. London: Tavistock Publications.

Christman, J.B. 1998. "Working in the Field as the Female Friend." *Anthropology and Education Quarterly*, 19(2): 70–85.

Hastrup, K. 1987. "Fieldwork among Friends: Ethnographic Exchange within the Northern Civilization." In *Anthropology at Home,* edited by A. Jackson, 94–108. New York: Tavistock Publications.

Narayan, K. 1993. "How Native Is a 'Native' Anthropologist?" *American Anthropologist*, 95: 671–86. https://doi.org/10.1525/aa.1993.95.3.02a00070.

9.5. "Gone Anthropologist": Epistemic Slippage, Native Anthropology, and the Dilemmas of Representation (2013)

Bernard C. Perley

It all began so innocently. How did a nice self-respecting Native American man working on a career in architecture become an anthropologist? Regarding innocence, don't we all say that when [we] find ourselves mired in existential and, apropos for this chapter, epistemic dilemmas? As for my decision to become an anthropologist, I do have to plead some innocence. I was unaware of how broadly Vine Deloria Jr.'s 1969 publication of his critical essay "Anthropologists and Other Friends" struck a resonant chord in Native American communities across North America. In that essay Deloria states, "Many Indians have come to parrot the ideas of anthropologists because it appears the anthropologists know everything about Indian communities" ([1969] 1988, 82). Not only were Native Americans "parroting" anthropologists, many were "going anthropologist" while pursuing degrees and careers in anthropology. However, what it means to have "gone anthropologist" has changed over time. At first, native anthropology conformed to social scientific conventions in the pre-Deloria period (before the 1969 essay); then discourses shifted to postcolonial critiques of the discipline during the Deloria period and shifted again to a post-Deloria period (let's call it the "indigenous turn") of global indigenous self-making.

EPISTEMIC SLIPPAGE

"Going anthropologist" represents concurrent and seemingly contradictory practices of epistemic discovery – or epistemic slippage. When anthropologists represent Others, they draw from fieldwork experiences as participant observers, which in turn extends their experiences of epistemic slippage. The firsthand accounts of personal experiences become the sources for ethnographic speaking and writing. The practice of representing Others through the authoritative voice of qualified and objective disseminators of Other ways of knowing – be it as professors teaching anthropology classes or through ethnographic accounts – is a practice of slipping into Other systems of knowing. Such slippage is characteristic of the discipline's Enlightenment heritage.

[…] Fabian argues that anthropologists "became serious about epistemology, that is, about the specific conditions of producing anthropological knowledge based on empirical work we call, not quite appropriately, ethnography," and that the "literary turn" made us more scientific because it sharpened our awareness of the epistemological significance of presentation and representation (13–14). Those specific conditions prompt Fabian to argue, "Anthropological practices happen in events and movements. They don't acquire their collective identity from subscribing to a single discourse but from having to face a common predicament: they must let themselves be constituted by facing a world that is non-anthropological" (15).

More important for this chapter, Fabian states, "I deeply believe that a realistic view of our discipline must acknowledge that our kind of science is practiced in the presence of other kinds of knowledge production" (15). In short, disciplinary practice is grounded in epistemic slippage, the process of knowing.

The presumption that anthropologists are authorized to present and represent Others, or, more radically, to present and represent as Others, not only is an uncritical Enlightenment stance of privileging the Western scientific episteme over Other epistemes, but is itself a form of Othering. In summarizing his argument presented in Time and the Other, Fabian states:

> Anthropology has its empirical foundation in ethnographic research, inquiries which even hard-nosed practitioners (the kind who liked to think of their field as a scientific laboratory) carry out as communicative interaction. The sharing of time that such interaction requires demands that ethnographers recognize the people whom they study as their coevals. However – and this is where the contradiction arises – when the same ethnographers represent their knowledge in teaching and writing they do this in terms of a discourse that consistently places those who are talked about in a time other than that of the one who talks. (1983, 22)

The discourse places Others not only in another time but also in another place, thereby relegating Other epistemes to secondary status. Does such Othering perpetuate a Manichaean dichotomy between primary and secondary epistemes such that primary epistemes are the at-home knowledge systems that serve as the ground for knowledge production and the secondary epistemes, as the Other epistemes, are waiting to be discovered? What happens when the epistemic stance is inverted? For a native "going anthropologist," will the native episteme invert the knowledge production privilege? What kinds of epistemic slippage must be negotiated when a native goes anthropologist? Does the native lapse into "reason"? […]

[…] Native Americans who chose anthropology as a career continue to benefit from a discursive and practical space from which to work as carved out by native anthropologist forebears. Continuities, such as the commitment to finding applications from the discipline's knowledge systems supportive of community self-determination and engaging in meaningful dialogue, continue to resonate with native anthropologists. The continuing dilemmas lie at the heart of representation. Academic requirements compel native anthropologists to publish texts that serve the discipline's conditions of merit, but all too often those texts are too specialized in terminology, research focus, and methods of dissemination to be of practical use for the communities from which those academic texts derive. From the perspective of the communities, such studies and scholarly texts are inaccessible and of limited value to the community. Such texts provide evidence that the native has slipped too far into the anthropology episteme. In other words, the native has "gone anthropologist." On the other hand, texts that communities understand and draw significant benefit from may not be accepted by the discipline because they lack scholarly merit. The dilemma facing native anthropologists is determining how far one can slip from one episteme into another and maintain balance, being native and anthropologist simultaneously. One strategy is to produce two sets of texts, one set for the anthropology discipline and one set for the community. Unfortunately, the two sets of texts are often separated from one another. Can there be a middle space where both epistemes may come together to promote mutual slippage toward each other's episteme? As a native anthropologist I offer a possible solution to this representational dilemma.

ALTERNATIVE EPISTEMIC SPACE

As a member of Tobique First Nation and an anthropologist, I have grappled with the dilemmas of representing the important issues and consequences of Maliseet language endangerment to both anthropological and Native American audiences. To accommodate the discipline's merit requirements, I have published peer-reviewed texts such as articles (Perley 2006), book chapters (Perley 2009, 2011a, 2012a, 2012b), and a monograph (Perley 2011b). To satisfy the community's need for practical solutions to prevent Maliseet language loss, I have produced illustrations for Maliseet texts; made artistic productions linking language and landscape; and designed, wrote, and produced a graphic novel reintegrating Maliseet language with Maliseet oral tradition and contemporary issues. These works will not meet academic, peer-reviewed merit requirements. These are two different sets of texts for two different audiences reflecting two different epistemes. Is it possible to bring the two epistemes together onto a common ground from which the members of the two epistemes can understand one another by slipping into a common epistemic world? My solution to this quandary was to bring the two audiences into an alternative epistemic space.

An important first step was to rethink ethnographic representation. In my dual position as a scholar working on language endangerment and language revitalization issues and as a native who has personal experience with the trauma associated with language loss and cultural alienation (Perley 2009, 2011b, 2012a), my academic texts seemed inadequate in conveying the visceral emotive experience when grappling with language and cultural oblivion. I sought to produce an alternative ethnography that graphically represented the trauma of language death, the desperation of language maintenance, and the optimism of language revitalization. The graphic ethnography was presented to my colleagues, and they received it with appreciation. However, their perception of the work was through their experiences viewing artwork rather than viewing ethnography. Undeterred, I produced additional graphic ethnographies that reintegrated language, stories, and landscape, and some of the ethnographies created alternative ethnographic spaces. Figure 6.2 [omitted here] is a photograph of a 360-degree primordial landscape with twelve verses of a Maliseet prayer of "giving thanks." The space integrates an oral traditional story with a construction of a particular point on the reservation and the incorporation of the Maliseet prayer in the Maliseet language. The installation can be experienced by anthropologists as an ethnographic space, while members of the Maliseet community can experience it as a sacred space. Most important, both audiences can experience the installation as ethnographic and sacred space simultaneously. As these various pieces of my graphic ethnography were completed, it became important to assemble the graphic work into an alternative ethnographic space that integrated my textual ethnographies with my graphic ethnographies.

In the fall of 2008 I organized an exhibit of creative work that addressed issues of Maliseet language endangerment, Maliseet cosmogony, and Maliseet "texts." [...] The collected works were presented in a university gallery space and arranged to prompt viewers (readers) to see (read) the connections between the textual and graphic ethnographies. My goal was to represent my collected ethnographies of Maliseet language death, maintenance, and revitalization as one intertextual, intermediated, and interdiscursive event so that the participants approached the exhibit as a graphic, spatial, and experiential ethnography. More important, the ethnographic texts are simultaneously representations of epistemic slippage as well as invitations to engage in epistemic slippage by immersing visitors in an alternative epistemic space.

My ethnography is about two hundred pages of specialized vocabularies, theories, and analyses that will be of interest to academics and perhaps some members of the community (Perley 2011b). Along with my other publications, it will serve as a marker of "merit," indicating that this native has "gone anthropologist" enough to satisfy the requirements of the discipline. However, over two hundred pages of "pure reason" were not enough to capture the visceral impact of the tragedy of language death and subsequent cultural loss that I suffered as a child. Nor will it adequately represent the potential trauma the community faces with Maliseet language and cultural loss. The text is ill suited to convey the vitality and beauty of language, oral traditions, and landscape that is interwoven into an integrated Maliseet cosmogony. My solution was to create alternative texts that conveyed the emotive force of language and cultural loss. Furthermore, the spatial and experiential ethnography created an alternative space for experiencing my representation of Maliseet epistemic space in its textual, graphic, spatial, and integrated complexity. The spatial ethnography provided the visitor an opportunity for multimodal slippage into Maliseet language, culture, and landscape. Rather than invite the viewers to "read" Maliseet ethnography, it invited the viewers to experience Maliseet ethnography by creating a space into which they could slip into a Maliseet world that I conceived, constructed, and re-presented.

EPISTEMIC SLIPPAGE AND EMERGENT REPRESENTATIONS

[…] Going anthropologist is a mode of epistemic slippage that has changed and continues to change according to the contingencies of emergence (Perley 2009). Epistemic slippage […] focuses on agency rather than system, on process rather than structure. To what purpose do anthropologists engage in epistemic slippage? Fischer argues that "it is a form of knowledge, ever evolving, urgently needed today" (49). The experimental systems approach to epistemic slippage is important as a system that produces "epistemic things" from emergent cultural "models."

But, as Fabian argues,

> historically and theoretically, our subject matter (an object made at least as much as found) has been peoples we represented as an Other. We may regret and lament the fact, as I do, that this critical insight is in constant danger of evaporating in clouds of fashionable talk about "othering" … but this should not make us abandon a vision of agency that is in essence dialectical. Anthropology may be what anthropologists do (as someone from my teachers' generation once defined the discipline); but anthropologists do what they do by doing it with, perhaps sometimes onto, others. (Fabian 2007, 5)

For anthropological knowledge to grow, Fabian argues that it requires a dialectical exchange with Other knowledge systems. Anthropological agency, then, is based on "our claims to validity on fieldwork, on direct interaction with those whom we study. Ethnographic authority may be said to rest on 'having been there,' that is, on our presence. But what would our presence count if it were not matched by the presence of those whom we study? Neither presence, ours or theirs, is a natural, physical fact (nor is intersubjectivity as a condition of communicative interaction); it must be achieved and it is always precarious" (Fabian 2007, 5). […]

[T]he opposition between anthropologist and native was never simple and […] there have always been anthropologists studying "exotics" at home. American anthropology has a long history of studying Native American communities. Furthermore, many anthropologists trained in anthropology programs in US universities have done and continue to do fieldwork "at home." The slippage between anthropologist and native was always precarious, but more recently the slippage has become more complicated in its directionality as well as the degrees of accepted slippage. Equally complex are the emergent representations of such slippage.

Epistemic slippage, as a process of knowing others, is the contested ground from which ethnographic representations emerge. The juxtaposition of a set of texts for anthropologists and a set of texts for the communities from which (and for whom) the texts are produced make possible the rekeying (Fischer 2009) of how we think of ethnographies. The standard model of disciplinary merit, the ethnographic text, need not limit the kinds of representation we as anthropologists can produce. Graphic ethnographies can convey other kinds of knowledge and can encourage other kinds of slippage. Assembling the various "texts" into alternative epistemic spaces can enhance slippage between worlds through multimodal slippage. The alternative ethnographic space I propose is the collected and arranged ethnographies produced by an ethnographer and based on the representations of epistemic slippage from working with (as Fabian stated) a community of knowers. It is a public invitation to anthropologists and to natives to evaluate, appreciate, contest, and know something of Other worlds. It is more than a collection of ethnographies or an "epistemic thing." The space represents ethnography as process. As process it is a catalyst for epistemic slippage. And, in turn, epistemic slippage provides the critical ground for our future in anthropology.

REFERENCES

Deloria Jr., Vine. 1988. "Anthropologists and Other Friends." In *Custer Died for Your Sins: An Indian Manifesto.* Norman: University of Oklahoma Press.

Fabian, Johannes. 1983. *Time and the Other: How Anthropology Makes Its Object.* New York: Columbia University Press.

Fabian, Johannes. 2007. *Memory against Culture: Arguments and Reminders.* Durham: Duke University Press.

Fischer, Michael. 2009. *Anthropological Futures.* Durham: Duke University Press.

Perley, Bernard C. 2006. "Aboriginality at Large: Varieties of Resistance in Maliseet Language Instruction." *Identities: Global Studies in Culture and Power*, 13: 187–208. https://doi.org/10.1080/10702890600698587.

———. 2009. "Contingencies of Emergence: Planning Maliseet Language Ideologies." In *Native American Language Ideologies: Language Beliefs, Practices, and Struggles in Indian Country*, edited by Paul V. Kroskrity and Margaret C. Field, 255–70. Tucson: University of Arizona Press.

———. 2011a. "Language as an Integrated Cultural Resource." In *A Companion to Cultural Resource Management*, edited by Thomas F. King. Malden: Wiley-Blackwell.

———. 2011b. *Defying Maliseet Language Death: Emergent Vitalities of Language, Culture, and Identity in Eastern Canada.* Lincoln: University of Nebraska Press.

———. 2012a. "Zombie Linguistics: Experts, Endangered Languages, and the Curse of Undead Voices." *Anthropological Forum*, 22 (2): 133–49.

———. 2012b. "Last Words, Final Thoughts: Collateral Extinctions in Maliseet Language Death." Invited chapter for the edited volume *The Anthropology of Extinction: Essays on Culture and Species Death*, edited by Genese Sodikoff. Bloomington: Indiana University Press.

Section Nine Glossary

citizen anthropology An approach to anthropology that incorporates social responsibility and contribution to a wider community as an integral component of research practice.

situated knowledge The notion that knowledge is highly situated, dependent upon the conditions in which it was produced, and shaped by the social position of the knowledge producer.

SECTION TEN

On Theorizing Globalization

THE SOCIAL CONTEXT

While socioeconomic interconnectedness and exchange are enduring features of humankind, the last two decades of the twentieth century ushered in a period of rapid global spread of capitalist modes of production – what is often termed "neoliberal" capitalism or even just "globalization." This penetration was spurred by several factors, including the breakdown of Soviet regional hegemony and "opening up" of capitalist markets in post-socialist nations; the role of **structural adjustment policies** (SAPs) in compelling national economies in "developing" regions to adopt global capitalism; and the West's use of embargoes and military invasion to pressure hold-out nations to open their economies to free market capitalism. Policy tools of global capitalism's growth, including **free trade policies, free trade zones,** and SAPs, resulted in widespread **depeasantization**, dispossession, migration, and postindustrialization, and these processes brought people around the world together in new and highly unequal relationships.

Within anthropology, discussions emerged over the degree to which global capitalism would result in global sociocultural homogenization (and if so, what would that mean for anthropology's *raison d'etre* as disciplinary specialist in "the other"?). Macro-level theories of economic globalization emerged, as did meso-level theories of "**glocalization**" that emphasized the ways in which people differentially adapt to and understand local forms of capitalism. More broadly, incorporating globalization into anthropological scholarship required rethinking often taken-for-granted conceptions of space, place, culture, and inequality. The selections in this section advance important contributions to our theorizations of globalization.

THE CONVERSATION

Our first essay is by Arjun Appadurai, who is probably best known for his theorization of transnational cultural flows. The piece we chose advocates a theorization of place and locality in anthropology. Appadurai argues that "place" and "culture" have been considered intrinsically connected in anthropological scholarship, with certain world regions coming to symbolize particular cultural issues. But this connection, Appadurai argues, has been assumed and not adequately theorized, leaving a host of potential analytical limitations unchecked.

Reading 10.2, by Akhil Gupta and James Ferguson, turns our attention to space as a key analytic of contemporary anthropology. While anthropological descriptions of "culture" assume spatial boundaries that produce cultural distinctiveness, Gupta and Ferguson (harkening back to Wolf and Hau'ofa) argue that spatial interconnectedness, not division, more accurately characterizes the human condition. Theorizing space, they claim, allows us to perceive and thus question how we formulate differential definitions of "local," "national," and "global" in the first place.

Aihwa Ong is the author of Reading 10.3, which advances a conceptualization of citizenship in an increasingly "deterritorialized" political world. Complicating the dichotomy between citizenship and statelessness, Ong points to the "flexible" ways in which political subjects negotiate access to rights and resources. In particular, Ong argues that global markets, human rights discourses, cyber spaces, and NGO networks break the monopoly of territorialized states over subjects and create emergent and unequal forms of political membership.

Our fourth piece, an excerpt from Faye V. Harrison's book *Outsider Within: Reworking Anthropology in the Global Age*, urges scholars to attend to gendered dimensions of global inequalities. Analyzing gender requires anthropologists to push beyond site-specific foci, Harrison argues, to better comprehend transnational experiences with neoliberal politics. These experiences are shaped not only by gender, but racial and class positions, as well. In particular, Harrison shows that gendered stereotypes of women push them into some of the worst-paid jobs of global capitalist production schemes, where they subsidize the cost of globalized goods and services with their underpaid labor.

Gustavo Lins Ribeiro, the author of Reading 10.5, theorizes "non-hegemonic" forms of globalization that have emerged in response to global capitalism. Focusing on anti-globalization activists, Ribeiro argues that "grassroots" mobilizations of anti-globalization (or alternative globalization) activists constitute a politics of anti-corporate capitalism. This non-hegemonic politics is not affiliated with particular nation-states, parties, or social groups, but rather is cohered by a shared determination to build a more equitable world.

THREE QUESTIONS FOR THE READINGS

1 How did processes of globalization draw attention to the theoretical concerns raised in these pieces?
2 Are these concerns applicable only to contemporary globalization, or are they relevant to earlier and other periods of social thought as well?
3 In addition to place, space, time, inequality, and "posts," what other concepts might require analysis in a context of globalization?

ON THE COMPANION WEBSITE

Life and debt in Jamaica, additional readings, and more.

www.anthropologicaltheory.com

10.1. Theory in Anthropology: Center and Periphery (1986)

Arjun Appadurai

Like the purloined letter, place is so much in the foreground of the anthropological consciousness that its importance has been taken for granted and its implications have not been systematically explored. Whatever else might be in dispute, the idea that culture is a *local* dimension of human behavior is a tenacious and widespread assumption. Though this assumption is itself overdue for critical appraisal, this is not the appropriate format for arguing that need. What does however seem appropriate is that the systematic analysis of locality, as a conceptual issue, and place, as the empirical counterpart to it, be undertaken by those who are concerned about the future of anthropological theory. The comments that follow do no more than sketch out a series of themes (with a minimal set of examples) that suggest why it is worth looking at the history of anthropological theory from this point of view.

At least since the latter part of the nineteenth century, anthropological theory has always been based on the practice of going *somewhere,* preferably somewhere geographically, morally, and socially distant from the theoretical and cultural metropolis of the anthropologist. The science of the other has inescapably been tied to the journey elsewhere. But the question of what kind of elsewhere is tied in complicated ways to the history of European expansion, the vagaries of colonial and postcolonial pragmatics, the shifting tastes of Western men of letters. In turn, changes in anthropological theorizing, influenced in ill-understood ways by these shifting loci of investigation, have themselves influenced fashions in anthropological travel. Places (i.e., particular areas, locations, cultures, societies, regions, even civilizations) are the objects of anthropological study as well as the critical links between description and analysis in anthropological theory.

Let me start with an observation with which few will quarrel. Though all anthropologists traffic in "otherness," we may note that it has always been true that some others are more other than others. From the start, the ethos of anthropology has been driven by the appeal of the small, the simple, the elementary, the face-to-face. In a general way, this drive has had two implications for anthropological theory. The first is that certain forms of sociality (such as kinship), certain forms of exchange (such as gift), certain forms of polity (such as the segmentary state) have been privileged objects of anthropological attention and have constituted the prestige zones of anthropological theory. The second result has been that the anthropology of complex non-Western societies has, till recently, been a second-class citizen in anthropological discourse. This second effect involves a kind of reverse Orientalism, whereby complexity, literacy, historical depth, and structural messiness operate as disqualifications in the struggle of places for a voice in metropolitan theory.

Yet this characterization of the role of complex traditional civilizations in anthropological theory is too simple and conspiratorial. The fact is that the anthropology of complex civilizations does exist, but in a peculiar form. In this form, a few simple theoretical handles become metonyms and surrogates for the civilization or society as a whole: hierarchy in India, honor-and-shame in the circum-Mediterranean, filial piety in China are all examples of what one might call gatekeeping concepts in anthropological theory, concepts, that is, that seem to limit anthropological theorizing about the place in question, and that define the quintessential and dominant questions of interest in the region.

Though such gatekeeping concepts are especially slow to change in regard to complex traditional civilizations, there is something of this effect in anthropological theorizing in general. Thus it is that Africa becomes the locus of many classical social forms, such as the lineage or the segment; tropical south America the arch representative of dual organizations and structured mythological discourse; Melanesia the principal exhibit for the manipulation of bodily substances in the management of society and the cosmos; aboriginal Australia the supreme example of the tension between structural simplicity and classificatory complexity; Polynesia the central place for the mechanics of reciprocity, and so forth. This is not to suggest that such issues are never raised in contexts other than their classical ones, but rather that the original loci retain a special authority in regard to the theoretical issue in question. Nor is it to suggest that this tendency to see whole societies through some particular conceptual vantage point is an ahistorical matter, without dynamic, context, or explanation.

The point is that there is a tendency for places to become showcases for specific issues over time, and that the sources and implications of this tendency are poorly understood. This tendency, especially pronounced in the case of complex societies, has two implications. One is that the discussion of the theoretical issues tends (surreptitiously) to take on a restrictive local cast, while on the other hand the study of other issues in the place in question is retarded, and thus the overall nature of the anthropological interpretation of the particular society runs the risk of serious distortion. Here, of course, the central questions anthropologists have to ask themselves regarding anthropological theory over time, and at any point in time, concern whether these gatekeeping concepts, these theoretical metonyms, really reflect something significant about the place in question, or whether they reveal a relatively arbitrary imposition of the whims of anthropological fashion on particular places. [...]

If places become guardians of particular cultural features or of particular forms of sociality, does this not affect the way these cultural features and forms of sociality are analyzed in other places? Do cities, by definition, tend to be characterized excessively by networks, brokerage, ethnicity, and entrepreneurs as a result of the original African copyright? Do all forms of culturally organized inequality begin to be seen excessively through the trope of caste? Does the special connection of nature and culture in mythological discourse in tropical South America, and its binary ideology, get imputed freely to places where it is less legitimate? Did the African model of segmentation excessively dominate accounts of social structure in the Middle East, the New Guinea highlands, and elsewhere?

Yet another problem is the relationship, in anthropological theory, between place, comparison, and generalization. To the degree that anthropological theorizing has been unwittingly affected by the shifting loci of its production, comparison becomes difficult, for a critical dimension of variability (not just in the data but in the relationship between observer and observed) is left unexamined. Where comparison (and generalization) have been successful in anthropology, they have occurred most often in the context of small-scale societies and have involved highly schematized aspects of social life, such as kinship terminology. As the societies under consideration become more complex, literate, and historical, the kind of decontextualization that facilitates generalization becomes harder to accomplish. Comparison also becomes difficult when theoretical interest focuses on qualitative, subjective, and experiential aspects of social life, rather than on quantitative, objective, or structural phenomena. Thus, the "interpretive turn" in cultural anthropology, which dates from the early 1970s, and the recent interest in the historicity of small-scale societies, both remarked by Ortner, tend to carry on an old tilt in anthropology, which is to localize the human condition. On the other hand, the other recent trends in anthropology discussed by Ortner, which focus on practice and on political economy tend, for all their differences, to look for cross-cultural regularities. [...]

The central fact here is that what anthropologists find, in this or that place, far from being independent data for the construction and verification of theory, is in fact a very complicated compound of local realities and the contingencies of metropolitan theory. Needless to say, all the social and human sciences share this problem regarding the relationship between theory and data, observer and observed, subject and object. What I am suggesting is that the "place" aspect of this problem is greater for anthropology than for any of the other human sciences, with the possible exception of history, and that the degree of attention accorded to this factor by anthropologists so far is in inverse proportion to its importance. In the cases of anthropology and history, given their idiographic, qualitative, and narrative orientations, place is not just a trivial contingency associated with data gathering, but a vital dimension of the subject matter of the disciplines. Since a great deal of what I have said so far has been schematic and rhetorical, I conclude with two examples, one which focuses on place and the other on theory.

In regard to place, let us consider the case of India. By and large, anthropological studies of India have focused, both ethnographically and theoretically, on the institution of caste and on its ideological framework – hierarchy. There have been important minority voices, both empirical and theoretical, that have discussed tribes, cities, families, temples, ascetic groups. So also there have been those who have looked at other ideological problems, such as authority, legitimacy, privacy, and domesticity (rather than just hierarchy and its twin – purity/pollution). Yet when India is referred to in the central zones of anthropological theory, it is rarely that caste and hierarchy are not the sole points of interest. In fact, in the last few years, a very complex set of anthropologies has emerged in South Asia, in which classical concerns with hierarchy play some part but do not dominate the proceedings. Yet it is my guess that it will be a long time before these local anthropological contributions will be able to gain a place in metropolitan anthropological discourse. India remains a stellar example of the anthropological black hole, where a variety of ideas, findings, and possibilities vanish from the metropolitan gaze.

Ortner is quite right to note that "history" and "practice" are important symbols of recent anthropological theory. Part of the significance of the idea of practice, especially as discussed by Pierre Bourdieu, is that it encourages us to examine the peculiar complicities between subject and object in anthropological activity. The revived excitement about history has itself a very complex relationship to the theme of this essay, for in different places this excitement takes very different forms. For one thing, certain independent theoretical fashions, involving the conjuncture of history and structure, the nature of theatricality in politics, and the problem of ethnographic time, which are of especial interest in the Pacific and in Southeast Asia, might convey the erroneous impression that the problem of dealing with history has not been significantly engaged by anthropologists working in other areas (such as India, Africa, the Middle East, native North America, or China), who might have quite other theoretical agendas. Thus, the geographical loci of the "new" interest in history do themselves conceal the fact that anthropology as a whole has shifted theoretically in ways that make the older modes of, and spatial contexts for, handling history seem less exciting. In fact, the conjunctures that are occurring between the practice of anthropology and history reflect a large number of variations, some of which have to do with older interests and methods in both disciplines in different empirical locations. Thus the dialogue of history with anthropology is very different, depending on whether one eavesdrops on it in Indonesia, India, Africa, Mesoamerica, or Europe, for reasons that have as much to do with the history of anthropology as with what Marshall Sahlins calls the anthropology of history.

Today, thus, place has a dual, even contradictory, relationship to theory in anthropology. On the one hand, as certain kinds of theorizing in anthropology become cryptophilosophical, the original place of origin of ethnographic descriptions becomes quite irrelevant. On the other hand, there is a growing tendency to produce careful, ethnographically based regional collections whose aim is to build theory out of a genuinely multidisciplinary and comparative picture of large regions and civilizations. The arbitrary hegemony of one region or regions over others in the making of anthropological theory is likely to be reified by the first tendency and discouraged by the second. As to which is the more likely possibility, that will depend at least in part on our willingness to be self-conscious about the problem of place in our own theorizing.

10.2. Beyond "Culture": Space, Identity, and the Politics of Difference (1992)

Akhil Gupta and James Ferguson

Representations of space in the social sciences are remarkably dependent on images of break, rupture, and disjunction. The distinctiveness of societies, nations, and cultures is based upon a seemingly unproblematic division of space, on the fact that they occupy "naturally" discontinuous spaces. The premise of discontinuity forms the starting point from which to theorize contact, conflict, and contradiction between cultures and societies. For example, the representation of the world as a collection of "countries," as in most world maps, sees it as an inherently fragmented space, divided by different colors into diverse national societies, each "rooted" in its proper place (cf. Malkki 1992). It is so taken for granted that each country embodies its own distinctive culture and society that the terms "society" and "culture" are routinely simply appended to the names of nation-states, as when a tourist visits India to understand "Indian culture" and "Indian society," or Thailand to experience "Thai culture," or the United States to get a whiff of "American culture."

Of course, the geographical territories that cultures and societies are believed to map onto do not have to be nations. We do, for example, have ideas about culture-areas that overlap several nation-states, or of multicultural nations. On a smaller scale, perhaps, are our disciplinary assumptions about the association of culturally unitary groups (tribes or peoples) with "their" territories: thus, "the Nuer" live in "Nuerland" and so forth. The clearest illustration of this kind of thinking are the classic "ethnographic maps" that purported to display the spatial distribution of peoples, tribes, and cultures. But in all these cases, space itself becomes a kind of neutral grid on which cultural difference, historical memory, and societal organization are inscribed. It is in this way that space functions as a central organizing principle in the social sciences at the same time that it disappears from analytical purview. [...]

[... C]hallenging the ruptured landscape of independent nations and autonomous cultures raises the question of understanding social change and cultural transformation as situated within interconnected spaces. The presumption that spaces are autonomous has enabled the power of topography to conceal successfully the topography of power. The inherently fragmented space assumed in the definition of anthropology as the study of cultures (in the plural) may have been one of the reasons behind the long-standing failure to write anthropology's history as the biography of imperialism. For if one begins with the premise that spaces have *always* been hierarchically interconnected, instead of naturally disconnected, then cultural and social change becomes not a matter of cultural contact and articulation but one of rethinking difference *through* connection.

To illustrate, let us examine one powerful model of cultural change that attempts to relate dialectically the local to larger spatial arenas: articulation. Articulation models, whether they come from Marxist structuralism or from "moral economy," posit a primeval state of autonomy (usually labeled "precapitalist"), which is then violated by global capitalism. The result is that both local and larger spatial arenas are transformed, the local more than the global to be sure, but not necessarily in a predetermined direction. This notion of articulation allows one to explore the richly unintended consequences of, say, colonial capitalism, where loss occurs alongside invention. Yet, by taking a preexisting, localized "community" as a given starting point, it fails to examine sufficiently the processes (such as the structures of feeling that pervade the imagining of community) that go into the construction of space as place or locality in the first instance. In other words, instead of assuming the autonomy of the primeval community, we need to examine how it was formed *as a community* out of the interconnected space that always already existed. Colonialism, then, represents the displacement of one form of interconnection by another. This is not to deny that colonialism, or an expanding capitalism, does indeed have profoundly dislocating effects on existing societies. But by always foregrounding the spatial distribution of hierarchical power relations, we can better understand the process whereby a space achieves a distinctive *identity* as a place. Keeping in mind that notions of locality or community refer both to a demarcated physical space *and* to clusters of interaction, we can see that the identity of a place emerges by the intersection of its specific involvement in a system of hierarchically organized spaces with its cultural construction as a community or locality. [...]

People have undoubtedly always been more mobile and identities less fixed than the static and typologizing approaches of classical anthropology would suggest. But today, the rapidly expanding and quickening mobility of people combines with the refusal of cultural products and practices to "stay put" to give a profound sense of a loss of territorial roots, of an erosion of the cultural distinctiveness of places, and of ferment in anthropological theory. The apparent deterritorialization of identity that accompanies such processes has made Clifford's question (1988:275) a key one for recent anthropological inquiry: "What does it mean, at the end of the twentieth century, to speak ... of a 'native land'? What processes rather than essences are involved in present experiences of cultural identity?" [...]

The irony of these times, however, is that as actual places and localities become ever more blurred and indeterminate, *ideas* of culturally and ethnically distinct places become perhaps even more salient. [...]

As Malkki (1992) shows, two naturalisms must be challenged here. First is what we will call the ethnological habit of taking the association of a culturally unitary group (the "tribe" or "people") and "its" territory as natural, which is discussed in the previous section. A second, and closely related, naturalism is what we will call the national habit of taking the association of citizens of states and their territories as natural. Here the exemplary image is of the conventional world map of nation-states, through which schoolchildren are taught such deceptively simple-sounding beliefs as that France is where the French live, America is where the Americans live, and so on. Even a casual observer, of course, knows that not only Americans live in America, and it is clear that the very question of what is a "real American" is largely up for grabs. But even anthropologists still talk of "American culture" with no clear understanding of what that means, because we assume a natural association of a culture ("American culture"), a people ("Americans"), and a place ("the United States of America"). Both the ethnological and the national naturalisms present associations of people and place as solid, commonsensical, and agreed upon, when they are in fact contested, uncertain, and in flux. [...]

As an alternative to this way of thinking about cultural difference, we want to problematize the unity of the "us" and the otherness of the "other," and question the radical separation between the two that makes the opposition possible in the first place. We are interested less in establishing a dialogic relation between geographically distinct societies than in exploring the processes of *production* of difference in a world of culturally, socially, and economically interconnected and interdependent spaces. The difference is fundamental, and can be illustrated by a brief examination of one text that has been highly praised within the "cultural critique" movement.

Marjorie Shostak's *Nisa: The Life and Words of a !Kung Woman* (1981) has been very widely admired for its innovative use of life history, and has been hailed as a noteworthy example of polyphonic experimentation in ethnographic writing (Clifford 1986, 1988:42; Marcus and Fischer 1986:58–9; Pratt 1986). But with respect to the issues we have discussed here, *Nisa* is a very conventional, and deeply flawed, work. The individual, Nisa, is granted a degree of singularity, but she is used principally as the token of a type: "the !Kung." The San-speaking !Kung of Botswana ("the Bushmen" of old) are presented as a distinct, "other," and apparently primordial "people." Shostak treats the Dobe !Kung as essentially survivals of a prior evolutionary age: they are "one of the last remaining traditional gatherer-hunter societies," racially distinct, traditional, and isolated (1981:4). Their experience of "culture change" is "still quite recent and subtle," and their traditional value system "mostly intact" (1981:6). "Contact" with "other groups" of agricultural and pastoral peoples has occurred, according to Shostak, only since the 1920s, and it is only since the 1960s that the isolation of the !Kung has really broken down, raising for the first time the issue of "change," "adaptation," and "culture contact" (1981:346).

The space the !Kung inhabit, the Kalahari desert, is clearly radically different and separate from our own. Again and again the narrative returns to the theme of isolation: in a harsh ecological setting, a way of life thousands of years old has been preserved only through its extraordinary spatial separateness. The anthropological task, as Shostak conceives it, is to cross this spatial divide, to enter into this land that time forgot, a land (as Wilmsen [1989:10] notes) with antiquity but no history, to listen to the voices of women, which might reveal "what their lives had been like for generations, possibly even for thousands of years" (Shostak 1981:6).

The exoticization implicit in this portrait, in which the !Kung appear almost as living on another planet, has drawn surprisingly little criticism from theorists of ethnography. Pratt has rightly pointed out the "blazing contradiction" between the portrait of primal beings untouched by history and the genocidal history of the white "Bushman conquest" (1986:48). As she says,

> What picture of the !Kung would one draw if instead of defining them as survivors of the stone age and a delicate and complex adaptation to the Kalahari desert, one looked at them as survivors of capitalist expansion, and a delicate and complex adaptation to three centuries of violence and intimidation? [Pratt 1986:49]

But even Pratt retains the notion of "the !Kung" as a preexisting ontological entity – "survivors," not products (still less producers), of history. "They" are victims, having suffered the deadly process of "contact" with "us."

A very different and much more illuminating way of conceptualizing cultural difference in the region may be found in Wilmsen's devastating recent critique of the anthropological cult of "the Bushman" (1989). Wilmsen shows how, in constant interaction with a wider network of social relations, the difference that Shostak takes as a starting point came to be produced in the first place – how, one might say, "the Bushmen" came to be Bushmen. He demonstrates that Sanspeaking people have been in continuous interaction with other groups for as long as we have evidence for; that political and economic relations linked the supposedly isolated Kalahari with a regional political economy both in the colonial and precolonial eras; that San-speaking people have often held cattle; and that no strict separation of pastoralists and foragers can be sustained. [...] Moreover, he shows that the "Bushman/San" label has been in existence for barely half a century, the category having been produced through the "retribalization" of the colonial period (1989:280); and that "the cultural conservatism uniformly attributed to these people by almost all anthropologists who have worked with them until recently, is a consequence – not a cause – of the way they have been integrated into the modern capitalist economies of Botswana and Namibia" (1989:12).

[...] Where Shostak takes difference as given and concentrates on listening "across cultures," Wilmsen performs the more radical operation of interrogating the "otherness" of the other, situating the production of cultural difference within the historical processes of a socially and spatially interconnected world.

What is needed, then, is more than a ready ear and a deft editorial hand to capture and orchestrate the voices of "others"; what is needed is a willingness to interrogate, politically and historically, the apparent "given" of a world in the first place divided into "ourselves" and "others." A first step on this road is to move beyond naturalized conceptions of spatialized "cultures" and to explore instead the production of difference within common, shared, and connected spaces – "the San," for instance, not as "a people," "native" to the desert, but as a historically constituted and de-propertied category systematically relegated to the desert.

The move we are calling for, most generally, is away from seeing cultural difference as the correlate of a world of "peoples" whose separate histories wait to be bridged by the anthropologist and toward seeing it as a product of a shared historical process that differentiates the world as it connects it. [...]

REFERENCES

Clifford, James. 1986. "On Ethnographic Allegory." In *Writing Culture: The Poetics and Politics of Ethnography*, edited by James Clifford and George Marcus, 98–121. Berkeley: University of California Press.

———. 1988. *The Predicament of Culture*. Cambridge: Harvard University Press.

Malkki, Liisa. 1992. "National Geographic: The Rooting of Peoples and the Territorialization of National Identity Among Scholars and Refugees." *Cultural Anthropology* 7 (1): 24–44. http://doi.org/10.1525/can.1992.7.1.02a00030.

Marcus, George E., and Michael M.J. Fischer. 1986. *Anthropology as Cultural Critique: An Experimental Moment in the Human Sciences*. Chicago: University of Chicago Press.

Pratt, Mary Louise. 1986. "Fieldwork in Common Places." In *Writing Culture: The Poetics and Politics of Ethnography*, edited by James Clifford and George Marcus, 98–121. Berkeley: University of California Press.

Shostak, Marjorie. 1981. *Nisa: The Life and Words of a !Kung Woman*. Cambridge: Harvard University Press.

Wilmsen, Edwin N. 1989. *Land Filled with Flies: A Political Economy of the Kalahari*. Chicago: University of Chicago Press.

10.3. Mutations in Citizenship (2006)

Aihwa Ong

We can trace mutations in citizenship to global flows and their configuration of new spaces of entangled possibilities. An ever-shifting landscape shaped by the flows of markets, technologies, and populations challenges the notion of citizenship tied to the terrain and imagination of a nation-state (Anderson, 1991[1983]). Mobile markets, technologies, and populations interact to shape social spaces in which mutations in citizenship are crystallized. The different elements of citizenship (rights, entitlements, etc.), once assumed to go together, are becoming disarticulated from one another, and re-articulated with universalizing forces and standards. So while in theory political rights depend on membership in a nation-state, in practice, new entitlements are being realized through situated mobilizations and claims in milieus of globalized contingency.

New connections among citizenship elements and mobile forms suggest that we have moved beyond the idea of citizenship as a protected status in a nation-state, and as a condition opposed to the condition of statelessness (Arendt, 1998[1958]). Binary oppositions between citizenship and statelessness, and between national territoriality and its absence, are not useful for thinking about emergent spaces and novel combinations of globalizing and situated variables. For instance, market-driven state practices fragment the national terrain into zones of hyper-growth. These spaces are plugged into transnational networks of markets, technology, and expertise.

Meanwhile, strict discriminations between the citizens and foreigners are dropped in favor of the pursuit of human capital. Such modes of governing engender a checkerboard patterning of the national terrain, thus producing an effect of graduated or variegated sovereignty (Ong, 2000). Some sites and zones are invested with more political resources than others. Meanwhile, rights and entitlements once associated with all citizens are becoming linked to neoliberal criteria, so that entrepreneurial expatriates come to share in the rights and benefits once exclusively claimed by citizens. The difference between having and not having citizenship is becoming blurred as the territorialization of entitlements is increasingly challenged by deterritorialized claims beyond the state.

Universalizing market interests, technologies, and NGOs become articulated with citizenship orders, creating new sites for the making of new claims for resources from state as well as non-state institutions.

We used to think of different dimensions of citizenship – rights, entitlements, a state, territoriality, etc. – as more or less tied together. Increasingly, some of these components are becoming disarticulated from each other, and articulated with diverse universalizing norms defined by markets, neoliberal values, or human rights. At the same time, diverse mobile populations (expatriates, refugees, migrant workers) can claim rights and benefits associated with citizenship, even as many citizens come to have limited or contingent protections within their own countries. Thus, the (re)combinations of globalizing forces and situated elements produce distinctive environments in which citizens, foreigners, and asylum-seekers make political claims through pre-existing political membership as well as on the grounds of universalizing criteria.

Given this scenario of shifting "global assemblages" (Ong and Collier, 2005), the sites of citizenship mutations are not defined by conventional geography. The space of the assemblage, rather than the territory of the nation-state, is the site for new political mobilizations and claims. In sites of emergence, a spectrum of mobile and excluded populations articulates rights and claims in universalizing terms of neoliberal criteria or human rights. Specific problematizations and resolutions to diverse regimes of living cannot be predetermined in advance. For instance, in the EU zone, unregulated markets and migrant flows threaten protections associated with liberal traditions. In emerging Asian sites, the embrace of self-enterprising values has made citizenship rights and benefits contingent upon individual market performance. In camps of the disenfranchised or displaced, bare life becomes the ground for political claims, if not for citizenship, then for the right to survive. In short, instead of all citizens enjoying a unified bundle of citizenship rights, we have a shifting political landscape in which heterogeneous populations claim diverse rights and benefits associated with citizenship, as well as universalizing criteria of neoliberal norms or human rights.

MARKET BLOC AND POLITICAL LIBERALISM

In the West, the European Union has been one of the most ambitious attempts to form a market zone by assembling various polities and cultures. With the rapid expansion of the bloc, the articulation of market interests with political rights has crystallized long-standing ambivalence over the erosion of cultural traditions and liberal norms associated with post-war European citizenship. In the region, global market forces and neoliberal criteria have come to articulate entrenched political norms and entitlements. For instance, opening markets to migrant labor – guest workers and illegal aliens – has ignited fierce debates about the integration of diverse foreign communities. On the one hand, there is talk about the need to balance diverse immigrant populations of non-European origins with an imaginary of European civilization. On the other, pro-human rights movements talk about "disaggregating" citizenship into different bundles of rights and benefits, so that European states can differently incorporate migrants and non-citizens. Such bundles of limited benefits and civil rights thus constitute a form of partial citizenship, or "postnational" political membership for migrant workers (Soysal, 1994). This political resolution, it is argued, can accommodate cultural diversity without undermining European liberal democracy and the universals of individual civil rights. But ambivalence remains, as a strong groundswell against the possible inclusion of Muslim Turkey in the bloc has fueled resistance to EU expansion.

Another dimension of the articulation between citizenship and deregulated markets is widely viewed as a threat to what Jürgen Habermas has called the "democratic achievements of European societies" – inclusive systems of social security, social norms regarding class and gender, investment in public social services, rejection of the death penalty, and so on. To counter the market-generated "democratic deficit" in public life, Habermas calls for the creation of a Europe-wide public sphere and constitution that can give symbolic weight to the shared political culture underpinned by the cluster of European welfare features (Habermas, 2001). The spring 2005 French and Dutch votes against the ratification of the existing European constitution delivered powerful statements about the primacy of national interests over the unity to be wrought through neoliberal policies. The rejection of the constitution by major members reflects popular sentiments against the widespread adoption of market-based criteria, as well as a positive affirmation of national regimes that preserve elements of social citizenship and protection for their people. There is now profound doubt about the feasibility of a Europe-wide solidarity built primarily on principles of market efficiency and competitiveness.

ZONES OF ENTITLEMENT

In contrast to the Euro zone, emergent sites of growth in Asia currently display less ambivalence over the adoption of neoliberal values in policies shaping citizenship. These sites recognize that articulation with transnational networks and global professionals is crucial for their emergence as centers of global capitalism. Transnational itineraries and practices enhance the capacity of professionals and investors to negotiate national spaces, while the desire for talented actors has induced changes in immigration laws. Complex affiliations by elite mobile actors allow for temporary, multiple, and partial ascription, thus creating conditions for expatriate populations to claim citizenship-like entitlements.

The concept of "flexible citizenship" describes maneuvers of mobile subjects who respond fluidly and opportunistically to dynamic borderless market conditions. Global markets induce such activities, so that "flexibility, migration, and relocations, instead of being coerced or resisted, have become practices to strive for rather than stability" (Ong, 1999: 19). Furthermore, nation-states seeking wealth-bearing and talented foreigners adjust immigration laws to favor elite migrant subjects. Thus a new synergy between global capitalism and commercialized citizenship creates milieus where market-based norms articulate the norms of citizenship.

This premium on flexible, self-enterprising subjects originated in advanced democracies that had steadily adopted market-driven rationality in politics. Such neoliberal ideas stem from Frederic von Hayek's theory of the *homo economicus* as an instrumentalist figure forged in the effervescent conditions of market competition. The ideas of individual economic agency as the most efficient form for distributing public resources were embraced under the "neo-conservative" policies of Thatcherism and Reaganomics.

This shift toward a neoliberal technology of governing holds that the security of citizens, their well-being and quality of life, are increasingly dependent on their own capacities as free individuals to confront globalized insecurities by making calculations and investments in their lives.

For instance, in Tony Blair's New Britannica, citizens are generally governed "through freedom," or an inducement for formally free subjects to make calculative choices on their own behalf. Government is no longer interested in taking care of every citizen, but wants him/her to act as a free subject who self-actualizes and relies on autonomous action to confront globalized insecurities. There is thus a fundamental shift in the ethics of subject formation, or the ethics of citizenship, as governing becomes concerned less with the social management of the population (biopolitics) than with individual self-governing (ethico-politics) (Rose, 1999). Such ethics are framed as an animation of various capacities of individual freedom, expressed both in the citizen's freedom from state protection and guidance, as well as freedom to make choices as a self-maximizing individual. In the USA, administrative practices that govern through the aspirations of subjects especially target the urban poor, immigrants, and refugees who are viewed as less capable of self-improvement. But as neoliberal values of flexibility, mobility, and entrepreneurialism become ideal qualities of citizenship, they also undermine the democratic achievements of American liberalism based on ideals of equal rights (Ong, 2003). Tensions between neoliberal values of citizens as economic agents, and liberal ideals of citizens as defenders of political freedom continue to roil American political life.

Neoliberal ideas and practices migrate and are taken up in new zones of hyper-growth. In democratic, socialist, and authoritarian Asian settings, citizens are urged to be self-enterprising, not only to cope with uncertainties and risks, but also to raise the overall "human quality" of their societies. Thus, in East and South Asian environments, neoliberal ethics of self-responsible citizenship are linked to social obligations to build the nation. In India and Malaysia, discourses about "knowledge workers" and "knowledge society" urge citizens to self-improve in order to develop high-tech industries. In Singapore, the accumulation of intellectual capital as an obligation of citizenship is most extreme. Ordinary citizens are expected to develop new mindsets and build digital capabilities, while professionals are urged to achieve norms of "techno-preneurial citizenship" or lose out to more skilled and entrepreneurial foreigners and be reduced to a second-class citizenry.

In short, neoliberal values of self-management and self-enterprise have different implications for citizenship, depending on interactions with particular political environments. While the tendency in Britain and the USA is to focus on the self-governing and technologically savvy citizen as a participant in civil society, in Asian growth zones, the discourse of the self-improving and entrepreneurial citizen is linked to "civic society," or the building of national solidarity. The common feature is that across these diverse milieus, the stakes of citizenship are raised for the majority. Especially in hyper-capitalist zones, those who cannot scale the skills ladder or measure up to the norms of self-governing are increasingly marginalized as deviant or subjects who threaten the security of the globalized milieu. Thus, the articulation of neoliberal criteria and situated citizenship regimes undercuts the protection of citizenship entitlements and blurs political distinctions between citizens and talented foreigners.

ARENAS OF POLITICAL CLAIMS

But the mix of market-opportunism and citizenship has also engendered conditions for greater political activism. In non-democratic countries embracing market-driven policies, new arenas are opening up for ordinary people to claim justice, accountability, and demo-cratic freedoms. The confluence of market forces and digital technologies have pried open cracks in the interstices of highly controlled societies, thus creating conditions for exciting outbursts of popular demands for democracy by ordinary people. [...]

SHEER SURVIVAL

[One] arena of political mobilization is the space of endangerment and neglect. Here the question is whether political resolutions to the plight of imperiled or abject bodies are framed in terms of the binary opposition between citizenship and statelessness. Giorgio Agamben draws a stark distinction between citizens who enjoy juridical-legal rights and excluded groups who dwell in "a zone of indistinction." Only the erasure of the division between People (political body) and people (excluded bodies), he maintains, can restore humanity to the globally excluded who have been denied citizenship (Agamben, 1998: 177, 180). Such views are reflected in claims that the human rights regime is capable of transforming millions of people enduring a bare existence in Africa, Latin America, and Asia into citizens, thus actualizing their humanity. But the rhetoric of ethical globalization operates at too vast a scale to deal with specific milieus of exclusion and endangerment. Furthermore, the focus on citizenship and human rights gives short shrift to other modes of ethical reflection and argumentation. It is by no means clear that the right to survival will everywhere be translated into citizenship or merely legitimized on the grounds of common humanity, or relevance to labor markets. Let me briefly cite three situations of interventions on behalf of the injured or threatened body, and their different resolutions in relation to citizenship.

In recent decades, health-based claims have become an important part of citizenship rights in the West. In the aftermath of the Chernobyl accident in the Ukraine, sufferers claimed biomedical resources and social equity, thus giving rise to a notion of "bi-ological citizenship" (Petryna, 2002). In France, migrants have recently made health the ground for claiming asylum. Didier Fassin argues that the suffering body of the

HIV-infected migrant reverses public perception of his biopolitical otherness rooted in race and alien status. Increasingly, some form of legal recognition is awarded in the name of humanity, i.e. the right to a healthy body, regardless of the citizenship of the patient (Fassin, 2001).

The explosive growth of NGOs is an index of the humanitarian industry that seeks to represent the varied interests of the politically dispossessed. Increasingly, such voluntary groups are shaped by specific interests, affiliations, and ethics, forming themselves into socio-political groups in order to make particular claims on states and corporations. Thus, the language of universal human rights is often superseded by more specific categories finely tuned to the criteria of state or philanthropic organizations. In the non-state administration of excluded humanity, groups and individuals are sorted into various categories, in relation to particular needs, prioritized interests, and potential affiliations with powers-that-be. These are "counter-politics of sheer life" – a situated form of political mobilization that involves ethical claims to resources articulated in terms of needs as living beings (Collier and Lakoff, 2005: 29).

The politics of sheer life is emerging in Southeast Asia, where a vast female migrant population – working as maids, factory workers, or prostitutes – is regularly exposed to slave-like conditions. Feminist NGOs invoke not the human rights of female migrants but something more minimal and attainable, i.e. biological survival, or "biowelfare." The claims of a healthy and unharmed migrant body are articulated not in terms of a common humanity, but of the dependency of the host society on foreign workers to sustain a high standard of living. NGOs invoke the ethics of reciprocity or at least recognition of economic symbiosis between migrant workers and the affluent employers who feel entitled to their cheap foreign labor. Where citizenship does not provide protection for the migrant worker, the joining of a healthy body and dependency on foreign workers produces a kind of bio-legitimacy that is perhaps a first step toward the recognition of their moral status, but short of human rights.

A simple opposition between territorialized citizenship and deterritorialized human rights is not able to capture the varied assemblages that are the sites of contemporary political claims by a range of residential, expatriate, and migrant actors. The confluence of territorialized and deterritorialized forces forms milieus in which problems of the human are crystallized and problems posed and resolved. Diverse actors invoke not territorialized notions of citizenship, but new claims – postnational, flexible, technological, cyber-based, and biological – as grounds for resources, entitlements, and protection. These various sites and claims attest to the contingent nature of what is at stake in being human today. Such political mobilizations engage but also go beyond human rights in resolution to situated problems of contemporary life. In addition to the nation-state, entities such as corporations and NGOs have become practitioners of humanity, defining and representing varied categories of human beings according to degrees of economic, biopolitical, and moral worthiness. Diverse regimes of living are in play. In short, global assemblages crystallize specific problems and resolutions to questions of contemporary living, thus further disarticulating and deterritorializing aspects of citizenship.

REFERENCES

Agamben, G. 1998. *Homo Sacer: Sovereign Power and Bare Life*, trans. by Daniel Heller-Roazen. Stanford: Stanford University Press.

Anderson, B. 1991[1983]. *Imagined Communities,* 2nd ed. London: Verso.

Arendt, H. 1998[1958]. *The Human Condition*, with an introduction by Margaret Canovaan, 2nd ed. Chicago: University of Chicago Press.

Collier, S.J., and A. Lakoff. 2005. "Regimes of Living." In *Global Assemblages: Technology, Politics, and Ethics as Anthropological Problems*, edited by A. Ong and S.J. Collier. Malden: Blackwell.

Fassin, D. 2001. "The Biopolitics of Otherness," *Anthropology Today* 17 (1): 3–23. http://doi.org/10.1111/1467-8322.00039.

Habermas, J. 2001. "Why Europe Needs a Constitution," *New Left Review* 11 (Sept–Oct): 5–26.

Ong, A. 1999. *Flexible Citizenship: The Cultural Logics of Transnationality*. Durham: Duke University Press.

Ong, A. 2000. "Graduated Sovereignty in Southeast Asia," *Theory, Culture & Society* 17 (4): 55–75. https://doi.org/10.1177%2F02632760022051310.

Ong, A. 2003. *Buddha is Hiding: Refugees, Citizenship, the New America*. Berkeley: University of California Press.

Ong, A., and S.J. Collier (eds.). 2005. *Global Assemblages: Technology, Politics, and Ethics as Anthropological Problems*. Malden: Blackwell.

Petryna, A. 2002. *Life Exposed: Biological Citizens after Chernobyl*. Princeton: Princeton University Press.

Rose, N. 1999. *Powers of Freedom: Reframing Political Thought*. Cambridge: Cambridge University Press.

Soysal, Y. 1994. *The Limits of Citizenship: Migrants and Postnational Membership in Europe*. Chicago: University of Chicago Press.

10.4. Global Apartheid at Home and Abroad (2008)

Faye V. Harrison

FROM URBAN TO GLOBAL APARTHEID

Recent trends in anthropology point to the usefulness of conducting research across multiple sites. This especially makes sense in light of the fact that anthropologists are increasingly thinking with deterritorialized concepts of culture and nation and are more apt to organize research around analytical units such as diasporic and transnational social fields (Appadurai 1991; Basch, Schiller, and Blanc 1994; Gupta and Ferguson 1992). As the beneficiary of multisited analyses, anthropological inquiry and applications must reject "the false dichotomy between First and Third Worlds" (Nash 1994, 9). As June Nash (1994, 9) writes, we must recognize "the commonalities in the welfare problems faced by women trying to feed their families and keep their children alive, whether they live in drug-war-devastated inner cities of industrialized [or deindustrialized] countries or in militarized countries where conflicts are exacerbated by U.S. arms shipments." On a similar note, Owen Lynch (1994, 37) argues that in light of the current globalized context, "what [anthropologists learn] about those living in one city often has implications or linkages of space-time distanciation with those living in another." He goes on to state that "it behooves ... anthropologists to take time-space [distanciation] into account and not remain with the localized fragmentations of place and identity to which postmodernism has so forcefully, but narrowly, redirected our attention" (49).

Social analysts who are taking the implications of globalization seriously are able to see that the Contract with America (advocated by controversial Speaker of the House Newt Gingrich during the Bill Clinton administration), and, before it, Reaganomics, the "Daddy Bush ditto" and continuities through Clinton and George W. Bush, are the U.S. variants of a broader process of structural adjustment, which, as I suggested earlier, is more than just the institution-specific programs and conditionalities that the International Monetary Fund (IMF) mandates debt-ridden economies in the Third World to follow (Sparr 1992).

Beyond these, structural adjustment is an international and transnational policy climate and development strategy informed by a neoliberal macroeconomic paradigm and worldview, which valorize laissez-faire capitalism. This worldview assumes that free-market forces will automatically lead to efficient and productive economies in the long run. According to this logic, the less government regulation and the more privatization, the better. Structural adjustments, then, are put into place to redefine and redirect the role of the state and to expand the rule of the market, which supposedly has the capacity to meet all needs. Consequently, government subsidies of goods and services are eliminated or drastically reduced. Neoliberalism underpins export-led industrialization in free trade zones around the world, IMF agreements and conditions, World Bank programs, the North America Free Trade Agreement (NAFTA), as well as former president Clinton's so-called welfare reform, the Hopwood decision delegitimating affirmative action, and the fact that more money is being channeled into the military and prisons than into public schools.

Although the effects of structural adjustment have not been uniform overall, they have exacerbated global apartheid and the structural violence it unleashes against the well-being and sustainability of people and ecosystems alike. Global integration has resulted in the growing erosion of subsistence security in both the North and South (Nash 1994). As sociologist William Robinson (1996, 22) has written, "[u]nder globalization there has been a dramatic growth of socioeconomic inequalities and of human misery.... The gap between rich and poor is widening with each country, in both the North and South. Moreover, inequalities between North and South have increased sharply." While the divide between North and South is growing, increasingly the human species has come to be stratified along transnational class lines, and, nationally as well as internationally, class is segmented and stratified by race and gender. As a consequence, racially subordinated peoples all over the world are disproportionately represented in labor's most vulnerable lowest strata, both in the United States and abroad.

The current global regime of export-led development, structural adjustment policies, and debt servicing – which could perhaps be characterized as a second primitive accumulation and an era of recolonization – are resulting in massive economic dislocations and the creation of a vast pool of men and women desperate for jobs, even at wages below subsistence levels. Under these conditions, many developing – or underdeveloping – countries have been converted into cheap industrial labor reserves, the most recent versions of imperialism's colonial frontiers (Mies, Bennholdt-Thomsen, and von Werlhof 1988), where women are often especially earmarked for factory work paid at nearly slave wages. For example, according to information from several years ago, Haitian women workers at the Disney factory earned only 28 cents per hour, nowhere near a living wage by either Haitian or U.S. standards (National Labor Committee 1996).

It should not be surprising that women bear the brunt of global apartheid. Seventy percent of the world's absolute poor are women, and these women disproportionately subsidize the production and accumulation of wealth and development with their unwaged and waged labor – labor that is socially constructed and ideologically defined as cheap or, in unwaged contexts, free. Women are especially vulnerable to the ideological and physical assaults of nationalist militarization, economically induced environmental degradation, and the economic restructuring and political realignments mediated by neoliberal policies. Increasingly, women's as well as their families' and communities' subsistence security and human rights are being eroded in a post-Cold War climate in which capitalism appears to have triumphed over its alternatives and is projecting its model of development as an inevitable course of history and regime of truth. That regime of truth legitimates an international division of flexible labor that depends on the naturalization of gender and racial hierarchies, as manifested in so-called women's work and men's work (Alexander and Mohanty 1997, 5). These categories are undergirded by the patriarchal assumptions that tasks such as sewing, assembling electronic components, or pursuing home- and community-based informal activities are extensions of women's natural activities requiring no special skills, training, or compensation and that skilled jobs belong to men who, as natural breadwinners, deserve greater remuneration for their special strength and training. With their labor socially constructed in these terms, poor women of the world – whether as participants in export industrialization, informal-sector activities, or other spheres of work – subsidize the production and accumulation of the world's wealth, which, more than ever, is being concentrated at the top of a transnational ladder. This upward redistribution of wealth is made possible at least in part by cultural production, a process of producing discourses and images through which presuppositions about subordinate womanhood, sexuality, domesticity, and marriage are mobilized. This discursive practice naturalizes women's subordination and helps lower their wages and benefits. According to Aihwa Ong (1991, 289), "reinventing principles of male and racial superiority, this process of cultural production rests upon the articulation that transnational labor relations have with local norms, including the norms expressed in the policies and practices of the postcolonial state."

Following feminist political scientist Cynthia Enloe, we know that gendered meanings, relations, and practices are thoroughly infused in international politics and political economy. Established forms of power depend on assumptions and expectations of masculinity and femininity (Enloe 1989, 4). For instance, the international order, as evidenced in its current structural adjustment strategy of development, depends on "ideas about masculinized dignity and feminized sacrifice." As a consequence, the politics of international debt, for instance, does not impact only women. It works in the first place because of widespread expectations and gender-role hierarchies that ensure that women will be shock absorbers taking up the slack when jobs and social safety nets are slashed or eliminated (Enloe 1989; Sparr 1992, 1994). According to economist Pamela Sparr, "women [around the world, North and South] have mortgaged their lives helping nations weather the painful adjustments" (Sparr 1992, 33). A UNICEF report for the Americas pointed out "that if it were not for poor women working harder and longer hours, the poorest third of the population in that region [women, men, and children] would not be alive today" (Sparr 1992, 33–4; UNICEF 1989).

Feminist research on women in development demonstrates that globalization in its neoliberal form is fundamentally a gendered phenomenon marked by a patriarchal logic. From the interventions that multiracial and postcolonial feminisms have made, we know that this masculinist logic is informed by racialized assumptions and meanings. Present-day strategies to facilitate capital accumulation implicate a racialized gender ideology and politics that legitimate the superexploitation of the productive and reproductive labor of women, with women of color bearing the heaviest burdens and being the most vulnerable targets of structural violence. These women are concentrated in the Southern Hemisphere. Disproportionately but not exclusively, they occupy subordinate racial, ethnic, and class statuses grounded in diverse histories of inequality that are context specific but, at the same time, cross culturally comparable and connected by continuities related to "the logic and operation of capital in the contemporary global arena" (Mohanty 1997, 28).

Gender, as only one axis in a more complex matrix of domination (Collins 1991, 1998), is inextricably tangled up with other hierarchies and processes of difference making. In view of the intersection of multiple axes of inequality and power, and the injustices accompanying them, it is not a coincidence that the superexploited Haitian workers to whom I referred earlier are black and second-class citizens of the poorest nation in the Western Hemisphere. Consequently, their bottom-level position in the international hierarchy is conditioned by their race, gender, class, and national status. Although all these dimensions of difference and inequality are flagrantly marked in Haiti's case, the international racial ranking of human subjects extends well beyond Haiti and is not always as visibly marked; "the [neoracist] order of power relations [does not necessarily] proceed through readily apparent notions of superiority and inferiority" (Gilroy 1991, 40; Balibar 1991) nor through explicitly articulated notions of race.

Implicit or coded articulations of race, and of race's intersection with gender, may appear in the language of "heightened nationalism" (Williams 1996, 7), which can have the effect of racialization. In the former Yugoslavia, the ethnonational conflicts that have erupted are expressed in a language emphasizing irreconcilable, immutable cultural/political differences that can be resolved only through ethnic cleansing. In the context of this violent conflict, full-scale military strategies have been inflicted on tens of thousands of women whose racially marked bodies have become battlefields (Kesič 1996, 51). The heinous campaign of ethnocide and its equivalents elsewhere (e.g., Rwanda) are being deployed by violating women's bodies and, through their bodies, destabilizing the assaulted nation's moral integrity and reproduction. To this horrendous end, the "wombs of nationalist respectability" and the prospects for preserving "racial patrimony" have been violated (Williams 1996, vii). In this case and in many others, rape is being deployed as a masculinist weapon not only against individual women but against their families, communities, and supralocal solidarities that dare to assert their right to self-determination and to imagine a future of national sovereignty.

In this context, rape is deployed as a means of racialization, "a means of imposing a permanent partition between territories as well as two previously co-existing and symbiotically related peoples" (Harrison 2000, 51).

CONFRONTING APARTHEID: LOCAL AND TRANSNATIONAL STRATEGIES

Local Responses with Global Implications

Whether encoding personal or social criticism in their songs or oral poetry (Price 1993 [1984]; Abu-Lughod 1986), being possessed and attacked by spirits on the factory floor (Ong 1987), or organizing a needed rural cooperative or a human rights organization to fill important gaps (Harrison 2004), racially situated women's agency is not precluded by the weight of the multiple oppressions with which they live. Interlocking oppressions are often discussed in the additive terms of double or triple burdens, evoking either an image of a poor black or indigenous woman overwhelmed by the weight of oppressions or a romanticized image of a superwoman exhibiting remarkable strength. Ethnographic analysis of ordinary women corroborates the practice theory notion that within structures of domination, no matter how severe, there exist constraints on as well as spaces and opportunities for resistance and contestation. Agency assumes a variety of forms that are influenced by historically specific circumstances shaped by the interplay of such factors as local culture and community power dynamics, state policies, and the local workings of transnational capital as played out in varying economic sectors, including the informal or underground sector (cf. Ong 1991, 296). [...]

REFERENCES

Abu-Lughod, Lila. 1986. *Veiled Sentiments: Honor and Poetry in a Bedouin Society*. Berkeley and Los Angeles: University of California Press.

Alexander, M. Jacqui, and Chandra Talpade Mohanty. 1997. "Introduction: Genealogies, Legacies, Movements." In *Feminist Genealogies, Colonial Legacies, Democratic Futures*, edited by M. Jacqui Alexander and Chandra Talpade Mohanty, xiii–xlii. New York: Routledge.

Appadurai, Arjun. 1991. "Global Ethnoscapes: Notes and Queries for a Transnational Anthropology." In *Recapturing Anthropology: Working in the Present*, edited by Richard G. Fox, 191–210. Santa Fe: School of American Research Press.

Balibar, Etienne. 1991. "Is There a 'Neo-Racism'?" In *Race, Nation, Class: Ambiguous Identities*, edited by Etienne Balibar and Immanuel Wallerstein, 15–28. New York: Verso.

Basch, Linda, Nina Glick Schiller, and Cristina Szanton Blanc. 1994. *Nations Unbound: Transnational Projects, Postcolonial Predicaments, and Deterritorialized Nation-States*. Langhorne: Gordon and Breach Sciences.

Collins, Patricia Hill. 1991. *Black Feminist Thought: Knowledge, Consciousness, and the Politics of Empowerment*. New York: Routledge.

Enloe, Cynthia. 1989. *Bananas, Beaches, and Bases: Making Feminist Sense of International Politics*. Berkeley: University of California Press.

Gilroy, Paul. 1991. *There Ain't No Black in the Union Jack: The Cultural Politics of Race and Nation*. Chicago: University of Chicago Press.

Gupta, Akhil, and James Ferguson. 1992. "Beyond 'Culture': Space, Identity, and the Politics of Difference." *Cultural Anthropology* 7 (1): 6–23. https://doi.org/10.1525/can.1992.7.1.02a00020.

Harrison, Faye V. 2000. "Facing Racism and the Moral Responsibility of Human Rights Knowledge." *Human Academy of Sciences* 925: 45–69. https://doi.org/10.1111/j.1749 -6632.2000.tb05583.x.

———. 2004. "Global Apartheid, Environmental Degradation, and Women's Activism for Sustainable Well-Being: A Conceptual and Theoretical Overview." *Urban Anthropology and Studies of Cultural Systems and World Economic Development* 33 (1): 1–35.

Kesič, Vesna. 1996. "Never Again a War: Women's Bodies are Battlefields." In *Look at the World through Women's Eyes: Plenary Speeches from the NGO Forum on Women, Beijing 95*, edited by Eva Friedlander, 51–3. New York: Women, Ink.

Lynch, Owen M. 1994. "Urban Anthropology, Postmodernist Cities, and Perspectives." *City and Society Annual Review*: 35–52.

Mies, Maria, Veronika Bennholdt-Thomsen, and Claudia von Werlhof. 1988. *Women and the Last Colony*. London: Zed Books.

Mohanty, Chandra Talpade. 1997. "Women Workers and Capitalist Scripts: Ideologies of Domination, Common Interests, and the Politics of Solidarity." In *Feminist Genealogies, Colonial Legacies, Democratic Futures*, edited by M. Jacqui Alexander and Chandra Talpade Mohanty, 3–29. New York: Routledge.

Nash, June. 1994. "Global Integration and Subsistence Insecurity." *American Anthropologist* 96 (1): 7–30.

National Labor Committee. 1996. *Disney Goes to Haiti*. Video. New York: National Labor Committee.

Ong, Aihwa. 1987. *Spirits of Resistance and Capitalist Discipline: Factory Women in Malaysia*. Albany: State University of New York.

Ong, Aihwa. 1991. "The Gender and Labor Politics of Postmodernity." *Annual Review of Anthropology* 20: 279–309. https://doi.org/10.1146/annurev.an.20.100191.001431.

Price, Sally. 1993. *Co-wives and Calabashes*. 2nd ed. Ann Arbor: University of Michigan Press.

Robinson, William. 1996. "Globalization: Nine Theses on Our Epoch." *Race and Class* 38 (2): 13–31. http://doi.org/10.1177/030639689603800202.

Sparr, Pamela. 1992. "How We Got Into This Mess, and Ways to Get Out." *Ms.*, March/April, 19–35.

UNICEF. 1989. *The Invisible Adjustment: Poor Women and the Economic Crisis*. Santiago, Chile: The Americas and the Caribbean Regional Office, Women in Development Regional Office.

Williams, Brackette. 1996. "Introduction." In *Women Out of Place: The Gender of Agency and the Race of Nationality*, edited by Brackette Williams, 1–36. New York: Routledge.

10.5. Non-hegemonic Globalizations: Alternative Transnational Processes and Agents (2009)

Gustavo Lins Ribeiro

Hegemonic globalization has been characterized by multinational and transnational agents' actions to seek out neoliberal capitalist goals: state reduction, structural adjustment, privatization and support for private enterprise and capital, redirection of national economies toward foreign markets, free global trade, weakening labor legislation, scaling down or phasing out the welfare state, etc. Financial capital and transnational corporations are often considered as the main agents of globalization. Indeed, the discussion on globalization tends to focus on processes commanded by powerful agents and agencies in a top-down perspective, thus ignoring other processes. Nonetheless, there is a growing body of literature on "globalization from below," almost exclusively focused on political resistance movements to neoliberal globalization. [T]his bias hinders researchers from seeing other forms of non-hegemonic globalization, especially the one I call grassroots globalization, a form of "globalization from below" that is more linked to globalization's economic aspects than to its political ones. Grassroots globalization involves non-hegemonic economic globalization processes.

I want to shed light on the hidden side of globalization's political economy, the one in which nation-states' normative and repressive roles are heavily bypassed both in the political and economic spheres. With a view to understanding "other globalizations," I will explore alternative political *and* economic processes and agents.

POLITICAL NON-HEGEMONIC GLOBALIZATION: THE ANTI/ALTER-GLOBALIZATION MOVEMENT

The 1992 UN conference in Rio, the most important mega global ritual of transnational elites in the late 20th century, was also an important structuring moment for the alternative globalization movement. It provided a particularly strategic and pioneering opportunity for environmentalist NGOs and social movements to meet at a parallel event, the Global

Forum, precursor to the World Social Forums, and the first occasion on which global civil society met in real public space (Ribeiro, 2000). Environmental activism's transnational characteristics provided the basis for discussions on notions of transnational citizenship and, more importantly, for articulations of transnational networks as a regulating power against neoliberal globalization.

Rio-92 also provided a template that was to shape the scenarios where pro- and anti-globalization networks would meet. This template is a triangle made up of (1) the meeting of the global and transnational establishment and managers (in Rio this was the United Nations Conference on the Environment and Development, held at a convention center in Jacarepaguá); (2) the meeting of global civil society's transnational elite (in Rio, the Global Forum meeting); and (3) transnational activists' street demonstrations against neoliberal globalization.

Since 1992, political counter-hegemonic efforts regarding globalization have increased. The plural composition of movements and coalitions – as well as the diversity of ideological and agenda goals – may be conceived in terms of two major parties: one is identified with anti-globalization and the other with alternative globalization or *altermondialization*, as the French call it. This internal division echoes that which existed within the alternative development camp. The difference in positions reflects radical and reformist perspectives. Those who believe that globalization is not inevitable, that it can be stopped or radically changed, comprise the anti-globalization movement. This movement usually expresses itself through ad-hoc coalitions that organize street demonstrations.

There are also those who believe that "another world is possible," that eventually globalization can and must be tamed. These make up the alternative globalization movement and have mostly been linked to the world of NGOs, understood as "the new political subjects" of the 1980s and 1990s. In fact, they are part of transnational political elites that have consistently evolved after the Second World War in an environment saturated with networking among NGOs themselves; NGOs and multilateral agencies, notably the United Nations and multilateral banks; and among NGOs and national governments. [...]

STREET DEMONSTRATIONS

Neoliberalism and global trade without barriers fuelled the shrinking of the world under the hegemony of flexible capitalism. The time was ripe for new institutions to congeal. This is typically the case with the World Trade Organization, a global institution committed to fostering, administering and overseeing global trade as well as to settling disputes among member countries. The WTO was established in 1994. It began operations in 1995 and rapidly became, together with the post-Second World War institutions (World Bank, International Monetary Fund and the United Nations), one of the most powerful members of the global management select club. WTO presents itself as "the successor to the General Agreement on Tariffs and Trade (GATT) established in the wake of the Second World War." Notwithstanding this genealogical relation, the World Trade Organization's reach in keeping with the hegemony of electronic and computer capitalism went well beyond that of GATT's since it included not only trade in merchandise goods but also in services (international telephone services, for instance) and intellectual property protection. The WTO's power caught the attention of a growing anti-globalization activism.

Since the late 1990s, anti-globalization street demonstrations have proliferated, always closely monitored and often repressed by the police. From 18 May through 20 May 1998, thousands of protesters marched through Geneva's streets in protest against the World Trade Organization's 50th anniversary celebrations. One hundred and seventeen people were arrested. From 18 to 20 June 1999, 35,000 marchers took to the streets of Cologne, Germany, during a G7 meeting to demand the cancellation of poor countries' foreign debt. On 30 November 1999, the street demonstration in Seattle against WTO's ministerial conference, the organization's top-level decision-making body, took place. This was, for many, the anti-globalization movement's foundational event. It was surely a prominent moment, but there were other important antecedents in the global South such as the protests against IMF Structural Adjustment Programs which started in the late 1970s, "peaking perhaps in the 1989 Caracas uprising" (Yuen, 2001: 6), and the Zapatista rebellion, in 1994, a source of inspiration for an "increasingly militant movement of global resistance to neoliberalism" (Callahan, 2001: 37). [...]

The year 2000 was particularly busy. There were demonstrations on 29 January, against the World Economic Forum, in Davos, Switzerland; in February, in Bangkok, against the Tenth Summit of the United Nations Conference on Trade and Development (UNCTAD); on 15–17 April in Washington, DC during an IMF meeting; on 14 June, in Bologna, against the Organization for Economic Cooperation and Development's (OECD) meeting; on 21–23 June, demonstrators protested in Okinawa, during a G7 meeting, for the cancellation of Third World debt and the withdrawal of the American base; in September between ten and thirty thousand people demonstrated in Melbourne, against a meeting of the World Economic Forum. That same month, on the 26th, during the Fifth Global Action Day, activists from many countries were focusing on the demonstrations that were to take place in Prague against a joint IMF–World Bank meeting. In the capital of the Czech Republic, environmentalists, religious groups, unionists, socialists, communists, anarchists and punks surrounded the convention center and engaged in skirmishes with the police. Simultaneously, different demonstrations happened around the world. In Brasilia, for instance, a small group of punks demonstrated in front of Brazil's Central Bank. In São Paulo, students, environmentalists, and unionists demonstrated in front of the stock market. In other Brazilian cities, such as Fortaleza and Belo Horizonte, protesters gathered in front of such "capitalist symbols" as a Citibank branch and a McDonald's. In tune with escalating police repression of these demonstrations, in July 2001, in Genoa, Italy, during an anti-G-8 demonstration, a young man, Carlo Giuliani, was killed by the police.

September 11th, 2001, undoubtedly posted a new warning on the horizon. Anti-terrorism became a major preoccupation for powerful state elites and the agenda became heavily marked by the threat of war. In the United States, the Bush administration passed stringent security laws. But that did not imply, especially outside the United States, that the anti-globalization movement had come to a halt (see Aguiton, 2003). In Europe, in Florence, there was another great demonstration in November 2002. Almost one million people went to the streets on the last day of the gathering of the European Social Forum. There were also the second and third editions of the World Social Forum (see below), in Porto Alegre, in January 2002 and 2003, which brought together more than 50,000 people from many different countries. Also, 20,000 participants attended the Asian Social Forum in Hyderabad, India, in January 2003. At the same time, after September 11th, the possible invasion of Iraq unleashed a movement for peace that resulted in the largest global demonstration ever. Cyberspace's instrumentality in transnational articulation proved again its effectiveness during the organization of the "greatest anti-war demonstration in history," according to the Brazilian newspaper *Folha de São Paulo* (16 February 2003). On 15 February 2003, more than 5 million people in about 60 countries took to the streets to protest against the United States' war against Iraq.

The anti-globalization movement's international expansion has increased its heterogeneity and brought new political challenges for its reproduction. Its heterodox diversity, highly praised for its effectiveness and novelty, also means a more complex political environment in which political alliance problems abound. Suffice it to enumerate the different actors that come together in these scenarios: punks, anarchists, students, unionists, environmentalists, peasants, feminists, human rights activists, scholars, intellectuals, and politicians. Most have progressive leanings and come from a different array of countries. Nevertheless, different combinations of such actors may vary according to where the demonstrations take place. In Europe, especially in countries with strong socialist traditions, socialist politicians, for instance, may also take part in these events.

[…] Anti-globalization is a movement in which young people make up the majority. They are well aware of the new media's effectiveness in the mobilization effort. The Internet has been crucial to the movement's articulation on the global level while cell phones are often used to organize street demonstration tactics. In addition to flexibility and horizontality in the decision-making process, some of the main characteristics of the movement's organizational structure are related to an overall but not complete adhesion to (1) "the tradition of mass civil disobedience commonly known as Non-Violent Direct Action" and (2) a commitment to direct democracy (Yuen, 2001: 8). Its organizational forms include, besides decentralized spokes-council meetings, "affinity groups" and consensus processes. […]

[…] Awareness of the media's importance in contemporary politics was inherited from such political actors as Greenpeace, Earth First! and the Zapatistas. It led the anti-globalization movement to value political action regarding the media and to look for alternative media practices. Struggling for a critical planetary citizenship, the movement is a particularly relevant constituent of the transnational virtual imagined community, the basis of the global civil society propitiated by the diffusion of the Internet as a means of interactive communication (Ribeiro, 1998). Another pertinent aspect of the movement's effectiveness is related to invading the world system with alternative mediascapes, with news that competes with information from global media corporations and chains. This is why demonstrations and forums are held in situations where not only global elites but the global media are present and perform a global media event. It is never too much to stress the role that environmental activism has played in the trend: from "think globally, act locally" to the awareness that the struggle against oppressive racist and environmentally destructive globalization needs to be fought in the global-fragmented spaces where transnational elites and managers perform their global integration rituals. A sensitivity to the role of information was already present in the Rio-1992 conference when the Internet was widely used to mobilize the transnational virtual imagined community by means of the Association for Progressive Communication's work. Faithful to this trend, the anti-globalization movement has fostered the creation of Independent Media Centers worldwide. The first indymedia was established by various independent and alternative media organizations and activists in 1999 for the purpose of providing grassroots coverage of the WTO protests in Seattle.

Street demonstrations are communication devices. Their purpose is to affirm the existence of a new political subject and to invade real and virtual public space with alternative messages on globalization. Quantity and quality play strategic roles in these scenarios. The size of the movement is a quantitative measure of its power. The effectiveness of the alternative discourses can be measured by its global visibility and dissemination, a proof of the quality of the movement's message. Diversity, closely related to quantity and quality, gives an idea of the movement's scope, complexity and representativeness. It is transclassist, transgender, transethnic, transnational, trans-ideological, trans-utopian and trans-behavioral. Form and organization are crucial because they show, in practice, a different collective identity that is plural and combative. The global media's attention is captured by the costumes some activists wear, the carnival like atmosphere of some demonstrations, the dramatization of parades and by the eminent and often real risk of violent street battles. Attracting the media is a role especially well performed by punks and by the massive display and use of repressive power.

The police are the most evident state representatives, expressions of local and national levels of power, at these demonstrations. City and federal authorities know that the world is watching them. Street demonstrations as counter-hegemonic mega global events are thus informed by the same triangle that structures other non-hegemonic global events attracting worldwide attention: (1) the rich and powerful gather in impressive scale; (2) the alternative trans-national agents meet in impressive scale; (3) national and local authorities try to control their public spaces, in order to control the mediascapes that are produced from their territories.

These demonstrations have occurred in different cities around the world and gained media visibility at global and national levels. They have reinforced the idea that another world is possible. This is, indeed, the motto of the World Social Forums.

REFERENCES

Aguiton, Christophe. 2003. *Le monde nous appartient.* Paris: Éditions Plon.

Callahan, Manuel. 2001. "Zapatismo and the Politics of Solidarity." In *The Battle of Seattle: The New Challenge to Capitalist Globalization,* edited by Eddie Yuen, George Katsiaficas, and Daniel Burton Rose, 37–40. New York: Soft Skull Press.

Ribeiro, Gustavo Lins. 1998. "Cybercultural Politics: Political Activism at a Distance in a Transnational World." In *Cultures of Politics/Politics of Culture: Revisioning Latin American Social Movements*, edited by Sonia Alvarez, Evelina Dagnino, and Arturo Escobar, 325–52. Boulder: Westview Press.

Ribeiro, Gustavo Lins. 2000. *Cultura e política no mundo contemporâneo*. Brasília: Editora da Universidade de Brasília.

Yuen, Eddie. 2001. "Introduction." In *The Battle of Seattle: The New Challenge to Capitalist Globalization*, edited by Eddie Yuen, George Katsiaficas, and Daniel Burton Rose, 3–20. New York: Soft Skull Press.

Section Ten Glossary

depeasantization   Transition from a largely agrarian to a largely wage-based subsistence strategy in the context of capitalist nation-states. Depeasantization often accompanies broader political economic shifts associated with modernization, such as land consolidation and privatization, and results in land dispossession and rural-to-urban migration.

free trade policies   Multinational treaties that facilitate capitalist exchange by removing barriers to "free" trade such as tariffs, subsidies for local producers, and regulations. Often touted as part of economic development, free trade policies tend to reproduce existing unequal relationships among states.

free trade zones   Areas of concentrated manufacturing, typically assembly, in which foreign companies can take advantage of lax labor, environmental, and tax laws to produce goods more cheaply than they could in "developed" nations with relatively highly paid and unionized labor forces.

glocalization   An approach to understanding globalization that focuses on local adaptations and interpretations of globalized practices.

structural adjustment policies (SAPs)   Policies that compel "developing" economies to adopt global capitalist production strategies in exchange for loans from the International Monetary Fund or World Bank. Structural "adjustments" typically include reductions in public spending, privatization of natural resources, eliminating barriers to "free" trade, and encouraging production for export.

On Environment, Pluriverse, and Power

THE SOCIAL CONTEXT

In 2004, an Indian Ocean tsunami barreled across coastlines, killing more than 200,000 people in 14 countries and displacing countless more. A hurricane that struck the US Gulf Coast in 2005 killed more than a thousand people and destroyed entire neighborhoods of disproportionately low-income Black residents. In 2010, a Haitian earthquake leveled much of Port-au-Prince, killing some 300,000 people and leaving another million without adequate shelter or basic necessities. In 2016, Indigenous water rights activists were tear-gassed at the Standing Rock Indian Reservation in North Dakota for protesting construction of an oil pipeline through their sovereign territory. All of these events reveal the rising catastrophic environmental consequences of capitalist industrialization and its unevenly distributed global effects.

While questions about human–environment relations have been around since the birth of anthropology, most trace the emergence of environmental anthropology to the mid-twentieth century, a time when anthropologists like Julian Steward began attending to the role of the environment in shaping sociocultural characteristics. At its inception, ecological anthropology dealt largely with studies of adaptation and cognition, asking questions about how societies related to their environments. Examples of these early theoretical orientations include **cultural ecology**, or the study of human adaptations to the environment, and **ethnoscience**, which focused on documenting local perceptions, knowledge, and experiences of the environment.

Ecological anthropology studies of the 1960s and 1970s largely comprised close studies of local communities (human and nonhuman) and elided concerns with power and politics. The emergence of **political ecology** in the 1980s provided a sharp corrective by attending to the relationships between the political economy and ecology. Political ecology, with its focus on analyzing interactions of power, economic interests, and social relations in relation to environmental change and decision making, came to dominate and unify much of the work of environmental anthropologists through the turn of the twenty-first century and continues to be an important theoretical current today.

Political economy and poststructuralism's attention to power flows introduced new constructs to frame and describe human–environment relations. Such interventions extend to the nonhuman world, decentering human exceptionalism and positing questions about the perspectives and agency of nonhuman life. With the emergence of **posthumanist anthropology** and **multispecies ethnography**, today's environmental anthropologists pay close attention to the ways in which local and global actors – human and more-than-human – assemble together in affective, agentive, and emergent relations with one another. Coinciding with this **ontological turn** are efforts to decolonize environmental anthropology by upending the Eurocentric, modernist perspective that nature is a set of resources to be exploited for their economic potential, embracing instead a pluriverse focus on alternatives, relationality, and the voices and perspectives of Indigenous scholars.

THE CONVERSATION

This section opens with a classic piece by Julian Steward that introduces the theoretical orientation of cultural ecology, a perspective that came to play a central role in ecological anthropology studies of the 1950s through 1970s and influenced the **processual approach** within archaeology. Steward describes cultural ecology as both a theory and a method for analyzing the adaptive relationship among a given culture's technological development, behavior, and environment.

The second reading fast-forwards through the emergence of political ecology to point to some of its pitfalls. In "Translation, Value, and Space" (Reading 11.2), Paige West argues that while political ecology raises important questions about power, capital, and social inequalities, it also relies on a view of socioecological relations in which people *act on* biological diversity rather than *interact with* nonhuman beings. Her piece reminds anthropologists of the central role they play in translating human relationships to biological diversity and stresses the importance of not taking for granted that all people everywhere value the natural world as a set of resources to be commodified or exploited. Drawing on decades of work with Gimi-speaking peoples of Papua New Guinea who have been a part of a conservation and development project, West presents another way of viewing human–environment relations that places Indigenous epistemologies at the forefront. Considering hunting and song, West explores how the Gimi understand their forests as a series of transactive dialectical relationships that produce and shape personhood, society, space, and sustenance.

Zoe Todd's "Indigenizing the Anthropocene" (Reading 11.3) moves West's caution against Eurocentric environmental assumptions forward through a reflective account of her experiences as a Métis scholar who questions the academy's approach to human–environment relationships. Todd considers the connections among art, the **Anthropocene**, and the academy, each "white public spaces" in which Indigenous experiences and ideas are appropriated or obscured by non-Indigenous artists, theorists, and scholars. She introduces the work of Papaschese Cree scholar, Dwayne Donald, as a means to indigenize and decolonize the discourse that shapes public understandings of art and the Anthropocene. Her piece reflects the posthuman, multispecies, and ontological turn in anthropology, infusing these theoretical interventions with the ideas and practices of Indigenous scholars.

The final two pieces round out the section by advancing a political ontology that rethinks human exceptionality and considers a future in which all beings exist in relationality and radical interdependence. Reading 11.4 by Arturo Escobar, "Designs for the Pluriverse," outlines this argument, presenting ontological design as a way to break free from the hegemonic one-world ontology to reckon with a pluriverse in which multiple ways of worlding or socionatural configurations are possible.

Finally, in "Complicity and Resistance in the Indigenous Amazon" (Reading 11.5), Alaka Wali puts the theoretical interventions of West, Todd, and Escobar to work in detailing her 15 years of engagement with Indigenous communities in the Peruvian Amazon who have been embedded in a neoliberal market economy. Wali documents an applied case study in which Chicago's Field Museum worked with Indigenous communities, NGOs, and government actors in a participatory assessment and planning process that demonstrated and reinforced the *economía indígena* in protected area conservation. This case study serves as a powerful example of a semi-autonomous population only partially incorporated within a capitalist mode of production, and where there is evidence of both complicity with and resistance to this mode of being; thus, the case offers a strong example of another form of worlding – evidence of the value of a pluriverse approach.

THREE QUESTIONS FOR THE READINGS

1 What conceptual threads can you identify across these pieces? How are they in conversation and where do they diverge?

2 How does the ontological turn in anthropology shape understandings of human–environment relations? What are its limitations?

3 What are some methodological strategies and challenges for conducting posthuman and multispecies ethnography?

ON THE COMPANION WEBSITE

Fieldnotes from Svalbard, a progressive environmental anthropology, additional readings, and more.

www.anthropologicaltheory.com

11.1. The Concept and Method of Cultural Ecology (1955)

Julian Steward

CULTURE, HISTORY AND ENVIRONMENT

While the human and social ecologists have seemingly sought universal ecological principles and relegated culture in its local varieties to a secondary place, anthropologists have been so preoccupied with culture and its history that they have accorded environment only a negligible role. Owing in part to reaction against the "environmental determinists," [and] in part to cumulative evidence that any culture increases in complexity to a large extent because of diffused practices, the orthodox view now holds that history, rather than adaptive processes, explains culture. Since historical "explanations" of culture employ the culture area concept, there is an apparent contradiction. The culture area is a construct of behavioral uniformities which occur within an area of environmental uniformities. It is assumed that cultural and natural areas are generally coterminous because the culture represents an adjustment to the particular environment. It is assumed further, however, that various different patterns may exist in any natural area and that unlike cultures may exist in similar environments.

[...] Since cultural differences are not directly attributable to environmental differences and most certainly not to organic or racial differences, they are merely said to represent divergences in cultural history, to reflect tendencies of societies to develop in unlike ways. Such tendencies are not explained. A distinctive pattern develops, it is said, and henceforth is the primary determinant of whether innovations are accepted. Environment is relegated to a purely secondary and passive role. It is considered prohibitive or permissive, but not creative. It allows man to carry on some kinds of activities and it prevents others. The origins of these activities are pushed back to a remote point in time or space, but they are not explained. [...]

CULTURAL ECOLOGY

Cultural ecology differs from human and social ecology in seeking to explain the origin of particular cultural features and patterns which characterize different areas rather than to derive general principles applicable to any cultural-environmental situation. It differs from the relativistic and neo-evolutionist conceptions of culture history in that it introduces the local environment as the extracultural factor in the fruitless assumption that culture comes from culture. Thus, cultural ecology presents both a problem and a method. The problem is to ascertain whether the adjustments of human societies to their environments require particular modes of behavior or whether they permit latitude for a certain range of possible behavior patterns. Phrased in this way, the problem also distinguishes cultural ecology from "environmental determinism" and its related theory "economic determinism" which are generally understood to contain their conclusions within the problem.

The problem of cultural ecology must be further qualified, however, through use of a supplementary conception of culture. According to the holistic view, all aspects of culture are functionally interdependent upon one another. The degree and kind of interdependency, however, are not the same with all features. Elsewhere, I have offered the concept of *cultural core* – the constellation of features which are most closely related to subsistence activities and economic arrangements. The core includes such social, political, and religious patterns as are empirically determined to be closely connected with these arrangements. Innumerable other features may have great potential variability because they are less strongly tied to the core. These latter, or secondary features, are determined to a greater extent by purely cultural-historical factors – by random innovations or by diffusion – and they give the appearance of outward distinctiveness to cultures with similar cores. Cultural ecology pays primary attention to those features which empirical analysis shows to be most closely involved in the utilization of environment in culturally prescribed ways. [...]

Cultures do, of course, tend to perpetuate themselves, and change may be slow for such reasons as those cited. But over the millennia cultures in different environments have changed tremendously, and these changes are basically traceable to new adaptations required by changing technology and productive arrangements. Despite occasional cultural barriers, the useful arts have spread extremely widely, and the instances in which they have not been accepted because of pre-existing cultural patterns are insignificant. In pre-agricultural times, which comprised perhaps 99 percent of cultural history, technical devices for hunting, gathering, and fishing seem to have diffused largely to the limits of their usefulness. Clubs, spears, traps, bows, fire, containers, nets, and many other cultural features spread across many areas, and some of them throughout the world. Later, domesticated plants and animals also spread very rapidly within their environmental limits, being stopped only by formidable ocean barriers. Whether or not new technologies are valuable is, however, a function of the society's cultural level as well as of environmental potentials. All pre-agricultural societies found hunting and gathering techniques useful. Within the geographical limits of herding and farming, these techniques were adopted. More advanced techniques, such as metallurgy, were acceptable only if certain preconditions, such as stable population, leisure time, and internal specialization were present. These conditions could develop only from the cultural ecological adaptations of an agricultural society.

The concept of cultural ecology, however, is less concerned with the origin and diffusion of technologies than with the fact that they may be used differently and entail different social arrangements in each environment. The environment is not only permissive or prohibitive with respect to these technologies, but special local features may require social adaptations which have far-reaching consequences. Thus, societies equipped with bows, spears, surrounds, chutes, brushburning, deadfalls, pitfalls, and other hunting devices may differ among themselves because of the nature of the terrain and fauna. If the principal game exists in large herds, such as herds of bison or caribou, there is advantage in cooperative hunting, and considerable numbers of peoples may remain together throughout the year, as described in Chapter 8. If, however, the game is nonmigratory, occurring in small and scattered groups, it is better hunted by small groups of men who know their territory well (Chapter 7). In each case, the cultural repertory of hunting devices may be about the same, but in the first case the society will consist of multifamily or multi lineage groups, as among the Athabaskans and Algonkians of Canada and probably the pre-horse Plains bison hunters, and in the second case it will probably consist of localized patrilineal lineages or bands, as among the Bushmen, Congo Negritoes, Australians, Tasmanians, Fuegians, and others. These latter groups consisting of patrilineal bands are similar, as a matter of fact, not because their total environments are similar – the Bushmen, Australians, and southern Californians live in deserts, the Negritoes in rain forests, and the Fuegians in a cold, rainy area – but because the nature of the game and therefore of their subsistence problem is the same in each case.

Other societies having about the same technological equipment may exhibit other social patterns because the environments differ to the extent that the cultural adaptations must be different. For example, the Eskimo use bows, spears, traps, containers and other widespread technological devices, but, owing to the limited occurrence of fish and sea mammals, their population is so sparse and cooperative hunting is so relatively unrewarding that they are usually dispersed in family groups. For a different but equally compelling reason the Nevada Shoshoni (Chapter 6) were also fragmented into family groups. In the latter case, the scarcity of game and the predominance of seeds as the subsistence basis greatly restricted economic cooperation and required dispersal of the society into fairly independent family groups. [...]

THE METHOD OF CULTURAL ECOLOGY

[...] Three fundamental procedures of cultural ecology are as follows:

First, the interrelationship of exploitative or productive technology and environment must be analyzed. This technology includes a considerable part of what is often called "material culture," but all features may not be of equal importance. In primitive societies, subsistence devices are basic: weapons and instruments for hunting and fishing; containers for gathering and storing food; transportational devices used on land and water; sources of water and fuel; and, in some environments, means of counteracting excessive cold (clothing and housing) or heat. In more developed societies, agriculture and herding techniques and manufacturing of crucial implements must be considered. In an industrial world, capital and credit arrangements, trade systems and the like are crucial. Socially-derived needs – special tastes in foods, more ample housing and clothing, and a great variety of appurtenances to living – become increasingly important in the productive arrangement as culture develops; and yet these originally were probably more often effects of basic adaptations than causes. [...]

Second, the behavior patterns involved in the exploitation of a particular area by means of a particular technology must be analyzed. Some subsistence patterns impose very narrow limits on the general mode of life of the people, while others allow considerable latitude. The gathering of wild vegetable products is usually done by women who work alone or in small groups. Nothing is gained by cooperation and in fact women come into competition with one another. Seed gatherers, therefore, tend to fragment into small groups unless their resources are very abundant. Hunting, on the other hand, may be either an individual or a collective project, and the nature of hunting societies is determined by culturally prescribed devices for collective hunting as well as by the species. When surrounds, grass-firing, corrals, chutes, and other cooperative methods are employed, the take per man may be much greater than what a lone hunter could bag. Similarly, if circumstances permit, fishing may be done by groups of men using dams, weirs, traps, and nets as well as by individuals. [...]

The third procedure is to ascertain the extent to which the behavior patterns entailed in exploiting the environment affect other aspects of culture. Although technology and environment prescribe that certain things must be done in certain ways if they are to be done at all, the extent to which these activities are functionally tied to other aspects of culture is a purely empirical problem. I have shown elsewhere (Chapters 6, 7, 10) that the occurrence of patrilineal bands among certain hunting peoples and of fragmented families among the Western Shoshoni is closely determined by their subsistence activities, whereas the Carrier Indians are known to have changed from a composite hunting band to a society based upon moieties and inherited statuses without any change in the nature of subsistence. In the irrigation areas of early civilizations (Chapter 11) the sequence of sociopolitical forms or cultural cores seems to have been very similar despite variation in many outward details or secondary features of these cultures. If it can be established that the productive arrangements permit great latitude in the sociocultural type, then historical influences may explain the particular type found. The problem is the same in considering modern industrial civilizations. The question is whether industrialization allows such latitude that political democracy, communism, state socialism, and perhaps other forms are equally possible, so that strong historical influences, such as diffused ideology – e.g., propaganda – may supplant one type with another, or whether each type represents an adaptation which is specific to the area. [...]

THE METHODOLOGICAL PLACE OF CULTURAL ECOLOGY

Cultural ecology has been described as a methodological tool for ascertaining how the adaptation of a culture to its environment may entail certain changes. In a larger sense, the problem is to determine whether similar adjustments occur in similar environments. Since in any given environment, culture may develop through a succession of very unlike periods, it is sometimes pointed out that environment, the constant, obviously has no relationship to cultural type. This difficulty disappears, however, if the level of sociocultural integration represented by each period is taken into account. Cultural types therefore, must be conceived as constellations of core features which arise out of environmental adaptations and which represent similar levels of integration.

Cultural diffusion, of course, always operates, but in view of the seeming importance of ecological adaptations its role in explaining culture has been greatly overestimated. The extent to which the large variety of world cultures can be systematized in categories of types and explained through cross-cultural regularities of developmental process is purely an empirical matter. Hunches arising out of comparative studies suggest that there are many regularities which can be formulated in terms of similar levels and similar adaptations.

11.2. Translation, Value, and Space: Theorizing an Ethnographic and Engaged Environmental Anthropology (2005)

Paige West

As an environmental anthropologist, I am often asked to translate (Zerner 2003) and make legible (Scott 1998) the actions and beliefs of one set of actors for another. In terms of explaining actions, [the Gimi-speaking peoples in the Eastern Highlands Province of Papua New Guinea (PNG)] wish that I could make the seemingly bizarre behaviors of tourists make sense, biologists ask me to explain Gimi forest-related practices, and gold miners ask me to clarify biologist's behaviors. In terms of explaining beliefs, tourists wish to know if Gimi have "magical" ways of relating to forests, biologists want to know if Gimi "value" plants and animals, and Gimi want to know why outsiders are interested in their land.

[... M]any environmental anthropologists attempt to make conservationists understand and value local knowledge by translating it into categories that scientists can easily understand and assimilate into their epistemologies. They do this because scientists who do not see the value of local knowledge are much more likely to suggest conservation policies that are not socially equitable (Harper 2002). But environmental translations that portray people as rational, neutral, and economically minded, and their socioecological actions as resource use (see Paulson et al. 2003), often miss the fact that human relations with the natural world are aesthetic, poetic, social, and moral. [...]

[... W]hen local knowledge and local social life are rendered legible, a "generification of culture" takes place. The complex and special character of knowledge and of the social practices it engenders are shaped to fit already existing categories of "otherness," thus softening the edges of difference so that it can be controlled and consumed by powerful outsiders (Errington and Gewertz 2001). On-the-ground knowledge and practice begin to look like the outside renderings of them, thus erasing the vernacular and creating a situation in which local social structures begin to conform to imposed models and ideologies (Carrier and Miller 1998; see West and Carrier 2004). This has material consequences for people and their environments.

Political ecologists [...] tend to translate socioecological agency in ways that generify it (Errington and Gewertz 2001). A political ecology "actor-centered" approach, although well intentioned, suggests a view of socioecological relations in which people act on biological diversity, as opposed to interacting with plants and animals, and on each other, as opposed to acting with each other in dialectical productive relationships. In turn, people are acted on by the environment and extralocal structures (Paulson et al. 2003). This approach reduces local socioecological lives and does not leave room for complex understandings of the dialectical creation of "self" and "other," central concepts to ethnographic understandings of the relations between people and environments. [… E]nvironmental anthropologists need to carefully consider how we allow fundamentally Western concepts and modes of explanation to dominate practices of translation. I am not simply arguing for a return to the universal versus relativist debate, because I am not claiming that Gimi ways of being are not translatable. Rather, I am saying that translations need to take into account indigenous understandings of knowledge and practice. […]

CONSERVATION ON GIMI LANDS

Since 1994, Gimi have taken part in an ICDP [Integrated Conservation and Development Project] that encompasses their land, labor, and lives. The spatial and social manifestation of this project is the Crater Mountain Wildlife Management Area (CMWMA), a 2,700-square-kilometer area […]. The ICDP was initially based on the idea that Gimi would begin to "value" and then work to "protect" biological diversity if their economic livelihood was directly connected to it. The Biodiversity Conservation Network (BCN) – a component of the Biodiversity Support Program (BSP), a short-term program that was funded by USAID and the World Wildlife Fund (WWF) – funded and helped to design the ICDP at Crater Mountain. […] The driving ideology behind the BCN was one of economic valuation. […]

Each project funded by the BCN was defined using the spatial metaphor of "site," and all the people involved in the projects – local landowners, biologists, U.S. Peace Corps volunteers, and others – were termed "stakeholders." The "sites," "stakeholders," and "ecological enterprises" were given a temporal dimension in that they were funded and assessed over a period of four years (Salafsky et al. 2001:1587). As part of its "scientific" approach, BCN devised a "core hypothesis" postulating that "if local communities receive sufficient benefits from an enterprise that depends on biodiversity, then they will act to counter internal and external threats to that biodiversity" (BSP 1996:1). […] The BCN staff, like many ecologists and economists, took as their starting point the assumption that the environment is simply livelihood for rural peoples (Tsing 2003:24). Given this assumption, they thought the most rational way to convince local communities to conserve was to link their forests to market-based enterprises. In Maimafu, these enterprises were handicraft production, ecotourism, and the training of local people to work for scientific researchers as paid employees.

Inherent in the original design of the CMWMA, and directly connected to the BCN view of environment as biological capital and people as economic actors, was the idea that Gimi are a threat to their forests (West 2001). […] Gimi are thought to threaten their forests through their land-use practices of gardening, cutting trees for fuel and constructing houses; their hunting practices; and through the pressure put on their forests because of their increasing population. Portrayals of Gimi use of the forests also imply that Gimi value them because of the money to be made off the "natural resources" within. Assuming as much, conservation practitioners, hence, created local ecological enterprises, turning bits of biological diversity into commodities that could be used to "increase the average annual per capita income of clans" (Johnson 1997:397). In doing so, they demonstrated that they did not understand that Gimi relations with their forests are social in nature.

MAKING GIMI, MAKING FORESTS

For Gimi, everything is a "gift" from the forest as it is the physical incarnation of their ancestors' life force (Gillison 1980, 1993). People and forests will always be – and have always been – in a constant transactive relationship, making and remaking each other over time. Gimi believe that people are made up of flesh, which is made by their social relations and transactions with the living, and auna, which is made by their social relations and transactions with the dead. Auna can be translated as "soul," "power," "vital spirit," "familiar spirit," and "life-force" (see Gillison 1993:365 and Glick 1963:201). Auna is the

> invisible animating aspect of a person, ghost (kore), animal, or plant manifested in breath, voice, pulse, heart beat, etc., and in the capacity for growth, and present in all body exuviae (urine, feces, sweat, tears, hair, blood, etc.) and discarded scraps of food or tobacco. [Gillison 1993:365]

[...] The human life force, forests, and animals are intimately tied. When a person dies, his or her auna "clings to its body" and must be helped along toward the forests (Gillison 1993:122). People must sing to a corpse, sit with it, and wail in their sorrow so that it does not cling to the body or hamlet forever. But slowly, "over time, auna penetrates the deep forests and is gradually transformed entirely into kore, taking up residence in giant trees, high mountain caves, and every kind of wildlife" (Gillison 1993:122). Once the auna goes to the forests and begins to infuse itself into wildlife, it becomes part of not only the forest but also the never-ending cycle of Gimi mythology. When the auna "penetrates" marsupials, animals that it seeks out in particular, it reenacts events from traditional women's mythology and comes to be part of this mythic cycle (Gillison 1993:92–5, 122). Marsupials can also be used in divination rituals: After a person's wandering kore has been "housed" (Gillison 1993:122) in an animal, it can help living relatives find his or her killer through divination rituals involving the live animal being questioned by elder men. So marsupials are not simply animals to Gimi, they are the literal embodiment of ancestors; what has been translated as "environment" is not simply a place filled with floral and faunal resources waiting to be used or made into commodities, it is a place of social relations between the living and the dead. [...]

DIALECTICS OF PERSONHOOD AND SPACE

The Gimi world is produced through social relationships between beings. These beings are people, ancestors, spirits, and animals. These social relations are not neutral and economic; they are familial and poetic. In societies based on gift exchange, like Gimi society, identity and personhood are made through social relationships with others. People's capacities are seen as they relate to others and their identities are understood as comprised of the sources that went into making them (Strathern 1988:131). Personhood is located at the confluence of relationships that encompass certain knowledges, social capacities, and practices that can only be expressed and utilized with reference to others. Because people are constantly entering into new social relationships, they are always making and remaking identity because that identity – the idea of who they are at any given time – is only realized through their relations and transactions with others (Strathern 1988:128). For Gimi, these generative transactions include transactions with nonhuman animals. [...]

When Gimi think about and interact with the forests, there is a constant dialectical relation between organism and environment (Ingold 2000) that is directly connected to how Gimi make themselves and others through transactive relationships (Strathern 1988) and through the sort of "mutual recognition" that creates subjectivity (Robbins 2003:10). This mutual recognition takes place on three levels: (1) between individuals, (2) between people and their ancestors, and (3) between people and animals. Tim Ingold (2000) develops the idea of "organism-in-its-environment" and contrasts it against the more traditional idea of organisms in an environment. For Ingold, the environment is only in relation to the organism, and the organism is only in relation to the environment (Ingold 2000:172). I want to push Ingold's argument to include the kind of mutual recognition that Robbins (2003) reads in Hegel [...]; for example, with no Gimi there is no tree kangaroo and with no tree kangaroo there is no Gimi. Ancestral spirits enliven Gimi forests, but it is, in part, the mutual recognition between Gimi hunters and hunted animals that creates subjects, produces space, and lies at the heart of Gimi politics of environment.

This transactional being-in-the-world, in which subjectivity is constantly being produced, is the way that Gimi see "self" and "other" – be that other another person, an ancestor's spirit, or a tree kangaroo. Gimi are in existence in relation to their forests and their forests are in existence in relation to Gimi; there is no Gimi without forest and no forest without Gimi. This being-in-the-world as a generative transactional relationship takes place on five levels for Gimi: through (1) the movements and transactions of their auna (life force) and kore (spirit) during conception, in dreams, and after death; (2) the hunting and eating of animals; (3) the meaningful human action that transforms forests into clan property; (4) relations between humans, animals, and spirits that literally created the Gimi universe and that are retold through a concert of male and female myths; and (5) reproductive labor. By viewing Gimi as a threat to their forests on the basis of an assumption that Gimi value them only as natural resources and potential commodities, conservation, indeed, "got it wrong." Further, by using similar categories to translate social life among Gimi to conservation-related actors, environmental anthropology would generify culture, failing to explain that Gimi cosmology creates a conceptual divide that makes the establishment of "values" impossible.

CONCLUSION

[...] Gimi understand their forests to be a source of personhood, society, and sustenance, in which the spirits of ancestors infuse life into rivers, trees, birds, marsupials, and humans (Gillison 1980:143). I argue that the translations of these socioecological understandings, and the subsequent actions of the BCN, are neither accurate nor particularly productive if the goal is to "conserve" forests held by Gimi. Such translations define Gimi as rational economic actors who value forests because of their potential as commodities and status as resources. This misunderstanding forms the basis for the interventions – specifically ecotourism, handicraft production, and attempts to regulate hunting practices – associated with the Crater Mountain ICAD project, which has neither brought money to Gimi nor curtailed the practices termed as "threats" (see West 2000, 2001, 2006; West and Carrier 2004). [...] I explore a more nuanced translation: In opposition to ecological and economic ways of knowing the environment in which humans are seen as a threat to nature, Gimi ways of knowing view humans as generative of and generated by social relations with what the Western world (but not the Gimi) categorizes as "nature."

The BCN wanted "stakeholders," "sites," and "eco-enterprises" – categories into which Gimi were translated. Afterward, the categories were monitored to measure their integration into global markets for ecoproducts. Over the course of four years, these categories were to be integrated in a way that encouraged development and contributed to conservation. The initial use of these categories called for a generification of culture – a translation of local social life that split Gimi being-in-the-world into "people," "plants and animals," and "environment." Part of this generification or production of ordered and easily consumable difference, with regard to conservation in PNG, is directly connected to the BCN's neoliberal approach to conservation. The categories used by the BCN also produce a particular kind of space and a certain kind of person who is located in place, and encode an economic rational view of people's relations with their environment. Gimi ways of making "self" and "other" and of being-in-the-world produce a fundamentally different space.

[...] I assert that environmental translations should not take for granted that people everywhere approach biological diversity as if it were composed of potentially commodified matter to be used rationally and neutrally or as if it were a "resource" provided by nature. My worry is that environmental anthropology in the guise of political ecology – in its rush to show how external structures affect local socioecological lives – has begun to translate local environmental understandings and actions in ways that generify them and that fail to show them to be aesthetic, poetic, and deeply social. Thus, political ecology is in danger of falling into the same trap as BCN did – failing to understand and demonstrate the nuances of how people come to know, produce, and be a part of environments, and missing aesthetic practices that may well be important political claims with material consequences. [...]

REFERENCES

Biodiversity Support Program (BSP). 1996. Biodiversity Conservation Network 1996 Annual Report: Stories from the Field and Lessons Learned. Washington, DC: BSP.

Carrier, James G., and Daniel Miller. 1998. *Virtualism: A New Political Economy*. Oxford: Berg.

Errington, Frederick, and Deborah Gewertz. 2001. "On the Generification of Culture: From Blow Fish to Melanesian." *Journal of the Royal Anthropological Institute* (n.s.) 7 (September): 509–25. https://doi.org/10.1111/1467-9655.00075.

Gillison, Gillian. 1980. "Images of Nature in Gimi Thought." In *Nature, Culture and Gender*, edited by Carol MacCormack and Marilyn Strathern, 143–73. Cambridge: Cambridge University Press.

———. 1993. *Between Culture and Fantasy: A New Guinea Highlands Mythology*. Chicago: University of Chicago Press.

Glick, Leonard B. 1963. Foundations of a Primitive Medical System: The Gimi of the New Guinea Highlands. Ph.D. dissertation, Graduate School of Arts and Sciences, University of Pennsylvania.

Harper, Janice. 2002. *Endangered Species: Health, Illness and Death among Madagascar's People of the Forest*. Durham: Carolina Academic Press.

Ingold, Tim. 2000. *The Perception of the Environment: Essays on Livelihood, Dwelling and Skill*. New York: Routledge.

Johnson, Arlyne. 1997. "Processes for Effecting Community Participation in the Establishment of Protected Areas: A Case Study of the Crater Mountain Wildlife Management Area." In *The Political Economy of Forest Management in Papua New Guinea Monograph*, edited by Colin Filer, 391–428. Boroko, PNG: National Research Institute.

Paulson, Susan, Lisa L. Gezon, and Michael Watts. 2003. "Locating the Political in Political Ecology: An Introduction." *Human Organization* 62 (3): 205–17. https://doi.org/10.C.62.3.e5xcjnd6y8v09n6b.

Robbins, Joel. 2003. "Properties of Nature, Properties of Culture: Possession, Recognition, and the Substance of Politics in a Papua New Guinea Society." *Suomen Anthropologi* 1 (28): 9–28.

Salafsky, Nick, and Eva Wollenberg. 2001. "A Systematic Test of an Enterprise Strategy for Community-Based Biodiversity Conservation." *Conservation Biology* 15 (6): 1585–95. http://doi.org/10.1046/j.1523-1739.2001.00220.x.

Scott, James C. 1998. *Seeing Like a State: How Certain Schemes to Improve the Human Condition Have Failed*. New Haven, CT: Yale University Press.

Strathern, Marilyn. 1988. *The Gender of the Gift*. Berkeley: University of California Press.

Tsing, Anna. 2003. "Cultivating the Wild: Honey-Hunting and Forest Management in Southeast Kalimantan." In *Culture and the Question of Rights: Forests, Coasts and Seas in Southeast Asia*, edited by Charles Zerner, 24–55. Durham, NC: Duke University Press.

West, Paige. 2000. The Practices, Ideologies, and Consequences of Conservation and Development in Papua New Guinea. Ph.D. dissertation, Department of Anthropology, Rutgers University.

———. 2001. "Environmental Non-Governmental Organizations and the Nature of Ethnographic Inquiry." *Social Analysis* (November) 45 (2): 55–77.

———. 2006. *Conservation Is Our Government Now: The Politics of Ecology in Papua New Guinea*. Durham, NC: Duke University Press.

West, Paige, and James G. Carrier. 2004. "Ecotourism and Authenticity: Getting Away from It All?" *Current Anthropology* 45 (4): 483–98.

Zerner, Charles. 2003. "Moving Translations: Poetics, Performance, and Property in Indonesia and Malaysia." In *Culture and the Question of Rights: Forests, Coasts and Seas in Southeast Asia*, edited by Charles Zerner, 1–23. Durham, NC: Duke University Press.

11.3. Indigenizing the Anthropocene (2015)

Zoe Todd

> The language of postmodernism is ethnocentric and insufficient.
>
> — Guillermo Gómez-Peña

> Art is supposedly well within the digital age of fusion, beyond boundaries and anthropology.
>
> — Loretta Todd

A CRISIS IN SEARCH OF A NAME

In a time of anthropological engagement with diverse and urgent environmental crises, current academic discourses in the Euro-Western academy have coalesced around the notion of the Anthropocene as a narrative tool. Popularized by Paul Crutzen in 2002, and subsequently taken up by the humanities, the Anthropocene references an epoch in which humans are the dominant drivers of geologic change on the globe today. As a Métis scholar, I have an inherent distrust of this term, the Anthropocene, since terms and theories can act as gentrifiers in their own right, and I frequently have to force myself to engage in good faith with it as heuristic. While it may seem ridiculous to distrust a word, it is precisely because the term has colonized and infiltrated many intellectual contexts throughout the academy at the moment that I view it with caution. However, my distrust is well-founded: Swedish scholars Andreas Malm and Alf Hornborg, among others, highlight the manner in which the current framing of the Anthropocene blunts the distinctions between the people, nations, and collectives who drive the fossil-fuel economy and those who do not. The complex and paradoxical experiences of diverse people as humans-in-the-world, including the ongoing damage of colonial and imperialist agendas, can be lost when the narrative is collapsed to a universalizing species paradigm. […]

As an Indigenous scholar working both in Canada and the UK, I am intensely aware of how discourse is deployed within and between geographies, disciplines, and institutions.

Whenever a term or trend is on everyone's lips, I ask myself: "What other story could be told here? What other language is not being heard? Whose space is this, and who is not here?" With the prevalence of the Anthropocene as a conceptual "building" within which stories are being told, it is important to query which humans or human systems are driving the environmental change the Anthropocene is meant to describe. [...] And, finally, who is dominating the conversations about how to change the state of things?

[...] A number of other scholars have critiqued current popular trends in the Euro-Western humanities: posthumanism and the ontological turn have all been queried and challenged as Eurocentric. These critiques re-center the locus of thought, offering a reconfiguration of understandings of human-environmental relations toward praxis that acknowledges the central importance of land, bodies, movement, race, colonialism and sexuality. [...]

In critiquing the locus of agency, and by re-centering motion, bodies, spirit, race, and sexuality [... such critiques] plainly demonstrate the dangers of a Eurocentric conception of ontology and posthumanism. What do these critiques of posthumanism have to do with the Anthropocene? Put simply: both threads of inquiry, posthumanism and the Anthropocene, share a terrain, even if they do not have in common the same central emphasis in their respective discourses. Posthumanism (and, more specifically, its concurrent stream of work on multispecies ethnographies) "aims to decenter the human" in Euro-Western scholarship, whereas the Anthropocene is *intensely pre-occupied with the human, the anthropos*. [...]

So, the Anthropocene narrative gathers discursive steam, dominating contexts where other discourses struggle to circulate. And, it dominates in what is an undeniably *white* intellectual space of the Euro-Western academy. It is perhaps unsurprising for popular thought to be Eurocentric when the institutions and structures within which it is generated continue to be largely heteropatriarchal, Eurocentric, and white. [...]

[...] For Brodkin, Morgen, and Hutchinson, anthropology in America is "white public space" because it operates both to: a) physically and procedurally discriminate against people of color in anthropology departments; and, b) conceptually discriminate by minimizing or denying experiences of racism within departments. So, the "buildings," or "white men as buildings" that Ahmed describes, within which ideologies are produced, serve to both literally and figuratively reinforce whiteness. If the academy's structures reproduce whiteness, what can we expect of the stories it is telling about the Anthropocene and our shared struggles to engage with dynamic environmental crises on the planet? [...] I argue that in order to enliven and enact active scholarship and praxis as responses to the Anthropocene, the academy must dismantle the underlying heteropatriarchal and white supremacist structures that shape its current configurations and conversations.

However, academia is not the only white public space; Guillermo Gómez-Peña describes the appropriation of the bodies/aesthetics/epistemologies of people of color/Latinos, and the uncritical centralization of whiteness of the American art world. [...]

As Gómez-Peña demonstrates, the erasure of Latino/Latina bodies and the sanitization of rage or dispossession in contemporary art obscures the visceral, racialized, gendered, and geographically distinct experiences of socio-political and environmental crises in the world today. [...]

[...] Martineau and Ritskes both highlight the ongoing whiteness of mainstream art praxis, positing Indigenous art as a counter-narrative to the heteropatriarchy and white supremacy that informs artistic discourses. They argue that "the task of decolonial artists, scholars and activists is not simply to offer amendments or edits to the current world, but to display the mutual sacrifice and relationality needed to sabotage colonial systems of thought and power for the purpose of liberatory alternatives." I would add that the non-human must also be incorporated into this equation. [...]

INDIGENIZING THE ANTHROPOCENE: DWAYNE DONALD'S "ETHICAL RELATIONALITY" AND INDIGENOUS MÉTISSAGE

Thankfully, there are ways to counter the Eurocentrism of the academy and the art world and its discourses about global environmental crises. I investigate here how Indigenous scholarship can accomplish what anthropological and arts discourses struggle to do: de-colonize the academy and its contemporary concerns, including the Anthropocene. As dis-courses of the Anthropocene heat up across and within various disciplines, Papaschase Cree scholar Dwayne Donald, who teaches and writes about education in Canada, has called for an "ethical relationality." [...] He advances two related ideas that can serve as strong responses to the current structures and frameworks that shape discussions about the Anthropocene, and indeed our complex existence on the planet. The first idea is "ethical relationality," which in a 2010 talk he defined as:

> an enactment of ecological imagination. Ethical relationality doesn't deny that we're different, so it's not a way to say we're all the same. But it seeks to understand more deeply how our different histories and experiences position us in relation to each other. It puts those at the fore-front: who you are, where you come from, what your commitments are, what your experiences have been. So, it's a desire to acknowledge and honour the significance of the relationships we have with others, how our histories and experiences position us in relation to each other, and how our futures as people in the world are similarly tied together. It is an ethical imperative to see that despite our varied place-based cultures and knowledge systems, we live in the world together and must constantly think and act with reference to those relationships.

Donald envisions ethical relationality as rooted in what he defines as our "ecological imag-ination." At its core, Donald's approach to our position as humans on this fraught planet is rooted in balance and reciprocity:

> I use that term "ecology," and this comes from, I guess, the little bit I know about Cree and Black-foot philosophies, which I know are connected in this way. And of course, I use ecology not in the sense I use it, typically, in Science. I don't mean "ecology" in that you study the environment separate from where we live or who we are as people. Actually, ecology, the way I think of it – the way I've been taught to think about it – is: paying attention to the webs of relationships that you

are enmeshed in, depending on where you live. So, those are all the things that give us life, all the things that we depend on, as well as all the other entities that we relate to, including human beings.

In turn, his notion of "ethical relationality" also "seeks to understand more deeply how our different histories and experiences position us in relation to each other," and provides an Indigenous framework through which to read the discourses of the Anthropocene. Donald unambiguously emphasizes the relationality between all things, all relationships. Though humans may drive some changes on the planet, Donald's framework re-centers how these connections are enmeshed in "webs of relationships."

The second idea that Donald advances is that of Indigenous Métissage, which he defines as "a place-based approach to curriculum informed by an ecological and relational understanding of the world," one that fosters reciprocal discourse between colonizer and colonized. In outlining the logics and praxis of Indigenous Métissage, Donald reminds readers that in order to mobilize Indigenous Métissage, there must be an "ethic of historical consciousness."

This ethic holds that the past occurs simultaneously in the present and influences how we conceptualize the future. It requires that we see ourselves related to, and implicated in, the lives of those yet to come. It is an ethical imperative to recognize the significance of the relationships we have with others, how our histories and experiences are layered and position us in relation to each other, and how our futures as people similarly are tied together. It is also an ethical imperative to see that, despite our varied place-based cultures and knowledge systems, we live in the world together with others and must constantly think and act with reference to these relationships. Any knowledge we gain about the world interweaves us more deeply with these relationships, and gives us life.

An orientation toward Donald's philosophical framework helps to address the shortcomings that Malm and Hornborg identify in the current framings of the Anthropocene, which currently acts as white public space and erases the differential histories and relationships that have led to current environmental crises. Historical consciousness, ethical relationality, and Indigenous Métissage – rooted in reciprocity, relationships, and responsibility – are among many principles the Eurocentric academy struggles to address in current framings and responses to the Anthropocene. […] His ethical relationality and Indigenous Métissage are processes through which to move away from human-centric discourses about the Anthropocene, and to envisage ourselves as rooted in reciprocal, ongoing, and dynamic relationships that are informed by Indigenous legal orders and our embeddedness in the meshworks that connect us through an "ecological imagination." Such relationality can inform decolonizing approaches to both art and anthropology in the Anthropocene. […]

CONCLUSION

[…] In order to engage in global conversations about the state of the world, such as the current discourse of the Anthropocene, there must be a concomitant examination of where such discourses are situated, who is defining the problems, and who decides the players involved. Rather than engage with the Anthropocene as a teleological fact implicating all humans as equally culpable for the current socio-economic, ecological, and political state of the world, I argue that we should turn to examining how other peoples are describing our "ecological imagination." To tackle the intertwined and complex environmental crises in which the world finds itself, a turn toward the reciprocity and relationships that Donald addresses in his writings and talks must be seriously considered, as locally informed responses to in situ challenges around the globe cannot be constructed using one philosophical, epistemological, or ontological lens. Art, as one mode of thought and praxis, can play a role in dismantling the condos of the art and academic world and help us build something different in their stead. The Anthropocene, after all, need not gentrify our discourses of outrage at the state of things when there are so many other ways to engage with our shared plight as beings on this planet. In order to resist the hegemonic tendencies of a universalizing paradigm like the Anthropocene, we need joyful and critical engagement through many forms of praxis. I see Indigenous thought and practice – including art – as critical sites of refraction of the current whiteness of Anthropocene discourses. [...]

11.4. Designs for the Pluriverse: Radical Interdependence, Autonomy, and the Making of Worlds (2018)

Arturo Escobar

[A] critique of dualities (mind/body, self/other, subject/other, nature/culture, matter/spirit, reason/emotion, and so forth) is arising from many different intellectual and activist domains, not just academic critiques. My argument is that the convergence of these tendencies is fostering the creation of an ontological-political field that questions anew, and goes beyond, these dualisms. The multisited emergence of such a field is making progressively perceptible – theoretically and politically – a range of alternatives, increasingly conceptualized in terms of the notion of relationality. This concept offers a different, and much-needed, way of re/conceiving life and the world [...]

[...] I present ontological design as a means to think about, and contribute to, the transition from the hegemony of modernity's one-world ontology to a pluriverse of socionatural configurations. [...]

Does the concept of the pluriverse, and the field of political ontology that attends to it, have a future with futures? [...] The answer will depend on the extent to which the notions of the pluriverse and political ontology can sustain their effort to disentangle themselves, perhaps not completely, but significantly, from the modern episteme. [...] I would like to offer a few [...] comments from the perspective of how worlds relate to each other and to the limits of modern knowledge's ability to understand what makes the modern and the nonmodern different yet not entirely separate, partially connected yet also divergent in relation to each other.

The concept of partial connection is useful to enable the analysis of how worlds appear to be shaped, and even encompassed, by each other while remaining distinct (de la Cadena 2015, 33). It provides a conceptual means to understand the ontological complexity of "really existing" partially connected worlds, of how worlds can be part of each other and radically different at the same time. It is necessary to start by emphasizing that radical differences is not something "indigenous people have" (275) but designates relationship existence under conditions of partial connection, where every world is more than one (not complete or total unto itself) but less than many (that is, we are not dealing with a collection of interacting separate worlds); all worlds are, in short, within the pluriverse. The question remains, however, of how to make explicit the onto-epistemic politics of translation going on between worlds under conditions of partial connection that are also asymmetrical relations.

One way to think of this difference [...] is in terms of the ontological excess that subaltern worlds continue to exhibit in relation to dominant worlds. There is, for instance, much in Andean indigenous worlds that does not abide by the divide between humans and nonhumans, even if the divide is also present in many of their practices. The question thus arises of how to understand worlds that clearly live partly outside of the separation between nature and humanity but who also live with it, ignore it, are affected by it, utilize it strategically, and reject it – all at the same time. A pluriversal attitude in relating to indigenous groups who defend mountains or lakes on the basis that they are "sentient beings" or "sacred entities" (our modern translation) would allow mountains or lakes to be what they are, not mere objects or independently existing things; above all, it would suspend the act of translating these arguments into "beliefs," which is the main way in which moderns can accommodate them from the perspective of an ontology of intrinsically existent objects or nonhumans. [...]

A timely question for all those worlds that never wanted, or no longer want, to abide by allegedly universal rules is that of how to relate with dominant worlds that do not want to relate. [... To] quote Mario Blaser [...]:

> Political ontology is intended neither as a pedagogic project to illuminate a reality that deficient theorizing cannot grasp, nor as a proselytizing project to show the virtues of other, nonmodern blueprints for a good life. Such readings would confuse an attempt to carve out a space to listen carefully to what other worldings propose with an attempt to rescue and promote those worldings as if we knew what they were about. Political ontology is closer to hard-nose pragmatism than to the liberal desire to understand everyone; the *pax moderna* no longer holds (if it ever truly did), and dominance without hegemony is a costly proposition when ontological differences become politically active. (2013, 559)

Political ontology is thus not a new approach for another realist claim on the real [...]. Political ontology is a way of telling stories differently, in the hope that other spaces for the enactment of the multiple ontologies making up the pluriverse might open up.

As the scale and pace of destruction continue to expand through the massive extractive operations needed to keep the capitalist industrial system going, these issues take on added meaning. Environmental conflicts are often ontological conflicts; patriarchal capitalist modernity entails the ontological occupation of the existential territories of humans and nonhumans; and people's struggles are thus ontological struggles. [...]

FROM CRISIS TO REEXISTENCE

[...We turn now to] the idea of the bifurcation taking place regarding the question of "posthuman" futures. [...] This bifurcation involves two paths, which we may call "return to Earth" and "the human beyond biology." By the first I mean – in the company of the many sages, activists, and intellectuals from territorialized communities; wise elders from "an alternative West"; and ecological and feminist thinkers – something more than merely ecological or environmentally correct living. Returning to Earth implies developing a genuine capacity to live with the profound implications entailed by the seemingly simple principle of radical interdependence. To return to the notion of the biology of love ([...] for its proponents this is not a moral precept but a way to name the structural dynamics of interdependence they discover at the foundation of all life; call it "care" if you prefer): "The biology of love, the manner of living with the other [human and nonhuman] in the doings or behaviors through which the other arises as a legitimate other in coexistence with oneself, and in which we human beings take total responsibility for our emotions and for our rational doings, is not a coexistence in appropriation, control or command" (Maturana and Verden-Zöller 2008, 118).

Living with the Earth within the biology of love supposes a mode of existence in which relations of mutual care and respect are *spontaneously realized* – a mode of living that involves our whole life and that can take place only within what we have called the communal. It means cultivating this principle not only theoretically but by living it autonomously. It means being actively cognizant of how "patriarchality through mistrust and control, through manipulation and appropriation, through domination and submission, interferes with the biology of love, pushing humans away from the domain of collaboration and mutual respect towards the domain of political alliances, mutual manipulation, and mutual abuse" (119). Sound familiar, right? "*And as the biology of love is interfered with, our social life comes to an end*" (119, emphasis added). This is because the biology of love is the principle of all successful sociality. [...]

Let us now look at the second scenario, by most counts the most likely to gain the upper hand. This is the overcoming and total transcendence of the organic basis of life dreamed up by the technopatriarchs of the moment. This scenario necessitates an ongoing legitimation of the ontology of separation. It would not have such a hold on the popular imagination were it not for the fact that its pivotal constructs – the individual, markets, expert knowledge, science, material wealth – are paraded every night for hours on end on CNN and the like and in the annual rituals of the Davos men and World Bank and International Monetary Fund economist, as if they *truly represented the fundaments of human life*. Be that as it may, the technological imagination is powerful, even more so perhaps when depicting the final alchemic fantasy of a world that no longer depends on nature. The entire panoply of biological, material, and digital technologies is placed at the service of this imaginary. Sure, the bodies of animals and plants might tolerate a high level of manipulation if certain fundamental cellular features are respected, so to this extent these developments may justifiably be seen as feasible. The corollary of this possibility, however, is literally earth-shattering. A question becomes imperative: "in doing all this, will humanness be conserved or lost?" (Maturana and Verden-Zöller 2008, 116). These authors continue:

> [...] If technology becomes the most fundamental and central feature of human endeavors, then indeed it does not matter that in the technological expansion and complication of human activities human beingness as *Homo sapiens-amans* should be lost to be replaced by the conservation

of some new being like *Homo sapiens agressans,* or *Homo sapiens sapiens arrogans,* for example. The conservation of some new *Homo sapiens* identity will change the course of history, and human beingness as *Homo sapiens-amans* shall disappear, or it will remain hidden in some distant pockets of primitive life.... But if loving humanness remains important and valuable for us as human beings, then technology will not determine human life, and the biology of intimacy [interconnectedness] will not be lost or destroyed but will be conserved. (119)

We are confronted here with the rise of a posthuman quite different from that envisioned by posthumanist social theory. The human would not disappear as such, as many environmentalists dread (rightly so), but would mutate into another type of being. The stakes are clear. How shall ontologically oriented design face the quandaries of life beyond biology? Will designers be able to resist the seduction of this powerful imaginary? For the technoworlds created by these imaginations are unfailingly loaded with the promise of unlimited growth, novelty, power, adventure, and wealth (as if these were the ultimate criteria of a good life), albeit at the cost of alienating us ever more from our participation in the life of Earth. [...]

Many people, doubtlessly many environmentalists, feel an immense sadness when confronted with the devastation of life. How can one accept a life without the anaconda, the jaguar, or the elephant, or so many birds and millenarian trees, rivers, landscapes, and snowy peaks, or even the smallest living beings that go unnoticed altogether? How can one think about reconstructing the House of Life (the Ecozoic) so as to avoid such futures? Can one bring back beauty and harmony into the world, so undermined in the name of urban comfort and efficiency? There is no doubt that beauty – which for some theorists has actually been an important piece of evolution, perhaps even its telos (Goodwin 2007; Lubarksi 2014) – has been a major victim of the Anthropocene; in fact, one may posit that the systemic exile of beauty from modern life is one of its most salient dimensions. [...]

REVISITING THE STAKES

At the other extreme from the views of the techno-fathers and the markets, we find complexity theory biologist Brian Goodwin's vision of "the great transformation":

> I am optimistic that we can go through the transition as an expression of the continually creative emergence of organic form that is the essence of the living process in which we participate. Like the caterpillar that wraps itself up in its silken swaddling bands prior to metamorphosis into a butterfly, we have wrapped ourselves in a tangled skin from which we can emerge only by going through a similar dramatic transformation. In the world of insects, this transformation occurs as a result of a self-digestion, a meltdown of the caterpillar in which only a few living foci of living tissue, the imaginal discs, remain intact. It is from this that the legs, wings, antennae, body segments and other structures of the adult form emerge as an integrated, transformed being, the butterfly. What the cultural correspondences of this metaphor might mean we can only speculate. (2007, 177)

For some indigenous and other subaltern peoples in Latin America, this great transformation is none other than the *pachakuti*: a profound overhaul of the existing social order, not as a result of a sudden act or a new great synthesis of knowledge or novel agreements, but of an expansive and steady, albeit discontinuous, effort to permanently unsettle and alter the established order. The pachakuti, or the great cycles of the Mayan calendar, are long-standing concepts of peoples who are strictly contemporaneous, that is, peoples for whom "there is no 'post' nor 'pre' because their vision of history is neither linear nor teleological; it sketches a path without ceasing to return to the same point" (Rivera Cusicanqui 2014, 6). The pachakuti "evokes an inversion of historical time, the insurgency of a past and a future that might culminate in catastrophe or renewal.... What is experienced is a change of consciousness and a transformation in identities, modes of knowing, and modes of conceiving of politics."

It seems daring to apply these concepts to the transitions into which we are being thrown at the present, but I find in them a more constructive way of thinking about human futures than in the prescriptions in vogue given to us by established institutions, such as the impoverished post-2015 sustainable development agenda or, even less so, the technological alchemies of the day, which would most certainly cause even greater destruction of the Earth with their offering of illusive futures.

Perhaps we can hear rumblings of the pachakuti in the transition initiatives and grassroots struggles for autonomy in so many parts of the world, as in Arundhati Roy's poetic evocation of it, "*Another world is not only possible, she is on her way. On a quiet day, I can hear her breathing*" (quoted in Macy 2007, 17). For this process to take off on a surer footing, albeit in unpredictable directions, the dream of fitting all worlds into one has finally to be put on hold.

REFERENCES

Blaser, Mario. 2013. "Ontological Conflicts and the Stories of Peoples in Spite of Europe: Towards a Conversation on Political Ontology." *Current Anthropology* 54 (5): 547–68.

de la Cadena, Marisol. 2015. *Earth Beings: Ecologies of Practice across Andean Worlds*. Durham: Duke University Press.

Goodwin, Brian. 2007. *Nature's Due: Healing Our Fragmented Culture*. Edinburgh: Floris Books.

Lubarksi, Sandra. 2014. "Living Beauty." In *Keeping the Wild*, edited by George Wuerthener, Eileen Crist, and Tom Butler, 188–96. Washington, DC: Island Press.

Macy, Joanna. 2007. *World as Lover, World as Self: Courage for Global Justice and Ecological Renewal*. Berkeley: Parallax.

Maturana, Humberto, and Gerda Verden-Zöller. 2008. *The Origin of Humanness in the Biology of Love*. Charlottesville: Imprint Academic.

Rivera Cusicanqui, Silvia. 2014. *Hambre de huelga: Ch'ixinakax Utxiwa y otros textos*. Querétaro, Mexico: La Mirada Salvaje.

11.5. Complicity and Resistance in the Indigenous Amazon: *Economía Indígena* under Siege (2020)

Alaka Wali

THE PERUVIAN CONTEXT

In the Western Amazon, the dominant form of neoliberalism is extractive capitalism: a capitalist mode of production based on mining the regions' natural resources – forests, minerals, fossil fuels and the like, for short-term profit at the expense of the environment (Acosta, 2013). Extraction as a mode of production is singularly characterized by cycles of boom and bust. This mode is not new, but under neoliberal regimes, it has intensified and accelerated. Intensification of resource extraction has come in successive waves – or booms, from the early days of the Conquistadores, searching for gold, throughout the succeeding centuries, but successively more frequent after World War II, when Peru, in like-mind with other countries that had large Amazonian "frontiers" began to build the infrastructure (roads, dams) that provided unparalleled access to the remotest parts of its territory. The booms made commodities out of nature: rubber trees exuded their resin, rivers coughed up gold, forests yielded centuries' old hardwoods or were cut down in huge swaths to make space for monocultivation of cash crops. The booms and their social and environmental consequences have been amply documented in the literature (Davis, 1977; Fearnside, 2008; Rodrigues et al., 2009). Ultimately, these boom times were intense periods of cultural loss when Amazonian indigenous peoples were subjected to severe oppression including displacement from their homelands. The latest booms affecting the region are oil exploration, logging for hardwoods, and African oil palm mono cultivation (Finer et al. 2008; Gutiérrez-Vélez, 2011; Kimmerling, 1991; Rodrigues et al., 2009). In different parts of the region, each one of these has held sway and been a driver of forest destruction.

Yet, the inevitable end of the booms as the commodity loses its cache in the market, or becomes too expensive to extract, or is simply exhausted, causes the market forces and apparatus to recede, leaving people behind. Additionally, the vast size of the Amazon offers an escape for people who can flee the destroyed areas or the labor subjugation to more remote refuges. It is in these interstitial moments that communities reestablished the alternative pathways discussed by Escobar, Tsing, and others. These bust times are the critical periods when Amazonian people draw on their reservoirs of ecological knowledge and cultural practices to regain a sense of autonomy and control over their lives, finding ways to re-privilege a subsistence mode of livelihood (through small scale cultivation, hunting and fishing and using forest resources), that while diminished as a sustainable source of support, remained essential even during boom times. Even as they were forced or recruited into supplying labor and natural resources for the supply chains of capitalist accumulation, Amazonian peoples still depended on a subsistence strategy as their primary source of livelihood. Reliance on what Eric Wolf termed a "kinship mode of production" (1982) and only partial integration into extractive work in the Amazon region permitted people to stay attached to place and to critical cultural resources that during the bust times when work for extraction ended or diminished, reemerged and expanded again to become a dominant form of structuring life ways. This mode of production is what Indigenous organizations today term the *Economía Indígena* (Indigenous Economy). The *Economía Indígena* has a millennial history in the Amazon as archeological research has revealed (Erickson, 2006; Heckenberger, 2008; Roosevelt, 1996 and c.f. Mann 2005 for a good summary). Although most of the research on indigenous Amazonian people's lifeways in pre-Columbian times has focused on Brazil, it can also be applied to understanding the antecedents of indigenous strategies in the Western Amazon. The depth of ecological knowledge and its sustenance has been documented by Peruvian scholars (Gashé, 2011) for example.

By the time I began to work in the Amazon region of Peru, in the early 2000s, however, the boom cycle of extraction was taking hold once again. In this time period, which is extending to the present day, a diverse array of extractive practices threatens large-scale degradation of forest habitats. Although logging for prized commodity woods such as Mahogany is not so feasible, timber extractors continue to seek hardwoods that are less lucrative but still in demand. In select parts of the region, there is wide-scale mining for gold and other precious minerals that is a mix of so-called artisanal and more industrial in nature. In addition, oil companies have secured large concessions across the region. Finally, there has been an escalation of monocultivation of cash crops such as palm oil, rice, coffee and cacao spurred in part by the United States funding of eradication of coca cultivation and substitution with acceptable cash crops. These booms are once again drawing larger numbers of people into the extractive sphere and creating greater vulnerability for land tenure for Amazonian communities. Throughout this period, the Peruvian Government (especially the Administration of Alan Garcia from 2006–2011) largely froze land titling for indigenous communities and encouraged the extractive enterprises by granting mining and timber concessions, among other actions.

In the face of this boom, both national and international environmental conservation organizations grew alarmed at the rapid pace of deforestation and contamination of watersheds. Researchers had identified the Western Amazon as a biodiversity hotspot, perhaps even more critical for species conservation than the Brazilian Amazon (Ceballos et al., 2006; Soares et al., 2006). However, the major conservation organizations were focused on

Brazil, which contained the largest amount of Amazon forests and were not investing much resources into protection for Western Amazon sites. Additionally, the relationship between large conservation organizations and indigenous peoples or other long-time forest dwellers was tenuous at best (see Chapin, 2004 for a detailed history). Conservation organizations, as Chapin pointed out, were reluctant to support indigenous land rights and human rights struggles and indigenous organizations became hostile to environmental organizations' agendas (c.f. Wali, 2012). Although much of the tension between environmental and indigenous organizations was happening at national or international levels, local communities felt the consequences. As protected areas were declared, or as extractive activities increased, these communities became ever more precarious. [...]

In the face of these pressures from both extractors and conservationists, indigenous and forest-dwelling communities faced difficult choices as to how to forge livelihoods. In our work we encountered villages in a range of positions vis a vis integration into the market economy or participation in conservation efforts. A distinct pattern, not surprisingly, was that those communities with the least access to urban centers were less engaged with extractors but more likely to work with conservationists, while those communities that were closer to urban circuits felt the need for cash more urgently and had significant factions in the community opposed to conservation efforts. Yet, those that were participating in either or both of these processes did not completely invest in them. Rather, most people we encountered in the course of our work in Peru tried to maintain a foothold in the *Economía Indígena*, perceiving it as a security against the precariousness of the market economy. Especially women maintained a kinship mode of production, exchanging resources with their relatives and extended village networks, cultivating their gardens and demanding men to do the work of helping to provide food and shelter. The daily acts of caring for children, cooking, maintaining the household tied both men and women to the land. Forms of social relations built over centuries were not abandoned entirely, even in cases where villages were fast losing access to natural resources and becoming more and more dependent on cash income for livelihood. Those living close to protected areas still regularly entered them to hunt or fish for subsistence purposes. Those communities in close contact with extractors rarely relied solely on cash derived income to meet subsistence needs. Only in the direst circumstances, where forest resources had become so scarce that people could no longer viably hunt or fish and could only farm on smaller plots, did people depend more on cash income than forest resources for livelihood.

Although these active efforts to maintain a hold on subsistence-generating livelihoods were not obvious forms of resistance to extractivists and conservationists, they nevertheless signaled a persistent desire to maintain a degree of autonomy and not completely capitulate to capitalist modes of production. This form of "everyday" resistance could also take an emotional and social toll because it entailed countering the narrative of "backwardness" and insisting on retaining a different worldview and transmitting it to children and grandchildren. I would argue that this form of resistance laid the groundwork for more overt political acts of resistance that erupted at specific historic moments. In the contemporary moment, from the 1970s to the present, indigenous peoples across the Amazon have formed organizations to advocate for greater representation, adherence to the International Labor Organization Treaty 169 (ILO 169) and later the United Nations Declaration of Indigenous People's Human Rights (2007), demand titling of Native Lands, and halt the construction of large scale infrastructure such as dams and roads that would permanently destroy their homelands (Hearn, 2008; Romero, 2009). The political argument that indigenous communities have made is centered on the right to cultural and political autonomy that is grounded in the livelihood strategy anchored in the Economía Indígena. Indigenous organizations, such as AIDESEP (*Asociación Interétnica de Desarrollo de la Selva Peruana* – Interethnic Association for the Development of the Peruvian Rainforest) claim that Amazonian indigenous communities have the right (under ILO 169) to develop their territories in accordance with their cultural traditions that privilege their worldview and stewardship of their resources. Because the everyday forms of resistance are central to the political work, maintenance of the *economía indígena* is of vital importance to any chance that indigenous and forest-dwelling people might have to not be completely swallowed up by the extractivist economy. But how can this resistance be strengthened and the autonomy to pursue well-being along a pathway that avoids maximal extraction expanded?

THE FIELD MUSEUM INTERVENTION

[... T]he Field Museum program has [facilitated] the creation of protected areas in the Western Amazon, funded in large part by private foundations. By 2019, the efforts of the team had led to over 30 million acres under protection. The Field Museum's team was small (never more than 12 people), in contrast to the large footprint of international conservation organizations who by the early 2000s had offices and staff around the world, large public relations campaigns, and financial support in the hundreds of millions (Wali, 2012). The small size of the team, and its location in a scientific institution with a large collection of both biological and cultural heritage from the Amazon allowed it to be flexible in its approach to conservation. [...]

As a founding member of the social science team, I have used anthropological perspectives on political ecology and the power differential between indigenous communities and external organizations to create interventions designed to give voice to local communities in the design of the protected area and to invest resources in empowering them to maintain subsistence livelihood strategies based on their conception of well-being and grounded in the *economía indígena*. Elsewhere, my colleagues and I have described our methodologies (Wali, 2016; Wali et al., 2017). Our approach is grounded in the theoretical underpinnings of the "pluriverse" [... (Escobar 2000, 2008, 2018)]. In the case of Peruvian indigenous communities, we find convincing evidence that the retention of a worldview (*cosmovision)* that radically departs from capitalist modes of production is at the heart of the *economía indígena,* as it is practiced in the communities where we have worked. Our approach surfaces both the worldview and the daily practices of subsistence that undergird it through a participatory assessment exercise. This exercise lays the foundation for a planning process which privileges community priorities rather than extractive-intensive activities. To date, we have used this approach in over 50 communities during rapid inventories and 40 communities in longer-term efforts with communities adjacent to protected areas.

At the core of the exercise is a community reflection process which creates a facilitated space where community members can discuss difficult choices, express anxieties and take stock of what they value. Reflection does not happen in a vacuum, but rather is guided by the information gathered during the participatory assessment. The information is deliberately focused on identifying the strength of cultural practices, ecological expertise, and the health of the natural resource base. As the community assesses the value of their way of life based on the subsistence economy, members find themselves feeling less anxious about earning a cash income and priorities for improving quality of life can shift to actions necessary to sustain the *economía indígena*.

Equally important as the work in communities is the work that the Field Museum team does with local partner NGOs and with the government actors involved in safeguarding protected areas. These local NGOs and protected area staff are often comprised of professionals trained in forestry, agronomy, or other technical expertise, but not experienced in working with indigenous communities. We have often found that these actors, however well intentioned, do not perceive indigenous communities as capable of managing their natural resources sustainably or able to withstand the pressures of the extractivists. Here too, in workshops we facilitate where community members and NGO or Protected Area staff come together, we create spaces for reflection that can shift the perspective of the external actors. They come to understand that their role is to accompany the process of community decision-making but not to dictate the terms of engagement. The shift in perception is aided by the data gathered in the participatory assessments which demonstrates the vitality and sustainability of the *economía indígena* and how reinforcing its maintenance can work to the benefit of environmental conservation. In this process, external actors we have worked with de-emphasize offering services and "development" projects to communities and instead support community driven priorities that can include such activities as language revitalization, vigilance of forest resources, small-scale horticulture, or improved infrastructure for potable water and sanitation.

In sum, the Field Museum program has attempted to put into action what anthropological theory indicates might be a viable alternative to neoliberal regimes of extraction. The challenge in the next phase of work will be to expand the effort systematically across the Peruvian Amazon. To accomplish this, we have been collaborating with the Peruvian Protected Area Service (SERNANP), which has adopted the methodology and intends to use it in a wide variety of protected areas. We are cognizant of the frailty of political and social processes and the continued power of extractivists in determining policy and practice for the Amazon. However, our experience has been that both within the government, NGOs, and in indigenous communities, a desire to push against the path of capitalist exploitation and toward an alternative pathway to well-being can be catalyzed to create measurable change. [...]

REFERENCES

Acosta, Alberto. 2013. "Extractivism and Neoextractivism: Two Sides of the Same Curse." In *Beyond Development: Alternative Visions from Latin America*, edited by Miriam Lang and Dunia Mokrani, 61–86. Quito: Rosa Luxemburg Foundation and Amsterdam: Transnational Institute.

Chapin, Mac. 2004. "A Challenge to Conservationists." *Worldwatch Magazine*. Worldwatch Institute. November–December, 17–31.

Davis, Shelton. 1977. *Victims of the Miracle*. Cambridge: Cambridge University Press.

Erickson, Clark L. 2006. "The Domesticated Landscapes of the Bolivian Amazon." *Time and Complexity in Historical Ecology: Studies in the Neotropical Lowlands*: 235–78.

Escobar, Arturo. 2000. "Beyond the Search for a Paradigm: Post-Development and Beyond." *Development, Journal of the Society for International Development* 43 (4): 11–14. https://doi.org /10.1057/palgrave.development.1110188.

Escobar, Arturo. 2008. *Territories of Difference: Place, Movements, Life, Redes*. Durham: Duke University Press.

Escobar, Arturo. 2018. "Transitions Discourses and the Politics of Relationality: Toward Designs for the Pluriverse." In *Constructing the Pluriverse*, edited by Bernd Reiter, 63–116. Durham: Duke University Press.

Fearnside, Philip M. 2008. "The Roles and Movements of Actors in the Deforestation of Brazilian Amazonia." *Ecology and Society* 13 (1). www.jstor.org/stable/26267941.

Finer, M., C.N. Jenkins, S.L. Pimm, B. Keane, and C. Ross. 2008. "Oil and Gas Projects in the Western Amazon: Threats to Wilderness, Biodiversity, and Indigenous Peoples." *PLoS ONE* 3 (8): e2932. https://doi.org/10.1371/journal.pone.0002932.

Gashé, Jorge. 2011. *Sociedad Bosquesina*, vol 1. Iquitos: Instituto de Investigaciones de la Amazonia Peruana.

Gutiérrez-Vélez, V., et al. 2011. "High-Yield Oil Palm Expansion Spares Land at the Expense of Forests in the Peruvian Amazon." *Environ. Res. Lett.* 6: 4–40.

Hearn, K. 2008. "For Peru's Indians, Lawsuit against Big Oil Reflects a New Era." *Washington Post*. http://www.washingtonpost.com/wp-dyn/content/story/2008/01/31/ST2008013100037.html.

Heckenberger, Michael J., et al. 2008. "Pre-Columbian Urbanism, Anthropogenic Landscapes, and the Future of the Amazon." *Science* 321 (5893): 1214–17.

Kimmerling J. 1991. *Amazon Crude*. New York: Natural Resources Defense Council.

Mann, Charles C. 2005. *1491: New Revelations of the Americas before Columbus*. New York: Alfred A. Knopf.

Rodrigues, A., R. Ewers, L. Parry, C. Souza, Jr., A. Veríssimo, and A. Balmford. 2009. "Boom-and-Bust Development Patterns Across the Amazon Deforestation Frontier." *Science* 324 (5933): 1435–7. https://doi.org/10.1126/science.1174002.

Romero, S. 2009. "Protesters Gird for Long Fight over Opening Peru's Amazon." *New York Times*. www.nytimes.com/2009/06/12/world/americas/12peru.html.

Roosevelt, Anna C., et al. 1996. "Paleoindian Cave Dwellers in the Amazon: The Peopling of the Americas." *Science* 272 (5260): 373–84.

Soares, B.S., D.C. Nepstad, L.M. Curran, G.C. Cerqueira, R.A. Garcia, et al. 2006. "Modeling Conservation in the Amazon Basin." *Nature* 440: 520–3.

Wali, A. 2012. "The Arc of Justice: Indigenous Activism and Anthropological Intersections." *Tipití: Journal of the Society for the Anthropology of Lowland South America* 9 (2): Article 2.

Wali, A. 2016. "Contextualizing the Collection. Environmental Conservation and Quality of Life in the Buffer Zone of the Cordillera Azul National Park." In *The Shibibo-Conibo: Cultures and*

Collections in Context, edited by Wali and Odland, 21–33. Fieldiana Anthropology. The Field Museum of Natural History.

Wali, A., D. Alvira, P.S. Tallman, A. Ravikumar, and M.O. Macedo. 2017. "A New Approach to Conservation: Using Community Empowerment for Sustainable Well-Being." *Ecology and Society* 22 (4): 6. https://doi.org/10.5751/ES-09598-22040.

Wolf, E.R. 1982. *Europe and the People without History*. Berkeley: University of California Press.

Section Eleven Glossary

Anthropocene   A term used to refer to the current geological period characterized by human influence over the earth's environment and climate.

cultural ecology   The study of how human groups adapt biologically and culturally to different environments and climates.

ethnoscience   The study of non-Western scientific knowledge and practice.

multispecies ethnography   Ethnography that encompasses the study of human and other-than-human life, including viruses and bacteria, nonhuman animals, and plants.

ontological turn   A shift in the study of reality that expands our understandings of "nature" and the "world" to allow for multiple realities.

political ecology   The study of relationships between environment and political economy.

posthumanist anthropology   An approach to anthropological study that "de-centers" human beings to overcome anthropocentric interpretations of human/nonhuman interactions. Some argue that we are in a transhuman period and cannot be posthuman until we give up our corporeal selves.

processual approach   Processualism is an archaeological theory that draws on cultural evolutionism to study social change in the material record of past human societies in response to environmental factors.

SECTION TWELVE

On State Power

THE SOCIAL CONTEXT

State societies are highly unequal by definition, with power concentrated in a political elite that largely controls structures of state society including law, bureaucracy, and military forces. These structures are designed to uphold state society – including its highly unequal nature – through various mechanisms of power, including violence. Indeed, Max Weber, who you read in Section One, defined the state as an organization that monopolizes the legitimate use of physical force in a given territory. In contemporary times, this territory is a nation, and state force is largely mobilized in the form of police agencies and military bodies whose actions are legitimated by law. And even though people who are not police or military agents can and do enact violence, the state still determines whether that violence is legitimate or not through a system of laws, courts, and prisons.

Not everyone is equally subjected to state force. Perhaps unsurprisingly, members of the elite are unlikely to be arrested or killed by police during periods of political stability, while colonized, racialized, impoverished, and otherwise marginalized people are disproportionately likely to be detained, arrested, jailed, killed, imprisoned, and executed. Thus, state agencies that govern violence and law are not divorced from broader sociopolitical contexts of inequality (and why would they be?), but rather deeply tied to them.

States and nations have long been units of anthropological analysis, and anthropologists are well suited to challenge their **naturalization**. And as anthropologists identify social stratification – enduring and hierarchical categorical inequality – as a defining feature of state society, we also critique reform measures that do not address underlying causes of inequity at local, national, and global scales. For example, after a rash of high-profile police killings of unarmed Black people, the Association of Black Anthropologists issued a 2020 statement that read in part:

White supremacist violence is at the heart of the founding of the United States. While the extreme manifestations of this genocidal violence take many forms, and ebbs and flows, the structures remain in place. For Black people, this has meant incalculable racial terror and a continuous struggle against numerous systems of oppression – the policing and carceral apparatus, the inequitable health care system, the education apparatus, social and economic hierarchies, and neoliberal policies among others. Our resolve and determination against these systems of tyranny cannot be understated. But we are aware that *there is no way forward if this foundational anti-Blackness is not acknowledged and reckoned with, in this country.* [emphasis added]

Exercises of state power, and their inequitable effects, are the subjects of this section's essays.

THE CONVERSATION

We begin this section with a 1977 essay by sociologist Pierre Bourdieu. In it, Bourdieu theorizes symbolic power – or symbolism that can be wielded to cultivate particular forms of knowledge and that tends to reproduce hierarchical relations of power. These forms of knowledge become authoritative, Bourdieu argues, because symbolism masks their politically constituted nature and makes them appear as given, natural, and inevitable.

Our second piece, by Begoña Aretxaga, analyzes an important site of nation-state power: policed border zones. Aretxaga shows how the border that divides Northern Ireland from the Republic of Ireland is a "spectacle of state control" that reinforces national, gendered, and class inequalities forged by the longstanding colonization of Ireland by Great Britain. Moreover, Aretxaga argues, for Irish nationalists, the border has become a symbol of colonialism and fractured Irish nationhood, which throws the legitimacy of the border itself into question.

Reading 12.3, by Katherine Verdery, examines postsocialist decollectivization efforts in Romania to explore interactions among local and central forms of power. Seeing "like a Mayor," Verdery argues, offers novel insights into local workings of power that can complicate and even contradict state mandates. Ethnographic attention to local politics introduces necessary nuance into treatments of the state as a monolithic or abstract actor.

Our fourth piece is by Achille Mbembé, who theorizes interactions among politics, sovereignty, and death. Mbembé's formulation of "necropolitics" introduces life and death as a central analytic of power and conceptualizes sovereignty as political control over death. Although we had to reduce this essay in size, Mbembé historicizes the exercise of necropolitical power in different contexts, including chattel slavery, colonialism, and war.

Christen Smith explores racialized, sexualized, and gendered police violence in Brazil in Reading 12.5. Rather than viewing police brutality – in particular, police complicity with death squads – as rogue or extra-legal, Smith argues that anti-Black violence is better understood as "an integral part of state security" in Brazil. Like Mbembé, Smith also emphasizes the transnational and historical nature of racialized police violence grounded in African slavery, colonialism, and globalized US practices of torture and assassination.

THREE QUESTIONS FOR THE READINGS

1 If borders, police, and military forces uphold state power, and states are inherently unequal, can these forces also promote equity, stability, and safety?

2 Aretxaga, Mbembé, and Smith all argue that racialized violence should be understood as part of, and not outside of, the exercise of state power. What does this analysis suggest about the long-term legitimacy of state society?

3 Intersectional analyses allow us to perceive gendered and classed experiences with racism, as well as racialized experiences with heteropatriarchy and capitalism. How do ideas about gender, race, and class differentially shape the life experiences of the people profiled in these essays?

ON THE COMPANION WEBSITE

"Black Lives Matter," "Race, Class, and Marxism," additional readings, and more.

www.anthropologicaltheory.com

12.1. Symbolic Power (1977)

Pierre Bourdieu

FIRST SYNTHESIS

"Symbolic systems" are instruments of knowledge which exert a structuring power insofar as they are structured: Symbolic power is a power to construct reality which tends to establish a gnoseological order; the immediate meaning (sens) of the world (particularly of the social world) presupposes what Durkheim calls logical conformism, i.e. "a homogeneous conception of time, space, number, and cause which makes agreement possible between intelligences." Durkheim – or, after him, Radcliffe-Brown, for whom "social solidarity" rests on the sharing of a symbolic system – has the merit of explicitly pointing to the social function which is not reducible to the structuralists' communication function. Symbols are the instruments par excellence of social integration: as instruments of knowledge and communication (cf. Durkheim's analysis of the feast), they make possible the consensus on the sense of the social world which makes a fundamental contribution toward reproducing the social order; "logical" integration is the precondition of "moral" integration.

"SYMBOLIC SYSTEMS" AS INSTRUMENTS OF DOMINATION

The Marxist tradition privileges the political functions of "symbolic systems," at the expense of their logical structure and their gnoseological function (though Engels speaks of "systematic expression" apropos of law). This functionalism (which has nothing in common with structural functionalism a la Durkheim or Radcliffe-Brown) explains symbolic productions by relating them to the interests of the ruling class. Unlike myth, a collective product collectively appropriated and consumed, ideologies serve particular interests which they tend to present as universal interests, common to the whole group. The dominant culture contributes to the real integration of the dominant class (by ensuring immediate communication among all its members and distinguishing them from the other classes); to the fictitious integration of the society as a whole, and hence to the demobilization (false consciousness) of the dominated classes; and to the legitimation of the established order by the establishment of distinctions (hierarchies) and the legitimation of these distinctions. The dominant culture produces its specific ideological effect by concealing its function of division (or distinction) under its function of communication: the culture which unites (a medium of communication) separates (an instrument of distinction), and legitimates distinctions by defining all cultures (designated as sub-cultures) in terms of their distance from the dominant culture (i.e. in terms of privation), identifying the latter with culture (i.e. excellence).

SECOND SYNTHESIS

To refute all forms of the "symbolist" error which reduces relations of force to relations of communication, it is not sufficient to note that relations of communication are always, inseparably, relations of power which depend, in their form and content, on the material or symbolic power accumulated by the agents (or institutions) involved in those relations and which, like the gift or the potlatch, may enable them to accumulate symbolic power. It is as structured and structuring instruments of communication and knowledge that "symbolic systems" fulfill their political function as instruments of domination (or, more precisely, of legitimation of domination); they help to ensure the domination of one class over another (symbolic violence), adding the reinforcement of their own force to the relations of force which underlie them and so contributing, in Weber's phrase, to the "domestication of the dominated."

The different classes and class fractions are engaged in a specifically symbolic struggle to impose the definition of the social world that is most consistent with their interests; the field of ideological positions reproduces the field of social positions, in a transfigured form. They may pursue this struggle either directly, in the symbolic conflicts of daily life, or vicariously, through the struggle between the specialists of symbolic production (full-time producers), for the monopoly of legitimate symbolic violence, i.e. the power to impose (and even inculcate) instruments of knowledge and expression (taxonomies) of social reality, which are arbitrary but not recognized as such (Weber, 1968; Bourdieu, 1971b and c). The field of symbolic production is a microcosm of the symbolic struggle between the classes: it is by serving their own interests in the struggle within the field of production (and only to that extent) that the producers serve the interests of the groups outside the field of production.

The dominant class is the locus of a struggle for the hierarchy of the principles of hierarchization (Bourdieu, 1971a). The dominant fractions, whose power is based on economic and political capital, seek to impose the legitimacy of their domination either through their own symbolic production (discourse, writings, etc) or through the intermediary of conservative ideologists who serve the interests of the dominant fractions – but only incidentally, i.e. only to the extent they thereby serve their specific interests as professional producers.

These ideologists always threaten to divert to their own advantage the power of defining the social world which they hold by delegation. The dominated fraction always tends to set cultural capital – to which it owes its position – at the top of the hierarchy of the principles of hierarchization. (This remains true of those whom the logic of the struggle within the field of cultural production leads to serve the interests of the dominant fractions.)

To insist that instruments of communication and knowledge are, as such, instruments of power is to insist that they are subordinated to practical functions and that the coherence which characterizes them is that of practical logic (contrary to the structuralist error which, attending only to the logical and gnoseological function, overestimates the internal logic of "symbolic systems" and "ideological systems," elliptical and allusive quasi systematizations oriented by ethical and political dispositions) (Bourdieu, 1972).

Instruments of domination that can structure because they are structured, the ideological systems which specialists produce through and for the struggle for the monopoly of legitimate production reproduce the structure of the field of the social classes in a misrecognizable form, through the intermediary of the homology between the field of ideological production and the field of the social classes.

"Symbolic systems" differ fundamentally depending on whether they are produced and, by the same token, appropriated by the whole group or, on the contrary, produced by a body of specialists and, more precisely, by a relatively autonomous field of production and circulation. The history of the transformation of myth into religion (ideology) is not separable from the history of the constitution of a corps of specialized producers of religious rites and discourses, i.e. the progress of the division of religious labor, which is itself a dimension of the progress of the division of social labor, and hence the division into classes (Weber, 1968; Bourdieu, 1971b); its consequences include the dispossessing of the laymen from the instruments of symbolic production.

Ideologies owe their structure and their most specific functions to the social conditions of their production and circulation, i.e. to the functions they fulfill, first for the specialists competing for the monopoly of the competence in question (religious, artistic, etc), and secondarily and incidentally for the non-specialists. When we insist that ideologies are always doubly determined, that they owe their most specific characteristics not only to the interests of the classes or class fractions which they express (the "sociodicy" function) but also to the specific interests of those who produce them and to the specific logic in the field of production (usually transfigured into the ideology of "creation" and the "creator"), we obtain the means of escaping crude reduction of ideological products to the interests of the classes they serve (a "short-circuit" effect common in "Marxist" critiques), without falling into the idealist illusion of treating ideological productions as self-sufficient and self-generating totalities amenable to pure, purely internal analysis (semiology).

The specifically ideological function of the field of ideological production is performed quasi-automatically on the basis of the homology of structure between the field of ideological production, organized around the opposition between orthodoxy and heterodoxy, and the field of struggles between the classes for the maintenance or subversion of the symbolic order. This struggle is organized around the opposition between the dominant ideology, a structured, structuring medium tending to impose apprehension of the established order as natural (orthodoxy) through masked (and hence misrecognized) imposition of classificatory systems and mental structures objectively adjusted to the social structures, and heterodox (or critical) discourse, a symbolic power to mobilize and subvert which actualizes the potential power of the dominated classes by destroying the false self-evidences of orthodoxy (the fictitious restoration of doxa), and so neutralizing the power to demobilize which it contains.

The homology between the two fields causes the struggles for the specific objectives at stake in the autonomous field automatically to produce euphemized forms of the ideological struggles between the classes (Bourdieu 1975b). The fact that the correspondence is only ever effected between one system and another masks, in the eyes of the producers themselves, as well as in the eyes of the profane, the fact that the internal classificatory systems reproduce the directly political taxonomies in a misrecognizable form and that the specific set of implicit axioms in each field is a transmuted form (transmuted in accordance with the specific laws of the field) of the fundamental principles of the division of labor. (For example, the university classificatory system makes explicit in a quasi-systematic form, and so legitimates, the objective divisions of the social structure and especially the division of labor – theory and practice – converting social properties into essential properties – Bourdieu, 1975d.) The specifically ideological effect consists precisely in the imposition of political systems of classification in the legitimate guise of philosophical, religious or juridical taxonomies. Symbolic systems owe their specific force to the fact that the power relations expressed in them only ever manifest themselves in the misrecognizable form of sense relations (displacement).

Symbolic power – power to constitute the given by stating it, to show forth and gain credence, to confirm or transform the world view and, through it, action on the world, and hence the world itself, quasi-magical power which makes it possible to obtain the equivalent of what is obtained by (physical or economic) force, thanks to its specific mobilization effect – is only exerted insofar as it is recognized (i.e. insofar as its arbitrariness is misrecognized). This means that symbolic power does not lie in "symbolic systems" in the form of an "illocutionary force" but that it is defined in and by a determinate relationship between those who exercise power and those who undergo it, i.e. in the very structure of the field within which belief is produced and reproduced. The power of words and commands, the power of words to give orders and bring order, lies in belief in the legitimacy of the words and of the person who utters them, a belief which words themselves cannot produce (Bourdieu, 1975c).

Symbolic power, a subordinate power, is a transformed – i.e. misrecognizable, transfigured, and legitimated – form of the other forms of power. A unified science of practices must supersede the choice between energy models which describe social relations as relations of force, and cybernetic models which make them relations of communication, in order to describe the transformational laws which govern the transmutation of the different forms of capital into symbolic capital. The crucial process to be studied is the work of dissimulation and transfiguration (in a word, euphemization) which makes it possible to transfigure relations of force by getting the violence they objectively contain misrecognized/recognized, so transforming them into a symbolic power, capable of producing effects without visible expenditure of energy (Bourdieu, 1970).

(translation by Richard Nice)

REFERENCES

Bourdieu, Pierre. 1970. *La Reproduction*. Paris: Minuit.

Bourdieu, Pierre. 1971a. "Champ du pouvoir, champ intellectuel et habitus de classe," *Scolies* 1: 7–26.

———. 1971b. "Genese du structure du champ religieux," *Revue fran aise de sociologie* XII: 3.

———. 1971c. "Une interpretation de la sociologie religieuse de Max Weber, " *Archives Europeennes de Sociologie* XII (1): 3–21.

———. 1972. *Esquisse d'une theorie de la pratique, Paris-Geneva, Droz; (Eng. trans. Outline of a Theory of Practice)*. London: Cambridge University Press.

———. 1975b. "L'ontologie politique de Martin Heidegger." *Actes de la Recherches en Sciences Sociales* 5–6 (November): 109–56.

———. 1975c. "Le langage autorise. Note sur les conditions sociales de l'efficacite du discours rituel." *Actes de la Recherches en Sciences Sociales* 5–6 (November): 183–90.

———. 1975d. "Les categories de l'entendement professoral." *Actes de la Recherches en Sciences Sociales* 3 (May): 68–93.

Weber, Max. 1968. *Economy and Society* (3 vols). New York.

12.2. What the Border Hides: Partition and Gender Politics of Irish Nationalism (1998)

Begoña Aretxaga

On 23 September 1989 I drove my old car from Belfast to Dublin crossing the border that separates Northern Ireland from the Irish Republic. Traveling with me were four women from the Belfast working class Catholic district of Falls Road, well known as a stronghold of the Irish Republican Army (IRA). As we approached the border at the town of Newry we held our breath and rode into its military fortress with the barbed wire, the observation post, the gray corrugated iron, the fully armed soldiers of the British army dressed in their combat fatigues, and the no-less-armed Royal Ulster Constabulary (RUC), the Northern Ireland police, imposing in their black uniforms and bullet proof vests.

Now that the Berlin wall has disappeared, the Irish border has possibly become the most militarized and surveyed frontier in Western Europe. It has been the scene of some of the worst political violence deployed by the security forces, loyalist paramilitary groups and the IRA. The countryside around Newry is strongly republican. Tightly knit rural communities, a difficult topography, and continuing violence have earned the area around Newry the name of "bandit country." The locals chuckle half ironically, half proudly, at the name which echoes the folklore of the heroic Irish bandit. Pushed beyond the pale into the arid terrain of bogs and forests of the north-west of the island by the forces of British colonization, the image of the dispossessed Irish was reconfigured into the dangerous figure of the kern and highway robber, an incarnation of the wild Irish for colonial authorities and of heroic resistance in the imagination of Irish folklore (O'Hogain 1985). The image of the heroic Irish bandit recreated through ballads and stories redefined the remote and wild woods, where the native Irish had been confined by the "civilizing" forces of British colonization, as a stage of rebellion. Much of the heroic folklore of the Irish bandit is bestowed upon the contemporary IRA guerrilla through the same expressive culture of songs and storytelling (McCann 1985). For the authorities of Northern Ireland, the spectre of surprise attacks by the IRA and the obsession to maintain the contested boundary between those variously "imagined communities" of the North and the Republic, of Protestant and Catholic, of colonial and postcolonial, has subjected the area around the Irish border to heavy militarization and intense surveillance. The border itself, with its paraphernalia of barbed wire and watch towers, is a spectacle of state control, a ritualization of authority that betrays a profound lack of legitimacy. Indeed, the border is the site where normality, the everyday order of things, is arrested into a state of subjection, a state of emergency that reveals the national order as one of "terror as usual" (Taussig 1992). The Irish border, I will argue in this article, is the site of troubled and troubling national imaginings.

Nationalists feel utterly vulnerable when they are stopped at the border. At best they expect to be subjected to questioning and scrutiny, at worst they can be harassed, arrested or even killed. Border "incidents" are part of everyday life for nationalists who are the ones who cross the border regularly. Unionists rarely go into the Irish Republic which they consider a permanent threat to their existence as Protestants and as members of the United Kingdom. For unionists, the border functions as a reminder of a permanent danger posed by the existence of the Irish Republic. For nationalists the border is a reminder of the incompleteness of the Irish nation and the unfinished business of colonization. Because the border is an unrecognized national boundary for nationalists, and because of the actual danger of crossing it, crossing the border becomes an act of defiance, filled at once with excitement and dread. Crossing the border is an act of transgression because in its back and forth movement it shows the porosity of the national frontier, its inherent instability. And in so doing, the back and forth movement of nationalists across the Irish border also questions its very existence and lays a national claim over the whole island, north and south. For if nation-states come to be formed through artifices like maps and national borders then it is at those sites that nations are not only imagined but also challenged. No wonder then that crossing the border triggers anxieties of different kinds for nationalists and the unionist security forces that guard it.

[...] National borders might be historical products of a particular kind of territorial imagination, as Benedict Anderson (1983) has suggested, but precisely because of that, borders are also the space where national imaginings are rendered unstable. What happens, for example, when national borders do not correspond with the outline of the imagined nation? What happens to national identity when an unimagined border forces a redefinition of the nation? The border might become then a space of instability, a space signifying what is lost, or left out of the imagined nation; a haunting presence that cannot be contained within the discourse of the existing nation-state but questions it by virtue of its presence. A national border of this kind – unimagined and forced by violence – becomes then a space of excess, the repository of what is denied or inarticulate in the discourse of the nation. In Ireland, such excess manifests itself in the hyper-visibility and hyper-vigilance of (Northern) state violence. Such visibility of violence iconized in the military paraphernalia that envelops the Irish border, mirrors the violence of the civil war that accompanied the birth of the Irish nation-state and which became the glaring absence in the discourse of official nationalism after partition. Once in place borders are not inert, they have a ghostly existence capable of producing concrete effects. They configure the lives of people circumscribed by their contours and give rise to particular subjectivities and identities. Things happened to people not only in those border zones, but also as a consequence of borders. If borders have the power to affect people so too do they affect the lives and identities of the nations they circumscribe. In other words, borders give rise to social and political imaginaries filled with dreads and desire. I want to insist on this because I think that it is the affective underpinnings of nationalism, its unconscious life if you wish, that Benedict Andersons's felicitous notion of "imagined communities" presumes but leaves unelaborated. [...]

[...] I think that a theory of nationalism must go beyond the discursive production of nationalism to explore its political imaginaries. We need to understand how particular political imaginaries articulate with the symbolic universe of nationalism in order to account for its affective power. Anderson has noted that this affective power stems from nationalism's skillful use of gender and familial metaphors. The power of metaphor to create affective states resides in the labor of condensation that taps into unconscious motivation to bring together different domains of experience (Fernandez 1986), that of romantic and filial love and political action, for example. It is this unconscious mechanism that permits the forms of identification and projection that often accompany nationalist discourse. In other words, the affective power of nationalism resides in its unconscious connection to formations of desire, in what is absent from its discourse yet crucial to its formation. The shifting constructions of gender and sexuality, and their entanglement with the tortuous and tortured process of national identity formation, constitutes the absent dimension of Irish nationalism, a dimension that is, however, central to the formation of the Irish nation. The Irish border is the site where such absent presences are crystalized in structures of feelings.

The [invasive and threatening] search at the border was a deeply humiliating experience for my friends, a humiliation loaded with a history of repetition. Harassment by the security forces is an everyday practice in the Catholic areas of Belfast. The feeling of being over powered experienced by working-class Catholics in Northern Ireland was inscribed at the border in the bodies of these women who felt poked and searched, manipulated and surveyed, and deprived of autonomy – just like the streets where they live were surveyed and controlled by the continuous occupation of the police and British army. And just as their bodies were appropriated by the security forces, these nationalist women also felt that the Irish nation – still under British control in the political imaginary of nationalists – was deprived of autonomy and held hostage within its own boundaries. This association between the body of women and the alienated space of nation was encapsulated by [my friend] Maura as we got into the car to leave, "that you have to be treated like this ... in your own country!" This association is not made in a representational vacuum, rather it resonates with a long history in Irish nationalist iconography, art, and literary production within which women have figured as allegories of the nation (Aretxaga 1997). Indeed, the inscription of the moral discourse of the nation in the body of women is common to nationalist discourse more generally and particularly post-colonial nationalist discourse (Mosse 1985, Mani 1990, Chatterjee 1989, 1993). For Maura the momentary dispossession of her body enacted the dispossession of the nation, a nation that the border materializes as an entity that simultaneously is and it isn't.

The whole episode at the border was for me a nasty experience that reminded me of similar forms of intimidation I had experienced at the hands of the Spanish police during the last years of Franco's dictatorship. But beyond the echoes of my own political experience, there was the rage, impotence and humiliation contained in Maura's voice; feelings sedimented through a collective history of exclusion from the Irish nation and of exclusion from the political structures of Northern Ireland, feelings unintelligible outside of that history. For Maura, as for the other women in my car, the search in Newry materialized the exclusions of nationhood at the very level of the feeling, gendered body. It marked the contours of a difference iconized in a border that makes the north the absence of the Irish nation, that which being part of the Irish nation as an "imagined community" is nevertheless excluded from it; a border which makes Northern Ireland the negation of the Irish nation, and paradoxically its very condition of possibility. The incident of the search brings to relief the border as the imaginary site and material place where the nationalist master narrative of the Irish nation is problematized through the operations of gender and sexual difference.

THIS NATION THAT IS NOT ONE

The search that I have described speaks of the effect of the border in configuring Catholic identities through practices of intimidation and violence, as well as in producing particular structures of feelings. In Northern Ireland, unlike in the south, one can be searched, or harassed for being Catholic (that is, nationalist). The meaning of Catholic identity is not pre-established, rather it is produced by discursive formations and histories of violence that have differed on both sides of the border. The politics of Catholic identity in the Free State and later on in the Republic are inscribed within the hegemonic discourse of state nationalism and the political dominance of the Catholic church. In Northern Ireland, however, the politics of Catholic identity are inscribed within the political dominance of the Protestant state that excluded Catholics from power structures. This difference in the politics of Catholic identity is also the difference between the meaning of ethnic identity and nationalism north or south of the border. Such difference within ethnic identity (Irishness), delineates two different forms of existence, and arises not from the overt contours of identity – being Irish – but from what is obliterated, eclipsed in the common definition of Irishness on either side of the border. In other words, the border constituted Irishness as a split identity, the product of simultaneous recognition and disavowal of the violence of partition by the emergent Irish state. For while the Irish state could only function by the recognition of the border as a national frontier, the official discourse of nationalism denied its legitimacy by claiming sovereignty over the whole of the island. This process reinforced the link between Irish identity and Irish nationalism in as much as the Irish nation was an unfinished project. In so doing the border constituted the difference in the meaning of Irish identity, North and South, as a residue of a proclaimed sameness of identity. And yet, that residue, that space of recognized and disavowed difference opened by the slippage in the meaning of nationalism north and south of the Irish border became precisely the kernel of identity, configuring it as permanently split and uncertain. What eludes identity in the formation of Irishness is precisely that which conforms it.

If the search at the border "speaks" of the aporetic configuration of Irish identity, it speaks also of the problematization of gender identity, and of the different realities that the border created for Irish women in the north and south. Difference among women, or if you will, difference within gender identity, has been the vexing question of feminist theory and politics. In Ireland, the question of difference within gender identity has been inextricably linked to the border and the unresolved issues of colonialism and nationalism that the border both manifests and hides. It was precisely the interrogation of this difference in being a woman north and south of the border that had led us to Dublin that September day.

The aim of the trip was a meeting between left-wing feminists, all working-class community activists from Dublin and Belfast. Disenchanted with liberal mainstream feminism, this group of women had been trying to articulate an "anti-imperialist" politics from within the arena of feminism. In using the term "anti-imperialist" they linked patriarchal oppression in Ireland to the lingering effects of British colonialism, and the neo-colonialism of multinational enterprises in Ireland. Any struggle for women's rights, from this perspective, had to tackle the unfinished business of colonialism.

The ineludible question for a feminist project critical of colonialism (or neocolonialist policies), and the central axis of the discussion in the Dublin meeting was the meaning and consequences of nationalism (which was to say colonialism) for women north and south of the border. This had been historically a thorny issue among feminists and there was a clear tension and unstated line drawn between northerners and southerners. At that meeting, the border was not just an issue of debate, it was embodied by the women present, materialized by social histories and structures of feelings that traced an invisible space between northerners and southerners, that hung there in the meeting room as a testament to incommensurability. The aporetic issue of Irish nationalism was at the center of that space.

[…] What was clear to all the participants was that, to evoke Luce Irigaray, Ireland was this nation *that was not one,* that is, a nation that cannot be encompassed by ontological definitions of identity as unified self-representation. Ireland's division in two parts destabilized unified representations of the Irish nation, producing a discourse of Irish identity that the border symptomatizes as still dependent on British colonialism. Nationalists had imagined Ireland as the whole territory of the island, yet its materialization as a nation rested on the exclusion of one part. The Irish nation-state came into being on the condition of losing the six counties that form Northern Ireland. From within the discourse of Irish nationalism, partition meant that the Irish nation came into being as a nation-state on condition of negating its self-identity as nation.

REFERENCES

Anderson, B. 1983. *Imagined Communities: Reflections on the Origin and Spread of Nationalism.* London: Verso.

Aretxaga, B. 1997. *Shattering Silence: Women, Nationalism and Political Subjectivity in Northern Ireland.* Princeton: Princeton University Press.

Chatterjee, P. 1993. *The Nation and Its Fragments: Colonial and Postcolonial Histories.* Princeton: Princeton University Press.

———. 1989. "Colonialism, Nationalism and Colonized Women: The Contest in India." *American Ethnologist* 16: 622–33. https://doi.org/10.1525/ae.1989.16.4.02a00020.

Fernandez, J. 1986. "Persuasions and Performances: Of the Beast in Everybody and the Metaphors of Everyman." In *Persuasions and Performance: The Play of Tropes in Culture,* edited by J. Fernandez, 3–27. Bloomington: Indiana University Press.

Mani, L. 1990. "Contentious Traditions: The Debate on Sati in Colonial India." In *Recasting Women: Essays in Indian Colonial History,* edited by K. Sangari and S. Vaid, 88–125. New Brunswick: Rutgers University Press.

McCann, M. 1985. *The Past in the Present: A Study of Some Aspects of the Politics of Music in Belfast,* PhD Dissertation, Queen's University.

Mosse, G. 1985. *Nationalism and Sexuality: Middle-Class Morality and Sexual Norms in Modern Europe.* Madison: University of Wisconsin Press.

O'Hogain, D. 1985. *The Hero in Irish Folk History.* Dublin: Hill and MacMillan.

Taussig, M. 1992. "Terror as Usual: Walter Benjamin's Theory of History as State of Siege." In *The Nervous System,* edited by M. Taussig. New York: Routledge.

12.3. Seeing like a Mayor; or, How Local Officials Obstructed Romanian Land Restitution (2002)

Katherine Verdery

In my opinion, only ethnography can adequately reveal the aftermath of socialism in Eastern Europe and the former Soviet Union, challenging the interpretations of analysts whose attention to actors and events at the center often leads them to miss the mark. They miss it, I think, partly because their methods remove them from the localized social processes through which central directives take shape and partly because they are not trained to question their ideological biases, as ethnographers attempt to do. In short, they are "seeing like a state" (Scott, 1998) – usually their *own* state. Because comparable limitations contributed to the earlier failure of most western analysts to foresee the collapse of socialism, I believe we are even more obliged not to repeat those errors. Ethnography is a necessary corrective: we understand postsocialist transformation better if we see less like a state and more like a mayor.

In this article, I dispute the opinion, widely held among both foreign observers and many educated Romanians, that decollectivization in that country proceeded so slowly because the government – particularly that of the post-communist party led by Ion Iliescu – wanted to retain collective agricultural forms and was obstructing their dissolution. From local ethnography we see that this vastly oversimplifies what was happening in villages. My argument also has implications for understanding changes in the nature of the state. Romania's unusually chaotic land reform reveals a marked disjuncture between what was legislated at the center and what happened in rural settings. In part this disjuncture resulted from the disestablishment of the Romanian Communist Party, which had organized politics from top to bottom. But the Party's central control was always weaker than it pretended to be; with the end of its formal monopoly, lower-level authorities became even harder to control than before. This was truer still given the frenzied scramble for power and resources that was unleashed at the national level; from it emerged a jumble of contradictory policies and utterances upon which local authorities could draw selectively.

In the general disarray of Romanian politics in the 1990s, I find evidence of a central power that was eroding, rather than of one scheming to keep agriculture socialist. Decollectivization contributed to that erosion by empowering lower – rather than higher – level authorities to implement the law. Focusing on these local actors, I argue that the design and implementation of Romania's land restitution process concentrated power in the hands of commune mayors, who had every interest in slowing things down. In arguing this, I find myself in reluctant agreement both with Romanian government ministers and with villagers, who blamed local authorities for the delay in completing restitution. My task is to show *why* this is a plausible interpretation, for otherwise it seems merely a rhetorical ploy to avoid taking responsibility for the mess. (Quite possibly, government spokesmen intended it thus; they might indeed be surprised by my analysis.)

[...] By the time Mayor Lupu was voted out of office in 1996, he had already been working land at "la Jigoaia" for four years and keeping the proceeds, and he stood every chance of receiving title to part of that area. Meanwhile, he had created chaos and social conflict by not resolving superimposed ownership claims in Vlaicu that would have required him to turn "his" land over to someone else. In Geoagiu he had avoided giving out titles altogether, a situation his successor perpetuated. He had also built a large villa in a nearby resort, apparently by illegal means, and would be able to rent it out for permanent income.

Lupu's actions, then, had a number of effects. First, they contravened the plans of the central government, which wanted landless households to receive land so they would be reliable supporters; for this it would happily have alienated a few Germans, who had little influence on national politics. But Lupu saw things differently. He coddled the Germans and alienated the landless, in pursuit of his own aggrandizement. Second, toward the same end he sacrificed social harmony. Discord in Vlaicu would serve him well by keeping the committee weak and the village unlikely to organize against him. Third, perhaps the most serious casualty of all was people's confidence in the restitution process. Instead of finding solutions that would uphold everyone's rightful claims to private property, even if only in part, he blatantly demonstrated his own prepotency, unchallenged by any legal sanction. He failed to do justice at a moment when justice was critical to consolidating the new order. If over the decade villagers across Romania became cynical (like those in Vlaicu) about the emerging private property regime, people like Lupu had much to do with that outcome. Mayor Lupu and his clique in Geoagiu commune, and others like them, did not just usurp the land of others: they compromised the very idea of a justly-acquired hectare of one's own guaranteed by the state and, thus, the very legitimacy of private property as an institution.

COMMUNE/CENTER RELATIONS

Why, we might wonder, could people like Lupu continue in this way? Part of the answer lies in the structural relations of communes with central authorities, particularly the institutional hiatus between national and local governments. In each election cycle, Romania holds two sets of elections, one for the president and parliament and another for mayors of communes and cities. The party or coalition that wins the national elections appoints, from above, the prefects of Romania's 40 counties, whereas the mayors are elected from below, by the people in the units they administer. More significant, however, was a feature of Law 18 and amendments to it: there were no sanctions if local officials failed to implement the law, and the reorganization of political responsibility had provided no alternative levers. Judges and lawyers with whom I discussed the question all agreed that this was the main problem with property restitution; so did Romania's Prime Minister in a television interview in 1993. Asked why the state did not enforce Law 18 more vigorously, he replied, "We ought to be firmer. But we have a separation of powers, especially at the local level. There's not much the prefects can do ... We no longer have direct government control [over what goes on]." The only way any sort of pressure had been put on the process was that as of about 1994, surveyors were no longer to be paid a regular salary but only a "piece rate" according to how many titles they had completed in a given month.

The entire enforcement mechanism returned final authority to the mayors and commune commissions. If a claimant brought suit against a commission and won, the courts or prefects referred execution of the sentence down to the mayor, for prefectures and county boards did not have the authority to award title. Interviewed by the popular weekly TV program "Village Life," a lawyer from the body investigating land-claims disputes admitted that there was little her office could do to prevent abuses: "There's no provision anywhere for the Ministry of Agriculture to intervene in the process of giving land back. We can't force local authorities to apply a judicial sentence." (Later she added, "Then again, if Law 18 had had sanctions for those implementing it, no one would have been willing to do so.") Although commissions could be sued, they were not liable for damages. As a judge told me, "I can find all sorts of infractions but have no means available to punish them." Another observed that she had resolved to fine the mayors who headed these commissions; then she learned that (unsurprisingly) many of them had not been reelected, and there was no way to extract a fine from them. In a 1996 conversation, an urbanite to whom local officials in his home village were refusing to allocate his land explained to me what he thought was happening. "There's a void of responsibility – not a void of power: power is well concentrated there, but responsibility is dispersed."

In short, local authorities were virtually unpunishable. When the political opposition came to power in 1996, it attempted to rectify this problem. It proposed amendments that would give judges full jurisdiction over land-rights cases, which they would no longer have to refer to commune land commissions for execution; fine recalcitrant mayors for every day of delaying the resolution of a property claim; assign penalties not only to mayors but to entire commissions; require all owners to declare the surfaces they held and to present documents justifying their ownership, with one- to three-year jail sentences if they could not; and so on. Passage of these amendments proved exceedingly difficult, however, because one of the coalition partners (the one representing the agrarian elite) bolted. Even after a version finally passed, implementing it, too, proved arduous, and when the coalition fell from power in November 2000, things reverted to the status quo ante. The state's momentary shift of vision had scarcely affected that of the mayors. [...]

STRONG STATE OR WEAK?

In closing, I wish to consider the implications of my argument for relations between the center and local authorities. Did commune officials exercise so much power in decollectivization because the center wanted them to, or because it could not control them – that is, did the state foresee the outcome or not? Most educated Romanians I spoke with asserted the former. They claim that the post-communist government of Ion Iliescu, which dominated politics between 1990 and 1996 and then again after 2000, never wanted to dismantle socialist agriculture. Although assessing that kind of claim requires ethnography of a kind different from mine, there is admittedly some support for this view. Most telling are President Iliescu's occasional statements throughout the decade that small-scale cultivation was non-viable and that larger-scale units were the way of the future – or even that private property was "silly," a remark he made shortly after his reelection in 2000. Then there was the government's failure to create the Agency for Rural Planning and Development that Law 18 required, and without which no land sales could occur. Additional evidence of dawdling was the snail's pace in setting up a cadastre. Those involved in the USAID project to help with surveying for it complained at the government's long postponement in providing the necessary seven cartographic points, which they saw as a delaying tactic.

Although I agree that one might interpret these and other events as evidence of a strong political center ordering its subordinate units to put the brakes on privatization, I remain doubtful that such an intention (if it existed) was so easily translated into practice. To think otherwise presupposes both a Romanian government with more power than I believe it had and a local sphere obedient to central directives (a laughable image). Understanding the motives for local officials to retard decollectivization makes it unnecessary to envision them as following Iliescu's every cue. Just as western analysts failed to perceive the signs of decomposition in socialism because they attended only to central Party policies, I think attributing too directive a role to state actors after 1989 leads to the same misperception. Instead, we should see much of the "evidence" of central footdragging as the results of fierce political battles over whether to modify Law 18 or not, battles in which the opposing forces were so evenly matched as to produce paralysis, rather than decisive direction. Although some political leaders might indeed have hoped to craft restitution plans that would have only a limited effect, success was unlikely given the necessary compromises, the pervasive uncertainty, and the constant improvisation characteristic of 1990s Romanian politics.

Assuming a weak state rather than a strong one seems to me to account for a number of aspects of Romania's postsocialist transformation. Central incapacity concerning the collection of revenues, for example, both contributed to and revealed state weakness – a point made frequently for Russia. In a 1996 TV interview, the head of Romania's Court of Accounts claimed that his office had found one trillion lei in the underground economy that should have gone to state revenues; he estimated that this was perhaps one-tenth of the actual amount owed. He added that if the hemorrhage of foreign currency out of the country were stanched, Romania would have no need of loans from the IMF and similar sources. That it continued indicates that there was no power strong – or interested – enough to prevent it. Similarly, I believe that open abuses of power in implementing Law 18 at the commune level imply the center's ineffectual control over its subordinates, if not its collusion. It had to collude because it could not control them, precisely because it could no longer offer them protection and benefits adequate to securing their allegiance as in the heyday of socialism (see Staniszkis, 1989).

In arguing for a weak rather than a strong state, I am not denying that members of the "new red bourgeoisie" represented by the party of Ion Iliescu (though not by his party alone) might have opposed dismantling the planned economy from which they had profited before. I deny, rather, that the forces opposing transformation were sufficiently concerted to achieve such an objective, and above all that they had the organizational means necessary for doing so *through the state*. The political field was too fragmented, with groups and individuals constantly shifting sides, coalitions, and party identities. Postsocialist Romanian politics bore the distinctive stamp of the Ceausescu period, its state not strong but weakened by parasitism, barely controlled anarchy, and scavenging on the part of virtually everyone – all features of the Romanian scene even as I write (October 2001).

[…] Decollectivization shows us [that] the reconfiguration of state power [hailed from the] necessity of empowering the local authorities without whom, given the magnitude of the process, restitution could not be implemented.

From this insight we might begin to wonder at the effects of the earlier process – collectivization itself – upon the attempt to create new socialist states in the 1930s and 1950s, for that immense undertaking too was impossible without empowering local cadres. Can we discern here sources of the relative weakness of those Party-states that western ideology presented as "totalitarian"? Is this further evidence of the problems inherent in research methods that overemphasize the view from the top? If so, then here is yet another reason to eschew "seeing like a state" in favor of the ethnographic work that enables us to see, instead, like a mayor.

REFERENCES

Scott, J. 1998. *Seeing Like a State: How Certain Schemes to Improve the Human Condition Have Failed*. New Haven: Yale University Press.

Staniszkis, J. 1989. *The Dynamics of the Breakthrough in Eastern Europe*. Berkeley and Los Angeles: University of California Press.

12.4. Necropolitics (2003)

Achille Mbembé

This essay assumes that the ultimate expression of sovereignty resides, to a large degree, in the power and the capacity to dictate who may live and who must die. Hence, to kill or to allow to live constitute the limits of sovereignty, its fundamental attributes. To exercise sovereignty is to exercise control over mortality and to define life as the deployment and manifestation of power.

One could summarize in the above terms what Michel Foucault meant by *biopower*: that domain of life over which power has taken control. But under what practical conditions is the right to kill, to allow to live, or to expose to death exercised? Who is the subject of this right? What does the implementation of such a right tell us about the person who is thus put to death and about the relation of enmity that sets that person against his or her murderer? Is the notion of biopower sufficient to account for the contemporary ways in which the political, under the guise of war, of resistance, or of the fight against terror, makes the murder of the enemy its primary and absolute objective? War, after all, is as much a means of achieving sovereignty as a way of exercising the right to kill. Imagining politics as a form of war, we must ask: What place is given to life, death, and the human body (in particular the wounded or slain body)? How are they inscribed in the order of power?

POLITICS, THE WORK OF DEATH, AND THE "BECOMING SUBJECT"

In order to answer these questions, this essay draws on the concept of biopower and explores its relation to notions of sovereignty (*imperium*) and the state of exception. Such an analysis raises a number of empirical and philosophical questions I would like to examine briefly. As is well known, the concept of the state of exception has been often discussed in relation to Nazism, totalitarianism, and the concentration/extermination camps. The death camps in particular have been interpreted variously as the central metaphor for sovereign and destructive violence and as the ultimate sign of the absolute power of the negative. Says Hannah Arendt: "There are no parallels to the life in the concentration camps. Its horror can never be fully embraced by the imagination for the very reason that it stands outside of life and death." Because its inhabitants are divested of political status and reduced to bare life, the camp is, for Giorgio Agamben, "the place in which the most absolute *conditio inhumana* ever to appear on Earth was realized." In the political-juridical structure of the camp, he adds, the state of exception ceases to be a temporal suspension of the state of law. According to Agamben, it acquires a permanent spatial arrangement that remains continually outside the normal state of law.

The aim of this essay is not to debate the singularity of the extermination of the Jews or to hold it up by way of example. I start from the idea that modernity was at the origin of multiple concepts of sovereignty – and therefore of the biopolitical. Disregarding this multiplicity, late-modern political criticism has unfortunately privileged normative theories of democracy and has made the concept of reason one of the most important elements of both the project of modernity and of the topos of sovereignty. From this perspective, the ultimate expression of sovereignty is the production of general norms by a body (the demos) made up of free and equal men and women. These men and women are posited as full subjects capable of self-understanding, self-consciousness, and self-representation. Politics, therefore, is defined as twofold: a project of autonomy and the achieving of agreement among a collectivity through communication and recognition. This, we are told, is what differentiates it from war.

[…] My concern is those figures of sovereignty whose central project is not the struggle for autonomy but *the generalized instrumentalization of human existence and the material destruction of human bodies and populations*. Such figures of sovereignty are far from a piece of prodigious insanity or an expression of a rupture between the impulses and interests of the body and those of the mind. Indeed, they, like the death camps, are what constitute the *nomos* of the political space in which we still live. Furthermore, contemporary experiences of human destruction suggest that it is possible to develop a reading of politics, sovereignty, and the subject different from the one we inherited from the philosophical discourse of modernity. Instead of considering reason as the truth of the subject, we can look to other foundational categories that are less abstract and more tactile, such as life and death. […]

BIOPOWER AND THE RELATION OF ENMITY

Having presented a reading of politics as the work of death, I turn now to sovereignty, expressed predominantly as the right to kill. For the purpose of my argument, I relate Foucault's notion of biopower to two other concepts: the state of exception and the state of siege. I examine those trajectories by which the state of exception and the relation of enmity have become the normative basis of the right to kill. In such instances, power (and not necessarily state power) continuously refers and appeals to exception, emergency, and a fictionalized notion of the enemy. It also labors to produce that same exception, emergency, and fictionalized enemy. In other words, the question is: What is the relationship between politics and death in those systems that can function only in a state of emergency? In Foucault's formulation of it, biopower appears to function through dividing people into those who must live and those who must die. Operating on the basis of a split between the living and the dead, such a power defines itself in relation to a biological field – which it takes control of and vests itself in. This control presupposes the distribution of human species into groups, the subdivision of the population into subgroups, and the establishment of a biological caesura between the ones and the others. This is what Foucault labels with the (at first sight familiar) term *racism*.

That *race* (or for that matter *racism*) figures so prominently in the calculus of biopower is entirely justifiable. After all, more so than class-thinking (the ideology that defines history as an economic struggle of classes), race has been the ever present shadow in Western political thought and practice, especially when it comes to imagining the inhumanity of, or rule over, foreign peoples. Referring to both this ever-presence and the phantomlike world of race in general, Arendt locates their roots in the shattering experience of otherness and suggests that the politics of race is ultimately linked to the politics of death. Indeed, in Foucault's terms, racism is above all a technology aimed at permitting the exercise of biopower, "that old sovereign right of death." In the economy of biopower, the function of racism is to regulate the distribution of death and to make possible the murderous functions of the state. It is, he says, "the condition for the acceptability of putting to death."

Foucault states clearly that the sovereign right to kill (*droit de glaive*) and the mechanisms of biopower are inscribed in the way all modern states function; indeed, they can be seen as constitutive elements of state power in modernity. According to Foucault, the Nazi state was the most complete example of a state exercising the right to kill. This state, he claims, made the management, protection, and cultivation of life coextensive with the sovereign right to kill. By biological extrapolation on the theme of the political enemy, in organizing the war against its adversaries and, at the same time, exposing its own citizens to war, the Nazi state is seen as having opened the way for a formidable consolidation of the right to kill, which culminated in the project of the "final solution." In doing so, it became the archetype of a power formation that combined the characteristics of the racist state, the murderous state, and the suicidal state.

It has been argued that the complete conflation of war and politics (and racism, homicide, and suicide), until they are indistinguishable from one another, is unique to the Nazi state. The perception of the existence of the Other as an attempt on my life, as a mortal threat or absolute danger whose biophysical elimination would strengthen my potential to life and security – this, I suggest, is one of the many imaginaries of sovereignty characteristic of both early and late modernity itself. Recognition of this perception to a large extent underpins most traditional critiques of modernity, whether they are dealing with nihilism and its proclamation of the will for power as the essence of the being; with reification understood as the *becoming-object* of the human being; or the subordination of everything to impersonal logic and to the reign of calculability and instrumental rationality. Indeed, from an anthropological perspective, what these critiques implicitly contest is a definition of politics as the warlike relation par excellence. They also challenge the idea that, of necessity, the calculus of life passes through the death of the Other; or that sovereignty consists of the will and the capacity to kill in order to live.

[…] If the relations between life and death, the politics of cruelty, and the symbolics of profanity are blurred in the plantation system, it is notably in the colony and under the apartheid regime that there comes into being a peculiar terror formation I will now turn to. The most original feature of this terror formation is its concatenation of biopower, the state of exception, and the state of siege. Crucial to this concatenation is, once again, race. In fact, in most instances, the selection of races, the prohibition of mixed marriages, forced sterilization, even the extermination of vanquished peoples are to find their first testing ground in the colonial world. Here we see the first syntheses between massacre and bureaucracy, that incarnation of Western rationality. Arendt develops the thesis that there is a link between national-socialism and traditional imperialism. According to her, the colonial conquest revealed a potential for violence previously unknown. What one witnesses in World War II is the extension to the "civilized" peoples of Europe of the methods previously reserved for the "savages."

That the technologies which ended up producing Nazism should have originated in the plantation or in the colony or that, on the contrary – Foucault's thesis – Nazism and Stalinism did no more than amplify a series of mechanisms that already existed in Western European social and political formations (subjugation of the body, health regulations, social Darwinism, eugenics, medico-legal theories on heredity, degeneration, and race) is, in the end, irrelevant. A fact remains, though: in modern philosophical thought and European political practice and imaginary, the colony represents the site where sovereignty consists fundamentally in the exercise of a power outside the law (*ab legibus solutus*) and where "peace" is more likely to take on the face of a "war without end."

Indeed, such a view corresponds to Carl Schmitt's definition of sovereignty at the beginning of the twentieth century, namely, the power to decide on the state of exception. To properly assess the efficacy of the colony as a formation of terror, we need to take a detour into the European imaginary itself as it relates to the critical issue of the domestication of war and the creation of a European juridical order (*Jus publicum Europaeum*). At the basis of this order were two key principles. The first postulated the juridical equality of all states. This equality was notably applied to *the right to wage war* (the taking of life). The right to war meant two things. On the one hand, to kill or to conclude peace was recognized as one of the preeminent functions of any state. It went hand in hand with the recognition of the fact that no state could make claims to rule outside of its borders. But conversely, the state could recognize no authority above it within its own borders. On the other hand, the state, for its part, undertook to "civilize" the ways of killing and to attribute rational objectives to the very act of killing.

The second principle related to the territorialization of the sovereign state, that is, to the determination of its frontiers within the context of a newly imposed global order. In this context, the *Jus publicum* rapidly assumed the form of a distinction between, on the one hand, those parts of the globe available for colonial appropriation and, on the other, Europe itself (where the *Jus publicum* was to hold sway). This distinction, as we will see, is crucial in terms of assessing the efficacy of the colony as a terror formation. Under *Jus publicum*, a legitimate war is, to a large extent, a war conducted by one state against another or, more precisely, a war between "civilized" states. The centrality of the state in the calculus of war derives from the fact that the state is the model of political unity, a principle of rational organization, the embodiment of the idea of the universal, and a moral sign. [...]

[In] this essay I have argued that contemporary forms of subjugation of life to the power of death (necropolitics) profoundly reconfigure the relations among resistance, sacrifice, and terror. I have demonstrated that the notion of biopower is insufficient to account for contemporary forms of subjugation of life to the power of death. Moreover I have put forward the notion of necropolitics and necro-power to account for the various ways in which, in our contemporary world, weapons are deployed in the interest of maximum destruction of persons and the creation of *death-worlds*, new and unique forms of social existence in which vast populations are subjected to conditions of life conferring upon them the status of *living dead*. The essay has also outlined some of the repressed topographies of cruelty (the plantation and the colony in particular) and has suggested that under conditions of necropower, the lines between resistance and suicide, sacrifice and redemption, martyrdom and freedom are blurred.

REFERENCES

Agamben, Giorgio. 1995. *Moyens sans fins. Notes sur la politique.* Paris: Payot & Rivages.
Arendt, Hannah. 1966. *The Origins of Totalitarianism.* New York: Harvest.
Foucault, Michel. 1977. *Discipline and Punish: The Birth of the Prison.* New York: Pantheon.
———. 1997. *Il faut défendre la société: Cours au Collège de France, 1975–1976.* Paris: Seuil.

12.5. Strange Fruit: Brazil, Necropolitics, and the Transnational Resonance of Torture and Death (2013)

Christen Smith

Bahia has the third highest rate of death squad murders in Brazil, preceded only by São Paulo and Rio de Janeiro. According to the United Nations the number of death squad murders in the state increased 212% from 1995 to 2005 (Ramos 2005). Death squads are egregious examples of police related violence in Brazil and the hallmark of police brutality in Bahia. Although death squads are not exclusively tied to the police, there is a strong correlation that is both historical and cultural. Many tie the emergence of death squads to Brazil's military dictatorship and the continued legacy of dictatorial repression in the nation. However, the genealogy of death squads in Latin America also implies a connection to the promulgation of United States' torture tactics. The United States' practice of teaching torture and killing methods to Latin American military and police officers has been well documented (e.g., Gill 2004; Huggins 1998). These multiple, layered connections suggest the need to re-situate death squad murders in Bahia as part of a transnational, cross-temporal web of necropolitical practices.

The images of bloody and often unrecognizable victims of death squad murders on the pages of Bahia's newspapers ignite a series of visual associations. Like a refracted mirror reflection, they resemble similar photographs of tortured and mutilated black bodies spectacularly put on display by vigilante groups in the United States one century before. On August 6, 1906, a lynch mob assassinated Nease Gillepsie, John Gillepsie, "Jack" Dillingham, Henry Lee, and George Irwin, thousands of miles away in Salisbury, North Carolina. Like the assassinations in Bairro da Paz, this image was forever preserved in a photograph that depicts a cruel and gruesome death (Allen 2000). These images, preserved in time, echo yet other moments as well: the infamous picture of an Iraqi prisoner standing on a tin can with a hood over his head and electric wires attached to his body. The ritual, spectacle, photographic display, racialized, gendered, and sexualized meaning of these moments demarcates a resonance between summary executions of Bahia, lynching in the United States, and the use of torture in the War on Terror. Far from a random connection, these cognitive associations mark an historical, political, and symbolic thread that strings each of these events together.

[...] Immediately after the controversy around the Abu Ghraib torture photos first erupted, televisions networks, newspapers, and magazines across the United States began to question how and why U.S. soldiers could torture inmates at Guantanamo, pose proudly next to their victims, and circulate the photos among their friends. In separate responses in the popular news media, Hazel Carby (2004) and Susan Sontag (2004) reminded us of the abhorrent legacy of lynching postcards and photography in the United States, and suggested that we should not be so quick to disassociate the Abu Ghraib torture photo incident from the history of racial violence in this nation. As many have noted since then, what U.S. military personnel did was not an aberrant act dissonant from the national identity. To the contrary, torturing and disfiguring racially "other" bodies, displaying them spectacularly and circulating images of these scenes as keepsakes simply represents the role racial terror has played in defining U.S. culture. However, in addition to being the reemergence of a tradition, this moment suggests that this historical legacy has also been passed down through the years, covertly (or maybe even overtly) institutionalized in practices of repression adopted by the state in order to discipline and fracture "terrorist" bodies, and socialized through transnational dialogues and U.S. Imperialism. [...]

The purpose of this article is to critically interrogate the epidemic of death squad murders in Salvador as a phenomenon imbued with multiple layers of racialized, gendered, sexualized and classed meaning, simultaneously territorialized as a continuous part of the landscape of inequality and black suffering in Brazil, and transnationally and cross-temporally defined by its connections to the geopolitical landscape of torture, the United States' war on terror, and legacies of colonialism and slavery in the Americas. Specifically, this article ties death squad murders in Bahia to the transnational exchange of torture practices between the United States and Latin America through foreign military and police training programs, the epistemological production of the black body as the "internal enemy" in Brazil and the United States, and the use of torture against "terrorist" Arab bodies in the War on Terror. I contend that what links all of these is a transnational "necropolitics" based on the logics of white supremacy that is not a state of exception but the state of affairs.

Achille Mbembe defines necropolitics as "contemporary forms of subjugation of life to the power of death" (Mbembe 2003:39). For him, the reality of wars rooted in the legacies of racism, colonialism, and slavery for which, "the political, under the guise of war, of resistance, or of the fight against terror, makes the murder of the enemy its primary and absolute objective" require that we rethink Foucault's notion of biopolitics in order to consider the central role death plays in the states' engagement with the bodies of its subjects (Mbembe 2003:12). The epidemic of police violence in Brazil, its economy of death, and its hegemonic racial logic, all suggest that the spectacular display of the mutilated, tortured, and dead body in Brazil is a symbol of the state's necropolitical tactics. It is this phenomenon that I analyze here.

[...] The black subject in Brazil has been constructed over generations as the internal enemy (captives, terrorists, criminals). Patterns of police violence demonstrate time and time again that the primary objective in the police's engagement with poor, black residents in peripheral neighborhoods is to kill first and ask questions later (Amnesty International 2005). According to an article published in *Correio da Bahia* on March 2, 2008, "[a] black [man], living in the periphery, unemployed, with an elementary school education, between the ages of 15–29, who easily speaks in slang, and generally has a tattoo on [his] body ... [is] marked to die" (Reis 2008). This death mark emerges from the hegemonic racial epistemology that frames policing, and the genealogy of police violence (including, by extension, death squad killings). A close reading of this genealogy, which links death squads to the military dictatorship and the CIA, suggests that racial profiling is not a deviation from the rule of law but an integral part of state security: maintaining the status quo. [...]

INSCRIBING BLACKNESS, WHITE SUPREMACY, AND TERROR IN BAHIA

There is a lack of comprehensive quantitative and qualitative information about the extent of police violence in Brazil. This indicates that the problem is even bigger than it appears. Most quantitative research on violence in Brazil has not examined sexuality. The focus has almost exclusively been on men and women assumed to be gender normative and heterosexual. This is a conspicuous oversight and curious given what we know qualitatively about race, violence, gender and sexuality. For example, *travestis* – transgendered men who often take hormones to enlarge their breasts and buttocks and acquire "feminine" body types but do not identify themselves as women – are frequently the victims of harsh police abuse (Kulick 1998). Working class *travestis* who mostly work as prostitutes in Salvador are also overwhelmingly black. Returning for a moment to the military dictatorship and the war on internal enemies, we know that one of the targets of police repression during this time were prostitutes (Pinheiro 1991). This coupled with the discourse of deviance and criminality points to the fact that sexuality plays a key role in police violence. Moreover, the gendered aspects of violence generally emphasize the need to take patriarchy and heterosexism into account when analyzing violence. As researchers note, although women are not nearly as likely to be the victims of homicide as men, most women who are killed are killed as the result of domestic disputes with their partners (Soares and Borges 2004). Moreover, the discrepancies in homicide rates according to gender reinforce hegemonic social scripts of patriarchy. Sexuality, gender, race, and class have a profound impact on experiences with violence.

Women are rarely taken into account in research on police violence. Analyses of general violence that aggregate race and gender are also rare. However, the statistics that exist on homicide rates and women according to race present predictable results. Black women are more likely to be the victims of homicide than white women (Soares and Borges 2004). Despite the lack of extensive numbers, we cannot comprehend police violence without taking the heterosexism and patriarchy of the hegemonic epistemology of white supremacy into account, as black, queer feminist scholars have argued for decades (Lorde 1984; Smith and Combahee River 1986). Throughout the course of my archival research on newspaper accounts of police violence in Salvador since 2001, I have frequently seen women listed among the dead, and most often these women are black and from the periphery. However, considering the numbers of women who are killed in police-related incidents miscalculates the issue. As sociologist Vilma Reis discusses, the mothers, wives, girlfriends, and children of the young men who fall victim to police violence are also victims (Reis 2007). Returning to the case of the three brothers who were killed by the police in Canabrava in 2009, their mother was dragged out of the house before they were killed. The mother's distraught face, wisps of hair desperately sticking out, hands outstretched crying and screaming at the camera, was the image that accompanied this story in *A Tarde* the next day. The wounds this black woman suffered by this loss, and the countless others whose lives are irrevocably altered by police abuse, will undoubtedly affect her health and her well-being for the rest of her life. How do we factor this violence into a discussion of the economy of death and the necropolitics of the state?

The image of this black mother returns us to the question of spectacle and performativity. Death squad assassinations, through dismemberment, torture, spectacle, and performance, both inscribe blackness onto the bodies of assassination victims and their communities, consequently severing the dead, their families, their friends, and their neighborhoods from the imagined social community. Anthropologist Alan Feldman, in his discussion of state violence in Ireland, contends that the interplay between violence and the body produces meaning in excess of repression and disempowerment during moments of state conflict. Bodies that are violated/violenced are not simply fractured by this violence but become through these violent acts coded with meaning. Specifically, "political violence is a mode of transcription; it circulates codes from one prescribed historiographic surface or agent to another" (1991:7). Competing transcripts define the black body in Brazil, fracturing it such that subjectivation is accelerated. One of these transcripts is police violence. The process of disfigurement, dismemberment, torture, and assassination is in part what constructs the black body as the internal enemy. When the police, either on-duty or off-duty, kill young black people in Brazil and place their corpses back into their communities in plain view, they separate the body from the whole of the community and reinscribe it with racialized social meaning. The individuality of the body is erased and the executed body becomes a metonym for black social space, an abstraction of blackness and a mark of death (as such, the individual racial classification of the body and its assassins is of little import). In the process of invading peripheral neighborhoods and homes and killing peripheral residents with impunity, the police inscribe racial inequality spatially into the periphery, marking this space and its residents as expendable. As Mbembe observes, "the ways of killing in massacres do not vary much, but nevertheless broadcast continual messages of the 'illusory rejection of a death that has already occurred' and 'the morbid spectacle of severing'" (2003:35). The spectacular display of these bodies is a death mark that conceals the necropolitics of the state. Death squads are not the counterpoint to just policing, they are the paradigm.

REFERENCES

Allen, James. 2000. *Without Sanctuary: Lynching Photography in America*. Santa Fe: Twin Palms.

Amnesty International. 2005. *Brazil: "They Come in Shooting": Policing Socially Excluded Communities*. London: Amnesty International.

Carby, Hazel. 2004. *A Strange and Bitter Crop: The Spectacle of Torture*. http://www.opendemocracy.net/debates/article-8-112-2149.jsp (accessed October 10, 2004).

Feldman, Allen. 1991. *Formations of Violence: The Narrative of the Body and Political Terror in Northern Ireland*. Chicago: University of Chicago Press.

Gill, Lesley. 2004. *The School of the Americas: Military Training and Political Violence in the Americas, American Encounters=Global Interactions*. Durham: Duke University Press.

Huggins, Martha Knisely. 1998. *Political Policing: The United States and Latin America*. Durham: Duke University Press.

Kulick, Don. 1998. *Travesti: Sex, Gender, and Culture Among Brazilian Transgendered Prostitutes, Worlds of Desire*. Chicago: University of Chicago Press.

Lorde, Audre. 1984. *Sister Outsider: Essays and Speeches, the Crossing Press Feminist Series*. Trumansburg: Crossing Press.

Mbembe, Achille. 2003. "Necropolitics." *Public Culture* 15 (1): 11–40.

Pinheiro, Paulo Sérgio. 1991. "Police and Political Crisis: The Case of the Military Police." In *Vigilantism and the State in Modern Latin America*, edited by M.K. Huggins. New York: Praeger.

Ramos, Cleidiana. 2005. "Maioria das Vítimas é Formada por Negros." *A Tarde*, July 20, 3.

Reis, Pablo. 2008. "Jovens Negros São Vítimas Preferenciais de grupos de Extermínio." *Correio da Bahia*, March 2.

Reis, Vilma. 2007. "O Estado Não pode Permitir uma Prática Policial Racista." *A Tarde*, March 6.

Smith, Barbara, and Collective Combahee River. 1986. *The Combahee River Collective Statement: Black Feminist Organizing in the Seventies and Eighties*. Freedom Organizing Series. Latham: Kitchen Table: Women of Color Press.

Soares, Gláucio, Ary Dillon, and Doriam Borges. 2004. "A Cor da Morte." *Ciência Hoje* 35 (209): 26–31.

Sontag, Susan. 2004. "Regarding the Torture of Others." *New York Times*, May 23, 25.

Section Twelve Glossary

naturalization   The process by which social phenomena appear natural, inevitable, fixed, or intrinsic. In the example of statehood, it is very hard for most of us to imagine a life without nation-states, even when we "know" that the overwhelming majority of human history has been characterized by non-state political organization. Naturalization of sociopolitical phenomena often has the effect of making opposition to power structures seem futile, a perception that tends to reproduce existing inequalities.

On Agency and Social Struggle

THE SOCIAL CONTEXT

Police killings of Black people in the 2010s catalyzed a wave of anti-racist community activism in cities across the United States, including Chicago, St. Louis, Baltimore, and New York. These protests against racist state violence have counterparts in US immigrant detention centers where Central American women have led hunger strikes; in Standing Rock, North Dakota, where Indigenous "water defenders" have been tear-gassed and shot with rubber bullets by police; as well as in mass social movements in Mexico, Palestine, Egypt, South Africa, and countless other places across the globe.

As the articles in the previous section attest, myriad forms of violence are central to the maintenance of state power. Anthropologists who work with people who are especially targeted for violence – such as Indigenous Peoples, racialized minorities, people who live in poverty, and migrants – have theorized the complex consequences of such power on people's lives. They have also shown that state power is never absolute but always negotiated, contested, resisted, and (to use Simpson's term) "refused." Thus, theories of the state must be complemented by theories of agency and struggle that explore how people actively respond to power and create social change. That is the work of the essays in this section.

THE CONVERSATION

Reading 13.1 is written by Saba Mahmood as part of a longer 2005 book, and it questions the role that liberal feminist notions of resistance or subversion play in conceptualizing women's agency. Drawing on her work with women in the Islamist Revival movement in Egypt, Mahmood argues that women's agency cannot be understood within frameworks of progressive liberal politics, but rather must be explored within its own cultural and political frames. Decoupling agency from resistance allows us to perceive and account for human actions that maintain and reproduce forms of hegemonic power, such as vigilante movements.

Our second reading, by Shalini Shankar, offers a linguistic anthropological analysis of how South Asian American youth use language styles to navigate racial, social, and class circumscription at their California high school. While these youth are not obviously politicized or resisting, their language play allows them to assert some control over their social bonds and negotiations with racial and class stereotyping in their school and wider community.

In the third essay, Victoria Redclift considers popular theorizations of camp-based or stateless people, as well as other disempowered people, as reducible to a "bare life," or physical existence devoid of social and political significance (cf. Agamben 1998). Redclift argues that "the camp" is a dynamic social and political space that is continuously negotiated by camp residents. These residents lack a formal legal relationship with a state, but nevertheless engage in meaningful claims-making behaviors that constitute the sociopolitical life of the camp itself. A characterization of their lives as "bare," Redclift argues, forecloses our ability to read the political and social life of the camp, robbing its residents of their sociopolitical personhood.

Reading 13.4 explores the possibilities of social media usage for creating novel terrain for the anthropological study of police violence. Yarimar Bonilla and Jonathan Rosa show how social media users deployed the Twitter hashtag #Ferguson to create an alternative discursive space about police brutality in the wake of Michael Brown's 2014 killing by police in Ferguson, Missouri. Treating #Ferguson as a field site, Bonilla and Rosa argue, allows ethnographers to cull a massive amount of digital information and explore how activists democratize information about police shootings to contest official police accounts and challenge state-sanctioned violence against Black people in the United States.

In the final essay of this section, Audra Simpson discusses her ethnographic work with Mohawk people, a community to which Simpson also belongs. Simpson argues that the people with whom she worked engage in a politics of refusal, in that they rebuff statist attempts to "incorporate" or "assimilate" them (attempts which undermine Mohawk sovereignty) under egregiously unequal terms. Simpson also theorizes her own "refusal" as an anthropologist, in which she decides not to disclose internal information about Mohawk struggles to her anthropological audience.

THREE QUESTIONS FOR THE READINGS

1 These essays conceptualize practices ranging from linguistic humor to organized political resistance. What are the advantages and limitations of theorizing such diverse practices together as responses to power? When and how does response become resistance?

2 How is human agency understood by these scholars (even implicitly)? What sorts of behaviors constitute agency? Does agency necessarily entail opposition to state power?

3 Escobar (Reading 11.4), Bonilla and Rosa, and Simpson all comment on the political position of anthropologists who work with people in struggle. In what ways do their insights build on and advance earlier essays on "native" and advocacy anthropology?

ON THE COMPANION WEBSITE

"The Infiltrators," accomplices over allies, additional readings, and more.

www.anthropologicaltheory.com

REFERENCE

Agamben, Giorgio. 1998. *Homo Sacer: Sovereign Power and Bare Life*. Translated by Daniel Heller-Roazen. Stanford: Stanford University Press. First published 1995.

13.1. The Subject of Freedom (2005)

Saba Mahmood

THE SUBJECT OF FREEDOM

Women's participation in, and support for, the Islamist movement provokes strong responses from feminists across a broad range of the political spectrum. One of the most common reactions is the supposition that women Islamist supporters are pawns in a grand patriarchal plan, who, if freed from their bondage, would naturally express their instinctual abhorrence for the traditional Islamic mores used to enchain them. Even those analysts who are skeptical of the false-consciousness thesis underpinning this approach nonetheless continue to frame the issue in terms of a fundamental contradiction: why would such a large number of women across the Muslim world actively support a movement that seems inimical to their "own interests and agendas," especially at a historical moment when these women appear to have more emancipatory possibilities available to them? Despite important differences between these two reactions, both share the assumption that there is something intrinsic to women that *should* predispose them to oppose the practices, values, and injunctions that the Islamist movement embodies. Yet, one may ask, is such an assumption valid? What is the history by which we have come to assume its truth? What kind of a political imagination would lead one to think in this manner? More importantly, if we discard such an assumption, what other analytical tools might be available to ask a different set of questions about women's participation in the Islamist movement?

In this book I will explore some of the conceptual challenges that women's involvement in the Islamist movement poses to feminist theory in particular, and to secular-liberal thought in general, through an ethnographic account of an urban women's mosque movement that is part of the larger Islamic Revival in Cairo, Egypt. For two years (1995–97) I conducted fieldwork with a movement in which women from a variety of socioeconomic backgrounds provided lessons to one another that focused on the teaching and studying of Islamic scriptures, social practices, and forms of bodily comportment considered germane to the cultivation of the ideal virtuous self. The burgeoning of this movement marks the first time in Egyptian history that such a large number of women have held public meetings in mosques to teach one another Islamic doctrine, thereby altering the historically male-centered character of mosques as well as Islamic pedagogy. At the same time, women's religious participation within such public arenas of Islamic pedagogy is critically structured by, and serves to uphold, a discursive tradition that regards subordination to a transcendent will (and thus, in many instances, to male authority) as its coveted goal.

[...] The pious subjects of the mosque movement occupy an uncomfortable place in feminist scholarship because they pursue practices and ideals embedded within a tradition that has historically accorded women a subordinate status. Movements such as these have come to be associated with terms such as fundamentalism, the subjugation of women, social conservatism, reactionary atavism, cultural backwardness, and so on – associations that, in the aftermath of September 11, are often treated as "facts" that do not require further analysis. While it would be a worthy task to dissect the reductionism that such associations enact on an enormously complex phenomenon, this is not my purpose in this book. Nor is it my aim to recover a "redeemable element" within the Islamist movement by recuperating its latent liberatory potentials so as to make the movement more palatable to liberal sensibilities. Instead, in this book I seek to analyze the conceptions of self, moral agency, and politics that undergird the practices of this nonliberal movement, in order to come to an understanding of the historical projects that animate it. [...]

AGENCY AND RESISTANCE

As I suggested at the outset, women's active support for socioreligious movements that sustain principles of female subordination poses a dilemma for feminist analysts. On the one hand, women are seen to assert their presence in previously male-defined spheres while, on the other hand, the very idioms they use to enter these arenas are grounded in discourses that have historically secured their subordination to male authority. In other words, women's subordination to feminine virtues, such as shyness, modesty, and humility, appears to be the necessary condition for their enhanced public role in religious and political life. While it would not have been unusual in the 1960s to account for women's participation in such movements in terms of false consciousness or the internalization of patriarchal norms through socialization, there has been an increasing discomfort with explanations of this kind. Drawing on work in the humanities and the social sciences since the 1970s that has focused on the operations of human agency within structures of subordination, feminists have sought to understand how women resist the dominant male order by subverting the hegemonic meanings of cultural practices and redeploying them for their "own interests and agendas." A central question explored within this scholarship has been: how do women contribute to reproducing their own domination, and how do they resist or subvert it? Scholars working within this framework have thus tended to analyze religious traditions in terms of the conceptual and practical resources they offer to women, and the possibilities for redirecting and recoding these resources in accord with women's "own interests and agendas" – a recoding that stands as the site of women's agency.

[... E]ven in instances when an explicit *feminist* agency is difficult to locate, there is a tendency among scholars to look for expressions and moments of resistance that may suggest a challenge to male domination. When women's actions seem to reinscribe what appear to be "instruments of their own oppression," the social analyst can point to moments of disruption of, and articulation of points of opposition to, male authority – moments that are located either in the interstices of a woman's consciousness (often read as a nascent feminist consciousness), or in the objective effects of women's actions, however unintended these may be. Agency, in this form of analysis, is understood as the capacity to realize one's own interests against the weight of custom, tradition, transcendental will, or other obstacles (whether individual or collective). Thus the humanist desire for autonomy and self-expression constitutes the substrate, the slumbering ember that can spark to flame in the form of an act of resistance when conditions permit.

[...] What [these perceptive studies] fail to problematize is the universality of the desire – central for liberal and progressive thought, and presupposed by the concept of resistance it authorizes – to be free from relations of subordination and, for women, from structures of male domination. This positing of women's agency as consubstantial with resistance to relations of domination, and the concomitant naturalization of freedom as a social ideal, are not simply analytical oversights on the part of feminist authors. Rather, I would argue that their assumptions reflect a deeper tension within feminism attributable to its dual character as both an *analytical* and a *politically prescriptive* project. Despite the many strands and differences within feminism, what accords the feminist tradition an analytical and political coherence is the premise that where society is structured to serve male interests, the result will be either neglect, or direct suppression, of women's concerns. Feminism, therefore, offers both a *diagnosis* of women's status across cultures and a *prescription* for changing the situation of women who are understood to be marginalized, subordinated, or oppressed (see Strathern 1988, 26–8). Thus the articulation of conditions of relative freedom that enable women both to formulate and to enact self-determined goals and interests remains the object of feminist politics and theorizing. Freedom is normative to feminism, as it is to liberalism, and critical scrutiny is applied to those who want to limit women's freedom rather than those who want to extend it.

[... M]y argument for uncoupling the notion of self-realization from that of the autonomous will is indebted to post-structuralist critiques of the transcendental subject, voluntarism, and repressive models of power. Yet, as will become clear, my analysis also departs from these frameworks insomuch as I question the overwhelming tendency within post-structuralist feminist scholarship to conceptualize agency in terms of subversion or resignification of social norms, to locate agency within those operations that resist the dominating and subjectivating modes of power. In other words, I will argue that the normative political subject of poststructuralist feminist theory often remains a liberatory one, whose agency is conceptualized on the binary model of subordination and subversion. In doing so, this scholarship elides dimensions of human action whose ethical and political status does not map onto the logic of repression and resistance. In order to grasp these modes of action indebted to other reasons and histories, I will suggest that it is crucial to detach the notion of agency from the goals of progressive politics.

It is quite clear that the idea of freedom and liberty as *the* political ideal is relatively new in modern history. Many societies, including Western ones, have flourished with aspirations other than this. Nor, for that matter, does the narrative of individual and collective liberty exhaust the desires with which people live in liberal societies. If we recognize that the desire for freedom from, or subversion of, norms is not an innate desire that motivates all beings at all times, but is also profoundly mediated by cultural and historical conditions, then the question arises: how do we analyze operations of power that construct different kinds of bodies, knowledges, and subjectivities whose trajectories do not follow the entelechy of liberatory politics?

Put simply, my point is this: if the ability to effect change in the world and in oneself is historically and culturally specific (both in terms of what constitutes "change" and the means by which it is effected), then the meaning and sense of agency cannot be fixed in advance, but must emerge through an analysis of the particular concepts that enable specific modes of being, responsibility, and effectivity. Viewed in this way, what may appear to be a case of deplorable passivity and docility from a progressivist point of view, may actually be a form of agency – but one that can be understood only from within the discourses and structures of subordination that create the conditions of its enactment. In this sense, agentival capacity is entailed not only in those acts that resist norms but also in the multiple ways in which one *inhabits* norms.

[…] Consider, for example, the women from the mosque movement with whom I worked. The task of realizing piety placed these women in conflict with several structures of authority. Some of these structures were grounded in instituted standards of Islamic orthodoxy, and others in norms of liberal discourse; some were grounded in the authority of parents and male kin, and others in state institutions. Yet the *rationale* behind these conflicts was not predicated upon, and therefore cannot be understood only by reference to, arguments for gender equality or resistance to male authority. Nor can these women's practices be read as a reinscription of traditional roles, since the women's mosque movement has significantly reconfigured the gendered practice of Islamic pedagogy and the social institution of mosques […]. One could, of course, argue in response that, the intent of these women notwithstanding, the actual effects of their practices may be analyzed in terms of their role in reinforcing or undermining structures of male domination. While conceding that such an analysis is feasible and has been useful at times, I would nevertheless argue that it remains encumbered by the binary terms of resistance and subordination, and ignores projects, discourses, and desires that are not captured by these terms (such as those pursued by the women I worked with).

[… Alternatively,] one may argue that the set of capacities inhering in a subject – that is, the abilities that define her modes of agency – are not the residue of an undominated self that existed prior to the operations of power but are themselves the products of those operations. Such an understanding of power and subject formation encourages us to conceptualize agency not simply as a synonym for resistance to relations of domination, but as a capacity for action that specific relations of *subordination* create and enable. [...]

First of all, as I hope I have made clear, I am not interested in offering *a* theory of agency, but rather I insist that the meaning of agency must be explored within the grammar of concepts within which it resides. My argument in brief is that we should keep the meaning of agency open and allow it to emerge from "within semantic and institutional networks that define and make possible particular ways of relating to people, things, and oneself" (T. Asad 2003, 78). This is why I have maintained that the concept of agency should be delinked from the goals of progressive politics, a tethering that has often led to the incarceration of the notion of agency within the trope of resistance against oppressive and dominating operations of power. This does not mean that agency never manifests itself in this manner; indeed it sometimes does. But the questions that follow from this relatively simple observation are complicated and may be productively explored, I would suggest, through the nexus of ethics and politics.

REFERENCES

Asad, Talal. 2003. *Formations of the Secular: Christianity, Islam, Modernity*. Redwood City: Stanford University Press.
Strathern, Marilyn. 1988. *The Gender of the Gift: Problems with Women and Problems with Society*. Berkeley: University of California Press.

13.2. Speaking like a Model Minority: "FOB" Styles, Gender, and Racial Meanings among Desi Teens in Silicon Valley (2008)

Shalini Shankar

In this article I examine how everyday performances of teenage linguistic style interact with broader meanings of class, race, and gender. Beginning with the media-ascribed category of the model minority, I examine the specifics of how it shapes meanings of race for Desi (South Asian Americans) teens in a Silicon Valley high school. Ideologies of multilingualism that prevail in South Asia travel with their speakers to an increasingly monolingual California, and such an ideological clash is managed differently by upwardly mobile, well-educated Desis and by middle-class families who have prospered from the tech boom but remain in assembly line jobs. Differences in the ways Desi teens conceive of and manage these ideologies are linked to how they regard their high school, their place in it, and the ways in which school spaces are understood to be public or private. I contrast two distinct Desi teen high school styles that embody these differences: the mainstream style of teens referred to as "popular"; and a marginalized style called "FOB," or "Fresh off the Boat." I focus primarily on FOB styles to examine how FOBs are judged by Desi peers as nonnormative, how they vary according to gender, and the ways they are received at school. In so doing, I analyze how racial meaning is constructed through language use, as well as how gender differently shapes linguistic norms for these speakers.

[...] In their multiracial, multiethnic school environment, teens who are called FOBs by popular teens for their style of speaking, dressing, and socializing are not actually brand new arrivals to the United States. Rather, FOB (pronounced as a word, not as individual letters) is a term that upper middle-class, popular Desi teens use to label second- and third-generation middle-class teens whose parents are nonskilled workers. So-called FOBs are middle-class Sikh Punjabis that popular teens marginalize and distance themselves from based on their ways of dressing, speaking, and comportment in school. To emphasize the connection between producers of particular ideological projects and their objects, Susan Gal (2007) has offered the term "clasp" as a way of relating how discourses are produced and linked to categories of individuals. She defines interdiscursive clasps as "speech registers (or registers of semiotic practice) that link those who create the category of a person-type and produce justifications for its indexical signs with those who are recruited to that person-type" (Gal 2007:6). FOB styles – the stereotypical ways in which FOBs are thought to speak – act as clasps between FOBby (FOB-like) and popular Desi teens.

[...] Although FOB styles of speaking include the use of Punjabi, English, Bollywood dialogue and song lyrics, hip-hop lyrics and lexicon, Desi Accented English, California slang, and Spanish, the stereotype that FOBs simply code switch loudly in Punjabi is what elicits negative judgment and enables popular teens to appear more model. In a school context, such practices of status making and exclusion are commonplace through talk and social activity (Goodwin 2006). Although I will discuss the numerous ways in which FOB styles are far more differentiated and nuanced than this, the racializing effect of the stereotype is ultimately what prevails (Roth-Gordon 2007; see also McElhinny 2001). For this reason, I use the terms *FOB* and *FOB style* to refer to the middle-class, marginalized Sikh Punjabi youth who engage in these marked language practices. *FOB style* is my analytical term, and I use it to contextualize their identity and style-making practices in the institutional setting of school and in the class-based inequities of the South Asian diaspora. [...]

FOB STYLES OF SPEAKING

FOB styles draw on English, Punjabi, Desi Accented English, hip-hop lexicon and lyrics, as well as Spanish and California slang. The following examples are drawn from tape recordings made by students featuring teens (*M* = male, *F* = female) speaking among themselves in my absence during March–April 2001. They exemplify that what may be overheard as simply code switching between English and Punjabi is, upon closer examination, a much more complex style. FOB styles include local California slang, such as *hella* (very), and *tight* (very cool), *dude*, and *bro*. Similar to "FOB accents" (Reyes 2007), "Mock Asian" (Chun 2001), and "Stylized Asian English" (Rampton 1995), which all refer to ways of speaking that ridicule the non-standard English associated with recent Asian immigrants, "Desi Accented English" (DAE) is a language variety I have identified through which teens index insider humor. DAE (formatted in boldface type below) is not simply an accent; rather, it is a way of speaking that indexes a lack of cultural knowledge about common aspects of American life and contains atypical grammatical constructions and lexical elements that may not be shared by other speakers of South Asian English. It may seem ironic that those called FOBs are performing a "FOBby" accent, but their sophistication in doing so is a reminder that FOB styles can indeed be seen in many instances as a stylistic variable. In the following example recorded during a morning break period, Manpreet (F) offers her friend Harbans (F) some of her Pop-Tart pastry. Munching on the snack while the conversation ensues, Harbans interrupts to inquire about the Pop-Tart's flavor, and Avinash (M) offers an explanation.

Example 1: S'mores

1　Harbans: Hey this is good; what is it?
2　Manpreet: S'mores.
3　Harbans: S'mores?
4　Avinash: You know that thing with **marshmallows and chocolate? Maarrsh-**
5　　**mallow,** that little white thing?

By using DAE (formatted in boldface) to respond to Harbans's confusion about a flavor inspired by an American campfire treat, Avinash indexes the lack of social knowledge generally associated with FOBs. His emphatic **maarrsh-mallow** especially elicits laughter, because it is not a foodstuff available in South Asia, and makes this ordinary American flavor seem exotic to the uninitiated. Like Avinash, FOB teens readily use DAE for humorous emphasis in the midst of California accented English. In a conversation where Manpreet disclosed to Ranvir (M) that she was taping their conversation for my research, Ranvir jokingly suggested that this amounted to "sexual harassment." Manpreet smilingly replied, **"It is very-very bad!"** Ranvir laughed and echoed, **"Very-very?"** Here, not just the accent but also the construction **very-very**, a common expression in South Asian English, index their knowledge of stereotypical ways in which actual FOBs speak, and indicate that they consider themselves to be far enough from this stereotype to use it humorously.

FOB style draws heavily on Punjabi (formatted in italic type below). This can include the use of expressions such as *Oh balle, balle!*, a multipurpose cheer uttered when dancing, as a rallying cry, and for surprise or exasperation, as well as *chak de fatte!* which teens translate as "let's go!" "raise the roof!" or "let's kick ass!" While sometimes used literally, they are also used sarcastically, as in this exchange between Jett (M) and KB (M).

Example 2: *"Chak de fatte!"* [Kick ass!]

1　Jett: Bend down, pick that up! All yous ready?
2　KB: Whaaaat?
3　Jett: *Chak de fatte!* [Kick ass!].
4　KB [sarcastically]: Thanks, bro.

In this exchange, the Punjabi phrase is used as a double entendre. In line 1, Jett tries to direct KB to pick up his bag and move along, but when KB takes his time doing so, Jett shouts, "*Chak de fatte!*" (line 3) as KB lackadaisically bends over to collect his belongings. The phrase is not just a rallying cry, but also a humorous suggestion that KB may require a swift kick in order to get moving.

Alongside Punjabi, California slang, and DAE, Spanish is also a resource for FOB style. San Jose's predominantly working-class Chicano population has exerted a visible influence on FOB styles. Latino and Latina styles of clothing and makeup, especially when markers of gang membership (Mendoza-Denton 2007), can also shape FOB styles of comportment and speaking. Spanish phrases can be quite humorous when inserted into conversational exchanges. In the following excerpt from a lunchtime conversation, Kuldeep (M) uses Spanish (formatted in an underlined typeface) in an exchange with Uday (M) and Simran (F).

Example 3: "*No Habla Inglés*" [I (sic) don't speak English]

1   Uday: *Saleya eh* **garbage** *can vai*? [Is this a garbage can, stupid?].
2   Kuldeep: <u>No habla Inglés</u> [I (*sic*) don't speak English]. [loud round of
3   laughter]
4   Kuldeep: **Don't know what you say ...**
5   Simran: Throw that fuckin' shit out!
6   Kuldeep: *Oh balle! Hon boleya!* [Oh wow! At least you're talking to me now!].

While Uday attempts to be discreet about Kuldeep's refusal to properly dispose of trash and reprimands him in Punjabi, Kuldeep rebuffs him with two different performances of misrecognition. In the first, he feigns ignorance by saying in Spanish that he does not speak English. This is met with a round of laughter in part because it is a clever retort to Uday's directive, and in part because Uday's statement in Punjabi does not require him to know English. Kuldeep's utterance could be read as an example of what Jane Hill (1995) has called "mock Spanish," but perhaps a more apt name for this would be "mocking Spanish." By occasionally speaking in Spanish in a school environment where they are routinely mistaken for Latinos, FOB boys use Spanish as a way to mock faculty who cannot easily differentiate between them and Latinos. Ridiculing this misrecognition is a continual source of humor for FOBby teens. The conversation continues when Kuldeep, encouraged by the laughter of his friends, chooses DAE (formatted in bold) to tell Uday that he does not understand him. Again, it is ironic that he uses a FOBby accent to communicate this, as a true FOB would have no trouble understanding Uday's Punjabi remark. When Simran reprimands him in English, Kuldeep responds to her sarcastically in Punjabi, and the joke has ended. While these teens studied Spanish in school and live alongside Mexican Americans in their neighborhoods, they rarely speak Spanish outside of these joking exchanges.

Similarly, FOB styles incorporate lexical elements from hip-hop without any political or social interests in black people. Blacks are concentrated in Oakland and other parts of the Bay Area but are a relatively minor presence in San Jose. Desi teens listen to commercial hip-hop but do not express interest in becoming hip-hop artists or forming social alliances with blacks. In the following example, the hip-hop shout out "West Siiiiide" is used by both KB (M) and Jett (M) to mollify a tense dynamic that develops between Uday and Kuldeep about the latter's neighbor.

Example 4: "*Dimag kharab hai, yaar*" [He is crazy, dude]

1   Uday: Oh man, listen to the bullshit.
2   Kuldeep: *Dimag kharab hai, yaar. Mera neighbor, yaar* [He is crazy, dude. My

3   neighbor, dude].
4   Uday: What has led you to this conclusion?
5   Kuldeep: *Dimag kharab hai!* [He is crazy!].
6   Uday: How do you know people don't say this about you?
7   Kuldeep: He is crazy, fool! Everybody says that, this fool really is crazy,
8   though.
9   Uday: Takes one to know one?
10 Kuldeep: Shut up!
11 Uday: *Main te ude hi karda* [I'm just kidding].
12 Jett: West siiiiide!
13 Kuldeep: *Aha ki karan lag peyan tu?* [What have you started doing?]. Ain't no
14   fuckin' California love, California thug …
15 KB: West Siiiiide!

When Kuldeep seems genuinely annoyed at Uday's needling, Jett steps in and offers a shout out that indexes the unified front of West Coast hip-hop. Kuldeep is hardly amused and snaps at Jett with a clever use of hip-hop lyrics from the then-popular song "The Next Episode" (line 13–14). KB reiterates Jett's shout out for unity, and the tension begins to diffuse. While such a use of hip-hop could be read as an attempt to "pass" for black or "cross" into this group (Bucholtz 1999; Cutler 2003; Lo 1999; Rampton 1995; Reyes 2005), Desi teens I observed did not use hip-hop lexicon for these purposes. FOB teens' overwhelming use of Punjabi and DAE, compared to their relatively infrequent use of hip-hop lexicon, underscores this point.

[…] FOB styles contribute to the creation of racialized meanings in the school context by disrupting the homogeneity of the model minority stereotype and playing a key role in racial formation (Omi and Winant 1994). In the struggle over who is and is not to be considered white, Desis, like other immigrant groups, have been consistently left in the blind spot of racial definition or fall subject to its aberrant nature. Scholars note the racial ambiguity that surrounds the category of Asian Americans (Okihiro 1994), and South Asians in particular (Prashad 2004; Radhakrishnan 2003; Visweswaran 1993). It has been suggested that as a model minority, Desis are poised to join white America (Prashad 2004). By engaging in normative uses of language that include speaking in English and minimizing profanity, popular Desi teens are rarely reprimanded by faculty for their styles of speaking and easily live up to the model minority stereotype. They distance themselves from FOB styles by meeting a normative standard and remaining linguistically unmarked, despite being racially marked as Asian American and brown. Popular styles can be understood as an ethnic variation on whiteness, in which a cosmopolitan, Bollywood-influenced style is showcased in performative contexts. Popular identity in school remains model in every way, including linguistically, and leaves these youth well positioned to integrate into wealthy white Californian communities.

Nonnormative use of language, combined with other unpopular speech practices such as quoting Bollywood, exchanging insults, and talking about fights codes FOBby teens as brown rather than white. FOBs distance themselves from popular Desis and instead align with Mexican American, Vietnamese American, and other teens with whom they feel an affinity in their neighborhoods. In Silicon Valley, these populations, like Desis, are not uniformly upwardly mobile and are subject to similar types of racializing judgments. Because boys and girls differently regard the school as more or less private based on the gendered standards of propriety they are expected to achieve in their communities, boys are far less self-censoring than girls in their language use. Both are marginalized by peers, but boys tend to be more conspicuous violators of school codes. The "brownness" of Indians, as [one teacher at the school] calls it, suggests that if Desis are not acting in model ways, they should be grouped with those who require reform. These social processes affect the positioning of South Asian Americans vis-à-vis other racial groups in the United States and underscore the role of language use in shaping racial meaning in diasporic communities.

REFERENCES

Bucholtz, Mary. 1999. "You da Man: Narrating the Racial Other in the Linguistic Production of White Masculinity." *Journal of Sociolinguistics* 3 (4): 443–60. https://doi.org/10.1111/1467 -9481.00090.

Chun, Elaine. 2001. "The Construction of White, Black, and Korean American Identities through African American Vernacular English." *Journal of Linguistic Anthropology* 11 (1): 52–64. https:// doi.org/10.1525/jlin.2001.11.1.52.

Cutler, Cecelia. 2003. "'Keepin' It Real': White Hip-Hoppers' Discourses of Language, Race, and Authenticity." *Journal of Linguistic Anthropology* 13 (2): 211–33. http://doi.org/10.1525/jlin .2003.13.2.211.

Gal, Susan. 2007. Circulation in the "New" Economy: Clasps and Copies. Paper presented at the 106th Meeting of the American Anthropological Association, Washington, November 29–December 2.

Goodwin, Marjorie. 2006. *The Hidden Life of Girls: Games of Stance, Status, and Exclusion*. Oxford: Blackwell.

Hill, Jane. 1995. "Junk Spanish, Covert Racism and the (Leaky) Boundary between Public and Private Spheres." *Pragmatics* 5 (2): 197–212. https://doi.org/10.1075/prag.5.2.07hil.

Lo, Adrienne. 1999. "Codeswitching, Speech Community Membership, and the Construction of Ethnic Identity." *Journal of Sociolinguistics* 3–4: 461–79. https://doi.org/10.1111/1467-9481.00091.

McElhinny, Bonnie. 2001. "See No Evil, Speak No Evil: White Police Officers' Talk about Race and Affirmative Action." *Journal of Linguistic Anthropology* 11 (1): 65–78. http://doi.org/10.1525 /jlin.2001.11.1.65.

Mendoza-Denton, Norma. 2007. *Homegirls: Language and Cultural Practice among Latina Youth Gangs*. Malden, MA: Blackwell.

Okihiro, Gary. 1994. *Margins and Mainstreams: Asians in American History and Culture*. Seattle: University of Washington Press.

Omi, Michael, and Howard Winant. 1994. *Racial Formation in the United States*. New York: Routledge.

Prashad, Vijay. 2004. *Everybody Was Kung-Fu Fighting: Afro-Asian Connections and the Myth of Cultural Purity*. Boston: Beacon Press.

Radhakrishnan, R. 2003. "Ethnicity in an Age of Diaspora." In *Theorizing Diaspora: A Reader*, edited by J. Braziel and A. Mannur, 119–31. Malden, MA: Blackwell.

Rampton, Ben. 1995. *Crossing: Language and Ethnicity among Adolescents*. New York: Longman.

Reyes, Angela. 2005. "Appropriation of African American Slang by Asian American Youth." *Journal of Sociolinguistics* 9 (4): 510–33. https://doi.org/10.1111/j.1360-6441.2005.00304.x.

———. 2007. *Language, Identity, and Stereotype among Southeast Asian American Youth*. Mahwah: Lawrence Erlbaum Associates.

Roth-Gordon, Jennifer. 2007. "Racing and Erasing the *Playboy*: Slang, Transnational Youth Subculture, and Racial Discourse in Brazil." *Journal of Linguistic Anthropology* 17 (2): 246–65. https://doi.org/10.1525/jlin.2007.17.2.246.

Visweswaran, Kamala. 1993. "Diaspora by Design: Flexible Citizenship and South Asians in U.S. Racial Formations." *Diaspora* 6: 5–29.

13.3. Abjects or Agents? Camps, Contests, and the Creation of "Political Space" (2013)

Victoria Redclift

The Universal Declaration of Human Rights (1948) states that "all people have the right to nationality." However, the number of people who are not considered nationals by any state under its laws ('*de jure*' stateless persons) is estimated at between 11 and 15 million across the globe (Refugees International 2008, Goris *et al.* 2009). These numbers only provide a partial picture. It is almost impossible to calculate all those who are unable to prove their nationality or, despite identification with a nation, lack the security and protection that citizenship can provide: refugees in camps, exiled minorities, internally displaced persons (IDPs) or those expelled or detained. These "dehumanized" individuals, without any political system to offer them protection, have been the subject of a growing body of scholarship and increasing academic concern. Variously portrayed as "bare life" (Agamben 1998, 2005), "human refuse" (Bauman 2004), "pariahs" (Varikas 2007) and "urban outcasts" (Wacquant 2007), this article attempts to give nuance to their representation and the understandings of "statelessness" it reflects. Agier describes "statelessness" as "a premonition, even a preparation, for complete 'human superfluity'" (2011, p. 18) in the sense in which the suppression of life is historically and politically prepared by the suppression of rights. In doing so, he suggests that the key question we face is that of the management of "the undesirable" on a planetary scale and the processes of "humanitarian government" at play in the many present forms of "encampment" across the globe today. Displaced, "stateless" and camp-based populations are likely to increase in line with global instability, growing regional inequality and international migration. "If all this continues camps will no longer be used just to keep vulnerable refugees alive, but rather to park and guard all kinds of undesirable populations" (Agier 2011, p. 3).

[...] This article argues that, while the reality of the world today may well be the reality of the camp, and this is a reality with prospects that are highly pessimistic (Agier 2011), "encampment" is a phenomenon of multiplicity and varied material, social and political realities. The Agambian logic, which renders abject subjects as "naked life," and the "jargon of exception" (Huysmans 2008) which this has spawned, suppresses a political reading of the camp, thus ignoring the complex social relations contained within. Thinking the camp "from below" is not to diminish its significance, but rather to underscore its power. It requires us to take the camp itself as a social and political space (Rygiel 2011) and to understand that, while it may be many things, it is not determined. It may both represent the most intense forms of intolerance and demonstrate the most intimate forms of cultural dialogue (Keith 2005). It may be abject and alienated, but it is not inert. It is a historically structured social and political space in which a "dynamic agonistic account of power-relations" (Walters 2008, p. 188) must be re-inserted. The "camp-dwellers" of this study are seen staking a claim and narrating themselves into the nation, and the camp, consequently, will always be a site of contested meaning.

Chatterjee's (2004) observation that citizenship will take on two different shapes, the "formal" and the "real," and that the negotiated instability the "real" represents may be exaggerated in post-colonial space, makes reference to a well-rehearsed duality evident in the citizenship literature. This takes the form of work that emphasizes a "formal" and legally coded status alongside more "substantive" examples of sociopolitical engagement. His concept of "the real" disrupts a reductive rationality in which "the latter is seen as a condition of possibility of the former" (Isin and Nielsen 2008, p. 2); however, the "negotiated instability" through which the "real" plays out remains insufficiently explored. Agamben's (1998, 2005) influential binary between "political beings" and "bare life" relies on a similarly crude and one-dimensional reification, which naturalizes citizenship. Reflecting upon times and spaces in which such a neat duality may not be very useful, this article argues that the exceptionality of the camp and the denials of "formal" legal status it conditions must be represented not only through the politics of control but also through the politics of resistance. In exploring the dynamic between individual agency and structural constraints, my research suggests that the camps of Bangladesh do not function as bounded physical or conceptual spaces, in which denationalized groups are altogether divorced from "the polity." Instead, "acts of citizenship" occur at the level of everyday life, as the moments, claims or contests through which "formal" status is transgressed. In asking how and when a "stateless" population is able to "access" citizenship, through which processes and by what means, we are able to identify the "non-citizens," "aliens" and "outcasts" who make claims to political subjectivity. Doing so reveals the tension, ambiguity and conceptual limitations of "statelessness" and citizenship, unearthing a reality of partial, shifting and deceptively permeable terrain.

This article therefore considers the camp in its double depiction: first, as an abject space whose subjects are excluded from the "formal" political domain and, second, as a site of claims-making in which the political can be created. It reveals the camp as a space of contestation and negotiation in which agents make strategic calculations even in the most difficult circumstances (Andrijasevic 2003). However, the article also questions the complex social processes through which political subjects are formed. In the context of irregular migrants in Northern France, Rygiel (2011) reflects upon social solidarities formed in camp spaces, which "decompose" traditional understandings of citizenship. I take this further to consider the fractured, ambiguous and highly discriminatory nature of claims-making processes too. Consequently, I do not propose to merely reclaim the camp through the agency of its subjects but to reveal the dissonance and discord (constitutive of an "us" and "them" divide) upon which political subjectivity may also rely. The camp is certainly a space of social relations, but these are formed through inequality as well as solidarity, through contest as well as through cohesion.

[…] "Urdu-speakers" in Bangladesh today exemplify some of the key problems facing uprooted populations. This article analyzes a very specific site of "camp" and "non-camp" based displacement to consider how citizenship status is affected by the spatial dynamics of settlement. In illuminating empirical and conceptual issues of relevance to lived spaces of "statelessness" across the world, it represents a critical evaluation of the way "political space" is contested at the local level and what this reveals about the nature and boundaries of citizenship. […]

ABJECT SPACES

Since 1972, the "Bihari" camps in Bangladesh have certainly functioned as "states of exception" in "formal" juridical terms. While those "Urdu-speakers" who retained their houses also retained their civil status, those living inside the camps were disenfranchised. [A] range of further economic and social rights have also been difficult [for camp residents] to access. In the words of the 2008 High Court ruling, those in the camps "are constantly denied the constitutional rights to job, education, accommodation, health and a decent life like other citizens of the country." The inability to access Government schools has been thought by many to have represented the most debilitating impediment to social mobility. In the absence of a Government alternative, the fees charged by non-Government schools would normally be too high. Government jobs have been even more of a chimera, but problems are not limited to Government employment alone. […]

Here in the camps, without formal recognition, political being has been enacted at a number of levels. Movement between physical spaces is one such example, and the position of those who have left the camps, straddling relationships and influences, inside and out, is therefore particularly illuminating. The data presented here not only speak to the camp as a political space, but also emphasize the idea of movement and mobility as an important element within the creation of such space (Rygiel 2011). It is, after all, very often through movement outside, or the pretense of such movement, that political subjectivity is achieved. As the quotation below suggests, movement outside the camps is about claiming citizenship and, as a result, achieving something more profound:

> We moved from the camp four years ago … we get many advantages living outside, like voter ID, and an address that I can give freely to people … We got self-respect from others living outside. (Timi, "in-between," 27 years old, Dhaka)

[…] The experience of "Urdu-speakers" requires us to ask how rights are taken and borders crossed, and in doing so disturbs some established rhetoric. The strategies people use to cross these boundaries are assorted and interlinked. They occur in all areas of daily life, as negotiations are made and statuses subverted:

> Acts of citizenship may be cultivated by, or may transgress, practices and formal entitlement, as they emerge from the paradox between universal inclusion in the language of rights ... and inevitable exclusion in the language of community and particularity on the other. (Isin and Nielsen 2008, p. 11)

They deconstruct the duality of sociopolitical engagement and emphasize the fluid and slippery reality of access. Here, non-citizens, aliens and outsiders are no longer simply helpless pawns; they demand a radical shift in focus. The object of attention becomes those moments, enactments and events "when a new identity, substance or relationship of citizenship is brought into existence" (Walters 2008, p. 192). This draws our attention to the contrast between citizenship, as it is "bestowed" upon "camp-dwellers" by the High Court ruling of May 2008, and citizenship, as it is "enacted" through movement outside the camps, through acquisition of a "fake" ID card and at the polling booth itself. It therefore allows us to better understand the space of citizenship and how those lacking formal rights occupy or negotiate that space.

Perhaps the "naked life" engendered through deportation, displacement or disenfranchisement, is not so naked after all? As Walters contends, what is needed is greater sensitivity to the diverse and often relatively minor ways in which "non-status" individuals are constituted, and constitute themselves, "not just as subjects capable of acting, but as political subjects" (Walters 2008, p. 191).

FRACTURED SOLIDARITIES: CONTESTATION AND DIFFERENCE

The growing interest in the emergence of alternative spaces of population control, management and detention has invigorated theorizing about the political action of subjects living in such spaces (Nyers 2003, 2008, Diken 2004). Within this body of work, it has been suggested that what is significant about migrant struggles over the meaning of the camp is fundamentally that it puts social solidarities back into this space (Rygiel 2011). This creates a vision of politics based on social relations, in which the rights and ability of migrants to build, and become members of, a "community" is a necessary step upon which to enact citizenship.

I contend, however, that in the fight for political subjectivity, it is very often disunity as much as unity that marks the creation of "political space," and there is danger in romanticizing the solidarity produced in abjection. As "Urdu-speakers" in Bangladesh navigate a complicated social world, and struggle to earn the economic, social and cultural capital to leave the camps, "outsiders" distance themselves not only from these spaces, but also from the friends and relatives within them. [...]

[...] The material presented here suggests that social solidarities and community cohesion are not the automatic by-products of subordination; the fight for rights is very often a fight indeed. It is necessary instead to attend to the variability of "abject spaces" (Walters 2008). From the hundreds of African IDP camps revealed by each new conflict, famine or natural disaster to the military-humanitarian camps holding Afghan asylum-seekers in Australia, the Palestinian refugee camps in Lebanon, Syria, Jordan and the occupied territories, or the transit centers, waiting zones or administrative detention centers emerging in Europe and North Africa, "the situations vary greatly and are always in flux" (Agier 2011, p. 38). The historical, spatial and material specificity of such sites determine the social and political relations that constitute them. Consequently, the creation of "political space" on the part of those excluded will often be a fractured, ambiguous and highly discriminatory process. The "acts of citizenship" produced will always be dependent on cross-cutting variables of gender, generation, social status and power. Citizenship functions to exclude and it is, therefore, very often born of contestation.

REFERENCES

Agamben, G. 1998. *Homo Sacer: Sovereign Power and Bare Life*. Stanford: Stanford University Press.

Agamben, G. 2005. *States of Exception*. Chicago: University of Chicago Press.

Agier, M. 2011. *Managing the Undesirables: Refugee Camps and Humanitarian Government*. Cambridge: Polity.

Andrijasevic, R. 2003. "The Difference Borders Make: (Il)legality, Migration and Trafficking in Italy among Eastern European Women in Prostitution." In *Uprootings/Regroundings: Questions of Home and Migration*, edited by S.A. Ahmed, C. Castaneda, A-M. Fortier, and M. Sheller, 251–72. Oxford: Berg.

Bauman, Z. 2004. *Wasted Lives: Modernity and Its Outcasts*. Cambridge: Polity.

Chatterjee, P. 2004. *The Politics of the Governed: Reflections on Popular Politics in Most of the World*. New York: Columbia University Press.

Diken, B. 2004. "From Refugee Camps to Gated Communities: Biopolitics and the End of the City." *Citizenship Studies* 8 (1): 83–106. https://doi.org/10.1080/1362102042000178373.

Goris, I., J. Harrington, and S. Kohn. 2009. "Statelessness: What It Is and Why It Matters." *Forced Migration Review* 32: 4–6.

Huysmans, J. 2008. "The Jargon of Exception: On Schmitt, Agamben and the Absence of Political Society." *International Political Sociology* 2: 165–83. http://doi.org/10.1111/j.1749-5687.2008.00042.x.

Isin, E.F., and G.M. Nielsen. 2008. *Acts of Citizenship*. London: Palgrave Macmillan.

Keith, M. 2005. "Racialization and the Public Spaces of the Multicultural City." In *Racialization: Studies in Theory and Practice*, edited by M. Karim and J. Solomos. Oxford: Oxford University Press.

Nyers, P. 2003. "Abject Cosmopolitanism: The Politics of Protection in the Anti-deportation Movement." *Third World Quarterly* 24 (6): 1069–93. http://doi.org/10.1080/0143659031000163 0071.

Nyers, P. 2008. "No One Is Illegal between City and Nation." In *Acts of Citizenship*, edited by E.F. Isin and G.M. Nielsen, 160–81. London: Zed Books.

Refugees International. 2008. *Futures Denied: Statelessness among Infants, Children and Youth* [online]. Washington: Refugees International. Available from http://www.refugeesinternational.org.

Rygiel, K. 2011. "Bordering Solidarities: Migrant Activism and the Politics of Movement and Camps at Calais." *Citizenship Studies* 15 (1): 119. https://doi.org/10.1080/13621025.2011.534911.

Varikas, E. 2007. *The Outcasts of the World: Images of the Pariah*. Paris: Stock.

Wacquant, L. 2007. *Urban Outcasts: A Comparative Sociology of Advanced Marginality*. Cambridge: Polity.

Walters, W. 2008. "Acts of Demonstration: Mapping the Territory of (Non)Citizenship." In *Acts of Citizenship*, edited by E.F. Isin and G.M. Nielsen, 182–206. London: Zed Books.

13.4. #Ferguson: Digital Protest, Hashtag Ethnography, and the Racial Politics of Social Media in the United States (2015)

Yarimar Bonilla and Jonathan Rosa

On Saturday, August 9, 2014, at 12:03 p.m., an unarmed black teenager named Michael Brown was fatally shot by a police officer in Ferguson, Missouri, a small town on the outskirts of St. Louis. Within the hour, a post appeared on the Twitter social media platform stating, "I just saw someone die," followed by a photograph taken from behind the beams of a small wooden balcony overlooking Canfield Drive, where Michael Brown's lifeless body lay uncovered, hands alongside his head, face down on the asphalt. Immediately following the incident, community members assembled to demand an explanation for why this unarmed 18-year-old had been seemingly executed while reportedly holding his hands up in a gesture of surrender, pleading "don't shoot." The impromptu gathering soon turned into a sustained protest marked by daily demonstrations and violent confrontations with highly armed local police – all of which were documented in detail across social media platforms like Twitter, Instagram, YouTube, and Vine.

Occurring on the heels of other highly publicized killings of unarmed black men – such as Eric Garner (who died as a result of an illegal chokehold by New York City police just weeks before the events in Ferguson), Oscar Grant (whose death was emotionally portrayed in the award-winning film *Fruitvale Station* released just one year prior), and 17-year-old Trayvon Martin (whose 2012 killing sparked national outcry and spurred numerous forms of activism) – the death of Michael Brown quickly captured the imagination of thousands across and beyond the United States. Protestors from around the nation flocked to Ferguson to participate in demonstrations calling for the arrest of the officer responsible for the fatal shooting. Television viewers tuned in across the country to watch live news coverage of the violent confrontations between the protestors and the highly armed local police. Images of these confrontations circulated widely in national and international news coverage, and news of these events quickly went "viral" across social media. During the initial week of protests, over 3.6 million posts appeared on Twitter documenting and reflecting on the emerging details surrounding Michael Brown's death; by the end of the month, "#Ferguson" had appeared more than eight million times on the Twitter platform.

[...] Much will also be written about the protestors who immediately gathered at the site of his killing and about those who remained, under intense police harassment, long after the media spotlight faded. But what are we to make of the eight million tweets? What do they tell us about this event, its place in the social imagination, and about social media itself as a site of both political activism and social analysis?

In 1991, a homemade VHS tape of Los Angeles resident Rodney King being brutally beaten by four police officers sparked outrage across the country and galvanized thousands in what is widely recognized as one of the most influential examples of citizen journalism in the United States (Allan and Thorsen 2009). Today, 56 percent of the U.S. population carries video-enabled smartphones, and the use of mobile technology is particularly high among African Americans. The increased use and availability of these technologies has provided marginalized and racialized populations with new tools for documenting incidents of state-sanctioned violence and contesting media representations of racialized bodies and marginalized communities. In many cases – such as police officers' use of a chokehold in the murder of Eric Garner – the use of mobile technology to record and circulate footage of events has played a key role in prompting public outcry. In the case of Ferguson, video footage of the fatal shooting of Michael Brown has yet to surface, but informal journalism was used to document the scene in the direct aftermath of his murder, to publicize the protests that ensued, and to bring attention to the militarized police confrontations that followed. Through social media, users were able to disseminate these accounts to a broad audience and to forge new mediatized publics that demand anthropological attention. In this essay, we explore how and why platforms like Twitter have become important sites for activism around issues of racial inequality, state violence, and media representations. [...]

CAN A HASHTAG BECOME A FIELD SITE?

[...] Is Twitter the ultimate "non-place" (Augé 1995) of super modernity, a transient site of fleeting engagement, or is it an instance of a "virtual world" (Boellstorff 2008), with its own set of socialities and forms of engagement? And is the study of an event through social media a return to a previous era of "armchair anthropology"? Or is hashtag ethnography the next logical step in an anthropology of the 21st century [...]? To answer these questions, it is necessary to begin by distinguishing the town of Ferguson, Missouri, from "hashtag Ferguson" and to recognize how each of these contributed to the formation of the larger "event" of Ferguson. As those familiar with Twitter know, the hashtag symbol (#) is often used as a way of marking a conversation within this platform. The hashtag serves as an indexing system in both the clerical sense and the semiotic sense. In the clerical sense, it allows the ordering and quick retrieval of information about a specific topic. [...] Similar to the coding systems employed by anthropologists, hashtags allow users to not simply "file" their comments but to performatively frame what these comments are "really about," thereby enabling users to indicate a meaning that might not be otherwise apparent. Hence, someone could write, "Decades of racial tension and increasing suburban poverty boiled to the surface last night" followed by the text "#Ferguson," as a way of creating a particular interpretive frame. Hashtags thus operate in ways similar to library call numbers: They locate texts within a specific conversation, allowing for their quick retrieval, while also marking texts as being "about" a specific topic.

In addition, hashtags have the intertextual potential to link a broad range of tweets on a given topic or disparate topics as part of an intertextual chain, regardless of whether, from a given perspective, these tweets have anything to do with one another. Thus, a tweet in support of Ferguson protestors and a tweet in support of Officer Darren Wilson could both be coded and filed under #Ferguson. Moreover, a tweet about racial disparity in Missouri, such as "racism lives here," and one about a night out on the town in St. Louis could both be marked #STL.

This insight requires anthropologists to carefully consider the variety of uses in play for any given hashtag as well as the stances and perspectives associated with any given use. In the case of #Ferguson, patterns emerged in which Twitter became a platform for providing emergent information about the killing of Michael Brown and for commenting on the treatment of the officer who shot him. For example, one user posted, "Prosecutors get real friendly when they have to adjudicate one of their own. But they'll move heaven and earth hunting POC down. #Ferguson." In contrast, other tweets recontextualized the situation in Ferguson as part of global affairs (e.g., "#Egypt #Palestine #Ferguson #Turkey, U.S. made tear gas, sold on the almighty free market represses democracy"), while others critiqued the appropriation of this event (e.g., "seriously though, @FCKH8 never posted ANYTHING on their Facebook page in support of #Ferguson until it was time to sell some t-shirts").

[...] In addition [h]ashtags also have the interdiscursive capacity to lasso accompanying texts and their indexical meanings as part of a frame. Linkages across hashtags and their accompanying texts – which comprise both other hashtags (e.g., #Ferguson, #MichaelBrown, #HandsUp, etc.) and additional commentary – frame #Ferguson as a kind of mediatized place. It is in this sense that much like one could go to the library, stand in front of a call number, and find texts on a particular subject, one could go onto Twitter, type #Ferguson, and find a large number of posts on the subject at hand. But what is the relationship between this mediatized place – as it is experienced from outside the boundaries of the geographical context with which it is associated – and everyday life in what might be understood as Ferguson proper? How does the mediatization of Ferguson, Missouri, through #Ferguson lead to the formation of new "ad hoc publics" (Bruns and Burgess 2011)?

The types of publics created by Twitter emerge from the hashtag's capacity to serve not just as an indexing system but also as a filter that allows social media users to reduce the noise of Twitter by cutting into one small slice. However, this filtering process also has a distorting effect. Social media create a distorted view of events, such that we only get the perspective of the people who are already in our social network (Garret and Resnick 2011; Pariser 2012; Sunstein 2009). This effect should signal one of the first cautions for anthropologists interested in social media: We must avoid the common slippage made by journalists and others who tend to represent Twitter as an unproblematized "public sphere" without taking into account the complexity of who is on Twitter, as well as how people are on Twitter in different ways (e.g., some are constant users, others tweet infrequently, some do so from their phone, some from their office, etc.).

Part of the problem of engaging in hashtag ethnography, then, is that it is difficult to assess the context of social media utterances. Moreover, a simple statement of fact – for example, that there were eight million Ferguson tweets – tells us very little. How many were critical of the police? How many were critical of the protestors? How many were posted by journalists (both professional and amateur)? Beyond knowing that people tweeted, we know little about what those tweets meant to their authors and their imagined publics. We do not know, for example, how many of the eight million tweets were aimed at a national audience (and thus appropriately hashtagged for quick retrieval and retweet) versus how many were aimed at a smaller group of followers with the contextual information necessary to assess both the explicit and implicit uses of hashtags and other references.

In thinking about the hashtag as a field site, these questions and the competing perspectives they highlight demonstrate the importance of reorienting social media ethnography from an emphasis on "network and community" toward a focus on individual experiences, practices, and socialities (Postill and Pink 2012:124).

[…] In the case of Ferguson, it is worth noting that, at least initially, the most common use of the #Ferguson hashtag was to convey information about the unfolding events. Before the mainstream media had caught up to what was happening, the mass of hashtagged tweets was a way of calling attention to an underreported incident of police brutality.

[…] Recognizing that hashtags can only ever offer a limited, partial, and filtered view of a social world does not require abandoning them as sites of analysis. Rather, we must approach them as what they are: entry points into larger and more complex worlds. Hashtags offer a window to peep through, but it is only by stepping through that window and "following" (in both Twitter and non-Twitter terms) individual users that we can begin to place tweets within a broader context. This kind of analysis requires us to stay with those who tweet and follow them after hashtags have fallen out of "trend."

[…] Twitter does not just allow you to peer through a window; it allows you to look through manifold windows at once. On #Ferguson, you could watch six simultaneous live streams. You could read what protestors were tweeting, what journalists were reporting, what the police was announcing, and how observers and analysts interpreted the unfolding events. You could also learn how thousands of users were reacting to the numerous posts. In the era of transistor radios and television sets, one did not necessarily know what listeners or viewers yelled back at their machines, but on Twitter one can get a sense of individual responses to mediatized events.

[…] It is important to examine how and why digital activism has become salient to particular populations. It is surely not coincidental that the groups most likely to experience police brutality, to have their protests disparaged as acts of "rioting" or "looting," and to be misrepresented in the media are precisely those turning to digital activism at the highest rates. Indeed, some of the most important hashtag campaigns emerging out of #Ferguson were targeted at calling attention to both police practices and media representations, suggesting that social media can serve as an important tool for challenging these various forms of racial profiling.

[...] The use of hashtags such as #HandsUpDontShoot, #IfTheyGunnedMeDown, and #NoAngel speak to the long history of inaccurate and unfair portrayal of African Americans within mainstream media and to the systematic profiling and victim blaming suffered by racialized bodies. Their use suggests that while social media might seem like a space of disembodied engagement, for many, social media can become an important site in which to foreground the particular ways in which racialized bodies are systematically stereotyped, stigmatized, surveilled, and positioned as targets of state-sanctioned violence. These hashtag campaigns, which seek to identify the insidious nature of contemporary racism, can thus be understood as a powerful response to the "racial paranoia" (Jackson 2008) associated with African Americans' ongoing experiences of abject inequality in an age of alleged colorblindness.

[...] Within this context, social media participation becomes a key site from which to contest mainstream media silences and the long history of state-sanctioned violence against racialized populations. Upon announcing the Ferguson grand jury decision, St. Louis prosecutor Robert McCulloch claimed that media coverage, and particularly social media, had posed "the most significant challenge" to his investigation. Social media cast a spotlight on this small Missouri township, but more importantly, by propelling Ferguson into a broader, mediatized, virtual space, social media users were able to show that "#Ferguson is everywhere" – not only in the sense of a broad public sphere but also in the sense of the underlying social and political relationships that haunt the nation as a whole.

REFERENCES

Allan, Stuart, and Einar Thorsen, eds. 2009. *Citizen Journalism: Global Perspectives*. New York: Peter Lang.

Augé, Marc. 1995. *Non-Places: Introduction to an Anthropology of Supermodernity*. John Howe, trans. New York: Verso Books.

Boellstorff, Tom. 2008. *Coming of Age in Second Life: An Anthropologist Explores the Virtually Human*. Princeton: Princeton University Press.

Bruns, Axel, and Jean Burgess. 2011. The Use of Twitter Hashtags in the Formation of Ad Hoc Publics. Paper presented at the European Consortium for Political Research conference, Reykjavik, August 25–27.

Garret, Kelly R., and Paul Resnick. 2011. "Resisting Political Fragmentation on the Internet." *Daedalus* 140 (4): 108–20. http://doi.org/10.1162/DAED_a_00118.

Jackson, John L. 2008. *Racial Paranoia: The Unintended Consequences of Political Correctness: The New Reality of Race in America*. New York: Basic Civitas.

Pariser, Eli. 2012. *The Filter Bubble: How the New Personalized Web Is Changing What We Read and How We Think*. New York: Penguin Press.

Postill, John. 2014. "Democracy in an Age of Viral Reality: A Media Epidemiography of Spain's Indignados Movement." *Ethnography* 15 (1): 51–69. http://doi.org/10.1177/1466138113502513.

Sunstein, Cass. 2009. *Republic.com 2.0*. Princeton: Princeton University Press.

13.5. Consent's Revenge (2016)

Audra Simpson

When I first conceived of the project that would become my book *Mohawk Interruptus: Political Life Across the Borders of Settler States* (Simpson 2014), my plan was a study of nationhood and citizenship among an Indigenous people in North America who are resolutely committed to jurisdiction over territories of various forms. Their own object was and is territory in a material sense, their land – but also ideas, the past, the present, the future, their membership within the polity itself. They make all of this effort as they travel across various borders and boundaries on their inherited and their claimed territories. They assert their histories in the face of the bordered contestation of those claims by liberal, democratic, and still-settling states. Because these are my own people, I had a very strong, a priori ethnographic sense of what was going on. However, I was *paying attention* differently for years before my formal fieldwork began. Our band council (tribal council) was evicting non-Native people from the community, the evictions were of a piece with a 50 percent blood-quantum requirement for membership that was vigorously debated, contested, embraced, defended. These processes were symptoms of something more than intolerance or liberal subject failure, and I wanted to know why. I looked for linkages between land, law, and governance within and beyond the reserve. The project turned into something else when I got into the archive and when I conducted interviews – when supposed observations and materials from the community took form in dense, identifiable lines of argument, of stances, of theories themselves. Suddenly I had something else, and that something was no easy answer. In fact, before me was a study in difficulty, a study of constraint, of contradictions, and I had no way to describe or theorize what was crucial. What was crucial were the very deliberate, willful, intentional actions that people were making in the face of the expectation that they consent to their own elimination as a people, that they consent to having their land taken, their lives controlled, and their stories told for them.

Refusal was a stance but also a theory of the political that was being pronounced over and over again. It emerged in my own writing through observation of Kahnawà:ke action, but also through their words. I would hear "enough is enough," "it's not us, it's them," "the white man put that there, not us" – on the international [US–Canadian] border. The people of Kahnawà:ke used every opportunity to remind non-Native people that this is not their land, that there are other political orders and possibilities. This meant longer waits at borders, awkward (to say the least) interactions with cashiers, as well as difficult personal decisions. I also saw that these matters of moral and political habit were articulated quite perfectly to larger actions by the Iroquois Confederacy through time, to broader efforts to demand recognition of existing agreements, as well as refusals to play various games. Among these games is citizenship: voting, paying taxes – actions that would move Mohawks out of their own sovereignty into settler citizenship and into the promise of whiteness. All of this pointed *analytically* to the deeply unequal scene of articulation that people were thrown into and remaking through the quotidian and the grand. This deeply unequal scene of articulation that I am describing may be understood as the settler-colonial present. How, then, do those who are targeted for elimination, those who have had their land stolen from them, their bodies and their cultures worked on to be made into something else articulate their politics? How can one articulate political projects if one has been offered a half-life of civilization in exchange for land? These people have preexisting political traditions to draw from – so how do they, then, do things? They refuse to consent to the apparatuses of the state. And in time with that, I refused then, and still do now, to tell the internal story of their struggle. But I consent to telling the story of their constraint.

This relationship between refusal and consent became the point to needle through and then stitch with. Part of the context for this argument is "let's not pretend that there is an even playing field for interpretation, let's not pretend that the Iroquois are not already prefigured, that their actions are going to be interpreted fairly *or* that we do not push on all of these processes in a *full-court press*." So I refused to be *that* thick description prosemaster who would reveal in florid detail the ways in which these things were being sorted out. As such, my ethnographic refusal operated at the level of the text: it was deliberate, it was willful, it was – like the people I was working with and the process I was documenting – very aware of its context of articulation. That context includes a settler suspicion of Indigenous peoples, and at times, as we saw during the so-called Oka Crisis of 1990, a deep hatred for Mohawks.

How then to describe or theorize that which is cognizant of its own space of articulation? The history that governs apprehension? This was also a way of listening that opened up a theoretical possibility for imagining and writing the political *ethnographically*. Here was a writing strategy and an analytic that stood outside the repetitive stance of resistance, which again overinscribed the state with its power to determine what mattered (Abu-Lughod 1990), which treated domination as an all-encompassing frame for action and treated engagements with it as one-up events, or concealed acts of sly, double-meaning subterfuge (Scott 1990). Here refusal offers its own structure of apprehension that maintains and produces sociality through time, manifest in a political posture of acute awareness of the conditions of this production. Settler colonialism is not eventful; it is enduring, it has its own structure and logic and refusal as well, operating like a grammar and posture that sits through time. It is a politics deeply cognizant of its own production, of the never-ending nature of inequity and the need to stay the course. So refusal availed itself through the research and helped as well in thinking beyond what counted through the channel of recognition (Coulthard 2014; Povinelli 2002; Simpson 2014) while pointing to the overly determined, effective capacity of the state.

The people I worked with and belong to know all this, and of course they know this in stratified ways. The condition of Indigeneity *globally* is to know this. Indigenous peoples are grappling with the fiction of justice while pushing for justice. So this is not particular to Kahnawà:ke or to Haudenosaunee peoples (McCarthy 2016) and can be found in Indigenous ethnography and cultural criticism elsewhere. In her book *The White Possessive*, Aileen Moreton-Robinson (2015) revisits the interpretive debate between Gananath Obesekeyere and Marshall Sahlins on the right way to think about Captain Cook's interpretation by Kanaka Maoli – was he a god, was he an invader? How did "the Natives" think about him? This was a tired exchange that met on the terrain of questions of structure. Moreton-Robinson revisits it with those that saw Cook and their stories of his arrival on another Indigenous coast. Her presentation and analysis of the narratives offer a gorgeous triangulation between accounts and a variance in interpretation. She centers the Bubu Gujin elder Hobles's version, as told to Deborah Bird Rose: "I know you been stealing country belong to mefellow, Australia. What we call Australia, that's for Aboriginal people. But him been take it away. You been take the land, you been take the mineral, take the gold, everything. Take it up this big England" (Moreton-Robinson 2015, 117). Suddenly "how 'Natives' think" (Sahlins 1995) is not a presumptive claim of interpretive ownership; it is a statement of theft, in raw form.

What does one do with this sort of knowledge? If such histories animate the consciousness of your people, do you then consent to notions of just law, of just governance? Of the *lawful* theft of your land? It is just this sort of cognizance of differing social and historical facts that make for the posture of refusal. Refusal holds on to a truth, structures this truth as stance through time, as its own structure and comingling with the force of presumed and inevitable disappearance and operates as the revenge of consent – the consent to these conditions, to the interpretation that this was fair, and the ongoing sense that this is all over with. When I deploy the term *revenge*, I am hailing historical consciousness. As such it is a manifestation of deep awareness of the past, of, for example, theft, in raw form. We see this with Hobles, who asserts this knowledge against the grain of presumed fairness, of justice, of settled affairs. As such this consciousness *avenges* the prior – the deep inequities of interpretation that structure the sense of settlement, of matters that are done. Revenge does not mean individuated harm inflicted on a perpetrator in a transaction that renders justice. In my usage here, I mean avenging a prior of injustice and pointing to its ongoing life in the present. This refusal to let go, to roll over, to play this game, points to its presumptive falsity of contractual thinking. With this, the notion of two parties knowingly abstracting themselves out of their own context to contract into an agreement. So-called treaties are the paradigmatic imagination of the social contract in the New World (North American variant) and are in many cases the foundational document of colonial recognition, the mechanism by which Indigenous nationhood is first recognized and affirmed.

The matter of *postcolonial* frankly eludes the North American case: "They" never left; the Native never disappeared. Treaties are central to contractual thinking in Native history and politics, regardless of the fact that most treaties were for land cessions, and many were signed under duress. These conditions were sometimes so forceful that if they were actually conditions of equal standing, they probably still would not have been signed in the first place. Yet they represent legal forms of incontrovertible rights to land, to resources, to jurisdiction. Regardless of intent, regardless of interpretation, they represent agreement and recognition; they are forms of covenant-making that bind. And that is where consent is bound with recognition and its refusal, symptomatic of truth itself and a mechanism for other possibilities.

I want to turn now to a different anthropological case to define and theorize refusal further. In *Barrio Libre: Criminalizing States and Delinquent Refusals of the New Frontier*, Gilberto Rosas (2012) takes on the structuring role of neoliberalism and capitalism in the production of criminals. His interlocutors are Mexican youth who are pushed and moved through borders not of their making. They move through sewers, through filth, in passages that are dangerous, and which hold nothing for them, it seems, but uncertainty on the other side. Yet they move, and their posture is one of nonconsent, as well as, at times, flagrant and ostentatious cruelty. They call themselves Barrio Libre, denizens of the free neighborhood. This is a space without constraint under conditions of "neo-liberal sovereignty-making" (Rosas 2012, 100), a sovereignty-making that is incomplete, that in its commitment to free trade and not people, cooks people in the desert. This militarization and violent precarity of life's passage (and possible death, horrible death, body-slicing death through or beyond the border) is what Rosas (2012, 105) names neoliberal sovereignty's incomplete but "violent affirmation." In spite of the precarity of life through the border, the youth with whom Rosas worked feel freedom – deeply, linguistically, behaviorally. Their own force on others is a manifestation of this unvanquished and internal script of refusal. Here Rosas (2012, 109) describes their geopolitics, their mapping, and their stance: "Barrio Libre was more than a free-floating geography, superimposed over a dominant one ... to belong to it was an expansive, furious refusal of normativity, an enraged subversion of the respective sovereignties of the U.S. and Mexico that seeped from under the new frontier."

What of these politics? Is this an agreed-upon resistance? Is this resilience, with lives and bodies contorting to withstand and accommodate pain and structures of injustice? They inflict pain. They walk through shit to get to where they are going. They get arrested. They get deported. They run and climb and get killed, fleeing from officers. Their refusal to see this condition as anything other than a state of freedom is a refusal for us of the easy answer, of a structure of consent, of ease. There is nothing easy in what I have charted out in this brief thesis on refusal. Rosas's interlocutors smash these categorical imperatives – what I want to call "the easy answers." The people I work with refuse the eliminatory efforts of the state. They operate as nationals in a scene of wardship and dispossession. They differ from Rosas's interlocutors, but they operate from a similar and flagrantly self-assured position, and from an impossible-to-record, or to analyze, easy answer. My ethnographic prerogative is to make the practice of ethnography itself a refusal in time with theirs.

REFERENCES

Abu-Lughod, Lila. 1990. "The Romance of Resistance: Tracing Transformations of Power through Bedouin Women." *American Ethnologist* 17 (1): 41–55. http://doi.org/10.1525/ae.1990.17.1.02a00030.

Coulthard, Glen Sean. 2014. *Red Skin, White Masks: Rejecting the Colonial Politics of Recognition*. Minneapolis: University of Minnesota Press.

McCarthy, Theresa. 2016. *In Divided Unity: Haudenosaunee Reclamation at Grand River*. Tucson: University of Arizona Press.

Moreton-Robinson, Aileen. 2015. *The White Possessive: Property, Power, and Indigenous Sovereignty*. Minneapolis: University of Minnesota Press.

Povinelli, Elizabeth A. 2002. *The Cunning of Recognition: Indigenous Alterities and Australian Multiculturalism*. Durham: Duke University Press.

Rosas, Gilberto. 2012. *Barrio Libre: Criminalizing States and Delinquent Refusals of the New Frontier*. Durham: Duke University Press.

Sahlins, Marshall. 1995. *How "Natives" Think: About Captain Cook, For Example*. Chicago: University of Chicago Press.

Scott, James C. 1990. *Domination and the Arts of Resistance: Hidden Transcripts*. New Haven: Yale University Press.

Simpson, Audra. 2014. *Mohawk Interruptus: Political Life Across the Borders of Settler States*. Durham: Duke University Press.

On Critical Theory for the Twenty-First Century

THE SOCIAL CONTEXT

If we do our jobs well, the next generation of anthropologists (that's you) will challenge us. You will build on the strengths of our work and address its limitations. You will broaden the relevance and responsibility of our discipline or dismantle it altogether. You will be bolder, clearer, and more critical. In recent years, graduate students in anthropology have opposed exploitative labor practices, questioned the politics of peer review and academic citation, and demanded better representation from their universities and textbooks, among many other things. How do the politics of academic work influence anthropological theory building and vice versa? And what directions do we (the older generation) envision for future critical anthropological theory?

The pieces in this section remind us that academic production in general, and anthropological work in particular, is fraught with the same hegemonic norms and political challenges that anthropologists research and write about. This context differently shapes anthropological products such that they can be more or less politicized, more or less reflexive, more or less critical, helpful, and generous. In the spirit of advancing our discipline in community-minded ways, the essays here offer some blueprints for future builders of anthropological thought.

THE CONVERSATION

The first piece, by our very own Lynn Bolles, traces a genealogy of Black feminist thought back to anthropology's earliest Black women scholars. Bolles shows how, even though many of these scholars did not directly address gender inequity in their research and writing, they laid a foundation for subsequent Black feminist anthropological theory. Bolles also discusses the silencing and erasure of Black women in anthropology, revealing the ways in which academic practices such as funding, mentorship, and citation can reproduce (or challenge) categorical inequalities.

Our second essay is by Leith Mullings, who urges anthropologists to undertake and value research and writing on racism and racial projects – those implemented "from above" as well as those cultivated "from below" – and to recognize the role that racism continues to play in shaping the discipline. Mullings also offers a compelling reminder that structural problems such as racism, while ubiquitous and powerful, are not inevitable but rather contingent upon human actions – our future rests on "the agency of people," she writes, with important implications for anthropological projects.

Ghassan Hage authored Reading 14.3, which argues that we should think of theoretical paradigms as sets of tools to be used selectively when helpful, rather than as ideologies that either demand allegiance or deserve disdain. Hage also encourages anthropologists to think "in terms of a labour theory of value" to encourage a respect of and generosity toward theory production.

The fourth essay, by Jeff Maskovsky, explores the meanings of home in relation to an "end-times" imaginary, in which it is increasingly difficult to envision or plan for an uncertain future. Contextualizing the neoliberal housing market, "bunker" mentalities, and antiforeclosure movements in a broader framework of end-times politics, Maskovsky attends to the political possibilities presented by a future-less present. As with the other pieces in this section, Reading 14.4 also asks us to consider anthropology's own "ends": both temporally, as in envisioning a future without anthropology, and in our ever-changing expectations for anthropological inquiry.

Our final essay is by Kim TallBear, who offers a critical appraisal of anthropological narratives that laud liberal multiculturalism and elide the central roles of Indigenous dispossession and genocide in the formation of modern settler states. Putatively progressive critiques of the "erosion" of US democracy, TallBear writes, nostalgically legitimize an idealized US nation-state, sustaining "that fundamental condition of US existence – ongoing Indigenous elimination." Rejecting such hegemonic temptations requires a radical rethinking of our approaches to social organization, such as cultivating kin relations – not national ones – among Indigenous and non-Indigenous peoples. TallBear ends with a reference to "radical hope," a term used by philosopher Jonathan Lear to describe a hope that transcends the boundaries of what is currently known to be possible.

THREE QUESTIONS FOR THE READINGS

1 Using Hage's strategy of selecting what's useful from a theory, choose some "tools" from this section's readings and apply them to your own interests. What can be easily accounted for using these theoretical frames? What is not so easily accounted for?

2 These readings represent the editors' interests and priorities for anthropology. What are yours? What would you edit out of our text and with what would you replace it?

3 Eventually, your generation will train the next generation of anthropologists. How do you anticipate your theoretical concerns and understandings developing over the course of the next 10 years? 20 years? How will you remain open to changing your stance, as Hage urges?

ON THE COMPANION WEBSITE

What it's like to f*ck up as an anthropologist of color, the best AAA presidential address ever, additional readings, and more.

www.anthropologicaltheory.com

14.1. Seeking the Ancestors: Forging a Black Feminist Tradition in Anthropology (2001)

A. Lynn Bolles

What would Black women anthropologists who have passed on, such as Caroline Bond Day, Zora Neale Hurston, Vera Green, and Irene Diggs, or the elders who are still among us, such as Katherine Dunham, say about being included in a discussion of Black feminist anthropology?[1] More likely than not, they would remind us that we cannot make the historical record say what it does not – nor can we make them say what they have not. Although each of these women clearly understood her situation as a woman, not all of them interpreted that experience as one of "domination"; rather, some saw being a woman as *difference* in its most mild form, or as a practice of social asymmetry, with each gender playing a traditional rule.

In this day of women and gender studies programs, such a perspective is untenable. Yet, the historical record tells us that for some women, in particular Black women, gender oppression has not placed high in their list of priorities, neither has it always served as the focal point of their scholarship and their activism. Despite this historical gender-neutral stance, the experiences and plights of these Black women anthropologists have been the seeds from which the current Black feminist tradition in anthropology has germinated. Further, whether or not they acknowledge themselves to be our intellectual forebears, those of us who consider ourselves Black feminist anthropologists have found inspiration and solace in their scholarship, and in the compromises and contradictions with which they were confronted for daring to declare themselves "Black" or "Negro" women anthropologists.

[...] For almost as long as there have been graduates of anthropology departments, there have been Black women who studied this field of inquiry. Most have yet to be acknowledged in the most recent canon-setting texts of the discipline, and few are recognized by the field – notwithstanding the election of the Black woman anthropologist Yolanda Moses in

---

1 Katherine Dunham was alive at the time this essay was written. She died five years later, on May 21, 2006.

1995 as president of the American Anthropological Association. [... From the 1840s] until the 1980s, the number of Black women in the discipline has not moved beyond the low double digits. Despite being few in number, Black women have been an integral part of the intellectual and knowledge production traditions of American anthropology, contributing innovations in innumerable ways.

[...] Before the 1980s, the presence of Black women in anthropology could be viewed as underscoring the liberal agenda of the field in general and the academy at large. This agenda contained enough symbolic land mines, however, to make most departments and institutions unhealthy places for these early pioneers. Their very presence raised havoc in a number of ways throughout departments across the country. What makes their story most poignant, though, is their silencing in the ways that "count."

[...] The intersection of the African American anthropological tradition and feminism has matured in the rather sophisticated way often fostered by oppression, and it is out of the ensuing tension that Black feminist anthropology has grown. In effect, Black women in anthropology came to feminism not because of what they found there, but because of what they felt they could contribute to the analysis of gender inequality. Most often this meant paying greater attention to the interactiveness and simultaneity of race, class, and gender. As products of the 1960s, and often as political workers inside and outside of the academy, Black feminists constructed an approach to race, class, and gender that brought it all home – linking anthropologists in a more integral way to the communities in which they worked and inviting the communities to speak back to anthropology. [Leith] Mullings asserts that it was her search for child care that brought class, race, and gender issues together in a very personal way, while for Johnnetta Cole it was conducting research in Cuba, where because institutional racism was outlawed, she was able to see sexism operating in more blatant, fundamental ways.

The thread that connects Black feminist theorizing both inside and outside anthropology is the concept of "the simultaneity of oppression." That is, race, class, gender are conceptualized as combining in various ways that are always historical and contextual. Following Rose Brewer's lead and the "simultaneity of oppression" mode, I suggest that to theorize about the simultaneity of oppression and struggle leads to an understanding of the embeddedness and relationality of race, class, and gender in a synergistic way. Furthermore, the analysis and description of the lived experiences, historical positioning, cultural perceptions, and social construction of Black women (who are enmeshed in and whose ideas emerge out of that experience) result in a feminism whose organizing principle is one firmly rooted in class, culture, gender, and race interacting. Black feminism, then, is an anthropologist's theoretical dream come true.

Contributing to this synergistic approach – yet complicating it too – is the fact that the researcher and those under study often have much in common as a result of these matrices of domination. Conducting fieldwork, especially with other Black or nonwhite women, demands that the Black feminist anthropologist be simultaneously analytical, political, and reflexive. Patricia Hill Collins's work on Black women's standpoint theory provides the necessary context for understanding this type of interaction between the Black feminist anthropological researcher and the women she encounters in the fieldwork situation. It is in the synthesis of the Black feminist concept of the simultaneity of oppression with the African American anthropological tradition that the foundation for contemporary Black feminist anthropology becomes evident. However, the time prior to the articulation of this gendered theoretical perspective is the entry point for Black women ancestors and elders. Trying to derive some meaning out of and some understanding of why [early Black women anthropologists Caroline Bond Day, Vera Green, and Irene Diggs] failed to prioritize gender or study sexual inequality enables us to historicize how theoretical perspectives are sometimes born out of omissions and silences.

[...] One thing that can be said about history is that it does not always cooperate. Trying to extract a feminist past from these women [Bond Day, Green, Diggs, and Zora Neale Hurston] may seem like an impossible task, for although they all might have agreed with the concept of simultaneous oppression, it is unlikely that they would have made use of this approach in their own scholarship. Yet, despite their unwillingness to position themselves within a feminist perspective, I argue that they can and should be claimed as predecessors to the existing Black feminist anthropology tradition that is alive and well in the discipline today. In claiming them, however, I realize that I risk accusations of revisionist history – but history is, after all, a matter of interpretations.

Nineteenth-century Black women public speakers and writers such as Ida B. Wells and Victoria Earle Matthews worked as individuals and leaders in the Black clubwomen movements, expressing their own personal sentiments about being Black and female. The next generation of Black women anthropologists heard the call to feminism – a personal and political stance – because of the circumstances of their own lives or as a result of fieldwork experience.

What is unique about the Black feminist perspective is its collective expression, which first surfaced in the early 1970s with Toni Cade Bambara's classic, *The Black Woman*. This anthology of writings by artists, social scientists, and activists examined how the Civil Rights movement was responsible for a heightened racial consciousness while the women's movement raised gender consciousness. As Blacks and as women, the contributors brought a new level of personal and political awareness to the forefront of thinking and activism.

In a chapter of her volume *Conversations*, aptly titled "Between a Rock and a Hard Place: On Being Black and a Woman," Cole provides observations, analyses, and specific reasons for how feminism can be understood within a Black American cultural context. Weaving together ideas rooted in history, popular culture, and sociocultural beliefs, Cole provides a useful framework for why feminism should not be viewed solely as a white woman's issue but rather as an ideology capable of encapsulating the experiences of Black women and other women of color. She posits that the issues addressed by feminism groups are ones that contribute to the welfare of all women. Commenting on the merits of the term *womanist*, coined by novelist Alice Walker, Cole argues that the word has cultural roots that make it more embraceable by Black women than the term *feminist*.

What separates the two terms is not the common goal of enhancing women's lives but the social and historical realities that differentiate Black women's and white women's lives. These differences do not make the task of finding a cure for racism and sexism any less difficult, but they do require different strategies. When Black women describe and analyze cultures and societies with a gendered approach, using the variety of tools, methods, and theories at their disposal, the differing realities of women and men surface. When the scholarship, lives, and experiences of Black women who are also anthropologists are examined using similar gendered understandings, the personal does become political. It is in the intensity and determination that these ancestors and elder [Katherine Dunham] directed toward finding a cure for racism that their work becomes a personal political act. When they entered a room, not only did the entire race enter but so did their womanhood and their anthropological expertise.

Women ancestors such as Day, Diggs, Dunham, Green, and Hurston can be claimed by those of us forging a Black feminist anthropology tradition because they had to contend with sexism as well as racism. Whether they chose to make the eradication of sexism a part of their activist scholarship is unimportant, given the historical period in which they lived and worked. Rather, what is most valuable is that even in the silence to which they were relegated by the discipline, the fact of their presence unlocked the door for subsequent generations of Black women intellectuals, trained as anthropologists and following in the African American vindicationist intellectual tradition, to enter the room and create their own place.

14.2. Interrogating Racism: Toward an Antiracist Anthropology (2005)

Leith Mullings

THE FUTURE OF RACE

Over one hundred years ago, African American sociologist W.E.B. Du Bois (1903) made the prescient observation that "The problem of the twentieth century is the problem of the color line – the relations of the darker to the lighter races of men in Asia and Africa, in America and the islands of the sea" (p. 8).

To what extent will race continue to be a central organizing principle in defining difference and rationalizing inequality in human societies?

Given the complexity and mutability of race and racism, it is not surprising that scholars disagree about its future. For example, although Winant (2001) predicts that race has become a permanent feature of human existence for the foreseeable future and that the most we can hope for is to reduce the degree of stratification and injustice that accompanies it, others emphasize racism's mutating, chameleonlike character (Fredrickson 2002, Gould 1996). Still others suggest that class will supersede race in social significance (Wilson 1978).

The contemporary global capitalist social order is characterized by competing and contradictory tendencies. As the redistributive functions of the nation state decline, and as millions of people cross borders to compete for limited jobs and resources in contexts of rising inequality and stratification, we have witnessed race making of various sorts intensify. Conversely, we are also confronted by corporate multiculturalism, "a global capitalism that draws no color line, because it seeks customers and collaborators from every race" (Fredrickson 2002, p. 148), although the real elite continue to be predominantly white and the disfranchised and socially stigmatized are predominantly racialized people.

The different logics of state capitalism, imperial interests, and transnational capital may work together or be at odds in race making. These conditions make it difficult to predict whether racialization will continue to be useful or even who will be racialized. If Harvey (2003) is correct that the coupling of nationalism and imperialism cannot be accomplished without resorting to racism, race making may mutate along lines of "civilizational conflicts" (Mamdani 2002). However, anthropologists have generally been fairly clear that the future of race is not predetermined: Ultimately the answer does not rest primarily on world structures but with the agency of people.

CONTEMPORARY ANTIRACISMS

Neoliberal racism, like neoliberalism, appears to be a hegemonic global project but is unstable and uneven. Within these spaces, contestatory projects emerge.

The enduring duality of race lies in the complicated fact that race is always simultaneously imposed from above and experienced from below; the imposition of race inevitably creates the structural context for producing oppositional sites of resistance as well as creative spaces for the articulation of subaltern consciousness, culture, and opposition. Race thus potentially becomes a space for resistance and counter-narrative. Although some observers of antiracism question the perceived contradictions of racially based mobilizations, most contemporary interpretations provide concepts that illuminate racism's complex reality. The concept of structural racism, "which refers to the dynamics of economic and social institutions through which racialised groups become systematically marginalized or excluded" (Stavenhagen 1999, p. 9) belies the easy distinction between "identity politics" or interest groups and movements directed toward transformative social change. Frequently, although not always, antiracist social movements combine class and race concerns. The notion of "racial project" (Omi & Winant 2002) captures the efforts of social groups to reorganize and redistribute resources along racial lines. This underscores the important point that racial projects may either reproduce or disrupt existing inequalities, opening up the space to define racial projects as resistance. Similarly, the distinction between "racial assignment" and "ethnoracial identification" allows for a more textured understanding of race (Brodkin 2001, p. 368).

Globalization also creates new possibilities for transnational antiracist organizing through building coalitions and alliances, networking, and implementing reform legislation. With the growth of an international labor force and the unwillingness and/or inability of states to address grievances through redistributive justice, there is an increasing awareness among antiracist movements that they must interface globally. The diversity of antiracist strategies and interventions derive, in part, from the local specificity of conditions but also from differing ideological perspectives among antiracist activists about the cause, nature, and future of racism, the level at which racism is shaped, and the most effective means of confronting it.

There is a wide array of coalitional activities, which address such issues as police harassment, racist violence, social services, voting rights, racist social movements, and immigration rights (e.g., Anthias & Lloyd 2002, Bowser 1995a). These projects have utilized a variety of antiracist strategies, policies, and practices, including individual antiracist interventions, public policy demands, and legislative reforms that may include specific compensatory measures, e.g., affirmative action, restitution (for example, of land rights), or reparations. Some have been controversial. Scholars have questioned the value of individual antiracist training and workshops in the absence of more structural interventions (Srivastava 1996). Similarly, demands for compensatory measures, such as reparations, are highly debated. Despite the successful campaigns for reparations on behalf of Jews and Japanese Americans, some experts raise doubts about African and African diasporic populations because, by contrast, they are thought to be unusually complex (Barkan 2000). Conversely, Corlett (2003) and Marable (2002) make a compelling case for U.S. reparations to Native Americans and African Americans. Recently, antiracist movements in Europe, drawing heavily on United Nations declarations and resolutions, have been involved in continental campaigns calling for the implementation of antidiscrimination policies. Although limited as remedies in themselves, such efforts have served as important organizing tools (Lusane 2004; see also Banton 1996).

In the 1980s and 1990s, counter-hegemonic social movements framed in the language of race and racism emerged, making claims on resources, forming unprecedented transnational alliances, and challenging racialization from above – a process we might call "racialization from below" (Mullings 1997, p. 4). The struggles against racism in the United States and South Africa have been important templates for other movements around the world and Afro-diasporic networks have significantly increased their scope, levels of activity, and transnational projects (e.g., Minority Rights Group 1995). The development of these organizations and movements has been particularly striking in areas such as Latin America, where ideologies glorifying race mixture and the lack of legal segregation have previously inhibited such movements, in contrast to the racial segregation of the United States and South Africa, where there have been longstanding movements for racial equality.

On the other side of the world, Australian aborigines are also incorporating a language of race to affirm their oppositional identity (Cowlishaw 2000). Within the United States, there is a growing movement among some Puerto Rican and Dominican youth to reaffirm belonging to an African diaspora, a Latin "double consciousness" (Flores 2002, p. 48; see also Aparicio 2004). Popular culture plays a strategic though controversial role, creating and sustaining Afro-descendant identities and establishing belonging to a larger African diaspora. The adoption and indigenization of popular cultural forms, such as hip-hop (Codrington 2001, Olavarria 2002, Wade 2002), and the incorporation and exchange of various musical forms of the diaspora provide mediums for diasporic communication and sometimes for counter-hegemonic organization.

Likewise, indigenous populations have become more successful in their attempts at hemispheric organizing since the pivotal 1991 meeting in Quito, Ecuador, attended by representatives of 120 indigenous organizations and nations (Delgado 2002). Clearly the role of new communications technology has been particularly important in the circulation of international production and mutual assistance. As a result of these activities and mobilizations, in the past two decades, many Central and Latin American nations, including Brazil, Bolivia, Colombia, and Nicaragua, have passed legislation recognizing their multicultural populations and, in some instances, granting constitutional rights and land titles (Wade 1997, 2002).

The 2001 United Nations World Conference Against Racism was an important point at which these nascent movements began to converge (see Turner 2002). One of the guiding themes of the conference, "global apartheid" (see Booker & Minter 2001) was notable in providing an analysis that eschewed an essentialist concept of race, utilizing a language that called for the global redistribution of resources. The Durban conference moved toward a perspective linking subaltern populations not by race but by the transnational processes of racialization (Mullings 2004, p. 8).

As states increasingly incorporate the language of the opposition through formulations of multiculturalism (see Benavides 2004), to what extent will emphasis on culture and representation overshadow demands for resources? Hale (2002) suggests that state-endorsed discourses of multiculturalism support the politics of recognition, while sidetracking movements that simultaneously contest representation and distribution: "[M]ulticulturalism, I contend is the *mestizaje* discourse for the new millennium ..." (p. 491). Anthropologists have been ambivalent about their complicated roles, and some have raised questions about the extent to which anthropological constructions have contributed to essentializing populations (Briggs 2001, Ramos 1998). Others suggest that subaltern populations have been able to use anthropological information to support their assertions of group distinctiveness in their bids for land and resources and that anthropological critiques of essentialist notions of race can also undermine ethnic mobilizations (Wade 1995).

Underlying these concerns is the complex challenge of forging antiracist work to the broader project of creating a more equitable society across borders of race, class, gender, and national identity. It is noteworthy that, although the Brazilian antiracist movement accelerated during the late 1990s under the centrist government of former President Fernando Henrique Cardosa, more recently, with the ruling leftist Workers Party, Afro-Brazilians have achieved major gains in recognition of discrimination, antidiscriminatory legislation, and affirmative action (Gilliam 2003).

ANTHROPOLOGY AND ANTIRACISM: AN AGENDA

What can we definitively say about racism? Racism is a relational concept. It is a set of practices, structures, beliefs, and representations that transforms certain forms of perceived differences, generally regarded as indelible and unchangeable, into inequality. It works through modes of dispossession, which have included subordination, stigmatization, exploitation, exclusion, various forms of physical violence, and sometimes genocide. Racism is maintained and perpetuated by both coercion and consent and is rationalized through paradigms of both biology and culture. It is, to varying degrees at specific temporal and spatial points, interwoven with other forms of inequality, particularly class, gender, sexuality, and nationality.

What must anthropologists address regarding racism and its consequences? First, we must begin to critically scrutinize our own discipline. Blakey (1994, p. 280) observes that "there is a tendency within the profession of anthropology for its practitioners to deny the pervasiveness of racism in its own history and to attribute racist thinking to aberrant individuals." Similarly Mukhopadhyay & Moses (1997) suggest that anthropology needs to confront its history of helping to "erect the ideological edifice of racism and biological determinism." Anthropology is one of the least integrated disciplines (Gonzalez 2002,

Shanklin 2000), with archeology (and no doubt physical anthropology) being 99.9% Euro American (Blakey 1997). In this regard, it is important for anthropologists to understand and act on the difference between diversity and affirmative action. Although both goals are laudable, diversity measures do not necessarily address the historical injustices of racism, although affirmative action does provide diversity.

It is also important to confront the manner in which race, class, and gender shape the production of knowledge. For example, Bolles (2001) asserts that even among some feminist anthropologists, the work of black feminists is undervalued because of its antiracist agenda. We must give attention to restructuring our textbooks and to interrogating our approaches to pedagogy. Shanklin's (1998) analysis of cultural anthropology textbooks found that only 4 out of 11 textbooks dealt with racism and that students in introductory courses may be taught about race but are generally not taught about racism.

All this will necessitate a radical reappropriation of the concept of culture. The limitations of the Boasian approach to culture, with its many confluences, its ahistoricity, and its lack of groundedness in processes of economy and power have allowed it to become essentialized, doing the work of race (Brodkin 2001, Visweswaran 1998). We see this in the culture of poverty or underclass concepts in the United States, in culture as irreconcilable difference embodied in the new racisms of Europe, in color blindness in the United States, as well as in the essentialism of liberal varieties of multiculturalism. An appropriate concept of culture must confront political economy and incorporate relations of power.

At its best, anthropology is uniquely positioned to make a decisive contribution to the critical interrogation of contemporary racism. With its emphasis on underlying social relations and the informal workings of structures, networks, and interactions that produce and reproduce inequality, anthropology has a set of theoretical perspectives and a methodological tool kit that lends itself to interrogation of new forms of structural racism and to unmasking the hidden transcripts of the process through which difference is transformed into inequality. This enterprise demands longterm ethnographic and historical research into the complicated representations, institutions, and practices through which racism is continuously reproduced, including employment practices, education, housing, environmental racism, and everyday practices, as well as the study of coercion in the form of police brutality and the prison-industrial complex and of consent and privilege in the form of whiteness. It must be grounded in a critical interpretation of race not as a quality of people of color, but as an unequal relationship involving both accumulation and dispossession.

Anthropologists must resist using the passive exonerative voice and name racism and the forces that reproduce it. This requires moving beyond noting that race is socially constructed to confront forthrightly the extent to which structural racism is pervasively embedded in our social system. Anthropological research has the potential to uncover the systemic and dynamic nature of racism and to identify the subterranean mechanisms through which racial hegemony is both perpetuated and deconstructed.

Finally, anthropologists must address the issue of public engagement and praxis. No matter how well we research racism, it will remain largely irrelevant unless we are able to get our analyses out of the academy and into public discourse. Anthropological analyses of antiracism have already effectively shaped contexts for activist initiatives such as desegregation and other social movements. As Baker (1998) observes, as these movements contested racial constructions, they also reshaped the boundaries of anthropology within the academy and presented a different reality to academics, permitting them to reimagine their concepts of race. We need to boldly build on this intellectual tradition and expand it.

REFERENCES

Anthias, F., and C. Lloyd, eds. 2002. *Rethinking Anti-Racisms: From Theory to Practice*. London: Routledge.

Aparicio, A.L. 2004. *Developing Politics in Quisqueya Heights: Local and National Trajectories of Dominican-American Organizing (New York)*. PhD thesis. City Univ. New York.

Baker, L.D. 1998. *From Savage to Negro: Anthropology and the Construction of Race, 1896–1954*. Berkeley: University of California Press.

Banton, M. 1996. *International Action Against Racial Discrimination*. Oxford: Oxford University Press.

Barkan, E. 2000. *The Guilt of Nations: Restitution and Negotiating Historical Injustices*. New York: Norton.

Benavides, O.H. 2004. *Making Ecuadorian Histories: Four Centuries of Defining Power*. Austin: University of Texas Press.

Blakey, M.L. 1994. Passing the Buck: Naturalism and Individualism as Anthropological Expressions of Euro-American Denial. In *Race*, edited by S. Gregory and R. Sanjek, 270–84. New Brunswick: Rutgers University Press.

Blakey, M.L. 1997. "Past Is Present: Comments on 'In the Realm of Politics: Prospects for Public Participation in African-American Plantation Archaeology.'" *Historical Archaeology* 31 (3): 140–5. https://doi.org/10.1007/BF03374237.

Bolles, A.L. 2001. "Seeking the Ancestors: Forging a Black Feminist Tradition in Anthropology." In *Black Feminist Anthropology: Theory, Politics, Praxis and Poetics*, edited by I. McClaurin. New Brunswick: Rutgers University Press.

Booker, S., and W. Minter. 2001. "Global Apartheid." *The Nation*, 9 July, p. 11.

Bowser, B.P., ed. 1995a. *Racism and Anti-Racism in World Perspective*. Thousand Oaks: Sage.

Briggs, C.L. 2001. "Modernity, Cultural Reasoning, and the Institutionalization of Social Inequality: Racializing Death in a Venezuelan Cholera Epidemic." *Comparative Studies in Society and History* 43 (4): 665–700. https://doi.org/10.1017/S0010417501004297.

Brodkin, K. 2001. "Diversity in Anthropological Theory." In *Cultural Diversity in the United States: A Critical Reader*, edited by I. Susser and T.C. Patterson, 365–88. Malden: Blackwell.

Codrington, R.G. 2001. *Sessions from the Big Smoke: Rap, Race and Class in London (England)*. PhD thesis. City Univ. New York. 296 pp.

Corlett, J.A. 2003. *Race, Racism, & Reparations*. Ithaca: Cornell University Press.

Cowlishaw, G.K. 2000. "Censoring Race in 'Post-colonial' Anthropology." *Critique of Anthropology* 20 (2): 101–23. https://doi.org/10.1177%2F0308275X0002000201.

Delgado, P.G. 2002. "The Makings of a Transitional Movement." *North American Congress on Latin America Report* 35 (6): 36–8.

Du Bois, W.E.B. 2004 [1903]. *The Souls of Black Folk*, ed. C Lemert. 100th anniv. ed. Boulder: Paradigm.

Flores, J. 2002. "Nueva York-Diaspora City: U.S. Latinos Between and Beyond." *North American Congress on Latin America Report* 35 (6): 46–9.

Fredrickson, G.M. 2002. *Racism: A Short History*. Princeton: Princeton University Press.

Gilliam, A. 2003. "Globalization, Identity, and Assaults on Equality in the United States." *Souls: A Critical Journal of Black Politics, Culture, and Society* 5 (2): 81–106. https://doi.org/10.1080/714044630.

Gonzalez, R.J. 2002. "'Top 10' Anthropology Departments and Underrepresented Minorities." *Anthropology News* Oct., p. 21.

Gould, S.J. 1996 [1981]. *The Mismeasure of Man*. New York: Norton.

Hale, C. 2002. "Does Multiculturalism Menace? Governance, Cultural Rights and the Politics of Identity in Guatemala." *Journal of Latin American Studies* 34 (3): 485–524. https://doi.org/10.1017/S0022216X02006521.

Harvey, D. 2003. *The New Imperialism*. Oxford: Oxford University Press.

Lusane, C. 2004. "Regionalism against Racism: The TransEurope Struggle for Racial Equality." *Souls: A Critical Journal of Black Politics, Culture, and Society* 6 (2): 51–63. http://doi.org/10.1080/10999940490507040.

Mamdani, M. 2002. "Good Muslim, Bad Muslim: A Political Perspective on Culture and Terrorism." *American Anthropologist* 104 (3): 766–75.

Marable, M. 2002. *The Great Wells of Democracy: The Meaning of Race in American Life*. New York: Basic Civitas Books.

Minority Rights Group, eds. 1995. *No Longer Invisible: Afro-Latin Americans Today*. London: Minor.

Mukhopadhyay, C.C., and Y.T. Moses. 1997. "Reestablishing 'Race' in Anthropological Discourse." *American Anthropologist* 99 (3): 517–33. https://doi.org/10.1525/aa.1997.99.3.517.

Mullings, L. 1997. *On Our Own Terms: Race, Class, and Gender in the Lives of African American Women*. New York: Routledge.

Olavarria, M. 2002. "Rap and Revolution: Hip-Hop Comes to Cuba." *North American Congress on Latin America Report* 35 (6): 28–30. https://doi.org/10.1080/10714839.2002.11722523.

Ramos, A.R. 1998. *Indigenism: Ethnic Politics in Brazil*. Madison: University of Wisconsin Press.

Shanklin, E. 1998. "The Profession of the Color Blind: Sociocultural Anthropology and Racism in the 21st Century." *American Anthropologist* 100 (3): 669–79. https://doi.org/10.1525/aa.1998.100.3.669.

Shanklin, E. 2000. "Representations of Race and Racism in American Anthropology." *Current Anthropology* 41 (1): 99–103. http://doi.org/10.1086/300105.

Srivastava, S. 1996. "Song and Dance? The Performance of Antiracist Workshops." *Canadian Review of Sociology* 33 (Aug.): 291–315.

Stavenhagen, R. 1999. "Structural Racism and Trends in the Global Economy." *International Council on Human Rights Policy* 25 (May): 1–17.

Turner, J.M. 2002. "The Road to Durban – and Back." *North American Congress on Latin America Report* 35 (6): 31–5.

Visweswaran, K. 1998. "Race and the Culture of Anthropology." *American Anthropologist* 100 (1): 70–83. https://doi.org/10.1525/aa.1998.100.1.70.

Wade, P. 1995. "The Cultural Politics of Blackness in Colombia." *American Ethnologist* 22 (2): 341–57. http://doi.org/10.1525/ae.1995.22.2.02a00070.

Wade, P. 1997. *Race and Ethnicity in Latin America*. London: Pluto Press.

Wade, P. 2002. "Music and the Formation of Black Identity in Colombia." *North American Congress on Latin America Report* 35 (6): 21–7. https://doi.org/10.1080/10714839.2002.11722522.

Winant, H. 2001. *The World Is a Ghetto: Race and Democracy Since World War II*. New York: Basic Books.

Wilson, W.J. 1978. *The Declining Significance of Race*. Chicago: University of Chicago Press.

14.3. Toward an Ethics of the Theoretical Encounter (2016)

Ghassan Hage

I often reflect with my graduate students on what it means to "encounter, read, critique and make use of theory." Sometimes I offer these reflections in the form of a research subject. Some of its content I deliver as a lecture. The idea of an "encounter" with theory is meant to interpellate those who meet it as they are working on their PhD, *en passant* as it were, and to differentiate such research subjects from those who come to their research already dwelling in a particular theory, reasonably knowledgeable of its beautifully lit spaces as well as its dark corners, its pitfalls as well as its potentialities. An encounter might initiate a dwelling. However, for most PhD students, indeed for most writers, the encounter might vary in duration and intensity, but it will remain just that. And so, it is a kind of practico-ethical disposition toward such an encounter that I try to instill in the students. I like to expand on a few pet ideas of mine, like: "A theory is not a generalization but a generative device"; "theory has exchange value and use value. It can be deployed for its own sake and it can be deployed analytically"; "whenever possible say, I don't find this theory useful, rather than I don't agree, or, this is wrong" – I encourage what I jokingly call a Facebook approach to theory: there's only a like button to use (at least that's how it was until recently). "If you don't like a theory just ignore it. There is no need to scream 'I don't like it' from the rooftops"; "a theory offers a tool or a set of tools. It is neither a church you adhere to nor a football team you support." There is more that I will come to later. A few years ago, I was in a Paris bookshop and by chance I came across Eduardo Viveiros de Castro's (2009) book *Metaphysiques Cannibales*. I began reading it in the bookshop and literally could not put it down. Some parts of it spoke to my concerns more than others, but on the whole I found it a breath of fresh air. Most importantly, I found a number of propositions in the book immensely productive. I could re-think some perennial issues concerning inter-cultural relations in the West and in Israel/Palestine with it and it could help me generate some new insights. I wrote a number of articles, now put together in a book (Hage, 2015), which at least partly touched on this. Slowly, I was being invited here and there to participate on panels discussing the "ontological turn." Almost immediately I found myself returning to my teachings around theory and their pertinence. Everywhere around the world there was always someone to hint with an accusatory tone that I was joining a religious sect called "the ontological turn." And if it is true that some "ontologists" behave like priests of theory, it is the case that some forms of anti-ontologism smack of religious fervor even more. How could I reconcile my known affinity to Bourdieu (1984) with the "ontological turn"? Have I not heard what Latour (2004: 228) and Bourdieu (2004: 26) think of each other? It was very hard to say "I found this or that idea or aspect of the ontological turn useful" without being put in a position where I had to answer a question formulated along the lines of "but how on earth can you believe in x and y," and where believing in x and y – often having something to do with essentialism – never occurred to me. It was as if I couldn't say that I liked the Christian conceptualization of love without being immediately asked "but how on earth can you believe in the Holy Spirit?"

This, of course, immediately brought to my mind that part of my course where I tell students not to think of theory as a church or a football team, but as importantly, it brought to mind the more difficult question that we also deal with: "If theorists think of their theories as a coherent whole, does that mean that it is not rigorous to pick whatever one wishes to pick from a theory?" I tend to tell students that if a theory is a set of tools, one can pick one particular tool from the set without being committed to use the whole set, as long as one understands the ramifications of the particular tool one is using.

Recently, Frederic Jameson (2015: 110) has proposed that if the hero of modernity is the orchestra conductor, the hero of post-modernity is the curator. He also argued that the curator is to the orchestra conductor what the theorist is to the philosopher. Even if it leaves out Marx's idea of the creative theorist as someone who creates fire by rubbing previously opposing theories against each other (Marx and Engels, 1976 [1847]: 320), I still find this idea of theory as a curated collection, as opposed to a symphonic whole, evocative and useful. At the same time, however, I find that it feeds the idea of theory as something one exhibits rather than something that one uses. One inevitably does both with theory but in my class, as most people would, I try to warn against the temptation for theoretical exhibitionism. I see it as partly behind one of the most negative aspect of theorizing, contributing to what I call, paraphrasing Marx, "theoretical fetishism" (1976 [1867]).

There is no doubt that theory is consumed like a commodity in a market-like space in the academic/intellectual world. Theories – like many other commodities – go in and out of fashion. Some become so fashionable that they become a must. Indeed, one can do a whole Bourdieu-ian analysis of the field of theoretical taste. There are orthodoxies and heterodoxies. There are forms of symbolic violence. There are dominant and dominated … and so on. What's more, people do not only make statements about themselves by being for or against theory in general, but they do so by choosing particular theories over others, and, perhaps more importantly, by the way they theorize: some are unsophisticated mimics of others' theories, some are avant-garde theorizers who break new ground and open new horizons. And so, as in any field, and again, as Bourdieu (1984: 467) states, one is classified by their classification. Or to paraphrase this, theorists end up being theorized by their theorization.

Accumulated in the form of cultural capital, theory is more often than not experienced phallically, as a valued possession that one can "show off." And we can move from Bourdieu to Freud's (1961 [1930]: 61) conception of "the narcissism of small differences" for a useful understanding of some of the incredibly affective and over-the-top rivalries that mar the world of theory. The way both some of the producers and consumers of theory differentiate themselves "theoretically" from others, one would think that the fate of the earth is at stake. In Arabic there is a word called "*takhween*," which refers to the tendency to make of any-one we disagree with a traitor of some sort or another such that the differences between us become automatically incommensurable and a matter of life and death. It strikes me that there is a fair bit of that in theoretical positioning. I've gone back to some of my own writ-ings and I can't say that I am not guilty of that too sometimes.

But a Bourdieu-ian or Freudian approach to the marketplace of theory are not the only ones that are productive here – and I am doing a theory of theory here, exemplifying how a theory has to be useful and yield something. One can also usefully approach the "theory as commodity" reality from a Marxist perspective, for theories' appearance on the market and the logic of their production and consumption makes them akin to capitalist commodities. Not least because they are experienced fetishistically in the way Marx analyzed the capitalist commodity in his famous conception of "commodity fetishism." That is, theories appear as relating to each other and are valorized against each other in the very same way Marx under-stood the production and power of the fetish. For him, the world of the capitalist commodity is such that "the products of the human brain appear as autonomous figures endowed with a life of their own, which enter into relations both with each other and with the human race" (Marx, 1976: 165). So, it is with the world of theory, which is the product of human labor (reading, thinking, writing, editing, printing, etc.) but is experienced fetishistically as a prod-uct with intrinsic power that has no relation to the labor that has produced it. It remains a mystery how we academics, who should know from experience how long and how much work it takes to produce a decent sentence on anything, let alone a decent theory, allow our-selves five minutes of reading someone else's work to declare it "rubbish" or "I agree." As with Marx, this fetishism is not the simple product of a mental mistake: once I know "the truth" I'll stop behaving this way. Fetishism for Marx was more like the experience of the sun rising. It was, and I am sorry to use the word if you happen to be sensitive to it, an ontological form of mystification. This was different from the "ruling ideas are the ideas of the ruling classes" con-ception of ideology that invites an epistemological conception of mystification. The latter can be argued and debated against. But with fetishism, no matter how much we are taught that it is the earth orbiting the sun, we will still experience the sun rising. Or as Godelier (1975: 337) put it long ago: "It is not the subject that deceives himself, it is reality that deceives him."

To take this critical approach to theory on board means that it is not so much by preach-ing the right attitude to theory that a diminishing of the unhelpful fetishistic tendencies listed above can come about. Rather, what is needed is a different mode of interaction and a different mode of experience of theory that can allow us to begin the process of de-fetishization. It is in this context that I attempt to workshop theory in a way that high-lights its use value.

First, I encourage researchers to ask: "what has this theory helped me see, understand or explain that I otherwise would not have seen?" At a most immediate level, this is to oppose a common tendency among PhD beginners to use a quote from a theoretician at the end of a paragraph à la "this shows that Ranciere is right when he argues…." Such a form of quoting makes it appear as if the main aim of one's study is to prove a theoretician correct. This is particularly infuriating in anthropology when a thesis is about Africa or the Middle East, as this form of quoting theory at the end of a theory-free account implicitly implies something like: "this shows that Badiou or Bourdieu or Butler well understood the situation in Mozambique without ever bothering to go there."

Second, I encourage people to think in terms of a labor theory of value of the theoretical works they are reading to learn to be respectful of them as works of labor, not as something that just pops up on the theoretical market for your instant enjoyment in a commodity fetishist-mode: "Think how much it takes you to write an idea. Do you like someone reading a couple of paragraphs you have spent many days writing in the two to three minutes it takes to read them, and in those few minutes judging them to be 'wrong,' 'bad' or 'meaningless,' let alone 'stupid' or 'idiotic'?" This labor can be accumulated labor too. Not everyone is as well read and philosophically sophisticated as everyone else. I often sound elitist saying so but I do tell students: "If you are reading a well-established thinker and you feel they need to be given a 101-type lecture in 'social causality,' 'essentialism' or whatever else, you should think twice and three times before doing so, as there is a high chance you have not understood them and it might be useful to read them again."

At the same time, I try to make them read writers who live up to an ethic of critical respect, who even while critical of others respect and value the labor of others and see them as engaged with them in a common pursuit. Not surprisingly this ethic is more present among women/feminist writers – Lauren Berlant (2011), Judith Butler (1990) or Marilyn Strathern (1988) – than in the spaces offered by the Badious, Bourdieus and Latours of the world. I also have my favourites in terms of works that combine respectful attitude to the labor of others and a generative conception of theory attentive to its explanatory yield. I find Evans-Pritchard's (1934) critique of Lévy-Bruhl exemplary in this regard. I also particularly like George Steinmetz's (2007) introduction to his *The Devil's Handwriting* and the way he plays Said (1978) and Bourdieu and Lacan (1991) against each other to help elucidate the logic of German colonialism.

Meanwhile I am continuing with developing what I feel is useful for me to develop with regards to the "ontological turn." First, I am reviewing classic anthropology and sociology to see how the tension between epistemological and ontological perspectivism is played out in those texts. I am hoping that this exercise can help me refine what it means to have an "ontological disposition" both ethnographic and theoretical. Second, I want to continue working on developing the analytical ramifications of "multi-realism": what does it mean to think the co-existence of a multiplicity of realities? There is clearly a multiplicity of ways of thinking that multiplicity: for example, there is a multiplicity based on the senses where hearing, smelling, visual, etc., realities co-exist in a variety of ways. There is multiplicity based on multiple forms of sociality, as I have argued elsewhere using Viveiros de

Castro, Mauss and Lévy-Bruhl (Hage, 2012). There is a multiplicity which is a multiplicity of ecologies, etc. Third, there is an interesting question around how these multiple realities are conceived to co-exist: are they parallel to each other, do they interpenetrate and/or do they intersect? All of these questions themselves are helping me think productively [on] my empirical work on nationalism, racism and multiculturalism and on the diasporic lifeworld.

REFERENCES

Berlant, L. 2011. *Cruel Optimism*. Durham: Duke University Press.
Bourdieu, P. 1984. *Distinction: A Social Critique of the Judgement of Taste*. Cambridge: Harvard University Press.
Bourdieu, P. 2004. *Science of Science and Reflexivity*. Cambridge: Polity.
Butler, J. 1990. *Gender Trouble: Feminism and the Subversion of Identity*. New York: Routledge.
Evans-Pritchard, E.E. 1934. "Levy-Bruhl's Theory of Primitive Mentality." *Bulletin of the Faculty of Arts* 2: 1–36.
Freud, S. 1961. *Civilization and Its Discontents*. New York: W.W. Norton & Company.
Godelier, M. 1975. "Structure and Contradiction in Capital." In *Ideology in the Social Sciences*, edited by R. Blackburn, 334–68. London: Fontana/Collins.
Hage, G. 2012. "Critical Anthropological Thought and the Radical Political Imaginary Today." *Critique of Anthropology* 32 (3): 285–308. http://doi.org/10.1177/0308275X12449105.
Hage, G. 2015. *Alter-Politics: Critical Anthropology and the Radical Imagination*. Melbourne: Melbourne University Press.
Jameson, F. 2015. "The Aesthetics of Singularity." *New Left Review* 92: 101–32.
Lacan, J. 1991. *The Seminar of Jacques Lacan. Book 1: Freud's Papers on Technique, 1953–1954*. New York: W.W. Norton & Company.
Latour, B. 2004. "Why Has Critique Run Out of Steam? From Matters of Fact to Matters of Concern." *Critical Inquiry* 30: 225–48. http://doi.org/10.1086/421123.
Marx, K. 1976. *Capital: A Critique of Political Economy – Vol. 1*. Harmondsworth: Penguin Books.
Marx, K., and F. Engels. 1976. *Collected Works, Vol. 6: Marx and Engels: 1845–1848*. New York: International Publishers.
Said, E. 1978. *Orientalism*. New York: Vintage.
Steinmetz, G. 2007. *The Devil's Handwriting: Precoloniality and the German Colonial State in Qingdao, Samoa, and Southwest Africa*. Chicago: University of Chicago Press.
Strathern, M. 1988. *The Gender of the Gift: Problems with Women and Problems with Society in Melanesia*. Berkeley: University of California Press.
Viveiros de Castro, E. 2009. *Métaphysiques Cannibales*. Paris: Presses Universitaire de France.

14.4. At Home in the End Times

Jeff Maskovsky

This essay explores the politics of "home" in the context of the temporal register of the "end times." By the end times, I mean the current moment of worry, fear, and uncertainty during which the future seems so hopelessly doomed that it is easy to detect a growing sense, across major social and political divisions, that we all might just be better off dwelling only in the present (Žižek 2011). Whereas "home" in the United States was once tied to a future imaginary in which investment and sacrifice were encouraged to generate a future of economic security and familial stability, today home is increasingly disconnected from a prosperous future. Instead, it is seen more and more frequently as an isolated and securitized space, a defensive outpost positioned against a broad range of potentially catastrophic incursions, from cyber bullying to home mortgage default to social upheaval. Micaela di Leonardo has urged scholars to "engage with the details of home in American history" (2004: 140) in order to shed light on the current social order. Building on this insight, I explore the ways that home and homeownership have become freighted to an "end times" imaginary. In particular, I consider what a future-less present might mean politically in the United States, where the pursuit of home has been a dominant precept in a liberal imaginary, with its class- and racial-inflected struggles for rights, recognition, and resources, for well over a century. [...]

In the 2010s, pundits from across the political spectrum advocated for the disconnection of homeownership from the current day pursuit of, and desire for, "the good life" (cf. Berlant 2011; Mühlebach and Allison 2012). On the right, libertarians called for the end of government backing of the 30-year mortgage. In a 2013 editorial in the *Financial Times*, for example, the editorial board criticized then-president Barack Obama (2009–2017) for his support of government-guaranteed mortgages after the 2007 housing collapse. Mortgage subsidies, the editors claimed, give borrowers a "huge subsidy" that "helps insulate middle-class homeowners from the effects of monetary policy, forcing more of the burden of adjustment on to slenderer shoulders." The editors call for the government to get out of the mortgage business (Financial Times 2013). This would, it is imagined, allow the mortgage market to operate more dynamically, and presumably more robustly, on its own, allowing the country to avoid the kind of speculative bubble that contributed to the housing market collapse of 2007–2008. But it would also restrict homeownership to only the most affluent. For their part, pundits on the left also condemned middle-class reliance on home ownership. They worried about the ongoing dangers of predatory lending and, more generally, about the political inertia that is frequently associated with home ownership.

Yet, during the 2010s, there was little political will in the United States for enacting such a proposal or any major policy change, for that matter. Although some might take consolation from this, it is also suggestive of a broader crisis in political authority. Indeed, elected officials and policy makers seemed unable to take political and managerial advantage of crises. This impasse is captured in a 2011 Bloomberg Businessweek Magazine article by Peter Coy, who hoped for a different (more conservative) future of home ownership (Coy 2011). He wrote:

> You'd think the moment for radical thinking would be upon us. But despite daily reminders of the current cataclysm – new home sales are running at the lowest rate since the 1950s – there's a good chance that the future of mortgages will be just a slightly modified version of the present … the challenge is to use this housing crisis to achieve change as effectively as FDR used the last one. (Coy 2011)

Another related concern is what Wall Street analysts call "mortgage lock." This is the worry that the low mortgage rates – a major consequence of monetarist strategies used by the Federal Reserve after 2008 to boost the economy in the absence of robust fiscal stimulus – would "lock" homeowners into their present homes, once mortgage rates rise in the future. This will make future homes too expensive, producing a perpetually weak home mortgage market. More broadly, it threatens white collar mobility, which has been an essential prerequisite for economic dynamism and robust economic growth especially in the last 30 years and which was a cornerstone of Trump's economic policy.

Locked in time by the inability to imagine the future of the mortgage, and locked in place by mortgage lock, a bunker mentality is increasingly coming to define the American home in the present. Threats to the home abound. The alt-right blogosphere is full of images of armed families standing at the ready by their front doors. On the left, liberal versions of home security involve nanny cams, home security systems, gates, and other technologies designed to prevent predators from entering the home via virtual and other means. The most downloaded free app for 2012 was a sex offender locator app that mapped sex offender registries in residential neighborhoods. There is more overlap between these two defense regimes than might first appear: they both presume that there is an ever-present threat to the home and its contents. Only levels of comfort or discomfort with policing, vigilantism, and the expectations of home itself mark the difference between white nationalist and liberal forms of bunker-ism. [...]

It is possible to see here resonances with a broader end-times imaginary, which appear to emerge from a variety of widely disparate political and social locations. Indeed, it is not unusual to hear "end time" talk on both the left and the right, across the secular and religious divide, and in pop culture in a variety of places. In left quarters, for example, philosopher Slavoj Zizek uses the "end times" to refer to the current period of permanent ecological and political crisis and immanent global economic collapse (Zizek 2011). For many on the religious right, the signs that the "final days" are upon us are being fulfilled daily. And let's not forget the popular cultural obsession, now over a decade old, with the Zombie Apocalypse, the signs of which include an endless stream of popular movies, TV shows, and graphic novels. This kind of thinking became so pervasive that the Center for Disease Control felt compelled to launch a tongue and cheek campaign in 2011 to encourage "Zombie preparedness" because "If you are generally well equipped to deal with a zombie apocalypse you will be prepared for a hurricane, pandemic, earthquake, or terrorist attack" (http://www.cdc.gov/phpr/zombies.htm). The end times appear to be one of the few things that home finance experts, anti-capitalists, eschatologists, social marketers of public health, and *Walking Dead* fans can agree upon. But the point here is not just that some of the most resonant popular cultural, religious, and political themes of the present reflect deeply felt anxieties about an uncertain future. Nor is it that a dystopic zeitgeist has somehow taken hold and is unsurprisingly expressing itself through culturally distinct idioms. Rather, it is that, for many, both the idea and the ideal of the future – of any future, good or bad, utopic or dystopic – is now perhaps in question, and that we are increasingly forced to grapple, culturally and politically, with the prospect of living out our days in a perpetually future-less present (cf. Coronil 2011).

NEW FUTURE-LESS POLITICS ARE NOT NECESSARILY POLITICS WITH NO FUTURE

Yet this bleak view of the future-less home is not the end of the story, and new future-less politics are not necessarily politics with no future. Here I want to briefly discuss two cases of future-less politics. The first is the wave of anti-foreclosure and anti-eviction activism by groups like Occupy Real Estate and Take Back the Land, which were active in high-foreclosure areas across the country during the 2010s. With protesters attempting to block housing auctions of foreclosed homes, and take-over vacant homes, activists have attempted to reclaim and de-commodify privatized spaces – to convert them into various forms of common property. That these efforts are targeted at that most purportedly private of spaces – the home – gives them political and ideological weight that may reverberate far beyond their immediate or practical effects.

Importantly, much of this anti-foreclosure and anti-eviction activism is framed as an end-times endeavor. Drawing on Civil Rights era rhetoric, for example, Take Back the Land activists refer to their foreclosed housing reclamation efforts as "live ins," which, like "sit ins" before them, are conceived more as short-term political tactics than as long term "occupations." What is being emphasized here is the temporary use of vacant properties that the dispossessed must "live in" in order to project a more humane, de-commodified model of home than one rooted in the free market homeownership. Importantly, activists from these movements tend be less interested in long-term take-overs of foreclosed-upon homes than they are in elaborating a vision of affordable housing that transforms the question of ownership. Their goal is to pull unoccupied houses out of housing markets, with their boom-bust temporalities, and place them into land trusts that they imagine to be under *permanent* control of Black, Latinx and other low-income communities. The notion of permanence is quite interesting here. By taking housing out of the market *permanently,* activists are using end-times sensibilities to disrupt the temporal frames for free market homeownership.

And it is not just the left who is finding room for maneuver in the end times. On the East Shore of Staten Island, which has long been a bastion of right-wing urban politics and that was, in 2009, a staging ground for tea party activism, residents spent decades renovating old cottages to pass down to their children. In 2012, Hurricane Sandy destroyed many of them. What is surprising is that in the aftermath of the storm, residents did not ask for government aid to rebuild. Libertarian commitments were not behind this reluctance: in fact, the residents feel that the government misled them about environmental threats, and that because of this they deserve public compensation. But what they wanted instead was cash to buy new homes elsewhere, wherever they wanted. The antidote to catastrophe in this case was liberty exercised with government cash (Checker 2020). The willingness to junk one's home in response to crisis is growing, and we should not presume that it always has tragic consequences. Indeed, defaulting on a home mortgage is an important assertion of freedom, freedom from a debt relationship with a bank, and the fact that defaulting can be done (to some extent) on defaulters' own terms is a worry for many mortgage servicers (Maskovsky 2018). The trick, it seems to me, is not to conflate politics with temporality. In short, politics are not necessarily doomed because they are happening in the end times.

EPILOGUE: ANTHROPOLOGICAL END TIMES?

As with homeownership, anthropology may also be confronting its own ends. Proclamations of our obsolescence give the sense that the discipline may have outlived its usefulness. Many anthropologists defend the discipline in response to assertions such as these: We do good work, we say. And besides, Why should anthropologists join the ranks of the unemployed without a fight? We are certainly no worse on the whole than any other discipline, and far, far better than some. Still, defending anthropology has a price; we risk capitulating to the insidious workings of liberalism, white supremacy and empire by defending the discipline in its status quo form. Instead of defending anthropology, perhaps it might be better to admit the extent to which colonialism continues to haunt it, to consider emancipatory steps we might take to abolish the broader regimes of power of which anthropology is a part, and to repair a world shattered by colonial and imperial violence. This way of thinking has one distinct advantage over the "save the discipline before it dies" strategy: it forces us to ask overtly what parts of anthropology should live on, and in what form, and which we can do without. A bloodbath will surely ensue if we dare to ask about anthropology's virtues and deficits in these stark terms. Still, a new generation of scholars is rethinking anthropology from the ground up and reforming it in drastically new ways, in line with explicitly abolitionist intellectual and political imperatives [see, for example, Jobson (2020) for an influential survey of work done in this vein]. Anti-capitalist, queer, and feminist frames also demand that we reckon with the discipline and question its terms. As we engage with these demands, we might be better off asking what kind of intellectual life we want, rather than worrying narrowly about anthropology's own end times.

REFERENCES

Berlant, Lauren. 2011. *Cruel Optimism*. Durham: Duke University Press.

Checker, Melissa. 2020. *The Sustainability Myth: Environmental Gentrification and the Politics of Justice*. New York: New York University Press.

Coy, Peter. 2011. "The Mortgage of the Future." *Businessweek* (November 10). http://www.businessweek.com/magazine/the-mortgage-of-the-future-11102011.html#p4).

Coronil, Fernando. 2011. "The Future in Question: History and Utopia in Latin America (1989–2010)." In *Business as Usual: The Roots of the Global Financial Meltdown*, edited by Craig Calhoun and Georgi M. Derluguian, 231–92. New York: New York University Press.

Financial Times. 2013. "Junking America's Mortgage Subsidies: Bolder Reform Needed to Cure Addiction to Risky Debt." *Financial Times* (August 7). https://www.ft.com/content/a22281fa-ff6c-11e2-8f25-00144feab7de.

Jobson, R.C. 2020. "The Case for Letting Anthropology Burn: Sociocultural Anthropology in 2019." *American Anthropologist* 122: 259–71. https://doi.org/10.1111/aman.13398.

Maskovsky, Jeff. 2018. "Guilty Subjects: New Geographies of Blame in the Aftermath of the US Housing Market Collapse." In *Handbook of Anthropology and the City*, edited by Setha Low. Abingdon: Routledge.

Mühlebach, Andrea, and Anne Allison. 2012. "Post-Fordist Affect." *Anthropological Quarterly* 85 (2): 317–455.

Žižek, Slavoj. 2011. *Living in the End Times*. London: Verso.

14.5. Caretaking Relations, Not American Dreaming (2019)

Kim TallBear

AMERICAN AND CANADIAN DREAMING IS INDIGENOUS ELIMINATION

We must strike blows whenever possible to the dominant narrative of a multicultural and supposedly progressive (always progressing toward greater good) settler state. That narrative misguides us in our "genius" and in our ability to live with each other. [Author Junot] Díaz explains that he is a child of Blackness, and "Blackness was not meant to survive." Indeed, settler-state dreaming is predicated on the extraction of resources from Black bodies, until they are dead, and from Indigenous lands, thus requiring our death, either literally or symbolically, in order to dispossess Indigenous peoples of our life-giving relations with these lands. Yet just as Díaz reminds us that Black people have survived and sometimes thrive, so have Indigenous peoples.

Yet in the months following the [2016] US election [of Donald Trump], I have read denial after implicit denial of Indigenous presence and experience in this land, including by friends and esteemed colleagues, mostly in the United States but also in Canada. Neil McKay, Spirit Lake Oyate citizen, Turtle Mountain Chippewa descendent, and University of Minnesota Dakota language instructor, opened the American Anthropological Association (AAA) meeting in Minneapolis on November 26, 2016, with a traditional welcome. Just a couple of weeks after Trump's election, McKay pointed out that "our [Dakota] perspective is a little bit different because we have always been here." This moment was not new. He reminded the thousands of anthropologists in that cavernous auditorium of the *ongoing* US American genocide and occupation: "This is Dakota land and you are illegally occupying it." McKay spoke of treaties made between the Dakota and the United States – all violated by the Americans. He challenged people to learn about those treaties. Still, he welcomed people to our homeland, just as our ancestors did. It was so good to hear his words, many of them in Dakota. "We are still here."

The sound of his footsteps still echoed on the stage when the following speaker, an anthropologist in an AAA leadership position and with the greatest of progressive intent,

I am sure, took the microphone. She began to speak of this new and terrifying moment! Like so many other Americans – of all genders and races, religions and persuasions, in the press, on blogs, Facebook, Twitter – she spoke in an alarmist tone of regressed American democracy, of sliding backward, of needing to rally together in progressive action to recover what has been *lost*.

To lament the current moment in a way that dreams of US redemption is to sustain that fundamental condition of US existence – ongoing Indigenous elimination, a genocide that is simultaneously human and other-than-human and that has proceeded apace in the so-called Americas for 527 years and counting. To lament the Trump presidency via recourse to the dream of a better United States, or a better Canada, is to contribute to that elimination. These settler states and Indigenous genocide are co-constitutive. An *explicit* white supremacist inhabits the White House. Again. The United States and Canada celebrate many "founding fathers" who were of the same ilk. But Indigenous elimination did not cease under supposedly more enlightened, even antiracist, presidents or prime ministers. They have all defended inherently eliminatory settler states.

Settler colonialism as a structure must feed off Indigenous dispossession. It is not its only food, but it is a required nutrient. Without it, these states become weakened and will eventually pass away.

Cloaking oneself in a mascot caricature or myths of a Cherokee great-grandmother or Aboriginal ancestor several centuries ago does not undo complicity in eliminatory nationalism. It is yet more elimination. Representational appropriation, like appropriation of land and biological resources (our very DNA), is also a manifestation of White possessiveness, one that simultaneously renders us as fundamentally other according to a binary of alive versus dead/vanishing. [Indigenous Studies Professor Aileen] Moreton-Robinson explains, "At an ontological level, the structure of subjective possession occurs through the imposition of one's will-to-be on the thing that is perceived to lack will, thus it is open to being possessed." It is key to this line of thought that Indigenous people are often referenced as being "close to nature," for as Moreton-Robinson points out: "Being perceived as living in a state of nature relegates one's existence to being an inseparable part of nature and therefore incapable of possessing it." Instead, we Indigenous people *are possessed* like the land. Of course, we recognize our intimate relations in what others call "nature." What we reject is the possessiveness associated with the hierarchy of human and nonhuman. As Koyungkawi poet Linda Noel explains: "I don't mind being 'close to nature.' But I know what *they* mean when they say that, and it's not what I mean."

TWENTY-FIRST-CENTURY RELATIONS: MAKING KIN

If one refuses Indigenous elimination and a de-animating possession of us, then a new redemptive narrative, a different creative move, is required. If you/we are to live together in a good way here – as kin or as Peoples in alliance with reciprocal responsibilities to one another and to our other-than-human relatives with whose land, water, and animal bodies we are co-constituted – the American Dream in any form, whether White supremacist or "progressive," cannot be our guiding hope. An important part of dismantling US hegemony and oppression is turning our eyes away from that story and toward another. This is no sudden move, and US exceptionalism, though it has suffered hard blows [since Trump's election], will not be let go easily. Neither will Canadian exceptionalism be let go easily – especially with the big, bad threat to the south. We should be practicing in every possible moment small acts of visionary resistance and deep narrative and ontological revision that forgo the relentlessly violent love for the nation-state in favor of loving and caring for our relatives, both human and other-than-human, whose lives depend upon these lands.

Some may think that the twenty-first-century state has moved beyond coercive tactics that constructed nonwhites as "others" to be either killed or assimilated. We hear so much talk of diversity and inclusion. Ongoing US military and police violence against those others disrupts that fantasy. But even the state's "multiculturalism," in which we see small tolerances for, say, Indigenous languages, the beating of drums, and the burning of sage in carefully contained moments, represents the idea that Indigenous people should be *included in* a nation that is assumed to be a done deal, its hegemony forever established. Indigenous peoples tend to have less interest in incorporation *into* a (liberal) settler worldview than in pushing for thriving Indigenous societies.

I propose *making kin* as an alternative approach to liberal multiculturalism, for righting relations gone bad. I have recently listened more closely to colleagues who focus on Indigenous kinship. Robert Alexander Innes, author of *Elder Brother and the Law of the People: Contemporary Kinship and Cowessess First Nation* (2013), blurs the lines between Indigenous peoples as dynamic kin groups and as "nations," with the latter term implying more cultural or even biological/racial stasis. His work opens my mind to a new way of reading people-to-people relations as also potentially making kin. Gabrielle Tateyuskanskan, a Sisseton-Wahpeton Oyate citizen, writer, and artist, also asks us Dakota to pay more attention to kinship in our analyses of the historical tensions that led to the 1862 war between our Dakota ancestors and settlers in what is today Minnesota. Tateyuskanskan reminded us one summer at our annual Oak Lake Writers' Society tribal writers' retreat in Oak Lake, South Dakota, that Dakota and European descendants were already heavily entangled through marriage and family at that time. This could explain my ancestor Chief Little Crow's misplaced expectations of kinship from newer arrivals who became settlers. I have since revisited sources on the 1862 war and now see Little Crow's efforts to make kin with other Dakota and with settlers where I had previously overlooked them. Tateyuskanskan calls for a more complex analysis of 1862 that highlights the political economy of war and conflict. How did the big capitalists in the Twin Cities benefit from and foment racial strife? The Dakota-US War of 1862 can be read in relation to perpetual US warfare designed to maintain empire and with corporate profit at the heart of it.

Calling non-Indigenous people into kin relations as a diplomatic strategy is a new and discomforting idea to me, even while it may be an idea that was once common among my ancestors. While Indigenous families regularly make kin with white settlers and other non-Indigenous peoples, we do not anymore foreground this as diplomacy. We have focused since the early twentieth century more on tribal or Indigenous nation-building rhetoric and strategies that include reservation-based, urban, and national Indigenous institutions and self-governance structures. Making kin is making people into familiars in order to relate. This feels like a creative alternative to nationalist assertions of inherent sovereignty. It seems fundamentally different from negotiating relations between those who are seen as different – between "sovereigns" or "nations," especially when one of those nations is a heavily militarized and racist empire.

I recall Little Crow's kin-making a lot these days as I ponder the genocidal actions of the US settler state. I consider how things might have been different had more newcomers respected long-established ways of relating already in place. What if settlers had not been dead set on cultural evangelizing through governance, religion, and science? Making or creating kin can call non-Indigenous people (including those who do not fit well into the "settler" category) to be more accountable to Indigenous lifeways long constituted in intimate relation with this place. Kinship might inspire change, new ways of organizing and standing together in the face of state violence against both humans and the land. Thinking through the lens of kin in our understanding of relations between peoples, we might chip away at racial structures produced in concert with white supremacist states' nation-building, structures that kill Indigenous and other racialized and "othered" people. Like my Dakota ancestors, I am heartbroken at the world, both at home and abroad, that the racist settler state continues to build. I have come to see both kinship's historical veracity and its generous strategic advantage.

Harvard's Cornel West wrote in *The Guardian* on November 17, 2016, post-election:

> We [must] build multiracial alliances to combat poverty and xenophobia, Wall Street crimes and war crimes, global warming and police abuse – and to protect precious rights and liberties. [W]e must be a hope, a participant and a force for good as we face this catastrophe.

But Dr. West also spoke of "*our* democracy slipping away." In his recognition of the many diverse peoples in the United States and abroad who have been wronged by US neoliberalism, not once did he reflect on Indigenous peoples, though the dispossession of our homelands is fundamental to providing the literal ground on which he lamented democratic loss. Cornel West, like many of his fellow Americans, erases Indigeneity in the most inopportune times. Still, I stand with him in "multiracial alliance." But even more, I stand in alliance with relatives – both human and other-than-human – who suffer across the planet from the violence that is the American Dream.

In order to sustain good relations among all the beings that inhabit these lands, we must undercut settler (property) relations. Instead of killing the Indian to save the man, we must turn the ontological table. The twenty-first-century mantra must be to kill the settler and save us all. Or as my Indigenous studies colleague and Lakota relative Nick Estes put it in an email to me, we must commit "settler ontocide." This does not, of course, mean literal killing. It means ridding ourselves of the category of the settler along with its discourse of white supremacy and assertions of an inherent right to these lands and waters. This distinction is so obvious to Indigenous thinkers and the Black decolonial scholars we also cite, but as Menominee scholar Enaemaehkiw Kesīqnaeh writes, the settler has "a deeply ingrained fear that in the revolution all that they have done will be visited back upon them by the global majority with great ferocity." How lacking in imagination and radical hope is the settler and his state.

REFERENCES

Innes, Robert Alexander. 2013. *Elder Brother and the Law of the People: Contemporary Kinship and Cowessess First Nation*. Winnipeg: University of Manitoba Press.

Kesīqnaeh, Enaemaehkiw. 2016. "Indigenous Revengence: The White Fear of Savage Reprisal." *Maehkōn Ahpēhtesewen* (blog), May 26. https://onkwehonwerising.wordpress.com.

Moreton-Robinson, Aileen. 2015. *The White Possessive: Property, Power, and Indigenous Sovereignty*. Minneapolis: University of Minnesota Press.

Noel, Linda, Christine Hamilton, Anna Rodriguez, Angela James, Nathan Rich, David S. Edmunds, and Kim TallBear. 2014. "Bitter Medicine Is Stronger: A Recipe for Acorn Mush and the Recovery of Pomo Peoples of Northern California." In *The Multispecies Salon*, edited by Eben Kirksey, 159. Durham: Duke University Press.

West, Cornel. 2016. "Goodbye, American Neoliberalism: A New Era Is Here." *The Guardian*, November 17. https://www.theguardian.com/commentisfree/2016/nov/17/american-neoliberalis_m-cornel-west-2016-election?CMP=share_btn_tw.

Provocation: Going Native – A Satirical End to Anthropology Theory

> *Now I want* [1]
> *Spirits to enforce, art to enchant;*
> *And my ending* [2] *is despair*
> *Unless I be relieved by prayer,*
> *Which pierces so, that it assaults*
> *Mercy itself, and frees all faults.*
> *As you from crimes would pardoned be,*
> *Let your indulgence* [3] *set me free.*
>
> — Prospero, Epilogue, *The Tempest*

We conclude this conversation across the decades and across personalities with a polyvocal and intertextual project to bring lightness into anthropology's proclivity for seriousness by introducing *Going Native*. What does it mean to "go native" when you are "doing" anthropology? By way of "provocation" we share a series of comics conceptualized and drawn by Bernard Perley for the American Anthropological Association newsletter *Anthropology News*. We hope readers imagine and share their own depictions of the ironies, contradictions, and complexities inherent in "going native."

In 2015 Perley received an invitation from Natalie Konopinski, the managing editor for *Anthropology News*, to consider publishing satirical cartoons for the Association's

---

1 Lack (*The Norton Shakespeare*: based on the Oxford Edition, ed. Greenblatt et al. [1997], 3106).
2 Punning on the sense "death" (ibid.).
3 Approval; appeasement; remission for sin (ibid.).

news magazine. After months of productive meetings outlining mutual expectations, parameters, and legal matters, the inaugural cartoon was published in the September/October 2016 issue of *Anthropology News*. The title of the cartoon column, "Going Native," was selected because it allowed Perley to explore a broad range of issues related to anthropology and for its critical, satirical, and humorous possibilities. The cartoons are created to serve both Indigenous and non-Indigenous anthropologists/readers. Perley's goal for the "Going Native" column is to deploy humor as an effective tool in the "healing arts" (de Pré 1998). Keith Basso's seminal work on Western Apache imitations of white men (1979) is a key source of inspiration for his cartoons in terms of both analysis and practice. Basso witnessed a young Apache girl imitate a white teacher while scolding her puppy. Then, he observed the girl's mother respond. "Stop," she called firmly in Apache, "the dog will bite you again." And then, more sternly, she added, "Be careful how you joke. It's dangerous to imitate a Whiteman" (Basso 1979:10–11). The Apache girl's mother recognized the power of joking behavior to offend if the joking behavior is enacted in the wrong context.

This implies that there are socially constructed boundaries with deep histories, in which the actors may not have all the necessary knowledge to perform the satire to achieve the desired results. Basso states that "Western Apache jokers are properly regarded as more than purveyors of preexisting cultural forms. They are creators of culture as well, and serve in this capacity as active agents of cultural change" (1979:80). Drees and de Leeuw argue, "Satire, we proposed, plays with cultural forms and identities, it travels between media and through periods of time, it provokes critical reflection on authorities, tackles values, dogmas and taboos and disturbs power relations" (2015:5). "Going Native" is Perley's modest attempt to provide some small measure of healing for Indigenous Peoples who grapple with "being an anthropologist and remaining native" (Medicine 2001) and for non-Indigenous anthropologists who grapple with imperialist nostalgia (Rosaldo 1989). The cartoons blur boundaries, question assumptions, and challenge imperialist nostalgia to provoke critical reflection about our pasts, the present, and our futures so that more equitable power relations between Indigenous Peoples and non-Indigenous peoples can co-produce new possibilities for anthropology futures.

The comic strips that appear on the following pages were published together in the 2019 March/April issue of *Anthropology News*. This first comic strip recalls the period immediately following the publication of Vine Deloria Jr.'s important 1969 essay "Anthropologists and Other Friends" (subsequently published in his collected essays volume *Custer Died for Your Sins: An Indian Manifesto*, 1973). Postcolonial resistance to imperial powers were creating opportunities that would eventually bring Indigenous Peoples together to compare experiences of oppression and emancipation. The Indigenous Peoples of North America were grappling with continued colonial oppression on the one hand and imperialist nostalgia on the other. Anthropology had to come to grips with its legacy of imperialist nostalgia. (Note: Ranger is inept when roasting a marshmallow.)

The reaction to Vine Deloria Jr.'s diatribe was knee-jerk defensiveness in many cases, but other anthropologists were willing to reflect upon their participation in perpetuating

Credit: Bernard C. Perley

an anthropology of white privilege. The second strip tackles the reflexive moment in anthropology when discourses surrounding the privileged status of anthropologist was openly deliberated and created the impetus for reflexive statements in future ethnographies. The strip also identifies these deliberations as academic rather than practical by surrounding Ranger with books as he sits alone with his thoughts. (Note: the coffee cup has the AAA logo on its side.)

While non-Indigenous anthropologists were anguishing over their privileged status among their research subjects, Beatrice Medicine and her allies were meeting at the annual

Credit: Bernard C. Perley

AAA meetings to continue the critical evaluation of their place in a discipline that continued to marginalize their voices. By the 1990s the Association began to take note of growing conversations of postcolonial and decolonizing rhetoric and strategies. The third strip presents the dilemma inherent in any attempt to decolonize the discipline. From whose perspective does decolonization take place? In the strip Ranger's hat is a metaphor for anthropology. The hat does double duty; it hides the face of the "native" as well as presents a character in anthropological nostalgia. Apparel, contexts, and discourses serve similar functions. The reader suspends disbelief and accepts the symbol to represent the native's persona. In this case, Ranger's white hat is part of his identity. The white hat is the good guy in American cinematic Western films. Is decolonizing anthropology as simple as putting the whiteman's good guy hat on an Indigenous person? Tonto is clearly uncomfortable wearing Ranger's hat. It is not a good fit. But Ranger does not see with his eyes, he sees with his imagination. (Note: Ranger is the domestic character serving Tonto coffee.)

Is anthropology a good fit for Indigenous Peoples? The United Nations adopted the Declaration on the Rights of Indigenous Peoples in 2007, advocating on behalf of Indigenous communities. Meanwhile, anthropology directed its attention to its own future. The new millennium prompted retrospection in order to imagine emergent systems. Unfortunately, those ruminations continued to frame the "native point of view" as alien (Fischer 2009:48). (Note: the open book of "emergent systems" is closed to the future.)

The feedback loop of emergent systems grappled with poesis as new forms of life and epistemic things became actualized in subsequent formulations of anthropological research and social relations. Techno-science and social analysis created exciting new slogans and research projects; just as Vine Deloria Jr. warned us back in 1969 (Deloria Jr. 1988 [1969]:80). As we approach the end of the second decade of the twenty-first century, many of the strategies for addressing new life forms is to try to see things from the perspective of those life forms. It would seem boundaries are being blurred and voices are being harmonized. From the Indigenous perspective, the decentering of the human – especially white male – point of view sounds familiar. The Native American expression "all my relations" has been colonized to mask new ventriloquisms allowing non-Indigenous anthropologists to "play Indian." The fifth comic strip concludes with Tonto congratulating Ranger for his emergent indigeneity. Tonto knows the relations in the new anthropology will require more suspension of disbelief for readers, "natives," and ethnographers alike. Indigeneity is "on the move" (Gerharz, Uddin, Chakkarath 2018) and the anthropologies of the past are crossing a threshold of new relations.

It is 2020 at the writing of this Provocation. Current anthropological imaginaries suggest anthropologists see humans as one global-earth-autochthonous community and are beginning to dissolve the "native" and "anthropologist" boundaries. Everyone is becoming Indigenous and enacting varieties of a shifting target identity. What will happen to anthropology if there are no "others" out there? Techno-science may offer a solution. Perhaps, machines will become new "natives" for anthropological observation and engagement. The sixth comic strip speculates how anthropologists will discern human/machine relations. Perhaps they will create new nostalgias between humans and machines in which the next disciplinary imaginary will be humanity's immoral acts of control and subordination of the machines they create. Anthropology's imaginary may position humans as observers and machines as others. If so, will humans become future anthropologists while machines become new natives? If machines do achieve sentience, self-intelligence, and intentionality, will they become "oppressed natives" when they cease to submit to human will as human/machine relations create new ethnographic objects? Perhaps, *going native* cannot be anything but "an art to enchant" in need of a "prayer." (Note: H.A.L.'s quote-line in the center frame is Morse Code for SOS [Save Our Souls?].)

As we assess the inequities laid bare by the COVID-19 pandemic and as we look forward to restructuring equitable relations in the third decade of the twenty-first century, we are in a position to reimagine possible futures that will help us all cross the threshold of past tragedies in order to create an anthropology practice that enables and empowers both Indigenous and non-Indigenous community members to co-produce stories of healing. To help promote those futures we provide you with this provocation – a template for imagining and drawing your own *Going Native* comic strip (see Appendix I). The future of anthropology theory is in your hands. Please share your imaginings with us.

Bernard C. Perley

REFERENCES

Basso, Keith. 1979. *Portraits of the Whiteman: Linguistic Play and Cultural Symbols among the Western Apache*. Cambridge: Cambridge University Press.

Deloria Jr., Vine. 1988. "Anthropologists and Other Friends." In *Custer Died for Your Sins: An Indian Manifesto*. Norman: University of Oklahoma Press.

Drees, Marijke Meijer, and Sonja de Leeuw (eds.). 2015. *The Power of Satire*. Amsterdam: John Benjamins Publishing.

du Pré, Athena. 1998. *Humor and the Healing Arts: A Multimethod Analysis of Humor Use in Health Care*. Mahwah: Lawrence Erlbaum Associates.

Fischer, Michael M.J. 2009. *Anthropological Futures*. Durham: Duke University Press.

Gerharz, Eva, Nasir Uddin, and Pradeep Chakkarath (eds.). 2018. *Indigeneity on the Move: Varying Manifestations of a Contested Concept*. New York: Berghan.

Medicine, Beatrice. 2001. *Learning to Be an Anthropologist and Remaining "Native": Selected Writings*. Urbana: University of Illinois Press.

Rosaldo, Renato. 1989. "Imperialist Nostalgia." In *Representations* 6: 102–22.

Appendix I: Anthropological Futures

Ultimately younger generations, including readers of this book, will build and transform the intellectual structures of society. What might your theoretical futures look like? Is there a future for anthropology? Use the frames on the next page to draw your own cartoon and illustrate your vision of theoretical directions for the twenty-first century.

Appendix II: Websites and Syllabi Projects

To build the collection in this volume, we drew on the expertise of countless colleagues in anthropology and beyond. We also combed the internet looking at anthropological websites, many of which offer "syllabus projects," or curated lists of readings on a topic. Often these projects are aimed at diversifying, updating, and politicizing anthropological conversations. Some websites that were especially helpful to us as we put together this book include the following:

American Anthropological Association: americananthro.org/index.aspx
American Ethnologist: americanethnologist.org
Anthro{Dendum}: anthrodendum.org
Anthropology News: anthropology-news.org
Association of Black Anthropologists: aba.americananthro.org
Association of Latina and Latino Anthropologists: alla.americananthro.org
Association for Queer Anthropology: queeranthro.org
Society for Cultural Anthropology: culanth.org
Society for the Anthropology of North America: sananet.org

About the Editors

A. Lynn Bolles is a professor emerita in the Harriet Tubman Department of Women, Gender, and Sexuality Studies and was an affiliate faculty in anthropology, African American studies, comparative literature, and American studies at the University of Maryland, College Park. She served as president of the Association of Black Anthropologists, the Caribbean Studies Association, the Association for Feminist Anthropology, and the Society for the Anthropology of North America. She was also elected as a councillor for the American Ethnological Association, and to the executive council of the American Anthropological Association. Among her honors are the Graduate School Mentor of the Year and the Minority Faculty Member of the Year from the University of Maryland, the Association of Black Anthropologists Legacy Award, the Gender Equity Award from the American Anthropological Association, and the Distinguished Alumni Award from Syracuse University. She is the author of several important articles and books on Caribbean women, including *We Paid Our Dues: Women Trade Union Leaders of the Caribbean* (1996), *Sister Jamaica: A Study of Women, Work and Households in Kingston* (1996), and *Women and Tourist Work in Jamaica: Seven Miles of Sandy Beach* (2021). Dr. Bolles earned a BA from Syracuse University with a double major in anthropology and English, and an MA and a PhD from Rutgers University–New Brunswick.

Ruth Gomberg-Muñoz is an associate professor of anthropology at Loyola University Chicago and past president of the Society for the Anthropology of North America. Her community-based work explores how members of mixed-immigration-status families navigate law and society in the United States and Mexico. Her most recent project is a translocal collaboration with deportee rights activists in Mexico City and anti-deportation organizers in Chicago. Dr. Gomberg-Muñoz's work has been supported by four National Science Foundation grants, and she is the author of two books, *Labor and Legality: An Ethnography of a Mexican Immigrant Network* (2011, 2020) and *Becoming Legal: Immigration*

Law and Mixed Status Families (2016). Dr. Gomberg-Muñoz has additionally authored more than twenty scholarly articles and book chapters, including essays in *American Anthropologist*, *American Ethnologist*, *The DuBois Review*, and the *Journal of Contemporary Ethnography*, and also coauthored policy briefs, public reports, blogs, and news articles.

Bernard C. Perley is a member of the Maliseet Nation from Tobique First Nation, New Brunswick, Canada. He is the director of the Institute for Critical Indigenous Studies (CIS) at the University of British Columbia. He was an associate professor in the Department of Anthropology at the University of Wisconsin-Milwaukee, where he taught courses in linguistic anthropology and American Indian studies. Dr. Perley received his Bachelor of Fine Arts degree and a Master of Architecture from the University of Texas at Austin. He went on to receive his PhD in anthropology from Harvard University. The knowledge and experience he gained from the three programs have contributed significantly to his writing and advocacy for revitalizing Indigenous languages, cultures, and identities as place-based interdependencies. He has published broadly on topics ranging from Indigenous language endangerment and language revitalization to anthropology and Native American studies theory and practice. Dr. Perley has served on the executive board of the American Anthropological Association and continues his service to the discipline as the president for the Society for Linguistic Anthropology and through his work with the SLA's Language and Social Justice Group. Dr. Perley's ongoing research is dedicated toward revitalizing Indigenous languages and Indigenous sovereignty and survivance. His critical creativity is expressed through cartoons drawn for *Anthropology News* as well as his own personal series, "Having Reservations."

Keri Vacanti Brondo is a professor and chair of the Department of Anthropology at the University of Memphis. Dr. Brondo has research and teaching interests in conservation and development, tourism and local livelihoods, Indigenous land rights, feminist methodologies, and nature-based volunteerism. She is a National Geographic Explorer (2019–2021) and the recipient of several awards, including the Presidential Award from the American Anthropological Association, the Sierra Club's Dick Mochow Environmental Justice Award, and the Dunavant Faculty Professorship at the University of Memphis. Her international research focuses on the relationship between Indigenous rights, conservation, development, and local livelihoods, particularly on Honduras's north coast and islands. She is the author/editor of over 65 articles and 5 books, including *Voluntourism and Multispecies Collaboration: Life, Death, and Conservation in the Mesoamerican Barrier Reef* (2021), *Land Grab: Green Neoliberalism, Gender, and Garifuna Resistance in Honduras* (2013), and *Cultural Anthropology: Contemporary, Public, and Critical Readings* (2017, 2020). Her newest book project is the coauthored book (with L. Vivanco) *Nature, Culture, and Environmental Sustainability: Anthropological Perspectives*.

Sources

Selection 1.1: Apess, William. 1833. "An Indian's Looking Glass for the White Man." In *On Our Own Ground: The Complete Writings of William Apess, a Pequot* (University of Massachusetts Press), pp. 155–6, 157, 158, 159, 160–16. Public domain.

Selection 1.2: Douglass, Frederick. 1854. "The Claims of the Negro, Ethnologically Considered: An Address before the Literary Societies Western Reserve College, at Commencement, July 12, 1854" (Central Library of Rochester and Monroe County – Historic Monographs Collection), pp. 3, 6–9, 10, 14–15, 16–18, 19–20. Public domain.

Selection 1.3: Marx, Karl, and Friedrich Engels. 1872. "Bourgeois and Proletarians." In *The Communist Manifesto*. Marxists Internet Archive, https://www.marxists.org/archive/marx/works/1848/communist-manifesto/. CC BY SA 2.0, https://creativecommons.org/licenses/by-sa/2.0/.

Selection 1.4: Morgan, Lewis Henry. 1877. "Ethnical Periods." In *Ancient Society*. Public domain.

Selection 1.5: Parsons, Lucy E. 1905. "Afternoon Session, June 29th." In *Speeches at the Founding Convention of the Industrial Workers of the World*. The Anarchist Library. Public domain.

Selection 1.6: Weber, Max. [1905] 1958. "Introduction," "Religious Affiliation and Social Stratification," and "The Spirit of Capitalism." In *The Protestant Ethic and the Spirit of Capitalism*. Charles Scribner's Sons. English translation originally published by Allen & Unwin, 1930.

Selection 2.1: Sapir, Edward. 1912. "Language and Environment 1." *American Anthropologist* 14: 226–42, pp. 227–9, 230, 231–2, 233–5, 239. Public domain.

Selection 4.3: Wolf, Eric. 1982. "The World in 1400." In *Europe and the People without History*. Copyright © 1982, 1997, 2010 by The Regents of the University of California. Republished with permission of the University of California Press; permission conveyed through Copyright Clearance Center, Inc.

Selection 4.4: Stoler, Ann L. 1989. "Making Empire Respectable: The Politics of Race and Sexual Morality in 20th-Century Colonial Cultures." *American Ethnologist* 16 (4): 634–60. Republished with permission of the University of California Press; permission conveyed through Copyright Clearance Center, Inc.

Selection 4.5: Farmer, Paul. 2004. "An Anthropology of Structural Violence." *Current Anthropology* 45 (3): 305–25. Republished with permission of the University of Chicago Press; permission conveyed through Copyright Clearance Center, Inc.

Selection 5.1: Dunham, Katherine. 1946. "Twenty-Seventh Day." In *Journey to Accompong*. Republished with permission of ABC-CLIO, LLC; permission conveyed through Copyright Clearance Center, Inc.

Selection 5.2: Geertz, Clifford. [1972] 2005. "Notes on the Balinese Cockfight." *Daedalus* 134 (4): 56–86. Republished with permission of MIT Press and the American Academy of Arts & Sciences; permission conveyed through Copyright Clearance Center, Inc.

Selection 5.3: Rosaldo, Renato. 1989. "Grief and a Headhunter's Rage." In *Culture and Truth: The Remaking of Social Analysis*. © 1989, 1993 by Renato Sosaldo. Republished with permission of Beacon Press; permission conveyed through Copyright Clearance Center, Inc.

Selection 5.4: Abu-Lughod, Lila. 1991. "Writing against Culture." Reprinted by permission from *Recapturing Anthropology: Working in the Present*, ed. Richard G. Fox. Copyright © 1991 by the School for Advanced Research, Santa Fe, New Mexico. All rights reserved.

Selection 5.5: Boswell, Rosabelle. 2017. "Sensuous Stories in the Indian Ocean Islands." *The Senses and Society* 12 (2): 193–208. Reprinted by permission of Taylor & Francis Ltd., http://www.tandfonline.com.

Selection 6.1: Medicine, Beatrice. 2001. "Learning to Be an Anthropologist and Remaining 'Native.'" In *Learning to Be an Anthropologist and Remaining "Native": Selected Writings*, edited by Beatrice Medicine and Sue-Ellen Jacobs. University of Illinois Press. Copyright © Beatrice Medicine 1978, use courtesy Ted Sitting Crow Garner.

Selection 6.2: Said, Edward W. 1979. "Knowing the Oriental." In *Orientalism*, copyright © 1978 by Edward W. Said. Used by permission of Pantheon Books, an imprint of the

Selection 6.3: Krotz, Esteban. 1997. "Anthropologies of the South: Their Rise, Their Silencing, Their Characteristics." *Critique of Anthropology* 17 (3): 237–51. Copyright © 1997, SAGE Publications. Reprinted by permission.

Selection 6.4: Trouillot, Michel-Rolph. 2003. "Anthropology and the Savage Slot: The Poetics and Politics of Otherness." In *Global Transformations: Anthropology and the Modern World.* © Michel-Rolph Trouillot 2003. Republished with permission of Palgrave Macmillan; permission conveyed through Copyright Clearance Center, Inc.

Selection 6.5: Hau'ofa, Epeli. 2008. "Our Sea of Islands." In *We Are the Ocean: Selected Works.* © 2008 University of Hawai'i Press. Republished with permission of the University of Hawai'i Press; permission conveyed through Copyright Clearance Center, Inc.

Selection 7.1: Leacock, Eleanor Burke. 1972. Introduction. In *The Origin of the Family, Private Property and the State: In the Light of the Researches of Lewis H. Morgan.* © by International Publishers Co., Inc., 1972. Republished with permission of International Publishers Company, Inc.; permission conveyed through Copyright Clearance Center, Inc.

Selection 7.2: Yanagisako, Sylvia Junko, and Jane Fishburne Collier. 1987. "Toward a Unified Analysis of Gender and Kinship." In *Gender and Kinship: Essays toward a Unified Analysis,* ed. Jane Collier and Sylvia Junko Yanagisako. © 1987 by the Board of Trustees of the Leland Stanford Junior University. Republished with permission of Stanford University Press; permission conveyed through Copyright Clearance Center, Inc.

Selection 7.3: Amadiume, Ifi. 1987. From *Male Daughters, Female Husbands: Gender and Sex in an African Society.* Zed Books. Copyright © Ifi Amadiume, 1987, 2015. Used by permission of Bloomsbury Publishing Plc.

Selection 7.4: Anzaldúa, Gloria. 1987. "La conciencia de la mestiza / Towards a New Consciousness." In *Borderlands / La Frontera: The New Mestiza,* © 1987, 1999, 2007, 2012 by Gloria Anzaldúa. Reprinted by permission of Aunt Lute Books. www.auntlute.com.

Selection 7.5: Bourgois, Philippe. 1996. "In Search of Masculinity: Violence, Respect and Sexuality among Puerto Rican Crack Dealers in East Harlem." *The British Journal of Criminology* 36 (3): 412–27. Copyright © 1996, Oxford University Press. Reprinted by permission.

Selection 8.1: Foucault, Michel. 1976. Excerpts from *The History of Sexuality: Volume I: An Introduction,* translated by Robert Hurley, translation copyright © 1978 by Penguin Random House LLC. Used by permission of Pantheon Books, an imprint of the Knopf Doubleday Publishing Group, a division of Penguin Random House LLC. All rights reserved. Originally published in French as *La Volonté du Savoir.* Copyright © 1976 by Editions Gallimard. Reprinted by permission of Georges Borchardt, Inc., for Editions Gallimard.

Selection 8.2: Towle, Evan B., and Lynn M. Morgan. 2002. "Romancing the Transgender Native: Rethinking the Use of the 'Third Gender' Concept." In *GLQ: A Journal of Lesbian and Gay Studies* 8 (4): 469–97. Copyright © 2002, Duke University Press. All rights reserved. Republished by permission of the copyright holder, Duke University Press. www .dukeupress.edu.

Selection 8.3: Stryker, Susan. 2008. "Transgender History, Homonormativity, and Disciplinarity." In *Radical History Review* 2008 (100): 145–57. Copyright © 2008 MARHO: The Radical Historians Organization, Inc. All rights reserved. Republished by permission of the copyright holder, and the present publisher, Duke University Press. www .dukeupress.edu.

Selection 8.4: Allen, Jafari. 2012. "One Way or Another: Erotic Subjectivity in Cuba." *American Ethnologist* 39 (2): 325–38. Republished with permission of John Wiley & Sons; permission conveyed through Copyright Clearance Center, Inc.

Selection 8.5: Shange, Savannah. 2019. "Play Aunties and Dyke Bitches: Gender, Generation, and the Ethics of Black Queer Kinship." *The Black Scholar* 49 (1): 40–54. Reprinted by permission of Taylor & Francis Ltd., http://www.tandfonline.com.

Selection 9.1: Haraway, Donna. 1988. "Situated Knowledges: The Science Question in Feminism and the Privilege of Partial Perspective." *Feminist Studies* 14 (3): 575–99. Reprinted by permission of the publisher, Feminist Studies, Inc.

Selection 9.2: Jones, Delmos. 1995. "Anthropology and the Oppressed: A Reflection on 'Native' Anthropology." Reproduced by permission of the American Anthropological Association from *Annals of Anthropological Practice* 16 (1): 58–70. Not for sale or further reproduction. https://doi.org/10.1525/napa.1995.16.1.58.

Selection 9.3: Davis, Dána-Ain. 2003. "What Did You Do Today? Notes from a Politically Engaged Anthropologist." *Urban Anthropology and Studies of Cultural Systems and World Economic Development* 32 (2): 147–73. Reprinted by permission of The Institute Inc.

Selection 9.4: Becker, Heike, Emile Boonzaier, and Joy Owen. 2005. "Fieldwork in Shared Spaces: Positionality, Power and Ethics of Citizen Anthropologists in Southern Africa." *Anthropology of Southern Africa* 28 (3–4): 123–32. Reprinted by permission of Taylor & Francis Ltd., http://www.tandfonline.com.

Selection 9.5: Perley, Bernard C. 2013. "'Gone Anthropologist': Epistemic Slippage, Native Anthropology, and the Dilemmas of Representation." In *Anthropology and the Politics of Representation*, ed. Gabriela Vargas-Cetina. Copyright © 2013 The University of Alabama Press. Reprinted by permission.

Selection 10.1: Appadurai, Arjun. 1986. "Theory in Anthropology: Center and Periphery." *Comparative Studies of History in Society* 28 (2): 356–61. Copyright © 2009, Cambridge University Press. Reprinted by permission.

Selection 10.2: Gupta, Akhil, and James Ferguson. 1992. "Beyond 'Culture': Space, Identity, and the Politics of Difference." Reproduced by permission of the American Anthropological Association from *Cultural Anthropology* 7 (1): 6–23. Not for sale or further reproduction. https://doi.org/10.1525/can.1992.7.1.02a00020.

Selection 10.3: Ong, Aihwa. 2006. "Mutations in Citizenship." *Theory, Culture & Society* 23 (2–3): 499–531. Copyright © 2006, SAGE Publications. Reprinted by permission.

Selection 10.4: Harrison, Faye V. 2008. "Global Apartheid at Home and Abroad." In *Outsider Within: Reworking Anthropology in the Global Age*. Copyright © 2008 by the Board of Trustees of the University of Illinois. Used with permission of the University of Illinois Press.

Selection 10.5: Ribeiro, Gustavo Lins. 2009. "Non-hegemonic Globalizations: Alternative Transnational Processes and Agents." *Anthropological Theory* 9 (3): 297–329. Copyright © 2009, SAGE Publications. Reprinted by permission.

Selection 11.1: Steward, Julian. 1955. "The Concept and Method of Cultural Ecology." In *Theory of Culture Change: The Methodology of Multilinear Evolution*. Copyright © 1983 Jane C. Steward. Used with permission of the University of Illinois Press.

Selection 11.2: West, Paige. 2005. "Translation, Value, and Space: Theorizing an Ethnographic and Engaged Environmental Anthropology." *American Anthropologist* 107 (4): 632–42. Republished with permission of John Wiley & Sons; permission conveyed through Copyright Clearance Center, Inc.

Selection 11.3: Todd, Zoe. 2015. "Indigenizing the Anthropocene." In *Art in the Anthropocene: Encounters among Aesthetics, Politics, Environment and Epistemology*, ed. Heather Davis and Etienne Turpin. Open Humanities Press. CC BY NC ND 3.0, https://creativecommons.org/licenses/by-nc-nd/3.0/.

Selection 11.4: Escobar, Arturo. "Introduction" and "Conclusion." In *Designs for the Pluriverse: Radical Interdependence, Autonomy, and the Making of Worlds*, pp. 1–22, 202–28. Copyright © 2018, Duke University Press. All rights reserved. Republished by permission of the copyright holder. www.dukeupress.edu.

Selection 11.5: Wali, Alaka. 2020. "Complicity and Resistance in the Indigenous Amazon: *Economía Indígena* Under Siege." In *Terrestrial Transformations: A Political Ecology Approach to Society and Nature*, ed. Thomas K. Park and James B. Greenberg. Lexington Books. © 2020 by The Rowman & Littlefield Publishing Group, Inc. Republished with permission of Rowman & Littlefield; permission conveyed through Copyright Clearance Center, Inc.

Selection 12.1: Bourdieu, Pierre. 1979. "Symbolic Power." *Critique of Anthropology* 4 (13–14): 77–85. Copyright © 1979, SAGE Publications. Reprinted by permission.

Selection 12.2: Aretxaga, Begoña. 1998. "What the Border Hides: Partition and Gender Politics of Irish Nationalism." *Social Analysis: The International Journal of Anthropology* 42 (1): 16–32. Reproduced by permission of Berghahn Books Inc.

Selection 12.3: Verdery, Katherine. 2002. "Seeing like a Mayor; Or, How Local Officials Obstructed Romanian Land Restitution." *Ethnography* 3 (1): 5–33. Copyright © 2002, SAGE Publications. Reprinted by permission.

Selection 12.4: Mbembé, Achille. 2003. "Necropolitics." *Public Culture* 15 (1): 11–40. Copyright © 2003, Duke University Press. All rights reserved. Republished by permission of the copyright holder, Duke University Press. www.dukeupress.edu.

Selection 12.5: Smith, Christen. 2013. "Strange Fruit: Brazil, Necropolitics, and the Transnational Resonance of Torture and Death." *Souls* 15 (3): 177–98. Reprinted by permission of Taylor & Francis Ltd., http://www.tandfonline.com.

Selection 13.1: Mahmood, Saba. 2005. "The Subject of Freedom." In *Politics of Piety: The Islamic Revival and the Feminist Subject*. Copyright © 2005 by Princeton University Press. Republished with permission of Princeton University Press; permission conveyed through Copyright Clearance Center, Inc.

Selection 13.2: Shankar, Shalini. 2008. "Speaking like a Model Minority: 'FOB' Styles, Gender, and Racial Meanings among Desi Teens in Silicon Valley." Reproduced by permission of the American Anthropological Association from *Journal of Linguistic Anthropology* 18 (2): 268–89. Not for sale or further reproduction. https://doi.org/10.1111/j.1548-1395.2008.00022.x.

Selection 13.3: Redclift, Victoria. 2013. "Abjects or Agents? Camps, Contests, and the Creation of 'Political Space.'" *Citizenship Studies* 17 (3–4): 308–21. Reprinted by permission of Taylor & Francis Ltd., http://www.tandfonline.com.

Selection 13.4: Bonilla, Yarimar, and Jonathan Rosa. 2015. "#Ferguson: Digital Protest, Hashtag Ethnography, and the Racial Politics of Social Media in the United States." *American Ethnologist* 42 (1): 4–17. © 2015 by the American Anthropological Association. Reprinted by permission of John Wiley & Sons.

Selection 13.5: Simpson, Audra. 2016. "Consent's Revenge." Reproduced by permission of the American Anthropological Association from *Cultural Anthropology* 31 (3): 326–33. Not for sale or further reproduction. https://doi.org/10.14506/ca31.3.02.

Selection 14.1: Bolles, A. Lynn. 2001. "Seeking the Ancestors: Forging a Black Feminist Tradition in Anthropology." In *Black Feminist Anthropology: Theory, Politics, Praxis, and Poetics*, edited by Irma McClaurin. Reprinted by permission of Rutgers University Press.

Selection 14.2: Mullings, Leith. 2005. "Interrogating Racism: Toward an Antiracist Anthropology." *Annual Review of Anthropology* 34: 667–93. Republished with permission of Annual Reviews; permission conveyed through Copyright Clearance Center, Inc.

Selection 14.3: Hage, Ghassan. 2016. "Towards an Ethics of the Theoretical Encounter." *Anthropological Theory* 16 (2–3): 221–6. Republished with permission of Sage Publications; permission conveyed through Copyright Clearance Center, Inc.

Selection 14.4: Maskovsky, Jeff. 2015. "At Home in the End Times." Reproduced by permission of Jeff Maskovsky.

Selection 14.5: Tallbear, Kim. (2019). Excerpted from "Caretaking Relations, Not American Dreaming." *Kalfou* 6 (1): 34–9. Reprinted by permission of Temple University Press. © 2019 The Regents of the University of California. All Rights Reserved.

Index